THE STANDARD BOOK OF ETIQUETTE

LILLIAN EICHLER WATSON

The Standard
Book of Etiquette

GARDEN CITY, NEW YORK

Garden City Books

Acknowledgment with thanks is made to
Prentice-Hall, Inc., New York, for permission to
quote from *The Standard Book of Letter Writing*
by Lillian Eichler Watson.

Preface

MANY far-reaching changes have taken place in the world since I wrote the original *Book of Etiquette*. It is, in fact, an entirely different world in which we now live, and not the least of this difference is expressed in the behavior patterns of our everyday lives. For the events of the past few years have made such a tremendous impact upon our whole way of life that they have radically influenced our social and moral concepts. Much of what was once considered proper is now looked upon as stuffy and old-fashioned. Much of what was once good form and good practice is now clearly outmoded. Just as yesterday's standard of living would fail to meet our requirements today, so yesterday's standards of correct social behavior will not meet the demands of today's busy existence.

In years gone by, in an attempt to keep up with these swiftly changing trends, I revised the *Book of Etiquette* several times. But no mere revision of the old forms is adequate to meet the problems and conditions of modern life. I was delighted, therefore, when my publishers asked me to prepare a completely new and modern treatment of the subject. I welcomed the opportunity of writing the kind of etiquette book which I had long felt was needed: a book free of antiquated notions and customs, yet preserving all of the cherished traditions—a book which my own teen-age son and daughter would find pertinent, interesting and in step with their own lively generation, but which at the same time would provide them with a code of social behavior made up of the best of the past and the best of the present.

This then is not just another version of my original *Book of Etiquette*. It is a completely new book from the first page to the last. I have, of course, included all of the standard and useful information such as table manners, rules of precedence, wedding-day formalities, etc. In addition, I have tried to bring the manners and customs sensibly up to date by keying them to a basic philosophy of life rather than to an inflexible set of rules. Etiquette, after all, is a subtle blending of time-honored usage and modern practicability.

I have thoroughly enjoyed writing this book. It has not been an easy task but it has been, for me, a gratifying one. The results of the research always necessary in a work of this kind have more than confirmed my belief that etiquette is a living thing—not a system of fixed regulations but something which is based upon fundamental principles

v

of human relationship. It has been my intention to make *The Standard Book of Etiquette* not only a reliable reference but also a guide to a happier and more confident way of living.

LILLIAN EICHLER WATSON

Contents

PART I   BASIC SOCIAL BEHAVIOR   1
1. The Little Courtesies of Daily Life   1
2. Introductions   10
3. The Etiquette of Visiting   26
4. Visiting Cards and Their Uses   39
5. Table Manners   51

PART II   THE ETIQUETTE OF ENTERTAINING   69
1. The Gracious Home   69
2. An Outline of Servants and Their Duties   81
3. Modern Entertaining   94
4. Table Settings   100
5. How to Give Successful Dinner Parties   106
6. Luncheon and Supper Parties—Breakfasts and Buffets   117
7. Teas, Dances, and Debutante Parties   128
8. Bridge and Card Parties   140
9. Cocktail Parties   148
10. House and Week End Parties   150
11. Service of Wines and Liquors   155

PART III   ENGAGEMENTS, WEDDINGS, DIVORCE   173
1. Becoming Engaged   173
2. Wedding Plans   181
3. Wedding Invitations and Announcements   192
4. Of Special Interest to the Bride   212
5. Correct Dress for the Wedding Party   221
6. The Wedding Day   234
7. Divorce   249

PART IV   CHRISTENINGS AND FUNERALS   253
1. Births and Christenings   253
2. Deaths and Funerals   259

PART V   SOCIAL CORRESPONDENCE   269
1. Good Taste in Correspondence   269
2. Parts of a Letter   275
3. General Invitations, Acceptances, and Regrets   289

4. Dance and Party Invitations and Acknowledgments   305
5. Letters of Congratulations   316
6. Letters of Thanks   320
7. Letters of Condolence and Sympathy   326
8. Greeting-Card Etiquette   331

PART VI   THE SOCIAL GRACES   339
1. Conversation   339
2. Personal Appearance   352
3. Telephone and Radio Courtesy   362
4. The Qualities that Make You a Welcome Guest   369
5. The Qualities that Make You a Gracious Host or Hostess   372

PART VII   ETIQUETTE IN PUBLIC PLACES   379
1. On the Street   379
2. At Theaters and Other Public Amusements   389
3. Restaurant and Night-Club Etiquette
     The Meaning of French Words Frequently Seen on Menus   394
4. Smoking and Drinking Etiquette   404
5. Travel Etiquette   414
6. Hotel and Resort Etiquette   427

PART VIII   GETTING ALONG WITH YOUR FAMILY   435

PART IX   ETIQUETTE FOR CHILDREN   449
1. Growing up with Good Manners   449
2. Learning to Live Like a Grown-up   453
3. Children's Parties and Party Invitations   459

PART X   TEEN-AGE ETIQUETTE   471
1. General Teen-Age Etiquette   471
2. Some Special Teen-Age Problems   477

PART XI   CLUB ETIQUETTE   483
1. Club Etiquette   483

PART XII   BUSINESS ETIQUETTE   493
1. How to Be Well Liked in Business   493

CONTENTS

Part XIII HIGHLIGHTS OF MILITARY AND OFFI-
CIAL ETIQUETTE   509

Appendix FORMS OF ADDRESS   521

Index   541

THE STANDARD BOOK OF ETIQUETTE

PART I

Basic Social Behavior

1. THE LITTLE COURTESIES OF DAILY LIFE

CERTAIN things do not change, however the outward manifestations of our daily lives may change. They are basic as the earth, and fundamental as the air we breathe. Among these are the little niceties of conduct which characterize good will and kindly impulse—the little courtesies which "oil the cogs of everyday life and are the hallmark of good breeding."

Such courtesy, to be sincere, must stem from an *inner grace*, from an awareness of other people and a consideration for their rights and feelings. It goes far beyond the use of the right fork or the ability to introduce people properly. It reflects a feeling, an instinct, an attitude —call it what you will! But one thing is certain: It begins *within* you, begins with a liking for people and a desire to be liked by them in turn.

Good manners are simply the outward forms of this inner grace. They are the friendly expression of your liking for people. Both are important—the inner grace and the outward forms. And etiquette today is a pleasant blending of the two: courtesy *based on kindness*, and therefore instinctive and unstudied.

To be thoughtful of others, to be gentle and kind, to be generous, agreeable, friendly, and above all *fair*—that is the best manners anyone can have. Make that your guiding principle in all contact with others, social or otherwise. If you are kindly and well disposed in your attitude toward people, you are not likely to be rude or inconsiderate to anyone. And whether you abide by the exact letter of the law or not, if you are courteous and thoughtful to others, you are essentially *well bred*.

You Can't Get by with Bad Manners

One of the primary joys of life is to be accepted and approved by other people, to be *well liked*. And no one can be accepted and approved—no one can be well liked—who continually offends or affronts the sensibilities of others.

We are living in a world where we cannot be blind to those around us. We have a social duty even to the strangers we meet. People are quick to recognize courtesy and eager to respond to it. But they are just as quick to be repelled by rudeness and bad taste.

So don't underestimate the value of good manners. They are important any way you look at them. They smooth the rough edges, prevent friction, make new friends and endear old ones.

Manners may not make the man, but they certainly make things run more smoothly and pleasantly for him! Good manners are responsible for much of the beauty and graciousness of our daily lives, and much of the comfort. They are the means of avoiding conflict and collision with others, spiritually and actually.

You can't get by with bad manners. Observe the little courtesies of daily life; for courtesy is the magic passport to any company, and the basis of a popularity that is real and lasting.

It Pays to Be Polite

A great American once said, "Manners are the happy way of doing things."

Good manners as interpreted in this book are not merely for their effect or influence on others. They are for your own *happiness*, your own peace of mind.

It pays to be polite! A pleasant face and a courteous manner are your own best protection against the rudeness of other people. Courtesy is contagious. A conductor with good manners and a friendly smile can make a whole car of passengers feel neighborly. A courteous man or woman at a party can make everyone feel happy and at ease. Courtesy radiates good cheer, and good cheer is catching. It's like a magnet that irresistibly attracts the courtesy of others to you.

Just try being unusually polite to everyone for a week or so, and see what happens! You'll discover that everyone is being unusually polite and friendly to you. You'll be amazed to find that many of your own little personal anxieties are slipping away, that you feel happier and more content. And if you continue, you'll be well on the way toward a wonderful new peace of mind.

There are very few things that pay such enormous dividends in personal satisfaction as good manners—"the happy way of doing things." The world opens its doors widely to those who have the habit of simple friendly courtesy.

COURTESY IS CONSIDERATION FOR OTHERS

True courtesy is consideration for the rights and feelings of others. It goes far beyond the pat rules of procedure which guide the socially inept. A knowledge of these rules is of course essential, for without it you cannot feel confident and secure. But if etiquette is to be of more than trifling use to you, you must recognize its real purpose and meaning: to make you happier and more successful in your association with others—not only strangers and business associates, but those near and dear to you.

Whatever else etiquette may or may not be, a generous regard for others is its great underlying principle. It's no mere polish, no superficial charm, on the surface of your personality. It's a *basic philosophy of behavior*. It's the way you greet your neighbor in the morning. It's the way you listen to people with all your interest, not with a faraway look in your eyes. It's the way you give up your seat to a lady . . . and ask about an ailing child . . . and avoid smoking where it causes distress to others. It's the way you refuse to spread unkind gossip, or to laugh at another's blunder or embarrassment.

Reduced to its simplest possible form, etiquette is the application of the Golden Rule: Treat others as you would have them treat you. It's an *awareness* of others, and the ability to put yourself in their place. It's an open-minded fairness in all your dealings with people. It's tolerance for ways and customs different from your own. It's confidence and quiet dignity, integrity and self-respect, justice and fair play. It's all these quite as much as it's the knowledge of how to set a table or how to write a letter of condolence.

MANNERS IMPROVE WITH PRACTICE

No one is born polite. No one is born with the ability to get along with all people, under all circumstances. There are rules of courteous behavior to be learned, fixed methods of procedure tested by long experience and handed down by tradition to make life more pleasant.

It's easy enough for anyone to learn these essential rules of courtesy. But learning the rules is only the first step. The really important thing is to follow them faithfully, day after day. For like everything else, manners improve with practice; and it's only through continuous practice of courtesy that it becomes a natural, instinctive part of your personality.

So be *consistent* in your courtesy! Don't be polite today, impatient and uncivil tomorrow; morose and sulky at home, affable at the office; obliging toward your friends, gruff and unfriendly toward strangers.

Make frequent use of those simple expressions of courtesy which do so much to build good will: *"Please"*—*"Thank you"*—*"I'm sorry."* They smooth the rough edges of daily contact with people, often work magic with strangers. Get into the habit of using them, not only out in public and among business associates and friends, but at home among members of your household. Don't reserve your best behavior for special occasions. Courtesy should be so thoroughly ingrained in your personality that it's practically "second nature" for you to be polite to everyone.

Don't Have Two Sets of Manners

You can't have two sets of manners, two social codes—one for those you admire and want to impress, another for those whom you consider unimportant. You must be the same to *all* people, whether you meet them in the ballroom or on a bus.

Make it a point to be courteous to everyone you meet. Don't make snap judgments about people; they are frequently wrong. Above all, don't estimate people for what they possess, but only for what they are. The so-called "best people" today are not those with the most money and the most impressive houses, but those with the most gracious and likable personalities—the people it's fun to know and be with.

So don't look down on people—don't ever be guilty of snubbing or "cutting" anyone—except for some grave and serious cause. The truly well-bred are never snobbish or superior in their dealings with others; they know that courtesy is kindness and that kindness is no superficial deference to a favored few, but a *quality of the heart* that reaches out to all.

"I call no man charitable," says Thoreau, "who forgets that his barber and cook are made of the same human clay as himself."

Be Especially Courteous to the Disabled

At no time is courtesy more important than in association with people who are physically handicapped or disabled. Such people are usually more sensitive than others, quick of perception and easily hurt. Here, indeed, courtesy must stem from an inner kindness and grace —a desire to spare the unfortunate person any unnecessary anguish.

People who are disabled don't like to be reminded of it. They want to forget their handicap as much as they can; and the way to help them forget is to show by your attitude that you are *not remembering*. Don't turn and stare. Don't whisper about them to others. Don't ask embarrassing questions or make personal remarks.

The first time you meet someone after he has been injured or disabled, you naturally want to say something kind and helpful. Try to be as brief as you can about it. Just say, "I'd like you to know how sorry I am"—or "Everyone says how wonderful you've been." But don't elaborate on it! Don't go into personal detail. However shocked you may be by the extent of the injury, don't show it. Nobody wants to be pitied. Sympathy is no kindness when it becomes excessive or when it's clearly the result of an ill-concealed curiosity.

If you happen to be near someone who is in difficulty due to a physical handicap, you offer to help. But you do it as quietly as you can, without drawing conspicuous attention either to the person or to his handicap. For example, if you are seated at the table next to someone whose arm is in a sling, or perhaps who has no arm at all—and if you see that it's quite impossible for him to manage without help— you say: "Let me do that for you." Then you proceed to do whatever is required without further comment. In the same way, you hold a coat for a disabled person, or adjust his chair, or light his cigarette quite as a matter of course and without making a fuss about it.

Just be sure that any offer you make to help a handicapped person is tactful and well-considered. Be sure it doesn't focus attention on his disability and cause him embarrassment. The greatest kindness you can show the physically handicapped is to treat them exactly as you do everyone else—being helpful and considerate when necessary, but not setting them apart from others and making them forever aware of their handicap.

PATTERN FOR POLITENESS

There are countless small gestures of courtesy that distinguish the well-bred. Some are so obvious that they scarcely need mention. But all are part of the broad general *pattern for politeness* which guides us in our association with other people.

In this pattern the predominating motif is a strong sense of personal dignity. It keeps us from doing or saying anything to reflect discreditably upon our families or ourselves. It restrains us in our dress and speech, keeps us from being loud or coarse in our actions, keeps us faithful to our traditions of civilized living.

But beneath this motif is the basic design, clear-cut and unmistakable: a regard for others. We don't yawn in people's faces because it would be inconsiderate to do so. We don't cough or sneeze without covering the mouth because that, too, would be inconsiderate and rude. We don't open a window if it means putting others in a draft, nor try to crowd ahead of people on a waiting line, nor play a musical instrument late at night if it's disturbing to neighbors.

Many other little courtesies make up the all-over pattern. For example, don't carry your umbrella carelessly—especially going upstairs. That's not only rude but dangerous.

Don't stand talking with friends you meet in the street, getting into other people's way. If you want to chat, walk on together—or get off to one side where you won't be obstructing traffic.

Don't glower at people who lurch against you accidentally in a crowded subway or bus. They can't help themselves. You are as much a part of the crowd as they are; so try to be pleasant and understanding about it instead of impatient and rude. A smile goes a long way toward making everyone feel better.

Don't unburden your woes in public, air your family affairs for strangers to hear, discuss people by name in a crowded elevator. It's definitely bad taste to talk about personal or private matters—your own or anyone else's—in a loud tone of voice.

Don't use chewing gum when it's likely to be offensive to others. Use it as much as you like when you are alone or when exacting standards of behavior are relaxed (as at picnics or sports events). And use it on planes, trains, ships, or in automobiles, if it makes you feel more comfortable and relaxed. But don't chew gum when you are at parties, when you are dancing or playing bridge, when you are visiting friends or carrying on a conversation with people.

The application of make-up in public is now permissible—but only if you don't try to do a complete and involved job of it. There's no objection to powdering your nose in a restaurant, if you do it briefly and inconspicuously. But if you want to make major repairs in your appearance—if you want to change your lipstick or comb your hair—a dressing room is the place for it.

It goes without saying that well-bred people never clean or file their nails in public. And even worse is to take out a mirror in a restaurant and carefully examine one's teeth for morsels of food! Such exhibitions are rude and offensive in the extreme.

Tact Is an Important Part of the Pattern

Tact is a generous courtesy born of kindness.

If an ambitious friend asks you how you like her voice and you tell her it's raspy and harsh, that's unkind. If you tell her it's beautiful when it's not, that's neither sincere nor helpful. But if you tell her you like the lovely soft quality of her voice, or the clear way she pronounces every word, or whatever you can find to admire with honesty and enthusiasm—that's *tact*.

Another example of tactful courtesy is to refrain from correcting a friend's misuse or mispronunciation of a word in the presence of others. If he says "integrate" when he means "correlate"—let it go! If you correct him publicly, you draw attention to his mistake and embarrass him. And what's more, you make it appear to the others as though you are trying to show off your own superior knowledge. So make it a point never to correct anyone except in private, and then only if you can do so without giving offense.

Don't invite someone to a dinner or party in the presence of others who are not to be included. Wait until you can take him aside and invite him without the others overhearing.

If someone starts telling a story you've heard before, let him tell it! It's more tactful to listen and laugh again than to spoil the fun for others.

Don't make fun of people. Don't ridicule their opinions and ideas, or the way they live. Don't gossip, spread false rumors, make damaging remarks. These are all part of the general pattern for politeness.

When in doubt, always remember that *whatever is more thoughtful and considerate of others is the polite thing to do.*

A Man's Courtesies to a Lady

Perhaps one of the most outstanding characteristics of a gentleman is his unfailing courtesy to a lady. It doesn't matter that the standards of today are much less exacting in this regard than they used to be, that many of the old familiar courtesies aren't even expected any more. A gentleman is *automatically* gracious and polite, observing the niceties of behavior whether they are firm rules or not—for they are natural and instinctive with him.

For example, a gentleman always rises when a lady comes into the room, and he remains standing until she is seated. He rises when a lady comes to his table in a restaurant; and remains standing until she either sits down or leaves. He also rises when a lady leaves the table, and again when she returns to it. These courtesies apply to his wife and grown daughters as much as they do to strangers and friends.

When a man meets a woman acquaintance on the street, he bows and lifts his hat. If they stop to talk, he removes his hat entirely; and he does not replace it until they either walk on together or go their separate ways. He does not stand talking to a lady with his hat on, no matter how cold or windy the day may be. However, the lady herself may thoughtfully suggest that he replace it, in which case he may do so. Needless to say, a gentleman never stands talking to a lady with a pipe, cigar, or cigarette in his mouth.

Lifting or "tipping" the hat is a conventional mark of courtesy and respect. It should always be accompanied by a nod of the head and a smile. The hat should be raised from the forehead, not merely touched —otherwise it's a lazy and halfhearted gesture. A stiff hat, like a derby, is lifted by the brim; a soft hat may be lifted by the crown.

A gentleman lifts his hat whenever he meets or takes leave of his wife or any other lady in public. He lifts his hat when he gives his seat to a lady, or picks up something she has dropped, or performs any other courtesy for her. Likewise he lifts his hat in acknowledgment of any courtesy shown the lady with him.

A gentleman lifts his hat when the lady he is with bows to someone, or is greeted by an acquaintance in passing.

He lifts his hat when a lady addresses him to request information or directions; and again when she thanks him for his help.

He lifts his hat when he must pass in front of a lady in a narrow passage, or hurry ahead of her through a door.

He lifts his hat if a lady makes way for him in a crowded subway or bus so that he can reach the door, rewarding her with a friendly nod or a polite "Thank you" as he passes by.

If he is thrown against another passenger by a sudden lurch of the train or bus, he lifts his hat (as soon as he regains his balance and is able to do so!) and says "Excuse me!"—"I'm sorry!"—or "I beg your pardon!" The condensed versions "Pardon" and "Beg pardon" are not good form and should be avoided. Only the complete sentence ("I beg your pardon") may be used.

When a lady enters the elevator of a hotel, apartment house, or club, a gentleman always takes off his hat and holds it in his hand. But in the elevators of an office building or store this is not necessary, as such elevators are considered as public as the street or the subway. However, even in the elevator of an office building a gentleman generally removes his hat when a lady he knows walks in.

It's more courteous, of course, for a man to step aside and let the ladies in the elevator get off first. But this is not always practical and convenient. If an elevator is very crowded, it's better to step out quickly, in turn, than to get in the way and block those behind in an effort to let the ladies go first.

Usually, however, it's "ladies first" going through doors, down aisles, into cars, planes, or trains, unless it is dark or there is some element of danger or uncertainty. In that case the man goes first to lead the way and assist the lady if necessary.

A man always *precedes* a lady getting out of a car or off a train or bus so that he can then turn and help her get off. He also goes first through a revolving door, as a rule, so that he can push it around for her. But it is also correct to hold the door until she gets in, then push it from behind.

On Offering One's Arm to a Lady

When walking in the street with a lady, a man does not link his arm in hers, nor grasp her firmly by the elbow and shove her along. Correctly they walk side by side, without holding on to each other. But he offers the protection of *his* arm when there is some obvious need for it.

For example, a man offers his arm to a lady when they are crossing a busy or dangerous street, or when there is likelihood of becoming separated in a crowd. He offers his arm when the pavement is uneven, or the road rough and bumpy, and there is a possibility of tripping. In a sudden shower he offers his arm to help her quickly to a place of shelter. If they come to a puddle of water, he crosses first and from the other side offers his hand to help her across. Or he may place his hand under her elbow to help her, if that seems more convenient. It is also correct to support a lady by the elbow in helping her up or down a difficult curb or into a car. But it is never correct to grasp her by the arm for any reason except a sudden emergency, to pull her out of the way of danger.

A gentleman always offers his arm to an elderly lady, an invalid, or anyone who has difficulty walking.

On Giving up One's Seat

It is emphatically not the behavior of a gentleman to make a dash for a seat in a subway or bus when there are women standing. Even if the seat directly in front of him becomes available, he steps aside and lets one of the women passengers take it.

On the other hand, in this day it is no longer expected that a man give up his seat to a young woman in a crowded subway or bus during the rush hours. At other times of the day he gives up his seat or not, as he likes; there's no hard and fast rule about it. But naturally a gentleman *always* offers his seat at once to an elderly woman, or to a woman with a child in her arms.

When a man gives up his seat to a lady, he should do so willingly and with a smile. To give up a seat with resentment is only half a courtesy, likely to make the woman who accepts it feel uncomfortable.

But uncomfortable or not, the lady who accepts a gentleman's seat should be gracious and appreciative about it! It's extremely rude for anyone—man or woman—to accept a courtesy without expressing thanks.

2. INTRODUCTIONS

THE purpose of an introduction is to make strangers known to each other; and modern etiquette requires that this be done easily and graciously, and without too much ceremony.

There is not much to learn, really—as the method of making introductions is much simpler today than it used to be. There are just a few basic rules; but it's important to learn these rules and abide by them, for the ability to meet people easily and well is one of the most useful assets you can have.

How to Introduce

For all ordinary purposes, the simplest and most acceptable form of introduction is the mere pronouncing of the two names: "Mrs. Pratt —Mrs. Simpson!"

For formal introductions, the phrase "may I present" is generally used. "May I introduce" is also correct, but the word "present" is somewhat more ceremonious.

A man is always introduced *to* a woman, and her name is mentioned first. For example, "Mrs. Curtis, may I present Mr. Pratt?" Or less formally, "Mrs. Curtis—Mr. Pratt!" The man's name is spoken first only if the preposition "to" is used: "Mr. Pratt, may I introduce you *to* Mrs. Curtis?"

A younger woman is introduced to an older one, an unmarried woman to a matron: "Mrs. Curtis, may I present Miss Brown?"

The same distinction may be made when introducing two men, the name of the older or more notable person being mentioned first. But this is no longer considered important. The typical introduction today, suitable for all but the most formal occasions, is simply "Mr. Thomas—Mr. Burke!" in no special order and with no particular emphasis on either name.

If you are introducing someone to a very special friend, you might say: "Mary, I want you to meet Mrs. Jones" (or "I'd like you to meet Mrs. Jones"). Then looking at Mrs. Jones and smiling, you tell her Mary's name: "Mrs. Thorpe."

Another form of introduction which is frequently used, and which helps put strangers on an easy and friendly basis, is "Mrs. Curtis, you know Mr. Pratt, don't you?" Or, "Mrs. Curtis, do you know Mr. Pratt?" It is also correct to say, "Mrs. Curtis, have you met Mrs. Smith?" or "Mr. Pratt, you have met Mrs. Curtis, haven't you?" All these are good form. But don't say "do you not" or "have you not" in making introductions, for such elongated phrases sound affected, and all affectations are bad form.

For a more friendly and intimate introduction than any of the above, you might use the phrase *"this is,"* particularly if you are introducing young people to each other. "Mary, this is Bob Jones!" has a certain warmth and enthusiasm that more formal introductions lack.

SOME PHRASES TO AVOID

There are a number of phrases frequently used in introductions which are in poor taste and should be avoided. Chief offender is that awkward phrase: "make you acquainted with." Never be guilty of announcing to someone that you want to make him acquainted with someone else! And avoid that equally offensive form of introduction: "Mr. Peters, shake hands with Mr. Green."

The word "meet," used alone, is not considered good form in making introductions. Don't say: "Mr. Peters, meet Mr. Green." Only the complete phrase is acceptable: "Mr. Peters, I'd like you to meet Mr. Green" or "I want you to meet Mr. Green."

When using just the names of the individuals being introduced, it isn't necessary to repeat the names back and forth, like a refrain: "Mr. Peters—Mr. Green! Mr. Green—Mr. Peters!" It's sufficient to say each name once, provided, of course, it's pronounced clearly and distinctly so that each person gets the other's name at once and without difficulty.

For true courtesy, avoid the use of the phrase "my friend" in making introductions. You can say "my sister" or "my son," if you like, but don't say "my friend." To introduce two persons and single out one of them as a friend is to imply that the other is not.

INTRODUCING RELATIVES

A well-bred woman does not introduce her husband socially as "Mr. Davis." She introduces him to her friends as "Tom" and less informally to acquaintances as "my husband."

A man introduces another man to his wife, and always refers to her as such, not as "Mrs. Davis." For example: "Mr. Thomas, may I present you to my wife?" or, "Mr. Thomas, I'd like to introduce you to my wife."

A husband might say to an old friend: "Ted, I want you to meet my wife." And then to his wife, "Mary, this is Ted Barrett" (or "Mr. Barrett").

The edict against "Mr." and "Mrs." applies to social introductions only. In business introductions, the use of "Mr. Davis" and "Mrs. Davis" is correct and permissible.

It goes without saying, of course, that "meet the wife" is a comic-strip vulgarism that no gentleman ever uses, even in jest.

A mother introducing her daughter to a visitor would say: "Mrs. Kingsley, you know my daughter, don't you?" or "Mrs. Kingsley, this is my daughter Mary." If her daughter is married, she would say: "Mrs. Kingsley, may I present my daughter, Mrs. Fair?"

A man introducing a distinguished visitor at his home to an unmarried daughter would say: "Mr. Creighton—my daughter Joan." Or if she is married—"my daughter, Joan Wright" (or "Mrs. Wright").

Introducing a younger man, the father might say: "Fred, have you met my daughter? This is Fred Evans, Joan." Or more formally, "Joan, I'd like to introduce Mr. Evans. My daughter, Fred."

A daughter introducing a young woman to her mother would say: "Mother, this is Miss Harris" or simply, "Mother, Miss Harris." If it's a young girl she is introducing, she would be more likely than not to use her first name: "Mother, this is Mary Harris."

A young man is introduced the same way: "Mother, may I present Mr. Jones?" or "Mother, this is Mr. Jones." Informally, he might be presented to both parents in this way: "Mother, Dad—this is Alan Jones."

A bride introduces her mother-in-law as "Jim's mother," "my husband's mother," or "my mother-in-law," whichever she prefers. There is no reason for self-consciously avoiding the use of the phrase "mother-in-law," as it can sound either coolly aloof or warmly affectionate, depending on the tone in which it is said. For intimate family introductions, "Mother Grainge" may be used (but never "Mrs.

Grainge"!). One might say, "Mother Grainge, this is my Aunt Edna" or "Aunt Edna, this is Mother Grainge." To an old friend one might say, "Claire, I'd like to introduce you to Jim's mother."

A woman introduces her son's wife formally to friends and acquaintances as "my daughter-in-law" or "my son's wife." To relatives and intimate friends, she would be more likely to say "Bob's wife." To an old friend she might say informally: "This is Julia, Bob's wife"— or even more affectionately, "This is Bob's wife—my new daughter!"

When introducing other relatives-in-law, always try to be as specific as you can. Instead of a vague, "This is my sister-in-law," explain that "this is my husband's sister" or "this is my brother Paul's wife."

GROUP INTRODUCTIONS

It is no longer the custom, at large parties, to take each newly arrived guest on a grand tour of the room and introduce him to every other guest. That kindly intentioned procedure usually ends up with the hostess rushing off to greet new arrivals while the uncertain guest, left with no group in particular but with only a blur of strange names and faces, must fend for himself.

A far better plan, at large parties, is to introduce a stranger to one small group of guests and leave him or her with them. It is then up to the newcomer either to remain with the group and join in the conversation, or to wander off and introduce himself to others.

At any large function where there are many guests, individual introductions are not considered necessary and are rarely made. It is assumed that those who meet under a friend's roof and share the same hospitality are automatically "introduced"; and they are expected to talk to those near them whether they know their names or not.

At a *small* luncheon or party, however, a stranger is usually introduced to everyone in turn. Unless the occasion is a very formal one, the introductions need not be made individually. One person may be introduced to a group in this way: "Mrs. Thompson—Mrs. Reade, Miss Sherill, Mr. King, Mr. Brent." If the group is a large one of six or more persons, it's a good idea to pronounce the newcomer's name again at the end as someone in the group may have missed it.

Today it's the genial, informal custom of young people to introduce all friends by their first names. Arriving at a party with a friend who is a stranger to the others, a girl might say: "Hello, everybody—this is Jane!" Introductions among younger groups are almost always without title—no "Misters," no "Misses." But even with all this informality, one courtesy must be observed: a young man is always introduced *to* a girl and not the other way around. "Jane, this is Bob Fellows." Or to a group: "Jane—Ruth Harrow, Bob Fellows, Jim Brown." The chances are they will start calling her "Jane" right away to show she is accepted as a member of the group. But as a stranger and a newcomer among them, she must wait until they start calling her by her first name, before she starts calling them by theirs.

INTRODUCTIONS TO DISTINGUISHED PEOPLE

Though you may rarely have occasion to introduce persons of high rank or title, you naturally want to know how to do so without doubt or confusion when that rare occasion does arrive.

The correct introduction of either a man or woman to the President of the United States is: "Mr. President, I have the honor to present Mr. [Mrs.] Cushing." A man nods, a woman bows when presented to the President, but neither offers his hand unless the President himself does so.

Introductions to a reigning sovereign require much formality beforehand, lists being submitted and names "accepted" before any actual presentation takes place. But the presentation itself is quite simple. Nothing is said to the king or queen except the person's name: "Mr. Franklin!" or "Mrs. Miller!" Mr. Franklin bows or bends his knee, whatever the court custom is. Mrs. Miller bows deeply; and if the king offers to shake hands, she bows again as she gives her hand to him.

A woman is always presented to a member of a reigning family: "Your Royal Highness, may I present Mrs. Kent?" A foreign ambassador, however, is always presented to a woman: "Mrs. Kent, may I present His Excellency, the British Ambassador?"

To a cardinal, the proper introduction is: "Your Eminence, may I present Mrs. Clark?" To an archbishop: "Your Grace, may I present Mrs. Clark?" But a priest, as a rule, is presented to a woman: "Mrs. French, may I present Father Kelly?" (though it is not incorrect the other way around.)

A duke is not addressed socially as "His Grace," nor a lord as "his lordship." A hostess introducing such persons of title would say: "Mrs. Brent, may I present the Duke of Kenmore?" or "Lord Fenton, may I present Mr. Smith?"

A doctor, dentist, judge, or bishop is addressed and introduced by his title. So are army and navy officers.

A senator is always addressed and introduced as "Senator Judd"— even when he is no longer in office. But a former President of the

United States is addressed simply as "Mister" (*never* as Ex-President!)

When in doubt, always remember that *"may I present"* is the most formal and ceremonious introduction possible, that the name of the more notable person is spoken first, and that a man is always presented *to* a woman unless he is a dignitary of the church, a royal personage, or President of the United States.

WHEN TO INTRODUCE

The question of whether or not to introduce people to each other can sometimes be awkward and puzzling. In general, it is best not to introduce strangers unless you are reasonably sure they would like to meet each other, or unless the occasion and circumstances require an introduction.

If you are walking with friends in the street, or are in the lobby of a theater or some other public place, it is not necessary to introduce an acquaintance who happens to pass by and greet you. If the newcomer stops for a moment to chat, you may introduce him or not, as you like—depending on whether it's convenient to do so and likely to be agreeable to all concerned. But there are other times when you have no such choice or leeway, when courtesy demands that an introduction be made.

Guests at a small luncheon, dinner, or card party in your home should, of course, always be introduced to each other. It's one of the first duties of a gracious hostess to make each newcomer feel at once a welcome and accepted part of the company and the conversation.

Although it is not necessary to introduce every guest at a large party or dance, the hostess should make it a point to introduce those who are to sit together in a small group—such as those who are to be at the same luncheon or supper table, or those who are to play bridge or some other game at the same table. No one should ever be left to wander self-consciously at the fringe of a party, looking for a familiar face.

When a dinner or party is given in honor of someone like a debutante or a visiting celebrity, everyone who attends must be presented to the guest of honor. The person who arrives late at such a function, after the receiving line has ended, should seek out the guest of honor and present himself. It is considered a great rudeness to go to a dinner or party in honor of someone and fail to "meet" that person.

At a large formal dinner, it is the duty of the host to see that every gentleman either knows the lady who is to be his dinner partner, or is presented to her. If possible, he should also be presented to the lady who is to sit at his left. If this latter introduction is overlooked, strangers seated beside each other at the table may introduce themselves. It's awkward and rude to sit beside someone all through a dinner and not talk. In fact, although many of the rules of etiquette today are conveniently elastic, adjusting themselves to changing conditions and circumstances, this one rule remains firm and unbreakable: *All persons who find themselves seated together at table must talk, out of courtesy to each other and to their hostess.*

Occasionally an invitation to a dance or reception is requested for a visiting friend or relative. On arrival, the guest should go at once to the hostess and present the stranger for whom the invitation was requested. He says, "Mrs. Blank, this is Mr. Roberts whom you said I might bring." The hostess should be especially cordial to such a guest, to make him feel welcome and at ease. She should offer her hand, smile and say: "How do you do, Mr. Roberts! I'm so glad you came!" (or "I'm delighted to see you").

If you are dining with friends in a restaurant and an acquaintance stops at the table for a moment to say "Hello," it is not necessary to introduce him to the others. But if he stays longer than a moment, if he stays to chat with you for a little while, introductions are in order.

If you are in a box at the theater or opera and a friend comes over during intermission to exchange greetings, it is courteous to introduce him to the others in your party.

The friend you take to your club need not be introduced to anyone (except special friends you may meet there) unless you are proposing him for membership. In that case, he should be introduced to the chairman and to the members of the nominating committee.

The newcomer at a place of business should be introduced as soon as possible to all who will be his immediate associates.

When Not to Introduce

A good rule is never to introduce people in public places if it disturbs or inconveniences others to do so.

If you are in the theater with friends and you see other friends a few aisles ahead, just greet them and let it go at that. On a busy street, at a crowded airport, or in a railway station, don't stop to introduce friends if it means getting in the way of others. The great common denominator of all good manners is simply this: *consider others, and avoid whatever is unfair, unpleasant, or unkind.*

Chance meetings on the street do not call for an introduction, unless the newcomer is invited to join the others and decides to walk on with them. When two people are walking together and they meet a third who knows one of them, the one who is not acquainted with the third person does not wait for an introduction but slowly walks on. A friend met by chance this way in the street or in a public place should not join a group unless specifically asked to do so, but if he or she is invited, the introduction is then made.

One should be careful about making introductions on shipboard, at resorts, or wherever close daily proximity makes it difficult to avoid new and perhaps uncongenial acquaintances. It's best not to introduce strangers in public places unless you feel sure they will enjoy knowing each other. This applies especially to people of note or prominence who certainly will not thank you for introducing strangers they don't care to know, and who turn out to be too presuming in their demands upon their time.

It is not good form to interrupt people for the purpose of making an introduction. A hostess should not interrupt an animated conversation between two guests to introduce a third one. Nor should she bustle about introducing latecomers while a speaker, singer, or pianist is entertaining the company. She should wait until she can introduce them without the rudeness of interruption to others.

Strangers who meet briefly in the sick room or hospital room of a friend are not, as a rule, introduced. If they remain together in the room any length of time (which they should not!) they may casually introduce themselves. Or if they leave together, a relative or mutual friend may introduce them outside the door.

Introducing Oneself

There are a certain few occasions when it is proper to introduce yourself.

At a large luncheon or dinner, for example, you may find yourself seated next to a stranger. It is not only proper but expected that you introduce yourself. There is no hard and fast rule about who speaks first. The lady might turn to the gentleman beside her, smile, and say: "I am Mrs. John Kendricks." Or the gentleman might glance at her place card and say: "How do you do, Mrs. Kendricks? I am James Smith."

At a wedding, tea, reception, garden party, or any large social function, you talk to those near you whether you know them or not. But you do not introduce yourself unless the circumstances seem to call for it. If you recognize the bride's favorite aunt from photographs you have seen, you might say to her: "You're Betty's Aunt Edna, aren't you? I'm Claire Hunt. I was Betty's roommate at school." Or if you overhear the young man seated near you addressed as "Dr. James," you might say: "Aren't you the Dr. James who interned with Ted Bailey at St. Lukes? I'm his brother, Arthur Bailey."

There's never any objection to introducing yourself, provided there's a good reason for it, and provided, of course, you are not presuming on too meager a basis for acquaintance. If you happen to see someone you once knew, but who apparently doesn't recognize you (perhaps because you have grown up since he saw you last!) it's permissible to say: "Aren't you Peter Rankin?" I'm Jane Marlowe . . . you used to go to school with my brother Bob." Or if it's a friend of your mother's: "Mrs. Benton? I'm Alice Faire, Mrs. Talbot Faire's daughter. I believe you're a friend of my mother's." To which Mrs. Benton is likely to reply: "Indeed I am! I'm so glad you spoke to me."

THE INDIRECT INTRODUCTION

Whenever it is desirable or convenient to include someone in your conversation without making an introduction, you can use the so-called *indirect* method.

For example, Dr. Brown is giving an informal chat on a subject in which everyone is interested. Mr. Smith, a stranger to Dr. Brown, arrives. The hostess does not interrupt to make an introduction but says: "Do go on, Dr. Brown! I'm sure Mr. Smith will enjoy hearing the rest of your talk." The newcomer is thus drawn into the group without interruption to the others. Later on the hostess can make a more formal introduction, if she likes, though that isn't necessary.

Or suppose you are talking with a decorator about doing over your living room, and a friend comes to call. You greet your friend, then include her at once by saying: "Mr. Thorpe suggests that I use scenic paper on one wall and paint the others a solid color. What do you think, Martha?"

Servants are rarely introduced, unless they have been with the family for a long time and are fondly regarded. However, maids, butlers, chauffeurs can be indirectly introduced to guests of a household merely by mention of name. To a chauffeur: "Peters, take Mr. and Mrs. Rogers to the railroad station. They are making the ten o'clock train." Or when a house guest arrives: "Berta, here are Mrs. Thompson's keys. I'd like you to unpack her bags and help make her comfortable."

ACKNOWLEDGING INTRODUCTIONS

In acknowledging an introduction, you say whatever is appropriate to the circumstances and to the nature of the introduction. If it's a simple exchange of names, you say a simple: "How do you do?" But if the introducer says: "Mary, you remember Bill Hutchins, don't you? Well, this is his brother Mark"—you make a more personal and friendly reply: "Of course I remember Bill Hutchins and I'm delighted to meet his brother!"

For all formal occasions—and, in fact, whenever you don't know what else to say—"How do you do?" is correct and acceptable. However, it's more complimentary to add the person's name, so make it a point to *listen carefully* when you are introduced and repeat the name in your acknowledgment: "How do you do, Mrs. Barton?" This is not only more flattering to a stranger, but pronouncing the name immediately after hearing it helps you to remember it.

For a more friendly and informal response to an introduction, you might say: "I'm delighted to know you." Or if it's someone you've heard a great deal about and wanted to meet: "I'm so glad to meet you!" Often the acknowledgment can be made the opening wedge to conversation: "I've heard so much about you, Mrs. Carter!" Or, "My brother has so often talked of you!"

But never say "Pleased to meet you"—one phrase which is strictly tabu. Avoid also the use of "Charmed," "It's a pleasure" and "Pleased to make your acquaintance."

WHEN TO RISE

A hostess always rises to greet her guests and introduce newcomers.

A gentleman should rise when introduced to anyone, man or woman. He remains standing until all the ladies, including the hostess, are seated.

A lady remains seated, rising only when introduced to an elderly or distinguished man, a guest of honor, or an elderly woman. However a group of young ladies sitting together should not rise *en masse* when introduced to an older woman; this merely causes confusion and (what is worse!) draws attention to the newcomer's advanced years.

SHAKING HANDS

Gentlemen always shake hands when they are introduced to each other, crossing the room if necessary, to do so.

Women customarily do not shake hands when introduced, though there's no reason why they shouldn't. Shaking hands is a genial and friendly custom, not to be discouraged.

It is a woman's privilege to offer her hand or not to a gentleman when they are introduced. She of course gives a man her hand at once if he offers his. Custom or not, no kindly and well-intentioned gesture of friendliness should be rebuffed.

The way to shake hands is with a quick, firm clasp—neither pumping furiously up and down nor letting your hand lie limp as a lump of clay in the hand of the other. Let it be a sincere and confident handclasp, as though you really mean it! Look at the person directly, and smile.

A man should remove his glove before shaking hands with a lady, if he can quickly and conveniently do so. But a lady does not take off her gloves to shake hands. The phrase "Excuse my glove" is obsolete and should be avoided.

IF THE NAME IS NOT HEARD

Where a person's name is concerned, it's always better to ask and be correct than to guess and be corrected. People are proud and possessive about their names and don't like to hear them mispronounced.

So if the name is a difficult one, or if the hostess didn't pronounce it clearly in the introduction, ask to have it repeated. You might say: "I'm sorry, but I didn't hear the name distinctly. Did you say Mrs. 'Counterway'?" On being informed that the name is "Countway," you turn to the lady with a smile and say: "How do you do, Mrs. Countway?"

AVOIDING THAT AWKWARD PAUSE

Sometimes there is an awkward pause between strangers who have just been introduced, who know nothing about each other and therefore find it difficult to get started on a friendly, conversational basis. But there needn't be, if one or the other is a good trouper and gets the show started. The important thing is not to wait self-consciously for the other person to take the lead. Of course if he does, that's fine; you can take it from there. But if he doesn't, make some remark that graciously opens the way to easy conversation between you. It needn't be anything clever or important. Any simple casual remark will do for your opening gambit—don't scorn even the weather! Just start the talk somewhere, anywhere, and let it flow where it will. If you concentrate on being friendly and attentive, there'll be no awkward pause.

A really deft hostess always tries to give some helpful information to people she is introducing, to smooth the way to conversation between them. She might say: "Mr. Rogers, I'd like to introduce Mr. Harding. You and he have the same hobby—tropical fish!" Or, "Mrs. Martin, this is Miss Pierce who is just as enthusiastic about gardening as you are!" When cues like these are given, they should naturally be used to "break the ice" and make the plunge into small talk.

Taking Leave of a New Acquaintance

When you take leave of someone you have met for the first time— man or woman—you either shake hands or not (as you choose), and say "Good-by" or "Good-night." If you want to be more cordial, you add some such phrase as: "I'm glad to have met you," "I enjoyed our talk very much," or "I hope we shall see each other soon again." To someone who has been especially interesting, or who is a notable or outstanding personality, you might say: "It's been a great pleasure to meet you!" Or, if it's true, "This has been a thrilling experience!"

In answer to any such cordial or complimentary remark, a simple "Thank you" is all that's ever necessary. But if you prefer, you can reply more effusively with: "It's been a pleasure meeting you, Mrs. Travers!" or "I've enjoyed telling you about it, Mr. Evans."

A gentleman generally waits for a lady to offer her hand first, when they part after an introduction. And he leaves it up to *her* to say she is glad to have met *him*, rather than the other way around. There's no longer any fixed rule about it, as people are now inclined to be informal and spontaneous about such things. But it's always more gracious to let the lady (or the older or more distinguished of the two men or two women) take the lead in shaking hands and making some pleasant remark about the meeting.

When taking leave of a large group of strangers to whom you have been introduced, it isn't necessary to bid each one "good-by" individually. You simply nod to all who happen to be looking your way, and let your cordial "good-by" take in everyone.

On Meeting Again

It was once the privilege of the lady, or of the older or more distinguished person, to accept or reject a new acquaintance by giving the first sign of recognition at the next meeting. But this rude custom is no longer looked upon with favor. Good manners today do not permit the deliberate "cutting" or snubbing of anyone, man or woman, except for the most grave or serious cause.

There are always some people you like more than others. But whether you like them or not, all new acquaintances *must be greeted* the next time you meet them. The greeting can be as reserved or as enthusiastic as you like. But to ignore a friendly smile or nod of recognition, to stare blankly and pretend you never saw the person before, is a great breach of civility—crude and unkind.

Of course you may not remember the person's name. That can be rather awkward, especially if he says: "You don't remember me, do you?" You could be truthful about it and say, "No, I don't," but that would sound abrupt and unflattering. You could say, "I remember your face, but what's your name?" but people very much *dislike* being asked point-blank what their names are. The most courteous procedure is to say, "Of course I remember you—how nice to see you again!" and hope you'll discover his name during the conversation, or get it later from a third person.

If it's the other way around—if you meet someone who has forgotten your name—don't act aggrieved or offended about it. Give the embarrassed person a bit of help. Just say: "I'm Martha Westley. I met you at the Barton's last summer." To which a suitable reply would be: "Of course! How do you do, Miss Westley? I'm delighted to see you again."

Sometimes a new acquaintance, meeting you again after the initial introduction, either mistakes or mispronounces your name. There is no objection to correcting him. ("My name is Grayson, not Graham.") But say it *courteously*—and with a smile.

If you are introduced to someone you have already met, don't hesitate to recall the previous introduction (unless, of course, there's some reason why that would embarrass your hostess). You might say, "I had the pleasure of meeting Mr. Lewis last week," or more directly, to Mr. Lewis himself, "I believe we've met before—at the Holbrook's." Mr. Lewis shakes hands and makes some such courteous response as: "How do you do, Mr. Brown—I'm glad to see you again!"

Introduction by Letter

If you have a friend who is going to some distant city, or to any place where you have other friends, and if you believe it would be mutually pleasant and agreeable for these people to meet, you may offer to write a letter of introduction. It is not considered good form to request such a letter, even from an intimate friend. But you should offer to write it if you feel that the persons involved would enjoy meeting and knowing each other.

Just bear in mind that an introduction by letter imposes obligations far more binding than any spoken introduction. It's a demand upon a distant friend's courtesy, hospitality, and time. Therefore never write a letter of introduction for someone you know only casually—someone who may turn out to be an insufferable nuisance or a bore.

The letter itself should be brief and to the point, giving the name of the person being introduced, the reason for the introduction, and whatever other information may be required. But there should be nothing of an intimate or personal nature in a letter given one friend to be presented to another. The letter is usually written in the presence of the person to be introduced, and is always handed to him unsealed. However, a second and private letter may be written and sent by mail, giving more detailed information about the person who is on the way with the letter of introduction. Following are examples of these two types of letters:

To Be Presented in Person

Dear Helen:

This letter will introduce James Preston, a great friend of ours, who is going to be in Chicago the week of April tenth. I want very much to have you meet him, as you are both interested in the same thing: child welfare.

I have told Mr. Preston about the wonderful work you are doing among the underprivileged children of Chicago, and he is eager to talk with you about it.

I'm sure you'll enjoy meeting him, and I'm equally sure he'll be delighted and charmed to meet you.

Affectionately,
Edith

To Be Sent by Mail

Dear Helen:

You will receive a call, sometime in the next day or two, from a Mr. James Preston. Mark and I have known him for many years and are very fond of him. He expects to be in Chicago for the week of April tenth and I have asked him to get in touch with you. He has a letter of introduction.

Mr. Preston is a lawyer by profession; but he is especially interested in juvenile delinquency, and right now is planning a book about delinquent parents. He was quite excited when I told him about the work you are doing, and he said he'd like very much to talk with you about it while he's in Chicago and has the opportunity.

So do see him if you can, Helen. I'm sure you and Fred will enjoy meeting him—he's interesting and very likable.

When are you two coming to New York again? It seems ages since we saw you!

Affectionately,
Edith

A Man's Introduction by Card

A man introducing one man to another often uses his card instead of writing a letter. He simply inscribes it as follows, and gives it to the person to be introduced:

Introducing Dr. Paul Gibson

Mr. Jayson Lothrop Gordon

A card of introduction calls for a private letter by mail, preparing the other person for the visit and explaining the reason for the introduction.

Presenting a Letter of Introduction

When a friend writes a letter of introduction the correct procedure is to thank him—and seal the letter at once, in his presence. It is not good form to take the letter out of its envelope and read it.

A man who has a letter of introduction to a lady goes to her house as soon as he arrives in her city. He leaves the letter with his card at her door, without asking to see her. If she comes to the door herself, as is frequently the case, he introduces himself and gives her the letter, leaving as soon as he graciously can. This initial visit is solely for the purpose of presenting the letter and introducing himself; it's up to the lady to make any subsequent arrangements.

If the letter is to a man, it is mailed to his house, either with a card or with a brief note. This is better than presenting it in person and standing by while he reads it. Of course if it's a business letter, one goes to the man's office and sends in the letter with his card. Then he waits in the reception room until he is admitted or is told when to call.

A woman with a letter of introduction to another woman, either calls at her home and leaves the letter with her card or mails it to her. But if the letter is to a man, she has no choice; she *must* mail it to him as it would be improper to call and present it in person. This refers to a letter of social introduction only; a business letter may be presented in person at the man's office.

ACKNOWLEDGING A LETTER OF INTRODUCTION

A written introduction imposes certain definite obligations on the person who receives it. That's why a letter of introduction should be written only for those you feel sure will enjoy each other's company.

A woman who receives a letter of introduction from a man should at once invite him to tea or dinner, or for an evening of bridge.

A woman who receives a letter of introduction from another woman, should either call formally at her home and leave a card or telephone informally and acknowledge the letter. She is expected to show the stranger whatever courtesy she can, inviting her at least once to her home for luncheon, tea, or dinner.

A man who receives a letter introducing another man calls him on the telephone and asks how he can be of service. He usually invites him to his house for dinner, or to his club or to a hotel for lunch.

A man who receives a letter of introduction from a woman, calls on her at once and invites her to luncheon or tea. He does whatever he can to make her visit to his city interesting and pleasant, perhaps offering to show her the places of interest or inviting her to the theater.

The obligations of a written introduction are such that only illness, or being out of town, can excuse the person who receives the letter from showing kindness and hospitality to the visiting stranger. If for these reasons, or any other, a letter of introduction cannot be honored, courteous notes of explanation should be written to the stranger and to the mutual friend.

If for some reason a letter of introduction is not presented, an explanation is certainly due the person who was generous enough to write it.

AN INDIRECT LETTER OF INTRODUCTION

A visitor in a strange city is soon gone again, and the obligation quickly ended. But when people come to live permanently in a new neighborhood, letters of introduction may involve those who receive them in burdensome and perhaps unwelcome responsibilities. Under such circumstances, an *indirect* letter of introduction is better than a direct one. It is sent by mail, without the knowledge of the person it introduces and therefore imposes no obligation on anyone.

If you write to a distant friend and say, "My former neighbors, the Nortons, are going to live in your city and I think you'd enjoy knowing them," it's up to the distant friend to decide whether or not she wants to know them. She takes the initiative, saving the newcomer this embarrassment. And inasmuch as the letter was not presented personally, she is free to make advances or not, as she likes. Following is an example of this type of letter, giving the strangers an opportunity to meet and become acquainted, but imposing no obligation:

Dear Claire:

I have just learned that my very good friends and former neighbors, Bill and Mary Norton, are now living in Philadelphia. They're at 148 Parma Road, practically next door to you!

The Nortons are charming people, and I feel sure you and Fred would enjoy knowing them. I told them all about you; so if you call them, they'll recognize the name right away and know who you are.

I hope you *will* call them, Claire. They're really wonderful people to know, and lots of fun to be with. They like bridge and play it well; and Mary's hobby is the same as yours—gardening.

Bob sends his best to you and Fred, and joins me in hoping you'll meet the Nortons and enjoy them as much as we always did when they lived here.

Affectionately,
Aileen

3. THE ETIQUETTE OF VISITING

THE days of formal "duty" calls, and of visiting cards left decorously on the entrance table, have vanished almost completely from our busy new way of life—along with many another quaint but archaic custom of the horse-and-buggy era. Visits of empty form, with elaborate and ceremonious card-leaving, are now practically obsolete, except in official and diplomatic Washington.

But there are still times when paying a visit is a social obligation, and should be regarded as such. For example, you are expected to call on a bride whose wedding you attended, soon after she has returned from the honeymoon and is settled in her new home. You are expected to call at once when there has been a death in the family of a friend, leaving your card if you are unable to see any member of the immediate family. You are expected to call on neighbors who have returned from a long absence, on a friend who is convalescing, on the mother of a new baby.

If you live in a small community, you are expected to make the first call on a new neighbor, introducing yourself and extending a friendly welcome.

If you are a young man who has been entertained several times during the season, you are expected to make a formal call on your hostess, not necessarily asking to see her, but leaving your card with flowers, books, or some other evidence of thoughtful appreciation.

If you are a close relative of a young man who has just announced his engagement, you are expected to go as soon as possible to see his fiancée. If she is out when you call, you leave your card; and soon afterward you invite her and her mother to your house.

Once it was the custom for well-bred people to call and leave cards after being entertained—especially after lunching or dining for the first time in the home of a new acquaintance. But people are much more casual about such things nowadays. Few in private life now acknowledge hospitality by formal visiting and card-leaving. The modern way is to write a note of thanks instead—or to follow up in a short time with a return of hospitality.

The Hours for Formal Visiting

The proper time for paying formal visits is between three and five o'clock in the afternoon. If the lady of the house has a regular "at home" day, those are the hours she sets aside for receiving her guests and serving tea. If there is no regular "at home" day, three to five in the afternoon is still the best time for making social calls of obligation.

Condolence calls should be made at a time most likely to be convenient to the bereaved persons of the household—usually around four o'clock in the afternoon, or eight o'clock in the evening. Sick calls should be made in the early afternoon or evening if the patient is at home, at the regular visiting hours if he is in a hospital.

A man can escape the obligation of formal visits during the day by having his wife make them for him. But a call of inquiry upon a friend who is ill, or a call of condolence on a friend who has had a death in the family, should be made in person. Such calls can be made on Sunday afternoons, or on any convenient evening during the week between eight and nine o'clock.

Businesswomen may also make their calls in the evening. However in these days, when most people must carefully plan and budget their time to take care of all their many interests and activities, it's courteous to telephone before making an evening visit. The hostess may have other plans in progress, and would be inconvenienced even by a ten-minute visit.[1]

FORMAL VISITS SHOULD BE BRIEF

Formal visits, whatever their nature or purpose, should be brief. They should rarely last more than fifteen minutes—twenty minutes at the most. Under certain circumstances (as when the person you have come to see is very ill) the visit should last no more than four to five minutes.

On the hostess' day at home, guests remain longer than ordinarily, as tea or coffee is generally served. But this is more in the nature of a friendly visit than a formal call.

A good rule to remember when making formal calls is never to outstay guests who arrive after you. You should try to leave before them; but if not, at least get up to leave when they do. On the other hand, don't wait for guests who were there when you arrived to leave before you get up to go. They may be intimate friends, making an informal visit.

It's bad manners to arrive in a flurry, announce you can stay only a minute or so, and then sit tensely on the edge of your chair as though dashing off again were the only thing on your mind. Whether you stay two minutes or twenty, sit back and relax—join in the conversation and enjoy the visit. Don't fidget. Don't chatter nervously. Don't keep looking at your watch and making remarks about leaving. When you think it's time to go, get up, say "good-by," and leave at once. Don't linger on in the doorway making last-minute conversation—a trait of the socially inexperienced. Above all, don't make parting apologies like, "I hope I haven't stayed too long" or "I hope I haven't bored you with my chatter." Such remarks merely betray self-consciousness and a lack of poise.

[1]For informal "dropping in" see page 36.

ARRIVING TO MAKE A FORMAL VISIT

Nowadays when so many people live in apartments, without maids or butlers, it's more likely than not for the hostess herself to open the door. If she recognizes the visitor, she says "How do you do, Mrs. Peters" or "Hello, Jean," as the case may be. They usually shake hands; then the hostess invites her into the house, leading the way into the living room and introducing her to any strangers who may be there.

If the hostess does not recognize her visitor, which is sometimes the case, it's up to the latter to introduce herself. She says, "How do you do, Mrs. Knight. I'm Betty Grayson—Mrs. Harold Grayson's niece." She does *not* hold out a visiting card, like a card of admission, and stand by while the hostess reads it. That is very bad form. Visiting cards, when they are used at all, are placed on a tray and carried by a maid or butler to the lady of the house to announce the visitor; or they are left on a tray in the entrance hall as evidence that one has been there to pay a call of obligation. They are never handed personally to the hostess.

Remember, we are now discussing *formal visits*—the calls of social obligation—not the gaily casual visits of old friends. People who know each other well do not make ceremonious calls on each other. They are in and out of each other's houses frequently and informally, without regard for whose "turn" it may be or what social obligation must be met.

If the lady of the house is upstairs when you come to pay a visit, the servant or whoever opens the door for you leads the way into the foyer or reception room and asks you to have a seat while she announces you. If you happen to be one of those few very punctilious individuals who still use visiting cards, you give one to the maid to take to her mistress. Otherwise you just tell her your name, take a seat . . . and remain seated until the hostess comes into the room. Then you rise at once to greet her, taking her hand if it is offered, and saying simply, "How do you do?" or "Good afternoon." Effusive greetings are not in good taste when one comes to make a formal call.

Ladies do not remove their coats and hats for a brief formal visit. If it's the hostess' day at home and tea is served, they remove their coats but not their hats. As a rule, ladies remove their hats only when visiting friends informally.

A gentleman, however, removes all his outer accoutrements in the entrance hall or foyer—unless of course there's some question about whether or not he can be received. For example, if it's a call of condolence, or a call of inquiry on someone who is ill or has had an accident, the gentleman visitor waits in the foyer or reception room with his hat in his hand, but without taking off his coat or gloves. When the maid, or whoever opened the door, returns and says, "Come this way, please," or announces that the lady of the house or some other member of the family will be down in a moment, he takes off his coat and gives them to her with his hat and gloves. But if the maid says: "Mrs. Carter isn't well enough to see anyone," he leaves a message for her (either written on his card, or to be delivered verbally) and departs at once.

"Not at Home"

No slight is intended when the person who opens the front door to a visitor lets it be known at once that "Mrs. Brown is not at home." This is not a discourtesy, but a polite phrase of convenience. It doesn't necessarily mean that Mrs. Brown is out; it means that she is ill, indisposed, very busy, or for some other equally good reason not at home to visitors at that particular time. No offence is meant, and none should be taken.

But if the visitor is admitted, and the person who opened the door says, "I'll see if Mrs. Brown is home"—that's a different story! To return and say, "Mrs. Brown is out" is like saying, "Well, I took your card [or your name] to Mrs. Brown and she doesn't want to see you." That cannot fail to offend even the most thick-skinned visitor.

The only way to avoid such rebuffs to friendly social callers—and at the same time preserve privacy when it's important to do so—is to leave exact instructions with whoever attends the front door. That person should know before opening the door whether the lady of the house is at home to visitors or not. And if not, she should say so promptly, right at the door. Once a visitor has been admitted, and his name or card taken upstairs, it's unnecessarily rude and unkind not to receive him.

Calling on a New Neighbor

That fine old American custom of calling on a newcomer in the neighborhood has vanished completely from busy city life—where apartment dwellers often don't even know the people who live right next door! But in many small towns and intimate closely knit communities, the custom still lingers on.

So if you live in a small community and you want to visit a new neighbor, by all means do so! It's a kindly and gracious gesture. But be sure to wait until the stranger has had a chance to get settled in her new surroundings. Don't rush over the first week or so when your visit—however well-intentioned and however gratifying to the newcomer—may be inconvenient and even embarrassing.

When you ring a new neighbor's bell and she opens the door—or you are admitted to her presence by a servant—you introduce yourself at once. You say, "How do you do, I'm Mrs. Thompson—I live in the red brick house on the corner." She will be very cordial of course, for it's pleasant to be welcomed by old residents when one is new and strange in a community. She will probably say, "How do you do, Mrs. Thompson. It was sweet of you to come!" Or "Good afternoon, Mrs. Thompson. How nice of you to visit me!"

But however cordial she may be, don't stay long this first time you visit her. Just sit and talk for ten or fifteen minutes, telling her whatever you think may be of particular interest to her as a newcomer— then get up to go. In leaving, you may want to tell her how much you enjoyed meeting her (unless she is considerably older than you are, in which case it's more courteous to let her say she was glad to meet you). Or you may want to wish her happiness in her new home, among her new neighbors. But don't get "chummy" . . . and don't stay for tea. Calling on a new neighbor is good form only if the visit is brief, formal, and courteously reserved.

The stranger herself does not call on her new neighbors but waits for them to make the first call on her. She is cordial and friendly to such visitors, but not excessively so. She keeps the conversation impersonal, doesn't ask prying questions about people in the community—some of whom may be her visitor's intimate friends. She doesn't offer refreshments the first time a neighbor calls; nor does she urge her to stay when she gets up to leave. But she thanks her for coming; and if the visitor says, "Now do come and see me soon!" she graciously replies, "Thank you! I'll be glad to."

The newcomer who receives a visit from a neighbor should return the courtesy promptly—either by making a brief call of the same kind, or by an invitation to luncheon, tea, or bridge. After that it's up to the ladies themselves whether they continue the social relationship. But the first visit must be returned.

VISITING A BRIDE

By courtesy and long tradition, a bride and groom are entitled to the first visit from relatives and friends after their return from the honeymoon. Everyone invited to the wedding is expected to call as soon as the young couple is at home and receiving visitors.

A customary procedure is for the bride and groom to issue "at home" cards—either enclosing them with the wedding announcements, or mailing them separately after the return from the honeymoon. These are small cards (about the size of a visiting card) giving the address of the bride and groom, and specifying the date after which they will be at home and ready to receive relatives and friends.[2]

When a man marries a girl from a distant place—especially another country—courtesy requires that all his relatives and friends go to see her as soon as she is settled and "at home." She is rightfully entitled to a first visit from all of them; but it is a thoughtful and kindly gesture on her part to visit elderly or infirm members of the family instead of waiting for them to come to her. If she likes, she can return the visits of her new relatives and friends by inviting them all to a dinner or party—instead of visiting each one in turn. Hospitality serves the same friendly purpose as a return visit, and cancels the need for it.

CALL OF CONGRATULATION ON A NEW MOTHER

The only time you can really be said to enjoy a visit to a hospital is when you go to congratulate a happy new mother on the birth of a child. But if you want the mother to enjoy the visit, too—don't go too soon! Only members of the immediate family should go to the hospital on the first and second days. It's time enough for others to go on the third day, or later, when the mother has regained some of her strength and is ready and eager to "hold court" for well-wishing relatives and friends.

When you visit a new mother in the hospital, observe the rules. Find out what the visiting hours are, and come at those hours only. It's inconsiderate—and therefore bad manners—to arrive at a hospital any old time and expect to be admitted.

If there are three visitors at the bedside, wait outside until at least one of them leaves. More than three visitors at a time is contrary to the regulations of most hospitals as it's tiring to the convalescent mother.

Don't stay too long. A brief visit is kinder and more kindly remembered. Stay only fifteen or twenty minutes at most, unless you are a close relative like a mother or sister.

It's customary to take a gift for the baby when you make your call

[2]For examples of "at home" cards, see pages 48 and 49.

of congratulations. But do not take gifts of food or candy for the mother. They may cause a digestive upset which is particularly bad if she is nursing her baby.

Nowadays most hospitals have glass-enclosed nurseries for displaying infants to their proud papas and grandparents. Other visitors should not ask to see the baby, but should be satisfied with the mother's glowing description of her offspring. The time to inspect the baby is not when you call to congratulate the mother, but a week or two after her return from the hospital when she and the baby both are comfortably "at home" to interested visitors.

Don't go to see a new mother when you are ill, though it may only be a slight cold. Write a note, send flowers or a gift—but keep away! People in a weakened physical condition are susceptible to germs; and your visit may endanger not only the mother but other patients in the hospital as well.

Don't take children under twelve to the hospital with you, unless you leave them outside or in the reception room. Small children are not allowed to visit patients in hospitals.

If you are visiting a new mother at home, try to be as careful and considerate as you would have to be in a hospital. Don't come at an inconvenient hour of the day when the mother is likely to be busy, or tired, or having luncheon or dinner. Plan the visit for her convenience as well as your own. And make it brief!

Visiting the Sick or Injured

From the standpoint of the convalescent, there are just two types of visitors: those who are welcome, and those who most emphatically are not.

The welcome visitor is thoughtful and considerate, comes at a reasonable time and doesn't stay too long, is tactful and encouraging, interested but not curious, sympathetic but not overly so—a restful person to have near when one is ill and perhaps in pain.

But the unwelcome visitor is just the opposite—breezing in with a fixed smile and a flurry of questions, eager for intimate details of the illness or accident, and curious about every other patient on the floor. The unwelcome visitor is nosy, noisy, and tiresome; he stays too long and leaves the patient exhausted.

But even with the best intentions in the world, friends sometimes cause distress to a patient without meaning to. Here are some things to avoid when you visit a sick friend:

Don't stand at the foot of the bed, leaning on it and perhaps giving it little shakes or knocks. That can be very distressing to the patient.

Don't sit on the bed, or put your coat or any other possessions on it. In fact, don't touch the bed at all.

Don't fidget! Don't walk up and down, handling things in the room. Tension or nervousness in a visitor is often transmitted to the patient; so sit as quietly as you can, getting up only to leave.

Don't talk to the patient from across the room, making him strain himself to answer you. Sit close to him and in his direct line of vision, if possible, so he can talk without turning his head or raising his voice.

It goes without saying that the etiquette of the sick-room does not permit smoking. Nor is it good form to nibble continuously at the fruit or candy you brought—or to take one of the patient's flowers to wear when leaving.

If you really have the patient's interest at heart, don't give advice! Don't go into a long discourse on your own illnesses, past and present. Few things provoke a sick person more than to be told about other people's ailments. He wants your attentive sympathy and understanding—not your reminiscences.

When visiting a friend who has been in an accident, be careful not to ask a lot of distressing or disturbing questions. If you are shocked by the nature or extent of his injuries, try not to show it. As soon as you can, ease the conversation away from the accident and talk about mutual friends, about things happening outside the sick-room, about important developments in the news—anything that's likely to interest the patient and take his mind away from his troubles.

Several brief visits and a lot of amusing or encouraging messages or cards are more helpful to the patient (and much more appreciated!) than a single long visit that may be boring or tiring to him. So, if you can possibly manage it, go to see your sick or injured friend several times—for ten or fifteen minutes each time. And in between visits, send him cards, messages, magazines.

It's customary to take a gift when you call on a friend who is ill. Flowers are always acceptable; but too many flowers can be a great burden to the nurse or whoever else takes care of them. So if the patient is very popular and always has a lot of flowers in the room, don't add to them. Take a basket of fruit or a box of cookies instead (unless the nature of the illness prohibits gifts of food), or take an amusing game the patient can play by himself or a book to take his mind off his troubles. One of the nicest gifts of all, when practical, is a pair of tickets for a good play a month or two ahead . . . to show you are certain the patient will be up and around, and well enough to go to the theater at that time. It gives the sick person something pleasant to think about and anticipate.

CALL OF CONDOLENCE

When death comes to the house of a relative or friend, it's necessary to make a condolence call. Intimates of the family come at once, as soon as they hear the news. Others wait until after the funeral, calling sometime during the first week, if possible, to express their sympathy and sorrow.

Casual acquaintances who do not wish to intrude on the grief of a family may call and leave a card or flowers at the door, without asking to be admitted, or they may write a note of condolence and send it by mail.[3] A neighbor may ring the bell and leave a box of home-baked cookies or some other delicacy for the family, without coming in.

But all relatives and close friends must make a personal call, however trying it may be. The bereaved need their friends near to comfort them and share their grief . . . but *not* to increase their burden of sorrow by tactless questions or gushy sentiment.

So when you make a condolence call, try not to be emotional or demonstrative. That can only be upsetting to the bereaved, not consoling. Be very careful what you say. It's better not to say anything at all than to reopen the floodgates of grief by a careless or thoughtless remark. A simple "I'm sorry" is often the best thing of all to say. Or even a wordless handclasp can be more comforting, can say more and mean more, than a lot of empty phrases.

Unless you are a relative or intimate friend, don't stay long when you pay a condolence call. Twenty minutes are ample. And don't ask questions; don't inquire about the details of the illness or death; don't talk about your personal affairs. There can be no rudeness more unkind than to obtrude selfishly on another's sorrow.

It is not good form for a woman to make a call of condolence on a man. She may write a note of sympathy, or send flowers for the funeral, but she should not visit him personally.

WHEN VISITS ARE RETURNED

It is not necessary to return the call of a friend or relative who comes to see you when you are ill. A note of thanks is courteous and customary, but not actually required. Nor is it necessary to return visits of condolence.

However, a first call on a newcomer in a community must be returned. Failure to do so is an affront, implying you don't care to know

[3] For examples of condolence letters, see pages 326 to 330.

or continue seeing the neighbor who was kind enough to call. That is unnecessarily rude to a well-meaning stranger. You should either visit her briefly some time in the next week or ten days, or invite her to a bridge or luncheon at your home. After that there is no obligation; but well-bred people always return the first visit of a neighbor or new acquaintance.

Old friends, of course, visit each other as they like, whenever they feel so inclined, without formality and without thought of obligation. It is only *first visits* that are made and returned with precise formality.

INFORMAL VISITING

Although visiting among good friends is on a much more casual and informal basis today than it has ever been, certain long-established customs and traditions still remain. These "unwritten laws" of courteous and considerate visiting must be observed if you want to be a welcome and well-liked guest in other people's houses.

For example, however relaxed the etiquette of informal visiting may be, one still doesn't "barge in" on friends at meal times, nor when the baby is being bathed, nor when others are being entertained. Well-bred people do not make a habit of invading the privacy of others, not even their most intimate friends. They do not arrive at a house sooner than expected, nor remain later than convenient.

Well-bred people try to be at their most gracious and agreeable best in company, friendly and pleasant, holding up their end of the conversation and making the hostess' task of entertaining easier. They are careful where they put their lighted cigarettes and wet glasses, always more careful of their friends' possessions than their own. They never turn on the radio, nor use the telephone, nor even open a window without first asking the hostess' permission. They never make themselves at home in any house except their own—never forget they are guests, with all a guest's traditional obligations of courtesy and consideration.

The whole keynote of courteous informal visiting among friends can be summed up in a single word: *unselfishness*. Whether you drop in for five minutes to say "Hello" or come by invitation for dinner and to spend the evening, remember that unselfish, considerate behavior is the outstanding quality of a well-liked guest.[4]

[4]For other qualities which make a man or woman a well-liked guest, see pages 369 to 372.

DROPPING IN ON FRIENDS

Many young, gay, social-minded people love to have their friends drop in any hour of the day or evening. They are delighted to stop whatever they are doing, at any time, to "visit" with a chance caller. And there are those many others—the shy newcomers in a community, the invalids and shut-ins, the *lonely* people of the world—who long for visitors and eagerly welcome them at any time.

But at the other extreme are the people with busy, well-ordered lives, people whose time is strictly budgeted to include all their many interests and activities. To such people, privacy is a precious thing. They can be greatly distressed by even a brief unexpected visit that upsets the carefully planned routine of the day; but they may be too polite to show it.

Unexpected visits are good form only if you are reasonably sure you are welcome, that you are not interrupting or intruding, and most important of all, *that you are not keeping your friends from other things they want to do.*

WHEN *NOT* TO STAY

It's very important to be observant when you drop in on people. Read the unmistakable signs that say whether or not you are welcome. Here, as in every other social contact, the quick perception and understanding of other people's feelings is the most useful asset you can have.

If your friend's face lights up when she sees you at the door, if she exclaims, "How wonderful! Come in!"—and you can detect the unmistakable ring of sincerity in her voice—you can assume she is glad to see you and that you have not come at an inconvenient time. But if the smile is a little weary, the "Hello" a little absent-minded, ask quickly, "Are you busy?"

A good friend will be frank about it. If she is expecting guests, or going somewhere, or busy, or tired, or just out of sorts . . . she will say so. But if she doesn't, it's up to you to notice such things as a table spread with letters or papers, a book reluctantly closed and placed aside, a coat ready and waiting to be put on.

Then you should say at once, "We were out for a walk and we just stopped to say 'Hello.' We're not staying—we'll come back some other time."

Your friend may put on a fine show of cordiality, begging you to stay, but the chances are she doesn't mean it. Nobody likes to be interrupted in the middle of writing a letter or getting ready to go out. But if she brightly insists that you stay (even though you can see for yourself you've come at a most inconvenient time) don't stand at the door and argue about it. Come in and stay for a little while—but *only a little while*. Then your friends won't feel they've been rude or ungracious toward you, and you won't feel you've seriously upset or disturbed their plans.

Don't Drop in at Inconvenient Hours

There's still another factor in connection with unexpected calls: Nobody likes to be seen, even by intimate friends, in housedress and curlers. Therefore any dropping in should be done at a sensible time of the day, when people are likely to be dressed and presentable, and the house ready for visitors. If you have reason to visit someone in the morning or late evening, it's best to telephone beforehand and ask if it's convenient. It takes only a minute to telephone—and it may save a lot of embarrassment.

How Long to Stay

Knowing when to leave is important in *any* kind of visit. Be constantly alert to signs of weariness or restlessness in your hosts. If you notice them glancing at the clock, don't naively ask, "Are we keeping you from something?" Of course you are—but they're likely to be too polite to admit it! So if you have any reason to believe your host and hostess are tired, or have something else to do, or—to put it plainly—would like to see you go, *get up and say "good-by."* Never risk outstaying your welcome.

No one can tell you how long an informal visit with friends should last. That depends entirely upon you and your friends—and upon the particular circumstances. If you drop in for the afternoon and your friends insist that you stay for dinner and the evening, there's no rule against staying. Just be sure that the invitation is sincerely meant and is not just a courteous gesture. You can tell. There's a big difference between a polite "Will you stay for dinner?" and an exuberant, "Look! You're staying for dinner—and that's that!"

If you *do* stay, accept the situation as graciously as though you had received an engraved invitation! It's a mistake to keep harping on the fact that you were not previously invited: "Are you *sure* you want us to stay? Are you *sure* we're not intruding?" That's no way to repay your good friends for their hospitality. Instead, try to contribute so much to the pleasure and enjoyment of the occasion that your friends are delighted with your company and very glad indeed you consented to stay.

An unexpected guest who stays for dinner should offer to help with the dishes if there's no maid to do them. But she should not insist if her offer of help is refused.

DROPPING IN ON FRIENDS IN THE COUNTRY

For some reason, people who wouldn't dream of intruding on their relatives or friends in the city seem to think it's perfectly all right to descend—bag and baggage—on friends in the country. But it's neither courteous nor fair to impose on people just because they happen to have country houses.

No one should ever arrive at a beach or country house expecting to spend the day or be "put up" for the night without having been specifically invited. Although it was once the custom for people living in the country to keep open house for their friends, the rules of hospitality have now changed to conform with our busier lives and broader interests. Today it's a fixed rule that guests come only when invited and remain only as long as they are asked to stay.

Of course dropping in for a brief visit is friendly and pleasant when you happen to be in the vicinity of someone you know and like. But staying for an entire day, or expecting to stay overnight, is an imposition that well-bred people do not practice.

4. VISITING CARDS AND THEIR USES

ORIGINALLY the visiting card was intended for one purpose only: to be left behind as evidence of one's presence at the home of another. It was, as the name implies, a card for visiting.

But gradually this original and principal use of the visiting card has gone out of fashion; and very few people, nowadays, go about making "duty calls"—leaving cards as proof that their social debts have been paid.

However, although visiting cards are now rarely used for visiting, they serve many other useful purposes. They are enclosed with gifts and flowers, used for messages of condolence and congratulation, even used for informal invitations and acknowledgments. But before we discuss these modern convenient uses of the visiting card, let us consider their correct form and appearance.

Good Form in Visiting Cards

Visiting cards should be engraved in plain black on white. Tinted cards are not in good taste, nor are cards engraved in color. Sometimes a delicate gray or cream-colored card is used; this is not objectionable if the card is neatly and simply engraved in black. But a gray card engraved in blue, or a pale blue card engraved in red (and we have actually seen such specimens!) is in bad taste and should be avoided.

The correct visiting card is made of plain unglazed bristol board, with no border and no decorations. There's a newer-type card of thin parchment which is also in good form, and which is convenient because a larger quantity can be carried easily. But nothing else may be used. Originality in visiting cards may be interesting—but it's not good taste.

The cards should be engraved, not printed. Block, shaded-block, and script lettering are all suitable, but should not be too large or ornate. Simple, legible lettering is always the best. Any good stationer will help you make your selection.

A visiting card is engraved with the person's name; and usually, but not necessarily, the address. If the address is given, it's in the lower right corner of the card in very small letters. A bachelor may use a club address instead of a home address, if he prefers.

Correct Sizes of Cards

As in everything else, styles in visiting cards vary from season to season—though never radically. Exact sizes therefore cannot be given, but must depend on the current vogue and on personal preference. Following are the approximate sizes:

A woman's card is generally about 2⅞ by 2 inches. If the name is unusually long, a somewhat larger card may be used.

A man's card is narrower in shape than a woman's, the size generally approximating 2⅞ by 1½ inches.

The joint card of a husband and wife, or of a mother and daughter, is larger than an individual card. It is generally about 3⅛ by 2¼ inches.

A young girl's card is slightly smaller than that of her mother.

Names and Titles

Names should be spelled out in full on visiting cards when possible. Initials should be used only when the name is too long to make a good-looking card. For example, "Mr. Alexander Corbett Huntington" would be justified in using either "Mr. A. Corbett Huntington" or "Mr. Alexander C. Huntington" on his cards. But "Mr. A. C. Huntington" would not be good form. A short name like "John Alan Smith" should always be spelled out in full.

A wife's cards should conform with her husband's. If his cards read "Mr. Alexander C. Huntington" her cards should read "Mrs. Alexander C. Huntington"—*not* "Mrs. A. Corbett Huntington."

Visiting cards always carry the person's title. The use of the name alone without Mr., Mrs., Dr. or whatever the title may be, is incorrect.

A doctor, a clergyman, a judge, a military or naval officer still in the service—all have their cards engraved with their titles: Dr.[1] John Henderson (or John Henderson, M.D.), The Reverend William Haines, Judge Thomas Brandt, Colonel James Vinson.

The joint cards of such individuals would read: Dr. and Mrs. John Henderson, The Reverend and Mrs. William Haines, Judge and Mrs. Thomas Brandt, Colonel and Mrs. James Vinson.

A woman does not use her husband's title on her own personal cards. The wife of a doctor, judge, general, admiral of the fleet, or President of the United States is just plain "Mrs. John Doe."

Socially, a woman doctor uses her husband's name. On her own personal cards she may use "Dr. Martha Hale" or "Martha Hale, M.D." But on a joint card with her husband the customary form is "Mr. and Mrs. Thomas Hale" . . . with no indication of her professional rank. The only other alternative is a two-line card reading:

MR. THOMAS HALE

DR. MARTHA HALE

which is awkward and cumbersome, but not necessarily incorrect.

When husband and wife are both doctors, their joint card reads, "Dr. James and Dr. Helen Crain."

College degrees or special degrees are not indicated by letters on personal visiting cards.

A widow continues to use her husband's name on her cards and in her social correspondence. She remains "Mrs. Franklin P. Jenson";

[1]Either "Dr." or "Doctor" may be used. Both forms are correct, although it's considered somewhat better form to engrave titles in full on cards used for social purposes.

she does not use "Mrs. Elizabeth Jenson" except in business or legal matters.

A woman who is divorced may continue using her former husband's name, if she likes. But the usual procedure is to combine her *own* last name with *his* last name. If her name was Mildred Cary before her marriage to John Smart, she uses the name "Mrs. Cary Smart" on her visiting cards. She does *not* use "Mrs. Mildred Smart," unless, due to business or professional activities, that is the name by which she is best known to her associates and friends.

Nicknames and pet names, and abbreviations like "Sid" for Sidney" and "Dot" for Dorothy are in bad taste, and should never be used on visiting cards.

Use of "Jr." and "2nd"

The word "Senior" (or "Sr.") is not ordinarily used on a visiting card. The elder of two persons having the same name is entitled to the use of it. But the younger of the two adds "Junior" (or "Jr.") to his name to avoid confusion.

The use of "Jr." following a name does not eliminate the need for "Mr." preceding it. Therefore a card should not be engraved "John Hayes, Jr.," but "Mr. John Hayes, Jr."[2]

"Jr." is properly used only by a son whose name is the same as that of his father, as, for example, "Mr. John D. Rockefeller, Jr." His wife should use the same name on her cards: "Mrs. John D. Rockefeller, Jr." As a rule, the use of "Jr." is discontinued after the death of the older person, unless there is some reason for keeping the two identities separate (as when father or son, or both, are famous personalities.)

If a man is named for a grandfather or uncle, he is not "Jr." but "2nd." His visiting cards are engraved "Mr. Paul Hartley, 2nd." Or if he is the third in the family to be given that name, his cards read "Mr. Paul Hartley, 3rd."

Traditional Use of Visiting Cards

For those who want to know about formal ceremonious card-leaving, even though the custom is now practically obsolete, here are the rules:

[2]The use of "junior" after a name (with a small letter) is an affectation, not recommended. Either "Junior" (with a capital) or "Jr." should be used.

Women are supposed to visit women only; men visit both women and men. When leaving cards, therefore, a woman leaves her own for the women of the family—her husband's for both the men and women.

For example, a married woman making a formal call on Dr. and Mrs. Blank, at whose home she and her husband have recently dined for the first time, leaves one of her cards and two of her husband's. Her own card is for Mrs. Blank; her husband's are one for Dr. Blank and one for Mrs. Blank.

A woman calling at a household where there is a mother and two grown daughters may either leave three separate cards (one for each of the ladies) or she may leave just one card, saying to the maid or whoever answers the doorbell, "For all the ladies."

A husband and wife visiting a household where there are grown daughters or a daughter-in-law may leave joint Mr. and Mrs. cards for the ladies, plus the husband's individual cards for the men of the family.

The seemingly complex matter of card-leaving can be reduced to these three simple rules:

1. Women do not call on men, therefore leave cards for the ladies only.
2. Men leave cards for all members of the household, men and women both—but no more than three of any one card should ever be left. (If there are more in the family, the maid or butler is told that the cards are "for all the ladies" or "for all the gentlemen.")
3. Joint cards are left only for the ladies of a household; men leave their own cards for the men.

Bending down the corner of a card simply means it was left at the door personally, not sent by mail. This is now as obsolete as the custom of card-leaving itself is rapidly becoming.

Modern Uses of Visiting Cards

Nowadays visiting cards are used as a convenience, not a formality. They are used mostly to enclose with gifts and flowers, and to leave at the door or send through the mail with brief messages written on them.

For example, if you call on people you know fairly well and are sorry not to find them at home, you write "So sorry to have missed you!" on your visiting card and leave it in the mailbox or slip it under the door.

Or if you call to see a friend who is ill, and there is some reason why you cannot be admitted at the time, you leave your card with whoever opens the door. Across the top of it you write, "To inquire how you are" or "I hope you are feeling better."

When you call at a house of mourning to express sympathy, but feel you don't know the people well enough to intrude on their grief, you leave your card at the door with "Deepest sympathy" written on it. A message of condolence may also be written on your visiting card and sent with flowers to the funeral.

A card with "Congratulations" across it may be sent with a gift to the parents of a new-born child, or with flowers to a graduate, or to a young singer or dancer on the occasion of her professional debut. A personal note is more gracious and friendly of course, but the use of a visiting card is correct . . . and very convenient.

The joint card of a man and wife is sent with a wedding or anniversary gift—or any gift that comes from both. The card may be used simply to identify the senders; or it may have a personal message of congratulations and good wishes written on it. No signature is required to such a message; the name on the card takes its place.

When a visiting card is sent with a gift, and the card is used only to identify the sender, no change is made in it. But if a message is written on the card—even if it's nothing more than "Best Wishes" or "Bon Voyage"—a line should be drawn through the "Mr." or "Mrs." The message should be written in ink, preferably above the name but above and below it if necessary.[3] Following are typical examples:

> *We hope you have a marvelous crossing!*
>
> *Mary and* ~~*Mr. and Mrs.*~~ *John Gray*
>
> *Eighty Park Avenue*

---

[3] It is not incorrect to write messages on the back of a visiting card; but it's wiser to write on the face of the card, as a message on the back may be overlooked.

> *My love and congratu-*
> *lations to you both —*
>
> ~~Miss~~ *Mary Evelyn Browning*
>
> *on your tenth anniversary*

> *With deepest sympathy*
>
> ~~Mr.~~ *Alan Powell, Jr.*

Visiting cards are frequently used to notify friends of a change of address. The new address is simply written in ink on the card, with a notation that "This is my new address" or "Here's where I'll be after June fifth."

Cards are also sent, with a temporary address written in ink, when one is staying for a while in a distant place . . . to let friends know where to write.

Men should not use their business cards for any of these social purposes.

THE P.P.C. CARD

This is an ordinary visiting card with the initials P.P.C. (*pour prendre congé* [to take leave]) written in ink in the lower left corner.

It is sent by mail to relatives and friends to let them know one is leaving on a journey and to say good-by. No acknowledgment of the card is necessary; but special friends generally send *bon voyage* gifts and are on hand to see the travelers off.

Nowadays, with people darting about from place to place with almost incredible speed, P.P.C. cards have outlived their usefulness and are only rarely used. But if you do happen to receive a visiting card with P.P.C. written in ink in the corner, you'll know what it means.

CARDS FOR A DEBUTANTE DAUGHTER

When no special coming-out entertainment is planned for a debutante daughter, visiting cards may be used to let people know she is "grown up" and ready to receive invitations. These are joint cards engraved with the daughter's name underneath that of her mother, as follows:

```
Mrs. John S. Huntington
Miss Helen Jean Huntington




                                    Riverside  Terrace
```

Where card-leaving has not gone entirely out of fashion, the debutante makes a round of calls with her mother—leaving cards like the above to announce her social "coming of age."

The name of a daughter never appears on the double card used by a husband and wife. It would be incorrect, for example, to have cards reading:

Mr. and Mrs. John Cary
Miss Helen Cary

However when a motherless girl lives with her father and attends social functions with him, a joint card is a convenience and is permissible. Her name is engraved underneath his on the card.

LEAVING A CARD FOR A FRIEND AT A HOTEL

Nowadays one frequently has occasion to call upon a friend who is stopping at a hotel. One should always be announced before going up.

If the person you have come to see is not in, you may want to leave your card. In doing so, be sure to write the person's name clearly across the top of the card, otherwise it may go astray. Just write "For Mrs. John Blank" above your name, and leave the card with the desk clerk. If you write a message on the card, don't leave it exposed for everyone to read. Slip the card into an envelope, seal it, and address it to the person for whom it is intended. People of good taste do not leave personal messages displayed on cards at a hotel.

INDICATING THE DAY AT HOME

The custom of setting aside one day a week for remaining at home to receive and entertain guests is out of tune with our busy times. But there are still some charming hostesses who cling to this fine old custom . . . receiving their friends and ceremoniously serving tea one specified afternoon a week. The day is indicated on the visiting card, as follows:

Mrs. John S. Huntington

Tuesdays   15 West Terrace

This card means that Tuesday is the day of the week Mrs. Huntington is "at home" to guests, and her friends respond accordingly.

A Bride's "At Home" Cards

A bride and groom often send "at home" cards to their relatives and friends, to let them know where they will live after the return from the honeymoon. As a rule these cards are sent out with the wedding announcements, being enclosed in the same envelope with them. But it is also correct to send them out separately after the bride and groom are settled in their own home and ready to receive visitors.

The typical "at home" card of a bride and groom is about the size of a visiting card and reads:

Mr. and Mrs. James Fox
will be at home
after the first of August
at Ten Little Plains Road

Or a joint visiting card of the new "Mr. and Mrs." may be used, with the address indicated in the lower right corner:

Mr. and Mrs. James Fox

Ten Little Plains Road

"At home" cards engraved with the bride's new name should not be sent out before the ceremony—for the reason, of course, that she has not yet acquired her new name. Such cards should be sent after the ceremony, either with the announcement or on the return from the honeymoon. However cards *without any name* may be sent before the ceremony, enclosed with the invitations. These would read:

At Home
after the first of August
Ten Little Plains Road

THE USE OF VISITING CARDS FOR INVITATIONS

Many people use visiting cards for informal invitations—simply writing the necessary few words in the lower left corner or across the top of the card.

It's a rather careless and "sloppy" social custom, we think. Originally intended as a convenient substitute for engraved third-person forms, visiting card invitations have a curt and unflattering connotation. They sound *hurried*. They have neither the dignity of formal engraved invitations, nor the warmth and charm of friendly informal notes.

However, inasmuch as visiting cards are still widely used for invitations—and you will no doubt continue to receive them from time to time—you should know what kind of function they represent, and what kind of acknowledgment you are expected to write.

If you receive an invitation like one of the following, you can expect a not-too-formal party, somewhat more important socially than a simple little supper or dance for intimate friends would be, but not important or elaborate enough to warrant engraved invitations:

Mr. and Mrs. Charles Putnam Newhall

Buffet Supper
Sunday at 8

R. S. V. P.
Four DeCamp Road

Mr. and Mrs. John Holt

Dancing at 10
Tues. June 14   *45 Park Avenue*

To meet
Mrs. Joel Jamison

Mrs. Frederick Arthur Hewitt

Wed. June 6.
Bridge at 4   509 West End Avenue

These invitations should be answered at once, whether a reply is requested or not, and they should be answered by personal note. It may be more convenient to write "Delighted! I'll be there Sunday at eight" on your own visiting card and send it to your hostess. And actually that is no more incorrect than the invitation itself; so if you want to respond on your personal card, you may. But it's so much more courteous to write a friendly note . . . just as it would have been more courteous to write a friendly *note of invitation* instead of sending a visiting card.

The Double Card or "Informal"

A type of card much used today is a double or fold-over card, called an "informal." It is somewhat larger than an ordinary visiting card; and since it is used for correspondence, it comes with its own envelope.

The outside of the "informal" is engraved with the person's name, just as a visiting card is. The address may be engraved in the lower left corner, if desired; but as a rule only the name appears on the front of the card. The inside is blank and may be used for any type of informal message or invitation. This may be just a few words, like a message on a visiting card; or it may be written like a letter with a salutation (Dear Mary:) and a complimentary close (Affectionately yours,).

The "informal" is simply a modern and convenient substitute for note paper. It is not intended to be used in place of visiting cards when making calls.

Visiting Cards During Mourning

Black borders were once used on visiting cards during the period of mourning. But nowadays one rarely sees black-bordered cards, and their use is rapidly disappearing.

For those who want to observe the custom, a very narrow border of black is recommended—no more than ⅛ of an inch. Wide black borders are needlessly conspicuous and in bad taste.

5. TABLE MANNERS

MUCH of the old rigid formality about the etiquette of eating has been relaxed in recent years. Nobody is greatly shocked nowadays by some trifling blunder at the table. Far more important than exact observance of every little rule and regulation is being gracious, friendly, and entertaining, and contributing to the general enjoyment and well-being of the company.

Not that table manners are any less important than they have always been! Nowhere are rudeness and lack of social training more quickly and cruelly betrayed than at the table. But the emphasis today is on dignity and self-restraint, rather than precise little rules—on consideration for others and the same broad, general principles of courtesy which make all social contacts more agreeable and satisfying. The emphasis today is on *common sense*—on eating neatly and quietly, without offending the sensibilities of others, and with the poise and assurance which make even a blunder seem of no great consequence.

Ease Is Essential

Good manners at the table should be an instinctive part of your personality—as natural and unstudied as saying "Hello." Only by being sure of yourself, by knowing what is right and what is wrong, can you acquire this fine free ease of *manner*, this sophisticated graciousness, which comes from within and without which dining in company can never be fully enjoyed.

Ease is essential at the table—and the only way to acquire it is to learn the rules. Learn them, and forget about them! The idea is to be so familiar with the little niceties and courtesies of dining that you don't even need to think about them at the table. You may not always observe every rule down to the smallest detail (so few people do!); but confidence in your knowledge will give you the ease that is so important.

For example, the socially inexperienced are often dismayed and confused when they sit down before an elaborate array of silver. But there is no need for anyone ever to pick up the wrong fork or spoon. For the rule is clear and simple: You just use the silver in the order it is placed on the table, beginning at the outside and working in.

That's all you need to know; but if you are still uncertain about it, watch your hostess and take your cue from her. And even if you make a mistake, remember—it's no great crime! Just take it in your stride. If you remain poised and at ease, the chances are no one will even notice it.

General Table Behavior

Always walk slowly and leisurely into a dining room. Don't rush. Don't be the first to seat yourself. Wait until all are present, and until the hostess tells you where to sit.

Don't sit on the edge of the chair. Pull it in and sit back comfortably. Keep your hands in your lap when they are not occupied (not on the table or the back of the next chair); and keep your feet firmly on the floor. The person who sits up straight at the table presents a better appearance—and a much more courteous attitude toward the hostess.

Try to keep your elbows close to you at the table. Don't wing them out and crowd the people next to you. Jabbing a dinner partner with your elbow is clumsy and inconsiderate.

At a small luncheon or dinner where there are just a few guests, it is courteous to wait until everyone is served before you start eating. But at a very large formal dinner, or at a buffet party where you serve yourself, it's permissible to start eating at once.

Bear in mind that the dinner hour is not just a time for eating, but for *social contact*—for talking, exchanging opinions, sharing experiences, enjoying one's family and friends. Always make a conscious effort to be "good company" at the table. Don't just sit and eat; join in the conversation (but don't monopolize it!) Save your best anecdotes, your most amusing jokes, to tell when you are a dinner guest. Don't talk about unpleasant things at the table; keep the conversation cheerful, entertaining.

Food should be eaten in a leisurely, matter-of-fact way, with a certain fine disregard of it—as though it were merely incidental to the conversation and not the most important business of the moment. It's all well and good to eat one's food with zest and pleasure; but there's a vast difference between the enjoyment of fine food and a mere greedy delight in eating. The true sophisticate does not relish food for itself alone, but rather as the pleasant accompaniment of good talk and good company.

There are, of course, a few basic details of eating etiquette which should be taught in the nursery and which, through daily observance, should become as familiar and commonplace as one's own right hand:

Don't try to talk when your mouth is full of food. Don't wave your fork or spoon in the air for emphasis. Don't tap on the edge of a glass or plate, or click the salt cellars together, or play with the silver. Don't reach in front of people at the table. Don't blow noisily on food to cool it. Don't smack your lips, or gulp food, or make other unnecessary noises. Keep your lips closed as much as possible while chewing. Remember that noisy, untidy, greedy, careless, or hurried eating offends the sensibilities of others at the table.

It is not good manners to probe food carefully with your fork before eating it. That's clearly an affront to your hostess. So is tasting food and then pushing it aside, or seasoning it vigorously with salt and pepper, or showing in some other conspicuous way that you don't like it. If you take a mouthful of food and discover that it's distasteful to you, swallow it anyway. It's offensive in the extreme to take it out with your fingers, or to spit it out on the fork or in a corner of the napkin (as some people actually do!) You don't need to continue eating something you don't like, but neither do you need to make a face about it or expel the one mouthful you have taken.

If you find something unpleasant in your food, don't draw everyone's attention to it. Why embarrass the hostess and spoil everyone else's appetite? The gracious way is to put your fork down quietly and engage in conversation to hide the fact that you are not eating. If you are so nauseated by what you find in the food that you are unable to control yourself, leave the table at once—and explain later that you felt suddenly ill. But it isn't necessary to explain why.

Don't talk about your personal likes and dislikes in food. Well-bred people don't have pronounced food quirks . . . or at least they don't talk about them. They try to eat a little of everything that is served; but if it's something they thoroughly dislike, or which disagrees with them, they just say, "No, thank you"—and let it go at that. They don't follow with an elaborate account of their tastes and allergies.

However, it is *not* bad manners to talk about how delicious the food is, how well-prepared, how delightfully served. There isn't a hostess living who doesn't enjoy such compliments! But be brief about it; don't enthuse to the point of sounding insincere.

FINGER FOODS

There are certain foods that do not require the use of knife, fork, or spoon. These foods are known as "finger foods"—and most familiarly included in this category are olives, pickles, radishes, celery, nuts, mints, popcorn, potato chips, small sandwiches, cookies, and crackers.

All types of bread and rolls are, of course, finger foods. It is not good form to butter a whole slice of bread, or an entire roll, and bite into it. The proper way is to break off a small piece at a time—enough for one or two mouthfuls—and butter each piece individually.

Dry cakes (like sponge cake, coffee cake, buns, etc.) may be eaten with the fingers. But "gooey" cake made with an icing or a soft filling —and all pastries—should be eaten with a fork.

Shoestring potatoes may be eaten with the fingers, like potato chips. But french fried potatoes are not a finger food. They are always eaten with a fork; and if the pieces are too large, they are cut to convenient size with the edge of the fork—not bitten in half in mid-air.

When possible, bacon should be eaten with a fork. But when it's so dry and crisp that it shatters into small fragments at the touch of the fork, fingers are permissible.

Many fresh fruits like plums, grapes, and cherries—and dried fruits like figs, dates, and raisins—are eaten with the fingers. So are berries when they are served with their hulls.

When eaten at the table, fresh peaches and pears are usually quartered and eaten with the fingers (or with a fork if the fruit is juicy). Apples eaten at the table are also quartered and eaten with the fingers. Oranges are sometimes served sliced and are eaten with a knife and fork. If they are served whole, they may be cut in half and eaten with a fruit spoon (like grapefruit); or peeled, divided into sections and eaten with the fingers. Fresh pineapple served in long spears may also be taken up in the fingers; but if it's sugary or juicy, it's better to use a fork.

A banana eaten at the table should be peeled down a little at a time, and small pieces broken off with the fingers. Or it can be peeled completely, placed on a dessert plate, and eaten with a fork. Both ways are correct.

The best way to eat watermelon is with a knife and fork. However, it can also be cut into mouth-size pieces and eaten with the fingers. Biting into a large slice of watermelon is messy and unsightly—and suitable only at picnics.

All fruits, when served at the table, are accompanied by a small fruit knife and fork. These should be used whenever necessary to manage the fruit with neatness and dispatch.

Corn on the cob and artichokes are finger foods; asparagus is not. For the handling of these and other "difficult" foods, see pages 59 to 61.

USE OF THE SPOON

The more familiar "spoon foods" include grapefruit, all fruits and berries served with cream, stewed fruits like prunes and apricots, custards and puddings, cereals, soups, ice cream and ices, and boiled eggs.

The spoon should be held lightly, as you would hold a pencil. When eating ice cream or pudding, take just enough on the spoon to make a mouthful. Don't take a huge heaping spoonful and lick it off a little at a time.

When eating soup, dip the spoon away from you; and sip (silently!) from the side. Don't fill the spoon right to the rim, as it's impossible to lift a full spoon to your mouth without spilling some of it. And you must lift it, as bending way over the plate to reach the spoon is bad manners.

Don't blow on soup that's too hot; just take a little on the spoon and wait until it cools. A little cools quickly. Don't crumble bread or crackers into soup, except at the home table. If oyster crackers are served and you help yourself to some, put them on the bread and butter plate or on the table and drop two or three at a time into the soup.

Don't go after the last drop of soup, tipping the plate and scraping the bottom. Take what you can gracefully, without tipping the plate, and leave what little remains. But if you simply must get that last mouthful, tip the plate very slightly, and tip it away from you.

Bouillon served in a cup may be sipped from a spoon or you may drink it right from the cup, as you prefer. The usual procedure is to sip a few spoonfuls and then, when the bouillon is cool enough, drink the rest of it from the cup. It's always best to hold the cup by one handle; if you hold it by both, the tendency is to prop yourself up by the elbows—and that's a careless, sloppy way of eating.

If soup is served in a plate, you leave the spoon right in the plate when you are finished eating. But if it is served in a bouillon cup, you remove the spoon and place it in the saucer.

One of the principal uses of the spoon is for mixing and stirring. It should, of course, always be removed from the cup or glass when drinking and placed in the saucer. It should never be used for sipping coffee, chocolate, or tea spoonful by spoonful from the cup. Long-handled spoons used for iced drinks may be placed on the bread and butter plate or the dinner plate, if they seem likely to fall off the saucer and spot the tablecloth.

USE OF THE KNIFE AND FORK

All meats, vegetables, fish, salads, soft cakes, and pies are "fork foods." Whenever possible they are eaten with the fork alone, the blunt edge being used to break them into mouth-size pieces. But when necessary, the knife is used for cutting.

There are two methods, or techniques, for using the knife and fork to cut food. One is the American method, the other is the European method. Both are correct; but our preference is for the familiar American way.

This is the procedure of cutting food with the fork in the left hand, the knife in the right; then putting the knife down on the plate and transferring the fork to the right hand to lift the food to the mouth. When cutting, the prongs of the fork point downward to hold the food in place. When lifting the cut morsel of food to the mouth, the prongs of the fork point upward.

The European way is to lift the food directly to the mouth with the fork held, prongs down, in the left hand. The knife is retained in the right hand, ready to cut the next piece.

Whichever method you use, try to be as deft and skillful in your handling of the knife and fork as possible. Try to acquire the ease which comes with sustained effort and practice, and which makes even the awkward switching of the fork from one hand to another appear smooth and graceful.

Never use a knife for any purpose but cutting food (except, of course, the small knife which is used for spreading butter, jam, or cheese). Never, never use a knife for conveying food to the mouth! When necessary, it's permissible to use the knife as a barricade against which to push the fork to get food on it more easily. But don't use a knife to load layers of food on the back of the fork—a childish and most unattractive eating habit.

Another unattractive habit is to cut a whole chop or a whole slice of turkey into small pieces. It looks messy, and it is messy, to cut up a whole plateful of food. The proper way is to cut just one or two mouthfuls at a time.

Always use your fork for cutting food when you can. For example, soft foods like meat cakes, fish, fried oysters, and waffles are easily cut with the edge of the fork and save much unnecessary manipulation of the knife. A good rule is to eat with the fork alone whenever the type of food permits and to use the knife as little as possible.

Don't take a larger piece of food on your fork than you can manage in one mouthful. It isn't good manners to bite part of the food from a fork held in mid-air. And don't hold a forkful of food poised in front of your mouth while talking to someone. The least movement may send the food toppling on the tablecloth or on your neighbor's clothes.

Never hold a knife and fork in the same hand at the same time. When not in use, one or both should be on the plate—not resting against it with the handles on the table, but entirely on the plate. If the plate is passed for a second helping, the knife and fork should be left on it, carefully placed so they won't fall off. Silver that has been used should not be placed back on the tablecloth for any reason whatever. Place both knife and fork on the plate when you are finished eating. The knife should be on the outside, with its blade facing in, and the fork should be nearer the center of the plate, with its prongs turned up.

CONCERNING BREAD AND BUTTER

We have already discussed the proper way to eat bread and rolls: breaking off and buttering one small piece at a time. The piece should be held against the rim of the bread-and-butter plate while it is being buttered—not held awkwardly in the air or against the palm of the hand. If there is no bread-and-butter plate, it should be held against the rim of the plate from which one is eating.

The butter knife is generally found across the rim of the bread-and-butter plate when you take your place at the table. And there it should be returned after each use during the meal—across the bread-and-butter plate, not propped against it or against the edge of the dinner plate. The butter knife is used to spread butter on bread, rolls, biscuits, crackers, muffins, and toast, on waffles and on griddle cakes, and on corn on the cob. It is also used to spread jellies, jams, and most types of soft cheese.

When no butter knife is provided, the dinner knife—or any other convenient knife—may be used for these purposes. But one should be very careful not to smear particles of food from the side of the dinner knife on to the butter—as that presents an offensive sight to others, and whatever is offensive at the table is bad manners.

If there is a dinner roll between the folds of the napkin when you take your place at the table, put it on the bread-and-butter plate if there is one—otherwise put it on the table beside the service plate. Bread also may be put directly on the table if no plate is provided for it. Butter is put on the edge of the dinner plate when there is no bread-and-butter plate.

Never reach out and "spear" a roll or slice of bread with your fork. If the bread tray is too far to reach, ask the person nearest to pass it to you, and help yourself with your fingers. Bread and rolls are never taken with a fork.

Hot biscuits and popovers are broken open, not cut with a knife. If they are small, each half may be buttered immediately—as that's the way they taste best. But if they are large, it's better manners to break off a moderate-sized piece at a time, as you do with rolls and bread.

A piece of bread may always be used to push a piece of bacon, or the last of the meat or vegetables, on your fork. It's also permissible to sop up gravy with a piece of bread—provided it's done properly. The right way is to put a small piece of bread in the gravy and eat it with the fork, as though it were a piece of meat. It is *not* good manners to smear a piece of bread around the plate with your fingers to clean up the last of the gravy.

Butter is not put on potatoes, rice, or vegetables (except corn on the cob) with a butter knife—or *any* knife. The proper way to mix butter and seasoning in vegetables is with a fork.

On Picking up Bones

Modern etiquette is lenient about many things—but not about gnawing bones in public! It may be no great offense to pick up a small chicken bone in the privacy of one's own home, or at a picnic. But brandishing a drumstick in public, attacking a large and greasy bone without benefit of silverware, picking up a chop and biting pieces from it—surely such conduct is neither polite nor fastidious. Those who condone it on the grounds that "nibbling a bone is good for the teeth" aren't necessarily concerned about the unpleasant impression it makes on others. *Picking up a bone and greedily chewing the meat off it is bad manners, and is never anything else.*

So when you are eating chicken or chops, get off all the meat you can with your knife and fork—and let the rest go.

How to Eat Sandwiches

Sandwiches are meant to be eaten with the fingers. But that can be a very difficult feat when a sandwich is made up of several layers and is soft and "drippy." If it's an ordinary sandwich that can be easily managed by hand, pick it up. If necessary, it can be cut diagonally in half for easier and daintier handling. But if it's a huge club sandwich or one of those towering whole-meal sandwiches, use your knife and fork.

In other words, eat all sandwiches (not only at picnics, but *everywhere*) whatever way is neatest, easiest, and most convenient.

Difficult Foods

Some foods, more difficult than others to manage, are often a source of embarrassment to those who are not sure of themselves. Of course, it is always possible to watch the hostess and follow her lead. But it's better to know the rules, especially when there is some controversy as to how a food should or should not be eaten.

Artichokes

Artichokes are eaten with the fingers. One leaf at a time is pulled off, and the bottom or edible part dipped in sauce and eaten. The inedible part of the leaf is laid on the side of the artichoke plate. The rough thistle part at the center is scraped away with the knife or fork, and the "heart" is then eaten with the fork.

Asparagus

Asparagus is *not* a finger food. It is unsightly and offensive to take up a dripping stalk of asparagus in the fingers, hold it suspended in the air, and suck it into the mouth! *Asparagus should be cut and eaten with the fork.* The hard end of the stalk which cannot be cut may be picked up in the fingers, but only if it is comparatively dry and won't drip juice down one's arm and over the table. Fastidious people prefer to leave the stalk rather than display messy manners.

Baked Potato

Baked potatoes, white or sweet, are usually eaten right from their skins. If they are not already open when served, they are broken open with fork and fingers, not cut open with a knife. Butter is added *with a fork*, to all the potato at once or to a little at a time, as desired. At informal meals, potatoes may be pressed from the skins or scooped out with the fork, and mixed with seasoning and butter on the plate. Those who eat skin and all merely cut the potato into pieces of eatable size with the knife and fork.

Corn on the Cob

This is a very difficult food to eat neatly and gracefully. It should be served at family and informal meals only. Corn on the cob should never be broken in half at the table; it should be served in pieces small enough to be handled conveniently. Butter a little at a time; buttering a whole ear at once makes fingers and face unnecessarily messy. Hold the ends of the corn in both hands—either with the fingers or by means of the small silver handles which are sometimes provided—and *eat as neatly and quietly as possible.* Some people hold an end of the corn in one hand and manipulate a fork with the other, prying off a mouthful at a time with the prongs of the fork turned upward and slipped deftly through the kernels. This is really the neatest and most efficient way to eat corn, once you acquire the knack. Practice it in private; it's easier than you think—and lots more fun than to attack it with your teeth and get yourself all messy!

Lobster

Broiled lobster is eaten with a tiny, short-pronged fish fork and with the fingers. Whatever meat can be lifted out with the fork is cut into mouth-size pieces, dipped into butter sauce, and eaten. The claws and legs must be taken up in the fingers as it's the only way to get at the meat inside them. Usually the claws are cracked in the kitchen; but if not, a claw cracker is provided for this purpose. You crack open the claw, dig out the meat with the little fork, and cut as required with the knife. It's difficult—almost impossible—to eat lobster daintily, but at least one doesn't need to eat it greedily, sucking at every last tiny morsel!

Olives and Cherries in Cocktails

Don't attempt to get the olive or cherry out of a cocktail until you have drained the glass. Then just tip the glass and let the olive or cherry drop into your mouth. But if the olive is very large and too much for one mouthful, you may lift it out with your fingers and eat it in two or three bites.

Pie Alamode

Pie alamode and ice-cream cake are eaten with a fork. But a spoon may properly be used to scoop up whatever sauce or melted ice cream the fork leaves behind.

Salads

There can no longer be any controversy about whether or not salads may be cut with a knife. For now, in most well-appointed homes, salad knives are placed right on the table—and are used or not, as one pleases. If not, the salad may be cut with the edge of the salad fork, or with the dinner fork, or even with the dinner knife, if one wishes. In fact, the salad may be handled any way that is neat and convenient.

Spaghetti

Spaghetti is usually cut into convenient mouthfuls with the blunt edge of the fork. But it may also be handled Italian style, with the fork in the right hand and a dessert spoon in the left hand. You place the tines of the fork into the spaghetti, bring the dessert spoon up close to it, then start turning the handle of the fork slowly. This winds several long strands of spaghetti around the fork and makes it easy to eat.

REMOVING PITS AND FISH BONES FROM THE MOUTH

Pits and seeds should always be eaten as clean and dry as possible in the mouth before they are removed. The stones and seeds of fruits such as stewed prunes and cherries which are eaten with a spoon should be returned to the spoon from the lips and placed on the edge of the plate. Other pits may be removed with the fingers or dropped into the cupped hand held close to the lips. They should *not* be spit into the hand or on to the plate. Olive pits are placed on the bread-and-butter plate, and the pits of grapes, cherries, peaches, etc., on the fruit or dessert plate.

Fish bones should be removed with the fingers, between compressed lips . . . and without comment. Whenever *anything* must be removed from the mouth for any reason whatever, it should be done as quickly, quietly, and inconspicuously as possible.

USE OF NAPKIN AND FINGER BOWL

A small napkin is usually opened completely; but a large dinner napkin is opened only half way and placed double across the knees. It should not be taken by one corner and snapped open to its full length, nor should it be used all neatly folded up, like a mop.

Use the napkin frequently during the meal to keep your lips and fingers free of grease and food particles. Always use it before drinking, to keep the water glass from becoming scalloped with greasy rims. There's no need to use the napkin vigorously, like a bath towel. Just touch it gently to your lips. Wipe the finger tips only, not the entire hand. When not in use, the napkin should be on the lap and out of sight.

When eating an endangering mouthful that may spatter or spill, a man or woman may momentarily lift the napkin in the left hand and hold it as a shield against suit or dress. But it should *not* be tucked unromantically into one's vest or under one's chin!

In strictly formal service, the finger bowl is brought in *after* the dessert on a small service plate. But for informal service, the finger bowl is brought in *on the dessert plate*, resting on a doily, and with the fork and spoon for dessert on the same plate. The guest removes the fork and spoon at once and places them on the table, one on either side of the plate. The finger bowl, with the doily under it, is slipped off the plate and set aside to be used at the end of the meal. It is placed a little above and to the left of the dessert plate. At the end of the meal, the fingers are dipped lightly into the bowl and dried on the napkin, one hand at a time.

Finger bowls brought to the table *between* courses (following lobster, corn on the cob, etc.) are used at once and removed before the next course is served.

Avoiding "Service Jitters" at the Table

People accustomed to informal maidless service at home are sometimes uncertain and confused when food is passed by servants. But they needn't be, for there are just a few important things to remember.

In the first place, food is always served from the left. Therefore one should wait until the serving dish or platter is presented at the left, and not make the mistake of turning in one's chair and trying to help oneself ahead of time from the right.

A serving dish or platter is usually presented with both a fork and spoon for helping oneself. The spoon is taken in the right hand and pushed under the portion of food to be taken; the fork is used to keep it from toppling off the spoon. If a serving spoon only is provided, it's permissible to use one's own dinner fork to help launch the serving safely to one's plate. The fork is then not placed back on the tablecloth but allowed to remain on the plate, prongs up.

In serving yourself, the nearest and most convenient piece should be taken. It isn't good manners to pick and choose. Don't turn your head to talk or listen while serving yourself. Pay careful attention to what you are doing. Put the serving spoon and fork back on the platter gently, and be sure they are far enough on the platter so they won't slip off on the next person's lap.

Don't try to cut or separate foods presented in individual portions on the serving platter. Take what you are supposed to take, and leave what you don't want on your own plate. Food served on toast should be lifted off toast and all. Food served with parsley or a slice of lemon should be taken exactly as presented, not carefully cleared of its garnishes.

When you help yourself to gravy, put it right on the meat; but condiments and jelly should be placed at the side of the meat, fish, or whatever it is they accompany. Olives and celery are put on the bread-and-butter plate, but if there is none, they are placed on the edge of the dinner plate. Mints and salted nuts are put right on the tablecloth.

It isn't necessary to say "Thank you" each time you are served. But it is necessary to say "No, thanks" when you decline something that is offered to you. Just shaking your head without comment is rude.

ACCIDENTS AT THE TABLE

Accidents happen at the table, as everywhere; and when they do, one should take them as quietly and calmly as possible. Becoming flustered and upset only adds to the confusion; and confusion never helps any situation—it only tends to emphasize it.

So if you have an accident at the table, don't make a fuss about it. Just say you are sorry (and show by your voice and manner that you mean it!)—then drop the subject. Profuse and continued apologies are in poor taste, and can be more annoying than the accident itself.

The guest who breaks a valuable cup or plate may want to replace it, either exactly or with something similar. Though this is not an obligation, it's the courteous thing to do. When the tablecloth or rug is stained, a personal note of regret may be written to the hostess a day or two later. Damage to another guest's clothes is regrettable, but there's nothing much that can be done about it except to say that one is sorry . . . and to be more careful about avoiding such accidents in the future.

If a spoon or fork is dropped in a home where servants are in attendance at the table, it's better not to pick it up but let a servant do so, as there's less commotion that way. But if there are no servants, the person who drops a piece of silverware should pick it up at once, with as little disturbance as possible to those on either side of him. In a restaurant it's generally advisable to let the waiter pick up any silverware that has dropped to the floor.

If you take a mouthful of food that's too hot, don't spit it out as that's offensive to others. Just take a swallow of cold water, quickly. If you choke on a fish bone, or something "goes down the wrong way," get up and leave the table at once. Don't try to explain while you are coughing and choking.

USE OF THE TOOTHPICK

It's bad enough to use a toothpick in public. But it's even worse to try to hide its use behind a napkin. The use of a toothpick is permissible in private only. The fact that prominent people may once have picked their teeth quite openly and unconcernedly does not make this offensive habit right or proper today.

As for digging food from one's teeth with a fingernail, that is of course the very height of vulgarity!

Leaving the Table

When you get up from the table, leave everything just where it is. Don't push the plate back. Don't stack things, or push them together. The napkin should be dropped loosely on the table, to the left of the plate. Don't fold it, or smooth it out, or crumple it into a tight ball. Just fold it once to hide the used spots, and lay it with apparent carelessness on the table.

The way to get up quickly and quietly, and with the least commotion, is to put both hands on either side of the chair seat and push back. Do not brace yourself against the edge of the table and shove back chair and all. That's hard on the floor, the furniture, and the hostess' nerves! It isn't necessary to push the chair back into place unless it's out so far that it's in the way of others.

Questions Frequently Asked About Table Manners

Question: When an ice is served with a meat course and on the same plate with it, how should it be eaten?

Answer: With the same fork as the meat. But you may use a spoon if you would rather do so.

Question: Is it proper to drink the leftover juice of a fruit cocktail right from the glass?

Answer: No; use the spoon.

Question: Should the lettuce leaves be eaten when a chicken, fruit, or shrimp salad is served?

Answer: Yes, indeed! The lettuce is part of the salad, not a decoration.

Question: From which side of the chair do you seat yourself at the dining table?

Answer: Either side—whichever happens to be more convenient.

Question: Should a little food always be left on the plate "for manners' sake"?

Answer: That's an old-fashioned idea, now considered foolish and wasteful. Today one eats everything on the plate.

Question: Is it rude to wipe off silverware at the table?

Answer: In a private home—yes! In a restaurant, if the silver doesn't look entirely clean, one may wipe it quickly with one's napkin—under the table's edge. There's no need to make a public demonstration of it.

Question: Is "dunking" permissible?

Answer: Only at home with the family, at informal picnics, etc.

Question: What should one do when greasy food particles are dropped on the tablecloth—try to remove them or let them remain?

Answer: Pick them up with a clean knife blade and put them on the rim of the plate. *Don't* try to wipe out the spots with water.

Question: Is it bad manners to refuse a type of food one has never tasted before?

Answer: Not bad manners—only provincial and rather childish. The true cosmopolitan enjoys tasting all kinds of unusual and unfamiliar foods—never hesitates to try something new.

Question: Does a latecomer at a dinner party begin at the beginning—or with the course then being served?

Answer: In a private home where there are only a few guests, the hostess will probably insist that the latecomer begin with the first course and "catch up" with the others. But at a large or ceremonious dinner, the guest who arrives late begins his meal with whatever course is then on the table.

Question: When you sit down at the table, do the rolls at the right or the left of the setting belong to you?

Answer: At the left.

Question: Are parsley and watercress meant for decoration only, or can they be eaten?

Answer: They can certainly be eaten—and nowadays they usually are.

Question: Is it permissible to squeeze half a grapefruit to get the juice?

Answer: Only in private—not when you are dining in company. However you can easily squeeze the juice out of a grapefruit with the back of your spoon, without the danger of spraying someone across the table.

Question: If there is no spoon in the salt dish, what is the proper way to help oneself to salt?

Answer: Either with the tip of a clean knife, or (if it's an individual salt dish) with one's fingers.

Question: Where do you put the salt into which you dip celery—on the tablecloth or on your plate?

Answer: Never on the tablecloth! Either on the bread-and-butter plate, or on the rim of the plate from which you are eating.

Question: Is it necessary to apologize when you sneeze or blow your nose at the table?

Answer: Yes, but only briefly and quietly to those nearest you—not to the entire table.

Question: Is it always bad manners to put elbows on the table?

Answer: Only while eating. During conversation, especially at small tables, it is often more graceful and convenient to lean forward on one or both elbows to talk to the person opposite. That is entirely permissible.

PART II

The Etiquette of Entertaining

1. THE GRACIOUS HOME

EVERYBODY loves to entertain; but many people hesitate to do so because they feel their homes are not fine enough. That is not the true spirit of hospitality, and never will be. We entertain our friends because we want to see them and be with them. We can entertain them as delightfully in a modest apartment as in a lavish house—if the spirit is to *please*, not merely impress.

Naturally you want your surroundings to have charm and beauty, to provide a gracious setting for your parties. But you don't need elaborate or costly possessions. You don't need Minton plates, or heirloom silver—or even a dining room, for that matter! It's fine to have them, of course. It's very gratifying to own beautiful gleaming linen, sparkling crystal, expensive furniture and rugs, but if you don't have them, it doesn't really matter.

In the final analysis, it's not the material accumulations that count for most in a house; *it's the people who live in it*. If you are a person of charm and grace, of good taste and good judgment, your simplest possessions will reflect it unmistakably.

The subject of interior decorating is, of course, outside the province of this book. If you feel you need help in this direction, your first step should be to provide yourself with a few good, authoritative books on the types and periods of furniture, color harmony, correct house furnishings, and related subjects. The few basic suggestions included in this chapter concern appointments as applied to service, and are chiefly for the purpose of helping you make your house more attractive and convenient for the entertaining of guests.

THE FOUR MAJOR POINTS TO CONSIDER IN SELECTING FURNITURE

Any one of a dozen different factors may finally govern your choice of a particular table, chair, or cabinet. But regardless of any other factor, here are the four major points to consider in buying furniture:

1. Period or style
2. Proportion
3. Color harmony
4. Quality

The period or style is entirely a matter of personal taste. Some people like the clean, simple, austere lines of modern furniture. Others prefer the homey comfort of French Provincial, or the classic dignity of eighteenth century, or the simple homespun loveliness of Early American. But whatever the style, keep it consistent. Don't combine the gay bright motifs of Pennsylvania Dutch with heavy Elizabethan oak, the delicacy of Hepplewhite or Sheraton with the massive incongruity of modern. An occasional odd or unusual piece can be very attractive in a room and add distinction to it. But if it's conspicuously out of place, if it clashes outrageously with everything else and practically shouts, "Look at me—I'm different!" it's not right for the room, and you should resist the temptation to buy it.

So don't let yourself be carried away by a chair or sofa that has nothing in common with the rest of your furnishings. Think of it in terms of the entire room, not as a unit by itself. *Be sure it's appropriate before you buy it.* Will it fit in with the other things you have —or will it stand out like a sore thumb? Is it in harmony with the tone and spirit of the room—or will it seem like an intruder? Furniture that clearly doesn't "belong"—that clashes unhappily in color, feeling, or design—is not in good taste.

The factor of proportion depends, to a great extent, upon the size of the room. Don't put huge overstuffed pieces into a tiny room, or a pair of tiny gilt chairs in a huge foyer that calls for massive, important-looking pieces. When you select a piece of furniture, visualize its position in the room for which it is intended; and consider its size not only in relation to the room itself, but in juxtaposition to other things. Any room in which guests are entertained should be friendly, uncluttered, comfortable. Often a single massive piece of furniture—such as a large leather lounge chair or an outside desk or table—can throw a whole room out of proportion and make it look crowded. Don't cling to a piece of furniture for sentimental reasons if it's obviously out of proportion to the room and everything in it. If you *must* use it, try to place it where it won't destroy the charm and comfort of the room.

Avoid tall chests or cabinets in a low-ceilinged room. Avoid large sofas or tables in a room with little wall space. Avoid small chairs lined like lonely sentinels against the walls and in the corners of a large room; arrange them in friendly "conversational" groups so that guests automatically sit and talk together. An experienced hostess never puts chairs in corners of a room, where shy or timid guests may be tempted to sit apart from others during a party.

The whole secret of creating a lovely environment in which you are proud and happy to entertain your friends is to combine things that go beautifully together. This may sound simple and elementary, but it's nevertheless one of the basic principles of successful decorating. Unless you are satisfied to have a nondescript home, a hodgepodge with neither character nor charm, you must combine things that go well together. And this means *color harmony* as much as anything.

If you are a bride just starting out, be sure that you have a color scheme and a definite plan in mind for your entire house before you buy a single chair. Even if it's only a one-room or two-room apartment you are furnishing, have a color scheme in mind and be guided by it in shopping. It isn't necessary for all the colors in a room to match; but they must harmonize. They must combine well and complement each other.

An inexperienced bride can easily avoid mistakes by using a favorite painting—or a good print of a painting—as her color guide. Making it the focal point of interest in a room, she can choose all other furnishings for that room—chairs, sofas, rugs, lamps, draperies—to blend with the colors in the painting. The floor covering should be selected first, for it's always easier to match fabrics to floor coverings than the other way around; and it should be examined both by day and artificial light, as colors are often deceiving. If it's an all-over carpeting, a small piece of it can be taken along when selecting furniture; otherwise some other convenient means of matching or blending the floor covering and furniture fabrics should be devised. Colors that clash are even worse than designs that clash, for they are more obvious to the average eye and more cruelly betray bad taste. Every purchase made for a room should be carefully considered in terms of the room as a *whole.*

If you are not just starting out but merely refurnishing or refurbishing parts of your house, try to find things that not only harmonize with what you have, but are also *adaptable.* For example, in selecting new chairs for your bedroom or guest room, choose colors and fabrics that go well with the furnishings in your living room. Then you can bring them in when you give a big party, and supplement the seating capacity of the living room without spoiling its effect. Nowadays many people plan color unity between rooms for this purpose, and they find it works out very well when extra chairs are needed.

The fourth factor in selecting furniture—and in many ways the most important one—is *quality.* Don't be satisfied with second-best; wait until you can afford to invest in a really good piece of furniture, rather than accept inferior quality or workmanship. Your way of life may change from time to time. You may live in a one-room efficiency apartment now, a suburban cottage five years from now, a big house by the time the children are grown. But wherever you live, whatever your way of life—furniture that is beautifully designed and made will always be a joy to own and a pleasure to use.

In buying furniture, be sure to select good basic things that will not "date" quickly. If you follow the fashion trends at all, follow them in general principle only. Avoid oddities and novelties in furniture, or anything that tends to be extreme. You can get very tired of looking at them after a few months. Any investment in furniture is sounder if you are careful to select good design and good workmanship. The décor of a room can always be changed through the years by slip-covering chairs, repainting or repapering the walls, changing the draperies. But good basic furniture can and often does last a lifetime.

Make it a point never to buy an important piece of furniture the first time you see it. Go back and look at it a second time. You may be surprised at how much less you like it when you see it again. Remember—you'll have to look at that sofa or chair, that console or cabinet, day after day for years. So don't buy it until you are sure it's exactly what you want.

From one important standpoint, buying furniture today does not pose the problem it used to. For it's no longer necessary to buy complete suites, unless you want to. Nowadays good furniture, like good china and silver, is available in open stock groups. You can mix and match pieces as you please. The modern way is to buy only what you wish. You select two or three good pieces to make the nucleus of a really distinguished room, adding matching or harmonizing pieces from time to time as you find what you want—or as your budget permits. In this way even a simple home can have originality and flair.

BASIC SILVER FOR THE WELL-APPOINTED HOUSE

Fine silver is a symbol of gracious living and one of the most essential requirements of every well-equipped house. It isn't necessary to have sterling; but whether your silver is sterling or plate, quality is very important. Since silverware is a long-term investment great care should be given to its selection. Weight, quality, pattern, finish—all should be taken into consideration.

Sterling silver is solid silver throughout, with only a small amount of other metal added to increase the wear. It comes in several weights —light, medium, and heavy—and the weight generally determines the cost. Lightweight sterling is not advisable for flat ware that will be used frequently through the years, as it isn't likely to wear well. Heavyweight sterling is too cumbersome, and as a rule is used only for heavy-duty pieces. Medium weight is the safest and most practical choice. Your best assurance of quality is buying from a reputable firm. Always look for the word "sterling" on each piece; it's your protection by law.

Plated silver differs from sterling in that it's merely a surface layer of silver applied to some base metal or alloy, like nickel. The thicker the plating, the better the quality of the silverware—and the longer it lasts. Much of the modern plated ware is as lovely in finish and design as solid silver; and if it's heavy plate, it lasts a lifetime. So although sterling silver is the heart's desire of every woman who loves beautiful things, don't feel you must have it. A table can be set just as beautifully, and every bit as correctly, with plated ware as with sterling silver.

The amount of flat silver required for a well-set table is variable, of course. In a big house where there is a great deal of formal entertaining, two dozen of everything is not too much. But in a tiny apartment where entertaining is simple and unpretentious, six or eight of everything is usually adequate. The ideal is twelve of everything one may need for smart, correct service. The following check list is for a complete set; but not every household needs every one of these items. Entrée or luncheon forks may be used also for salads and desserts. Dessert spoons may double for cream soup and bouillon. Dessert knives may be used as butter spreaders. Oyster forks, after-dinner spoons and iced-tea spoons can be eliminated, and often are. If you cannot start out with a complete set, start out with what you need and must have (marked with a star in the list below)—adding the other pieces gradually. The modern trend is to buy one complete place setting at a time, adding to it for birthdays and anniversaries until one has a complete service for eight or twelve. But it seems more practical to start out with a minimum set for four (only the most essential items), since minimum silver for four can be used for a simple dinner or luncheon, while a complete place setting for one must be put aside until other place settings are added to it.

Use this check list to help you select adequate silver for correct service in your household, according to your particular style of entertaining.

*12 dinner forks
*12 entrée or luncheon forks
12 salad forks
12 dessert forks

12 oyster forks
*12 soup spoons
12 cream-soup spoons
*12 teaspoons
12 after-dinner coffee spoons
12 dessert spoons
12 iced-tea spoons
*12 steel-blade dinner knives
*12 entrée or luncheon knives
12 dessert knives
12 butter spreaders
3 serving spoons
3 serving forks
1 large carving set
1 small carving set
1 gravy ladle
1 sugar spoon
1 cake server

ESSENTIAL CHINA FOR THE WELL-SET TABLE

There is practically no limit to the amount of china one can use in a gracious home where friends are frequently entertained; for more than any other table appointment, china sets the tone of a party and gives it personality.

For example, you wouldn't use the same type of china for a gay little luncheon on the terrace as you would for an important dinner by candlelight; nor would you be likely to use the same china for an afternoon tea that you would use for an informal Sunday night buffet. There is endless and fascinating variety in table ware—from delicate bone china to bright Mexican pottery, from fragile and precious porcelain to simple, inexpensive earthenware. Any hostess so inclined can indulge her taste for many different types of table settings.

Although it certainly isn't necessary to be equipped with different kinds of china for all the kinds of entertaining one may do, every well-appointed house *does* have at least two kinds. There is always an adequate supply of gay, colorful china suitable for luncheons, buffets, and casual parties, and more formal china, finer in quality and more conservative in pattern, suitable for company dinners and other important occasions. As a rule there is also an inexpensive earthenware or pottery set for everyday family use. But whatever other china there may be depends on the needs and desires of the hostess, the type of entertaining she likes to do, and the degree to which she wishes (and can afford) to express her originality and ideas in table settings.

Much of the finest china comes from England and France, but there is also fine American china—as beautiful in workmanship and quality as any that comes from overseas. The best china is known by name; and you will find the name, or its symbol, on the back of every piece. Choice is a matter of taste—and of cost. There is a tremendous range in price in china, from a few dollars for a gay pottery set to hundreds of dollars for fine bone china. To buy intelligently, one should have at least a general knowledge and understanding of the different types.

Although the word *china* is used to refer to any kind of dinnerware, technically it means a special kind of ware—vitrified at very high temperature to produce a translucent quality and a hard, non-absorbent finish. This is what is known as vitreous or "real china" in this country, "porcelain" in Europe. When tapped with a pencil, it rings with a clear bell-like tone. When held up to the light, the shadow of dark objects can be seen through it.

Bone china is a variety of English china, the formula for which was discovered late in the eighteenth century. As the name implies, it contains animal bone, ground in with the clay to give greater strength and translucency. The bone content also produces an excellent finish, or texture, for glazing and decorating. Because of its combined delicacy and durability, English bone china is recognized as one of the finest of dinnerware chinas.

Earthenware is fired at lower temperature than china, and is known also as "semivitreous" or "semiporcelain." It does not ring when tapped, and is not translucent. Fine earthenware is hard and strong, resistent to chipping, comes in beautiful patterns, and may be used for practically every purpose that fine china is used.

Pottery is soft-bodied and porous, usually coarse and thick, and is more subject to chipping than earthenware or china. It is clearly an informal type of table ware, often crude in finish and decoration, and should not be used for dinners or other important entertaining.

In china, as in every other table accessory, pattern is a highly individual matter. Women of good taste try to choose a pattern that harmonizes with their other possessions, and isn't likely to clash with the decorative scheme of the house even if it should later be changed.

It isn't wise to select extreme designs or vivid colors for your best china. Indulge your taste for gay patterns in everyday or casual ware that you change from time to time. But when buying expensive china that you expect to use for many years for your most important entertaining, it's best to be conservative.

Nowadays it is considered smart to vary one's china after the meat course, instead of using the identical pattern throughout. Some hostesses buy salad and dessert plates in odd dozens, and use them to add interest and originality to the progress of the meal A very popular hobby today is to collect odd cups and saucers of fine bone china, either in after-dinner or regular size.

It isn't advisable for a young hostess just starting out to stock up with large quantities of china. The better way is to start out with one comparatively inexpensive but well-chosen set that can be used for practically every purpose. Then when she knows exactly what she wants and needs, she can start accumulating good china that fits in with her other appointments and that meets her own particular requirements for entertaining. Brides on a modest budget often begin with a "starter" set of fine china, consisting of service for four, adding to it as convenient and gradually filling in with patterns and other odd pieces that add to the beauty and convenience of service. To accumulate china in this way, one must naturally choose an open stock pattern which isn't likely to be discontinued before the set is completed. All expensive china should be purchased from open stock patterns rather than in complete sets.

To attempt a list of china for basic everyday use, for breakfast, luncheon, buffets, and casual entertaining, isn't very practical—for every household has its own requirements and they vary greatly. But for dinner, and for important luncheons and parties, here is a list of essential requirements. (Purchase in quantities of eight instead of a dozen if the family is small, and if you rarely entertain twelve people at a time at luncheon or dinner.) The most practical size for dinner plates is 10 inches—for luncheon plates, 7½ inches. If you don't have a silver coffee service, add a sugar bowl and cream pitcher to this list:

12 soup plates
12 luncheon plates
12 dinner plates
12 bread-and-butter plates
12 salad plates
12 dessert plates
12 cups and saucers
1 large platter
1 small platter
3 vegetable dishes
1 gravy boat
1 relish dish

Of course if you are fortunate enough to own silver platters and vegetable dishes, you may wish to eliminate the china ones to match your set.

ESSENTIAL GLASSWARE

In glassware, as in china, there is an almost unlimited range of quality, price, type, and pattern—from dime-store tumblers to flawless hand-cut crystal. For ordinary everyday use, and for casual entertaining, always keep a supply of inexpensive glassware on hand. For this purpose, any type of glassware that appeals to your taste is acceptable —plain, decorated, crystal, colored—anything that pleases your fancy and is at least reasonably in keeping with the occasion and with the other appointments on your table. Nowadays there is such a wide and tempting variety of glassware that it's possible to have all sorts of gay and amusing changes for informal table settings, to harmonize with every type of china and every imaginable color scheme.

But for company dinners and other important entertaining, when you use your best china and your finest linen damask, crystal glassware is still traditional . . . and still the best taste. It doesn't matter particularly whether it's stemmed, footed, or tumbler-shaped—whether it's inexpensive machine-made glass or costly hand-cut crystal. If it's bright and sparkling, and in keeping with the furnishings of the room and the china and silver on the table, it's right and proper for the occasion.

Good crystal glassware has clarity, brilliance, smooth edges, and a bell-like tone. To test its clarity, hold it up to the light and look through it. It should be absolutely free of waves, bubbles, specks, or any other imperfections. To test its brilliance, hold it against a pure white background; it should be clear and sparkling . . . with no cloudy bluish or greenish tinge. To test its smoothness, run your finger around the edge; if it's rough or scratchy, it's an inferior quality glass. To test its tone, tap it lightly with your knuckle or fingernail; it should have a clear, rich ring.

Following is a list of the essential glassware to go with one's best china, for a well-set table at luncheon or dinner. Reduce the number to eight of each if your dinner service is for eight:

> 12 water tumblers (for luncheon or buffet)
> 12 water goblets (for dinner)
> 12 fruit juice glasses
> 12 sherbets (for fruit cup, desserts, etc.)

    12 tall glasses (for iced coffee and tea)
    12 finger bowls
    12 glass plates (for under finger bowls;
        may be used also for salads or desserts)

If liquor is customarily served in your household, you need the appropriate glassware for the purpose. To your list of essential glassware, you would add any or all of the following that you may have occasion to use:

    12 cocktail glasses
    12 highball glasses
    12 old-fashioned glasses
    12 wine glasses
    12 brandy glasses
    12 liqueur glasses
    12 champagne glasses

LINEN REQUIREMENTS FOR THE WELL-APPOINTED HOUSE

Household linens fall into four general classifications: table linens, kitchen linens, bedroom linens, and bathroom linens. The best assurance of quality is to buy well-known brands or to accept the advice of a reputable store.

The qualities to look for, whether buying linen, cotton, or percale, are fine weave, straight hems well fastened at the corners, and guaranteed fast colors. The way to judge these qualities is to *feel* the fabric, hold it up to the light and *look* through it, *examine* the selvage and the hems, and carefully *read* the labels for size, shrinkage, color guarantee, etc. If when you rub a corner of a sheet or tablecloth it feels stiff, and a white powdery film comes off on your fingers, it means the fabric contains a starchy filling, or sizing, to give it body and is therefore of an inferior quality. The sizing washes out in the first laundering and leaves the fabric limp. White linens should be sparkling white, not greyish or yellowish. The hems should be deep and straight, and well-finished. The selvage of properly woven linen feels thick and substantial. When held up and examined through the light, the threads of a good quality fabric look fairly uniform, do not show a marked variation from thin to thick.

Table linens are important as the background for lovely silver, china, and glassware. For breakfast, luncheon, and informal entertaining, you use what you like—from gaily colorful cork mats to fine, delicately embroidered cloths. For dinner, gleaming white linen damask is best, with an overhang of from 12 to 15 inches around the table. For formal dinners and buffets, or any important entertaining, a lace or embroidered banquet cloth is the most effective and the most suitable. Banquet cloths usually have a deeper overhang than ordinary linen dinner cloths, often reaching nearly to the floor.

Any list of essential linen must, of course, be based on average standard requirements. A bride in a tiny apartment who entertains very simply (mostly on bridge tables!) obviously doesn't need large damask dinner cloths or lace banquet cloths—but a busy hostess in a big house may need quite a few of them. The following lists approximate the essential requirements of a well-appointed house; but here, as in the choice of china and glassware, one must be guided by individual requirements.

Essential Table Linens

4 everyday breakfast cloths with napkins
2 17-piece breakfast sets
4 everyday luncheon cloths with napkins
2 17-piece luncheon sets
1 special linen or embroidered luncheon cloth with napkins
2 large damask dinner cloths with napkins
1 large lace or embroidered banquet cloth with napkins
2 to 4 bridge cloths with napkins
1 or 2 fine tea cloths
12 tea napkins
12 general utility napkins
12 to 24 cocktail napkins
12 finger-bowl doilies
linen, plastic, or cork mats
tray cloths

Essential Kitchen Linens

12 linen glass towels
12 linen or cotton dish towels
12 cotton-mesh dish cloths
6 hand towels for kitchen use
4 pot holders

Essential Bedroom Linens

6 sheets per bed
3 pillowcases per pillow

    2 bedspreads per bed
    2 mattress covers per bed
    1 pair of winter blankets per bed
    1 pair of summer blankets per bed
    1 down comforter per bed
    1 blanket cover per bed

Essential Bathroom Linens

    (For each bathroom)
    12 bath towels
    12 washcloths to match
    12 linen hand towels
    12 Turkish hand towels
    12 linen guest towels
    2 bath mats
    2 bathroom rugs
    1 shower curtain (unless bathroom has stall shower)

THE IMPORTANCE OF ACCESSORIES

In addition to the basic requirements outlined in the preceding pages, every well-appointed house needs the interesting extras, the accessories, that complete the picture. Accessories are either decorative or functional, or they are both. In any case, they are the important final touches that give character and distinction to a room and make it more liveable.

Every well-appointed house has plenty of ash trays, wastepaper baskets, trays, book ends, candy dishes—and all the many useful little accessories that add to general comfort and convenience. Every well-appointed house has plenty of lamps shedding good light where it is needed, a place to keep books and magazines, a place for cards and score pads, and any other essential paraphernalia of entertaining.

Never buy a decorative accessory on the basis of its own charm and appeal alone. Consider it in relationship to the room as a whole—its effect on the general appearance and basic color scheme. Accessories should be to a room what lovely jewels are to a costume—the final note of beauty and perfection. So be careful to avoid using ornaments or decorations that merely clutter up a room and add nothing to it.

2. AN OUTLINE OF SERVANTS AND THEIR DUTIES

No ONE can attempt to analyze the service needs of the modern household. Too many factors are involved, not the least of which is the difficulty nowadays of assembling an efficient, well-organized staff. The most important considerations, of course, are the size of the house, the manner of living, and the frequency and style of entertaining.

Assuming that one is in a position to maintain as large a staff as is necessary for complete or "perfect" service, a staff of three should be adequate for all but very large and pretentious houses where much lavish entertaining goes on all the time. The ideal staff of three consists of cook, butler (or waitress), and housemaid. They alternate for each other, providing complete service at all times. With a staff of three, there is always someone on duty in the kitchen to prepare meals, always someone to serve the meals, to answer the telephone and doorbell, to serve tea in the afternoon if required, to keep the house dusted and shined, and to take care of all the many other duties of the household.

Where there are young children in the family, the housemaid on a staff of three usually functions as nursemaid as well. The arrangement should be made with her at the time she is employed, so that there will be no misunderstanding later.

The duties expected of every servant in a household should be clearly stated and explained at the time they are hired.

Many large households are well-managed with two servants—one to prepare the food and the one to serve it, with the care of the house divided agreeably between them. The staff of two may consist of a cook who takes care of the downstairs work, and a waitress who takes care of the upstairs work (or any other fair and practical division of the household duties). Or the two may consist of a couple—man and wife—who function as cook and housemaid, butler and houseman. In some households, especially in the country, the man also serves as chauffeur. If it's a simple household where there is very little entertaining, he may help with the gardening as well. All this depends on the type of household and its requirements, and of course on whatever arrangements are made with the couple beforehand.

The household with a cook and waitress can expect fairly complete service, in the sense that one is always on hand to prepare and serve meals, answer the doorbell, etc., as arrangements are usually made for one to substitute for the other on days out. However it is not quite so simple with a couple. As a rule they ask for and are given time off together; and unless other arrangements are made with them in the beginning, the mistress of the house must be prepared to take over in their absence.

Obviously one cannot expect complete or perfect service with one maid. This doesn't mean that the one-maid household cannot function smoothly and efficiently, with charm—and even with distinction. But it does mean that the mistress must understand the limitations of her household and be guided by them. She should not attempt large formal dinners, or any type of lavish entertaining for which she is not equipped. She should not expect from one maid the impressive results that in other households are accomplished through the combined efforts of a well-organized staff. Unless she can count on additional help from the outside, she should plan only such types of entertaining as she and her maid can manage easily and well.

In fact, most households today are managed with no servants at all, and guests are beautifully entertained with no apparent effort. It's all a matter of intelligent organization and planning, and of utilizing the many fascinating new ideas for saving time and work. Modern aids to efficient housekeeping make maidless entertaining no very great problem, nowadays—not even to the businesswoman who likes to turn hostess after hours.

THE STAFF OF A BIG HOUSE

Each year sees fewer and fewer "great establishments" with large staffs of servants functioning behind the scenes with the precision of a small army. Such households are rapidly becoming a thing of the past. But no book of this kind would be complete without at least a broad, general outline of the types of servants likely to be employed by a large establishment, their duties and responsibilities, and their employer relationships.

The Housekeeper

When the mistress wishes to be relieved of responsibility in the management of a large, elaborately staffed household, the details are often placed in the hands of an efficient, experienced housekeeper who manages the servants and superintends the entire house exactly as the mistress herself would in a smaller establishment. She engages and dismisses servants, prepares the menus, is responsible for the marketing, takes charge of all linen and bathroom supplies, and in general assigns and supervises the work of all servants. In other houses, however, the housekeeper is in charge of the housemaids, parlormaids, and laundress only. She has no authority over the cook, butler, nurses, governesses, or lady's maid. Her sole responsibility, in this case, is the appearance of the house and the appearance and conduct of the maids who come under her supervision.

The housekeeper in a big establishment has her own quarters, usually consisting of a bedroom, bath, and sitting room. She does not wear a uniform but dresses in simple clothes, dark and conservative. As a rule her meals are brought to her in her own quarters by a kitchen maid or footman.

The Butler

In large establishments where there is no housekeeper, the butler usually functions in this capacity: He orders the supplies, keeps accounts, engages servants, and manages and supervises the details of the household. He is in full authority and is responsible for the smooth efficiency of daily routine, as well as all the details of entertaining.

In the houses of greatest size, management is often divided into several departments—each under a separate head. In such households, the butler has charge of the dining room and pantry, is responsible for the wines, chooses the china, linen, and glassware for every meal, and supervises the service of meals. Sometimes he is in charge of the entire main floor of the house except the kitchen, which is under the managment of the cook.

In smaller households, the butler does less supervising and more of the actual work himself. Where there are few other servants, he is required to polish silver, serve at table, assist with the downstairs cleaning, answer the doorbell and telephone. Often he combines his work with that of chauffeur and valet.

The butler does not wear livery. In the morning he wears a black or dark-blue suit with an inconspicuous tie. For luncheon in a formal household, and when he is on duty at the door, he wears a tail coat and black waistcoat with a wing collar and black four-in-hand tie. At six o'clock he changes into evening clothes, with black waistcoat and white tie. In simpler informal houses the butler wears a white, washable coat with dark trousers, day and night. The employer ordinarily furnishes the butler's clothes, but in some households he provides his own.

The Footman

In houses of great ceremony, the menservants who assist the butler are known as footmen, and they usually wear matching livery of some color distinctive of the household. This regulation livery is worn day and night, whenever the footmen appear in the front part of the house. At their work, which consists largely of cleaning, they wear an apron and shirt sleeves.

The duties of house footmen include cleaning the dining room and pantry, the entrance hall and vestibule, sidewalk, windows, mirrors, and fireplaces. They clean all brass and silver, and help with the dishes. They also set the table, assist in serving, answer the door when required, and take care of any special duties assigned them by the butler.

When guests are entertained formally in a fashionable household, one or two footmen are stationed at the door to admit guests. The butler waits in the front hall to conduct guests into the drawing room and announce them.

The first footman in a large household functions as deputy butler. He takes over the responsibilities of the butler when he is off duty.

The Chauffeur

In the city, a chauffeur does not usually live with the family. He is expected to provide his own board and lodging, except when traveling. When they are away from home, the employer always pays for the chauffeur's room and lodging for the entire period.

In the country there are usually quarters above the garage or elsewhere on the premises for the chauffeur and his family. If he is a single man, arrangements are generally made for him to eat with the servants in the kitchen.

A chauffeur's hours and duties are irregular. He must always be available to drive members of the family, or their guests, where they wish to go. A considerate employer tries to maintain a reasonable schedule so that the chauffeur has some regular free time he can count on for his own life and his own family. If a long trip is contemplated, the employer lets his chauffeur know well in advance.

The duties of a chauffeur include the washing and care of the car or cars. On a large estate there are often garage helpers to do this work, but otherwise it is the chauffeur's responsibility. In the city, chauffeurs are often employed for driving only, the car being washed and cared for in a public garage.

As a rule, the chauffeur's uniform is provided by his employer. It is usually dark in color, though it sometimes matches the footmen's livery. It may be worn either with trousers or puttees. The cap generally matches the uniform.

A well-trained chauffeur always gets out of the car and opens the door for his employer. He touches his cap when he receives orders, unless he is driving. In this case he nods to show he has understood. He does not smoke while he is on duty.

The Cook

In a large household with many servants, the cook does nothing outside the kitchen. This is her private domain and over it she rules supreme. She has several assistants and kitchen maids under her, to help in the preparation of food and to keep the kitchen clean. In some households, the cook does the marketing, prepares the menus for the day, and submits them to the butler or to the mistress of the house for approval, whichever the custom of the particular household may be. The approved or corrected menus are returned to the kitchen and are usually tacked up where the butler and footmen can refer to them before setting the table for luncheon or dinner.

In smaller establishments, the cook has considerably less executive responsibility. As a rule, the mistress of the house plans the meals and orders the supplies herself. The sole duty of the cook is to prepare the food attractively and well. She is sometimes required to take care of the kitchen and pantry, and perhaps do some of the other downstairs work, in addition to the cooking.

In a small informal household where there is just a cook and one other in help, the work of the household is of course divided between them. The arrangements are made when they are engaged, a schedule of duties convenient to the household being worked out by the mistress and strictly adhered to.

A cook who does nothing but cooking traditionally wears all white. But a cook who helps with the housework often wears a colored morning dress with a white apron.

The Kitchen Maid

The duties of a kitchen maid vary with the household. She is always under the supervision of the cook, and assists her in any way required with the preparation of food, washing of dishes, cleaning the kitchen, etc. She acts as waitress to the servants, and in some households she prepares the food for them. Often she is required to take care of the housekeeper's room; and if there are other kitchen maids, she alternates with them in taking care of the rooms of the butler and cook.

Kitchen maids may wear white uniforms, or they may wear cotton dresses matching the uniforms of the other maids in the house.

The Parlor Maid

In households where there are no footmen, one or more parlor maids assist the butler in such duties as waiting on the table, answering the door and the telephone, and keeping the downstairs floor in order. In some houses the parlor maid takes up the breakfast trays; and when there is no butler, she performs all of his duties, including the serving of afternoon tea.

Parlor maids generally wear cotton "work" dresses in the morning, with white collar and cuffs, and a large white apron with a bib. In the afternoon they wear black or gray uniforms of whatever type and fabric the mistress likes, with organdie or dotted swiss collars, cuffs, and aprons. Caps are sometimes worn, but not nearly as much as they used to be.

The Waitress

All uniforms for all maids in a house are provided by the employer; and in large, well-appointed households, all maids, particularly all downstairs maids, are dressed alike. Parlor maids and waitresses must be dressed for the afternoon by lunch time.

The waitress, like the parlor maid, wears a colored cotton uniform or "work" dress in the morning. This is changed before luncheon to a black or gray dress of rayon or silk with a daintier apron. If the mistress prefers a color to harmonize with the background of the dining room, there is no objection to it; but in that case the parlor maid and all other downstairs maids should have afternoon uniforms of the same color.

A good waitress is quick, neat, pleasant, and immaculate. Her hands and nails are spotless, her person beyond reproach. Her hair is neatly arranged, without ornaments, and with a net to keep it in place if necessary.

The duties of a waitress are to serve at all meals, assist in the kitchen with the preparation of salads, butter forms, dressings, beverages, etc. When there are no kitchen maids, she helps the cook with the dishwashing and cleaning up. Of course in small households where there are just a cook and a waitress, they divide the responsibilities of the house between them and the waitress generally does the upstairs work.

The Housemaid

Housemaids are what were once called, and in some houses are still called, chambermaids. They do all the chamber, or bedroom, work—making the beds, cleaning and dusting the bedrooms, polishing the silver on the dressing tables and the fixtures in the bathrooms, and in general keeping the upstairs clean and in order. A large establishment with many guest rooms may require as many as half a dozen housemaids—though nowadays there are few such pretentious households still remaining.

Housemaids dress as parlor maids and waitresses do, in "work" uniforms for the morning, more formal uniforms for the afternoon and evening.

The Lady's Maid

The duties of a lady's maid are to look after her mistress's person and her clothes. She must be able to shampoo and dress her hair, and manicure her nails. She must know how to remove spots from clothes, sponge and press them, mend and make minor repairs. A lady's maid lays out her mistress's clothes, draws the water for her bath, and helps her dress. Unless instructed otherwise, she waits up for her at night to help her undress, brush her hair, and take care of any other personal services that may be required. As a rule, a lady's maid washes the delicate stockings and lingerie that cannot be entrusted to an ordinary laundress. She always packs her mistress's bags and trunks when she goes visiting or traveling.

A lady's maid generally wears her own clothes, though in some families her dresses and aprons are provided. The correct outfit is an all-black dress, with or without white collar and cuffs, and a plain or pleated black taffeta apron. In summer a gray dress with a dainty white apron may be worn. When traveling with her mistress, a lady's maid wears a simple and inconspicuous suit or dress.

The Children's Nurse

A nursemaid should be chosen with great care, not only for her competence but for her kindness and sunny disposition. Anyone who is sullen, irritable, or short-tempered has no business taking care of children and should not be tolerated a day longer than absolutely necessary.

A children's nurse takes care of all the physical needs of her young charge or charges. She dresses them, gives them their meals, takes them out, safeguards their health and their well-being. She keeps them clean, neat, busy, and content, takes care of their clothes, takes pride in their good manners and good behavior, and does her best to make them happy.

In the house, a children's nurse wears at all times a white uniform and white shoes and stockings. When she goes out with the children, she wears a simple blue or gray coat over her uniform and a simple felt hat. Or she wears the regulation nurse's cape and the hat which goes with it.

The Governess

Strictly speaking, a governess is not a servant. She is a companion to the children of the household, and her chief duty is to supervise their manners and guide their developing young minds and personalities.

Ordinarily the governess has breakfast and lunch with the family. But if the children are still quite small, she has dinner with them in the nursery. If they are half-grown teen-agers, and the family like to be together at dinner to discuss their own intimate and private affairs, arrangements are made for the governess to be served elsewhere, perhaps in her own sitting room if she has one.

When a governess dines with the family, she is pleasant and agreeable, but self-effacing and tactful. She does not try to lead or dominate the conversation, speaks only when spoken to (except to the children) and keeps the relationship with her employers on a strictly professional basis. After dinner she withdraws to her own quarters, leaving the children to enjoy their parents' company, unless she is asked to stay or unless her professional duties require her presence with the children at that time.

A governess does not dine with the family when guests are at the table, unless specifically invited to do so. When introduced to guests at the table, she is cordial and polite, but does not enter into lengthy conversation with them. She leaves the dining room when the children do, under no circumstances joining the family and their guests in the drawing room. This is not a matter of snobbishness but of good judgment and good taste. The guests are there to see and talk with their friends, not their friends' employees.

A governess does not wear a uniform. She wears simple, conservative clothes of good quality and good taste. In voice, speech, dress, manner, and personality, she must be a shining example to the young persons in her charge.

The Valet

The valet is the personal servant of the man of the house. He attends to all his personal needs and comforts. He lays out his clothes, draws his bath, shaves him, helps him dress. He keeps his clothes in perfect order, brushing and pressing every suit after it has been worn. He packs his bags and trunks, buys his tickets, attends to his luggage, makes himself generally useful. He takes no part in general household routine, except in an emergency. However, he is expected to unpack the bags of gentlemen guests when they arrive, and serve them in any personal capacity they may wish while they are there.

The valet does not wear livery. At all hours of the day or evening, whether at home or traveling with his employer, he wears a dark, inconspicuous business suit with a black tie.

Addressing Servants

In a dignified, well-managed household, servants are addressed courteously. No well-bred man or woman is ever deliberately rude or curt to a servant, or permits a child to be insolent. Requests are made politely; and those gracious little phrases, "please" and "thank you", are never forgotten.

Maids are generally addressed by their first name in this country. (In England just the opposite is true—maids are addressed by their last name.) A pleasant "Good morning, Margaret" starts the day right for the mistress and maid. It is not considered good taste to call a maid by her nickname—such as Lizzy for Elizabeth or Maggie for Margaret.

The housekeeper in a large establishment is always called Mrs. or Miss. So are the children's governess and any professional members of the household staff such as tutors, secretaries, or registered nurses.

Butlers, chauffeurs, and all menservants are usually addressed by their last name. But a butler or chauffeur who has been with the family for many years is often called by his first name. So are menservants whose last names are too difficult to pronounce. Nowadays there is no longer any hard or fast rule about it.

The Average House Today Has One Maid—or None

In these times most households do not have large staffs of servants. They have only one maid—if, indeed, any at all! The subject of the one-maid household must therefore be given special attention.

For a small apartment, the best arrangement is to have a cook who prepares attractive meals and keeps the kitchen immaculate, and who can be depended upon to serve nicely when there are guests. The marketing and the care of the rest of the apartment would be the responsibility of the mistress.

In a house, the best one-maid arrangement is a good houseworker who can take over most of the responsibility of cleaning and keeping the place in order, leaving the mistress free to do the marketing and prepare the meals. When guests are entertained, extra help should be brought in from the outside, if possible—preferably a waitress, as a well-served meal is always more enjoyable.

Of course every household has its own particular needs. Where there are two or three small children, for example, the maid who is "wonderful" with youngsters usually is a great deal more useful than a maid who can cook and serve well when there are guests. The first and most important step is to find the kind of maid best suited to your needs and to the routine of your household.

The next step is to have a definite and clear-cut plan, or system, for running your household. Not even a tiny apartment can be managed efficiently on a haphazard hit-or-miss basis. There must be an established daily routine, clearly understood by the maid from the start, and agreeable both to her and to the mistress. Strict adherence to this schedule is the only way friction can be avoided and a satisfactory mistress-maid relationship established.

It is very important for the mistress of the household to know exactly how everything should be done. She should be able to show or explain to her maid how she wants the door opened for guests, the dinner served, or the telephone answered. She should not expect the maid to know the ways and customs of the household instinctively, or to pick them up gradually. She should explain everything carefully and in detail, and make any necessary corrections courteously and in private, not before guests or other members of the family.

Only one person in the household should give instructions to the maid. Children should not be permitted to give orders, or to interfere with the maid's routine schedule of duties.

The room and board a maid receives are part of her pay, and it is the responsibility of the employer to provide adequately for her comfort and well-being. She is entitled to a comfortable bed and pleasant surroundings, suitable bathroom facilities, and good meals. As a rule she is also provided with the uniforms and aprons she is expected to wear.

How to Engage a Maid

The best way to acquire a maid is to go to an employment agency and interview applicants. Agencies usually have the widest choice and best candidates; and most agencies are reliable. In New York City, and many other large cities, agencies must be licensed; and to protect themselves, as well as their clients, all applicants are carefully investigated. But whether you secure your maid through an agency, through advertising, or through the recommendation of a friend, *always check her references personally.*

When interviewing a maid in regard to a position, look at her references first. If they are not satisfactory, there is no point in interviewing her further. The references should be fairly recent, and should be specific as to character, personal qualities, and capabilities. An evasive reference is not a good reference.

If the written references seem satisfactory, talk to the maid about your household—the number of people in your family, the habits and customs regarding meals, the usual daily routine. Tell her about time off, about the accommodations she will have, the salary you are willing to pay. You can generally tell a great deal about her by the questions she asks and the remarks she makes. And you can judge from her appearance, too; if she is sloppy and untidy in her person, she isn't likely to keep your house looking neat and clean.

On your part, be straightforward and fair. Give a true picture of the job. Don't conceal any unusual or difficult aspects of your household; but on the other hand, don't exaggerate the problems unnecessarily. Just state clearly and accurately what the conditions are, what will be expected of her, and what you offer in return.

How to Get Along with a Maid

Much of the smoothness and efficiency in running a household, and much of the comfort and well-being of the family, depend on the relationship between mistress and maid. The relationship can be a very pleasant and agreeable one, but it calls for understanding and fairness on both sides.

A well-bred mistress is kind and considerate, but *firm*. She does not make unreasonable demands, nor blame a servant for her own mistakes or mismanagement. But neither does she allow carelessness or laxity in appearance, behavior, or the performance of duty. When the mistress of a house meets and fulfills her obligations to a maid, she has every right to expect competent service in return. *Both* sides of the bargain must be kept, otherwise the relationship cannot be a successful one.

A well-bred mistress never loses her temper, and especially never scolds or corrects a servant in the presence of guests. When correction is necessary, she talks to the maid privately, in a pleasant and helpful manner. She is consistently fair and just, never imposes on her maid or takes advantage of her, doesn't encroach on her free time, or expect favors without making some adequate return. She is appreciative of work well done, and doesn't hesitate to give praise when it is deserved. She makes it convenient for her maid to go to church on Sunday, if she wishes, and permits her to receive an occasional visitor in the kitchen or in her own quarters if she does not abuse the privilege in any way. This last is especially important if the maid has no other home, and therefore no suitable place to receive her friends.

Correct Dress and Behavior for a Maid

Neat appearance and good manners are just as important in a maid as efficiency in her work. She should be immaculate in her clothes and on her person, soft-spoken and restrained in speech, unfailingly polite to members of the family and to all visitors who come to the house.

A maid's uniforms and aprons are provided by her employer, but it's her own responsibility to take care of them, to keep them clean and in good order. She should dress as the mistress wishes—usually in cotton "work" dresses in the morning, more formal uniforms in the afternoon and evening, and always a crisp, freshly laundered apron. Aprons should be changed daily, morning uniforms every second day, and formal or serving uniforms as frequently as required.

A well-dressed maid wears black shoes and dark stockings, no elaborate jewelry, no perfume, and very little make-up. She wears her hair simply and neatly. Caps are very formal and rarely used nowadays; but if the mistress wishes her maid to wear a cap, she should of course comply graciously. When an employer provides the uniforms, she is entitled to that much co-operation.

A courteous, self-respecting maid does not shout upstairs or from one room to another. She does not open closed doors without knocking, listen to private family conversations, gossip about the household and its affairs with outsiders. She does not use the family radio or television, or make personal telephone calls without asking permission to do so. She doesn't sulk; if she has something on her mind, she talks to the mistress about it. She doesn't resent well-meant advice or criticism; she welcomes it as a means of improving herself. She doesn't impose on the people who employ her or take unfair advantage of them in any way. She keeps her own room neat and clean, and ready for inspection at any time. She takes pride in being trustworthy, dependable, fair-minded, and conscientious.

In a formal household, a maid addresses her employers as "madam" and "sir." But in a simple, informal household, the employer's name is used instead—as for example, "Yes, Mrs. Smith" or "Good morning, Mr. Smith." Young children are called by their first names; but half-grown sons and daughters are properly addressed as "Miss Jane" or "Mr. Richard."

A reliable maid gives at least a week's notice before leaving. She always tells her employers why she is leaving. She owes them that courtesy—just as they would owe her the courtesy of an explanation if she were dismissed.

How to Dismiss a Maid

Sometimes a maid is dismissed because the family is moving to smaller quarters, or perhaps to another city. Under these circumstances it is kind to let her know well ahead of time, to give her an opportunity to find another position. As the fault is not hers, it isn't fair to put her to any loss or hardship, if it can be avoided. Some employers feel their responsibility in this matter so keenly that they undertake to advertise and find another position for a well-liked maid when they can no longer keep her in their employ.

But when a maid is dismissed for being unsatisfactory, a week's notice is all that is required. If having her around for another week is likely to be unpleasant, she may be given a week's extra pay and asked to leave in the next day or two. Of course a maid who is dishonest, or commits some other serious offense against the family, is dismissed at once—without notice and without extra pay.

If a maid is dismissed for being lazy, careless, irresponsible, personally unpleasant, it's only fair to tell her the truth, as kindly and courteously as possible. She is entitled to know why she is being dismissed. If she knows what her faults are, she can make an effort to correct them, and perhaps be more satisfactory to her next employers.

It is never wise to act impulsively, to dismiss a maid in a fit of temper. Always give yourself time to think it over, and perhaps talk it over with the family. If it's agreed there are grounds for dismissal, handle the situation with dignity and restraint and with as much kindness as possible. Explain to the maid how or why she has failed to come up to expectations, or to meet the needs of your particular household—and suggest that she is likely to be happier elsewhere. Tell her you are giving her a week's notice, and that you will give her a reference for the *good qualities* you have found her to have. That takes some of the unpleasantness from the situation, and is a much more satisfactory procedure than losing your temper and getting all the accumulated "'peeves" off your mind. It doesn't necessarily obligate you to give her a good reference; all you need to do is enumerate her desirable qualities and omit the undesirable ones.

On Giving a Reference

No maid should ever be refused a reference, unless she has been dismissed for dishonesty or some equally serious fault. References carry a great deal of weight when applying for a job; and refusal to give a former maid a reference because of dissatisfaction with her work may keep her from earning a living.

Naturally it wouldn't be fair to the next employer to misrepresent. But you can always find one or two good qualities to mention without stretching the truth.

In writing a letter of reference for a worthy, completely satisfactory servant, always put in every good quality you can think of. Omission of a quality may imply *lack* of it. All good references should include mention of honesty, sobriety, capability, disposition, reliability, and such personal traits as neatness, cleanliness, and agreeable manners. The reason for leaving should always be given.

Don't begin a letter of reference with *"To whom it may concern."* That phrase is no longer in good taste or good usage. Avoid also the phrase, *"This is to certify."* The correct way to write a letter of reference is without a salutation, as follows:

257 Park Avenue

Mary Johnson has been in my employ for three years as cook and general houseworker.

She is immaculate in her person, industrious and cooperative, and of amiable disposition. I can recommend her as honest and sober, and completely reliable in every way.

She is leaving of her own accord, as she prefers living in the country, and I sincerely regret losing her.

I recommend Mary Johnson very highly, and shall be glad to answer any inquiries concerning her.

Margaret Preston
(Mrs. George T. Preston)

June, 1949

3 . MODERN ENTERTAINING

The days of great estates and lavish parties, with dozens of trained servants to handle every detail with precision and skill, are now largely a thing of the past. The general trend today is toward less pretentious living; and the whole keynote of modern entertaining is on a correspondingly simpler and more informal scale.

Nowadays it doesn't matter whether you live in a two-room apartment or a 20-room house—whether there's a jewel of a maid in the kitchen or no one at all to help you. If your surroundings reflect good taste and gracious charm, if your friends are congenial, the talk stimulating, the food well-prepared and attractively served, your parties gay, lively, and relaxing . . . you are a *successful hostess.*

THE TREND TODAY IS FOR SIMPLE ENTERTAINING

The most important single factor in successful entertaining is not to attempt anything for which you do not have the room and facilities. It may be generous, but it is by no means *good hospitality,* to invite more people than you can comfortably and conveniently take care of. So don't attempt pretentious dinners or parties in a small apartment without adequate help—and especially without adequate experience. Start with simple little suppers and buffets, and try more elaborate parties as you gain more confidence in yourself.

Don't make the mistake of thinking you can give a formal dinner for twelve just because you happen to have a dozen beautiful service plates and a dozen fine-cut crystal goblets! You need far more than the required amount of silver, china, and glassware. You need a dining room that comfortably seats your guests. You need (at the very least) a cook to prepare the dinner, and a well-trained butler or waitress to serve it.

The sensible way, if your house is small and your facilities limited, is to entertain smaller groups more frequently. Concentrate on informal card parties, colorful and imaginative buffets, intimate Sunday night suppers. Try to perfect one particular type of entertaining so that you can do it supremely well. It's far better to acquire the reputation for delightful *little parties* that you can handle smoothly and without apparent effort, than to try to impress people with large, elaborate functions which are poorly managed.

HOW TO ENTERTAIN ATTRACTIVELY WITHOUT SERVANTS

Entertaining in a servantless home can be gracious and charming, and not too great a burden on the hostess. It's simply a matter of intelligent organization and planning: of selecting the *right type* of function in the first place and then making all preparations well in advance. The more that can be taken care of before the guests arrive, the better. When the house, the food, the table, the step-by-step details of the party are all taken care of, the hostess should have at least an hour (more if possible) to relax and refresh herself before the guests arrive.

Next to basic simplicity of function, and careful planning and preparation beforehand, the factor that counts most in entertaining successfully without servants is *imagination*. There are almost endless possibilities nowadays for entertaining one's friends in amusing and charming ways, without too much effort or too great expense. A clever hostess can make the simplest foods appear glamorous and exciting by the way she serves them . . . can make an ordinary little Sunday night supper seem like a gala occasion by the originality of menu or service.

Some hostesses concentrate on chafing-dish specialties. They make a hobby of tracking down and collecting unusual chafing-dish recipes, and of inviting select groups of friends to help them sample each new "discovery." Guests are always delighted to be included in such parties. It makes them feel like gourmets. The menu, as a rule, consists of little more than fruit juice served from a tray, the chafing-dish specialty, a salad and simple dessert—all very easy to prepare and no trouble at all to serve.

Some hostesses cook and serve on oak planks, acquiring a reputation among their friends for wonderful planked steak and planked fish dinners. The whole dinner (except for appetizer and dessert) is arranged on one large plank, or on individual planks for each guest. Oak planks for cooking are available in many department stores, and directions for preparing planked dinners can be found in most good cookbooks. Food prepared this way not only looks and tastes delicious, but is quick and easy to serve and saves the hostess many steps. The planks can be arranged beforehand, ready to pop into the oven at the proper time. When ready, they are taken directly from the oven to the table —without the need for extra serving plates. With fruit or tomato juice served from a tray as the first course, and dessert served from a utility table arranged conveniently beside the hostess, everything can be handled smoothly and efficiently, without a lot of jumping up and down. The auxiliary table used for serving should have a shelf where the hostess can stack the used dishes. A tea wagon on wheels is very convenient for a hostess who does her own serving.

Among the many easy, informal ways of entertaining without servants—and a favorite nowadays—are "kitchen parties" after the theater or after an evening of bridge. Cold cuts, fillings for sandwiches, salads, etc., are spread out on a counter or on a table in the kitchen, and guests help themselves to what they want—making their own sandwiches, experimenting with their own combinations, and having a lot of fun doing it. The guests either gather around the kitchen table or carry their plates into the living room or dining room. Dessert is usually cake, to which the guests also help themselves; but if coffee is served, the hostess should take care of this responsibility herself.

Some hostesses delight in casserole cookery, some specialize in smörgasbord tables, some like to cook electrically at the table, some are expert in outdoor barbecues and picnics. And of course there are always buffet dinners and suppers, still one of the most convenient and enjoyable ways to entertain. These, and many others, are all pleasant, informal ways of entertaining which are easily managed without help.

When to Give Parties

People often ask, "When is the best time to give a party?" Actually there is no "best" time, unless it's a time that synchronizes with the best moments of your house. If you have just had the living room repainted, if you have just had an interesting new scenic wallpaper put in your dining room, or if you have just installed television or sound movies—that's a good time to stage a party. Or in summer when your peach tree is in fabulous bloom, or your rose garden at the peak of its beauty, this is the time to invite your friends so that they may enjoy its fleeting loveliness with you.

But in general, any time you want to be with your friends and enjoy their company is a good time to invite them to your house. Try to do your most important entertaining when you are not occupied with too many outside interests—when you are relaxed and can make your plans leisurely and without pressure.

All special events—like birthdays and anniversaries—are, of course, occasions for special entertaining. Holidays like Thanksgiving, Christmas, and New Year are traditional for party-giving—and many hostesses plan their important entertaining to coincide with these gala days of the year. The holiday season is a fine time for open-house hospitality, with friends dropping in all through the afternoon or evening—as specified in the invitation. Refreshments may be just eggnog and fruitcake, or an elaborate buffet that is kept constantly replenished for new arrivals.

Preparations for a Party

As soon as you issue invitations for a luncheon, dinner, buffet, bridge, or any kind of party, your preparations for it should begin.

The first step is to outline all details in your mind, or write them down on a sheet of paper, so that you know exactly what needs to be done and can proceed systematically with your arrangements. There should be nothing for you to think about on the day of the party but last-minute essentials which cannot be taken care of in advance.

Decide well ahead of time what you are going to wear, so that you can put that matter out of your mind. Know exactly where you are going to put the guests' wraps. Plan the menu, and make a list of the supplies you will need. Decide on the linen; and give some thought to the centerpiece and the kind of flowers you would like to use. If it's to be a dinner party, make a table chart and plan the seating.

The week before the party is the time to shine up the house and put it in apple-pie order. Don't leave everything for the last day or two; a final dusting is all the house should need just before the guests arrive. See that all the brass is polished (including the knocker on the front door, if you have one). See that the flatware, silver vegetable dishes, silver coffee service and whatever else you plan to use are bright and polished. See that the glassware is clean and sparkling, ready to put on the table. All of these are time-consuming jobs which should not be left until the last day.

Preparations for a party should include a thorough cleaning of rugs, draperies, lighting fixtures, mirrors, windows if necessary, and of course all woodwork and furniture. The house should be made to look as clean, fresh, and attractive as possible; and on the day of the party there should be flowers, greens, or growing plants in the party rooms to make them look "dressed up" and festive.

The hostess who must do everything herself is wise to plan a menu she can prepare at least partially the day before, so that she'll be free to spend most of the time with her guests—and not in the kitchen. It's always best for the food supplies and flowers to be in the house the day before the party. Usually the dessert can be made and stored in the refrigerator; and certainly the lettuce for the salad can be washed and wrapped in a napkin or dish towel, ready for use.

When You Prepare for One Party—It's Smart to Give Two

Many hostesses have learned from experience that giving two parties, one right after the other, is easier and more economical per party than one. For the most difficult part of entertaining is the preparation that precedes it.

When two parties are given, *the same preparations serve both.* There is just one super-shining of the silver and glassware—one thorough cleaning of the house—one shopping expedition. The same flowers and the same centerpiece can be used for both parties. All that's necessary is to empty the ash trays, dust the furniture, freshen the rugs and carpets, and the house is ready for the next batch of guests. You can even serve the identical menu, if you want to. You can prepare most of the food for both parties at the same time, if you plan wisely and well—and if the parties are just a day apart.

So when you plan one party, plan two. It's the smart, efficient way to take care of your social obligations.

PLANNING THE MENU

Guests who are invited to your house expect food and drink of some kind to be served, and much of your reputation as a hostess depends on how you meet this responsibility.

A hostess wise in the ways of entertaining usually has two or three "specialties of the house" on which she can count for party fare. These are special, perhaps unusual, dishes which she (or her cook) has learned to prepare supremely well. Many hostesses have one "perfect menu" which they count on for parties, changing it only in minor details.

Unless one has a very competent and trustworthy cook in the kitchen, it's important to supervise the preparation of food personally. A gracious hostess does not serve haphazard refreshments; she makes certain that everything is well prepared and attractively served. It isn't necessary to serve elaborate or expensive food. Even the simplest refreshments can be made to look festive with just a little extra thought and care.

The hostess who does not have servants to help her should plan an interesting but *convenient* menu, one which won't keep her in the kitchen most of the evening. She should try to serve dishes that can be prepared beforehand, instead of being rushed into preparation at the last moment. She should, of course, avail herself of all the modern time-saving conveniences such as frozen foods, instant cake and biscuit mixes, soluble coffee, ready-to-freeze ice cream, etc. The time saved in preparation can be put to good use in garnishing the dishes in some new or unusual way.

As a final word, any entertaining you do at home should be reasonably simple in plan, menu, and service—with the emphasis on congenial company rather than creating an impression. The trend today is definitely away from formality toward gay and relaxed entertaining.

4. TABLE SETTINGS

A BEAUTIFULLY appointed table can make the simplest refreshments seem festive and important.

Beautiful appointments are not necessarily expensive ones. The three essentials of an attractive table—whether it's lavish or very simple and modest—are *harmony, good taste*, and a *shining, immaculate sparkle* to everything, from linens to glassware.

Though closely allied, harmony and good taste in table settings must be considered separately. For although each thing on the table may be in exquisite taste individually, together they may present an inharmonious whole.

As an example, a plaid homespun cloth may be colorful and charming in its own right; but when it is combined with the formal elegance of fine bone china, the effect is incongruous. So watch texture, pattern, colors, design when you choose table linens to go with your silver and china. Don't combine things which obviously do not belong together. A table may be elegant or gay, homey or formal, quaint or classic. But whatever it is, it should be *consistently* so—in china, glass, silver, linen, and decorations. All things on the table should harmonize, should be as lovely *together* as they are by themselves, presenting a pleasing and inviting all-over picture to the eye.

Good taste calls also for harmony with the surroundings and with the type of function. You wouldn't use a lace cloth on the terrace, for example, nor a printed cotton cloth for an important formal dinner. A table setting may be as imaginative and original as you like, but it must be *suitable* as well. It must conform with the tone and spirit of the occasion, and be in keeping with the type of meal to be served.

Needless to say, much of the beauty and distinction of a table setting depends on its shining condition. The silver should be bright and polished, the linen fresh and crisp, the china and glassware sparkling. It has been said that one can often tell more about a woman by the appearance of her table than by her dress or speech. Nothing should ever be put on the table without a wiping or polishing—or a good dousing in hot soapsuds, if necessary. China or glassware that has been put aside for some time should always be washed thoroughly before use.

A well-set table is never cluttered with unnecessary appointments, nor burdened with unnecessary decorations. Only what is actually required should be used. The fewer things that appear on the table, the more beautifully the china, silver, and glassware show to advantage.

CORRECT TABLE COVERINGS

There is great variety in table coverings, from simple plastic place mats to fabulous banquet cloths luminous with metal threads or hand decorated in elaborate designs. But for the dignified formality of an important dinner or luncheon, a snowy white linen damask cloth with matching napkins is still the most acceptable choice. The table should be completely covered; and there should be an overhang of at least twelve inches all around.

A damask cloth should be placed on a silence cloth of felt or cotton. It should be laid very carefully so that the long center crease runs exactly down the center of the table. If possible, large linen dinner cloths should be kept on cardboard rollers so that there is only one crease lengthwise down the middle. Otherwise the hostess should try to smooth the cloth as much as possible in laying it, and make sure that all creases run at right angles to the edge of the table.

Never use all-white or almost all-white china on a white table cloth. The effect is deadly, and makes even the most wonderful food look pallid and uninteresting. If your best china is white or nearly white, use a delicately tinted linen cloth for your dinners and important luncheons. You'll find that a tinted cloth makes a much more effective background for your table setting.

If you use a lace, net, embroidered, or sheer organdie cloth, place it directly on the table with no silence cloth underneath. In general, the finer the fabric of the table covering and the more elaborate its workmanship, the more formal it becomes, calling for matching formality in appointments and in service. Lace and embroidered cloths usually overhang the edge of the table more than damask, sometimes almost reaching to the floor.

For informal table settings, one may use practically any type of covering that is effective and suitable. Runners and place mats, now widely used instead of cloths, have many advantages. They are easier to launder and to keep looking fresh and crisp, and they show up the lovely polished surface of the table. Cork, plastic, and straw place mats are very practical, as they are just wiped clean after use. But they should be used only for breakfast and for very simple, informal entertaining.

When place mats are used, one should be at each cover, close to the edge of the table and with no pads underneath. There should be ample space between each mat, and of course they should be arranged geometrically, around the table. The most inflexible rule of table setting is that everything should be perfectly spaced and balanced.

A runner to match the place mats is generally used in the center of the table. But it can be omitted if it crowds the table or interferes with the individual covers.

TABLE DECORATIONS AND CENTERPIECES

In planning a centerpiece, always bear in mind that people like to see each other across the table, and that a tall ornament or towering arrangement of flowers which obstructs the view is not desirable. Keep the center ornament low and unobtrusive, so that people can see and talk with each other freely across the table.

It's a mistake to overdecorate the table to the point of making it look crowded or cluttered. A large table can naturally take more decoration than a small one; but large or small, the table looks best when the centerpiece is simple and restrained in motif.

Cut flowers are by far the most effective decoration for any table, regardless of the occasion. Try to select flowers that go well with your china and linen; and it's wise to provide yourself with a book on flower arrangements so that you can make the most effective possible use of even a few fresh-cut blossoms. If you have only a few wispy flowers left in your garden, try putting them on a mirror with some dainty porcelain figures around them, and see what a charming effect you can achieve.

Never use wilted flowers for your centerpiece. Flowers must be fresh and fragrant to be effective, and no flowers at all are better than droopy, half-dead ones. Avoid also the use of artificial fruit or flowers. They may look all right from a distance, but they are never effective on the table. If no fresh flowers are available, use one of your cheerful little house plants, or ivy growing in a colorful bowl, or even an amusing figure or group of animals. Anything is acceptable that suits the occasion and the type of table appointments, and that does not obstruct vision or interfere with conversation across the table.

When candles are used on the table, only new ones will do. It is not good form to use half-burned candles on a guest table. The glare of candles burning at eye level, or below eye level, can be very annoying—so be sure they are tall enough. The flame should be at least fifteen inches above the table.

A clever hostess uses the slightest fragment of an idea for a theme for her table. If the guests of honor are going abroad, for example, the focal point of interest might be a ship sailing on a mirror plateau, decorated with blue chalk to look like the sea. Or if a guest has just returned from Mexico, the use of a Mexican motif as the centerpiece is not only flattering but colorful and effective as a form of decoration.

Holidays and special occasions offer many possibilities for amusing and interesting table decorations. For Christmas, one might use a sheer organdie cloth over shining red oilcloth, with a miniature Christmas tree, or a bowl of colorful Christmas tree ornaments as the centerpiece. For St. Valentine's Day, a snowy white cloth with a heart-shaped centerpiece of red roses is striking and memorable. For Hallowe'en, a scooped-out pumpkin may be filled with flowers. For Thanksgiving, a centerpiece of fresh fruit and autumn leaves is effective. For birthdays, anniversaries, and showers, the most inspired table decorations are always those which take their theme from the occasion.

Basic Procedure for Setting the Table

When the table is covered and the centerpiece arranged, the next step is the setting of the places. Each place, or setting for one person, is called a cover. It includes china, silver, glasses, napkin, chair, and accessories. All covers should be identical, they should be evenly spaced around the table, and if possible directly opposite each other.

Following are the step-by-step directions for setting a dinner table properly. The same procedure applies to luncheon tables, except that smaller plates are generally used—and naturally the silver and glassware depend on what is to be served. The only other important difference is that service plates are not used on luncheon tables; place plates are used instead to mark each individual cover.

1. Decide on the seating arrangement. The host and hostess sit at opposite ends of the table. The woman guest of honor is placed at the right of the host, the man guest of honor at the right of the hostess. Other guests are seated any way that is convenient and likely to be congenial, men and women alternating.

2. Mark each individual place at the table with a service plate. A service plate is somewhat larger than a dinner plate; and though it's usually different in design, it should harmonize in style and coloring. The purpose of the service plate is to mark each cover beautifully and decoratively. It may be removed when the first course is served, or it may be left in place and the first course served on top of it. Both procedures are correct. When service plates remain on the table for the first course, they are replaced by the hot plates for the main course or entrée. Service plates should be spaced evenly on the table, about twenty-four inches apart from center to center, and about one inch from the edge.

3. Arranging silver on the table is simply a matter of placing it in

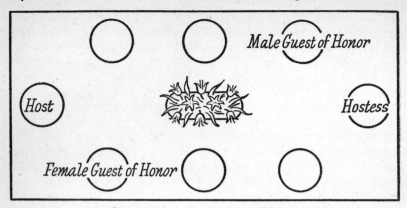

Seating Arrangement at Dinner

the order of its use, from the outside toward the plate. Forks are always at the left; spoons and knives at the right. There are only two exceptions to this rule: (1) The oyster fork is usually placed at the extreme right of the place setting—though it is not incorrect to place it at the left, if one wishes. (2) The butter spreader is not included with the other knives, but is placed on the butter plate.

The silver should be laid evenly on the table, the handles about an inch from the edge. The tines of the forks should be turned up, and the cutting edges of the knives faced in toward the plate. Only silver up to the dessert course is placed on the table. The dessert fork and spoon are brought in with the dessert plates. Three forks and three knives are the maximum number that should be included at one place setting. If additional forks or knives are required, they are brought in during the dinner.

4. For formal dinners, napkins are generally folded in squares and placed on the service plate. For all other occasions, napkins may be folded in squares, rectangles, or triangles, as preferred. They may be laid on the place plate, or at the left of the forks with the loose-edged corner facing in.

5. The correct position for the water glass is directly above the tip of the dinner knife. Whatever other glassware is included in the setting depends on what wines are to be served.[1] But two glasses in addition to the water goblet should be the maximum, even for an elaborate dinner. If more than two wines are served, the required glasses are placed on the table just before the wine is poured. Glasses are usually grouped on the table to form a triangle. The water glass and

[1]For the correct wines to serve with various courses, and the proper glassware to use, see pages 155 to 168.

First Course, Dinner

Soup Course

Main Course

Salad Course

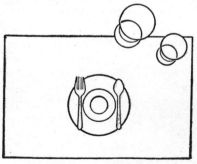

Dessert Course

first wine glass are in a parallel line—the second wine glass in back, forming the point of the triangle. Or the glasses may be in a straight line slanting downward to the right from the water goblet.

6. Bread-and-butter plates are placed at the left of the setting, above the forks. The butter spreader is placed along the edge of the plate, either horizontally or parallel with the forks.

Bread-and-butter plates are often omitted at a formal dinner, as butter is not served. An assortment of bread and rolls is passed during the soup course, guests helping themselves with their fingers and placing the bread or rolls right on the table. But bread-and-butter plates are useful and convenient even when butter is not served, for the bread, for relishes, etc., and nowadays it is considered courteous to provide them even though they do not traditionally belong on a formal table.

7. Individual salt and pepper shakers are desirable; but for a large group of people, one pair of salt and pepper shakers for each two guests is customary. Some hostesses use open salt dishes with tiny spoons in preference to shakers. Either is correct; but open salt dishes *must be freshly filled* each time they are used. Guests should never be served salt that has been standing exposed to dust for some time.

Salt and pepper shakers, individual nut dishes, ash trays and other smokers' items (if there is to be general smoking at the table) go at the top of the service plate—between the bread-and-butter plate and the glasses.

8. Nowadays place cards are used only for special occasions—like large Christmas or anniversary parties—or for formal, ceremonious dinners for ten persons or more. Plain white cards are considered the best taste, though very *simply* decorated cards are not objectionable. The name of the guest is written on the card in ink, with the title of Mr., Mrs., Miss, Senator, Judge, Doctor—or whatever it may be— preceding it. The correct position for the card is on the napkin (if the napkin is on the service plate) . . . or centered directly above the service plate with nothing in front of it to obscure the name. Guests should be able to see at a glance where they are to sit.

5. HOW TO GIVE SUCCESSFUL DINNER PARTIES

OF ALL formal entertaining, dinners are perhaps the most difficult and exacting, and to a novice the most formidable.

A formal dinner is a dinner of *ceremony*, calling for perfection in every detail of service. Obviously it should not be attempted by any-one who lacks the space, furnishings and great personal tact required to manage such functions properly.

Even for a very small dinner, with only four or six at the table, there must be at least two servants—one to be in the kitchen through-out the meal, and one to serve. With eight or ten people at the table, at least two are required to serve properly. Unless a formal din-ner can be absolutely correct in every detail of preparation and service, it's best to avoid it entirely.

Planning a Formal Dinner Party

To give a perfect formal dinner, whether for ten persons or two hundred, calls for a combination of many skills—not the least of which is inviting guests who are congenial, and seating them at the table to assure the maximum enjoyment of good talk and good fel-lowship.

Assuming that you have the space, appointments, and experience to give a gracious formal dinner, the first step is to set the date. Plans should be made well ahead of time, for invitations to a formal dinner must be mailed two or three weeks in advance.[1]

The customary hour for formal dinners in large American cities is eight o'clock. However dinner may begin as early as seven, if guests are going on to the theater or opera afterward; or it may be delayed until nine o'clock, if that hour is more convenient for the hosts or their guests.

In making up your guest list, try to choose people of reasonably similar interests and tastes. No dinner party can be a success if the guests are tactlessly chosen. A well-bred hostess does not knowingly invite to the same dinner party people who dislike or resent each other. Nor does she ever invite a man to dinner without his wife, nor a woman without her husband.

Arrival of Dinner Guests

In days gone by, the inevitable sign of an important formal dinner in a big house was an awning from front door to curb, with a red carpet beneath it. But nowadays awnings are rarely seen, except at weddings; and red carpets are used only for the most elaborate, cere-monious functions.

[1]For the wording of dinner invitations, formal and informal, see pages 289 to 301.

There should be someone on duty to admit and announce guests on formal occasions. If possible, there should be dressing rooms on the entrance floor, one for the ladies and one for the men; or at least some convenient place for guests to leave their wraps.

In most big houses, guests are announced at the door of the drawing room before entering. This is rightfully the responsibility of a butler; but in homes where there is no butler, a maid may be trained to announce guests as they arrive.

The correct procedure for announcing guests is as follows: As soon as guests arrive and have doffed their outer wraps, the butler (unless he knows them by sight) asks, "What name, please?" He addresses the question to whichever one is nearest him, man or woman, and that person answers, "Mr. and Mrs. Blank." The butler then proceeds to the door of the drawing room, takes a few steps inside to where the hostess is standing, and announces the guests in a clear but not too-loud tone of voice. If they enter together, he announces them as "Mr. and Mrs. Blank." If the husband falls behind his wife and they enter separately, it's better to announce them separately: "Mrs. Blank"—a pause, and then: "Mr. Blank."

Men of high executive rank (like the President of the United States and the Governor of a State) are always announced first at formal functions, and take precedence over their wives in entering the drawing room.[2]

The hostess must receive all guests personally and cordially, as they arrive. She stands just inside the door of her drawing room, and the host should be somewhere near by. As guests arrive, they both advance to greet them with a smile and a handshake. For a minute or two, the hostess gives the new arrivals her complete attention, making them feel welcome and desired. Then she relinquishes them to the host, who sees that they are introduced to others in the room and are courteously taken care of.

When there is no host, a woman may ask a brother, a male relative, or perhaps a close family friend to act as host and take over the traditional duties and responsibilities of a host at a dinner party.

WAITING FOR DINNER TO BE SERVED

As a rule, guests remain standing in little groups in the drawing room while waiting for dinner to be announced. The reason for this is that the hostess must remain standing near the entrance of the drawing room until all her guests arrive; and as their hostess is stand-

[2]For official etiquette, see Part XIII, pages 509 to 515.

ing, none of the men may sit down. Many of the women therefore also remain on their feet, as it's awkward for a woman who is sitting to talk to a man who is standing.

It's while guests are standing about chatting and waiting for dinner to be announced, that cocktails and hors d'oeuvres are generally served in the drawing room. They are prepared in the kitchen and offered on a tray, and may be served any time after the first guests arrive. One servant circulates among the guests with a tray of cocktails, and another with a tray of hors d'oeuvres; but if the household staff is limited, a tray of hors d'oeuvres may be placed where the guests can help themselves while a servant passes the tray of drinks.

How Dinner Is Announced

The butler or maid who admits the guests should know exactly how many are expected. When all have arrived, the butler (or maid) goes to the kitchen to make sure that dinner is ready, looks into the dining room, checks the table, and lights the candles if there are any. When he is satisfied that everything is exactly as it should be, he goes to the door of the drawing room, bows slightly to the hostess, and says, "Dinner is served." The announcement should be made quietly to the hostess, not to the room at large.

Entering the Dining Room

In large and formal households, an envelope containing the name of the lady he is to take in to dinner is usually handed to each gentleman on arrival. Here is the way it is done:

The names of the ladies are written on cards, slipped into envelopes, sealed and addressed to the gentlemen. They are then arranged on a silver tray, which is offered each man as he is about to enter the drawing room. He takes the envelope addressed to him, opens it as soon as convenient, reads the name, then slips it into his pocket.

In less formal households, and for less elaborate dinners, the hostess merely tells each man who his partner is to be.

When dinner is announced, each man seeks out the lady he is to take in to dinner and offers her his arm. The host leads the way into the dining room with the lady guest of honor,[3] followed by the others

---

[3]The lady who sits at the host's right at the table is the guest of honor, regardless of her personal distinction or importance. She may be a bride, the wife of a prominent guest, the person for whom the dinner is given, or just the oldest lady present.

in any order they find convenient. The hostess enters last with the gentleman guest of honor.

It is only at very large, ceremonious dinners that guests still maintain the rigid formality of a procession into the dining room. Nowadays the custom is to saunter in casually, in pairs or in groups, as soon as the host and the most important woman guest have led the way. There is no stiff "procession" in the true sense of the word.

In planning her dinner, the hostess should be careful to invite an equal number of men and women. Occasionally, however, it may be necessary to have one more woman than there are men. In this case, the hostess enters the dining room last, and alone. She does not join the last couple. But if there is an extra man at the dinner, the hostess enters last with a gentleman guest on each side of her.

At a formal dinner, place cards generally show the guests where they are to sit. But if it's a very small group, the hostess indicates the places—or has the butler do so.[4] Each gentleman seats the lady he escorted in to dinner. In most homes, the butler stands behind the chair of the hostess and helps her to be seated; but often she instructs him beforehand to seat the lady of honor instead.

THE GUEST WHO ARRIVES LATE

At a formal dinner, the hostess waits fifteen minutes for a tardy guest—no more. The guest who arrives while dinner is in progress goes directly to the hostess and apologizes briefly and simply. The hostess accepts the apology with a smile, extends her hand in greeting, but does not rise. The latecomer then takes his place with as little fuss and confusion as possible. He apologizes to his partner at the table for being late; and after dinner, when convenient, he offers a word of explanation to the host.

The tardy guest at a formal dinner always starts with the course then being served to the others. He is not served any of the courses which have already been removed from the table.

THE FORMAL DINNER MENU

The days of elaborate, many-coursed dinners are over—and happily for the figure and the digestion lighter meals are in order.

The basic menu for all dinners is soup, meat, vegetables, salad, and

[4]For seating arrangement see pages 103 and 104.

dessert. Other courses may be added (like a fruit or sea-food cocktail before the soup, or a fish course after it.) But the modern dinner, no matter how formal or ceremonious it may be, rarely consists of more than five courses, in addition to coffee and liqueurs.

It is important that hot dishes be served piping *hot*, on plates that have been warmed—and that cold dishes be served *cold*. Simple foods, well-prepared and properly served, are always more desirable than elaborate dishes planned more for show than for palatability.

SERVING THE DINNER

Water glasses are filled from the right of each guest, usually before the first course is served, though they sometimes are filled *after* the first course is on the table. Water glasses should never be more than three-fourths full, and should be promptly replenished as necessary during the progress of the dinner.

The lady guest of honor should be served first. In the old days, the hostess was always served first (and in some homes she still is). But this custom dates back to medieval times when the purpose was to prove to one's guests that the food was unpoisoned. Since it is no longer necessary to prove the food fit to eat, and since it is obviously more courteous to serve guests first, this is now the accepted practice.

All service at the dinner table, except the filling of glasses, is from the left. Serving dishes are presented on the palm of the left hand, steadied with the right hand if necessary. A folded napkin is used as a pad under a hot platter to protect the hand from being burned. An appropriate serving fork and spoon should accompany every dish. Vegetables such as peas, mashed potatoes, and rice, may be offered with a spoon alone at a simple, informal dinner; but at the formal table, both a fork and spoon are required. Two kinds of vegetables may be offered at one time in a double compartment dish, each with its own serving implements. But the server should not present two separate dishes at one time.

Used plates are removed from the left. An important rule of formal service is that at no time before dessert may the place before the guest be left bare. Either the next course, or a clean plate for the next course, should be placed before the guest when the used plate is removed.

The first course is generally placed on top of the service plate. In very formal houses, the service plate may be removed before any food is served; but more frequently it remains until it is replaced by the hot plate for the main course.

After the soup has been served, rolls or assorted breads are passed on a tray. The guest helps himself with his fingers and places the roll or bread right on the tablecloth (unless there is a bread-and-butter plate, which is not customary at a formal dinner).

Olives and celery are also passed during the soup course. Pickles are not served at a formal dinner. They are properly used as an accompaniment or garnish for cold meats, served at lunches, supper, buffets, barbecues, and picnics. Condiments, sauces, jelly, etc., are served with the foods they accompany, and are placed directly on the plate from which one is eating.[5]

If there is a fish course, it follows the soup course. When the fish plates are removed, the service plates are removed with them and a hot plate for the main course is placed before each guest. If gravy is served, it should be passed immediately after the meat, in a gravy boat on its own tray.

Following the main course, the salad is served. At a formal dinner, salad is always served as a separate course—never with the meat. The salad is arranged in the pantry and served on separate dishes; but the dressing is sometimes mixed at the table by the hostess and then passed by the butler or waitress.

After the salad plates are removed, and before dessert is served, the table should be cleared of everything except water and wine glasses, ornaments and nut dishes. All unused silver, china, salt and peppers, etc., should be removed. Crumbs should be brushed off the table onto a plate with a clean, neatly folded napkin.

The silver for the dessert course is ordinarily brought in on the dessert plate. But sometimes it is arranged beforehand on the sideboard, and is placed at the right of each guest just before the dessert is served.

In a strictly formal service, the finger bowl is brought in after the dessert on a small service plate. But for less formal service, the finger bowl is brought in on the dessert plate, resting on a doily. If the fork and spoon for dessert are on the same plate, the guest removes them and places them on the table, one on either side of the plate. The finger bowl, with the doily under it, is slipped off the plate and set aside to be used at the end of the meal. It is placed a little above and to the left of the dessert plate.

The wines served with dinner are determined by the menu.[6] Wine glasses, like water glasses, are filled from the right—and never more than three-fourths full. They remain on the table until the end of the meal.

[5]For the details of table etiquette, see Part I, Chapter 5, pages 51 to 67.
[6]For the correct wines to go with various types of foods, see pages 155 to 158.

Coffee Service at a Formal Dinner

Black coffee is always served after a formal dinner, in a tiny cup or demitasse. As a rule it is not served at the table, but in the living room or drawing room—with cordials or brandy.

At a large dinner, however, the men often remain in the dining room for their coffee and cigars. The ladies go to the drawing room where coffee, liqueurs, and cigarettes are brought to them.

After-dinner coffee should be very hot and black. The cups are generally brought in filled, on a tray, and passed by a butler or maid. There are some hostesses, however, who prefer to pour the coffee themselves and have their coffee service and cups brought to them on a tray. In most homes, cream and half-size sugar tablets are provided for those who have not acquired a taste for black coffee.

If the men remain in the dining room for their coffee, they of course rise when the ladies withdraw. They are expected to join the ladies in the drawing room in about half an hour. It is the host's duty to keep track of the time, and suggest rejoining the ladies at the proper moment.

Informal Dinners

In many of its essential features, informal dining is the same as formal dining. However the details of service are much simpler, and all ceremonious forms and procedure are dropped.

There is no precise receiving and announcing of guests at an informal dinner. There are no prearranged dinner partners; when dinner is announced, the guests go into the dining room in any order they please, the ladies often entering first and the men following. The hostess generally indicates the places, or, if it is a fairly large party, she may use place cards to facilitate the seating.

Unlike formal dining, informal dining may be kept as simple and easy as one wishes, with the emphasis on *convenience* rather than ceremony. There is much greater leeway and flexibility in the details of preparation and service. This doesn't mean that an informal dinner may be carelessly casual or haphazard. The requirements may not be as exacting as those for a formal dinner, but the food should be tempting and well prepared, and the service as smooth and impeccable as one can possibly arrange it.

The same general rules of table setting apply to an informal dinner as to the most formal, ceremonious function. The cloth may be simpler and the centerpiece less ornate; but the place settings are the same, and there should be the same immaculate sparkle to everything on the table. Service plates may or may not be used on an informal table. Dessert silver may be placed on the table with the other flat silver, or it may be brought in later on the dessert plate. And on an informal table a bread-and-butter plate, with a butter spreader across it, is placed just above the forks at the left of each cover.

Just before the guests are seated, the water goblets are filled and butter is placed on each bread-and-butter plate. If there is only one maid to prepare and serve the dinner, the first course may be on the table when the guests take their places. Bread and relishes may be served while the guests are eating the first course, as at a formal dinner; or they may be placed on the table beforehand and passed by the guests themselves.

At an informal dinner, soup is frequently served from a tureen. The tureen and plates are placed before the hostess, who ladles out the soup and hands each plate to the waitress to serve. Of course, soup plates should have another plate under them, even when they are placed on top of a service plate. Only one guest should be served at a time. However, if it expedites the serving of the main course, the waitress may remove two soup plates at a time by taking one in each hand. It is bad form to stack dishes when removing them from the table. The service of food is always made from the left; but at an informal table, used dishes may be removed from the right or left, whichever is more convenient.

In many homes, the carving of the meat is done at the table by the host. But if skilled carving is not one of the host's accomplishments, it's wiser and more practical to have it done in the kitchen. If the carving is done in the kitchen, hot plates are placed in front of each guest when the soup plates are removed (or the fish plates, if a fish course followed the soup.) Then the meat platter is passed by the waitress, followed by the gravy and the vegetables—exactly as at a formal dinner.

If the carving is done at the table, the soup plates and soup tureen are removed before the meat is brought in and placed before the host. A stack of hot plates is also placed before the host, and as he serves each plate the waitress lifts it and takes it to the person specified. If there is a second waitress, she serves the gravy and vegetables; otherwise they are passed after everyone has been served with meat. A double dish is practical and convenient for serving vegetables when there is only one maid. Anything that speeds up service, without destroying the gracious charm of hospitality, is desirable.

The salad may be served as a separate course, or as an accompaniment of the meat course. It is usually prepared and brought in on individual plates. In some homes, however, the hostess makes a pleasant rite of mixing and serving the salad right at the table.

After the salad course, the table should be crumbed and cleared of everything except the glasses and decorations, just as it is for a formal dinner. Dessert should never be served on a cluttered, untidy table.

When the table is cleared, the dessert plates are brought in with the dessert silver (if it is not already on the table). The finger bowls are usually brought in on the dessert plates and removed by the guests. However, they may be brought in later, while the guests are eating the dessert, if that is more convenient. The serving of the dessert depends upon what it is. It may be served in individual portions from the kitchen, or it may be served by the hostess from the head of the table. Demitasse or large cups of coffee are served, as preferred—either at the table or in the living room.

SERVING DINNER WITHOUT A MAID

The hostess who enjoys her friends should not hesitate to invite them to dinner simply because she lacks someone to do the serving. Naturally she should not attempt large or formal dinner parties, but entertaining small groups at simple, unpretentious dinners can be a most delightful and enjoyable type of hospitality.

If she plans wisely, preparing and serving dinner single-handed need be no great problem or strain upon the hostess. The most important factor is to plan a menu and arrange the mechanics of its serving so that she doesn't need to get up from the table more than once or twice during the course of the meal. This is best accomplished by means of a tea wagon, or any other type of small table, placed conveniently next to the hostess in the dining room. The table should have a lower shelf on which to stack the used dishes and silver to get them out of the way without taking them into the kitchen.

Entertaining without servants is the rule in most homes today, and often it has an intimacy and charm which are lacking in more formal and elaborate affairs. The five essentials for successful *hostess-alone* serving are:

1. A correct, beautifully set table.
2. A carefully planned menu, made up of three or four courses which can be prepared well ahead of time.

3. Food properly cooked, and as appetizing to look at as to eat.
4. A plan of service that is smooth, quick and efficient, with a handy table beside the hostess as a "base of operations."
5. Well-chosen guests who thoroughly enjoy one another's company.

The experienced hostess chooses something cold for the first course such as grapefruit, tomato juice, or fruit cup, which can be on the table ready to eat when the guests sit down. Arranged on the table beside her, in covered dishes to keep them warm, are the main course and the vegetables. It's best if the main course is something that can be served easily, without carving.

After the first course is eaten, the guests pass the used dishes to the hostess, who stacks them out of the way on the bottom shelf of the auxiliary table. Then she serves the main course and vegetables to the guests, who pass the filled plates from one to another around the table. Bread, butter, and relishes are on the table, and the guests help themselves. Up to this point it should not have been necessary for the hostess to leave her place at the table.

But if the main course is a roast which is to be carved at the table, the hostess must go to the kitchen and get it—placing it on the table before the host. Or it may be already on the table, waiting in a covered platter convenient to the host. He carves and serves the meat, passing the filled plates around the table. Gravy and vegetables may be added at the same time, or passed separately around the table in serving dishes. The hostess without a maid works out whatever plan best suits her own particular needs.

A pitcher of ice water on the bottom shelf of the tea wagon, or on the table near the hostess, enables her to keep the guests' glasses filled without making extra trips to the kitchen.

After the main course, the used dishes are passed to the hostess, who places them on the tea wagon. If the salad was not placed on the table at the start of the meal, it is now served—either from the sideboard or from the auxiliary table.

After the salad, all used dishes are wheeled or carried out, the table crumbed and cleared of everything but glassware and decorations. If a guest offers to help, the hostess should accept graciously; but she should not permit two or more guests to jump up and help her, as that disorganizes the table. There is usually less confusion if the hostess takes care of clearing the table herself. In many households, a teen-age daughter is trained to serve and to assist her mother at the table; but very young children should not be permitted to serve or to clear the table.

When the table has been cleared, the hostess wheels in her tea wagon again—this time with the coffee service on the top shelf, the dessert on the lower shelf, and whatever silver and china she will need. If she is not using a tea wagon, the next best arrangement is to bring in the dessert, and the china required for it, on a tray. Or if it's cake, it can be waiting on the sideboard, with plates and forks beside it, ready to cut and serve either right from the sideboard or from the hostess' place at the table, whichever is more convenient. Coffee is usually served at the table; but it's an increasingly delightful custom to serve it in the living room—even at very simple, informal dinner parties.

More and more the trend today is for *casserole dinners*. These are quick, easy, and very practical for the hostess who has no maid to do the serving. The first course is served before the guests take their places at the table. It is usually fruit juice, tomato juice, or eggnog served from a tray. The main dish is a casserole specialty, brought piping hot from the oven to the table, and easily served by the hostess from her place. Bread, butter, relishes, and salad are all arranged on the table beforehand so that there is no need for the hostess to get up until it's time to clear the table and serve the dessert. With a simple dessert ready and waiting on the sideboard, and coffee prepared in an electric percolator at the table, the mechanics of serving are reduced to a minimum. This is the favorite "little dinner" of many busy women who enjoy entertaining their friends but haven't much time to do so . . . and no maid in the kitchen to help.

6. LUNCHEON AND SUPPER PARTIES, BREAKFASTS AND BUFFETS

FORMAL luncheons, like formal dinners, are ceremonious in character—and are generally given for some important purpose like introducing a debutante daughter, honoring a bride, or presenting a distinguished visitor to one's friends.

As a daytime function, however, even the most elaborate luncheon is less formal and precise than a dinner would be. Usually luncheons are given by and for women, as men are too busy in the middle of the day for social affairs. But men are sometimes included on Saturday and Sunday, especially if it's a formal, ceremonious luncheon to celebrate some significant occasion. When men and women both are present, the menu and service are usually on a more pretentious scale.

The fashionable hour for an important formal luncheon is one o'clock, though it is sometimes scheduled for two o'clock, or even later if guests come from a great distance. But a formal luncheon never starts before one.

For a socially important luncheon engraved third-person invitations are sent out two to three weeks in advance.[1] But for simpler luncheons, especially if there are to be only eight or ten guests, first-person handwritten notes are correct. The invitations may even be telephoned, if one wishes. The name of the host does not appear on luncheon invitations unless he is to be present and men are to be included among the guests.

The hostess does not receive at the door, as she does for a formal dinner, but mingles with her guests and chats with them until all have arrived. However, she should try to sit where she can see the door so that she may rise to greet each new arrival and make any necessary introductions.

Cocktails are not ordinarily served at a luncheon by and for women only—though nowadays this is more a matter of personal preference than of form. Fruit juice or tomato juice is often served in the living room before luncheon. Sherry or chilled Dubonnet may be served if the hostess is familiar with her guests' tastes and knows they will enjoy it. When men are present, cocktails are generally served before a formal luncheon just as they are before a formal dinner.

There is no "procession" into the dining room, even at the most formal luncheon. Guests enter as they please, in any order that is convenient. If there is a guest of honor, she is given precedence and usually enters first with the hostess (or with the host, if men are present.) Otherwise there is no formality in entering the dining room.

DETAILS OF A FORMAL LUNCHEON

Tradition requires a formal luncheon table to be completely covered, as it is for a formal dinner, with a lace cloth or with a delicately colored damask cloth instead of a white one. But like many another old tradition, this too has given way to newer trends. Nowadays the hostess uses whatever most effectively dramatizes her table. Place mats and runners are used as much as table cloths, even for the most elaborate luncheons. Many hostesses like showing the polished wood of the table and prefer the effect of attractive place mats to the formality of a fully covered table.

For a truly feminine luncheon, the hostess can stress bright colors and lively appointments to her heart's content. She doesn't need to conform to custom as rigidly as for a formal dinner. The table decora-

[1]See pages 301 to 303 for correct luncheon invitations.

tions can be as gay and imaginative as she pleases. For a spring or summer luncheon, especially one given out of doors in the garden, a riot of color on the table is not only acceptable but exhilarating.

Flowers always make the most effective centerpiece for any table, and especially for a formal luncheon table. If fresh-cut flowers are not available, a colorful arrangement of fruit—or even a small growing plant flanked by silver, glass, or porcelain ornaments—makes an attractive substitute. Candles are not used on a luncheon table, unless the dining room is so dark that artificial light is required.

First Course, Luncheon

The places are set as for dinner, with silver arranged according to the menu. A place plate is used instead of the larger, more elaborate service plate; and the lunch napkin (which should match the table linen) is placed on top of it. Bread-and-butter plates, omitted at a formal dinner, are always included in luncheon table settings.

The menu of even a very ceremonious formal luncheon rarely consists of more than four courses. These are usually a first course of soup, melon, shrimp cocktail or tomato juice, an entrée or hot meat course with vegetables, salad, and dessert. The beverage is coffee or tea, served at the table or in the living room. In summer it is often served iced instead of hot.

There should not be too much food at a luncheon; but what is served should be appetizing and substantial, not merely fussy. A simple chicken or sea-food casserole served with a green vegetable is so much more tempting than the fancy salads and appalling sandwich concoctions some hostesses seem to think are appropriate for luncheon.

The formal service of luncheon is the same as for dinner. Differences are in minor details only, and concern the menu rather than the service. The luncheon menu is simpler than the dinner menu, is served on smaller plates, calls for less silver at each place, and is a less precise and exacting ritual throughout. But the basic principles of arrangement, setting, serving, and removal of courses are identical.

Soup at luncheon is generally served in two-handled cups instead of soup plates. It is eaten with a bouillon spoon, or drunk from the cup.

To speed and simplify service, especially if bridge or a matinée is scheduled for the afternoon, the main course is sometimes brought in on individually filled plates from the kitchen. A more formal procedure is to present serving platters to the guests, who help themselves.

Salad plates for a formal luncheon are usually filled in the kitchen or pantry and served as a separate course. However it is not incorrect to serve the salad with the main course, as is often done at small informal dinners. The salad may be omitted entirely, if one wishes, as three courses are considered adequate even for a formal luncheon menu.

After the luncheon table has been cleared and crumbed, the dessert plate and silver for each guest are brought in. The finger bowl may be on the dessert plate, or it may be brought in later while the guests are eating the dessert or when the dessert service is removed.

Tea or coffee is served at the table, in the living room, on the terrace, or wherever the hostess wishes. Demitasse is sometimes served, as at formal dinners; but large cups of coffee are generally preferred at luncheon. The filled cups may be brought in from the kitchen on a tray, with spoons on the saucers, or the hostess may pour from a silver service. In the service of luncheon, as in the service of dinner, the hostess adapts traditional forms and customs to whatever best suits her particular household—and her own personal requirements.

INFORMAL LUNCHEON PARTIES

There is no more charming and delightful way for a woman to entertain friends informally than at luncheon. Simple and intimately casual, this type of party calls for little preparation and is almost always as enjoyable to the hostess as to her guests.

Invitations to an informal luncheon are issued a week to ten days in advance, and are usually in the form of brief, handwritten notes.[2] It is also proper to invite people informally by telephone. No more guests should be invited than can be easily and comfortably accommodated.

[2]See page 303.

As a rule, informal luncheons are composed entirely of women. The hour is the same as for a formal luncheon: between one and two o'clock. If bridge or gin rummy is scheduled for the afternoon, the guests remain until five; otherwise they leave between three and four.

Luncheon may be served at one large table or at several small ones. The table linens and decorations may be almost anything that appeals to the taste and ingenuity of the hostess, provided all appointments are consistent and in harmony. The general arrangement of each cover is the same as for an informal dinner, but the mechanics of serving are simplified in keeping with the friendly informality of this type of function. The food should be as temptingly prepared as for an important dinner, and the details of service, simple though they may be, should be correct and in good form.

The menu for an informal luncheon should not consist of more than three courses: soup or fruit cup, entrée or salad, dessert and coffee. Nowadays a first course of fruit juice or tomato juice is often served from a tray, before the guests sit down—only two courses and the beverage being served at the luncheon table. If a salad is served as the main course, it should be a substantial one—such as chicken or lobster salad—and hot buttered rolls should be served with it.

An informal luncheon before a bridge party is often served right at the bridge tables. Any type of small luncheon cloth may be used to cover the tables; but if possible all cloths should be exactly alike or should at least harmonize in color and design. Matching cloths on a group of small tables always presents a more charming effect than several different colors or types.

For luncheon served at bridge tables, it is best to concentrate on two courses. In winter, one might serve a hot dish like chicken pie, a casserole, or mushroom patties, dessert, and hot coffee or tea. In summer, a hearty salad, dessert, and iced coffee or tea would make a more acceptable menu. Sometimes the hostess serves sherry or a tomato-juice cocktail before the guests are seated, but this isn't really necessary at a simple, informal bridge-luncheon.

After luncheon at small tables, the cloths and decorations are removed and the bridge cards brought out. If there is a maid to clear the tables, coffee or tea might be served in another room while this is being done. Otherwise the beverage is served with dessert. The hostess then clears the tables as quickly and with as little confusion as possible, graciously accepting the help of her guests if it is offered. Small tables should be arranged for luncheon as they will be used for bridge, to save moving around and rearrangement afterward.

With gardening one of America's major hobbies today, garden luncheons have become increasingly popular. A large table on the terrace, under an awning for protection from the sun—and with an unobstructed view of the flowers and trees—makes a lovely setting for any type of luncheon. Those who do not have a terrace or an outdoor dining table can achieve a charming effect by dotting small tables under the trees.

Linen, china, and glassware for outdoor luncheons should be bright and colorful. The silver for each place should be rolled in a paper napkin, and the glasses should be turned upside down, to protect them from dust—at least until just before the guests are seated. At a quite informal luncheon they can be left so, the guests themselves unwrapping the silver—and the glasses being turned up when they are filled, by whoever does the serving.

An excellent menu for an outdoor luncheon, regardless of its size or degree of formality, might consist of a first course of melon or fruit cup, a main course served piping hot in a casserole or covered dish, with a simple green salad instead of a vegetable, dessert, and beverage. For the hot dish, one might serve lobster Newburg, chicken à la king, curried lamb, a glamorous sea-food casserole—whatever the hostess, or her maid, knows how to prepare superbly well, and can serve attractively. For a very simple garden luncheon, or on a particularly warm day, chicken, lobster, or salmon salad may replace the hot dish as a main course. A favorite for ladies' luncheons is fruit salad, served with assorted sandwiches, followed by ice cream or sherbert. This is a simple, easy-to-serve luncheon, especially suitable for out of doors. Both the salad and sandwiches can be prepared well in advance, leaving the hostess free to enjoy her guests . . . and her garden.

SUPPERS

One of the simplest and most enjoyable types of informal entertaining is the supper party. This may be the ever-popular Sunday night supper, traditional in many households—or it may be a late supper "snack" served after the movies or theater, or after an evening of bridge.

Supper parties are always informal; and the guests are usually either relatives or close friends. Invitations are as informal as the supper itself, and are invariably by word of mouth or by telephone. Written invitations are sometimes used for special or important supper parties —following a dance, or perhaps a theater party to celebrate a birthday or anniversary. Or visiting-card invitations may be used.[3] But supper is the most intimate and informal meal there is, and invitations should be in the same casual spirit.

[3]See page 50.

Supper parties, unless they follow an important evening dance or reception, are entirely free of ceremony. There are no set rules as to menu, service or table setting—except of course the general rules of good taste and good form which apply to every type of function. The hostess generally prepares and serves the food herself, especially at Sunday night suppers when the servants (if there are any) are more likely than not to be out. This is one occasion when the hostess may introduce any intriguing new idea she may have as to menu or service —being very careful, however, not to serve anything so rich or heavy that it's likely to interfere with sleep. It is also an occasion for the host to show what he can do, if he fancies himself a cook—a chance for him to star at the chafing dish or table grill.

The charm of informal supper parties is in their relaxed and friendly atmosphere—congenial people gathered around the table or at several small tables (or at no tables at all!) for good food and good talk. Sometimes supper is served in the dining room, with the table set as for an informal luncheon. Sometimes it is served at a counter in the kitchen or game room, or buffet style in the living room, with the guests helping themselves, or on individual trays brought in from the kitchen, the guests sitting where they please and eating from the tray. The hostess serves whatever she likes and thinks her guests will like, in any way that is easy and convenient for her.

Supper "snacks" are generally cold, consisting of salads, cold sliced meats, a dessert, and either cold drinks or hot coffee. For a more elaborate meal, and especially for Sunday night suppers, a hot dish is generally included. Perennial favorites are Welsh rabbit, creamed chicken, scrambled eggs with sausage, hot grilled sandwiches, and waffles. It isn't wise to attempt waffles for a party, however, unless one has a speedy, efficient iron which turns out two or more at a time.

Waffles and grilled or toasted sandwiches are always prepared after the guests are seated at the table. But cooked dishes, such as creamed chicken, lobster Newburg, and Welsh rabbit, should be prepared beforehand and practically ready to serve when the guests assemble at the table. They are either heated at the table in a chafing dish or brought in piping hot in a casserole or covered dish just before the guests are seated. When food is to be prepared at the table, the hostess should see to it that all ingredients and required utensils are at hand and everything is in readiness, so that there are no awkward delays once the guests are seated.

It is entirely proper for a hostess to ask one of her guests to help her at a supper party. But she should not ask a guest to do anything more difficult than attend the toaster or percolator, or perhaps cut and serve the cake while she is serving the coffee.

BUFFET SERVICE

By far the simplest and most convenient way to entertain large groups of people is with buffet service.

The buffet is a versatile type of serving that adapts itself to practically every type of hospitality—from Sunday brunch to midnight suppers, from formal teas to delightful informal dinners. It has many obvious advantages. It enables you to take care of many guests, to serve them a wide and interesting variety of food without anyone to wait on the table, for the food, and everything required for eating it, is laid out attractively on one large table and the guests help themselves.

The informality of a buffet is very pleasant. There is none of the stiffness and restraint which so often accompany a sit-down affair. Most men and women like the easy casualness of a buffet and enjoy helping themselves from the beautifully arranged and tempting platters, especially if there is a comfortable place to sit and to set one's plate afterward.

For a simple "stand-up supper," as many people call a buffet, invitations are either by word of mouth or by telephone. For a more important occasion, personal notes are written or visiting-card invitations are used. For a socially significant buffet supper, as to celebrate an anniversary or announce an engagement, engraved invitations are generally used.

The basic essentials of any buffet are a big table, a room large enough for guests to move around in, plenty of attractive serving platters and dishes, some of them covered to keep the food hot, and of course an interesting menu that delights the eye and appeals to the palate. The dining table may be used, with the sideboard serving as an auxiliary buffet for cold drinks, ice, liqueurs, and perhaps the dessert. Or any large table can be set for the buffet in the living room, on the porch, or even out on the lawn in the summer. A ping-pong table in a basement playroom, lavishly covered with a net or coarse lace cloth and with a dramatic centerpiece of fruit or flowers, makes an ideal foundation for a buffet.

There are no formal table-setting rules for a buffet, only a few general principles by which one should be guided. The table should be completely covered, preferably with white damask or lace—but almost any kind of cloth will do if it harmonizes with the room and with the appointments. The buffet table should have a center of interest, made up of fruit, flowers, ornaments, leaves, or a combination of any or all of these. This focal point of interest needn't be in the center of the table. It may be at the back of the table if it's against the wall, or at one end of it—depending on the position of the table in the room and how the guests will circulate around it to help themselves to food.

In setting a buffet table, strive for a balanced and pleasing effect. If you have a coffee service on a tray at one end of the table, have large platters of food at the opposite end, with the smaller dishes and platters in between. Try to arrange the food approximately as it would be served at a sit-down meal: fruit or hors d'oeuvres before the entrées or meats, meats before the salads, salads before the coffee service, etc. Plates are stacked near the food, with the required amount of silver arranged in rows beside them. Napkins are piled at one or both ends of the table; and rolls, relishes, salt and peppers, cream and sugar for the coffee, etc., are placed at convenient intervals around the table where guests can reach them easily.

The menu for a buffet—whether it's a dinner, luncheon, or supper —may be anything the hostess wishes to serve and thinks her guests will enjoy. However, the fact that guests do not sit down to individually laid places at the table doesn't mean the meal may be haphazard or carelessly planned. It's important to select foods that go well together, that look attractive on the buffet table, and that are easy to eat with fork alone.

At most buffets, there is at least one hot dish like creamed chicken, spaghetti or macaroni, curried shrimp, baked beans, or any casserole specialty in which the hostess or her cook excels. With this there is generally a variety of cold meats like ham, turkey, tongue, etc., salads, relishes, buttered rolls, and perhaps an assortment of small sandwiches.

Of course the more elaborate the buffet, the more elaborate the menu. When a ham, turkey, or impressive-looking roast beef is the mainstay of the menu, it should be put on the table whole—the host or a competent servant doing the carving. If there's no one to do the carving efficiently and well, it's fun—and entirely proper—to let each guest slice off his own portion. Just be sure the carving knife is very sharp and the platter very large, and that there is enough room for the guest to put down his plate while he serves himself.

Dessert isn't usually placed on a buffet table. It is placed on the sideboard or a separate table, with plates and silver; or it is brought in later and served to the guests wherever they are sitting.

Coffee is sometimes served to the guests individually, from the kitchen; but more often the coffee service is placed at one end of the buffet table and guests help themselves. The coffee should be very hot, and should be brought in when the guests are ready for it—not before. Cups and saucers are arranged on a tray, beside the service. The cups and spoons may be on the saucers or laid out in a row on the table, depending on how much space there is.

Guests generally use just one large plate to serve themselves at a buffet. No bread-and-butter plates are required, as rolls and bread are placed on the table already buttered. Separate salad plates are not used except at the most formal buffets where there are waitresses in attendance. Meats, salad, relishes, roll—all go on the same plate.

Each guest is expected to serve himself at a buffet. However at elaborate evening buffets, especially those following a dance, gentlemen frequently serve the ladies first—and then themselves.

The hostess should see to it that all guests have a suitable place to sit—not on a window sill or the bottom step of the stairs, but somewhere they can put their plate and cup conveniently. Since plate-juggling is difficult for the guest and dangerous to rugs and furnishings, there should be plenty of small tables where guests can sit while they eat and feel secure. Bridge tables serve the purpose very nicely; but any small table that stands firmly and seats two or more may be used.

For those who do not have an adequate supply of small tables to seat their guests, "tray buffets" are an increasingly popular form of service for simple, informal parties. Each guest is provided with a fairly large tray, which he uses to serve himself with whatever he wishes from the buffet table. Then he finds congenial company and a comfortable place to sit, and eats from the tray balanced on his lap. When he is ready for dessert and coffee, he disposes of the used dishes by placing them on a side table provided for the purpose and again uses the handy tray.

Much of the responsibility for the success of a buffet party rests with the hostess. She must keep a vigilant eye on everyone, see that plates are kept filled and conversation kept going. She must watch the buffet table and see that the platters and serving dishes are kept refreshed and replenished. Empty or untidy platters should be removed, and fresh ones brought in as required. Guests should be provided with water, cigarettes, ash trays, and whatever else they may need to make them comfortable.

BREAKFASTS AND BRUNCH

Breakfast to many people means a hastily swallowed cup of coffee with a roll or toast. But there is another breakfast, the social breakfast, which comes later in the morning and is attended by some of the ceremony that marks the luncheon hour.

There is, for example, the semiformal breakfast served to guests at a house or week-end party—for although the breakfast tray has become almost a tradition for house guests, not everyone enjoys eating alone in his room. Many guests prefer breakfasting with the family in the dining room. For such breakfasts, the hostess has her table looking its gayest and prettiest—with bright china, colorful linens, and a center-

Setting for Breakfast

piece of fruit or flowers. The menu generally consists of fruit, cereal, an egg or pancake dish (or waffles), ham or bacon, hot rolls, jelly or marmalade, coffee or chocolate.

The coffee service is always placed before the hostess at the breakfast table. The platter of bacon and eggs, or any other hot dish ready to serve, is placed before the host. Just before breakfast is announced, the first course of grapefruit or juice is placed on the table. In well-managed households, finger bowls are always provided following a fruit course, even at the breakfast table.

In large houses where guests are frequently entertained for week ends or longer, breakfast is usually served in the English manner. This is a convenient practice in any household when guests or members of the family come down at different times, and there is no regular hour for breakfast. The main courses—cooked cereal, eggs, fish, etc.—are placed on heaters or in steam dishes on the sideboard or on a side table. Orange juice or grapefruit is at each plate at the dining table. After eating this first course, the breakfasters get up, place their used plates on the side table, take a hot plate from the stack set ready for their use, and help themselves to whatever they wish. They then return with their filled plates to the dining table. In such homes a waitress or butler is generally in attendance, to bring in hot toast and rolls as required and to serve coffee.

Boiled eggs are a popular breakfast dish and are frequently served.

The English way of eating a boiled egg is to put it into the small end of an egg cup, cut off the top, and spoon the egg out of the shell with a teaspoon. The American way is to break the egg into the larger end of the cup, mix it with salt and pepper, and eat it with a teaspoon. Both ways are correct.

Little need be said about the family breakfast—a completely informal meal at which guests are rarely present. Our only suggestion is that the table be as pretty as possible, the appointments gay and colorful, the food well prepared and attractively served; for a good breakfast, nicely served in bright and cheerful surroundings, is a fine and zestful beginning to the day.

"Brunch" is a late Sunday morning meal, served later than breakfast is usually served, but earlier than lunch, and being in effect a satisfying combination of both. The table is set as for luncheon and, though breakfast foods are served, the menu is somewhat more elaborate than it would be for breakfast alone. There is a fruit course, usually a cereal or egg dish, and always some favorite specialty of the house such as creamed chicken served on waffles, pancakes made with jelly or cheese, a casserole of chicken livers, or corned-beef hash. In addition there are always rolls, muffins, and sometimes popovers—and plenty of good hot coffee. To invite guests to Sunday morning "brunch" is a delightfully intimate and informal means of entertaining, and it's becoming more and more popular all the time. At a country house, in the summer, "brunch" is a particularly charming way to extend hospitality to well-liked neighbors and friends.

7. TEAS, DANCES, AND DEBUTANTE PARTIES

IF YOU haven't the room, the servants, and the equipment to give important dinners and luncheons, you can always entertain simply and beautifully at teatime. For afternoon tea is now, as always, one of hospitality's most cherished traditions.

The tea hour today is used as the background for many kinds of parties, from the simplest meeting and mingling of a few intimate friends to an elaborate reception in honor of a debutante, a new bride, or a visiting celebrity. But the casual, unpretentious afternoon tea, requiring little preparation and imposing no great burden or expense, is perhaps the most charming "little party" of all.

SIMPLE AFTERNOON TEA

An afternoon tea is given for the purpose of seeing and enjoying one's friends, welcoming a new neighbor or a new bride home from her honeymoon, or repaying hospitality. Invitations are by telephone or personal note; and for this type of informal function, needn't be more than a few days in advance. The hour is between four and five in the afternoon; but if men are included (which isn't very usual for casual tea parties), the hour may be from five to six.

The hostess may serve in the living room or dining room, whichever is easier for her and likely to be more pleasant for her guests. There is no setting of individual places. The tea is just handed to the guests, who sit wherever they wish and put their plates and cups wherever convenient. Any hostess who entertains frequently at afternoon tea should have several small tables she can place strategically here and there around the room to hold cups, plates, ash trays and other teatime paraphernalia.

The tea things are arranged on a tray and placed on a low table in front of the hostess, who properly makes and serves the tea herself at a small party. If there is a maid, she brings in the tea service after the guests are assembled. Otherwise everything should be brought in and arranged before the guests arrive—except of course the cream, lemon, and hot water which are brought in at the very last moment.

The tea tray should be large enough to hold everything required for preparing and serving the tea properly. This means a complete tea service including a hot-water kettle and waste bowl, tea caddy, cream pitcher and sugar bowl, glass dish of sliced lemon, small silver lemon fork, sugar shell or tongs, and the cups and saucers. In other words, the tray should be large enough to hold everything except the platters of sandwiches and cakes, and the tea plates and napkins used by the guests for these refreshments.

Though there is nothing more beautiful than a silver tray and silver service for afternoon tea, a gracious hostess makes the most of what she has and entertains charmingly in whatever style she can. A large antique lacquer tray, or a handsome walnut or mahogany tray, is just as appropriate (if not as lavish) as a silver one. And a china tea service can be as appealing in its fragile loveliness as a costly silver one would be.

The tea table should be covered with a cloth before the tray is put on it. A plain white linen damask cloth is always acceptable and in good taste; but this being a purely feminine function, a dainty lace or embroidered cloth is perhaps more desirable. The favorite choice of many hostesses today is a sheer organdie cloth in a delicate pastel shade to match or harmonize with the china. As there is so little other preparation, the tea hostess should concentrate on making her table and tray look as beautiful as she can.

The tray is arranged and so placed that everything is handy to the hostess when she is ready to serve. At one side of the tea table, or on a separate small table near by, are the tea plates arranged in a pile, with the napkins folded between them. As each guest lifts a plate from the pile, she lifts a napkin with it. No silverware is necessary, as only finger foods are served. A spoon for the tea, the only implement required, rests on the saucer when the cup of tea is handed to each guest.

Preparing the Tea

A good hostess always uses good tea and sees that it is properly made.

The most important factor, more important even than the quality of the tea, is the use of *boiling hot water* in its preparation. Water that is merely hot won't do; it must be bubbling and boiling to produce really fine, fragrant tea.

The amount used depends on the quality of the tea, and on personal taste. In general, one can count on two rounded teaspoons yielding three cups of tea.

If the tea is made at the table—and many people think it's better if made on the spot—you put the required amount of tea into your silver or china pot and pour on enough boiling water to cover it about half an inch. You let it steep from three to five minutes, then add enough boiling water to fill the pot. The tea is now ready. For those who like it weak, you pour half tea, half boiling water. For those who like it strong, you pour it right from the pot into the cup.

If there are more than five or six guests, it is usually simpler and more convenient to have the tea prepared in the kitchen and brought to the table ready to serve. The important thing is to instruct whoever prepares the tea not to let it steep too long before pouring it off the leaves. Tea which has been allowed to steep too long acquires a bitter, rancid taste. See to it also that the teapot is rinsed with boiling water before the tea is poured into it, so that it will retain the heat better.

Correct Service for an Informal Tea

The hostess always pours at a simple, informal tea. Guests sitting or standing near by merely put out their hands to accept their cup of tea from the hostess. Others sitting farther off rise and come to the table for it (unless there is a maid or butler to carry it to them).

As each guest is served, the hostess generally asks her how she likes her tea. The guest answers, "Weak, please—with a little cream and one lump" or "Strong, please—with lemon but no sugar." The tea is poured and prepared according to the guest's wishes, and handed to her. She then returns to her chair, or finds herself a convenient place to sit, perhaps at a little table where she can put down her cup.

If there is a maid, she now serves the little cakes and sandwiches which usually go with afternoon tea. Or one of the guests is pressed into service to pass the trays of food. But more likely than not, the guests help themselves.

The food is arranged on the tea table, on one of those handy little three-tiered tables called a "curate" or "muffin stand," on a tea wagon, or on any convenient surface at all. After safely depositing her cup of tea somewhere, the guest takes a plate and napkin, serves herself to whatever she wishes, and returns with it to her chair and her cup of tea. If there is no table handy, she rests the plate on her lap and eats the food with her right hand—lifting the cup with her left hand to drink the tea. It may take a little maneuvering, but she must balance the plate, cup, and saucer as best she can.

The menu for an informal tea is strictly limited, with the emphasis on light, dainty refreshments—no rich or heavy foods. Only very small sandwiches, hot breads, cinnamon toast, muffins, cookies, and crackers are served—nothing more. The food should be small in scale, easy to pick up and eat with the fingers. Sticky, crumbly, or drippy foods, cakes with gooey icings or fillings, are not appropriate for tea as they are too messy to eat without silverware.

Some hostesses serve sliver-thin orange slices, candied cherries, and cloves with hot tea, in addition to the customary lemon. In summer, with iced tea, mint leaves, and pineapple spears are often served. An especially generous hostess may offer her guests a choice of tea or coffee—or even chocolate. But this isn't really necessary, as tea is of course the traditional beverage of the afternoon tea party.

THE FORMAL CEREMONIOUS TEA

A formal tea is today's substitute for the stiff Victorian "reception," but it is so much more friendly and inviting in spirit! It is generally given for some special social purpose like introducing a debutante daughter, presenting a new daughter-in-law, announcing an engagement, or honoring a house guest from another city. It provides an excellent way to entertain a large group of people without great expense or elaborate preparation.

Unlike most teas, which are given by and for women alone, the formal ceremonious tea is almost always given by "Mr. and Mrs." jointly—and men are included in the guest list. The invitations may be third-person handwritten notes, but usually they are engraved, especially if the tea is away from home, at a club, inn, or hotel.

Like a reception, the formal tea calls for a receiving line. The hostess receives at the door of her living room (or at the door of the assembly room, if it's in a club or hotel) with the person in whose honor the tea is given. Sometimes an intimate friend of the hostess or of the guest of honor receives with them. The ladies on the receiving line wear their most elaborate afternoon gowns, with gloves but no hat.

Guests arriving at a formal tea greet the hostess first, then the guest of honor. If they do not know the guest of honor, or any of the other ladies on the receiving line, the hostess introduces them. No other introductions are necessary. Guests at this type of function are expected to mingle and engage in conversation whether they know each other or not.

Refreshments for a formal tea are about the same as for a simple tea party—just a little more elaborate, perhaps, and more impressively served. A large table is lavishly laid with a lace or embroidered cloth; and there is generally a tea service at one end and a coffee service at the other, with the cups and saucers arranged conveniently beside them. Plates, spoons, and napkins are laid out in rows; and trays of tiny sandwiches, hot breads, little cakes, and other dainty finger foods are arranged attractively on the table.

As a rule, the dining room table is used for a formal tea. The chairs are removed to make plenty of room for the guests to circulate freely. But any large table may be used, where there is space enough for a big refreshment table and all the guests, too—in the living room, in the library, or even in a basement playroom if it is attractive and impressive enough for this type of formal function.

Although guests do not ordinarily sit down to tables at a formal tea, there should be plenty of small tables available here and there, so that a cup or plate can be put down conveniently. Otherwise guests are likely to put used dishes on the refreshment table and spoil its effect.

The hostess does not preside at the tea tray, nor pour for her guests, as she does at a simple tea. There is usually a maid or butler to take over this responsibility at a formal tea; and there should be another maid, if possible, to bring in fresh tea, hot water, and any other accessories or refreshments as needed.

If there are no servants, and the tea is a fairly large one with many guests, the hostess generally arranges beforehand with one or two of her friends to act as "table hostesses" for the occasion. The best plan is to have one person at each end of the table, to preside at the tea or coffee service and take charge of pouring the beverages.

At a reception of this kind, guests merely go to the table, ask whoever is pouring for coffee or tea, and help themselves to sandwiches or cakes. They eat standing at the table or near it, or find a convenient place to sit.

When a formal tea is held outdoors, on the terrace or in the garden, a large table is set up just as it is indoors, with smaller tables scattered here and there for the convenience of the guests. A maid should be in attendance to collect used dishes and bring out fresh ones. Nowadays the clever hostess who entertains out of doors provides each group of guests with a "tea spike." This is a small portable table of metal or wood which is stuck into the ground, wherever it is needed. It keeps fragile cups and plates from being set down carelessly on the grass.

INFORMAL DANCES

Dancing is one of the most popular modern pastimes, and therefore a favorite way to entertain. Anyone can give a small informal dance at home if there is enough space for it, and a good smooth floor to dance on. But no one should ever invite people to dance in a small carpeted living room, with no music to count on except what the radio is likely to offer.

The three essentials for a successful dance, whether it's for just a few intimate friends or for a large and impressive guest list, are (1) ample space to dance without crowding, (2) a smooth waxed floor, (3) good music. Refreshments and decorations are secondary. You can serve hot dogs and lemonade if you like, and forget the decorations entirely except for a few leaves and flowers. If the music is good and the dancing conditions agreeable, your guests will have a wonderful time.

It isn't necessary, or even practical, to engage an orchestra for a small dance at home, unless it's for a very special occasion. A good phonograph and a selection of new and popular dance records serve the purpose very nicely, particularly if the phonograph plays ten or more records at a time automatically.

Of course if you have a large basement playroom with a fine floor for dancing, where you can accommodate as many as forty or fifty guests at a time, that's another matter! With that much space, it's good practice to plan one large dance instead of several small ones (preferably during the holiday season) and engage a three- or four-piece orchestra for the occasion. It may be a quite informal dance with a simple buffet supper afterward. But it will enable you to discharge your social obligations with one grand gesture in a way your guests will thoroughly enjoy.

Invitations for an informal dance are by personal note or by telephone. As for all functions in a private home, guests should be limited to the number of persons one can take care of easily and comfortably. It's better social strategy to entertain a few people beautifully and correctly than a large group with confusion and strain.

If you invite friends to dance in your living room, and it's not a particularly *large* room, be sure to move all unnecessary furniture out of it for the occasion. Have all rugs taken up, of course, and the floor waxed and polished. Put a small table in one corner of the room, or just outside it, for a tray of glasses and a punch bowl or pitcher of something cold and refreshing to quench thirst between dances.

Refreshments at an informal dance may be anything from sandwiches and coffee to an elaborate buffet with a turkey or ham as the center of attraction. The most usual procedure is to put plates of sandwiches, salad, and cake on the dining room table and let the guests help themselves. Coffee is served in filled cups from the kitchen, or is poured from a coffee service at the table, whichever is more convenient. There is no formality. The guests make up their own small groups and sit where they wish. When there are no servants, the hostess generally asks one of the guests to help her serve the coffee.

FORMAL DANCES

The days of huge, gala "balls" with fortunes spent on extravagant decorations and lavish many-coursed suppers are over, and no one greatly regrets their going. For with them have gone much that was false and artificial in the ballroom of the past, much that was mere ostentation and display.

Today even the most formal "ball" is simply a *big dance*, light-hearted and gay, as a dance should be. The decorations are simple; and so are the refreshments, as a rule—often no more than sandwiches and punch. But there is light and space, music and fresh air. There are lovely gowns and smiling faces. And surely there can be no more delightful and satisfying way than this to celebrate an important social occasion!

A large formal dance is always for some special purpose, such as announcing an engagement or celebrating an anniversary. The invitations are engraved and are sent out well in advance.[1] If the house is large enough, the dance may be held at home. In this case, the hostess often places the responsibility for refreshments and service in the hands of a caterer. But for most functions of this type, a hotel ballroom is engaged, and the details of refreshment and service arranged with the manager. An orchestra is hired to provide the music. For a particularly large dance, two orchestras are sometimes engaged to provide music continuously.

Years ago, no "ball" was considered complete without an elaborate champagne supper following the festivities. Nowadays sit-down suppers only occasionally follow a big dance, and they are not nearly as grand as they used to be. Sometimes there is champagne, but rarely are there the many rich and varied courses people used to consume. Often there are only sandwiches and coffee, served buffet style. Or there might be one light supper course like creamed chicken or chicken salad, to which guests help themselves. Today, it is only for some special occasion like a debut dance or an anniversary celebration that a formal sit-down supper is served, with places set for each guest.

SUBSCRIPTION DANCES

A subscription dance is semipublic and is always held in a public ballroom. Instead of a host and hostess there are patronesses, or a specially appointed committee of prominent women who receive and welcome guests and make all necessary introductions.

Dances such as these are arranged by a group of men and women who appoint a committee to manage all details. A list of proposed guests is made out, and these people are invited to subscribe. The subscription generally entitles the guest to several tickets.

The committee attends to all details such as music, decorations, supper, attendants, and any special kind of entertainment. Money for all expenditures is appropriated from the subscription fees.

Most subscription dances are planned to include a supper, served either at one large table or several small ones. Guests are generally given table and seat numbers to enable them to find their places readily. Those who wish to sit together at supper should make the necessary arrangements beforehand with the committee.

[1]See pages 305 to 309.

A large public dance in honor of a visiting celebrity or distinguished guest is exactly like a private dance—except that a specially appointed committee fills the position and the duties of the host and hostess. At most such public balls, the committee members wear a badge, a flower, or some other distinguishing mark to indicate their position. They stand at or near the door (not necessarily in a precise receiving "line") to greet arriving guests and make them feel welcome. Later on they mingle with the guests, exactly as a host and hostess would at a private dance, seeing to it that everyone is comfortably taken care of.

When a public ball is given in honor of a celebrity, he (or she) must be met on arrival and presented at once to everyone on the reception committee. This guest must be specially attended throughout the evening, introduced to all strangers and made to feel welcome and honored. When he leaves, he is escorted to his car, train, or plane by one or all the members of the reception committee.[2]

Debutante Parties

One of the customs of the old order which still survives, though in greatly modified form, is the "coming-out party" to introduce a girl to society.

In the old days, no expense was spared to present a marriageable daughter impressively, and debutante parties were often unbelievably fabulous and extravagant. But the modern girl has little taste for such ostentation. Rarely nowadays are there great formal balls with everyone on the mother's list invited, regardless of age. The trend today is for simple entertaining, with the emphasis on gaiety and a good time instead of impressive display. The guest list is made up almost entirely of young people, except for the few older relatives who must be invited out of courtesy and respect.

A dance is of course the logical type of party for young people; and parents have their choice of three types of dances, all equally popular. The most elaborate is a dinner dance, given at home or in a club or hotel. Somewhat less elaborate is an evening of dancing followed by a simple supper, served at tables or buffet style. Simplest and often most enjoyable, especially at a country house or at a country club or inn, is a luncheon or afternoon tea with dancing. An afternoon party in the city should be planned for the week end or for a holiday so that all the young men who are invited can conveniently attend.

Group debuts are a recent development and are increasingly popular. A number of parents give one large dinner or dance for several

²For invitations to subscription dances and charity balls, see pages 311 and 312.

debutante daughters, issuing joint invitations and sharing the expenses equally. In cities like Chicago and New York, groups of debutantes are presented to society every season at large Christmas and New Year assemblies and balls. Most of the young ladies are feted individually at dinners held earlier in the evening at their homes or at hotels. The winter holiday season is of course the best time for debutante parties, as the young men are home from their schools and colleges.

DEBUT LUNCHEON OR TEA WITH DANCING

One of the simplest ways to introduce a debutante daughter is with a luncheon followed by an afternoon of dancing; or a formal tea dance, held indoors or outdoors depending on the circumstances. Outdoor debuts are charming in the country, either in one's own garden or on the grounds of a country club or inn. But winter debuts are considered smarter by fashionable society, and are therefore more popular.

In cities, a coming-out luncheon or tea with dancing may be given at home, but it is usually held at a club or hotel. Invitations are engraved, unless it's a very simple, informal type of party, in which case personal handwritten notes are acceptable. All of the debutante's young friends and the dancing brothers of her friends are invited, but not necessarily their parents.

The young lady in whose honor the party is given receives with her mother throughout the afternoon. She dances every dance, but returns to the side of her mother to receive and welcome guests during the intervals. They both wear gloves, but no hats. Old-time debutantes always held a bouquet of flowers as they received, but the modern girl is more likely to wear a corsage—and to wear it high on her shoulder where it won't interfere with her dancing.

When luncheon precedes dancing, no other refreshments are served during the afternoon. There is usually a table somewhere about with ice water and glasses, but that is all.

The preparations for a tea with dancing are much the same as for a formal tea, except that an orchestra and space for dancing are provided. Guests go to the table whenever they wish for whatever refreshments are offered. In addition there is usually a separate table with an enormous punch bowl and plenty of glasses where guests may quench their thirst during dances.

For an afternoon dance, whether in a public ballroom or at home, curtains are usually drawn and the room lighted as for an evening function.

DEBUT DINNER AND SUPPER DANCES

Nowadays few houses have ballrooms, and therefore few debut dances are held in private homes. When they are, special appurtenances like a red carpet to the curb (traditional symbol of an important social function), coat racks, ballroom chairs, the food and even waiters to serve it can be supplied by caterers or by a hotel.

The great majority of debut dances are held in hotel or club ballrooms, with the details of arrangement entrusted to a capable staff. For dancing followed by a supper, one set of invitations is sent out. For a dinner dance, two sets of invitations are required—one for the guests who are invited for dinner and dancing both, one for those who are invited for dancing only.[3]

The dinner at which a debutante is honored before making her formal bow to society is no different from any other important dinner party. Usually it's held at the same club or hotel where the dance is later to take place. But sometimes the dinner is given privately, at the debutante's house or elsewhere—dinner guests joining dance guests later on in the evening.

The dancing generally begins about ten o'clock, and the debutante stands beside the hostess and receives until most of the guests have arrived. She wears a gala evening gown which should be either white or a delicate pastel shade (never black, or a bright shade like red or green, for a debut!). She wears a corsage, or carries a bouquet, and wears gloves all evening, except when she is at dinner or supper.

Relatives and friends customarily send flowers to a debutante, and these are always banked around the place where she stands to receive her guests. Little else is required in the way of decoration, except perhaps a few ferns and palms. For large group debuts, however, there are often elaborate and impressive floral displays.

Supper following a debut dance is often in buffet style. Tempting platters of food are arranged on a long table and guests help themselves. If there is a sit-down supper, it's usually in a room adjoining the ballroom or in one of the private dining rooms of the hotel. The debutante goes in to supper with a young man of her own choosing, more often than not someone who has asked for the privilege. There is always a special table for the debutante in the center of the room. For this she makes up her own party of friends to sit with her at supper. Other guests generally make up their own tables too unless the hostess has used place cards to speed and facilitate the seating arrangements.

[3]For examples, see pages 307 to 309.

There should be no tipping of waiters at a debut dinner or supper in a hotel dining room, since for the time being it is the *private* dining room of the host and hostess.

ETIQUETTE OF THE BALLROOM

At a small dance where the hostess knows everyone intimately, she mingles with her guests and makes all necessary introductions. But at a large dance this is hardly possible. Guests are expected to introduce themselves, to enter into conversation and make themselves generally agreeable.

A man and woman who attend a dance together traditionally have the first dance together. Thereafter they dance with whomever they please, although a gentleman sees to it that the lady he has accompanied is not left without a partner while he dances with someone else. He returns to her between dances and attends courteously to her wants during the evening. If there is a supper after the dance, they go in together.

When the music stops, a man is expected to talk for a few moments with his partner before taking her back to her friends. He doesn't rush right off to claim his next partner, leaving her conspicuously alone in the center of the room. After he has escorted her back to her friends, he either remains to chat with them until the music for the next dance begins, or he says, "Thank you, Miss Blank," and leaves her to return to his own group.

A gently bred young lady does not seek out the man to whom the next dance is promised. She waits for him to come and claim her. Naturally she is guided by common sense, in this as in all other phases of etiquette. If she sees him looking for her, she may make her whereabouts known, provided it is done inconspicuously.

If a young woman does not wish to dance with someone, she should make some polite and courteous excuse to him. Then she should either sit out the dance or take that time to retouch a shining nose. It is needlessly rude to refuse one man and the next moment start dancing with someone else. Of course no young lady ever refuses to dance with a man unless she has some very good reason for doing so.

Though the practice of "cutting in" must at times be extremely annoying to young people enjoying a dance together, it is for some reason still accepted almost everywhere by the most fashionable society. So however we may disapprove of the procedure as rude, we must acknowledge it—for the time being, at least—as "proper."

Under the system of "cutting in," a stag on the sidelines simply approaches a couple on the floor and places his hand on the man's shoulder. By that gesture he claims the lady as his partner. She must change partners whether she wants to or not, and is expected to do so pleasantly. It's traditional to allow the person who "cuts in" the courtesy of dancing at least once around the room before he is "cut." Another point of etiquette is for the man who lost his partner to wait until she has still another partner before he himself "cuts in." It's considered discourteous for one man to "cut in" continually on the same man all evening.

8. BRIDGE AND CARD PARTIES

If you have a number of friends who like to play bridge or gin rummy, one of the easiest and most popular ways to entertain them is by means of a card party. It requires little preparation, the refreshments may be of the simplest, and there are few social diversions people enjoy more than playing their favorite card game in pleasant surroundings and congenial company.

Fads in games come and go, but bridge remains a perennial favorite. We shall therefore discuss *bridge parties* specifically; but the same broad, general rules of etiquette apply of course to all other card games.

No one should venture to entertain at bridge, nor accept a bridge invitation, who cannot play the game at least passably well. There are many excellent books available, and anyone who wants to learn how to play bridge can easily do so.

How Many Guests to Invite

In planning a bridge party, one should consider the space available for placing the tables and chairs. The hostess who wishes to entertain more guests than she can comfortably accommodate at bridge tables in her own house, should engage a private room at a hotel or club for the occasion. Many hostesses who live in the suburbs prefer to do this rather than put their guests to the inconvenience of traveling a considerable distance.

Since there are four players to each table, the number of guests invited to a bridge party should be some multiple of four. It is not wise to invite players and non-players to the same party, but if for some reason it is necessary to include a guest or two who doesn't play, the hostess herself must forego the pleasure of the game and devote herself to the non-playing guests. They should sit in another room, or at least far enough removed from the players so that they can talk without disturbing them.

When there is only one table of bridge, the hostess invariably plays with her guests. When there are two tables or more, she generally prefers not to include herself in making up her list. This leaves her free to attend to the final details of preparing and serving the refreshments. If there is sufficient help in the kitchen to take care of these details, she merely watches the game and occasionally circulates among the tables to see that her guests are comfortable, the candy dishes and cigarette boxes filled, the ash trays emptied. Furthermore, if a guest is unable to come at the last moment, the hostess who has not included herself in the list is able to fill in at the incomplete table.

BRIDGE PARTY INVITATIONS

Invitations to an informal bridge party are either by telephone or personal note. Many hostesses prefer to telephone their invitations, as this provides an immediate acceptance or regret from each guest and tables can be arranged accordingly. However, notes of invitation are a shade more gracious and give greater social significance to the occasion. If they are sent out well in advance and answered promptly, the hostess will have time to substitute if necessary, in arranging the right number of players for each table.

Dear Jane:
How would you and Fred like to play bridge on Friday evening, March the tenth? The Willards and the Bentons are coming—and as you know, they are excellent players.

I hope you and Fred have no other plans for that evening. We're starting at about eight-thirty. Do try and make it, Jane. We are looking forward to seeing you!

Affectionately,
Claire

An invitation calls only for an acceptance or regret, not for a long, chatty letter giving the local gossip and the family news. One who receives an invitation like the above should answer briefly and to the point, either accepting or regretfully explaining why it is impossible to accept.

To entertain more importantly than with a bridge party alone, many hostesses like to give a bridge luncheon. It may be quite informal in character, with invitations by telephone or word of mouth. But if it's a formal bridge luncheon at a club or hotel, engraved invitations are usually sent out. Below is the standard form for these invitations:

Mrs. Frederick B. Hayes
requests the pleasure of your company
at luncheon
Thursday, the twenty-first of September
at one o'clock
The Essex House

Please reply to
480 Park Avenue   Bridge

RESPONSIBILITIES OF THE BRIDGE HOSTESS

It is the responsibility of the hostess to establish the rules of play for her guests—not the rules of the game (which are of course standard), but the rules for playing the game (which are variable).

For example, the hostess may decide that each table will play four hands, that the scores will then be tallied and the winning team move to another table. Or she may decide that the same four persons will play together throughout, merely cutting or pivoting to change partners. It's up to her to decide on the method of scoring, especially if there are to be prizes. In order for prizes to be distributed equitably, all groups must play the same number of hands, play uniformly, and use the same method of scoring.

Frequently a bridge hostess is called upon to settle a table dispute, to decide on a point of scoring or a detail of play. The hostess who intends to entertain bridge players should have an authoritative text on the game ready for reference in case of a difference in opinion among the players.

PLAYERS SHOULD BE EQUALLY MATCHED

One of the most important responsibilities of the bridge hostess is to invite players who are fairly equally matched, and to arrange the tables not only according to their ability as players, but according to their temperaments and personalities.

An experienced hostess is careful not to place a brilliant player at the same table with indifferent, careless players who are satisfied with a second-rate game. She never pairs an expert with a beginner, a serious player with a chatterer, a fast player with one who is maddeningly slow. She does her best to match the players as to temperament and skill; for she knows that whatever else a card party may or may not be, it's a disappointment to the guests if they don't enjoy playing together.

At afternoon bridge parties made up of women who play together frequently, it's a good idea to let them make up their own tables— when the method of playing permits. In this way the hostess avoids seating at the same table women who do not enjoy playing together, and therefore cannot fully enjoy the party.

CORRECT BRIDGE EQUIPMENT

Next to a well-selected guest list—and equally important—is correct and comfortable equipment for the players.

The basic requirement is a good, firm, steady table for each group of four players. To sit down at a wobbly table which is likely to collapse during an exciting play—or one with a dense undergrowth of legs which one must straddle—is to get off to a bad start even before the game begins. An uncovered table is best for cards; but if a cover is used, it should be smooth and taut so as not to interfere with the playing. (When chips or mah jong tiles are used, a cover with a felt or quilted back is desirable as it absorbs much of the noise.)

The chairs should be of suitable height and comfortable for playing. Deep chairs into which one sinks are not desirable, nor are chairs which tower above the table and command a view of everyone's hand. Chairs that creak and squeak with every move can be a great annoyance to the players—and are certainly no credit to the hostess. A drop of oil will ease the creak from any chair.

For each table there should be two decks of clean new cards, four score pads and well-sharpened pencils, and plenty of ashtrays for the smokers. If drinks are served at the tables, coasters should be provided. Whatever is required for the comfort and convenience of the players, the thoughtful hostess is careful to provide. But she doesn't unnecessarily clutter the table, as that isn't pleasant for the players.

Lighting is very important at a card party, for poor or inadequate light handicaps the players. In the afternoon, the tables should be so arranged that they are neither in bright glare nor deep shadow. In the evening the tables should be softly illumined by bridge lamps—one for each table, if possible.

CONCERNING BRIDGE PRIZES

At parties where both men and women play, it is customary to award two prizes: one for the man with the highest score, and one for the woman with the highest score. Sometimes, at very large parties, a first and second prize for men and women are awarded.

When groups of four play together all evening without changing tables, a small prize is generally given for high score at each table. Some hostesses also give a "booby" prize to the player who turns in the lowest score of all.

Prizes should be attractively wrapped, and presented as soon as the scores are totaled and the winners announced. Those who receive prizes should open them, and express pleasure and appreciation to the hostess.

Although it is not the best social practice to play bridge for money at a party, some people cannot enjoy the game unless they do. If it's the guests' wish to play for money, the hostess should accede— whether she approves or not. But she should insist on low stakes, for surely it would be against all the rules of hospitality for a player to lose a large sum of money while a guest in her house.

GOOD MANNERS AT THE BRIDGE TABLE

It's a strange and sad fact that many people who are otherwise completely charming become impatient and bad-tempered at the card table. Since bridge is a social game, and so very much a part of social life, it's surprising that this should be so. It is meant to be a pleasant and relaxing pastime; but in many people the competitive spirit is unfortunately so keen that at times it becomes almost pathological.

Truly well-bred people, however, keep their tempers under control, do not permit themselves to become rude or abusive under any circumstances. They refuse to check their good manners at the door, and are as courteous and controlled in a card game as they are in a ballroom or at an afternoon tea. Not everyone can play bridge like an expert, but everyone can be courteous and considerate.

Avoid post-mortems, avoid endless arguments about how a hand should have been played. They slow up the progress of the game and often turn the bridge table into a battle ground of angry recriminations. The friendly discussion of an interesting or unusual hand after it has been played is a fine way to study the game and improve one's playing. But there's a vast difference between ill-tempered argument and the amiable exchange of theories and ideas.

Avoid also gratuitous instruction and unwelcome bridge lessons during the course of the game. Few things can be more irritating to a player, even a beginner, than loud and patronizing instruction from a more experienced player—given with a curt impatience which clearly says, "Why did I ever get stuck with a player like you?"

Of course, the greatest courtesy of all is to play a serious, intelligent game. People who take their bridge seriously—and most good players do—don't like to stop in the middle of an exciting hand to listen to a story or wait for a conversation to end. Most card games call for concentration, and this is especially true of bridge. Concentration is difficult when lively talk is going on around the table. It isn't necessary to be grim about it; any game is better for being spiced with a little good talk and a little laughter. But the talk should be *between hands*, during the dealing, when it doesn't interfere with the progress of the game.

The person who is dummy should remain at his own place, quietly observing the progress of the game but offering no comments or criticism. Being dummy doesn't give a player the right to stop the game to tell a story or relate an amusing incident.

There are many seemingly insignificant things that people do at bridge tables that can drive other players to distraction, and ruin the party for them. Whistling, for example, can be very irritating to a player trying to concentrate. Humming is equally annoying. Any nervous mannerism like drumming on the table or snapping the edges of the cards is disturbing to the other players. The ideal bridge guest is relaxed and at ease, plays quietly and attentively—and always with consideration for the other players at his table.

THE ETHICS OF THE GAME

In bridge, as in every other game, the well-bred man or woman plays fair. It is *not* fair to give one's partner illegal information by playing the cards quickly, or with hesitation, or with marked emphasis. It is *not* fair to ask leading questions, make pointed remarks, show sudden interest or elation—or in any way influence the play of one's partner or opponents.

An experienced bridge player cannot fail to be influenced by the little "signs" that give away another player's hand, and is almost instinctively guided by them in his bidding and playing. It is therefore very important to avoid such "signs"—to be guarded and noncommittal in one's facial expressions and remarks. Any useful information given to one's partner during the course of the game, whether deliberate or not, is clearly *unethical*.

For example, one should never make any such remark as, "Well, I guess I must pass again" or "I can't say a thing!" It doesn't take much cleverness to gather from such remarks that the hand is weak. Nor should a player pass with just one quick, disgruntled look at his cards —for that, too, indicates weakness. The bid should be made as promptly as possible, without undue emphasis or hesitation and without any subtle (or not-so-subtle!) side remarks. No information whatever should be given about the hand other than what is conveyed by the bid itself.

Once a bid has been made, it should not be retracted. To change a bid, or suddenly decide to make a bid after passing, is not an ethical practice, as it gives unfair information, and often an unfair advantage to one's partner.

During the bidding, a player should not call his partner's attention to the score, should not indicate approval or disapproval of a bid, pass, or double.

When hands are being dealt, players should not touch the cards or pick them up until the deal has been fully completed.

Each card should be played to the center of the table—without emphasis, without flourish, and without comment.

Rearranging one's hand after playing the last card in a suit is a give-away to everyone at the table—and a very amateurish way of playing bridge.

A player who has unwittingly been given useful information about another player's hand should disregard that information. To take advantage of it is poor sportsmanship.

REFRESHMENTS

The refreshments served at a bridge party depend on the type and nature of the function. A bridge luncheon generally begins at about one o'clock. The playing begins at two or soon thereafter, and no further refreshments are served during the afternoon except ice water or soft drinks. For an important, ceremonious bridge luncheon, the dining room or dining terrace is used. But for a simple party, luncheon is usually served at the bridge tables, conveniently arranged and in position for playing afterward. All that is necessary is to remove the dishes and linen, and the tables are ready for the game.[1]

[1]For details of the bridge luncheon, see pages 141 and 142.

A bridge tea is simply an afternoon of playing, generally from two to five—followed by a tea which may be as simple or elaborate as the hostess wishes and the occasion warrants. But it should never be so elaborate that it interferes with dinner. Tiny sandwiches and cakes, and tea or coffee, should be adequate for most occasions; but for a rather special party, something like fruit salad might be added.

Guests invited for a very simple, informal afternoon of bridge often prefer to play straight through until six, without stopping for refreshments—especially if they are bridge enthusiasts. In this case, the hostess sets up a small buffet table in a corner of the room where guests may help themselves to refreshments whenever they wish, which is usually when they are dummy. Only finger foods, like sandwiches and small cakes, are suitable; but with a little imagination they can be arranged temptingly and attractively. There may also be colorful little dishes of candy and nuts. Coffee or tea is served by the hostess or a maid; or cold drinks are made available to the guests to take back with them to the bridge tables.

In the evening, bridge often follows a dinner party. Of course when dinner is served to guests, no other refreshments are necessary during the evening. Ice water and mints are generally made available for guests who want them, and perhaps fruit or nuts for later in the evening. But certainly nothing else is indicated.

The dessert bridge is extremely popular nowadays, and is an easy, pleasant way to entertain. Guests are asked to eliminate dessert and coffee from their dinner at home. When all guests have arrived, and before any bridge is played, a gala dessert is served to them in the dining room—with large cups of coffee or demitasse, as they prefer. This gives the hostess an opportunity to show her table at its best, ablaze with lights and flowers, set for dessert with her finest silver and china. An impressive effect is achieved without the effort or expense of a dinner, and the hostess can relax and enjoy herself during the long evening of bridge for no further refreshments need be served.

Most popular of all types of bridge parties is the simple, informal evening with a congenial group of friends—followed by a light supper served either at the bridge tables, or buffet style from the dining room table. In summer there are usually salad and cold cuts, dessert and iced beverages. In winter there is usually a hot dish like creamed chicken, spaghetti, or an interesting "specialty of the house" served from a casserole or chafing dish, dessert, and hot coffee.

When refreshments are served at the card tables, they should be covered with bridge cloths. It's nice to have all the cloths match, if possible, as it gives a more pleasing effect to the room. All the silver, linen, china, and accessories for serving should be conveniently laid out and ready, so that the refreshments can be served without delay when the playing is over for the evening. At an informal bridge supper served late at night, guests usually help to remove the cards and score pads, set the tables, and otherwise assist the hostess.

9. COCKTAIL PARTIES

A COCKTAIL party is the smart, modern way to entertain guests without too much preparation or too much effort. Such parties are casual and informal, and as much fun for the hosts as for their guests.

The requirements for a successful cocktail party, whether for six guests or a hundred, are congenial people, good liquor, a tempting assortment of tidbits to go with the drinks, and music if convenient. There should always be at least one kind of non-alcoholic drink such as tomato juice or fruit juice for guests who do not drink liquor. Obviously a gracious hostess does not make a practice of inviting friends who never take alcohol to cocktail parties.

"Little" cocktail parties for a few special friends are intimate and lively, and a very easy way to entertain. The party is generally between the hours of five and seven, and guests are invited informally by telephone or personal note. In preparation, the hostess brings all the essential equipment, the glasses and the ingredients, into the living room on a large tray, and places the tray on a firm, steady table (unless, of course, the house is equipped with a bar, as so many are nowadays). There is usually a choice of at least two kinds of cocktails; and a generous host also provides scotch and soda for those who rarely drink anything else. For hors d'oeuvres, any little sandwiches, appetizers, and relishes that look tempting and taste good may be served. They are simply spread on platters and arranged attractively on the table or the bar, and guests help themselves. They should be foods that can be eaten with the fingers so that plates and forks aren't necessary; and other than the drinks and hors d'oeuvre, only tiny cocktail napkins need be provided. For an informal party of this type, paper napkins are considered appropriate. If the hostess is a busy woman, with no time to prepare special hors d'oeuvres, and no servant to do it for her, crackers and cheese, bowls of nuts, potato chips, carrot sticks, olives, etc., are also considered entirely appropriate and acceptable.

A ceremonious cocktail party, to celebrate a particular occasion like an engagement or an anniversary, naturally involves more preparation and is conducted with more formality. Often as many as a hundred guests are invited; and if space is limited, they may be invited in relays to avoid overcrowding. For example, some guests are invited to come from four to five, some from five to six, and some from six to seven. At a "little" cocktail party, guests stay from beginning to end. But at a large cocktail party, guests stay only for the time specified in the invitation. It's rude and discourteous for a guest invited from four to five to remain until seven.

For large cocktail parties—whether they are given at a club or hotel, or at home—engraved invitations are generally used. Visiting-card invitations (the word "Cocktails" and the date and hour written on the face of the card in ink) are also used, though not especially recommended. Invitations by telephone are appropriate nowadays for all but the most formal functions.

If the party is at a club or hotel, the details of service are taken care of professionally by the staff; and the most important concern of the host and hostess is to invite congenial people and see that they enjoy themselves. But if the party is at home, there is also the responsibility of providing suitable drinks and hors d'oeuvres, for these are as essential to the success of a big cocktail party as the guests who are invited to it. Therefore, unless the household servants include a butler proficient in mixing drinks, or unless the host himself is an expert, it's advisable to engage a bartender for the occasion. There should also be an adequate number of people to pass the trays of food, refill them as required, remove empty glasses, and otherwise attend to the needs and desires of the guests.

There should always be an assortment of drinks at a large and important cocktail party, as not everyone likes every type of drink. Guests are usually offered a choice of at least two different cocktails, and scotch or rye—or both. There is often champagne also, or sparkling burgundy or sauterne, for those who prefer wine to stronger liquor.

Hors d'oeuvres are more elaborate for this type of party. Both hot and cold canapés are generally served in as wide and fascinating a variety as the hostess wishes. A workable plan for a large group (unless one has many servants) is to pass the cold canapés once, and then put the trays down on a table where the guests can help themselves. After hot canapés are passed the tray is taken back to the kitchen to be replenished and passed again later. Hot canapés should not be left on a table for guests to help themselves, but should be kept coming hot and tempting from the kitchen at regular intervals.

Although some hostesses provide cocktail plates (about the size of bread-and-butter plates), they aren't really necessary. At cocktail parties, guests eat to complement their drinking, not to satisfy hunger. They properly help themselves to one canapé at a time, taking it with their fingers. Napkins should of course be provided; and for an important party, only fabric ones will do. Paper napkins are suitable only for simple, casual entertaining.

10. HOUSE AND WEEK-END PARTIES

HOUSE parties should be given only by those who have well-equipped homes and are able to make guests comfortable in every way. While it is pleasant to invite your friends to share the beach life, sailing, fishing, and other sports of your particular locality, you do not take them away from their own cozy homes for a week end or more to impose upon them the discomforts of a crowded house with limited bedroom and bathroom facilities. Not that you must have a big, lavish house by any means! But there should be a room for every guest invited, and enough bathrooms to avoid a long "waiting for turn" in the morning.

INVITATIONS FOR HOUSE AND WEEK-END PARTIES

Invitations for house parties, whether for a week end or longer duration, should be by letter. There are many things the guest needs to know, and these should be included in the invitation.

House guests must know the exact duration of the visit, when they are expected to arrive, and when they are expected to leave. They should be given some idea of the activities planned, so that they will know what clothes and sports equipment to take with them. Unless they have been there before, they should be told the best way to come —with marked roadmaps or timetables enclosed for their convenience.

A week-end visit is generally from Friday or Saturday until the following Monday morning. Guests should be invited two weeks in advance, to give them time to make all necessary arrangements. If several members of a family are invited, they should all be mentioned specifically by name. The thoughtful hostess mentions what other guests have been invited, to avoid the possibility of bringing uncongenial people together for a week end.

Dear Marjory:
I hope you and Ted haven't any plans for the week end of August twelfth, as we'd like you to spend it with us here at Glen Point.
I think we can promise Ted some real good fishing this year. The trout are biting better than ever! So bring your fishing clothes; and be sure to bring your tennis things, too, because the Martins are coming and I'm sure you'll want to get out on the courts with them.

There's a very good train Friday night; I've marked it in red on the timetable. It arrives about seven, which is just in time for dinner. You can get a late train back Sunday night, or there's an early express that Ralph usually takes on Monday morning.

Now don't let anything prevent you from coming, Marjory, as we're looking forward to your visit. And be sure to let us know what train you are taking so that Ralph can meet you at the station.

Affectionately,
Ellen

Such an invitation should be acknowledged promptly with a definite acceptance or regret. If one cannot accept, the reason should be given.

People who own big country places often invite friends to house parties that may last anywhere from three days to three weeks. The invitation must give the exact date of expected arrival and departure, so that there can be no question about the duration of the visit. Like the week-end invitation, it should indicate the best and most convenient way to come, the sports and activities planned, the clothes likely to be needed, other guests invited, and so on. House guests should never remain even one day longer than specified in the invitation.

THE GUESTS ARRIVE

It's an unwritten law of hospitality that house guests arriving by train or plane should be met, and transportation to the house provided for them. They should be met by their hosts, if convenient; otherwise by a servant or an intimate of the household. An old friend who is a frequent visitor at the house and knows exactly how to get there needn't be met every time—especially when many other guests, less familiar with the locality, are expected.

A good hostess personally inspects all guest rooms before her guests arrive, makes sure they are comfortable and inviting, equipped with all essentials, and made cheerful with fresh-cut flowers. If flowers are not readily available, a colorful bowl of fruit on the bedside table is a pleasant substitute.

Upon arrival at the house, guests are immediately shown to their rooms and given an opportunity to change their clothes and relax. They should be given at least an hour to rest and make themselves comfortable before meeting the other guests, or before being expected to appear for a meal. As a rule, guests arrive for a week-end or house party in the late afternoon, around teatime. The hostess may arrange to have her guests meet at tea; or they may not meet until the dinner hour.

THE FIRST EVENING

House and week-end parties should be made up of people who know each other, or at least people who have somewhat the same interests and enjoy the same type of things. As they will be in close association for several days or more, it is important that they be congenial. Guests who do not know each other should be introduced the first evening.

At dinner the hostess generally discusses plans and suggests interesting and pleasant activities for the next day or two. She doesn't try to blueprint every waking hour of her guests' stay in her house. Some of her guests will want to play tennis; some will want to spend most of their time on the golf course, or fish, or ride, or just loaf and relax. A good hostess does not insist on a planned routine of activity, but permits her guests to do pretty much as they please. She provides a flow of events and activities in which they can join or not, as they choose.

Needless to say, the good hostess makes a point of providing good food for her guests. She doesn't serve them a cold and meager supper after they have traveled for hours to reach her house. Dinner the night of arrival may be quite simple and casual. In fact, the party is more likely to get off to a good start if there is no formality the first evening. But the food should be hot and satisfying, tempting to the eye and to the palate . . . and there should be plenty of it. There's nothing like a good dinner and gay, lively talk around the table to make a guest feel welcome and at ease.

No special or elaborate plans should be made for the first evening, as guests may wish to retire early. There may be some bridge after dinner, or an hour or two of television; but when congenial people have come together in the house of a friend, conversation is frequently the most welcome kind of entertainment.

Before her guests retire for the night, the hostess lets them know what the habits of the household are in regard to breakfast, and learns their preferences. She sees to it that they have all the blankets they may need, in case the night turns cold, and, if she is especially thoughtful, she arranges for a tray of fruit juice or ice water and glasses to be placed in every room.

THE WELL-EQUIPPED GUEST ROOM

Much of the pleasure and comfort of a house guest depends on the sleeping quarters provided for him, and the good taste and good judgment with which the room is furnished and equipped. It may be the smallest room in the house. But if it's bright and cheerful, with good light, restful and inviting furniture, and the important essentials conveniently at hand, it is all any guest can ask for.

In general, there should be a room for each guest, or for each husband and wife who are guests. When the house is crowded, two brothers or two sisters may be asked to share a room. Otherwise guests should not be asked to "double up" except for a special occasion or in an emergency.

A guest room should be equipped with everything a guest needs to feel "at home"—including many of the things he is expected to bring along, but may forget. The bed should be comfortable, and placed so that it does not face the full glare of sunlight. There should be a bed table, a good light for reading, and some interesting books and magazines for those who are accustomed to reading themselves to sleep. There should be a writing desk or table with pen and ink, blotters, note paper, and envelopes, perhaps a little clock that doesn't tick too loudly, ash trays, and a handy wastepaper basket near by. There should be a bureau or dressing table with a mirror above it, and a little chair or bench before it. In a top drawer there should be small, useful articles such as a clothes brush, nail file, sewing kit, pins, hairpins, facial tissue, etc. In a bottom drawer, or on the top shelf of the closet, there should be one or two extra blankets. All guest closets should be empty, containing only the extra blankets and a generous supply of hangers. There should be a big, comfortable easy chair for lounging; and to be *completely* equipped, the guest room should also contain a radio and a luggage rack.

Though guests generally bring their own toilet articles, many hostesses provide face cream, bath crystals, body powder, toilet water, even shaving cream and toothpaste. Of course, there should be plenty of towels and washcloths, a fresh bath mat, and a new cake of soap for every guest. These are in the bathroom if it adjoins the guest room; but if the bathroom must be shared, these essentials are placed on a small table in the guest room itself.

A guest who needs something the hostess may have forgotten to provide should not hesitate to ask for it. But under no circumstances may a house guest ask to have the room assigned to him changed. The only possible excuse for such a request would be an illness aggravated by some condition of the room, such as excessive dampness. In this case the guest would carefully explain the situation to the hostess and ask to have the room changed *if possible*. The hostess graciously complies, if she can do so without inconveniencing too many other people. If a change of rooms is impossible, she does everything in her power to correct the condition and to make the guest more comfortable in the room assigned to him.

It goes without saying that a well-bred guest does not make selfish or unreasonable demands upon his hostess, but adapts himself to the conditions of the household and overlooks any little discomforts or inconveniences.

Making a House Guest Feel at Home

Since her guests' comfort and pleasure are her first consideration, the truly hospitable hostess does not lay down any hard or fast rules, especially as to rising and retiring. In most homes where house guests are frequently entertained, the breakfast tray sent to the room is practically an institution. This is not only for the indulgence of the guests, but also for the convenience of the servants. It keeps the guests in their rooms and out of the way until most of the morning duties are taken care of and the house made ready for the new day. In large, well-staffed houses, a butler or maid usually asks each guest what he would like for breakfast, and when he would like his tray sent up. In simple households, the hostess merely sends up what she thinks her guests will enjoy or tells them when family breakfast is served.

All house guests generally meet for luncheon. Many hostesses plan a beach picnic or backyard barbecue for the middle of the day, to gather their wandering guests together and enable them to eat informally in whatever clothes they are wearing. Dinner is, of course, the ceremonious meal of the day for which everyone must be present . . . and everyone must be *prompt*.

It isn't necessary for the host and hostess to spend every waking moment with their guests, nor to provide something to do for every hour of the day. Entertaining is best when it is relaxed and effortless. The most successful hosts are always those who *enjoy* their guests, and have just as good a time as they do.

The Qualities of a Welcome and Agreeable House Guest

Being a good house guest begins even before one arrives at the house. The invitation must be acknowledged promptly, with a definite acceptance or regret. It is ungracious to keep a hostess waiting for an answer, uncertain until the last moment of your presence at the week-end or house party she is planning.

A good house guest arrives on time, and exactly when expected.

He brings whatever clothes and equipment he will need, but doesn't arrive loaded down with an unreasonable amount of luggage. If he is courteous, he brings a gift for his hostess—nothing so elaborate that it seems like payment for her hospitality, but a small thoughtful gift that shows his appreciation. He does not bring candy for her small children, to impair their young digestions and spoil the fun. He knows that books or games to keep them occupied and out of mischief are more sensible.

A good house guest is ready to accept conditions as he finds them —to be pleasant and agreeable in any situation, even if he finds his former wife at the same party! He is co-operative and obliging, falls in with his hostess' plans, adapts himself to the routine of the household. He is punctual for meals, doesn't keep his hosts and fellow guests waiting for him, is careful not to keep the family up at night beyond their usual time. He accepts his share of responsibility for making the party a success, is good-tempered and cheerful, and does what he can to contribute to the general entertainment and fun. If he finds the visit unpleasant or disappointing, he doesn't show it.

A good house guest respects his hosts' property. He takes very good care of everything he uses, and puts things back in their proper places. He doesn't leave cushions, blankets, books, tennis rackets out of doors to be damaged by the dew or by rain. He watches where he puts burning cigarettes and wet glasses. He keeps his room orderly, and leaves it in the same condition he found it.

A good house guest does not overstay his welcome. He leaves when he is expected to leave . . . and does not forget to tip the servants before going. The size of the tip depends on the duration of the visit and the amount and type of service rendered. The average tip is about $2 a week to the maid who takes care of his room, and $2 or $3 a week to the butler or waitress who serves him at mealtimes. However, if special services are required, such as pressing a suit, a somewhat larger tip is generally given.

A day or two after he leaves, the guest should write an enthusiastic bread-and-butter letter to his hostess, thanking her for her hospitality.

11. THE SERVICE OF WINES AND LIQUORS

THERE IS, or should be, nothing very complicated or confusing about the use and service of wines. There are just a few basic principles with which one need be familiar.

All wines fall into five general classifications. These are: appetizer wines, red table wines, white table wines, dessert wines, and sparkling wines. There are literally hundreds of different "types" of wines and wine names; but all fall into one or another of these five categories.

To know the five basic wine types, and the foods with which they go best, plus a few simple details of proper handling and service, is all the information anyone needs for gracious hospitality.

A Brief Analysis of the Five Types of Wine

Appetizer wines, or *apéritifs,* are so-called because they are served before a meal, as cocktails are. Best known in this group are sherry and vermouth, but there are many others. In general, any light dry wine is acceptable. Some people prefer Dubonnet as an *apéritif,* especially before luncheon.

Red table wines are robust, full-bodied wines that are usually served with the main course of a meal—wines that go well with rich and hearty foods. They range from the lighter clarets, which complement lighter foods such as chicken and veal, to the deep red burgundies, which go well with red meats and highly seasoned foods. The most popular red table wines are claret, burgundy, bordeaux, and chianti.

White table wines aren't necessarily white, but range from a pale straw or greeny-gold color to a dark amber shade. In general, they are lighter and more delicately flavored than the red wines, and blend best with white meats, fowl, seafood, and creamed dishes. The best-known and most popular wines in this group are sauterne, chablis and rhine wine (sometimes called hock or moselle).

Dessert wines are rich, full-flavored wines which range from slightly sweet to very sweet, and from pale gold to deep red in color. As the name implies, they are the wines which are usually served with dessert. Actually, however, they are "all-occasion" wines which may be served with crackers and cheese, or with biscuits, any time friends drop in for a visit. The favorites are port, muscatel, marsala, sweet sherry, and tokay.

Sparkling wines are table wines which have been made effervescent by a second fermentation. Many people prefer them to *still* table wines, find their lively sparkle more exhilarating and enjoyable. The most popular are sparkling burgundy, sparkling sauterne, and of course champagne. Sparkling burgundy is a smooth, rather sweet wine, an excellent choice for luncheon. Champagne is a gay, festive wine which may be served all through dinner, if desired, or just with dessert, or afterwards in the drawing room to keep the party going. Champagne may be dry, medium sweet, or sweet. *Brut* on the bottle means dry, sec or demisec means medium, doux means sweet. A dry champagne is preferred for serving with dinner. All sparkling wines, red and white, are so-called "party" wines, suitable for special occasions, and may be served as appetizers, during the course of a meal, or any time during the evening for refreshment.

WINE AND FOOD

The subtle harmonies of flavor between wine and food are for the epicure to contemplate—a subject too highly specialized to fall within the boundaries of this book. But the average host and hostess who like to entertain properly and well, should know—at least in a broad, general way—which wines go with which foods. The following chart will serve as a handy reference.

Before Dinner

Dry sherry makes a splendid appetizer before dinner for those who do not wish to serve mixed drinks or cocktails. Madeira, dubonnet, vermouth, and light sauterne are also acceptable . . . and of course there's always champagne for special and important occasions.

Not all of the usual hors d'oeuvres are suitable to serve with wine. Anything with a very sharp or acid taste should be avoided. Mild cheese spread on crackers makes an excellent canapé to serve with wine; and caviar is almost traditional with champagne.

During the Meal

Your success as a hostess is not measured by the variety of wines you serve, but rather by the suitability of the one or two you wisely select. Certainly at a luncheon party, one wine is quite enough; more would only seem ostentatious. A light wine that blends with all the courses is best. One might serve dry sherry (the most versatile all-purpose wine of all), sauterne, or a light claret. For an informal dinner also, one wine is the usual custom—dry sherry or champagne being the ideal choice. Both of these wines, or any favorite sparkling wine, may be served from the beginning of a meal straight through to the end. Champagne is poured from its own bottle; sherry from the bottle or from an attractive decanter. Even for an elaborate formal dinner, two wines are generally considered ample, though three, and sometimes even four, are occasionally served in big houses with well-stocked wine cellars.

Following are the wines which blend best with various types of foods, the combinations which gourmets agree are most harmonious and acceptable:

OYSTERS OR CLAMS

Chablis
Rhine
Moselle
Dry champagne

MELON

Medium sherry
Sweet sauterne
Madeira

SOUP

Light dry sherry
White burgundy
Graves
Beaujolais

FISH

Moselle
Chablis
Rhine
White burgundy
Sauterne

ENTRÉES

Light claret
Chianti
Light red burgundy

ROASTS

Still or sparkling burgundy
Rich red claret
Zinfandel
Chianti

GAME

With wild duck—Burgundy
With rabbit—Claret or burgundy
With grouse—Burgundy
With partridge—Claret
With venison—Burgundy
With pheasant—Claret or burgundy
With quail—Champagne
With hare—Burgundy
With woodcock—Burgundy

POULTRY

With chicken—Champagne or sauterne
With turkey—Claret or medium burgundy
With duck—Rhine wine or burgundy
With goose—Burgundy or champagne
With squab—Champagne or sauterne

STEAKS AND CHOPS

Claret
Burgundy
Dry champagne

HAM

Claret
Champagne

SPAGHETTI

Claret
Chianti

SALAD

No wine

CHEESE

Claret } with mild
Burgundy } cheeses

Port
Sherry } with stronger
Madeira } cheeses
Tokay

DESSERT

Sweet champagne
Sweet sauterne
Port
Madeira
Muscatel

After Dinner

Brandy, cognac, and liqueurs are served in the drawing room after dinner, usually with the after-dinner coffee. They are sometimes served at the table with demitasse; but when the coffee is served in the drawing room, the brandy and liqueurs should be, too.

Brandy and cognac are potent, and as a rule are proffered the gentlemen only. But liqueurs, which are also called "cordials," are offered to the ladies as well as the gentlemen. The favorites are chartreuse, benedictine, cointreau and crême de menthe. To give them a glamorous "party" look, liqueurs may be served frappéed. This means they are poured over finely crushed ice in saucer-shaped champagne glasses instead of the usual tiny cordial glasses, and the guests sip them slowly through short straws.

When champagne is the only wine served at dinner, it is often served throughout the evening, especially at important family parties or celebrations. Sweet wines like marsala, madeira, tokay and port are also frequently served during the evening following a dinner party. A special favorite of the ladies is angelica, a cordial-type wine—mild and sweet, and an excellent accompaniment of fruit and nuts.

Any well-chilled dessert wine may be served for refreshment when friends drop in after dinner for an evening of cards or conversation. In fact a glass of port, with a piece of fruitcake or some biscuits, provides adequate and acceptable refreshment for an unexpected guest any time of the day—afternoon or evening.

THE SEQUENCE OF WINES

The order in which wines are served is important. Dinner wines should be chosen in relation to each other, as well as the foods they accompany.

When more than one wine is served at a dinner, white wines should be served before red wines, otherwise the flavors "go wrong" and are not fully enjoyed. Dry wines should be served before sweet wines—as after a sweet wine, a dry wine tends to taste sour. Lighter wines should be served before heavy, full-bodied wines; and young wines should be served before rare old vintage wines.

These are not mere foibles of the wine-fancier, but good common sense. The wrong sequence of wines mars not only their own tang and flavor but also that of the foods with which they are served. So remember:

—white wines before red   —light wines before heavy
—dry wines before sweet   —young wines before old

The Storage of Wines

Wine is a living thing, delicate and easily disturbed, and therefore should be gently handled and carefully stored. It reacts violently and unpleasantly to outside conditions and disturbances, even when tightly sealed in a bottle. And as wine is fit to drink only when it is clear and transparent, it must be protected from any conditions which may affect it unfavorably.

The three things which most seriously threaten the quality of stored wines are (1) vibration or constant disturbance, (2) excessive light, (3) extremes of varying temperature. So never store good wines in sunlight, or where they are likely to be moved about and disturbed, or where they will be subject to fluctuations of temperature. Never store them close to hot-water pipes or furnaces, or where there is excessive dampness or mustiness. The ideal storage place is dark and dry, with some ventilation, and with a fairly constant temperature of about 55 degrees.

The term "wine cellar" means a collection of wines, rather than a basement. The collection may be stored in a specially constructed closet or in an old chest of drawers; it may be in the kitchen or in the attic, but it's still a "wine cellar."

Of course a basement, if you have one, is a fine place to keep most wines. However it must be a dry, dark cellar, with a temperature that never ranges far on either side of 55 degrees—and there should be suitable racks or bins to hold the bottles in a horizontal position. All wines, except madeira, should be kept lying on their sides or tilted forward enough to keep the corks wet. If bottles are left standing upright, the corks dry out—and a dry cork may mean a spoiled wine, as it lets the air work itself in. Also dry cork breaks more easily, and small particles are very likely to drop into the liquid.

For those who have no cellar, a closet or chest of drawers will do for storing wines . . . if the temperature is cool and even, and the bottles will not be frequently disturbed. The drawers should be opened occasionally for ventilation. If space is limited or conditions unfavorable for storing wine, it's advisable to buy in small quantities, as needed.

The Care and Handling of Wine

Live wines throw off certain impurities and by-products which sink down to the side of the bottle. It's important, in handling a bottle of wine, not to shake or disturb this sediment so that it swishes back through the wine. The bottle should be lifted and carried, the cork drawn and the wine poured, gently and carefully, with as little agitation as possible. If the sediment has been obviously stirred up, the wine should be permitted to settle before it is served. A permanently cloudy wine which does not settle is unsound and not fit to drink.

It's in pulling the cork that the wine is most likely to be shaken up and disturbed. A corkscrew that works by leverage should be used, if possible. It's wise to hold the bottle in a napkin to avoid cutting your hands if the neck of the bottle should break. If bits of cork break off and drop into the wine, decant and strain at once.

Many wines deteriorate when exposed to the air—go "sour" and spoil, as milk does. The higher the temperature, the more quickly they spoil; therefore a partly empty bottle should be kept in a cool place, and the wine should be consumed within twenty-four hours after the cork is drawn. This applies particularly to *table* wines, which are delicate and perishable and will not keep in a decanter. *Dessert* wines, and some of the *appetizer* wines, are fortified with extra alcohol after fermentation, and do not become acid if allowed to stand after opening.

So serve your sherry, madeira, port from a lovely decanter, if you wish. But serve claret and burgundy from their own bottles, or if you decant them, use them up quickly. Champagne is always poured from the bottle to the glass; so are all other sparkling wines, and most of the white wines like sauterne, rhine wine and chablis. A bottle of table wine partly used and recorked will quickly spoil; so always use up what you have opened as soon as you can.

Wine from two different bottles should never be mixed in the same decanter.

CONCERNING WINE TEMPERATURES

The temperature at which wine is served is important. Cold brings out the fine bouquets of certain wines but tends to numb the flavor and bouquet of others.

In general, all dry white table wines are chilled. The sweeter the wine, the colder the temperature at which it is served. Red wines are served at room temperature. Champagne and sparkling wines are served at colder temperature than any other type of wine and are generally placed in buckets of cracked ice for twenty or thirty minutes before serving.

To chill white table wines, allow them to stand in the lower part of the refrigerator for about an hour. But never leave wine in the refrigerator indefinitely, as that destroys its finer qualities.

To bring a red table wine from cellar temperature to room temperature, simply let it stand in the room for several hours before serving. *Never place it in hot water or let it stand near heat.* Epicures always draw the cork from a bottle of claret or burgundy about a half hour before it is served, so that the wine can "breathe" and increase the fragrance of its bouquet.

To ice champagne or sparkling burgundy, take it directly from the cellar to the ice bucket. Be sure that the ice in the bucket is piled high enough to cover all the wine, but not to cover the neck of the bottle. If no ice buckets are available, champagne or sparkling burgundy may be chilled in the refrigerator until thoroughly cold.

Ice should never be placed inside a glass of wine. It kills the bouquet, and in the case of champagne and other sparkling wines, it flattens out the effervescence.

For handy reference, here is a list of some of the more familiar wines and how they are served:

Angelica	cool
Barsac	room temperature
Brandy	room temperature
Burgundy	room temperature (or slightly cooler)
Chablis	chilled
Champagne	very cold
Chianti	room temperature
Claret	room temperature
Dubonnet	chilled
Grâves	well chilled
Haut sauterne	cold
Madeira	room temperature
Marsala	room temperature
Moselle	chilled
Muscatel	cool
Port	room temperature
Rhine wine	chilled
Riesling	chilled
Sauterne	chilled
Sherry	room temperature
Tokay	cool
White bordeaux	very cold
White burgundy	slightly chilled

Most cordials and liqueurs are served at room temperature or slightly cooled.

CORRECT GLASSWARE

Gourmets who take their wine drinking seriously will tell you that wine must be served in the proper glass, otherwise it won't look or taste as it should. Skeptics go to the other extreme and declare that the glass makes no difference at all—that wine tastes the same from any glass. The truth lies somewhere midway between these two extremes.

Nowadays it isn't considered necessary to have a wide array of glassware for correct service. It isn't necessary to have a different size and shape for every type of wine. There's much greater latitude in the use of wine glasses than there used to be, even in formal service. Actually, only two kinds of glasses are required for the average household. These are large wineglasses (4 to 6 ounces) for table wines, and small glasses (2 to 3 ounces) for the appetizer and dessert wines. Even for the most elaborate service, only two more glasses need be included—a 3 to 4-ounce champagne glass, and a 2 to 3-ounce V-shaped glass for sherry. With these four basic types of wine glasses, a hostess is equipped to serve practically any kind of wine at any time.

But though the details of shape and design may have been simplified, certain other factors remain unchanged—and as important as they have ever been. For example, wine should never be served in opaque or colored glasses. Much of the enjoyment of wine comes from its own rich or tawny color. Therefore any glassware that tends to obscure the color is not suitable. Only brilliantly clear crystal glassware should be used, through which the color of the wine glows and reflects—delighting the eye.

Wineglasses should also be thin and fine, as delicate as one can afford. For delicate glasses greatly enhance the pleasure and satisfaction of wine, especially for guests who are connoisseurs. Through thin glass, the warmth of the hand can reach the wine, if desired—increasing the aroma and bouquet. But thick glass does nothing to bring out the enjoyable qualities of a good wine.

Stemmed wineglasses are desirable for two reasons: They add dignity and elegance to the dinner table, and they are pleasant to hold and turn in the hand. For formal service at a luncheon or dinner, all glassware should of course match in design.[1]

Large wineglasses, half or three-quarters filled, are preferable to small glasses filled to the brim. In a large glass the wine can be gently swished to release its full flavor and bouquet—one of the main sensations to be derived from drinking good wine.

[1]For the proper arrangement of glassware on the table, see pages 104 and 105.

These, then, are the main considerations in the choice of wine-glasses: They should be clear and transparent, thin, stemmed, and adequate in size. Tiny glasses are appropriate only for cordials and liqueurs—and for brandy, if one wishes. But really fine brandy is usually served in what is called a "snifter" or "inhaler"—a large, balloon-shaped glass which can be slowly turned and warmed in the hands to release the full, rich bouquet.

As for the shape and design of other glasses in which particular wines are served, they are dictated for the most part by tradition, and may or may not be observed, as one wishes. There are specially shaped glasses for claret, burgundy, and sauterne, but special glasses aren't really necessary. All table wines may be properly served in the same type of large 4 to 6-ounce wineglass. Sherry, too, is often served in its own specially shaped glass although an ordinary two-ounce wineglass is entirely correct. Champagne is traditionally served either in a glass with a shallow, saucerlike bowl or in a goblet with a hollow stem which fills as the bowl is filled. But unless it's a very formal, ceremonious occasion, champagne may also be served in the conventional large-size wineglass.

Customs and Traditions of Wine Service

Certain niceties and customs are observed in the service of wines . . . not important in themselves, but the traditional concern of a perfect host.

First is the matter of drawing the cork at the table, or at least in the dining room in the presence of the guests. This is a gesture of courtesy and a compliment to the guests, suggesting that a very fine and special wine is being opened in their honor. The mouth of the bottle is carefully wiped before the cork is drawn, to remove dust; and again after the cork has been drawn to remove any clinging particles. If the cork is swollen and has a pronounced musty smell, the wine is stale or otherwise unsound and should be discarded.

The courtesy of serving calls for a little wine to be poured into the host's glass first, so that he can judge its quality before it is served to his guests. Just a very small amount is poured into his glass; and as a conscientious host, he goes through the little ceremony of holding it to the light, examining it, and perhaps tasting it. As soon as he signifies that the wine is satisfactory, the guests are served. After all the guests have been taken care of, the host's glass is filled. The custom of pouring a little into the host's glass first also disposes of any particles of cork which may be lodged in the neck of the bottle, and which might otherwise get into a guest's glass.

Wine is sometimes decanted and served from the decanter at the table. Only a transparent crystal decanter should be used, through which the color of the wine can be seen and appreciated. But most table wines are served right from the original bottle. Champagne and sparkling burgundy are always poured from the bottle into the glass, a napkin being wrapped around the bottle to prevent moisture from dropping on the tablecloth or the guests' clothes.

It isn't customary to lift the glasses from the table when the wine is poured. The bottle is carefully tilted, and the wine poured slowly and gently into the glass as it stands on the table. Before pouring the wine, the butler (or the host) asks, "Claret, sir?" or "Claret, Bill?" If the guest does not wish to drink, the says, "No, thank you," or makes a slight gesture of negation with his head or hand. A gracious host never insists, never urges a guest to drink if he doesn't wish to.

A wineglass should be filled only a little more than half to permit full enjoyment of the bouquet. But it's a tradition of hospitality to refill the glass before it becomes completely empty, and to keep refilling it unless the guest signifies that he does not wish any more.

An attractive decanter of wine may be left on the table. But a partially empty bottle of wine should not be left standing on the table. It should be placed on the sideboard or the buffet.

A toast to a guest of honor should be brief and sincere, expressing the true sentiments of the person making it. The more spontaneous it is, the more likely it is to sound sincere. Everyone always rises to drink a toast. The guest of honor doesn't drink to himself, of course —but merely looks pleased, and says (or nods) "Thank you" to the assembled company.

COCKTAILS BEFORE DINNER

Apéritif is the name given to any beverage served before dinner. The favorite continental apéritif is a light dry wine. Sherry, vermouth, and champagne are the most popular. But in this country, the favorite apéritif is the cocktail—a typically American invention with special appeal for the American palate.

Cocktails served before dinner are meant to stimulate the appetite and prepare the palate for the enjoyment of fine food. Therefore sweet or syrupy cocktails should be avoided. A dry cocktail of simple mixture (such as gin and bitters or whiskey and vermouth) is the most desirable. Common sense suggests that the host who wishes to serve cocktails before dinner (or highballs after dinner) should acquire a dependable book of recipes and learn how to mix and prepare them properly.

In many homes it is traditional for the host to prepare the cocktails himself, in the presence of his guests, making a pleasant little ceremony of it. All the essential ingredients, including ice in a bowl or in a special ice bucket, are brought into the living room on a tray. It is supposed to add to the enjoyment of the drink to see it being measured, mixed and poured. However it isn't necessary for the host to mix the drinks himself. It's quite correct to have them mixed in the kitchen or pantry and brought in on a tray, ready to serve.

Either stemmed or footed glasses may be used for cocktails, and there are traditional sizes and shapes for the various types of drinks. A hostess who customarily serves cocktails before dinner should, of course, be equipped with whatever glasses are required to serve them properly.

Hors d'oeuvres—a selection of tiny sandwiches and relishes—are generally served with cocktails before dinner. They should be *really tiny*, just a mouthful; and there should be no more than three or four for each guest. Too many or too rich hors d'oeuvres spoil the appetite for dinner.

COCKTAIL PARTIES

For details of a cocktail party, see pages 148 to 150.

DRINKS SERVED IN THE EVENING

The word "highball," once socially taboo, is now a familiar and acceptable part of the American language. A highball is any mixture of whiskey, gin, rum, or brandy with soda or ginger ale. It is served with ice cubes in a tall glass like that used for iced tea; and is one of the most popular evening drinks to serve to guests.

Highballs are generally brought to the living room on a tray, ready to serve, especially if the guests are playing bridge or watching television. But if they are not so occupied, it's hospitable to mix the drinks in front of them and let each guest decide how much liquor goes into his particular glass. Behind scenes, of course, in the pantry, a jigger or measuring cup is always used; but in the living room, the whiskey is poured from the bottle into the glass. This is the courteous procedure: First, ice cubes are placed in the glass. Then the whiskey is poured by the host until the guest makes a gesture to stop. The glass is filled almost to the top with soda or ginger ale. The drink is then thoroughly mixed and handed to the guest on a coaster. It isn't customary to serve food of any kind with a highball.

Fizzes, flips, rickies, sours, mint juleps, all are appropriate drinks to serve in the evening. So are hot spiced drinks and toddies, wintertime variations of the highball. Their preparation belongs by tradi-

CORRECT BAR GLASSWARE

Top Row: (1) Pilsner beer glass (2) Beer goblet (3) Beer mug (4) 10-ounce highball (5) 5-ounce Delmonico or champagne tumbler (6) Hollow-stemmed sparkling wine glass (7) Saucer champagne (hollow-stemmed) (8) 9-ounce water goblet (9) 4-ounce claret glass.

Second Row: (10) Claret glass (11) Sherry glass (12) 2-ounce wine glass (13) Liqueur frappé (14) Line brandy (15) Liqueur glass (16) Pousse-café (17) 2-ounce cocktail glass (18) 2½-ounce cocktail glass (19) 3½-ounce cocktail glass (20) 5-ounce cocktail glass.

Third Row: (21) 6½-ounce fizz glass (22) 14-ounce Tom Collins glass (23) 12-ounce highball glass (24) 10-ounce highball glass (25) 5½-ounce side water glass (26) 8-ounce Old Fashioned glass (27) 6½-ounce Old Fashioned glass (28) Straight whiskey glass (29) 7-ounce highball glass (30) Hot toddy glass.

tion in the hands of the host; and a good host masters the recipes, perfects his technique, and prepares his guests' drinks with the flair that comes from skill and confidence.[2]

QUESTIONS FREQUENTLY ASKED ABOUT ENTERTAINING

Question: Are husbands and wives generally seated beside each other at a formal dinner table?

Answer: No; they are almost always separated.

Question: When linens are monogrammed, should the wife's maiden initials be used?

Answer: That's an old-fashioned custom, senseless and now considered poor taste. The married initials should be used.

Question: When soup or fruit cup is placed on a service plate, should a small plate also be used?

Answer: Yes.

Question: Is the evening meal called dinner or supper?

Answer: It depends on what is served. A dinner is called "dinner" regardless of whether it is served in the middle of the day or at night. Supper foods are simpler, and are served more casually than dinner foods. A meal consisting of cold cuts, salad, dessert, and a large cup of coffee is a supper. A meal consisting of appetizer, roast, vegetables, salad, dessert, and demitasse is a dinner.

Question: Are thick soups or clear broths considered more appropriate for dinner?

Answer: Clear, light broths are best for the dinner hour, as they are less likely to spoil the appetite for what is to follow. Thick creamed soups are more appropriate for luncheons.

Question: May coffee be served at an afternoon tea?

Answer: Tea is traditional, but there is no objection to coffee. Many hostesses serve both.

Question: Is it discourteous to attend a costume ball in ordinary clothes?

Answer: Not discourteous, but inconsiderate . . . and rather unfair to the hostess. If you accept her invitation, you should dress for the occasion. Of course a doctor, or anyone who is likely to be called away during the evening, is not expected to wear a costume. But all others should do so if they possibly can.

[2] For the details of drinking etiquette, see pages 410 to 414.

Question: Is it possible for a hostess to serve a complete guest dinner, smoothly and correctly, without once getting up from the table?

Answer: Yes—if the first course is on the table when the guests take their places, the roast and vegetables in covered dishes on the table near the host, and the salad and dessert on a separate small table beside the hostess. Used dishes are passed to the hostess who replaces them with clean dishes from the auxiliary table. Coffee is served later in the living room; or it can be served right at the table from an electric percolator.

Question: What should a lady say at the end of a dance when her partner thanks her?

Answer: It isn't necessary to say anything at all. A pleasant, friendly smile is adequate acknowledgment. If she feels she must say something a comment about the music is always in order.

Question: Should a hostess gift be acknowledged?

Answer: If the guest brings the gift with him, the hostess' verbal thanks are sufficient. If he sends the gift after returning from his visit, a note of thanks should be written.

Question: What is the correct way to take loaf sugar from a bowl if no sugar tongs are provided? May the fingers be used?

Answer: It isn't considered good form to put one's fingers into a bowl of loaf sugar. Any unused spoon may be used if the hostess fails to provide the required tongs.

Question: Should guests be allowed to help with the housework at a week-end party?

Answer: If you have no servants and your women guests offer to help with the dishes or the beds—let them! It makes them feel better about accepting your hospitality. But don't let them do too much; they came to relax and enjoy themselves—not to do housework.

Question: Is it proper to use a three-compartment dish at an informal dinner, for serving two vegetables and potatoes at the same time?

Answer: Yes. The modern hostess makes use of any convenient device for speeding up service and making it simpler and more efficient. Divided compartment dishes are meant for informal service, are very practical when there is no maid to help, and are entirely correct. Some hostesses use large trays which have a section in the center for the meat course, and separate sections on either side for the vegetables.

Question: Should sugar and cream for coffee be passed around the table, or should the hostess serve them from her own place?

Answer: The hostess serves them, after asking each guest's preference.

Question: When are paper napkins correct?

Answer: Never for formal entertaining, but at any other time that they are practical and convenient. They are especially appropriate, of course, for picnics, barbecues, and informal luncheons and suppers held out of doors.

Question: What is meant by "ushers" at a ball or dance?

Answer: Ushers are young men appointed by the hostess at a big dance to rescue the wallflowers, introduce shy young people, and keep everyone dancing. They wear white boutonnieres, and they have the "right" to talk to any girl—whether they know her or not—and to ask her to dance. Any stag called upon by an usher to dance with a girl who is standing or sitting alone must do so.

Question: May a bachelor who has a big house in the country invite unmarried women to week-end parties?

Answer: Yes, if there is at least one married couple in the group, or if his mother, sister, aunt, or some other female relative is living in the house with him.

Question: How long do guests remain after dinner, if no special diversion like bridge is planned for the evening?

Answer: As long as they find the conversation interesting and agreeable . . . and are certain that they are not overstaying their welcome. As soon as one guest leaves, the others generally rise to go. When there is a guest of honor, it is traditional for him (or her) to make the first move—though this custom is no longer as rigidly observed as it used to be. In general, dinner guests should spend at least one hour in conversation with their hosts and fellow guests before leaving a dinner party. To leave any sooner would be considered rude.

Question: Is the "head of the table" where the host sits—or the hostess?

Answer: The hostess. She is the *head of the table*—the host is the *head of the house.*

Question: Why is a folded napkin sometimes put under asparagus when it is served?

Answer: To keep water from collecting at the bottom of serving platter and making the food soggy.

Question: When you have been a house guest for a week in a big house, do you tip all the servants or only those who have served you personally.

Answer: Only those who have served you personally.

Question: Are dance programs still used?

Answer: Only at school and college balls and "proms." They are rarely seen nowadays at private dances.

Question: If two wines are served at a dinner party, what are the smartest two wines to use?

Answer: Sherry and champagne, if the dinner starts with soup; chablis and champagne if the dinner starts with oysters or other shell fish.

Question: How many drinks are served to each guest at a cocktail party?

Answer: There is no special number. Drinks are served continuously throughout the party. But the intelligent host and hostess who understand their responsibility to their guests, do not encourage excessive drinking.

PART III

Engagements, Weddings, Divorce

1. BECOMING ENGAGED

WHEN young people fall in love and become engaged, they share far more than their joy and devotion, far more than their own rosy dreams and hopes for the future. They share a new social responsibility—to their families, their friends, and themselves.

How and when a man proposes is, of course, a matter of the heart and has little to do with etiquette. It is safe to say that the proposal is rarely unexpected, and more often than not the young lady is prepared for her suitor's declaration of love. It is no longer customary to "ask father"; the formal proposal on bended knee and the formal consent of the young lady's father are things of the past, surviving for the most part in romantic novels and on the screen.

But well-bred young people are nevertheless careful to observe certain long-established customs of courtesy and good sense. As soon as they have definitely decided to marry, they go to the young lady's parents and ask their approval. Unless it has been romantic love at first sight, with courtship and betrothal all in a week, the parents will have heard all about the young man and know enough about him to have a definite opinion as to his acceptability. This is the time for them to ask him any questions they may wish about his business and his ability to provide for their daughter. To all questions he should reply with candor and courtesy.

If the parents disapprove of the engagement, they should not hesitate to say so—and to explain why. It is then up to the young couple to decide for themselves whether or not they will continue the engagement without the approval of the girl's parents. If it's some fault of character or personality the parents object to, or some condition that can be corrected or improved, they should discuss it frankly with the young man. They should give him an opportunity to correct the fault or prove his stability. In this day and age intelligent parents do not interfere in young people's lives without a very good reason for doing so.

ANNOUNCING THE ENGAGEMENT

An engagement always sets in motion a series of pleasant activities, not the least of which is spreading the news among ones relatives and friends.

Before public announcement is made, the young couple usually confide in close relatives and intimate friends. This is done by letter or telephone, or by personal visit. Of course the young man does not tell his friends about the engagement until he is quite sure his fiancée has told hers.

General announcement of the engagement is always made by the parents or guardians of the girl, never by the young man or his family. The announcement can be made in a number of different ways, all of which are acceptable. Often there is a party of some sort—a luncheon, tea, buffet supper, or perhaps a small dinner or dance—at which the young man and his parents are the guests of honor. The announcement is made by the bride-elect's father or older brother, usually just before dessert is served. Sometimes engraved announcements are sent to relatives and friends of both families, and all who are likely to be interested. Frequently the only public announcement is a notice sent to the local newspapers, all close intimates having been informed beforehand by personal letter or telephone call.

It has long been the custom to give the announcement of an engagement as nearly the appearance of "leaking out" as possible. This may be done in any clever or ingenious way the young lady and her mother can devise. Sometimes announcement scrolls are found at each place as the guests take their seats at the table. Sometimes the happy news is announced in the festive icing on a cake. Sometimes surprise corsages are presented to the ladies either just before or just after the dessert is served, a tiny card attached to each corsage announcing the engagement.

But however the announcement is made, it should be kept within the bounds of dignity and good taste. A simple announcement in the form of a toast to the young couple is more desirable than a too-obvious striving for effect. One should be especially careful not to be coy about an engagement everyone has been expecting for some time.

NEWSPAPER NOTICES

In small communities it's a fairly general custom to send notice of an engagement to the society editor of the local paper or papers.

But in large cities this is done, as a rule, only if one or both of the young people are prominent socially.

Notice of an engagement is generally printed the day after formal announcement has been made by the girl's family. Therefore if the announcement is to be made at a dinner or reception, the girl's mother should write or telephone the newspapers several days before the event takes place. If duplicates are sent to out-of-town papers they should be mailed well in advance, with a request that the announcement be withheld until the date it is scheduled to appear in local papers. A typical written notice follows this general form:

> Mr. and Mrs. Frederick Hay Coates of 56 Oakwood Terrace announce the engagement of their daughter, Emily, to Mr. Robert Walton, son of Mr. and Mrs. Douglas Walton of Stamford.

To this basic announcement may be added whatever details of family background are of general interest—the schools both young people attended, their clubs and fraternities—and the date of the wedding if it has been decided upon. No photograph should be sent unless the newspaper specifically asks for it. But just in case a photograph is requested, the bride-elect should have a fairly recent one available —preferably a glossy print—and she should remember to write her name and address on the back of it before sending it out.

THE ENGAGEMENT RING

It is customary (but not necessary) to seal the engagement pact with a ring. Traditionally it's a diamond solitaire, set in platinum or gold; but any other type of ring is acceptable. Very often an old family ring is used, a treasured heirloom . . . more precious than any modern gem could be.

It is by no means necessary for the young man to have the engagement ring at the time of the proposal, even though he's reasonably sure of being accepted. Many girls prefer to help select the ring, and this is entirely correct and permissible.

Naturally a young man in love wants to give his fiancée the most beautiful ring possible; but it is neither good taste nor good judgment to buy a more expensive one than he can afford. A watch or pin is sometimes substituted for a ring at the time of the engagement, and the purchase of a ring put off until a more convenient time.

The engaged girl should not wear an engagement ring publicly until the announcement has been made.

Meeting Each Other's Relatives and Friends

As soon as an engagement is announced, the parents of the young man call on the prospective bride and her family. Sisters and other close relatives are also expected to call and extend good wishes. Of course, if the young man's family lives in a distant city, letters may be written instead.

All such calls should be returned by the young lady and her parents as soon as possible, and letters from her fiancé's family and friends should be acknowledged at once.

Unless there is a party or reception at which they all meet, the bride-elect usually takes her fiancé to visit favorite relatives so that they may become acquainted before the wedding day.

There need be no formality about meeting one another's friends. A young lady may take her fiancé to visit her friends, and he may take her to visit his, just as they please. There are no specific rules that need be observed other than the general rules of courtesy and consideration which well-bred people always observe.

If the parents of the young man are in the habit of entertaining a great deal, they often give a luncheon or dinner in honor of their son's fiancée—at their home, or at a club or hotel—so that she can meet their circle of friends.

Behavior of an Engaged Couple in Public

There is perhaps no time when the rules of etiquette need to be so strictly observed as during the period between betrothal and marriage. Although there is far greater freedom among young people nowadays, and it is no longer considered necessary for a bride-elect to be chaperoned to within an inch of her life, the conventions and proprieties must still be observed. Now as always the behavior of an engaged couple in public must be beyond reproach, otherwise they are likely to get themselves talked about unpleasantly.

For example, however liberal and enlightened one's own family and friends may be about such things, it is certainly not wise for an engaged couple to make overnight trips together, nor to spend week ends in the country alone. They may, of course, stay at a country house together as the guests of a relative or friend; but they should not stay at a club or hotel unless there are others in the party—preferably a married couple.

Obviously it is not wise for a girl to visit her fiancé's apartment alone, nor to stay at his bachelor quarters overnight even when accompanied by a sister or friend. She may pride herself on being "modern"; but unless she is smart as well, she may expose herself needlessly to gossip. And gossip, even when untrue, is often harmful.

Being engaged does not give a young couple the right to enact love scenes in public. To make a display of one's intimate affections, to kiss and caress in the presence of others, is ill-bred . . . and can never be considered otherwise. It is particularly offensive for a girl to sit in her fiancé's lap all evening—or for both to sit cuddled in a corner, oblivious to everyone but themselves. Such conduct reflects bad taste and careless upbringing and is usually very embarrassing to those who must witness it.

At parties or receptions in their honor, an engaged couple have a special responsibility to those around them. They must mingle companionably with everyone—he with her relatives and friends, she with his. Devotion to each other does not excuse them from the courtesies and consideration due others.

ENGAGEMENT GIFTS

The announcement of an engagement does not necessarily call for gifts. But relatives and intimate friends generally like to present the prospective bride with something for her new home. Anything useful or decorative is in order—china, linen, and kitchenware being the three most acceptable choices. Expensive and elaborate gifts are not indicated for an engagement, except perhaps from an especially devoted relative.

Engagement gifts, like wedding gifts, are always sent to the young lady. She acknowledges them at once, expressing thanks for her fiancé and herself. Even when gifts are presented in person and thanks verbally expressed, it's gracious to follow up with a friendly note of appreciation.

It's customary and entirely proper for the prospective bride and groom to give each other an engagement gift. This needn't be anything very costly, but it should be something personal and lasting.

Sometimes the young man's parents present their future daughter-in-law with a treasured family heirloom—perhaps a fine old brooch or necklace, or a pair of antique vases for her mantel. Gifts like these are rich in sentiment and are worth far more than their intrinsic value. As such they deserve a girl's most affectionate appreciation.

BRIDAL SHOWERS

A shower is an intimate, informal party at which the bride-to-be is presented with a variety of useful gifts. Only close friends should be invited, as each guest is expected to contribute either to the "shower" of gifts, or to one large gift presented by the group collectively.

Bridal showers may be given any time after the engagement has been announced, but preferably not too close to the wedding date. During the last weeks before the wedding, the bride-elect is likely to be too busy to enjoy the party as much as she should. Showers should be given only by friends, not by members of the immediate family. Obviously it isn't good taste to ask for gifts for a daughter, sister, cousin, or niece!

The setting for a shower may be a luncheon, an afternoon tea, or any type of informal evening party like a dessert bridge or buffet supper. It may be at a club or hotel, but is usually at the home of the friend who plans the party and functions as hostess. Invitations are by personal note, by telephone or by any of the attractive shower cards which are available nowadays at stationers.

If possible, the bride-to-be should not know anything about the shower beforehand as the surprise element adds to the fun. She should be invited simply "to tea," "to luncheon," or "to a little party"—and her invitation should be for an hour later than the time set for the other guests to arrive. Elaborate decorations are not necessary; but most hostesses like to plan an original and attractive presentation of the gifts, appropriate to the occasion. As this is a completely informal occasion, whatever decorative treatment or idea appeals to the hostess is acceptable.

There are as many kinds of showers as there are imaginative and generous friends. The linen shower is a perennial favorite, as no bride can ever have too many linens with which to start housekeeping. Kitchen showers are practical and popular; they may include gifts of china, glassware, woodenware, cooking utensils, and gadgets. Apron showers are interesting; cookbook showers are always fun; lingerie showers add to the bride's trousseau—and there is always the miscellaneous shower which includes everything from garden tools to guest towels! It's always a good idea for friends to compare notes so that there is no exact duplication of gifts. Sometimes they pool their resources and buy a single important gift like a pressure cooker or an electric mixer, which they present collectively.

A shower gift is not a substitute for a wedding gift. An intimate friend may attend as many as three or four showers for a popular bride-to-be, but she still sends a wedding gift sometime during the last weeks preceding the ceremony.

Refreshments at a shower are provided by the hostess, and may be just as simple or elaborate as she pleases.

The girl who is given a shower by her friends should not only thank each guest personally at the party, but should later write individual notes of thanks. And of course a special note of thanks should go to the hostess who planned the party and provided the refreshments.[1]

How Long Should an Engagement Last?

Old-fashioned engagements sometimes lasted for years; but the trend today, especially in fashionable circles, is for short engagements.

Unless the bride is very young, or unless there is some other good reason for putting off the marriage date, the period between the engagement and the wedding need be no more than is required to assemble a trousseau, make wedding and honeymoon plans, and arrange for living quarters afterward. Three to four months are usually adequate; but the interval may be longer or shorter depending on circumstances.

When an Engagement Is Broken

A broken engagement is usually embarrassing and often painful. Well-intentioned friends should not ask probing questions, for the situation is unpleasant enough without making it more so. But unpleasant or not, if an engagement turns out to be a mistake, surely it would be an even greater one to let it culminate in marriage. Brief embarrassment is better by far than a lifetime of unhappiness or the ordeal of divorce.

When an engagement is broken, it's important for the girl to conduct herself with the utmost dignity and restraint. It isn't necessary for her to make explanations to relatives and friends. The matter concerns her alone, and no one has the right to discuss it or to ask questions—except, perhaps, her own parents. All that's necessary for people to know is that she and her fiancé have "broken up." Why they have decided to go their separate ways is strictly their own business.

A girl of good breeding never makes her private affairs the topic of a general conversation. She may wish to confide in a few intimate friends, of course; but even with them she is guarded and discreet. She is careful not to express bitterness or resentment, not only be-

[1]For examples of such notes, see page 322.

cause it's bad taste to do so, but because she's so likely to be carried away by her feelings and say things she doesn't mean and may later regret.

The young man, on his part, assumes all blame *regardless of the circumstances*. He does not discuss the matter, of course—either publicly or in private. He merely lets it be known among his friends that he is no longer engaged, but beyond that offers no explanation. He makes no unflattering remarks about his former fiancée, and refuses to listen to any criticism of her. He confides in no one, not even his closest friends, the reason for breaking the engagement.

The ring is returned, of course, when an engagement is broken—as are any other costly gifts the girl may have received from her fiancé. He also returns gifts received from her or her family. Both are expected to send back or destroy any intimate letters they may have received from each other and saved.

In any written or formal announcement by the girl's parents, the engagement is said to have been broken "by mutual consent." No further information or explanation is either necessary or desirable. If a notice of the engagement has been published in the newspapers, a brief announcement to the effect that it has been broken may be sent to the same papers, worded as follows:

> Mr. and Mrs. James P. Stephens announce that the engagement of their daughter, Suzanne, and Mr. Philip Carter has been ended by mutual consent.

If a reception has been scheduled, guests should be notified at once that the engagement has been broken and that the party will not take place. This is usually done by telephone, the calls being made by the girl's mother or by an older sister. Or brief notes are written by the mother, or by the girl herself to intimate friends. For example:

Dear Joan:

This is to let you know that Robert and I have reconsidered our engagement and have decided to call it off.

Will you therefore please disregard the invitation for Thursday evening.

Sincerely,

Margaret

It's rather awkward when an engagement has progressed to the point of wedding invitations being issued, and is then broken off. Fortunately that rarely happens; but when it does, the invitations must be recalled promptly.[2] If wedding gifts have been received, they should be returned. So should any costly engagement gifts. But shower gifts need not be returned, nor any gifts given jointly by a group of people.

[2] For recalling wedding invitations, see page 207.

Modern intelligent young people do not brood over a broken engagement. They turn to new interests, make new friends . . . face the future with courage and pride.

2. WEDDING PLANS

THE period of the engagement is usually a period of prenuptial parties, showers, and happy excitement; but it should also be a period of careful planning. The young couple should decide the time and place for their wedding, the number of persons each wishes to invite, the attendants, the type of reception—and the many other details that go to make up a beautiful and memorable wedding day.

A large and fashionable wedding, with all its cherished customs and traditions reaching back into the past, is one of society's most impressive rites. But an elaborate wedding isn't necessary, often isn't even desirable. To stage such a wedding is costly, and usually involves a staggering burden of detail and preparation. Unless a girl's family has the necessary resources and facilities, a simpler wedding is more sensible.

But large or small, formal or informal, at church or at home—the important thing is to know the correct procedure for the type of wedding planned, and to adjust the details to one's own particular needs. The simplest wedding ceremony is impressive if it has the quality of dignity and the charm of good taste.

SETTING THE DATE

The first step is to set the date. Traditionally a girl has the right to name her own wedding day, but as a rule she talks it over with her fiancé and they decide on the date together.

If it's to be a church wedding, the young couple (or the girl and her mother) visit the minister before the date is set, and talk things over with him. In a large city it may be necessary to engage the church and minister as much as three months ahead of time—especially if the wedding is scheduled for the busy month of June.

BRIDE'S FAMILY MAKES ALL WEDDING ARRANGEMENTS

The wedding is always given by the girl's parents. They supervise the many details of preparation and assume all financial responsibility. Though the groom-elect is generally consulted—and often helps with such details as addressing invitations and running errands for his busy bride-to-be—he takes no part in the actual arrangements. The girl and her mother make all plans: decide on the type of wedding, the floral decorations, the refreshments, the dress of the bridal attendants; order the invitations and announcements, the wedding cake, the champagne; assemble the wedding clothes and the trousseau the bride will take to her new home. The plans should be in keeping with the family's circumstances. No wedding should ever be more lavish than the parents can afford, even though their daughter may be marrying a man of great wealth.

In planning the type of wedding, the bride and her mother must decide whether it will be formal or informal, in church or at home, at a club or at a hotel—or perhaps in their own lovely garden. Of course, if a garden wedding is planned, alternate arrangements must be made for performing the ceremony indoors in case of rain.

The choice between a church and home wedding is entirely one of personal preference. A church wedding is usually more picturesque and impressive, and a greater number of people can be invited to the ceremony. But a home wedding, though less formal and ceremonious, is more intimate . . . and often a great deal more charming. A home wedding is especially desirable when there has been a recent death in the family of the bride or groom. It is also a better choice when there is a religious difference between the two families.

The ceremony may be planned for whatever time of the day best suits the bridal couple (and, if possible, the majority of their guests). A week-day morning is not advisable if it means that most of the guests cannot attend without absenting themselves from business. A late afternoon or evening wedding is best during the week. Morning or noon weddings should be planned for the week end or for holidays like Christmas and New Year.

Preliminary Plans for the Reception

With the date and hour set, the minister engaged, and the wedding planned in a general way, the bride and her mother start to think about the reception. This may be anything from a simple luncheon to an elaborate formal dinner. It may be a roof-garden supper at a fashionable hotel, a garden buffet at the country club, or just punch and wedding cake in the family living room to toast the bride and groom after the ceremony. But like any party, large or small, planning will make it run more smoothly; so the sooner the type of reception is decided upon and the details worked out, the better.

Obviously the reception depends to a great extent on the kind of wedding it is, and the time of the ceremony. A fashionable eleven o'clock church wedding is more likely than not to be followed by a formal wedding breakfast at a hotel or club. A noon wedding at home is generally followed by a luncheon; an afternoon wedding, at church or at home, by a dinner and dance in the evening. For an evening wedding, one generally plans a dinner or supper party—which may be as simple or as elaborately formal as one pleases. There is no firm rule about the type of reception required. The bride and her parents plan whatever is best and most acceptable for them.

Whatever the nature of the reception, however, there is always a wedding cake . . . and usually champagne, the traditional wine for weddings.

Making out the Guest Lists

Before reserving the rooms at a club or hotel for the reception—or the services of a caterer, if the reception is to be at home—it's important to have a rough estimate of the number of guests to be invited.

Both families make out lists of (1) those who are to be invited to the ceremony and reception, (2) those who are to be invited to the ceremony only, and (3) those who are to receive announcements. For a large church wedding, the invitation lists may include all relatives and friends of both families. But for a home or hotel wedding, the two mothers may find it necessary to get together and pare down their respective lists to a more manageable total.

The invitations should be ordered two months before the wedding, if possible. This allows ample time for engraving, which generally takes several weeks. It's helpful to have the envelopes delivered at once so that they can be addressed and ready to mail by the time the invitations are ready.

Invitations are always engraved for a large or formal wedding. But for a small wedding, personal notes of invitation may be written by the bride's mother.

Sending out the Invitations

Wedding invitations should be mailed four weeks before the big event, so that friends will "save the day." Last-minute invitations are unflattering, usually seem like an afterthought to those who receive them. Then, too, the sooner invitations go out, the sooner wedding presents start coming in—to be enjoyed and acknowledged more leisurely than if they arrived at the last moment.

Announcements are sent only to those who do not receive invitations. They are mailed on the day of the wedding or afterward.[1]

Choosing the Wedding Attendants

As soon as possible, the bride-elect and her fiancé should decide on their attendants and get their acceptances. Only intimate relatives and friends should be asked to participate in the bridal procession; and such persons, when asked, may not refuse without a very good reason.

Attendants may be married or single, but are usually single. The husband (or wife) of a married attendant must, of course, be invited to the ceremony and reception, and to all prenuptial parties in connection with the wedding except showers for the bride.

The number of attendants depends upon the size of the wedding and the degree of formality. For a simple, informal wedding, a maid of honor and best man are adequate. For a large church wedding there may be as many as a dozen attendants or more . . . though too many are to be avoided, as that may tend to make the procession seem theatrical.

The bride selects her attendants, and the groom selects his—though they naturally consult each other about their choices. The maid of honor is frequently a sister of the bride. If she is married she is called the matron of honor. If there are no sisters, a cousin or intimate friend is generally invited to be maid or matron of honor. She holds the bride's bouquet during the ceremony, and is expected to be generally attentive and helpful to her throughout the proceedings.

The bridesmaids are selected from among the bride's closest friends, and have no responsibility except to look their loveliest and most decorative. Often younger sisters of the bride and groom are included among the bridesmaids.

The best man is usually the groom's best friend or an older brother. He has many important duties and responsibilities; therefore only someone who can satisfactorily cope with responsibility should be selected. The best man calls for the groom on the day of the wedding, helps him dress, accompanies him to the place of the wedding. He sees to it that the ushers are dressed as they should be, that all have uniform ties, gloves, etc. He carries the wedding ring in a convenient pocket, and produces it at the proper moment. After the ceremony,

---

[1]For the complete etiquette of wedding invitations and announcements, see the following chapter.

and in private, he hands the minister his fee (in an envelope, given him beforehand by the groom). He mingles with the guests during the reception and sees that no one is left alone or allowed to feel neglected. And as a last gracious service to the newlyweds, he looks after their luggage and sees that they get away according to schedule.

Ushers are selected by the groom from among his intimate associates and friends. In addition to their part in the bridal procession, the ushers are expected to be generally useful to other members of the wedding party and to the guests. One of their most important responsibilities is to be at the church at least an hour before the ceremony, and to show guests courteously to their seats as they arrive. For a large wedding there should be a sufficient number of ushers on hand to avoid confusion and congestion.

Flower girls are customary only in large church weddings, and their function is purely decorative. They should *not* be used to scatter flowers but only carry them. One or two flower girls are sufficient for even the most elaborate wedding. They are usually young sisters, cousins, or nieces of the bride.

The use of a tiny boy as ring bearer is an English custom, ancient and picturesque . . . but no longer popular in modern fashionable weddings. If a ring bearer *is* included in the procession, he may be any small boy from either family. He carries the ring on a white satin pillow, to which it should be fastened by a thread or pin to prevent it from slipping off.

ORDERING THE WEDDING CAKE

Shopping for the wedding cake is one of the most pleasant duties of the bride and her mother during the busy weeks of prenuptial planning. They usually inspect pictures or samples at a bakery; or they consult a caterer who specializes in wedding cakes. The order should be placed at least five weeks in advance—or longer, if the cake is to be an especially fancy one.

For a small wedding, and a completely informal one, a wedding cake made in the family kitchen and lovingly decorated by the bride and her mother, has a charm all its own. But a simple cake won't do for a ceremonious wedding. It must be a work of art, created by a professional confectioner, elaborately iced and beautifully ornamented— perhaps with a bride and groom or some other appropriate symbol on the top. For the wedding cake is the *pièce de resistance*, and occupies the place of honor at the reception.

According to tradition, if a girl sleeps with a piece of wedding cake under her pillow she will dream of her future husband. Therefore two cakes are sometimes provided: one for eating, and one for the guests to take home as souvenirs in little boxes. The "Bride's Cake," cut by the bride and eaten at the party, is usually a white cake—towering and festive. The "Wedding Cake," to take home and sleep on, is usually a dark, rich fruitcake which is cut into small squares, packed in attractive little wedding-cake boxes, and tied with white ribbon. Of course, there's no law that says the same cake may not be used for both purposes; but the "Bride's Cake" is usually much too elaborate and impressive to cut into small pieces.

Planning the Music and the Floral Decorations

In making plans for the wedding, careful thought should be given to music and flowers, for they add much to the beauty and romance of the ceremony.

The floral decorations need not be elaborate, but they should be effective. Since white is the traditional bridal color, white flowers generally predominate—Easter lilies being a special favorite for church weddings. White tulips and lilacs are lovely for a Spring wedding, white peonies in May, white roses in June. Even daisies, simple as they are, make a charming decoration when combined with lacy ferns —especially for a country wedding. And in the fall, huge white chrysanthemums massed around the altar or pulpit make an ideal church decoration.

But any kind of flowers, and any colors that blend harmoniously with the wedding picture, are acceptable. The usual procedure is for the bride and her mother to consult a reliable florist and have him submit plans and estimates for decorating the church or house, or both. If the same florist is to provide the bouquets for the bride and her attendants, and the corsages for the two mothers, color samples of the gowns they are to wear should be given him, as that helps achieve a more beautiful all-over effect.

The bride and groom decide together on the music for their wedding. Organ music is, of course, traditional for church weddings. An orchestra consisting of piano, violin, and cello (the usual trio) is adequate even for a large and elaborate home wedding, and for a small, informal wedding at home, piano or violin alone is entirely satisfactory. Vocal solos are always acceptable, especially when the singer is an intimate friend of the bride. One or two favorite songs in the five- or ten-minute period just before the wedding march is the customary procedure. Often the soloist sings at the reception, too.

In making arrangements for a church wedding, it's gracious to consult the minister regarding the use of music during the ceremony. Obviously no popular music should be planned, as that is out of keeping with the background and the occasion. Any musical selections during the services should be classical or semiclassical in nature, muted and soft, contributing to the beauty and dignity of the ceremony—not detracting from it.

The entrance music as the bride approaches the altar is traditionally the "Bridal Chorus" from *Lohengrin*. The wedding march as bride and groom walk down the aisle together is the Recessional from *A Midsummer Night's Dream* by Mendelssohn. During the ceremony the selections most frequently heard are "Oh, Promise Me," "I Love You Truly," "Ah! Sweet Mystery of Life," "At Dawning," "Serenade" by Schubert, "Liebestraum," by Liszt, "Melody in F" by Rubenstein, and at Catholic weddings, "Ave Maria." There are many others, of course. The choice is a highly personal matter between the bride and groom—as most such details of the wedding are.

At the reception, the musical background should be planned so that it does not interfere with conversation. If there is dancing later, all the popular tunes of the day are generally played, with particular emphasis on the bride's and groom's favorites.

Buying the Wedding Ring

The purchase of the wedding ring brings the great day closer, and is always a significant occasion for the bride and groom. It's not at all unusual for them to select the ring together. As the bride will presumably wear it for the rest of her life, she should be allowed to choose the style and width she likes, or at least express her preference.

No one particular type of ring is required, though many seem to think a marriage isn't legal unless a plain gold band is used. A gold band is always in good taste, of course—and always a great favorite. But a diamond band, or any other type of band the bride prefers, is just as acceptable. Naturally a band set with stones cannot be marked with initials and date, or with a romantic sentiment, the way a plain gold band can—which is a detail the bride may wish to take into consideration.

If it's to be a double-ring ceremony, the bride usually buys the groom's ring at the same time he buys hers. As a rule, it's a simple gold band, somewhat wider than a woman's ring. But it may be any type of ring he prefers and she is able to buy.

Completing the Wedding Plans

There are so many things to think of in the last busy weeks before a wedding, so very many things to do, that the burden of preparation may seem overpowering to the bride and her family. It needn't be a burden at all if they go about it systematically, step by step, taking care of one thing at a time—and keeping a check list to remind them of what still needs to be done.

In addition to the plans already discussed, here are some matters that demand the attention of the bride and her mother. If they are wise, they will allow enough time to take care of all arrangements conveniently, in easy stages, to avoid any last-minute rush.

1. Decide definitely on the reception menu.
2. Order awning and carpet for the church or house, if they are to be used.
3. Order the wedding gown and consult with the bridesmaids about their costumes.
4. Order the mother's gown, and send a sample of the colors used to the groom's mother to guide her in her selection.
5. Assemble the trousseau, leaving the purchase of honeymoon clothes until the bride knows just where she is going and what she will need.
6. Arrange for bridal photographs, and engage the photographer.
7. Buy a wedding gift for the groom if the bride plans to give him one.
8. Buy gifts for the bride's attendants, and plan a luncheon or dinner for presenting them.
9. Record and acknowledge wedding gifts as they arrive, and display them for the admiration of guests.
10. See to it that satisfactory arrangements are made for out-of-town guests.
11. Arrange for the transportation of the bridal party and out-of-town guests from the house to the church.
12. Check delivery on all trousseau purchases and make sure everything is delivered at least a week before the wedding.
13. Pack the honeymoon luggage and have it ready, leaving clothes that crush to the last.
14. Plan a rehearsal for a night or two before the wedding.
15. Remember to invite the officiating clergyman and his wife to the rehearsal, the bridal dinner, and the wedding reception.

The Groom's Responsibilities

The groom is no mere bystander in all these busy preparations. He, too, has a full quota of duties and responsibilities in connection with the wedding, even though the bride and her parents make all the actual arrangements. Following is a check list of the groom's responsibilities:

1. He chooses his best man and ushers.
2. He provides a list of guests to be added to the bride's list—also a list of those who are to receive announcements.
3. He helps with the seating arrangements, suggesting where the important Mr. and Mrs. So and So should sit.
4. He buys uniform ties and gloves for his ushers; also some small but lasting gift for each—such as cuff-links, cigarette case, gold pen or pencil, etc.
5. He arranges all details of the wedding trip, makes plane, train, or boat reservations and gets suitable hotel accommodations.
6. He gets the marriage license . . . and if he's a true romantic, plans a delightfully intimate lunch or tea with his fiancée for that day.
7. He makes whatever arrangements are required for living quarters after the return from the honeymoon.
8. He orders the bride's bouquet, unless she and her mother prefer attending to this themselves (in which case he sends the "going away" corsage instead).
9. He orders corsages for the two mothers, and boutonnieres for the best man, the ushers, and himself.
10. He attends to his personal wardrobe and sees that everything is ready at least a week before the wedding.
11. He arranges for a change of attire at the bride's home or the place of reception, if the plan is to leave from there.
12. He buys the wedding ring and has it engraved; and also usually buys a wedding present for the bride.
13. He arranges for a bachelor dinner sometime during the week before his marriage.
14. He sends a letter or telegram to the bride's parents the day after the wedding, saying how nice it was and thanking them for it.

THE BRIDAL DINNER

Most important of the prenuptial parties is the bridal dinner, given by the girl's parents for the bridal party. It may be at home, but is usually at a club or hotel and is often followed by an evening of dancing. It is at this party that the bride presents her attendants' gifts.

The bridal dinner may be planned for any convenient evening during the last two weeks, but should not be too close to the wedding date. Sometimes it follows the rehearsal—but only if the rehearsal is several days before the wedding, not just a day or two before it.

If the bride's timetable is too crowded to permit a dinner party for her attendants, a farewell luncheon or tea may be given instead. This may be a quite simple, informal party, differing from an ordinary luncheon or tea only in the presentation of the attendants' gifts. Often a bride's cake containing tokens or "lucky pieces" (like miniature wedding rings, engagement rings, slippers, thimbles, etc.) is a feature of the bridesmaids' luncheon, adding to the fun and festivity.

The Bachelor Dinner

Sometime during the week preceding the wedding, but preferably not just the night before it, the groom gives a dinner for his best man and ushers—and perhaps a few of his most intimate associates and friends. This is strictly a stag affair; and though it is usually boisterous, it need not be rowdy. It's intended as a farewell party and should be like any other "gentleman's dinner"—gay and lively, but in good taste.

Always a feature of the bachelor dinner is the groom's toast to his bride, followed by the traditional smashing of the glass (so that it may never be used for a less honorable purpose). Also a feature of the occasion is the presentation of gifts to the ushers and the best man. This may be done any time before, during, or after the dinner that the host finds convenient and appropriate.

The Rehearsal

To be impressively beautiful and dignified, the wedding march should proceed without the slightest hitch, smoothly and with precision. This can be achieved only through careful rehearsal a day or two before the ceremony. The entire wedding party should be present, including the minister, sexton, organist, soloist—and all who are to participate in any way.

The bride herself does not take part in the rehearsal but appoints someone as a stand in. (It's supposed to be unlucky for a bride to participate in the rehearsal.) However she observes the proceedings attentively, supervises the arrangements, and sees to it that everything is exactly to her liking.

At the rehearsal, the minister, priest, or rabbi outlines the form of service, explaining to the attendants their part in the ceremony, showing them the positions they are to take and exactly what they are to do. He also shows the groom and best man where they are to stand and what they are to do during the ceremony. The ushers are given directions for seating guests, the soloist receives her cues, and the organist is given whatever instructions are necessary. This is the time to ask questions and clear up any doubts or uncertainties, so that there will be no confusion on the day of the wedding.

One of the most important details of the rehearsal is to practice the pace of the procession. It should be neither too fast nor too slow; and the only way to get it right is to practice with the bride and her family as audience, letting them decide the pace that looks best.

Summary

It's helpful in making plans for a wedding to know exactly what the bride's parents are expected to pay for, and what the groom's financial responsibilities are. The following check lists are a summary of general expenses in connection with a fashionable wedding.

The Bride's Parents Pay For:

—the wedding gown and veil
—the complete trousseau, including household linens
—the engraved invitations and announcements
—the bridal attendants' gifts
—the bridal dinner (or bridesmaids' luncheon)
—the aisle carpet and canopy for the church
—all other church expenses, except the clergyman's fee
—the music for the ceremony and reception
—the flowers and other decorations for the ceremony and reception
—the food and champagne for the reception
—the wedding cake
—the bridal attendants' bouquets
—wedding gift for the groom
—ring for the groom, if required
—cars to and from the church for bridal party and out-of-town guests
—orchestra for dancing
—bridal photographs

The Groom Pays For:

—the wedding ring
—the marriage license
—the bride's bouquet (optional)
—boutonnieres for the best man, ushers, and himself
—corsages for the two mothers
—uniform ties and gloves for the ushers and best man

—gifts for the ushers and best man
—wedding gift for the bride
—clergyman's fee
—bachelor dinner, including liquor
—all expenses in connection with the wedding trip
—all expenses in connection with providing a home

3. WEDDING INVITATIONS AND ANNOUNCEMENTS

EVERYTHING about a wedding should be in quiet dignity and good taste, including the invitations and announcements. Only white paper of finest quality should be used, and it should be entirely without decoration—except for a family crest or coat of arms embossed without color. But gilt edges, borders, monograms, entwined initials and the like are all in extremely bad taste.

Engraved invitations are traditional for all weddings, large or small, as they reflect the great importance of the occasion. But if it's a very simple, informal wedding for just a few intimates—or if it's a very quiet wedding due to a recent death in the family—invitations may be by personal note, or even by telephone. In this case, formal announcements are generally sent on the day of the wedding, or soon afterward, to everyone on the mailing list of both families.

Engraved wedding invitations come either in large double sheets which must be folded in half to fit the envelope or in smaller-size double sheets which slide right into the envelope without folding. Both are correct and in good form. But it is not good form to use single sheets or cards for wedding invitations.

The style of lettering used depends on what is fashionable at the moment. Script and Shaded Roman are always in good taste, but there are many other styles that are acceptable. It's a good idea to look at samples of invitations at a reputable stationery or department store before making your choice.

All wedding invitations and announcements are customarily enclosed in two envelopes. The inside envelope contains the invitation, the reception card, and whatever other cards or enclosures are necessary. This envelope is not sealed, and only the name of the guest or guests is written on it. (The names of children invited to the wedding may be written on this inside envelope, under the names of their parents).[1] The outside envelope is for mailing and carries the com-

[1]See page 288.

plete address. It protects the invitation and enclosures, and assures their delivery in the clean inner envelope.

SOME HELPFUL POINTERS

1. Invitations and announcements are issued by the bride's parents, even though she may not be living at home. If one parent is dead, the invitations are issued in the name of the remaining parent. If neither parent is living, the invitations are issued by the nearest relative—a married brother and his wife—or by a guardian. In rare cases, when there are no relatives and no guardian, the invitations may be issued by an intimate friend—or the bride and groom may send them out in their own names.

2. Parents who are separated may unite their names on the occasion of their daughter's wedding, if they so wish. Thus the invitations may be issued by "Mr. and Mrs. Harrison P. Gaylord"—even though "Mr." and "Mrs." have been living apart for many years. But if parents are legally divorced, and especially if one or the other has remarried, the invitations should be issued only in the name of the parent with whom the daughter has been living. If that parent has remarried, the invitations should be issued in the names of the parent and the new mate. When a bride has lived part of the time with one parent and part of the time with the other, the invitations are usually issued in the name of her mother.

3. The year is not necessary on wedding invitations, and it is not ordinarily used. But if it is used, it should be written as spoken: "Nineteen hundred and forty-nine." The form, "One thousand, nine hundred and forty-nine" is an affectation and should be avoided.

4. The year *should* be given on wedding announcements—also the city or town where the ceremony took place. This applies even after an elopement, regardless of the time that has elapsed between the marriage and the announcement.

5. Numbers, names, street addresses, and dates should be spelled out in full on an engraved invitation or announcement. Numerals may be used only if an address is unusually long and would look clumsy and unattractive spelled out on the invitation.

6. If necessary, the street address may be engraved under the name of the church. Also "daylight saving time" may be engraved after the time of day on an invitation, to avoid the possibility of mistake or confusion.

7. The word "to" is used between the names of the bride and groom

on announcements and on invitations to the ceremony. But the word "and" should be used instead of "to" on invitations to a wedding breakfast or reception—because by that time the bride and groom are already man and wife.

8. The words "honor" and "favor" are frequently spelled with a "u" on wedding invitations. But the modern Americanized form, without the "u," is now preferred.

9. The phrase *"request the honor of your presence"* is always used for church weddings. But *"request the pleasure of your company"* is considered more suitable for home, club, and hotel weddings, as such invitations include the reception following the ceremony.

10. Any wedding reception before one o'clock in the afternoon is called a "wedding breakfast." After one o'clock it is called a "reception."

11. At the typical wedding, family and intimate friends are invited to the reception and the ceremony; less intimate friends, neighbors, acquaintances, and business associates are invited to the church only. Two sets of invitations may be ordered for the two groups of guests: one for the ceremony only, the other for the ceremony and reception. Or the same invitation may be sent to all guests, with a separate card enclosed for those invited to the reception.

12. When an invitation is for the church ceremony only, a reply is not ordinarily required—and as a rule none is requested. But when the invitation is to both the ceremony and the reception following it, a reply is generally requested. The letters "R.s.v.p." or the phrase "Please reply" may be engraved in the lower left corner of the invitation; or a separate card to be filled out and returned by the guest may be enclosed.

13. Occasionally, when one of the bride's parents is an invalid, the wedding ceremony is very small and private, with only the immediate families present; but a big reception follows for all the relatives and friends. In this case, *reception invitations* only are issued. Invitations to the ceremony are either given verbally to the few who are to be present; or "Ceremony at three o'clock" is written on a small card and enclosed with the invitation to the reception.

14. Wedding announcements are never mailed before the ceremony has taken place. They are mailed on the day of the wedding or after it, and only to those who did not receive invitations.

INVITATIONS TO A CHURCH WEDDING

One may use either of the following two forms of invitation to a church ceremony:

Mr. and Mrs. Craig Halsey
request the honor of your presence
at the marriage of their daughter
Elaine
to
Mr. Paul Lockwood
on Wednesday morning, the sixth of June
at ten o'clock
St. Thomas Episcopal Church
New York

OR

Mr. and Mrs. Craig Halsey
request the honor of

Mr. and Mrs. Martin Beckworth's

presence at the marriage of their daughter
Elaine
to
Mr. Paul Lockwood
on Wednesday, the sixth of June
at ten o'clock in the morning
St. Thomas Episcopal Church
New York

For those who are to be invited to the reception also, a card like the following is included:

Mr. and Mrs. Craig Halsey
request the pleasure of your company
at breakfast
Wednesday, the sixth of June
at one o'clock
Nine East Sixtieth Street

Please respond

Or just a simple card like the following may be enclosed with the invitation:

Breakfast
immediately following the ceremony
Nine East Sixtieth Street

Please respond

The invitation for an afternoon or evening church ceremony is exactly the same as the invitation for a morning ceremony—except, of course, for the difference in time. The reception card may be like the one above (with the word "Reception" in place of "Breakfast")—or it may be the popular "fill-in" type of card with space left for the guest's name. For example:

Mr. and Mrs. Craig Halsey
request the pleasure of

Mr. and Mrs. Martin Beckworth's

company immediately following the ceremony
at the Carlstone

Please address reply to
Nine East Sixtieth Street

For guests who are not invited to the ceremony but to the reception only, one uses an invitation like the following:

Mr. and Mrs. Craig Halsey
request the pleasure of your company
at the wedding reception of their daughter
Elaine
and
Mr. Paul Lockwood
on Wednesday, the sixth of June
at four o'clock
The Carlstone

Please reply to
Nine East Sixtieth Street

When all guests, or most of them, are invited to both the ceremony at the church and the reception following, a combined invitation like this is generally used:

Mr. and Mrs. Craig Halsey
request the honor of your presence
at the marriage of their daughter
Elaine
to
Mr. Paul Lockwood
on Wednesday, the sixth of June
at twelve o'clock
St. Thomas Episcopal Church
New York
and afterwards at breakfast
at the Carlstone
Please reply to
Nine East Sixtieth Street

Occasionally a reception following the ceremony is given at the home of a relative or friend. The invitation should be in the name of the bride's parents, regardless of who gives the reception. Here is the correct wording for a card enclosed with the invitation to the ceremony:

Mr. and Mrs. Craig Halsey
request the pleasure of your company
at the residence of
Mr. and Mrs. Peter Blaine
Forty-Three Park Avenue
immediately following the ceremony

The reply to such an invitation is always sent to the parents of the bride, not to the people in whose home the reception is held.

CHURCH ADMISSION CARD

When the wedding is large, the church small, and the general public is not to be admitted, cards of admission are required for the guests. These are usually engraved in the same style as the invitations, and are enclosed with them. The wording is simply:

> Please present this card
> at St. Thomas Episcopal Church
> on Wednesday, the sixth of June

For members of the family and intimate friends, the number of the pew may be written on the admission card in ink. If they are not to occupy individually reserved pews but a special area "ribboned" off at the front of the church, the phrase "Within the ribbon" may be written in the lower left corner of the admission card. If admission cards are not necessary, "Pew No. 5" or "Within the ribbon" may be written on a small white card and enclosed with the invitation.

THE HOME WEDDING

The invitation to a church wedding is solely for the ceremony, which is why a separate invitation to the wedding breakfast or reception must be enclosed with it. But the invitation to a home wedding is for both the ceremony and the reception. Obviously a second invitation to stay on at a house to which the guest is already invited is unnecessary.

Here is the correct invitation for a wedding held at the home of the bride:

> Mr. and Mrs. James R. Tyler
> request the pleasure of your company
> at the marriage of their daughter
> Lois Anne
> to
> Mr. Raymond Dearborn
> on Monday, the first of June
> at four o'clock
> Twenty-One Lake Drive
> Chicago, Illinois

The favor of a reply
is requested

If the invitations are issued by the parents of the bride, but the wedding takes place in a home other than their own (like the home of a relative or friend), this is the form of invitation to use:

Mr. and Mrs. James R. Tyler
request the pleasure of your company
at the marriage of their daughter
Lois Anne
to
Mr. Raymond Dearborn
on Monday, the first of June
at four o'clock
at the residence of Mr. and Mrs. Thomas Courtney
Twelve Alburtus Road
Chicago, Illinois

If the ceremony is private and guests are invited to the reception only, the following form is used. Note that the word "and" is used instead of "to"—as by the time of the reception the bride and groom are already married:

Mr. and Mrs. James R. Tyler
request the pleasure of your company
at the wedding reception of their daughter
Lois Anne
and
Mr. Raymond Dearborn
on Monday, the first of June
at eight o'clock
The Kentmore
Chicago, Illinois
Please send reply to
Twenty-One Lake Drive

For an outdoor wedding, the same form of invitation is used as for any other home wedding, except that the phrase "in the garden" appears just above the address. For example:

on Monday, the first of June
at four o'clock
in the garden
Twenty-One Lake Drive
Chicago, Illinois

As a rule, a rain card is enclosed with the invitation to an outdoor wedding. This is a small card engraved to conform with the invitation, and reads simply:

> *In the event of rain*
> *the ceremony will be held*
> *at Saint Paul's Church*

Train and Direction Cards

When a wedding takes place at a country home, the transportation of guests is sometimes arranged by the bride's parents. They may have a special car added to a regular train for the convenience of the guests—in which case train cards are generally enclosed with the invitation and guests use them in place of tickets. Such cards are worded as follows:

> *A special car will be attached to the train*
> *leaving Pennsylvania Station, New York*
> *for Southampton at 10.40 A.M.*
> *and to the returning train*
> *leaving Southampton at 8.20 P.M.*
>
> *Please present this card in place of a ticket*

When transportation is not provided, a small card is often enclosed with the invitation to indicate the best trains to take. The information may be neatly written by hand on plain white cards; or engraved cards for the purpose may be ordered at the same time as the invitations. This is the usual wording:

> *Train leaves Pennsylvania Station*
> *for Southampton at 10.40 A.M.*
> *Returning train leaves Southampton*
> *for New York at 8.20 P.M.*

Route maps and direction cards are also frequently enclosed with the invitation to a country wedding. A simplified map may be printed or engraved on a card for all guests coming from a certain point, like New York. Or a direction card like the following may be used to help guests find their way to the wedding without too much difficulty:

> Automobiles from New York take
> Saw Mill River Road
> to
> Hawthorne Circle
> turn left at circle and follow
> Taconic State Parkway
> to
> Danbury
> turn right on Middle River Road
> continue about 5 miles to intersection
> turn left on Willow Road
> to
> Shady Acres

Train and direction cards do not need to be enclosed in separate envelopes. They are just slipped into the same envelope as the invitation. However, it's a good idea to use sheets of thin tissue between the cards and the invitation to prevent smudging. Suitable tissue for this purpose can be secured from your stationer.

WEDDING ANNOUNCEMENTS

Announcements are properly sent only to persons who were not invited to the wedding, to inform them it has taken place. They should therefore be mailed on the day of the ceremony or soon after it—never *before* the ceremony.

The announcement is made by the bride's parents or nearest relative, whether actually present at the ceremony or not. For example, even though the bride's mother may be a hopeless invalid confined to a nursing home—even though her father may be abroad at the time of the ceremony—the announcements should be issued in the names of both parents.

Formal announcements should have all the traditional beauty and dignity of wedding invitations—being engraved on good quality white paper and, like invitations, enclosed in two envelopes. Here is the correct wording:

Mr. and Mrs. James R. Tyler
have the honor of announcing
the marriage of their daughter
Lois Anne
to
Mr. Raymond Dearborn
on Monday, the first of June
Nineteen hundred and forty-nine
St. Paul's Church
Chicago, Illinois

It's correct to send engraved announcements even if the marriage was an elopement. Following is the form customarily used. Notice that the city or town in which the ceremony took place is given; but the name of the church where the ceremony was performed is not necessarily included.

Mr. and Mrs. Edmund Le Brun
announce the marriage of their daughter
Janet
to
Mr. Clive Galloway
on Tuesday, the second of June
Nineteen hundred and forty-nine
Carson City, Nevada

Enclosing "At Home" Cards with the Announcement

If the bride and groom want to let their friends know where they are going to live, they send them cards of address—or "at home" cards. These are usually enclosed with the announcements of the marriage; or they are sent out separately after the bride and groom are settled in their own home and ready to receive visitors.[2]

Wedding Invitations for Special and Unusual Circumstances

Not all weddings conform to type; and those involving special or unusual circumstances—such as the bride with one parent, the bride whose parents have remarried, the double wedding for sisters, and so on—require special wording of the invitation.

[2]For examples of "at home" cards, see pages 48 and 49.

The forms that follow are for these special cases; and though they are for invitations, they apply also to wedding announcements issued under the same circumstances.

INVITATION TO A DOUBLE WEDDING

Mr. and Mrs. Henry Ames
request the honor of your presence
at the marriage of their daughters
Joan Claire
to
Mr. Frederick Bains
and
Celeste
to
Mr. Jeremy Walden
on Tuesday, the third of April
at four o'clock
St. Bartholomew's Church
New York

Sometimes friends or cousins are married on the same day, at the same time, and invitations are issued jointly for both ceremonies. The wording of a double wedding invitation when the brides are not sisters should include the surnames of both brides to prevent confusion:

Mr. and Mrs. Robert Holt
and
Mr. and Mrs. James P. Mansfield
request the honor of your presence
at the marriage of their daughters
Nancy Holt
to
Mr. David Symonds
and
Muriel Mansfield
to
Mr. Arthur P. Owens
on Wednesday, the second of October
at four o'clock
Grace Church
Brookline, Massachusetts

THE BRIDE WITH ONE PARENT

If one of the bride's parents is dead, and the remaining parent has not remarried, the invitations are issued in the name of that parent alone.

But if the bride's mother has remarried and there is a stepfather, invitations should be issued in the names of both. Following are the two forms most frequently used. The bride's *full name* should always be given; and in the first of the two forms below, "her daughter" may be used instead of "their daughter."

> Mr. and Mrs. Franklin Thomas
> request the honor of your presence
> at the marriage of their daughter
> Anna Marie Thorpe
> etc.

> OR

> Mr. and Mrs. Franklin Thomas
> request the honor of your presence
> at the marriage of
> Mrs. Thomas' daughter
> Anna Marie Thorpe
> etc.

If the bride has a stepmother, the invitations may read "the marriage of their daughter," "the marriage of his daughter," or "the marriage of Mr. Crawford's daughter"—depending on which wording best suits the circumstances and the wishes of those most intimately concerned. In this instance, of course, the bride's full name does not need to be used as it is the same as the name in which the invitations are issued.

WHEN THE PARENTS OF THE BRIDE ARE DIVORCED

Parents who are divorced and remarried do *not*, under any circumstances, combine their different names on invitations or announcements for their daughter's marriage.

Invitations should be issued in the name of the parent with whom the bride has been living. If that parent has remarried, the invitations are issued in the names of the parent *and* the new mate. If the bride has lived part of the time with one parent and part of the time with the other, the invitations are usually issued in the name of the mother.

Here is the wording to use when the bride's mother is a divorcée who has not remarried:

Mrs. Morton Peters
requests the honor of your presence
at the marriage of her daughter
Elizabeth
etc.

Here is the wording to use when the bride's mother is a divorcée who has remarried:

Mr. and Mrs. Donald Farnham
request the honor of your presence
at the marriage of her daughter
Elizabeth Peters
etc.

OR

Mr. and Mrs. Donald Farnham
request the honor of your presence
at the marriage of
Mrs. Farnham's daughter
Elizabeth Peters
etc.

WHEN THE BRIDE HAS NO PARENTS

As a rule, when a bride has no parents the invitations are issued by her oldest brother, whether he is married or not. Or a sister, aunt, grandparent, or other close relative gives the wedding and issues the invitations. If there are no relatives and no guardian, the invitations may be issued by intimate friends. And in those rare cases when there are neither relatives nor close friends to issue the invitations, the bride and groom invite their own guests, using this form:

The honor of your presence
is requested at the marriage of
Miss Emily Randsome
to
Mr. Carl Evans Macvane
on Wednesday, the third of September
at twelve o'clock
St. Bartholomew's Church
New York

When friends give a wedding reception at their home for a bride
who has no parents, this is how the invitation should read:

Mr. and Mrs. Leigh Bascom
request the pleasure of your company
at the wedding reception of
Miss Claire Dunn
and
Mr. Frank Edmondson
at four o'clock
Twenty Surf Road
Huntington, Long Island

Please respond

INVITATIONS FOR A SECOND MARRIAGE

If a widow or divorcée is young, the invitations to her second marriage are issued in the name of her parents or nearest relative; and
the form is the same as for her first wedding except that the full
name is used:

Mr. and Mrs. Robert Crane
request the honor of your presence
at the marriage of their daughter
Nancy Crane Hassett
to
Mr. William Mitchell
etc.

If the bride is a mature woman, or if there are no close relatives or
old family friends to issue the invitations, this form is acceptable:

The honor of your presence is requested
at the marriage of
Mrs. Nancy Crane Hassett
and
Mr. William Mitchell
etc.

The name of the bride comes first on invitations and announcements
issued by the bride and groom themselves. And the prefix "Mrs." is
always used before her name.

A divorcée uses whatever name she has taken after the divorce. If
she has legally resumed her maiden name, it is entirely permissible for
her to use it on invitations and announcements of her remarriage.

WHEN THE GROOM IS IN THE MILITARY SERVICES

See pages 516 to 518.

RECALLING A WEDDING INVITATION

A sudden death in the family, serious illness or an accident, may make it necessary to recall the invitations issued for a wedding. If it's very close to the date set for the wedding, someone in the family should notify everyone immediately by telephone. But if there is time, small cards should be printed or engraved and sent to the list of expected guests. The announcement should be formal in wording, but not necessarily arranged with indented lines. The reason for recalling the invitation is always given:

> Owing to the sudden death of Mr. Raymond Dearborn's sister, Mr. and Mrs. James R. Tyler beg to recall the invitations issued for the marriage of their daughter, Lois Anne, on Monday the first of June.

OR

> Mr. and Mrs. James R. Tyler regret that owing to their daughter's illness they are obliged to recall the invitations to her marriage on Monday, the first of June.

When a wedding is broken off after the invitations have been issued, announcements should be sent out as quickly as possible. If comparatively few guests are expected, or if time is short, someone close to the bride—preferably her mother—should telephone the people who must be notified. No explanation need be given on the telephone or in the announcement; just a matter-of-fact statement that the wedding will not take place is all that's necessary:

> Mr. and Mrs. James R. Tyler announce that the marriage of their daughter Lois Anne and Mr. Raymond Dearborn will not take place.

HOW TO ACKNOWLEDGE WEDDING INVITATIONS

An invitation to a church wedding does not require written acknowledgment—unless a reply is specifically requested, or unless an invitation to the reception is included. But a prompt acceptance or regret *is* definitely required for a home, club, or hotel wedding, or for an invitation to a wedding reception.

The answer to a formal wedding invitation should *not* be written like a friendly note, but should be in formal third-person phraseology. It may be written in straight box form, without indented margins, if that is preferred; but the wording should follow the exact wording of the invitation—even to the repetition of date, place, and time. That helps prevent the possibility of a misunderstanding. A *regret*, of course, does not require repetition of the time, as that is unimportant if one does not plan to attend.

It's thoughtless and rude to wait until two or three days before the wedding to mail your acceptance or regret. Always write your reply and mail it *promptly*, within a few days after receiving the invitation. Write it by hand, on the first page of a double sheet of your best white notepaper.

Here is the correct form to use for acknowledging a formal invitation to a reception following the ceremony:

> *Mr. and Mrs. Edward Hopkins*
> *accept with pleasure*
> *Mr. and Mrs. James R. Tyler's*
> *kind invitation for*
> *Monday, the first of June*
> *at eight o'clock*
> *at the Kentmore*

Or it may be written *without* the indented arrangement of the lines. If it's a regret, however, be sure the reason for not being able to attend is given.

A combined invitation to the ceremony and reception would be acknowledged as follows:

> *Mr. and Mrs. Edward Hopkins*
> *accept with pleasure*
> *Mr. and Mrs. James R. Tyler's*
> *kind invitation to be present*
> *at the marriage of their daughter*
> *Lois Anne*
> *to*
> *Mr. Raymond Dearborn*
> *on Monday, the first of June*
> *at four o'clock*
> *and afterward at the wedding reception*
> *at the Kentmore*

Mr. and Mrs. Edward Hopkins
regret exceedingly that
owing to the illness of their son
they are unable to accept
Mr. and Mrs. James R. Tyler's
kind invitation to be present
at the marriage of their daughter
Lois Anne
to
Mr. Raymond Dearborn
on Monday, the first of June
and afterward at the wedding reception

The announcement of a wedding does not call for formal acknowl-edgment, as an invitation does. You may write a note of congratula-tion, if you like (see page 317). Or you may send a wedding gift if that is your generous impulse. But these are entirely of your own pleasure and volition; no response is required.

The Informal Wedding Invitation Written by Hand

For a small informal wedding, with only a few relatives and inti-mate friends invited, personal notes are generally used. They should be written by hand, on plain white paper—preferably double sheets like those used for engraved invitations.

Bride's Note of Invitation to a Relative

Dear Aunt Mary:
Jim and I are to be married at the Church of the Redeemer on Tues-day, May the twelfth, at noon.
We hope you can come to the ceremony, and also to a little wedding breakfast afterward at the Somerset. It's just for the immediate family and a very few close relatives—so don't disappoint us!
With love,

Ellen

To an Intimate Friend

Dear Muriel:
At last David and I have set the date! We're going to be married very quietly at the Community Church on Wednesday, June the tenth, at

noon. We're asking just our nearest relatives and a few special friends to come to the ceremony, and to a wedding breakfast afterward at the Pierre.

I'd like you to go to the church with us, Muriel; so can you come to the house about eleven? Francine will be here too, and we can all go together.

I'm hoping for a bright and sunny day on the tenth! With much love,
Betty

To a Business Associate of the Groom

The bride writes all the notes of invitation, including those to friends and business associates of the groom. If a business associate is married, the note should be addressed to his wife and mailed to their home, not the office. For example:

Dear Mrs. Brandt:
Arthur Wilton and I are to be married at my home on Tuesday, November the third, at eight o'clock in the evening.

Arthur has been so long and so happily associated with Mr. Brandt that the wedding just wouldn't be complete without him!

We do hope that you can both come, and that you will stay on for the small reception following the ceremony.
Sincerely yours,
Rosemary Allen

Acknowledging Informal Wedding Invitations

Following are informal notes of acceptance and regret:

Dear Janet:
Of course I'll come to your wedding on Sunday, June the eighth, at four o'clock—and stay on for the party afterward. In fact, I wouldn't miss it for anything!

Thanks, darling, for including me among the friends you like best. My best to you and Fred; and I hope the eighth is a bright, beautiful day for your wedding!
Affectionately,
Amy

Dear Miss Allen:
Mr. Brandt and I sincerely regret that we cannot accept your kind invitation for Tuesday, November the third.

It was sweet of you to ask us to your wedding, and we'd certainly like to come. But unfortunately we will be in Cleveland on the third for our grandson's christening, and it won't be possible to return in time for your wedding.

We hope to meet Arthur Wilton's bride very soon; and in the meantime, we send you both our best wishes for a lifetime of happiness together.

Sincerely yours,
Margaret Brandt

Invitations to Wedding Anniversaries

If the celebration of a wedding anniversary is simple and informal, the invitations are written by hand or are telephoned. Following is a sample note of invitation to a twenty-fifth anniversary buffet supper. Acknowledgment is made in kind, with a brief friendly note of acceptance or regret.

Dear Martha:

On Sunday, June twelfth, Jim and I will be married twenty-five years, and we're inviting our good friends to help us celebrate.

We're having a buffet supper, with dancing afterward—and we hope you and Fred can come. Supper will be at eight.

We'll be looking forward to seeing you on the twelfth.

Affectionately,
Cornelia

Invitations for a formal reception to celebrate a twenty-fifth or fiftieth wedding anniversary should be engraved. As a rule, the year of the wedding and the year of the anniversary are featured at the top of the invitation. These significant dates—or even the entire invitation, if so desired—may be engraved in silver for a twenty-fifth anniversary, in gold for a fiftieth anniversary. Following is the form generally used for an afternoon reception. The wording is the same for an evening reception, except for the time; and if it's a dinner or a supper-dance, that fact is of course specified.

1900–1950
Mr. and Mrs. Philip Britten
request the pleasure of your company
on the Fiftieth Anniversary of their marriage
on Thursday, the second of March
from four until seven o'clock
The Inn
Oakland, California

Acceptance or regret of the above invitation should be in the same precise, third-person phraseology, handwritten on plain white paper of good quality:

Mr. and Mrs. John Lord Cabell
accept with pleasure
Mr. and Mrs. Philip Britten's
kind invitation
for Thursday, the second of March
from four until seven o'clock
at The Inn
Oakland

4. OF SPECIAL INTEREST TO THE BRIDE

As soon as the invitations go out, the wedding gifts begin to come in . . . and how exciting it is for the bride to open each glamorous package as it arrives!

Wedding gifts are sent directly from the store where they are purchased, with the card of the donor enclosed. Only those who are invited to the wedding send gifts. Those who receive announcements are not expected to send anything but their good wishes, though they often send gifts anyway.

The bride should start writing her notes of thanks immediately, as each gift arrives. She shouldn't wait until the thank-you's to be written pile up and become a problem instead of a pleasure.

To facilitate the often enormous task of acknowledging wedding gifts, the systematic bride keeps a gift book. This may be one of the handsome little books published for the purpose and kept as a souvenir, or it may be just a blank notebook like those children use at school. As each gift arrives, she pastes a tiny numbered sticker on the bottom of it. (Such stickers are available at most stationers.) Then she enters this number in her gift book, along with a brief description of the gift, the name of the sender (and the address, if necessary), the store from which it came, and the date it arrived. When the thank-you note is written and mailed, she puts a check mark next to the gift in her record book. By means of this system she can always tell at a glance what gifts must still be acknowledged; and there is much less likelihood of error.

The Etiquette of Acknowledging Wedding Gifts

Courtesy requires a prompt and personal note of thanks for every gift received. The bride must write these notes herself. She cannot delegate someone to do it for her. Nor may she use printed or engraved cards of thanks for wedding gifts. Only a letter in her own handwriting will do; and it should be on formal note paper—not on cards or so-called "informals."

Wedding gifts should be acknowledged within a week of their receipt, or as soon thereafter as possible. The bride acknowledges all gifts, for the groom and herself—including gifts from friends or business associates of the groom whom she has never seen and doesn't know. Notes of thanks may be brief, but should be gracious and friendly.[1]

If the bride is swamped with gifts and it is impossible to acknowledge them all before the wedding, she may take her gift book along on the honeymoon and complete her note-writing while she is away. Of course, if she's only going to be away for a week or two, the notes can wait.

Often gifts arrive while the bride is away. If she will be gone for some time, her mother may acknowledge them—but only to let the sender know they were received. She might write, for example: "Joan had already gone when your beautiful candlesticks arrived. She will, of course, write and thank you for them as soon as she gets back."

A socially important and very popular bride may receive a thousand gifts or more, each one of which must be personally acknowledged. Under these circumstances, it is permissible to send out engraved cards to acknowledge receipt of the gifts. Such cards must, of course, be followed in due time by cordial handwritten notes of thanks. The card would read:

> Miss Joan Lois Creighton
> wishes to acknowledge the receipt
> of your wedding gift
> and will write a personal note of appreciation
> at an early date

A well-written note of thanks for a wedding gift does more than just acknowledge—it shows pleasure and appreciation. A note of thanks that sounds enthusiastic is always very gratifying to the person who sent the gift.

[1] For specimen notes of thanks, see pages 321 and 322.

Displaying the Wedding Gifts

A formal display of wedding gifts is customary, but not necessary. As a rule, when a bride receives many beautiful and impressive gifts, she enjoys displaying them . . . and her relatives and friends enjoy the opportunity of seeing and admiring them. The giving of gifts has always been an important part of the marriage proceedings, and a display of the gifts is meant as a tangible and eloquent expression of the affectionate interest of family and friends, as well as a gesture of proud appreciation on the part of the bride.

Gifts are most effectively displayed at the wedding reception where everyone can see them. But this is possible only if the reception is at the bride's home. Gifts are never displayed at a reception held at a club or hotel. If the reception is not at home, a tea may be given two or three days before the wedding and intimate friends invited by telephone to come and view the gifts.

The display may be in any convenient room, preferably a first-floor room like a library, study, or extra sitting room. If there is no such room available, an upstairs bedroom from which all the furniture has been removed is appropriate. A basement recreation room is, of course, ideal for the purpose. Obviously no formal display should be attempted if the bride lives in a tiny apartment, or if the house is so small that every square inch of it is required for the reception.

The gifts are displayed on long tables or tiers of shelves, generally rented for the occasion. The platforms should be covered with white cloths reaching to the ground, to provide a simple but effective background for the gifts . . . and it's important that the gifts be displayed tactfully. Duplicates should not be displayed side by side. Modest gifts of pottery or pewter should not be placed beside rare porcelains or costly silver—to make them appear even more modest by contrast. Each gift should be so placed that it looks attractive and appears to best advantage. As a rule, the most satisfactory effect is achieved by grouping similar types of things—like all gifts of silver in one group, all glassware in another, all electrical appliances in a third, and so on.

Cards are sometimes left on the gifts when the bride's family is especially prominent and the names of the donors are of public interest. But in general, it's considered somewhat better taste to remove the cards before the gifts are placed on display.

Bonds, checks, and gift certificates should not be displayed, nor the amount of a check discussed with anyone outside the immediate family.

MAY WEDDING GIFTS BE EXCHANGED?

Most people who send wedding gifts like to see them used and enjoyed in the new home. Therefore no gift should be exchanged without a good reason . . . particularly if it's known to have been selected with loving thought and affection.

Of course, a popular bride who is deluged with gifts is bound to receive duplicates—sometimes as many as five or six of the same thing. It is not considered improper for the bride to exchange such duplicates for something she wants or needs and did *not* receive. Clearly it would be foolish to keep half a dozen silver inkwells when she doesn't have even one cake knife!

But a wholesale exchange of gifts is ungracious, and not to be encouraged. Nor should an attempt be made to exchange gifts which have been engraved or marked in any way.

THE MODERN TROUSSEAU

The word *trousseau* is from *trusse*, which means "a little bundle." But it was no *little* bundle the bride of former times took with her to her new home! Often she began collecting linens and household effects long before she was even engaged, fond aunts and doting grandmothers adding to the "hope chest" at every opportunity. By the time she walked down the aisle in white gown and veil, she had usually accumulated an impressive trousseau, with linens and embroideries to last a lifetime.

But such elaborate trousseaux belong to the past. The modern young woman doesn't think in terms of long-range "hope chests." As a rule, she doesn't begin collecting things for her own home until the engagement has been announced and the wedding date set. And then she limits her trousseau to what she will need in the immediate future, not for years to come.

After all, it's no longer necessary—nor even very desirable—to lay by linens for the first ten years or so of married life. The modern bride can replenish her linen closet whenever she wishes, with no more effort than is required for a shopping trip to her favorite store. Today's intelligent bride starts out with the essentials, filling in gradually after she is settled in her own home and when she knows exactly what she needs and wants.

There is no such thing as a "perfect" or "ideal" trousseau. The requirements cannot be standardized, as they depend on highly individual factors. Over and above the basic consideration of how much she can afford to spend, the bride must consider the kind of life she will live after marriage, the size of the house or apartment she and her husband will occupy, their social position in the community, and the amount of entertaining they are likely to do. A trousseau that is adapted to her new life and its particular requirements—that provides the clothes and household linens she personally requires to make a good start in married life—is the ideal trousseau for her.

We have already discussed, in an earlier chapter, the essential requirements of the well-appointed house—the linen, silver, china and glassware a bride in average circumstances is likely to need.[2] A bride with unlimited funds at her disposal will naturally add whatever extras she likes. A bride on a budget will reduce her purchases to an absolute minimum, but will try to include a little of everything she needs to start housekeeping, counting on wedding and shower gifts to help round out the essentials. If she is wise, she will make a point of registering her silver and china patterns at the leading stores in town, so that relatives and friends can add extra pieces as wedding gifts.

The bride's personal trousseau is just as elaborate as she has need for, and can afford. In the selection of clothes for her honeymoon and afterward, she may indulge to her heart's content, selecting whatever makes her look her loveliest and most glamorous . . . for this is the most important wardrobe she has ever assembled.

It is customary for the bride's parents, or the bride herself, to furnish the personal trousseau. None of her clothes should be bought or given her by the groom. His responsibilities in this direction begin after the wedding.

The only essential requirements for a trousseau is that it be adequate for the bride's needs, and of as good quality as possible. Apart from the bridal gown, the most important item is the "going-away" outfit. Usually it's a suit, but it may be any other ensemble that meets her needs and pleases her fancy. Regardless of what it is, surely this costume should be chosen with special thought and attention. If necessary, it should be given a lion's share of the bride's trousseau budget. For in it she will make her first public appearance as a wife, will start out with her husband on their wedding trip. It should be smart and flattering: a costume that both will love and long remember.

In planning the rest of her trousseau, the bride should bear in mind that fashions are constantly changing and clothes soon go out of style. She should therefore limit her purchases to immediate needs, being careful not to overbuy. It's a good idea to choose colors that match or

[2]Chapter 1, Part II. Pages 69 to 80.

harmonize throughout, co-ordinating clothes and accessories so that everything can be worn interchangeably. It's wise also to take into account shower gifts of lingerie, which often go a long way toward making up the intimate trousseau. Here are some other important factors for the bride to consider:

1. What she already has and can continue using.
2. Where she is going on her honeymoon and what kind of clothes she will need there.
3. Where she will live later on, whether in a small town or large city.
4. The kind of life she will live, and what clothes she will need for it.
5. How active she will be socially, and how much formal dressing (if any) she will be required to do.
6. Her husband's financial status and social position, for it is not good taste to dress conspicuously beyond his means.

How to Monogram Silver and Linen

In days gone by, linens and silver were almost always marked with the bride's maiden initials—clearly a senseless and confusing custom. Nowadays all linen and silver, so integrally and intimately a part of the new household, are marked to include the married initial.

The monogram may correctly consist of one, two, or three initials. If it is one initial, it should be the first letter of the groom's family name (R for Robertson). If two initials are used, they usually consist of the first letter of the bride's family name (S for Smith) and the first letter of the groom's family name (R for Robertson)—or SR. If three initials are used, they are usually the bride's maiden initials plus the initial of her married name. (For example, LSR for Laura Smith Robertson. Sometimes the married initial is centered, with the bride's maiden initials somewhat smaller on either side of it l.R.s. Or the married initial is used below the first initials of the bride and groom $\frac{LJ}{R}$.) It's advisable to decide on a monogram as soon as the first linens and first pieces of silver are selected, so that all subsequent purchases can be marked to conform.

Gifts of silver are often left unmarked so that the bride can exchange them if she wishes, or have them engraved later in the style she likes best. Gifts of flat silver should not be engraved without first consulting the bride as to her choice of monogram (unless, of course, the jeweler knows exactly how she is having her other pieces marked).

"Something Old—Something New"

Most familiar of all the many ancient and well-loved bridal traditions that still survive, is the one which says a bride, on her wedding day, must wear:

> Something old,
> Something new,
> Something borrowed,
> Something blue—
> And a lucky sixpence in your shoe!

However a bride may scoff at superstition, she rarely forgets this age-old rhyme, and is usually very careful to observe its five conditions. For who wants to break a bridal charm that promises a lifetime of great joy and happiness?

The *something old* may be a cherished heirloom of lace from her grandmother's wedding gown, or her mother's lovely veil, or perhaps a tiny white bible that belonged to a family bride of long ago.

The *something new* is usually the wedding gown itself. But even when the bride wears her mother's gown, most of the accessories are new . . . and new, of course, is the bridal bouquet with its lovely white flowers and trailing ribbons.

The *something borrowed* may be a piece of lingerie, gloves, stockings, or a lace handkerchief from a friend's wedding.

The *something blue* is traditionally a blue garter. But it may also be a delicate blue monogram on her slip, or a small bow of blue ribbon attached to her gown inside the skirt.

A *silver sixpence* in the shoe is supposed to bring good fortune. But if a real English sixpence isn't available, a silver dime will do (and it may be tucked in the foot of the stocking, if it's likely to roll out of the bride's slipper during the ceremony!).

Some Other Popular Bridal Traditions

Many of the customs of modern marriage are rooted deep in history and tradition, and brides are often curious as to their origin and meaning. Here are a few of the more familiar ones:

Throwing the Bridal Bouquet

Throwing the bridal bouquet originated with the custom of scrambling for the bride's garter in early fourteenth-century France. In those days it was considered lucky to win the bride's garter, and everyone made a rush for it at the end of the ceremony. Brides wisely left one garter dangling where it could easily be reached, but even so they were often hurt in the scuffle.

The garter gave way to the stocking; and in the fifteenth century we find "stocking-throwing" a widespread custom. The bride would take off a stocking and throw it to the assembled guests, and whoever caught it was marked for good fortune during the year. But brides rebelled against throwing their stockings; it was too much trouble. They began throwing their bridal bouquets instead. Apparently the idea took on and gradually gained in popularity, until throwing the bouquet replaced entirely the awkward custom of stocking-throwing.

The modern bride, turning to toss her bouquet to her attendants, links herself to this chain that reaches back across the centuries. And lucky the bridesmaid who catches her bouquet, for tradition says she will be the next to marry!

Rice and Old Shoes

In ancient times, rice and grain were symbols of productiveness. Rice was used in early marriage ceremonies to symbolize "a fruitful union"—in other words, to wish the young couple many children.

The shoe was an ancient symbol of possession and authority. When a girl married, her father gave one of her old shoes to the groom—signifying she was now his property and that he had full authority over her.

So actually what friends are saying when they throw rice and old shoes after a departing couple is that they hope the bride will be fruitful and obedient! But the custom has lost its original significance, of course—and the rice and old shoes remain only as symbols of good luck. Nowadays confetti and rose petals often replace the rice and old shoes; the good wishes are just as sincere, the use of confetti much more considerate.

The Wedding Veil

Veils have been worn in wedding ceremonies since the earliest times. Though there are many conflicting stories concerning the origin of the custom, there seems to be little doubt that it began as an expression of sexual shyness on the part of women and the desire to hide themselves from view. Many of the ancient peoples believed that a bride should be shrouded from head to foot, completely hidden from her husband's gaze until after she was married to him. Others believed that a bride should be veiled to protect her from the influence of evil spirits. But whatever its original significance, the bridal veil remains an old and cherished tradition that makes the wedding ceremony more romantic and the wedding procession more picturesque.

Orange Blossoms

It's a popular custom for the bride to wear orange blossoms on her wedding day. These delicate and fragrant little blossoms have long been associated with happiness and good fortune in the marriage tie.

According to an ancient myth, Juno gave Jupiter a "golden apple" on their wedding day, and both Spenser and Milton say that the "golden apple" was an orange. This is very likely how the belief that orange blossoms bring happiness to brides originated.

"Happy Is the Bride
the Sun Shines on"

Primitive people recognized the great fertilizing power of the sun. They believed that a bride who married on a bright, sunny day would be prosperous and have many children. Among some ancient peoples, the bride was required to rise early on her wedding day and "look into the face of the sun." Among others, both bride and groom were required to rise and greet the sun together; and if it rained, the wedding day was put off—for rain was a sign of evil.

These old beliefs are immortalized in today's familiar tradition, "Happy is the bride the sun shines on."

Lifting the Bride
over the Doorstep

Among the ancient Romans, the threshold or doorstep of a house was held sacred to Vesta, the goddess of Virgins. If a bride, upon entering her new house, stumbled on the doorstep, it was considered a sign of bad luck, an omen that her marriage would not be happy. To prevent stumbling, the groom lifted the bride over the doorstep and into the house.

The old superstition has long since been forgotten, but the pleasant custom of lifting the bride over the doorstep still lingers on.

The Teacup Tradition

It's customary for the bridegroom's family to present the bride with the dinner service for her new home. Few may know it, but this custom originated in an old tradition—the "teacup" tradition.

Long ago a lover who was obliged to go away on an extended sea voyage gave his betrothed a delicate china cup, asking her to drink tea from it at a certain hour every afternoon. He said, "If I am unfaithful, the cup will fill to overflowing, the hot tea will pour over the sides and crack the thin china. Then you will know I have broken faith."

Today it's not just a teacup but a complete dinner service that the bride usually receives from her husband's parents—a curious survival of an old and beautifully romantic tradition.

5. CORRECT DRESS FOR THE WEDDING PARTY

THE wedding march is one of life's loveliest and most picturesque rites; and the costumes of the bride and her attendants do much to make it so.

The gowns of the bridal party should be ordered well in advance of the wedding date, to allow time for fittings and to be sure everything is completed and ready at least a week before the big event. Therefore as soon as the date has been set and the type of wedding decided on, the bride should start thinking about her bridal outfit, and consult with her attendants concerning theirs.

The maid of honor and the bridesmaids provide their own costumes, but they buy and pay for what the bride chooses. This is very important in making preparations for a wedding, a point we wish particularly to emphasize. It is the bride who decides on the dresses, hats, slippers, bouquets, and accessories of the attendants. She may, and usually does, consult her bridesmaids, and gets their opinions and ideas. But as a rule she knows exactly the picture or effect she wishes to create; and members of the bridal party must be guided by her decisions as to style, color, fabric, headdress, flowers, and all the other many details that go to make up their costumes.

As the attendants themselves pay for their outfits, a thoughtful bride will avoid gowns and accessories that are unnecessarily extravagant (unless the cost makes little difference to them). Or if she decides on very special and expensive outfits, she may present the dresses to her bridesmaids as gifts, though this is not usual. Ordinarily only the bridesmaids' bouquets or ivory-bound prayer books are provided by the bride.

Most department stores nowadays have bridal consultants who gladly help in planning the bride's and bridesmaids' outfits. Any girl who feels unable to cope with the responsibility herself should make use of this helpful service, letting an experienced consultant work out an effective background and color scheme for the ceremony.

All members of the bridal party must co-operate, if they are to present a beautiful and impressive picture on the day of the wedding. The bride should check up on all costumes for the bridal party a week or ten days before the wedding, to make sure everything is progressing according to schedule and that all deliveries will be made on time. It is the groom's responsibility to inform the best man and ushers as to their correct attire, and to check with them a week or so before the wedding to make sure they have everything they need. He provides the gloves, ties, and boutonnieres (and often, when they are worn, the waistcoats and spats). The ushers themselves provide all other clothes and accessories required for the occasion.

Ushers must be dressed identically alike, as if in uniform. For very fashionable weddings, typewritten lists are often sent to the ushers telling them exactly what kind of coat, trousers, shoes, socks, shirt, and collar to wear. Such lists are generally enclosed with the groom's gift of tie and gloves.

A conscientious best man will call the ushers a day or so before the wedding to make sure they are equipped and ready, so that no one appears on the day of the wedding in the wrong kind of coat or the wrong color shoes. Also a day or two before the wedding, the groom (or best man) should check the florist and make sure all corsages and bouquets will be delivered at the right time and to the right place. A telephone call a few days in advance may prevent distressing confusion or delay on the day of the wedding.

PLANNING THE BRIDAL OUTFIT

There is no more important person at a wedding than the bride. It is her day; and of course her costume is the most important one of all.

What the bride wears depends on the time, place, type of wedding, degree of formality—and above all, her own personal preference. Every girl, in romantic dreams of her wedding day, pictures herself as a misty vision in white gown and veil; and for almost every type of wedding—daytime or evening, formal or informal, house, church, club, garden or hotel—that dream can become a reality. There are just a few occasions when traditional white gown and veil are inappropriate and may not be worn.

But whether she is married in church with elaborate pomp and splendor, or quite simply before a justice of the peace, a bride has the right to look romantically glamorous on her wedding day. Whether she wears white gown and veil, a simple afternoon dress, or a tailored suit and hat, the wedding outfit is extremely important and deserves the careful attention it usually receives.

For a formal wedding during the daytime or in the evening, the usual costume is a formal wedding gown and a long or short veil. The formal gown usually but does not necessarily have a train.

A formal wedding adheres strictly to tradition; but for an informal wedding there is a much wider choice of costume. The bride may still wear a wedding dress and veil, if she wishes—especially if the wedding is in church. But if it's a very simple wedding to which just a few people have been invited by handwritten note or telephone, and to which all other members of the bridal party wear ordinary street clothes, white gown and veil are not indicated. An afternoon dress, suit, or ensemble would be more appropriate; and with it the bride would wear a hat and corsage. Bouquets are not carried when the bride and her attendants wear street-length dresses.

If the wedding is to take place in a judge's chambers, at the office of a registrar or justice of the peace, or in a clergyman's study, the bride may wear street-length clothes only. A long dress would be conspicuously out of keeping with this type of ceremony.

THE WEDDING GOWN

For her day of days, and her once-in-a-lifetime gown, the bride chooses whatever is most flattering to her, regardless of the prevailing fashions. She chooses a style of gown and type of fabric she knows are becoming to her, not what somebody else thinks she should have —a gown that expresses her personality and shows her to best advantage.

White is of course traditional for brides, for white is the age-old symbol of purity. But off-white or ivory shades are often preferred by brides who do not look their best in pure white. In fact, any delicate pastel shade—like a soft pink or blue—is acceptable nowadays for the bridal gown and veil, especially for a home or garden wedding.

The material for the wedding gown is a matter of personal preference. Satin has always been a favorite; but organdie, taffeta, crepe, net, chiffon, and lace are just as acceptable—and can be used as effectively. Today's bride has a wide and fascinating choice, and may use any fabric that suits the elegance and dignity of a wedding gown. She should, of course, consider the time of the year and choose a fabric appropriate to the season.

The bride's gown may be, and often is, decorated with fine old lace from her mother's or grandmother's wedding gown. If lace doesn't go with the style of the dress, it may be used as a trimming on the veil.

High neck and long sleeves were once practically a regulation for the bridal gown. But now the style may be just about anything the bride likes and finds flattering. Short sleeves are worn as often as long; and wedding gowns are often off-the-shoulder and décolleté. The most important point to remember in selecting the style is that it should reveal the bride's loveliness and not conceal it. A billow of dress so elaborately impressive that it eclipses the bride is not a good selection.

Frequently an ancestral wedding gown, worn by a grandmother or great-aunt, is offered to the young bride for her wedding. If it's a quaint period style, trimmed with exquisite lace and wonderfully becoming to her, she should consider herself lucky and accept the offer. But if it's just an ordinary gown, old-fashioned and unbecoming, and if the bride doesn't want to wear it, she needn't feel obligated to accept the offer. Of course she should be tactful and gracious about it, so as not to offend a well-meaning relative. A good way out is to explain that she always wanted her very own wedding dress and has planned it down to the smallest detail.

It is not good taste for a bride to wear elaborate or conspicuous jewelry with her wedding gown. A string of pearls, or perhaps a pin or clip which is the gift of the groom, is acceptable; but no other jewelry or ornaments should be worn. All accessories should be very carefully chosen, and make-up lightly and skilfully applied, so as not to mar an otherwise beautiful picture.

The Wedding Veil

A wedding veil may be long and flowing, or it may be short and sweet. "Short" may mean finger-tip length, shoulder length, or just reaching the chin. A floor-length veil is indicated when the wedding is very formal; but otherwise the bride may choose whatever length she likes and considers most flattering.

Any sheer, filmy material may be used for the bridal veil: net, tulle, lace, or any of the lovely shimmering new synthetic fabrics that fall and drape so beautifully. A combination of lace and tulle is particularly effective, with duchess or rose-point lace framing the bride's face. But plain net or tulle is preferable to a great deal of imitation lace trimming.

Fresh orange blossoms are traditional as a headdress for the bridal veil. But they are not always available, and replicas in wax are often used. However almost any flowers are acceptable; brides often wear a headdress of the same flowers used in the wedding bouquet. Or no flowers at all need be used, the tulle or lace alone being formed into a flattering cap or tiara arrangement.

The veil should be the same color as the gown, or blend harmoniously with it. White or ivory is customary; but if the gown is a pale pink or blue, the veil also may be that color.

Veils are worn at first weddings only. They are not worn by widows or divorcées.

THE BRIDAL BOUQUET

Any white flowers are bridal flowers; and any other blossoms the bride likes and wants to use are acceptable if they do not clash with her costume. White orchids, roses, and lilies of the valley are traditional favorites. The bouquet may be made up of one of these, or may be a combination of all three. Orange blossoms, bouvardia, gardenias, white lilacs, white iris, camellias, and Easter lilies are also very popular for bridal bouquets. There are many others from which to choose, depending, of course, on where the bride lives and the season of the year. Any fashionable florist will make interesting suggestions to meet the bride's needs, and to conform with her own personal ideas.

Although the bridal bouquet is generally all white, it need not be. A touch of color may be introduced if the bride wishes, but it should be a delicate pastel shade—nothing too bright or vivid. The bouquet is usually tied with ribbon or tulle (or both) to match the bride's gown and veil.

Sometimes the bride carries a white bible or prayer book instead of the usual bouquet. It may be decorated with a single white orchid or Easter lily; or there may be a spray or "shower" of small white blossoms hanging from it.

Or to complete the demure effect of a period gown, and especially if it's a midsummer wedding, the bride may carry a small pearled fan instead of flowers. If it's an heirloom fan of duchess or rose-point lace with a romantic family background, so much the better. But even if it's nothing more than a wire fan made by the local florist and covered with gardenias and lilies of the valley, it will do very nicely to carry out a Victorian wedding theme.

Bouquets, bibles, and fans are carried with floor-length wedding gowns only. When a bride is married in a street-length dress or suit, she wears a corsage.

Concerning Gloves

Once it was the custom for every bride to wear gloves, and the third finger of the left glove was always carefully ripped in advance so that the ring could be slipped on without difficulty. But times and customs change, and today the bride may wear gloves or not, just as she pleases.

Of course with a short-sleeved formal wedding gown, long gloves are smart, and in somewhat better taste than bare arms. But as one arm will be tucked in her father's anyway, and the other almost completely hidden by her bouquet, the absence of gloves is not likely to be noticed. Therefore unless she is wearing a period gown which calls for gloves to complete the picture, the bride may prefer *not* to wear them.

With a long-sleeved gown, the bride wears short gloves if she wishes, but is not obligated to do so. As short gloves can be quickly removed, they present no special difficulty during the ceremony; and many brides who like wearing gloves, and feel they must have them to complete the wedding costume, select a long-sleeved gown for this very reason.

Gloves are also optional when the bride marries in a street-length dress or suit. Most brides wear gloves to the ceremony but remove them just before, placing them to one side with the purse. Purse and gloves should never be held by the bride during any kind of wedding ceremony.

Bridal Costume for a Garden Wedding

Garden weddings are beautiful, especially in midsummer when everything is in bloom. Costumes should be appropriately light and airy, with the emphasis on simple charm rather than elegance.

What the bride wears depends on the degree of formality, as it does with any other type of wedding; but it also depends, to a great extent, on the location and the setting. If the setting is quaintly simple and rustic, an unpretentious ceremony in keeping with the background is indicated. But if the garden is large and beautifully landscaped, walled in by tall hedges or evergreens, with lovely borders of flowers and an ideal spot for the ceremony, the bride may make her plans just as she would for a wedding indoors (wisely including an alternate plan, just in case of rain!).

For a formal wedding in the garden, on a summer afternoon or evening, the bride wears the traditional long gown and veil, either white or pastel, and of a fabric appropriate to the season and the setting. The gown may be of any sheer, summery material such as organdie, cotton lace, piqué, or dotted Swiss, but not heavy satin or brocade. A bouffant dress of frothy tulle is especially charming and effective for a garden wedding, if the bride is slender and can wear it attractively. But any style of dress is acceptable; and it may or may not have a train, as the bride wishes, although a train is not very practical in the garden.

The veil for this type of wedding is usually of net or tulle, worn with a headdress of fresh flowers. It may be modestly trimmed with heirloom lace, if the bride is fortunate enough to have it. However, neither the gown nor the veil should be as elaborate as for a formal church wedding.

For an informal garden wedding, the bride has her choice of a wide variety of costumes. She may, and often does, wear a pastel wedding gown with veil to match. Or she may wear a white or pastel wedding gown *without* a veil. Often the bride and her attendants wear long, fluttery afternoon dresses in delicate tints, with picture hats to match, and carry small colorful bouquets—a very charming effect against the green of the outdoors. Even when the wedding is completely informal, with just a few guests invited by note or telephone, the bride can still manage to look festive and *bridal* in a street-length dress of white organdie, chiffon or *mousseline de soie*, with a headdress of fresh white flowers from the garden.

The Bridesmaids' Costumes

The purpose of the bridal escort is to provide a picturesque background for the ceremony, and the most satisfactory effect is achieved when the bridesmaids are identically attired, their gowns in exactly the same material—differing only in color. If they cannot be identical, at least they should be closely similar, for the most important factor in any bridal procession is *unity*.

In planning the costumes for her attendants, the bride should keep in mind the complete picture, or theme, she wishes to create . . . and adhere to that one theme throughout. If she plans a period gown for herself, she should plan the same period or style for the bridesmaids' dresses. If they are not the same style, they should be the same general trend or type—so that the picture as a whole is co-ordinated and in harmony.

The bride should give some thought, of course, to her bridesmaids' figures and personalities, avoiding any style or period of costume that few of them can wear well. But as previously emphasized, the bridesmaids must conform to her decision, regardless of their own wishes or preferences. They must wear the style, fabric, and color the bride selects, or drop out of the proceedings.

For a fashionable church wedding, the bridesmaids often wear exact replicas of the bridal gown, in varying pastel shades—with matching or contrasting hats and bouquets. The effect is charming and impressive. But the style may be completely different, if the bride wishes, just so long as it harmonizes with her own costume and provides a complementary background for it.

The fabric, too, may be the same as that used in the bridal gown. Or it may be a similar fabric that is easier on the bridesmaids' purses and more practical for use later on. For spring and summer, any sheer material such as chiffon, marquisette, *mousseline de soie*, net, tulle, and lace may be used effectively. For fall and winter, heavier fabrics like moire, satin, faille, velvet, and brocades are generally used.

There are many enchanting color possibilities; and it's the bride's privilege to work out any color scheme or arrangement that appeals to her. She may decide to have her bridesmaids all in one color, or in graduated tones of the same color, or perhaps paired in different colors. Or she may decide to have each individual gown in a different but harmonizing pastel shade. On her day of days, she may have any color scheme that appeals to her, that brings to life the picture she has long cherished in her heart and mind. The only colors to guard against are those which are too vivid to be in good taste, or too somber to suit the occasion.[1] She may even have an *all-white* wedding if she so wishes—with bridesmaids, maid of honor and flower girls all in dazzling white, like a lovely spun-sugar fantasy marching down the aisle.

The bridesmaids almost always carry flowers, though occasionally they carry prayer books, fans, or parasols instead. (Parasols are of course more appropriate for a garden or country-house wedding than a solemn church ceremony.) The bridesmaids' bouquets are sometimes made up to match or contrast with the individual gowns; but as a rule all the bouquets are exactly alike, with only different shades of ribbon to match the gowns or provide contrast.

The bridal attendants generally wear a hat or headdress of some sort to complete their costume. In some churches this is required, in others not, but covered heads always present a more charming effect. The covering may be anything that fits in with the general theme or

[1] A girl in mourning who cannot wear whatever color the bride wishes, should not participate as a bridesmaid.

picture, that looks attractive, and that is appropriate. Frequently seen
are small hats and veils to match the gowns, demure bonnets to go
with period costumes, large picture hats for outdoor summer weddings. Fresh flowers are always in good taste, and may be used singly
or in clusters, as tiaras or as half-wreaths across the back of the hair—
any way that is interesting and decorative. White ostrich plumes and
unusual hair ornaments are sometimes used, and there is no objection
to them if they fit in with the rest of the bridal picture. But in general, hats, brief veils, period caps or bonnets, and flower headdresses
are safer to use, as they are not so likely to create a bizarre or theatrical impression.

Gloves need not be worn by the bridesmaids unless they wish—or
unless the period of the costume particularly calls for it. Of course if
one bridesmaid wears gloves, all must do so.

As a rule it's better if the slippers match the gown instead of contrasting with it. Too many different colors in the procession tend to
look "spotty," and present a hodgepodge effect instead of a smooth,
co-ordinated one.

Daytime or evening, formal or informal, in house, garden, church,
or hotel, the attendants' costumes are always keyed to conform with
the bridal outfit.

What the Maid of Honor Wears

The function of the maid of honor in the bridal procession is to
immediately precede the bride and dramatize her entrance. She
should therefore make every effort to look lovely and impressive,
but without outshining the bride.

The maid of honor's gown is usually the same as those of the
bridesmaids, with only a difference in color or perhaps a slight variation in headdress or bouquet to distinguish her from them. Or her
gown may be entirely different in fabric and design, but conforming
to the same period and carrying out the same general theme.

A frequent procedure at fashionable weddings is for the maid of
honor to wear an exact replica of the bridal gown, but in a pastel
shade like peach or delicate blue, and for the bridesmaids to wear
gowns of a slightly different but harmonizing style. The effect is especially charming when all the bridal attendants wear identical hats,
in colors to match their gowns.

The excessive use of make-up is bad taste in a wedding procession,
and should be avoided by all who participate. It's up to the maid of
honor to set a good example to the bridesmaids by applying make-up

lightly and avoiding the use of costume jewelry that doesn't fit into the picture.

When the bride is married informally in tailored suit or street-length dress, with the maid of honor as her only attendant, they usually wear very much the same type of costume. A popular trend is for both to wear similar or even identical suits or ensembles—the bride with a festive white hat and corsage, the maid of honor with a less elaborate hat and corsage in some appropriate shade.

CORRECT DRESS FOR THE GROOM AND HIS ATTENDANTS

All men of the bridal party dress exactly alike. The groom and best man may wear a different type of tie or collar to distinguish them from the ushers, and the groom usually wears a somewhat more elaborate boutonniere. But otherwise all details of the men's outfits are identical, and are determined, of course, by the time of the day and the type of wedding.

As a rule the best man and ushers are informed in a general way what they are expected to wear at the time they are invited to participate, and are given more complete instructions later on.

Following is an outline of the correct attire for the groom and his attendants at various types of weddings:

Formal Daytime Wedding

There are very few occasions nowadays when men wear formal morning clothes, but a fashionable wedding is one of them. For a formal wedding any time in the morning or afternoon, the groom and his attendants (and any guests who have them) wear cutaways and gray striped trousers, with the appropriate accessories. These include wing collar, ascot tie,[2] black socks and shoes, gray vest and gloves, and high silk hat. If spats are worn, they should match the vest. The groom usually wears a boutonniere of lilies of the valley; the best man wears a white gardenia; and the ushers wear white carnations. If lilies of the valley are not available, the groom wears a white gardenia and his attendants wear white carnations or rosebuds.

If the men of the bridal party do not have cutaways and prefer not to buy them, oxford jackets may be worn with gray striped trousers, and with the regulation accessories for correct formal morning attire. But then all must wear the oxford jackets instead of cutaways, including the groom. He may not wear one type of coat and his attendants another.

[2] Or black silk bow tie with small white dots.

Informal Daytime Wedding

For an informal morning or afternoon wedding, with the bride in wedding gown and veil, the groom and his attendants wear a dark or oxford gray single or double-breasted coat with gray striped trousers, white shirt with stiff collar, gray four-in-hand tie and gloves to match, black shoes and hose, gray or black felt hat, and white boutonniere.

When the bride wears a suit or afternoon dress and no veil, the men of the bridal party may wear dark-blue or gray business suits, white fold collars, four-in-hand or bow ties, gray gloves, black shoes —and of course the inevitable white boutonnieres to mark it a gala occasion. The hat may be a Homburg or derby, as preferred, the tie any conventional color.

Formal Evening Wedding

An elaborately formal wedding after seven o'clock in the evening calls for traditional full dress. This means a formal tail coat, white stiff-bosomed shirt and wing collar, white bow tie, white waistcoat, black patent leather pumps or dress oxfords, white kid gloves, and either a high silk hat or opera hat.

If white tie and tails are not practicable for the men of the wedding party (and especially in smaller and less formal communities than New York) dinner jackets or tuxedos may be worn. The correct accessories in this case would be white stiff-bosomed or pleated shirt, wing collar, black tie, black waistcoat, black shoes and hose, gray gloves, and either a black or gray Homburg or an opera hat.

Informal Evening Wedding

What the bridegroom, best man, and ushers wear for an informal wedding in the evening depends on the bride's costume. If she wears a long dress, with or without a veil, the men of the bridal party wear semiformal clothes as described above: dinner jacket or tuxedo with black bow tie and appropriate accessories. If she wears a street-length dress or going-away suit, the groom and his attendants wear dark-blue or gray business suits, white fold collars, four-in-hand or bow ties, black shoes, gray gloves, and derby or Homburg.

Summer Wedding

Formal tails are not worn by fashionable society during the summer months, not even for the most elaborate weddings. Light tuxedo coats are worn instead, with appropriate accessories, for formal evening weddings.

For all informal summer weddings in the daytime or evening, a white linen or light Palm Beach suit is acceptable, worn with white shoes and hose, a light-colored tie, straw or Panama hat, no vest, and as a rule no gloves. With a white suit, the groom's boutonniere should have more than a touch of green to it, for contrast. The ushers usually wear flowers to match their ties when their suits are white or very light.

Also popular for informal summer weddings in town—and especially for country-house and garden weddings—are blue or gray coats with white flannel trousers. This outfit—worn with white shoes and hose, a blue or gray bow tie depending on the color of the coat, and a festive white boutonniere—is perfect for a midsummer garden wedding, regardless of the bride's costume.

Parsonage or Civil Wedding

For a completely informal wedding in a parsonage or clergyman's study, in a judge's chambers, or before a justice of the peace, the groom wears a dark-blue or gray business suit, not necessarily new but well-pressed and immaculate. With it he wears a white shirt with fold-down collar, four-in-hand tie of conservative color and pattern, black shoes, grey gloves, felt or derby hat, and of course a gay white boutonniere.

MEN'S GLOVES DURING THE CEREMONY

The groom may wear his gloves or leave them in the vestry, as he prefers. He should, of course, be ungloved when he places the ring on the bride's finger; therefore if he wears them, he must take an instant to remove them just before the ceremony begins. He hands them to the best man who puts them in his pocket.

As a rule if the groom leaves his gloves in the vestry, the best man does also. Otherwise he removes them inconspicuously during the ceremony, so that his hands will be free to find and give the ring to the groom without fumbling. He then replaces them, carries them, or keeps them in his pocket—whichever is most convenient.

The ushers always wear gloves at fashionable weddings, and keep them on throughout the ceremony.

THE BRIDE'S FATHER

The appearance of the bride's father is, of course, very important, for he plays a key part in the wedding procession. As he enters with the bride on his arm, *he* as well as she is under the full gaze of the assembled guests.

He dresses exactly as the groom and his attendants do, but with his own choice of tie and boutonniere. Any other deviation in his outfit from that of the other men in the wedding party would make him conspicuous and mar the otherwise perfect picture presented by the bridal procession.

THE TWO MOTHERS

Proud mothers and grandmothers, sisters who are not in the bridal party, and all others of the two immediate families—men as well as women—dress as befits so gala an occasion: in their best and most becoming clothes for the time of day and the type of wedding.

The two mothers sometimes have special gowns made for the occasion. It's considered gracious for the bride's mother to let the groom's mother know what style and color she plans to wear, so that she can choose a gown that harmonizes attractively. However this is strictly a personal matter, not a matter of etiquette.

In general, the mothers should wear smartly simple clothes, impressive but not elaborate. They should avoid any extreme style, or any fussy decorations, which tend to make them look and feel uncomfortably overdressed. Delicate and subdued shades are best; neither of the two mothers should wear brilliant colors. Black is much too somber for so festive an occasion as a wedding and should be avoided. If one of the mothers is in mourning, she should wear gray or lavender, or perhaps black-and-white—but not solid black or dark purple.

For a formal daytime wedding, the mothers wear long dresses with short or long sleeves as they prefer, hats and accessories to match or harmonize, and flower corsages. The corsages of both mothers should be exactly alike, or they should harmonize.

For an informal daytime wedding, when the bride wears a long gown and veil, the mothers generally wear long dresses, as they must receive with the bride and should wear the same length gown she does. But if it's a very small, simple wedding with no reception (or perhaps just a very informal one) afterward, they may wear any becoming afternoon dress with hat and corsage.

For a formal evening wedding, the two mothers wear evening gowns with shoes and accessories to match, long white gloves, and usually (but not necessarily) orchid corsages.[3] If the wedding is at home or in a hotel, no hat is worn; but at church a hat or headdress

[3]The mothers' corsages are a gift of the groom.

of some kind is usually required. It is also necessary to wear some covering over bare arms and shoulders in church, removing it later for the reception.

For an informal evening wedding, the two mothers are guided by the bride's costume. If she wears a long gown and veil, they wear long dresses; if she wears street-length clothes, so do they.

CHILDREN IN THE BRIDAL PROCESSION

The tendency is to overdress children in a bridal procession, which is a mistake of course as it makes them too conspicuous and detracts from the dignity of the bride's entrance. Overdressing also makes youngsters self-conscious and destroys their natural charm.

Flower girls should be dressed to conform with the general theme, in costumes that are sweet and charming rather than elaborate. The dresses may be long or short, but long skirts are more picturesque and generally fit in better with the all-over picture—especially if the bride and her attendants are in period gowns. Sometimes the flower girls wear miniature replicas of the bridesmaids' dresses, if they are suitable and not too elaborate. The children's dresses may be all white, or they may be any soft pastel shade.

A small boy in the bridal procession, like a ring bearer or page, is generally dressed all in white.

6. THE WEDDING DAY

HOWEVER radically other phases of social life may have changed, weddings still involve much traditional and time-honored procedure which probably will go on forever and ever.

For practically every type of wedding, wherever it may be held, this procedure is essentially the same—differing only in minor details. All weddings follow the same general form. All observe the same ancient customs and traditions.

But of all weddings, those which take place in church with solemn ritual and pageantry are the most beautiful and impressive. This is especially so when the wedding is well managed, when it moves with smooth precision from start to finish. Following is an outline of procedure for a perfectly managed church wedding—every important step from the time the bridal party leaves the house, until the bride and groom take leave of their guests at the reception.

LEAVING FOR CHURCH

On the day of the wedding, the members of the bridal party assemble at the house of the bride, where they usually receive their bouquets.

When it's time to go to the church, the bride's mother leaves first, either with someone from the immediate family or with one or two of the bridesmaids. As soon as she leaves, the bride's attendants follow in as many cars as are needed—bridesmaids, maid or matron of honor, flower girls, and any others who are to participate in the wedding procession. They are followed by members of both families and any out-of-town guests who may be at the bride's house.

Last of all to leave is the bride, who goes with her father. There should be no one else in the car with them. If the bride has no father, she drives to the church with her brother, uncle, guardian, or whoever is to give her away.

The timing should be so planned that the bride and her father arrive exactly on the hour set for the ceremony, or perhaps a minute or two later. By that time all guests will be seated, the groom's parents and members of the bride's immediate family will be assembled in the vestibule, the bride's attendants will be eagerly waiting for their cue . . . and the wedding will be ready to begin.

AT THE CHURCH

For a large church wedding, there are often as many as eight or ten ushers. One of their most important responsibilities is to greet guests as they arrive and show them to their places. Therefore they must be on hand early, at least an hour before the ceremony. They leave their hats in the vestry or coatroom, where they usually find their boutonnieres waiting if they have not already received them. If they are conscientious about their duties (which they certainly should be!) they will see to it that they are immaculately ready and waiting at the door before the first guest arrives.

It's important for guests to be seated promptly, to avoid crowding of the vestibule and aisles. The front pews on the *left* side of the church are reserved for the bride's family and intimate friends, those on the *right* for the groom's. These reserved seats are marked off with white ribbons. If a great many guests are expected, cards for numbered pews (or marked "Within the ribbon") are enclosed with the invitations.[1] Otherwise, to avoid possible confusion, each usher is given a list of the guests who are to occupy the reserved seats. Others are seated as convenient, in successive rows behind the ribbon —on the "bride's side" or the "groom's side," according to their preference.

In the meantime, while the ushers are seating guests and keeping things under control in the rapidly filling church, the bridegroom and best man have arrived, entering by the side door which leads to the vestry. In a perfectly planned wedding, they arrive fifteen to twenty minutes before the time set for the ceremony, and enter inconspicuously without being seen by any of the guests. They remain in the vestry, or clergyman's study, until the sexton or an usher comes to say the bride and her father have arrived—and the wedding is about to begin.

The ushers continue seating guests until the entire wedding party is in the church and ready for the ceremony. Then any brothers or sisters who are not to participate in the procession and are still in the vestibule, are taken to their places in the front pews. The groom's parents are ceremoniously escorted to their seats in the first pew on the right. Finally, the bride's mother enters on the arm of the head usher, and, as they walk down the aisle to the first pew on the left, the doors between the vestibule and the church are closed. *For the bride's mother is the last person to be escorted.* Her entrance is the signal to begin, and as she takes her place there is an expectant hush . . . and in a moment or two, the sound of music.

The Processional

At the first sound of music, the clergyman enters the chancel and takes his place. He is followed by the groom and the best man, who enter from a side door to wait at the altar for the bridal party. They will have been told previously, in the rehearsal, just where to stand. Usually it is on the right-hand side at the head of the aisle. The best man stands a little behind and to the right of the groom.

The wedding procession enters from the rear of the church. First come the ushers, walking slowly two by two, and about five or six feet apart. Then come the bridesmaids, also two by two and also exactly the same distance apart. They are followed by the maid or matron of honor, walking alone. If there are both maid and matron of honor in the procession, they may walk in together or the younger of the two may precede, whichever the bride prefers. Then come the

[1]See page 198.

THE WEDDING CHART

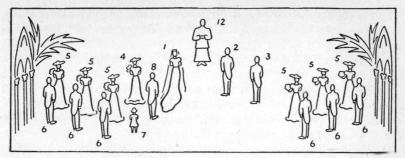

DURING THE CEREMONY

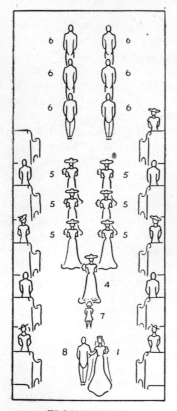

PROCESSIONAL

RECESSIONAL

(1) Bride (2) Groom (3) Best Man (4) Maid-of-Honor (5) Brides-maids (6) Ushers (7) Flower Girl (8) Bride's Father (12) Minister

flower girls, the ring-bearer, if there is one, and finally, at double distance from the last person to enter, the bride on the right arm of her father.

As the bridal procession reaches the altar, the ushers separate—one line going to the right and the other to the left. The bridesmaids do likewise, usually standing in front of the ushers. The maid of honor generally turns to the left and takes her position in front of the second and third bridesmaids. The flower girls also step to the left, the ring-bearer to the right, next to the best man.

As the bride approaches the altar, the groom steps forward to meet her. She relinquishes her father's arm, transfers her bouquet to her left arm, and gives her right hand to the groom. He either draws it through his left arm or holds it in his own hand. Together they walk up to the officiating clergyman.

DURING THE CEREMONY

At the altar, as the bride and groom stand facing the clergyman, the maid of honor steps forward so that she is standing behind and to the left of the bride, the best man, behind and to the right of the groom. The bride's father also remains standing behind and to the left. During the ceremony when the clergyman asks, "Who giveth this woman to be married?" her father steps forward and the bride turns very slightly to give him her right hand. He places it in the right hand of the clergyman and says, "I do." Then he turns and walks to the first pew on the left, taking his place beside his wife.[2]

Holding the bride's hand in his own, the clergyman now takes the groom's hand and places the two together, and the ceremony proceeds according to the rites and customs of the church. The maid of honor holds the bride's bouquet during the service; and the best man produces the ring at the proper moment. All details of procedure should have been so well rehearsed beforehand that there are no awkward pauses or fumbling.

THE RECESSIONAL

As soon as the ceremony is over, the bride retrieves her bouquet from the maid of honor, takes the groom's right arm, and together

[2]In the Catholic service, the father of the bride does not give her away. He merely escorts her to the chancel steps, then immediately takes his place in his pew beside his wife.

they lead the recessional—or the march from the altar. They are followed by the flower girls, the maid of honor on the arm of the best man, and the bridesmaids and ushers in couples. Or the bride may prefer to have the bridesmaids come down the aisle as they went up, two by two—followed by the ushers, two by two. In this case the best man does not accompany the maid of honor but quietly disappears into the vestry to give the clergyman his fee and get the groom's coat and hat.

Guests remain in their places until after the recessional. The ushers hurry back to escort members of the bride's family, and then the groom's family, to the vestibule. Then the white ribbons are loosened, and the guests disperse.

HOME WEDDINGS

Although a home wedding is much less formal and ceremonious than a church wedding, it is similar in most of its essential details.

Even at the smallest home wedding, the bride and her attendants remain out of sight until the ceremony. The bride's mother, as hostess, greets relatives and friends as they arrive, while her father mingles with the guests until it's time for the wedding to begin. But the bride herself does not appear until she makes an entrance on her father's arm, just as she would in a church wedding.

In planning a home wedding, some one spot should be selected that lends itself conveniently to the setting up of an "altar." This may be a quite elaborate and impressive bower of flowers, or it may be just a very simple arrangement of ferns and palms. Almost every house has at least one lovely spot that can be used as a background or setting for a wedding. A bay window is a good place or an arched doorway or alcove, or perhaps in front of a favorite fireplace. Here the improvised altar is set up; and the rest of the room is decorated with flowers and ferns to harmonize.

As a rule, a small space is marked off near the altar with white satin ribbons—for the two families. White ribbons are also used to mark off an aisle for the bridal party, and this aisle must be kept clear. In a very large house, benches are sometimes installed like pews in a church to accommodate the guests. But more often than not, no seats are provided—guests merely standing wherever they can find places behind the aisle ribbons. It is never wise to invite so many guests to a home wedding that the room in which the ceremony takes place is unpleasantly crowded.

When it's time for the ceremony, the bride's mother and immediate family gather at the left of the altar—the groom's family at the right. The clergyman enters and takes his place, followed at once by the groom and the best man. Music is provided by a small orchestra, or by a violinist or pianist alone. It may also be very effectively provided by phonograph records of organ and choir music made for weddings. As the wedding march begins, the procession advances through the aisle of white ribbons—down the stairs or from an adjoining room—to the altar. The ushers enter first, then the bridesmaids, then the maid of honor, and finally the bride on the arm of her father—just as in a church procession. But there are seldom as many bridal attendants at a house wedding as at church. Two or three bridesmaids and an equal number of ushers are adequate for the most elaborate home wedding, and usually there aren't even that many. At a very simple informal wedding, for example, there may be no more than one bridesmaid or the maid of honor.

The ceremony, of course, proceeds exactly as in church. But there is no recessional at a home wedding. At the end of the ceremony, the groom kisses the bride, the minister offers his congratulations, and the young couple turn to face the room and receive the best wishes and congratulations of their relatives and friends.

Garden Weddings

There is clearly a growing trend for garden weddings; and nowadays everyone who owns so much as a bit of lawn and a border of flowers wants to hold at least the reception outdoors. But even the ceremony can be very lovely under the trees; and can, in fact, be more easily managed outdoors than in the house if it is small and crowded. But a very important consideration is privacy. On no account should a garden wedding be planned if the proceedings will be exposed to the prying eyes of strangers, and the dignity of the services thereby rendered less impressive.

Another important consideration is the weather. In making plans for both the ceremony and the reception, everything should be so arranged that it is possible to shift to cover at the first hint of rain.

Otherwise the bride makes her plans exactly as for a wedding indoors. She may wear an elaborate gown and veil, if she wishes,[3] and have a procession in the full romantic tradition just as in the house or at church. A runner of canvas is generally stretched from the house to wherever the ceremony is to take place; and this runner functions as the "aisle" along which the bridal party proceeds. There may also

[3]For garden wedding costumes, see pages 226 and 227.

be white ribbons on rented standards, or pots of white flowers to accent the line of the bridal march.

An improvised altar is usually erected on framework in an appropriate corner of the garden; or an arbor or summer house may suggest itself as a lovely spot for the ceremony and be converted into a suitable "altar" for the services. A long cushion or bench is provided for the bride and groom if kneeling is part of the ceremony. Often an awning or marquee is erected for the protection of the bridal party in case of a sudden shower.

Etiquette is not left behind when the bride takes her wedding into the garden. The informal setting is no excuse for careless or casual procedure. The wedding march, the services, and the reception afterward should all be conducted with dignity and should be as meticulously correct as in any other setting.

A garden wedding may have a recessional, but usually does not. As a rule the bride and groom turn directly from the ceremony to greet their guests and receive their good wishes.

CLUB AND HOTEL WEDDINGS

The same general rules prevail for club and hotel weddings as for those held at home or in church. An altar is improvised and the ceremony performed in one room—the reception held and refreshments served in another. Details of service and management are handled by the club or hotel personnel, in accordance with the wishes of the bride and her parents.

WEDDING RECEPTIONS

Following a wedding, there is usually a reception of some kind for the young couple, so that they may receive the congratulations and good wishes of their relatives and friends. Afterward there are generally refreshments which range anywhere from wedding cake and coffee to an elaborate dinner or champagne supper.

The reception may be held anywhere that is convenient: at the bride's home, a restaurant, club or hotel, a relative's lovely garden, or somebody's spacious and specially decorated playroom. Usually everyone goes to the place of the reception right from the ceremony; but often the church ceremony is in the morning, the reception later in the day or in the evening.

If it's a very small, informal wedding, with no reception to follow afterward, the bride and groom sometimes remain in the vestibule of the church to meet their friends and receive their congratulations.

The reception is keyed, of course, to the time of day and type of wedding. If it's a fashionable church wedding in the morning or at noon, guests who have been invited to the reception go back to the house (or to a club or hotel) for a wedding breakfast, which isn't nearly as simple as the name implies. A wedding breakfast is a gala repast, often very formal and elaborate. An afternoon or evening wedding is followed by a luncheon, dinner, supper, or perhaps just a simple buffet collation of sandwiches, punch, and wedding cake served from long tables on the lawn or in the house. All guests at a home wedding are automatically invited to the reception and remain for whatever food and festivities follow the ceremony.

THE RECEIVING LINE

Following a formal wedding, there is almost always a formal reception with the bride and groom standing in line to receive the guests. The receiving line is formed near a door or entrance where the recep-

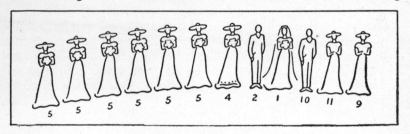

THE RECEIVING LINE

(1) Bride (2) Groom (4) Maid-of-Honor (5) Bridesmaids (9) Bride's Mother (10) Groom's Father (11) Groom's Mother

tion is held—or any other location that is convenient. There should be an attractive background of flowers and ferns for the bridal party, or perhaps a picturesque window or lovely draperies against which they may stand.

First in line as the hostess, and as the person likely to know most of the guests, is the bride's mother. Next is the groom's mother;[4] then the minister, if present; then the bride and groom, the maid of honor,

[4] It is optional whether both mothers receive, or just the bride's mother. Of course if the groom's parents are from out of town and strangers to most of the guests, they should be included in the receiving line.

and the bridesmaids. The bride's father does not ordinarily stand in the receiving line, nor do the ushers and best man. They mingle with the guests, make introductions, and see to it that everyone is made to feel welcome and happy. (If the bride's father does receive, he stands second in line, beside his wife.)

As guests arrive, they go at once to the receiving line and say a few words of congratulation and good wishes—perhaps remarking to the bride's mother about how beautiful the wedding was. Introductions are made if necessary to those next in line, but guests do not linger to chat as that would hold up the proceedings. The receiving line remains until all guests have passed; then the bride and groom lead the way to the bridal table. Members of the bridal party, the two sets of parents, and the minister and his wife are always seated, even when others are served buffet style.

THE BRIDAL TABLE

A wedding reception in a private home—unless it's an immense house with a large staff of skilled servants—is furnished by caterers

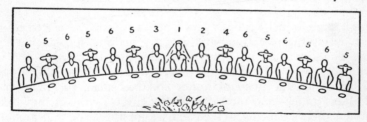

THE BRIDAL TABLE

(1) Bride (2) Groom (3) Best Man (4) Maid-of-Honor
(5) Bridesmaids (6) Ushers

who bring all the food, tables, chairs, napery, china, and glass, as well as the necessary waiters. Arrangements for table decorations are made separately with a florist. The bridal table is always elaborately decorated, often with a magnificent lace cloth; and the flowers are generally all white, while those on other tables are various pastel shades.

As a rule only the bridal party is seated at the bridal table. The parents of the bride and groom and other members of the intimate family, and the minister and his wife, are seated at a separate table near by. Guests are seated at small tables as convenient, with some thought given to placing together those who are likely to be most congenial.

At the bridal table, the bride and groom sit next to each other of course—she at his right. The maid or matron of honor sits at the groom's left, the best man at the bride's right. The ushers and bridesmaids alternate around the rest of the table.

The wedding cake is always centered on the bridal table, in front of the bride and groom. It is traditional for the bride to cut the first piece and serve it to the groom before a waiter takes over and cuts and serves the rest of it.

Champagne is the wine of weddings, though any other beverage may be used. As soon as the first glass is poured, the best man proposes a toast to the bride and groom. Everyone rises to drink to their happiness, while they smile in acknowledgment and say "Thank you" to those around them. Others may then propose toasts, if they wish—but all toasts, and any speeches, should be brief and sincere. The best man acts as toastmaster during the reception and, in addition to his many other duties, reads aloud any telegrams which arrive for the bride and groom.

The Bride and Groom Take Leave

For a large formal wedding, an orchestra is usually engaged to play music during the reception—and, if space permits, for dancing afterward. The bridal couple always has the first dance. No one else should get on the floor until they have had this traditional first dance together. Then the maid of honor and best man, the bridesmaids and ushers follow—and thereafter all the guests join in as they please.

When there's dancing, it's customary for the bride and groom to stay with their guests until the crowd thins—unless they have a plane or train to catch. Just before she must leave to change into her going-away costume, the bride lets her bridesmaids know; and they gather at the foot of the stairway. She tosses her bouquet to them from about midway up the stairs . . . and tradition says the girl who catches it will be the next bride.

As soon as the bride leaves the reception to change into her going-away clothes, the groom goes to the room reserved for him and changes into the suit brought there previously by himself or by the best man. When he and the bride are ready to leave, they say their goodbyes to relatives and friends, and especially all who participated in the wedding procession. Any who are missing must be sent for. It would be ungracious in the extreme, for example, to leave without saying goodbye to the maid of honor, or to one of the ushers or bridesmaids.

With all their personal goodbyes taken care of, their bags in the car, and the guests eagerly assembled at the door to see them off—the bride and groom make a dash for it under a shower of rice or confetti. The best man helps them into the car, slams the door, and they're off for the honeymoon.

QUESTIONS FREQUENTLY ASKED ABOUT ENGAGEMENTS AND WEDDINGS

Question: If a girl has no parents and no near relatives, who announces her engagement?

Answer: In the rare case when a girl has no relatives and no guardian, a close friend may make the announcement.

Question: If one is invited to a shower and cannot attend, is it necessary to send a gift?

Answer: It isn't necessary, but most friends like to send a gift anyway.

Question: May a bridal shower be given by a member of the groom's family?

Answer: Preferably not. Showers should be given by friends of the bride-elect.

Question: Is there any objection to announcing an engagement at a cocktail party?

Answer: No—especially when the guest list includes business and professional friends who find the cocktail hour more convenient than other times of the day.

Question: At a dinner to announce an engagement, who proposes the toast to the prospective bride and groom?

Answer: The girl's father. His toast makes the announcement official.

Question: If the groom has two sisters, may one be invited to be a bridesmaid and the other not—or would that be considered rude?

Answer: If both are intimate friends of the bride, both should be invited; but if it's just a matter of courtesy to the bridegroom, only one need be asked.

Question: May a group of the groom's friends give the bachelor dinner?

Answer: They may, of course, but it isn't the usual procedure. The groom himself is supposed to give and pay for his farewell dinner.

Question: If a bride is asked what she would like for a wedding gift, should she answer—or should she evade the question?

Answer: There's no objection to telling a friend what she would like for a wedding gift, if she is specifically asked.

Question: What happens to the church decorations after the wedding? Are they just left there?

Answer: Yes; however arrangements are sometimes made to remove the flowers and send them to a hospital after the wedding.

Question: What is the usual fee for the officiating clergyman at a wedding?

Answer: The amount of the fee depends on the financial status of the groom. From $50 to $100 is the fee usually paid at large and fashionable weddings. For a smaller wedding, $25 is an average fee. It should not be less than $10.

Question: Do the bride and groom always kiss at the altar, after the ceremony?

Answer: Not always, but usually. They should decide this between them beforehand.

Question: When is the best time to have the wedding portraits made?

Answer: In advance of the wedding, if possible. Arrangements can be made for a photographer to be present at the last fitting of the wedding gown, or at the rehearsal, or at the house on the wedding day before leaving for church.

Question: Should a bride wear white gown and veil if she's in mourning?

Answer: It's considered better taste to marry very simply and quietly, in ordinary street clothes.

Question: If a bride wears long gloves, should they be removed during the ceremony?

Answer: No; long gloves are never removed. The third finger of the left glove is carefully ripped in advance, so that it can be turned back and the ring slipped on the bride's finger at the proper moment, without confusion or delay.

Question: Does the bride take off her engagement ring just before the wedding band is slipped on her finger, or is the wedding band placed above the engagement ring?

Answer: The bride leaves her engagement ring at home on the day of the wedding, or she wears it on the right hand until after the ceremony.

Question: May gold slippers be worn with a wedding gown?

Answer: No. Gold or silver slippers, or slippers with ornate trimming, are not appropriate. They should be plain white, or an off-white or ivory shade, to match the gown.

Question: How many attendants does a bride have at a simple, informal home wedding?

Answer: One, as a rule—but never more than three. More than three attendants puts a wedding in the formal class.

Question: How does an informal wedding differ from a formal one?

Answer: The basic plans and procedure are the same, but everything is on a simpler scale. The hour is usually in the morning or early afternoon.

Question: Is more than one rehearsal necessary for an elaborate wedding?

Answer: One really serious rehearsal is usually adequate.

Question: What are the duties of the bride's father on the wedding day?

Answer: He escorts his daughter to church, accompanies her to the altar, and at the proper moment gives her to the groom in marriage. At the reception, he sometimes stands in line beside the bride; but usually he acts as host, mingling with the guests, making introductions, and seeing that no one is alone or neglected.

Question: May a young woman who is divorced act as matron of honor at her sister's wedding?

Answer: Yes, if the rules of the church do not forbid it.

Question: Is a wedding reception ever held after the return from the honeymoon?

Answer: Yes, if for some reason it cannot be held right after the ceremony.

Question: Should a widow discard her first husband's rings when she remarries?

Answer: Not necessarily; but it's better taste not to wear them during the ceremony. Afterwards she may wear them on her right hand, if she wishes . . . and if her new husband does not object.

Question: If there is no reception following a church ceremony, where do the bride and groom receive the congratulations of their relatives and friends?

Answer: In the vestibule or any small assembly room of the church. Arrangements are generally made when the church is engaged for the wedding.

Question: For how long after the ceremony is a girl called a bride?

Answer: One year.

Question: If a wedding is indefinitely postponed, should gifts be returned?

Answer: No; gifts are returned only when the engagement is broken and the wedding called off.

Question: May the groom's father act as best man?

Answer: Yes; that is not at all unusual.

Question: Who carries the ring for the groom in a double-ring ceremony?

Answer: The maid or matron of honor. She hands it to the bride at the proper moment during the ceremony.

Question: Should wedding invitations be sent to persons who are known to be unable to attend—like invalids and friends in mourning?

Answer: Yes, and even to relatives and friends living thousands of miles away. An invitation is a compliment. It clearly says, "We'd love to have you with us, if it were only possible!"

Question: May brides "attend" each other at a double wedding?

Answer: It isn't usual, but neither is it incorrect. Each in turn would hold the other's bouquet during the ceremony. (As a rule there are a maid of honor and bridesmaids for each bride at a double wedding.)

Question: If a bride has no other male relative, may her sixteen-year-old brother walk up the aisle with her and give her away?

Answer: Yes.

Question: Is it correct to have ushers at a church wedding when there are no bridesmaids?

Answer: Yes; ushers are always correct at a church wedding whether there are bridesmaids or not.

Question: Should the bride's personal trousseau be displayed with her wedding gifts?

Answer: In large cities like New York, Philadelphia, Washington, Boston, etc., it has never been considered good taste to display the bride's personal trousseau and household linens. However, it is often done in smaller communities; therefore the bride should be guided by the custom of the locality in which she lives.

Question: May a married business associate be invited without his wife?

Answer: Only if it's a general invitation sent to an entire staff or office group. When invitations are sent individually, they should be addressed to the home—and both husband and wife included.

Question: If a couple should discover soon after their marriage that it was a mistake and they decide to part, should the wedding gifts be returned?

Answer: No. The presents are the possession of the bride and hers to keep—with the possible exception of those few typically "male" gifts which came from his own intimate friends and which he wishes to take with him.

Question: Is it bad form for a divorcée to wear her first husband's rings when she goes to the altar to be married for the second time?

Answer: Yes. The rings should be removed as soon as she becomes engaged again. Later, after her marriage, she may have her first engagement ring reset, if she wishes, and wear it on her right hand.

Question: How does the marriage of a widow differ from that of a girl who has not been married before?

Answer: It is much simpler. The bride does not wear white, does not wear a veil, and usually has only one attendant. The bride's father gives her away, just as he did at the first marriage.

Question: When a girl's parents are divorced and have remarried, who gives her away?

Answer: No one blanket answer can cover all the circumstances which may be involved. Only the bride's own happiness need be considered, and either her own father or her stepfather may give her away *as she herself prefers.*

7. DIVORCE

WE CANNOT here discuss the moral or emotional issues involved in divorce, as clearly they do not fall within the scope of etiquette. However there are certain matters of form and propriety which those who are divorced or expect to be divorced should know about.

In the first place, divorce is a highly personal matter, and should be so regarded. When a man and woman find they cannot live happily together and decide to separate, the situation is one that concerns them and their near relatives intimately, but that should concern no one else at all. It is bad taste to discuss the details of one's private life outside the immediate family.

FIRST PROCEEDINGS

When the decision is reached that a marriage has been a mistake and should be dissolved, the first step is to place the matter in the hands of a competent lawyer. Whenever possible, the woman should be allowed to bring suit; and she should try not to make the basis of the suit any more unpleasant than necessary, especially if children are involved. Her lawyer will tell her exactly what must be done and how to proceed. She should be guided by his specialized knowledge, and not by the well-meant but often misleading advice of relatives and friends.

During the course of divorce proceedings, the participants should be careful to conduct themselves with dignity and restraint. This is no time to let their emotional reactions so influence their behavior that they do and say things which hold them up to public censure —and perhaps have an adverse influence on their case in court. Both should make an effort to conclude the proceedings quickly and quietly, and with as little unpleasantness as possible.

Obviously an estranged couple cannot be expected to be cordial or friendly when they meet in a courtroom. But neither should they be rude or resentful toward each other. They should be as tactful as possible when they meet in public, maintaining the same polite reserve they show toward strangers.

After the Divorce Is Granted

It is not proper to issue formal announcements of a divorce. The principals let it be known among their friends that their marriage has been dissolved, but they make no explanations and give no reasons—beyond, perhaps, a general statement that they were not happy together and decided it was best to separate.

A gentleman does not say unkind or unpleasant things about his former wife; nor should she criticize or disparage him to her friends. There is nothing to be gained by such actions, and it's certainly no credit to the person who pursues such a childishly vindictive course.

There is no reason why divorced people cannot continue seeing each other if they wish. In fact, it is often desirable for them to do so. Well over half of all divorces occur in the first few years of marriage, and often for comparatively unimportant reasons. A period of separation following divorce sometimes proves to these young people how trifling the cause was, and shows the divorce to have been a mistake rather than the marriage. Not infrequently this results in a remarriage and a new chance for happiness together. But obviously if they avoided each other after divorce, this could not occur.

However, where deep-seated problems or animosities exist, or where a high moral issue is involved, it is usually best that a clean and permanent break be made after divorce, and that no further contact between the two be encouraged.

Division of Property

The division of money and property depends on personal and legal factors. It is always desirable to settle such matters outside of the courtroom, if possible. But whether in court or outside of it, an agreement as to the division of jointly owned property should be reached quickly and amicably, without unnecessary bickering.

The wedding and engagement rings are not returned but remain the property of the divorced wife. She may continue to wear them, if she wishes; or she may prefer to remove them as soon as she is legally free. Often the wedding ring is discarded, and the engagement ring worn on the right hand. When a divorcée remarries, she either discards the rings of her first husband permanently—or she removes them for the wedding and thereafter wears them on her right hand.

The Divorcée's Name

A divorcée generally continues to use her former husband's surname, with her own surname prefixed. For example, if her maiden name was Mary Blair and her former husband's name was John Cummings, she uses the name Mary Blair Cummings. However if she intends to return to the business world that knew her by her maiden name, or if for some other good reason she prefers to resume her own name after the divorce, she may do so legally by making that stipulation during the proceedings.

On Meeting Socially Following Divorce

Mutual friends should be careful not to invite divorced people to the same party. Occasionally, however, people who are separated or divorced meet at a social function; and when they do, it's important that they rise above their own personal feelings and conduct themselves with dignity and poise. They should greet each other as politely as they would any acquaintance, stopping to chat for a few moments if they feel so inclined. But they should not pointedly "cut" each other or make a public display of bitterness or resentment, as that only adds to the awkwardness of the situation. Nowadays when people often separate for nothing more serious than incompatability or a difference of temperament or interests, it is not at all unusual for a man and woman to remain friends following a divorce.

When Children Are Involved

The most bitterly unhappy family relationship is that in which parents are divorced and children are shuttled back and forth between them. This cannot fail to be spiritually and emotionally upsetting to young people; and however parents may dislike or disapprove each other, they should make an effort to conceal it from their children and spare them as much distress as possible.

It is, of course, up to the courts to determine the custody and disposition of the children in a divorce case, and to authorize the visiting privileges of the parent who does not receive custody. If the mother receives custody of the children, she should not try to exercise undue influence on them—should not try to alienate their affection for their father.

Children who love both parents and are forced to listen to unflattering or uncomplimentary remarks about one from the other suffer more than most adults realize. The personality and even the character of an impressionable child can be seriously impaired by remarks made by his divorced parents in anger or resentment—and especially by rude, curt, or unkind behavior toward each other in his presence. Mature men and women should be able to control their feelings to the extent of sparing their children unnecessary distress—and undesirable influence.

When divorced parents meet in the presence of a child, they should make every effort to be courteous and friendly toward each other. To meet as sullen, unspeaking strangers is not only bad taste but a great unkindness to the child. To quarrel, criticize, ridicule, or condemn is selfish and unthinking, for it subjects the child to unnecessary anguish and tension.

Divorced parents may disagree as radically as they wish on everything else in the world, but on this one point they should be in full and unselfish accord: The children in the family must not be hurt any more than can be helped. The children must not be exposed to unpleasantness, must not be made to suffer unnecessarily for their parents' mistakes and shortcomings.

No child should be made the unhappy pawn in a personal feud between parents who have separated. Both should be big enough to subordinate their own interests and desires in the interests of the child. Unless there is some real reason for it, a child should not be kept from seeing either parent—and enjoying the love, guidance, and companionship of both.

PART IV

Christenings and Funerals

1. BIRTHS AND CHRISTENINGS

As soon as a child is born, the parents have the responsibility of notifying all who may be interested. This involves several different types of announcements.

The father always telephones or telegraphs close relatives at once, giving them the news. Then a notice is generally sent to the newspapers, announcing the baby's arrival. And as soon as convenient, the parents send birth announcements to all relatives and friends.

The most formal type of announcement is a tiny white card printed with the baby's name and attached with narrow white ribbon to the Mr. and Mrs. card of the parents. (If preferred, pink or blue ribbon may be used.) The date of birth is given in the lower right corner of the baby's card; but there should be nothing else—just "*Robert Brent Mitchell, Jr.*" and "*June fourth.*" On the parents' card there should be nothing but their names: "*Mr. and Mrs. Robert Brent Mitchell.*"

For those who prefer a more informal announcement, there are many enchanting little cards available at any stationer. These are generally signed "*Robert and Julia Mitchell*" instead of "*Mr. and Mrs.*"

Announcing a Birth Under Special Circumstances

1. When Living Abroad

If a child is born while its parents are living in a foreign country, cablegrams or radiograms are sent to relatives; and a notice of the birth is sent to home-town newspapers. But no other announcements are required, unless of course the proud parents particularly wish to write letters or send cards to their friends back home.

2. When the Parents Are Divorced

It's a tragic circumstance when parents are divorced before a child is born; but it sometimes happens. When it does, the birth is announced by the mother alone. She signs the birth announcements with her divorced name: her own first name and the surname of her ex-husband.

3. When the Child Is Adopted

It's entirely proper to send out announcements of an adopted baby, if one wishes. However the announcements should not be sent out during the proceedings—only after the child has been *legally* adopted. The announcement cards should read:

> Mr. and Mrs. Thomas Blaire
> are happy to announce
> the adoption of
> Thomas, Jr.
> Age ten months

Such announcements are acknowledged just as any others are, with cordial notes of congratulation and good wishes . . . and often with gifts for the baby.

CONCERNING GODPARENTS

The number of godparents is determined by the customs of the parents' church, and by their own particular preference. As a rule there are two godmothers for a girl and one for a boy—two godfathers for a boy and one for a girl. They are chosen from among intimate friends and favorite relatives; and should be asked in plenty of time to make sure of their acceptance before the christening.

Only those who can reasonably be expected to take special interest in the child, and be willing to accept the obligations and responsibilities involved, should be asked to serve as godparents. They should be asked in person, whenever possible; otherwise a letter or telegram may be sent. For example, a telegram like the following might be sent to a friend in another city on the day of the baby's birth, or very soon afterward:

"Baby girl born yesterday. Will you be godfather?"

A letter asking someone to be a godparent might be worded as follows:

Dear Katherine:

Our son is to be christened at Grace Church on Sunday, May the tenth, at four o'clock. We have decided to call him "Peter."

Will you be Peter's godmother, Katherine? It would make Jim and me very happy. We spoke of it once, months ago—remember?

We are planning to have a small dinner party at the house after the service, and we expect you to join us. Jim and I are both looking forward to seeing you.

Affectionately,
Helen

The purpose of godparents is to provide "substitute parents" or guardians for the child, should it be left alone in the world. To be selected as a godparent is therefore an honor, for it is clearly an expression of trust and confidence. The request cannot very well be refused; on the contrary, it should be accepted with obvious pleasure and pride, and with an appreciation of the responsibilities involved:

Dear Helen:
I'm happy and proud to be chosen as godmother for little Peter!
I warn you I shall take very seriously my share of the responsibility for your son's welfare, and shall keep a careful eye on the young man in the years ahead.
I plan to be at your house about three o'clock on Sunday so that I can go to the church with you, and perhaps be of some help on the way. It will be good to see you and Jim, and to become acquainted with my young godson!

Affectionately,
Katherine

It is expected, of course, that godparents attend the christening; but this isn't always possible. If a godparent cannot be present, someone else may act as proxy.

INVITATIONS TO A CHRISTENING

There was a time when christenings were great social events; many people were invited and formal engraved invitations were sent out. But nowadays a christening is considered strictly a family affair, and is usually quite simple and informal. Only relatives and a few very intimate friends are invited.

Invitations to a christening are now usually telephoned, or friends are asked when they come to see the mother. But informal notes of invitation are also correct, and may be used for either church or home christenings. They should be brief and friendly:

Dear Aunt Jane:
The baby is to be christened at Grace Church next Sunday, May the tenth, at four o'clock. Come and see him make his first public appearance! We're planning to call him "Peter"—I hope you approve.
Jim and I will be looking for you on Sunday, so be sure to come.

Affectionately,
Helen

Dear Margaret:

Our new baby is to be christened on Wednesday, April the eighth, at three o'clock. The ceremony will be at home, and we hope you and Frank can come. We look forward to seeing you.

Sincerely,
Joan Whitney

CHURCH CHRISTENING

The hour and date of a church christening must be arranged between the parents and the clergyman who will officiate. It may take place on Sunday at the close of the regular service; or on a weekday at an hour when the church is not being otherwise used.

In the Catholic Church, a child is usually christened not later than the third Sunday after birth. But in other churches the ceremony may take place any time the mother feels equal to it and the child's condition permits. If one or the other is in delicate health, the christening may be delayed for several months.

The church may be decorated for the christening, but decorations should be simple and unpretentious. Palms and a few flowers around the font are customary.

As guests arrive, they seat themselves in the pews nearest the font. At the designated time, the baby's coat and cap are taken off, and the godmother who is to hold the child takes it in her arms and stands directly in front of the clergyman. (A very small or delicate baby is usually carried on a pillow.) The other godparents, and the parents, stand on either side of her during the ceremony—close to the font, but not so close as to interfere with the proceedings.

As a rule, the baby's name is written on a slip of paper and given to the clergyman beforehand, to avoid any possibility of mistake. Nevertheless the godmother should pronounce it very carefully and distinctly, for it's the name the child will carry throughout life.

As soon as the ceremony is over, everyone goes to the house of the parents or grandparents where a tea or dinner party has been arranged.

A gift or donation is presented privately to the clergyman by the baby's father, either just after the christening or at any other convenient time.

HOME CHRISTENING

There is little difference between a home and church christening, except in the setting.

For a home christening, a "font" must be provided. This is usually a handsome silver bowl, though any presentable china one will do just as well. It is placed on a small high table which is covered with lace or any attractive fabric, and is sometimes decorated with flowers. Cut flowers arranged in vases around the room help to give the occasion a festive air.

As at a church christening, the godmother holds the child and clearly pronounces its name at the proper moment. The other godparents stand near her; and the guests either form a semicircle behind them or are seated wherever convenient in the room. At the end of the ceremony, the child is taken back to the nursery, and the guests are served christening cake and "caudle"—a hot eggnog served in small punch cups. Champagne or any other beverage may be used in place of the traditional "caudle" to toast the baby's health and prosperity.

Certain courtesies toward the clergyman must not be overlooked. A room should be placed at his disposal for changing into his vestments if he wears them for the ceremony. And if there is to be a tea or luncheon afterward, he should of course be invited to remain.

What Mother and Baby Wear for the Christening

The baby is always dressed in white for the christening. If there's a precious heirloom christening robe in the family, once worn by a parent or grandparent, it should certainly be used again. But otherwise a long dress or special "christening robe" isn't necessary. Any dainty little white dress trimmed with lace or embroidery is acceptable; and with it—for the trip to and from church—the baby wears a white coat and cap.

At church, the mother wears conservative afternoon clothes, with hat and gloves. At home she may wear a long tea gown or hostess gown, if she wishes.

Women guests at a church christening always wear hats; but at a home ceremony they may wear them or not, as they please.

Baby Gifts

As soon as relatives and friends learn of the birth of a baby, they send letters or telegrams of congratulation—and sometimes flowers or baskets of fruit. Visits should not be made until after the second or third day, except by very close relatives; and all visits to a new mother should be brief.[1]

The custom of "gifting" infants is an ancient one. Among many people in early times, babies were ceremoniously presented with gifts of money and food, to insure prosperity throughout life. In medieval days, the traditional gift was a silver spoon with the figure of an apostle on the handle—from which we get the familiar phrase "to be born with a silver spoon in one's mouth." Rattles, today intended solely for the baby's amusement, were once meant to frighten away evil spirits and keep the infant safe from harm.

Nowadays friends rally with gifts of silver mugs and porringers, silver spoons and forks, wearing apparel, blankets, crib and carriage covers—in fact, any useful or attractive gift the mother is likely to need and appreciate. All who visit the mother generally bring something for her or for the child; and certainly all who attend the christening should give a present to the baby if they have not already done so. Godparents give especially impressive gifts, if they can afford it. The godmother, for example, often presents the christening outfit of dress, coat, and cap. Godfathers usually give a gift of silver, like a cup or bowl, which is engraved:

> Marjory Winston
> from her godfather
> James Paul Norton

Every gift should of course be acknowledged by a cordial, informal note of thanks, as soon as convenient.[2]

BABY SHOWERS

Baby showers are given by intimate friends, usually before but sometimes after the baby's arrival. They are generally held in the afternoon, but may be in the evening if that is more convenient. The health and well-being of the mother must be taken into consideration, and nothing planned that may be a burden to her. A simple afternoon tea or informal supper party is best, with the baby gifts presented in any charming way that suggests itself to the hostess. Guests are generally limited to eight or ten, as large parties are too trying to a new or expectant mother.

[1]See pages 32 and 33.
[2]For examples of thank-you notes for baby gifts, see pages 324 and 325.

2. DEATHS AND FUNERALS

THERE is greater dignity and restraint, less pomp and ceremony, in the treatment of death nowadays. Funerals are simpler; mourning is worn only for a very short period, if at all—and many of the old meaningless customs and traditions seem to have given way to clear-eyed common sense.

Naturally death brings with it great sorrow and pain, and it is not within the province of etiquette to say how those so stricken shall react. The purpose of this chapter is not to obtrude on grief, but to suggest the best procedure for those close to the bereaved family, so that they may be spared any further pain through the confusion or thoughtlessness of relatives and friends.

WHEN DEATH OCCURS

As soon as death occurs, a close relative should take charge—not several relatives, but just one person who is given full authority to do whatever is necessary. It is this person's most important responsibility to see that the family's privacy is respected, and that members of the family are not burdened with the unhappy details of arrangement. It is also his responsibility to see that relatives and friends are notified, and that the funeral ceremony is carried out in strict accordance with the family's wishes.

Of course members of the family must decide such important matters as the time of the funeral, whether it's to be at church or at home, the place of burial, and so on. And nearest of kin have the sad duty of selecting the undertaker and the casket. But all actual arrangements are made by the person in charge. As soon as he knows the wishes of the family, he sees the clergyman, interviews the funeral director, telephones or telegraphs the friends selected as pallbearers, orders the casket and the wreath or flowers for the door, and attends to all the details of the service and the burial. Usually friends come to the house to offer their services, and he accepts whatever help he may need at the moment and they are competent to give.

ANNOUNCING THE DEATH

As quickly as possible after death occurs, intimate relatives and friends are notified by telephone or telegraph. Others are informed of the death by means of paid announcements in the obituary columns of the newspapers. Such announcements generally read about as follows:

> CREIGHTON—In Boston, April 5, John Hale Creighton, husband of Margaret (Benton) Creighton. Funeral services from his late residence, 277 Park Avenue, at 2:30 P.M. April 8.

> RADCLIFF—At her residence, 410 West Fiftieth Street, Rose Speyer Radcliff, daughter of James and Helen Wilson Speyer, wife of Robert L. Radcliff. Funeral services in the Chapel of St. Bartholomew's Church, Park Avenue and Fiftieth Street, New York City, on Saturday morning, 11 o'clock. Interment at Waterbury, Conn.

When announcements like the above appear in newspapers, all friends and associates of the family who wish to do so may attend the funeral services without further notification. If the funeral is to be private, the notice will clearly say so, and neither the time nor place will be given.

Often the family prefers to avoid the complication of flowers; and when the notice requests that no flowers be sent, the wish should be respected. This is particularly important if the service is being held in a Catholic or "high" Episcopal church, or in an orthodox Jewish synagogue, to which flowers are not admitted. However "Please omit flowers" does not mean that friends may not send them after the funeral with a warm and comforting message of sympathy.

AT THE HOUSE

One of the first things to do at the house is to draw the blinds and lower the shades. If possible, all bells should be muffled. Someone should be stationed at the door to see that only intimates of the family are admitted. Others may leave cards or messages, but should not try to make a condolence call until after the funeral.

If there are small children in the family, it is usually advisable to send them elsewhere until after the funeral. However this is something for the bereaved themselves to decide. The presence of children can often be a great comfort in time of sorrow.

The purpose of crepe or ribbon streamers on the door is to indicate there has been a death in the house, and to keep persons who may not know about it from intruding. This traditional symbol of death may be used or not, as the family wishes. Either the funeral director is instructed to attend to this detail, or the person in charge at the house orders the flowers from a florist. It is customary to use white flowers with white ribbon streamers for a child; white or purple flowers with purple ribbon for a young man or woman; purple flowers with black crepe or black ribbon streamers for an elderly person.

THE WOMEN OF THE FAMILY

As a rule, the women of the family stay in seclusion until it's time for the funeral. This is not a matter of etiquette, but of common sense. It's much easier for them to remain in seclusion than to expose themselves to emotional upsets in the presence of visitors, who are sometimes cruelly tactless without meaning to be. It isn't necessary for the women of the family to see anyone before the funeral except very close relatives . . . unless they wish to.

An intimate friend or relative should make any necessary purchases for the women members of the bereaved family. It isn't good taste for them to be seen out shopping before the funeral. A dressmaker may be summoned to the house if orders must be given for mourning clothes.

CONDUCT OF FRIENDS AND NEIGHBORS

It is customary for friends of the deceased to call at the house to offer sympathy and help. But only those close to the immediate family should ask or expect to be admitted. Others just write a message on a card and leave it at the door. They might write, for example, "With deepest sympathy" or "My heartfelt sympathy—please let me know if I can help."

Friends who cannot call in person should write a letter of condolence to the family. The letter should be brief, but warm and friendly . . . and as comforting as possible.[1]

Flowers are the traditional tribute of sympathy and affection to the memory of a friend; and unless the newspaper notices specifically request that flowers be omitted, most people send them. They are sent to wherever the funeral services are to be—the house, church, or fu-

[1] For examples of condolence letters, see pages 326 to 330.

neral home; and they are addressed either "To the funeral of ———— [name of the deceased]" or to the nearest relative. A card is enclosed with a brief message of sympathy.

Neighbors often call and leave a cake or basket of fruit at the door for the bereaved family, but do not ask to be admitted. This is more customary in small towns and suburban areas than in large cities.

All friends and neighbors pay their last respects by attending the funeral services, unless the newspaper notices read, "Funeral Private." In that case, only friends who receive a message from the family attend the services. But otherwise anyone who wishes may go to the church or funeral home without being personally notified. Funerals at the house, however, are private—and as a rule only relatives and very intimate friends are asked to attend.

Friends and neighbors who attend the funeral services should dress appropriately—not necessarily in black, but in dark and inconspicuous clothes. Bright colors and extreme styles are in poor taste.

Well-bred people enter quietly, find a seat at once, talk very little —and then only in a soft tone of voice. Only relatives and intimate friends sit with or near the family; others take seats toward the rear of the church.

PALLBEARERS

If there are to be pallbearers, the person in charge of funeral arrangements makes up a list with the family's approval and invites those who are to serve. Nowadays pallbearers function mostly as an escort of honor, attending the casket but not carrying it.

The usual number of pallbearers is six, or perhaps eight; but for a man who has been prominent in public life, there may be as many as twelve or more from among his political or business associates. Pallbearers are unusual for a woman unless she is a celebrity, in which case an escort of honor may be selected from among her personal friends.

As a rule, only friends and close business associates of the deceased are asked to serve as pallbearers. Relatives are rarely included. The request is made by telephone, telegraph, or personal visit, and it's impossible to refuse except for reasons of ill-health.

The pallbearers are instructed when and where to assemble, and of course they must be on time. There are few things more rude and thoughtless than to keep a funeral waiting. Usually they meet at the house, but sometimes they meet in the vestibule of the church or the funeral home—depending on the arrangements. They wear dark clothes, black ties and shoes.

Formerly it was the duty of the pallbearers to carry the cloth or velvet pall that covered the coffin—hence the name. Later their duty was to carry the casket into and out of the church. Today they may still carry the casket if the family so wishes; but usually that task is left to the undertaker's trained assistants, and the pallbearers accompany the casket as a guard of honor.

Following is an outline of procedure for honorary pallbearers on the day of the funeral:

1. They assemble at the house (or in the vestibule of the church or funeral home).
2. At the house, they walk out two by two in front of the casket, which is carried by the undertaker's assistants.
3. They stand reverently at the side of the hearse as the casket is put in place, their heads uncovered.
4. At the church, they form a lane through which the casket is carried; and if there is a processional, they precede the casket up the aisle.
5. After the services, they precede the casket down the aisle, and again form a lane outside through which the casket is carried.
6. They again stand reverently at the side of the hearse as the casket is put in place, their heads uncovered. They do not enter their cars until the hearse has passed on ahead.
7. At the grave or crematory, they precede the casket in double file.
8. Each pallbearer makes a point of saying a few words of comfort and sympathy to the bereaved family.
9. Each pallbearer makes a formal visit at the house of the deceased two or three days after the funeral, leaving a card but not usually asking to be received.

CHURCH FUNERAL

Relatives and friends who attend a church funeral assemble at the church, not at the house of the deceased. Only pallbearers and a very few intimates of the family assemble at the house.

Persons attending a funeral should make it a point to be in their seats at least fifteen minutes before the time scheduled for the services. This is one time when arriving late is inexcusably rude and unkind. Men and women both should wear dark clothes; and of course the women always wear hats.

During the services, the family occupies the front pews on the right of the center aisle. The pallbearers occupy the front pews on the left side of the aisle. Close relatives and intimate friends take any places they wish behind them. Neighbors and business associates take places toward the rear. There are no ushers at a funeral, and it is expected that people will seat themselves quickly and quietly, and where they properly belong.

If there is to be a procession, it forms in the vestibule. The choir generally leads, followed by the clergyman, and then the pallbearers walking two by two. The pallbearers always immediately precede the casket, which is covered by flowers and is carried by trained persons who are not likely to slip or stumble. The casket is followed by the chief mourners, two by two or any other way they find comforting. The women of the family should be supported on the arm of a male relative, whenever possible.

A widow walks immediately behind the casket on the arm of her nearest male relative—a son if she has one. Sometimes she walks between two sons, or perhaps a son and daughter. There can be no rigidly prescribed rules for a situation such as this.

A widower follows the body of his wife attended by his oldest daughter—or by a son if he has no daughter—or perhaps one on either side of him, if that's the most comforting way.

Often the immediate family does not walk in the procession at all, but enters the church at a side door and is seated just before the casket is carried in. Clearly their own wishes and feelings in this matter are all that need be considered.

Nowadays the trend is more and more to eliminate formal funeral processions as needlessly distressing to the family. Instead the coffin is placed on a stand at the foot of the chancel sometime before the services. At the appointed time, members of the family enter from the vestry and take their places in the front pews, and the services proceed at once with simple dignity.

After the services, the pallbearers precede the casket down the aisle, followed by the immediate family and then the other mourners in the order of their relationship to the deceased. Casual acquaintances and business associates should remain at their places until all relatives and close friends have passed. There should be no delays in the vestibule nor crowding at the door—and especially no intrusion on the family at this time to offer sympathy and condolences. The members of the family go at once into waiting cars, followed by those who will accompany them to the place of burial. All others remain considerately in the background so as not to interfere with the proceedings.

FUNERAL FROM THE HOUSE

A house funeral is simpler and more private than a church funeral, and usually much less of an ordeal for the family. Often the chief mourners do not appear at all, but remain in seclusion in a separate room where they can hear the services but cannot be seen.

The services are held in the living room or drawing room, from which all large pieces of furniture have been removed. The casket is placed on a draped stand in front of the mantel, between two windows, or in any niche or alcove that is convenient—but not too near the door. The undertaker provides as many folding chairs as are likely to be required, and they are arranged in two rows with an aisle between.

Only relatives and very intimate friends attend a house funeral. They begin to assemble about a half-hour before the time set for the services, and take seats at once—talking in whispers or not at all. They do not stand about in groups talking and "visiting," nor try to see members of the immediate family if they are in seclusion. All wear dark and preferably inconspicuous clothes. The women keep their wraps on; the men wear their overcoats or carry them in their arms, and hold their hats in their hands.

If the members of the family are to sit with their relatives and friends during the services, a row of seats is reserved for them near the casket. The women wear hats and veils, as in church, and generally do not come into the room until the clergyman arrives and the services are about to begin. The room may be darkened or not according to the wishes of the family.

Nowadays organ and choir records are available for use during the services in a house funeral; and it's entirely proper to use them if the family so desires.

When the services are over, it's customary for everyone to take a final look at the deceased—members of the immediate family being the last to do so. The casket is then closed and carried to the waiting hearse.

THE FUNERAL HOME

In recent years the funeral home or chapel is more and more taking the place of funerals at the house of the deceased.

The procedure is the same as for a house funeral, except that all the details of arrangement are taken care of by the funeral directors.

Flowers are sent to the funeral home, not the deceased's home. They are addressed "To the funeral of Mr. ——— [name of the deceased]." A card with a brief message of sympathy written on it is attached to the flowers; and someone responsible should be assigned the task of listing all floral tributes and the names of the senders so that they can later be acknowledged.

On the day of the funeral, relatives and friends go directly to the funeral home. No one goes to the house except the pallbearers. During the services, the family may either sit with relatives and friends in the chapel, or remain in seclusion in an adjoining room where they can hear but cannot be seen.

AT THE GRAVE

It is unusual for any but relatives and very close friends of the deceased or of the family, to attend the services at the grave. For these, and for the clergyman, transportation is provided; but if any others wish to drive their own cars in the funeral procession and accompany the family to the place of burial, there is no objection to it.

Those who go to the cemetery should wear black, or at least dark and inconspicuous clothes. The men remove their hats during the services unless the weather is very bad—in which case they generally keep their hats on but hold a hand at the brim as a gesture of respect.

If there are pallbearers, they precede the casket to the grave, walking two by two. They stand at one side as a guard of honor; the chief mourners stand opposite, their relatives and friends grouped behind them. The services at the grave are usually quite brief; and as soon as they are over, the family and their friends disperse. The family should not remain until the casket is lowered into the ground.

CREMATION

The funeral services are the same whether they are to be followed by cremation or interment. Up to the time of the disposition of the body, there is no difference whatever in the procedure at the church, house, or funeral home. Relatives and friends send flowers, and assemble for the funeral ceremony, just as they would for a burial.

After funeral services are held, the body is removed to the crematory; and those who would ordinarily go to the cemetery to attend the interment services, go to the crematory to attend the services there. These services are brief and usually very impressive.

AFTER THE FUNERAL

When the family returns to the house after the funeral, the blinds should be drawn up, and the house restored as nearly as possible to its normal condition. The ribbon and flowers on the door should be gone, all articles belonging to the undertaker out of the house, the furniture back in its usual order, and the belongings of the deceased put away. A relative or friend usually stays behind to take care of these important details.

Someone also arranges for coffee or tea to be ready for the family on their return, and something light to eat in case they want it.

But having done what they can to help, relatives and friends do not linger at the house. They realize it has been a very trying day for the family, and they leave them to rest and relax in privacy.

ACKNOWLEDGING FLOWERS AND NOTES OF CONDOLENCE

Acknowledgment of flowers and notes of condolence should be made by some member of the family as soon as convenient after the funeral. *These must be handwritten notes.*[2] Engraved cards of thanks are not good form and should not be used. The only exception to this rule is in the case of a person of great prominence whose family received so many tributes and messages it would be impossible to acknowledge them all personally.

MOURNING DRESS

Grief turns instinctively to the somber garments of mourning for the slight measure of comfort they give; and those who wish to wear black should certainly do so. But in this modern world we have adopted a very sane and liberal attitude toward mourning; and those who do *not* wear black need no longer fear criticism on that score. Today people wear mourning only if it gives them comfort to do so, not for show or effect.

There is no longer any rigidly prescribed etiquette of mourning, no longer any set period for seclusion from social life and for the wearing of black clothes. Prolonged mourning is, in fact, out of date. The once-familiar heavy crepe veils women used to wear are almost never seen any more, except perhaps on the day of the funeral as a shield from the gaze of the curious.

Parents who have lost a child generally wear black to the funeral, and dark or somber clothes for several months afterward. For a parent, or for a brother or sister, one generally wears mourning for a short period, though not necessarily unrelieved black. Some widows still

[2]For examples, see pages 325 and 326.

wear black for a year, but most start wearing black-and-white or gray after the first six months.

In general, it is now customary for those who have lost someone close to wear deep mourning at the funeral, and thereafter to dress soberly and remain in retirement from social functions for at least several months. Just as grief heals gradually, so do the grief-stricken gradually return to gaiety and bright colors.

Men, like women, wear mourning only if they wish to do so, not because they feel it is expected of them. For a member of his immediate family, a man wears a black suit on the day of the funeral, if he has one. Otherwise the darkest suit he owns, with black shoes and a black hat, are considered appropriate mourning clothes. After that, if he wishes to continue wearing mourning, he may do so by the simple expedient of putting a black band on his hat and on the left sleeve of his suit and overcoat.

Young children are, of course, never dressed in black—even for parents.

PART V

Social Correspondence

1. GOOD TASTE IN CORRESPONDENCE

APART from the pleasure and satisfaction that a wide correspondence with friends can mean to you, letter writing is an important social asset. The ability to write good letters can be as useful to you socially as the ability to talk well or entertain successfully.

Letter writing helps facilitate all social activities—often saves you much time, trouble, and inconvenience. Your letter goes to the hospital to cheer a sick friend. It goes to your hostess to thank her for entertaining you. It conveys your best wishes, congratulations, condolences, when you are unable to do so in person.

Naturally, what you write in a letter—its message, the tone and spirit of its contents, the news you tell, and the friendliness and cheer you radiate—these are of first importance. But almost equally important is the appearance of your letter. It should not only be interesting to read, but attractive and inviting to the eye.

CORRECT STATIONERY FOR SOCIAL AND PERSONAL CORRESPONDENCE

For your *formal* correspondence—such as invitations, acknowledgments, formal notes of thanks, condolence, etc.—plain white unruled paper of good quality is best. The paper should be a double sheet of standard size and shape that folds once into a matching envelope.

For *informal* correspondence—such as friendly letters, family letters, informal notes of invitation, thanks, congratulation, etc.—there is a much wider scope for personal choice. In stationery, as in everything else, there are new styles almost every season, and you may indulge your fancy as you like. There are no inflexible rules; just be sure to avoid extremes of size, shape, color, or style. Any extreme that makes your letter conspicuously different from others is in poor taste.

If you like color in your stationery, choose a delicate, subdued shade such as ivory, tan, or gray. Even a very light shade of blue or pink is permissible, if your taste runs that way. But avoid the loud, gaudy shades. And remember, white is always acceptable, always in good form, for every type of correspondence. Giddy borders and decorations are for the very young only, and for the immature in taste. Keep your stationery simple and dignified. Envelope linings of contrasting color may be used provided they are not too vivid and conspicuous.

Double or folded sheets are still the most widely used, and are best for the general run of personal correspondence. However, if you like to write long letters, if your handwriting is very bold and large, or if you use a typewriter for your personal correspondence, single sheets are more convenient. Both types are equally acceptable for informal correspondence; but for formal purposes, only the conventional double sheet is correct.

It's not good form to use ruled stationery for your letters. Ruled paper is only for children learning how to write! If you can't keep your lines straight, use one of those handy dark-lined guides which are usually furnished with letter paper.

Always try to use stationery that fits the letter. For example, if you are writing a long, chatty letter with all the accumulated news of the past month, use fairly large sheets of paper. But if you are writing a short message, perhaps just a few words, use smaller-size paper. It is not advisable to use tiny cards or sheets that fit into very small envelopes. Undersize letters are not approved by the postal authorities as they present difficulties in handling and are easily lost or misplaced.

The use of office or hotel stationery for personal correspondence is not recommended, except in an emergency. The use of a sheet of paper from a child's school tablet, and any stray envelope that happens to be around, is never recommended under any circumstances! If you don't have suitable stationery available, put off writing the letter until you can get some . . . or if the message can't wait, telephone.

ENGRAVED AND MONOGRAMMED PAPER

Many people like to have their personal stationery engraved with their name and address. Others like to have an engraved monogram on their letter paper. Either is correct—but never *both*. If you use a monogram, be sure it's a simple one and that it appears on the paper only, not on the envelope. Don't use a crest unless such distinction rightfully belongs to your family. The use of a crest that doesn't belong to you is not far removed in principle from the use of a "phony" title.

Country-house stationery generally has the name of the place engraved at the top of the first page, centered or to the right. Other information to guide the visiting guest (such as railroad station, telephone number, telegraph, etc.) may be listed at the left. Small decorative illustrations like a tiny house, a hitching post, a palm tree—or anything symbolic of the place or its location—are often used, but for a big house with impressive grounds, plain paper engraved only with the name and address is more dignified.

It's always best to consult a reliable stationer when planning engraved writing paper, or engraved invitations or announcements of any kind. He can show you samples of paper and engraving and help you make a correct and satisfactory choice.

SHORT NOTES SHOULD BE HANDWRITTEN

Although the typewriter is being used more and more generally for personal correspondence, a handwritten note is always more gracious and personal. It's best to write brief notes by hand—especially those intimate messages of thanks, congratulation, and sympathy we are all called upon to write. But be sure they are written plainly and legibly.

Difficult, hard-to-read handwriting is usually just careless, indifferent writing which can be greatly improved. It takes time and practice, but it's well worth a few days of sustained effort. Try experimenting with types of pens, too. Often the type of point used makes a big difference in the smoothness and legibility of your writing. Write with deliberation and care, taking time to complete every word—to dot every "i" and cross every "t." Only in that way can you improve your penmanship to the point where writing clearly and legibly becomes habitual and "second nature" to you.

Always use pen and ink for handwritten correspondence. Never write in pencil unless you are ill, or are in a moving vehicle like a train or plane, or other circumstances make it unavoidable (in which case you should be sure to explain). Avoid the use of brightly colored ink. Black is the best; though dark blue and dark green are also ac ceptable. Such shades as violet, bright green, and red are not in good taste.

Make it a practice never to send out a slovenly letter. Remember, you are often judged more by the appearance of your letter than by its contents. It's much better to rewrite a messy and untidy letter than to let it go out and show you to disadvantage.

Longer Letters May Be Typed

Although a message in your own hand is more intimate and personal when writing to comfort a stricken friend, or to thank someone for a favor or a gift, all other personal and social correspondence may be typed. Today the use of the typewriter is accepted as socially correct for all but the most formal invitations and acknowledgments.

Just be sure you know *how* to type! Be sure your letters are neat, clean and well spaced, without errors or erasures. A well-typed letter, with its precise legibility, is inviting and attractive to the eye. However, much of its neatness and legibility depends on the condition of the machine; so be sure your typewriter is always in good condition. Change the ribbon as soon as the impressions begin to look light and faded. Brush the type faces occasionally to keep them sharp and clean.

All typewritten letters must be signed by hand, with pen and ink. A typed signature is discourteous.

The Spacing and Arrangement of a Letter

Whether your letter is typed or written by hand, it should "sit nicely" on the page. That means it should be well spaced and well balanced, with reasonably wide and straight margins.

When writing with pen and ink, leave adequate space *between* the lines as well as generous margins at the sides. An openly spaced letter is more inviting to the eye and easier to read than one which is carelessly crowded on the page.

If your letter is to be typewritten, give some thought beforehand to the approximate length of it, so you can plan its spacing. A letter that is typed grotesquely off-center on a page does not make a good impression. The final appearance of your letter, handwritten or typed, should be of a picture set neatly in a frame.

Don't use folded stationery for typing letters; it's neither convenient nor practical. Special paper for typing personal correspondence comes in single sheets about 7½ by 10 inches in size. That's slightly smaller than commercial letterheads which are 8½ by 11 inches. For a long letter that fills the page, there should be a margin of at least an inch and a half at the top, bottom and left-hand side— and approximately the same margin on the right-hand side. For short notes, the margins are proportionately wider.

It is not advisable to type on both sides of a sheet of paper. If you cannot get your letter on one sheet, use a second sheet to complete it.

SEQUENCE OF PAGES AND FOLDING THE LETTER

In writing social notes—like informal invitations, notes of thanks, condolence, etc.—it's considered better form to get all the message on one page instead of carrying it over. Therefore always try to keep such notes brief enough to go on the first page.

Personal letters that carry over to a second page of a double sheet should be written on pages one and three.

Long letters that fill all sides of a double sheet should follow the natural page order—one, two, three, four—with no backtracking or alternating. Skipping around in a letter from pages one to three and from two to four merely confuses and annoys the reader. Even when you write in the natural order of the pages, it's a good idea to number them. Writing sideways or crosswise in a letter is bad taste and should be avoided.

Always fold your letter neatly, with the edges even—as a carelessly folded letter implies indifference toward the person to whom you are writing. Both double and single sheets are folded evenly from the lower to the top edge, and are inserted in the envelope fold first. A sheet too large to go into the envelope with a single fold should be folded in three equal sections, and placed in the envelope with the closed end first.

THE WELL-WRITTEN LETTER

By all the approved standards of today, the most natural letters are the best letters. Therefore the first thing you should strive for in letter writing is a natural, spontaneous sincerity.

Just bear in mind that letter writing is a substitute for conversation, and that a good letter is primarily good "talk" on paper. The exchange of letters should be like the exchange of conversation—lively, stimulating, and enjoyable.

The whole secret is to write in an easy, natural way without self-consciousness. Make your letters sound as much as possible like your conversation. There's no reason why you should write to your friends any differently than you would speak to them—except, of course, in a strictly formal communication. To talk one way and write another is an affectation that betrays itself in forced and stilted language.

You'll find that letter writing is easier, and a lot more fun, when you get on to the knack of writing as you speak. There's really no great trick to it. The important thing is the message, not the words.

If you keep thinking of what you want to say, the words will take care of themselves. Don't grope for flowery ways of expression! Don't try to write any differently than you speak! Just write simply and naturally, letting your personality shine through and animate your letters exactly as it does your speech.

The well-written letter conjures an image of you on the page—brings your very voice and gestures to the mind of the reader. The well-written letter sounds the way you sound when you are talking with pleasure and enthusiasm to someone you like.

KEEP YOUR LANGUAGE SIMPLE—USE SHORT WORDS AND SENTENCES

The use of simple, understandable language is one of the most important factors in producing interesting letters—letters that have a friendly, conversational tone. The short crisp words of everyday speech are more vivid and expressive than long bookish words.

For example, if you were talking directly to someone, you wouldn't be likely to say, "I'll endeavor to converse with him." Then why write it that way in a letter? Write it the way you'd say it: "I'll try to talk to him."

So keep your language simple; keep it clear and concise. Whenever possible use a single vigorous word instead of an elaborate phrase. Avoid long rambling sentences, involved paragraphs. Short familiar words and fast-moving sentences make a letter more lively and readable.

TACT AND COURTESY IN LETTER WRITING

Answer all your correspondence promptly. If you are in doubt as to whether or not a letter requires an answer, answer it. You can never hurt anyone by writing a cordial, friendly letter; but sensitive people are easily wounded by apparent lack of interest on the part of friends to whom they have written and from whom they have had no reply.

Never say anything in a letter you wouldn't say to a person's face. Don't spread rumors, or repeat unkind gossip, or write anything that is confidential and shouldn't be revealed. Never express yourself in any way that sounds ungracious, unfriendly, or rude.

It's important, in letter writing, to avoid careless remarks that may be misunderstood. In conversation, a careless or thoughtless remark can always be retracted or explained, or made to seem unimportant by the friendliness of a gesture or a smile. But not so with a careless or thoughtless remark in a letter! It's there in black and white, cruelly repeating itself with every reading. It may have been meant as a jest; it may not have been meant at all the way it sounds. But you aren't there to explain.

A good idea is to read your letter aloud before mailing it, and listen to the way it sounds. *Listen through the ears of the person who is to receive it.* Make sure that person will not get any implications or shades of meaning that you do not intend. If there's even a single word or phrase that can be misinterpreted, write the letter over again.

Equally important is to avoid writing anything you may later regret. Make it a practice never to send out a letter written in anger or in a mood of depression or despair. Write it if you must! Pour out your heart on paper—for that's a wonderful way to overcome anger, worry, bitterness, or fear. *But don't mail it.* Put it aside until your anger has cooled. You may be very, very glad you didn't mail that letter!

Try to acquire the knack of putting yourself in the other person's place, and of writing with his interests and problems in mind. Failure to see things from the other person's point of view is the cause of most of the dull, tactless, and uninteresting letters that get into the mail. No one ever really enjoys a letter that is filled with "peeves" and gloomy complaints. So don't pour all your worries and troubles into your letters! Don't write of ill-health, or servant problems, of domestic difficulties, of business reverses. Avoid disagreeable or unpleasant things if you can—that is, of course, if you want your letter to be read with enjoyment.

People judge you by your letters, so be careful—be *critical!* Don't let any letter go out under your name unless you feel that it does you justice, that it's a credit to you, not only in its appearance, but in its tone and contents. It's far better not to send any letter at all than to send one that stamps you as crude, thoughtless or ill-bred.

2. THE PARTS OF A LETTER

ALL letters—social, business, and personal—are made up of five parts. Although it isn't necessary to follow exactly all details within each part, you must follow the general form if you wish to produce acceptable, well-constructed letters. The five parts are:

1. THE HEADING
   which is the address and date
2. THE SALUTATION
   which is the complimentary greeting

3. THE BODY OF THE LETTER
   which is the message
4. THE CLOSE
   which is the complimentary "good-by"
5. THE SIGNATURE

In addition to these five basic parts there is also the superscription —the outside address, written on the envelope.

The Heading

If the stationery you use has a printed or engraved address already inscribed, the heading consists of the date only. Otherwise it consists of your address and the date.

The heading is the first thing you write in a letter. It should be at least one inch from the top edge of the sheet. Start writing approximately in the center, so that the heading ends three quarters of an inch or so from the right margin. Here is the way the heading should look at the top of your letter:

> 277 Park Avenue
> New York, N.Y.
> November 10, 1949

The lines may be "stepped" or indented, if you prefer. But a straight edge is considered more modern and better form. Note that there are no commas at the ends of the lines, and no period after the date.

The date always goes below the address—never above it or on the same line with it. Don't abbreviate the month. Write it out; it looks better.

The Salutation

The salutation is the friendly "Hello!" of your letter—the complimentary greeting to your correspondent. It is placed at the left side of the sheet, about half an inch below the heading. The point at which you start the salutation will be your left-hand margin, as the body of the letter will be in a straight line with it. So start the salutation where you want the margin to be—usually one to two inches from the edge of the paper.

Long use and familiar custom have made "Dear John" or "Dear Mary" the popular form of address in letters. But that doesn't mean you cannot say "Dearest" or "Darling" or "My own precious Anne" in an intimate letter to someone you love. Just bear in mind that in routine everyday correspondence, standard forms of salutation are best and any sharp deviation from the customary and familiar should be avoided.

"My dear" is considered more formal than "Dear"—so if you are writing a friendly, informal letter, the salutation should be "Dear Frank" or "Dear Mr. Smith." But if you are writing a formal note, or if you are writing to someone you don't know well, the salutation should be "My dear Mr. Smith."

Certain forms of address are in bad taste and should be avoided. For example, never use "Dear Friend" or "My dear Friend" as your salutation. Equally undesirable are "Madame," "Dear Miss" and "Friend Tom." The use of the name alone as a salutation should also be avoided, as that is rude and abrupt. Never start a letter like this:

Mr. Martin Harris:
I have just returned from Paris where I had the great pleasure of meeting your brother, Fred. He asked me to write you on my return to New York and . . .

As a rule, the salutation is followed by a colon, although the use of a dash or a simple comma is also correct. But don't use a colon and a dash (:—) or a comma and a dash (,—) as these are obsolete forms.

THE BODY OF THE LETTER

Naturally the most important part of any letter is its body, or contents. And that is strictly your department! No one can tell you what to write in your letters. The most anyone can do is make suggestions.

Obviously one of the first requisites of a good letter is to have something to say. You aren't very likely to produce an interesting letter if there is neither the reason nor the inclination to write. So first of all, know why you are writing—and then be sure your letter accomplishes its purpose. Say what you have to say simply and to the point, leading naturally from one subject to another as though you were talking.

Try to get your letter off to a good start with something interesting in the very first sentence. Avoid the obvious, "I received your letter and am answering it." Avoid that old familiar apology (so trite, and so unflattering!)—"I meant to write sooner, but I've been busy." Avoid particularly starting your letters with any word that ends in "ing." Don't, for example, ever begin a letter like this:

Having heard that you are in New York, I am writing to . . .

OR

Learning of your illness, I hasten to write and . . .

Such leads almost always make a letter sound stereotyped and dull.

Before you start to write, organize your thoughts and decide what you want to say. Then plunge right in and say it! If it's to greet an old friend, sit down and write "Welcome to New York!" Just as cordially and spontaneously as you would say it in person. If it's to cheer someone who is sick, don't try to camouflage the purpose of your letter with a lot of unrelated opening remarks. Start off with the same sort of cheerful nonsense you might indulge in if you visited the patient's bedside: "What's the idea of being sick? Don't you realize how your friends all miss you?" Then go on to the next thought that logically presents itself, exactly what you would say if you were right there at the bedside, chatting with your friend. "No fooling, Fred—we just can't get along without you! So hurry and get well. You know our annual fishing trip is scheduled for early next month, and you just can't miss that!"

If it's a letter of thanks, be sure it's written promptly and for the purpose—expressing cordial and sincere thanks—not rambling on page after page about Aunt Tilly's tulips, or the feud with your next-door neighbor.

If it's a letter of condolence, don't write even briefly about some unrelated subject.

If it's an invitation, give only the essential facts: the time, the place, the occasion.

Bear in mind that all social communications are for a definite purpose. In a friendly letter you can ramble to your heart's content, and the more ground you cover, the more interesting your letter is likely to be. But in a social communication, written for a specific purpose, stay with the subject.

In writing the body of your letter, always start a new paragraph when you change to a new subject. Begin each sentence with a capital and end it with a period. Watch your spelling! Keep a dictionary handy and refer to it whenever you are in doubt about a word. Check your grammar and be sure it's correct. Remember that bad spelling, poor English, the misuse of words betray you even more cruelly in a letter than in speech.

THE CLOSE

The close of a letter is the complimentary greeting, or "good-by" before signing your name and slipping the letter into its envelope.

This closing phrase is written two or three spaces below the body of the letter, beginning at about the center of the page. Only the first word is capitalized, and a comma is used at the end.

The wording varies according to the type of letter, and according to the degree of friendship and intimacy with the person addressed. You wouldn't write "Devotedly yours" or "With deepest affection" to someone who is little more than a casual acquaintance. Nor would you write a cold and impersonal "Very truly yours" to an old and well-loved friend. Your closing phrase should be neither flowery nor curt, but friendly to the degree that you are friendly with your correspondent.

Business letters, letters to professional people, and very formal social notes generally close with "Yours truly" or "Very truly yours."

For informal social notes, and for the general run of friendly correspondence, the forms most frequently used are:

Sincerely yours
Yours very sincerely
Always sincerely yours
Yours cordially
Most cordially yours
Faithfully yours

Letters to intimate friends or relatives might close with any of these familiar forms:

Yours affectionately
Always affectionately yours
Lovingly yours
Your loving sister
Lovingly, your sister
With love

As for love letters, the wording is whatever the degree of affection inspires—from a simple "Fondly yours" to a fervent "Yours with the utmost devotion."

It's always best to conform to conventional closings in business and social letters. But you can "let yourself go," if you like, in your personal and family correspondence. Here you can use your own pet expressions, your favorite phrases of endearment. You can even eliminate formal openings and closings entirely if that is your preference. If you want to start your letter, *"I've been thinking of you all day, Joan darling"*—if you want to close your letter, "Good-by, my dearest one"—by all means write it just that way! Formal openings and closings are expected in formal correspondence; but in letters to your intimate friends, no tradition-bound rules need inhibit your natural, spontaneous expressions of greeting and farewell. Whatever helps to maintain the illusion of a face-to-face conversation makes your letter that much more delightful to receive.

The position of the word "yours" in a formal complimentary closing may be at the beginning or end of the phrase, as you prefer. There is no difference in meaning between "Yours sincerely" and "Sincerely yours." Strictly speaking, the use of an adverb ending in "ly" (like *truly* or *cordially*) calls for the use of the accompanying pronoun "yours" to complete the phrase. Therefore it's always better to include it in very formal correspondence. But in your friendly and informal correspondence, you may omit the pronoun if you like—closing with a simple "Sincerely" or "Cordially."

It is not advisable to use the word "Yours" alone—except, perhaps, at the close of a love letter where the word takes on special meaning and eloquence.

The phrase "Warmly yours" is bad form and should not be used. "Hastily yours" and "Yours in haste" are unflattering and rude.

"Respectfully yours" should be used only by a tradesman to a customer, or by an employee to an employer. It is often used when writing to a church dignitary or to a high public official; but "Faithfully yours" is more acceptable for that purpose.

It is correct to use "Gratefully yours" only when a benefit has been received. You might use it, for example, in a letter to a surgeon who has successfully operated on someone dear to you, or a lawyer who has won a difficult case, or a teacher who has given special attention to your child.

"Believe me, Sincerely yours" is an old English form still used by many people to express formality in the closing of a note. But it's a timeworn and cumbersome phrase and should be avoided, along with such other stilted expressions as "I beg to remain," "I have the honor to remain," "I remain, Your humble servant," "I am, Yours obediently."

"With best wishes" and "With kindest regards" are less offensive ornaments of expression—though these, too, date back to a more flowery age of letter writing than our own. Use them if you like; but bear in mind that the trend today is more and more toward simple, unadorned expression.

THE SIGNATURE

The signature of a letter is written below the complimentary close and somewhat to the right, so that it ends just about in line with the right-hand margin. These are the three important things to remember:

1. Always sign by hand, in ink.
2. Write *legibly*, so there can be no doubt as to the exact spelling of your name.
3. Sign your name without any accompanying title.

A gentleman does not write "Mr." before his name when signing a letter. He signs all formal social correspondence—and all business letters, unless the business associate is also a personal friend—with his full name but no title: "John Edgar Prescott." Informal social notes and letters to friends are signed simply "John" or "Jack"—or however he is fondly and familiarly known to his correspondent.

A married woman does not sign letters with "Mrs." preceding her name. In social correspondence, she uses her given name alone (Margaret), or the nickname by which she is affectionately known to her friends (Peggy), or her full name (Margaret Blair Prescott), depending upon the degree of intimacy between her and her correspondent. Under no circumstances does she sign a letter "Mrs. John E. Prescott." However, in a business letter or a letter to a complete stranger, she may wish to indicate how the reply to her should be addressed. In that case she adds her married name, *in parenthesis*, either directly below the signature or over toward the left, in line with the left-hand margin. For example:

Yours very truly,
Margaret Blair Prescott
(Mrs. John Edgar Prescott)

OR

Yours very truly,
Margaret B. Prescott

(Mrs. John E. Prescott)

In a letter to a tradesman or servant, a married woman may not wish to use her first name. In that case she signs "M.B. Prescott" (for

Margaret Blair Prescott) and adds her married name, in parenthesis, either below it or in the lower left corner.

An unmarried woman signs her social correspondence "Laura" or "Laura Prescott." In business letters she may use the form "(Miss) Laura Prescott."

A widow signs her social correspondence exactly as she did before her husband's death. Her business letters may also be signed as before, with "Mrs. John Edgar Prescott" in parenthesis below the signature. Or if she prefers, she may just put "Mrs." in parenthesis before her own name:

> Yours very truly,
> (Mrs.) Margaret Blair Prescott

Unless she has legally resumed her maiden name, a divorced woman[1] signs her social letters as before, with her own first name and surname, and her former husband's surname: "Margaret Blair Prescott." In business correspondence, instead of her former husband's name in parenthesis below the signature, she uses her own:

> Yours very truly,
> Margaret Blair Prescott
> (Mrs. Margaret B. Prescott)

A doctor signs his letters, "John Edgar Prescott" or "John Edgar Prescott, M.D."—never "Dr. John Edgar Prescott."

A minister signs his letters "Thomas Wilbur Crane" or "Thomas Wilbur Crane, D.D."—never "Rev. Thomas Wilbur Crane."

Whether a man is a college professor, a justice of the Supreme Court, or President of the United States—he signs his letters without any title or "handle" attached to his name. Of course in a business letter, a letter to an editor or colleague, or a letter of a professional or scientific nature, a man's title, position, affiliations, etc., may be required—to give substance and authority to his communication. In that case, the essential data is written *below the name*, not as a part of it. A physicist who writes a paper on atomic energy and sends it to the editor of a scientific journal for publication, would sign his covering letter:

> James R. Farnell, Ph.D.
> Professor, Department of Physics
> University of Maine

[1]For chapter on divorce, see page 249.

The use of a degree following the name is acceptable only when the nature of the communication calls for it—when it has some definite bearing on the subject of the letter and denotes authority to discuss that subject. Naturally one doesn't tack a degree to one's name when writing a letter of sympathy or acknowledging a dinner invitation.

Often, in a letter to a stranger, a degree following the name is helpful in indicating how the reply should be addressed. For example, earned degrees such as Ph.D., M.D., D.D., and D.D.S. entitle the person to be addressed as "Doctor." But holders of honorary degrees such as L.L.D. and Litt.D. are not ordinarily addressed as "Doctor." A bachelor of arts or science (B.A.) or a master of arts or science (M.A. or M.S.) is addressed simply as "Mr."

In all correspondence, business or social, it's important to avoid confusion due to incomplete or misleading signatures. Therefore while there are no hard and fast rules against the use of initials or abbreviations (such as "T. M. Blake" or "Mac"), it is always best to write out the name in full.

"Junior," or "Jr.," should be used only by a son whose signature is identically the same as that of his father . . . as, for example, "John D. Rockefeller, Jr." If a man is named for a grandfather or an uncle, he is "Peter Bliss, 2nd."—not "Peter Bliss, Jr." If he, his father and grandfather all have the same name, he is "Peter Bliss, 3rd."

As a rule, the "Jr." is dropped on the death of the father, and the son becomes simply "Peter Bliss." But it is often desirable to retain the "Jr." for business reasons, especially if the son has achieved prominence in some field and is known to many people by name and reputation. In that case the "Jr." must be regarded as a permanent part of his signature, and is used indefinitely in correspondence.

There is no problem of signature involved when a daughter's name is identically the same as that of her mother. In intimate correspondence, the contents of the letter naturally tell whether it's "Joan Cary" the daughter, or "Joan Cary" the mother writing. In all other correspondence, the daughter uses "Miss" in parenthesis before her name —the mother uses "Mrs. Frederick Cary" in parenthesis below her name—to differentiate between them and avoid confusion. There is no term similar to "Jr." that a woman may use; and since "Jr." is as masculine as "Mr.," it should certainly not be borrowed for the purpose. "Katherine Winston, Jr." is an incorrect form; and though it is used occasionally even by very prominent people, it is clearly an affectation.

How to Address the Envelope

If you want to insure swift, accurate delivery of your letter, and at the same time make a good impression on the person who receives it, be sure the envelope is addressed properly.

Begin writing the address slightly below the middle of the envelope, far enough to the left to permit the name to be written without crowding. If you are not using a typewriter, take enough time to write the name and address as legibly and precisely as you can. Give all the necessary data: name, number, street, town or city, zone, state—*and give it correctly!* If there's even the slightest doubt in your mind as to the name of the street, the number of the house, or the spelling of the town—look it up!

Try to arrange the writing on the envelope so that it "sits well"— looks balanced and inviting to the eye. Avoid crowding the name and address too high against the top of the envelope, or too low against the bottom edge. When completed, the block of writing or typing should tend toward the right-hand side of the envelope, slightly below the middle—and with at least a little white space to the right and below.

In writing the name and address, you may either use a straight margin, one line directly below the other, or you may indent each line in "step" fashion. Postal authorities prefer the slanting arrangement as it's easier to read. Here is the way a properly addressed envelope should look:

Mrs. John Edgar Prescott
277 Park Avenue
New York 23, N.Y.

It is not necessary to use punctuation on the envelope unless it helps prevent confusion or misdirection. For example, commas at the end of each line serve no useful purpose and are now rarely used. But a dash between a house number and a street number is always advisable (368–84th Street); and commas separating the zone number from the name of the city and state make for greater legibility and easier reading (New York, 23, N.Y.). So use only whatever punctuation helps the postman read the name and address correctly.

Always try to give the name of the person to whom you are writing *in full* on the envelope. If it's a very long name—like Burton Ellsworth Clint du Bois—you would naturally find it more practical to use middle initials, addressing the envelope: "Mr. Burton E. C. du Bois." But Mrs. James Cort Ewing should be addressed as such—not as "Mrs. Ewing" or "Mrs. J. C. Ewing."

Be sure to give particular attention to the spelling of the name when you are writing to a new acquaintance or a stranger. Some people deeply resent a mistake in the spelling of their name, looking upon it almost as a personal affront. So check and make sure! *Spell it right.* Don't address Mr. Rolfe as "Mr. Rolf"—or Mrs. Gambel as "Mrs. Gamble."

In social correspondence, a married woman is ordinarily addressed by her husband's name: "Mrs. John Edgar Prescott."

A widow remains "Mrs. John E. Prescott." She is not addressed socially as "Mrs. Margaret Prescott"—unless, due to business or professional activities, that is the name by which she is best known to her associates and friends.

A divorced woman continues to be addressed by her former husband's name; unless she has indicated, in her own correspondence, that she prefers to be addressed as "Mrs. Margaret Blair Prescott" or "Mrs. Blair Prescott" (*Blair* having been her maiden name). The way she indicates this preference is to write it in parenthesis in the lower left corner of her letters.

The way a woman writes her name in parenthesis below her signature, or in the lower left corner of her letter, is the way she wants to be addressed. But if you receive a letter from a woman who is a stranger to you, and she signs herself "Elizabeth Tucker" without any other name in parenthesis below it, you can assume she is unmarried and address her as "Miss."

A woman is never addressed by her husband's title—as, for example, "Mrs. Dr. John E. Prescott" or "Mrs. Professor James R. Fosdick."

Until recently, a married woman with the title of "Doctor" was addressed only professionally by her professional name. Socially, she was addressed by her husband's name. But a woman who has earned a doctor's degree has certainly earned the right to be addressed by her title, socially as well as professionally. Therefore she should be addressed *either* by her professional name (Dr. Mary Starr Cutting) or by her married name (Mrs. Harold Cutting)—based upon the judgment and discretion of the person writing to her.

A delicate situation arises when a woman who is a doctor, and her husband who is a layman, are both addressed on one envelope. In the past, the form "Mr. and Mrs. Harold Cutting" was always recommended for social use; and that form may *still* be used if, under the circumstances and in one's best judgment, it is the most desirable procedure. But if Dr. Mary Starr Cutting is a woman of great prominence and distinction in her profession, surely it would be more gracious to address her by her title. In that case the form to use would be: "Mr. Harold Cutting and Dr. Mary S. Cutting." Though this is a departure from long-established usage, it is common practice today —and certainly common sense.

A husband and wife who are both doctors may be addressed socially either as "Dr. and Mrs. Milton P. Brown" or as "Drs. Milton and Cynthia Brown."

A married woman who has a professional name but no professional title, like a writer or singer, is addressed by whatever name she is known to her correspondent. In her work, of course, it would be impractical to use any name but the one under which she functions and by which she is best known. In social life, however, she is customarily addressed by her married name.

A man is always addressed as "Mr." unless he has some other title —*in which case that title should be used*.[2]

Originally the word "Esquire" following a man's name denoted a *gentleman*, a person of education, substance, and social importance —as distinguished from an ordinary shopkeeper or clerk. In time it lost this significance and came to be just an ordinary courtesy title or form of address, like "Mr." It was never used in conjunction *with* "Mr." but *instead* of it—as "Winston Barton, Esq." However, the use of "Esq." is no longer common practice and it is not recommended— though one does still see it occasionally on a letter.

Note that the use of "Jr." following a man's name does not eliminate the need for "Mr." preceding it. "Mr." and "Jr." do not mean the same thing (like "Mr." and "Esq.")—therefore the use of both is not a duplication. In other words, you would not address your letter to "John Thompson, Jr." but to "Mr. John Thompson, Jr."

Always be sure to write the proper title before a man's name, as

[2]A list giving correct forms of address for public officials, church dignitaries, army and navy officers, etc., will be found on page 521.

it is highly uncomplimentary to address him without it. But do *not* use both title and degree at the same time. For example, a doctor is addressed *either* "Dr. John E. Prescott" or "John E. Prescott, M.D." He is *never* addressed "Dr. John E. Prescott, M.D." The title is usually abbreviated; but in very formal social communications, such as engraved invitations and announcements, it is somewhat better form to spell it out (Doctor John E. Prescott.)

A letter to a minister is addressed "Reverend (or Rev.) Thomas Wilbur Crane." If he is a doctor of divinity, he may be addressed either as "Rev. Dr. Thomas W. Crane" or as "Dr. Thomas W. Crane" without the "Reverend."

A letter to a priest is addressed "Rev. Father Francis G. Duffy."

A letter to a rabbi is addressed "Rabbi Joseph P. Wolfe" or "Rev. Joseph P. Wolfe." If he holds a doctor's degree, he is addressed "Dr. Joseph P. Wolfe."

A letter to a small boy is addressed "Master Richard Kenway." His young sister is addressed "Miss Patricia Kenway," regardless of age. No period should be used after the word "Miss" as it is not an abbreviation.

Letters to servants were formerly addressed, very rudely, by name alone—as, for example, "Berta Schiller" or "Carl Lundstrom." But today most people prefer to address servants more graciously as "*Miss* Berta Schiller," "*Mr.* Carl Lundstrom."

Two or more men are usually addressed as "Messrs.," which is an abbreviation of "Messieurs" and means "Misters." Thus unmarried brothers living at the same address and invited to the same function, or perhaps thanked jointly for a gift sent by both, might be addressed as "Messrs. Alan and Robert Hartwell."

A father and son, however, should not be lumped together as "Messrs." in social correspondence. They should be addressed individually, with separate invitations or notes of thanks sent to each. Or if they are addressed jointly, it should be as follows—with the name of the father at the top:

> Mr. *James Hartwell*
> Mr. *Alan Hartwell*
> *480 Park Avenue*
> *New York, N.Y.*

Sisters living together may be addressed individually or jointly, depending upon the occasion and the circumstances. For example, when sisters are invited to an important dinner or reception, *separate* invitations are more desirable for they imply a greater personal compliment to each. But it would be silly to send two identical announcements of a birth or marriage—or even two similar notes of thanks for a joint gift, or for hospitality received—to sisters living at the same address. One announcement, one letter of thanks to both is the usual procedure. The envelope may be addressed simply to "Misses Claire and Elsie Hartwell." Or, if you prefer, the full name of each may be written out—one below the other on the envelope, with the name of the older sister at the top.

Christmas cards and other holiday greetings may be sent to "Mr. and Mrs. Philip Hummert *and family*." But the phrase "and family" should never be used when addressing invitations, as it is no compliment to be tacked on unceremoniously—like an afterthought. Invitations should be addressed specifically to all members of a family who are invited. That doesn't necessarily mean *separate* invitations for every member of the family. Even formal invitations may be addressed to "Mr. and Mrs. Philip Hummert," with "Miss Julia Hummert" written below the names of her parents. If the Hummerts have two daughters, the names of both may be added. Or *two* invitations may be sent: one to "Mr. and Mrs. Philip Hummert," another to "Misses Julia and Marlene Hummert." If there is also a small son in the family, either a separate invitation is sent to him or "Master Robert Hummert" is written below the other names on the envelope.[3]

Unlike city names, the names of the state may be abbreviated—especially if it's a long name (like "Massachusetts" or "Pennsylvania") or if the abbreviation is well known and familiar (like "N.Y." or "N.J."). Following are the standard abbreviations for the names of the states and the territorial possessions of the United States. Use these abbreviations only, as others may result in confusion or delay:

Alabama — Ala.	Kansas — Kan.
Arizona — Ariz.	Kentucky — Ky.
Arkansas — Ark.	Louisiana — La.
California — Calif.	Maine — Me.
Colorado — Colo.	Maryland — Md.
Connecticut — Conn.	Massachusetts — Mass.
Delaware — Del.	Michigan — Mich.
Florida — Fla.	Minnesota — Minn.
Georgia — Ga.	Mississippi — Miss.
Idaho — Ida.	Missouri — Mo.
Illinois — Ill.	Montana — Mont.
Indiana — Ind.	Nebraska — Neb.
Iowa — Ia.	Nevada — Nev.

[3] A boy is addressed as "Master" until he graduates from Elementary School—or until he is about 13 years old. Thereafter the title "Mister" is used.

New Hampshire — N.H.
New Jersey — N.J.
New Mexico — N.M.
New York — N.Y.
North Carolina — N.C.
North Dakota — N.D.
Ohio — O.
Oklahoma — Okla.
Oregon — Ore.
Pennsylvania — Pa.
Rhode Island — R.I.
South Carolina — S.C.
South Dakota — S.D.
Tennessee — Tenn.

Texas — Tex.
Utah — Ut.
Vermont — Vt.
Virginia — Va.
Washington — Wash.
West Virginia — W.Va.
Wisconsin — Wis.
Wyoming — Wyo.
District of Columbia — D.C.
Alaska — Alas.
Puerto Rico — P.R.
Territory of Hawaii — T.H.
Virgin Islands — V.I.

3. GENERAL INVITATIONS, ACCEPTANCES AND REGRETS

ALL social correspondence falls into two general classifications: *formal* and *informal*.

Informal communications are simply handwritten notes, in the first person—like any little note you might write to an acquaintance or friend. They include the many brief notes of congratulation, appreciation, and condolence we are all called upon to write. They also include notes of invitation, acceptance, and regret for simple, informal social affairs like bridge parties, small dinners, and luncheons.

A formal invitation implies a large or elaborate social function, like a church wedding, a ceremonious dinner, an important reception or dance. Formal invitations are usually, but not necessarily, engraved. They are not written in the first person ("I would like you to come to dinner next Tuesday . . .") but in the *third* person ("Mr. and Mrs. John T. Bayles cordially invite you to dinner . . ."). They are not written like ordinary letters, but are arranged in a decorative, irregularly indented form on the page.

Some people still use visiting cards for semiformal invitations. The procedure is to write the occasion and the date in the lower left corner, as follows:

Dinner at Eight
September the Tenth

The card is then slipped into an envelope and mailed. Though this type of invitation is still widely used, it is considered rather curt and ungracious by modern standards and is not especially recommended.[1]

FORMAL DINNER INVITATIONS

Today there is considerably less formality in social life than ever before in the past. Invitations are now frequently made by telephone, and even more casually when friends chance to meet. But there are still occasions that call for formal announcements or invitations, and still the need to reply to such communications properly. One should be familiar with the forms that good usage has established and tradition preserved.

One occasion that still calls for a strictly formal invitation is the elaborate ceremonious dinner—as, for example, to honor a distinguished guest, introduce a debutante daughter, celebrate a wedding anniversary. If the dinner is at a club or hotel the invitations are usually engraved; but frequently they are written by hand, especially when the dinner is a small one. However, even when they are written by hand, formal invitations should follow exactly the wording and spacing of the engraved form.

Formal dinner invitations should be mailed two to three weeks in advance. If they are to be engraved, you must allow another week or more; so make your plans well ahead of time. And be sure to give the correct information to the engraver, for mistakes in spelling, in date, place, hour, etc., cannot be corrected once the form is run off.

ENGRAVED FILL-IN TYPE OF DINNER INVITATION

Mr. and Mrs. Thomas Lloyd Whitney
request the pleasure of

Mr. and Mrs. Frank P. Jenson's

company at dinner
on Wednesday, June the tenth
at eight o'clock
250 Park Avenue

[1]See pages 49 to 51.

ENGRAVED INVITATION TO A FORMAL DINNER

Mr. and Mrs. Thomas Lloyd Whitney
request the pleasure of your company
at dinner
on Wednesday, June the tenth
at eight o'clock
250 Park Avenue

HANDWRITTEN INVITATION TO A FORMAL DINNER

The Marlowe Apartments

*Mr. and Mrs. Thomas Lloyd Whitney
request the pleasure of
Mr. and Mrs. Frank P. Jenson's
company at dinner
on Wednesday, June the tenth
at eight o'clock*

Dinner Invitations Call for Prompt Acknowledgment

A dinner invitation should be acknowledged *promptly*—within twenty-four hours, if possible—and with a definite acceptance or regret. Follow the exact wording of the invitation, writing on the first page of the note paper only, and centering the message attractively so that it not only *reads* but *looks* formal. Here, for example, is the way an acceptance of the invitation above should look:

15 Sutton Place

Mr. and Mrs. Frank P. Jenson
accept with pleasure
Mr. and Mrs. Thomas L. Whitney's
kind invitation for dinner
on Wednesday, June the tenth
at eight o'clock

Nowadays many people write formal acknowledgments without indented margins, following only the wording and not the arrangement of the invitation. There is no objection to this form if you prefer it:

> Mr. and Mrs. Frank P. Jenson accept with pleasure Mr. and Mrs. Thomas L. Whitney's kind invitation for dinner on Wednesday, June the tenth, at eight o'clock.

If you cannot accept a dinner invitation, it's courteous to give the reason why. Following are typical "regrets" to a formal dinner invitation. These are written by hand, of course, on one's best white note paper:

> *Mr. and Mrs. Frank P. Jenson*
> *regret that a previous engagement*
> *prevents their accepting*
> *Mr. and Mrs. Thomas L. Whitney's*
> *kind invitation for dinner*
> *on Wednesday, June the tenth*

> *Mr. and Mrs. Frank P. Jenson*
> *regret exceedingly that they*
> *are unable to accept*
> *Mr. and Mrs. Thomas L. Whitney's*
> *kind invitation for dinner*
> *on Wednesday, June the tenth*
> *owing to illness in the family*

An acceptance always requires the repetition of both the date and the hour to prevent the possibility of a misunderstanding. But a regret requires the repetition of the date only.

DINNER IN HONOR OF A SPECIAL GUEST OR GUESTS

INVITATION

> *Mr. and Mrs. James L. Matthews*
> *request the pleasure of*
> *Mr. and Mrs. Roger B. Smith's*
> *company at dinner*
> *on Saturday, October the fourteenth*
> *at eight o'clock*
> *to meet Mr. Frederick West*
> 280 Park Avenue

ACCEPTANCE

Mr. and Mrs. Roger B. Smith
accept with pleasure
Mr. and Mrs. James L. Matthews'
kind invitation for dinner
on Saturday, October the fourteenth
at eight o'clock
to meet Mr. Frederick West

REGRET

Mr. and Mrs. Roger B. Smith
regret that a previous engagement
prevents their accepting
Mr. and Mrs. James L. Matthews'
kind invitation for dinner
on Saturday, October the fourteenth
to meet Mr. Frederick West

When the guests of honor are persons of particular importance or prominence, their names are generally placed at the top of the invitation. The words "To meet" may be used alone, as below; or the entire phrase, "To meet General and Mrs. Claude G. Alton" may be used as the first line.

INVITATION

To meet
General and Mrs. Claude G. Alton
Dr. and Mrs. John Edgar Prescott
request the pleasure of your company
at dinner
at the Stratmore
On Tuesday, September the third
at half past seven o'clock

ACCEPTANCE

To meet
General and Mrs. Claude G. Alton
Mr. and Mrs. Frank Curtis
accept with pleasure
Dr. and Mrs. John Edgar Prescott's
kind invitation for dinner
at the Stratmore
On Tuesday, September the third
at half past seven o'clock

REGRET

Mr. and Mrs. Frank Curtis
regret that owing to illness
they are unable to accept
Dr. and Mrs. John Edgar Prescott's
kind invitation for dinner
On Tuesday, September the third
to meet General and Mrs. Claude G. Alton

DINNER TO CELEBRATE A SPECIAL OCCASION

INVITATION

Mr. and Mrs. Paul Davis
request the pleasure of your company
at dinner
on the Tenth Anniversary of their marriage
Sunday, the fifteenth of June
at seven o'clock
227 Lake Drive

ACCEPTANCE

Mr. and Mrs. Robert G. Trent
accept with pleasure
Mr. and Mrs. Paul Davis'
invitation for dinner
on the Tenth Anniversary of their marriage
Sunday, the fifteenth of June
at seven o'clock

Dinner to Introduce a Debutante Daughter

INVITATION

Dr. and Mrs. John Edgar Prescott
request the pleasure of your company
at dinner
in honor of their daughter
Miss Laura Prescott
on Saturday, the ninth of November
at eight o'clock
The Ritz-Crown

Please send reply to
227 Park Avenue[2]

REGRET

Mr. and Mrs. Maynard Knox
regret that they are unable to accept
Dr. and Mrs. John E. Prescott's
invitation for dinner
in honor of their daughter
Miss Laura Prescott
on Saturday, the ninth of November
as they will be abroad at that time

How to Postpone or Cancel Formal Dinner Invitations

Occasionally a dinner party must be canceled or postponed due to illness or other circumstances. If there is no time to write, the hostess (or someone representing her) telephones or telegraphs all guests. Otherwise brief notes like the following are written—in the third person, but not with indented spacing:

1. Dr. and Mrs. John Edgar Prescott regret that, owing to the severe illness of their daughter, the dinner arranged for next Saturday must be postponed.
2. Dr. and Mrs. John Edgar Prescott wish to announce that the dinner planned for next Tuesday, in honor of their niece, is temporarily postponed due to illness in the family.

[2]The letters R.s.v.p. (abbreviation for "Répondez s'il vous plaît") are still frequently used on invitations; but the preference today is for the simple English phrase, "Please reply."

3. Mr. and Mrs. Thomas L. Whitney regret that they are obliged to recall their invitations for Wednesday, June the tenth, because of the death of their nephew, Mr. James Carter Pell.

4. Owing to injuries sustained in an automobile accident, Mr. and Mrs. Peter Kenway regret that they must cancel their dinner planned for Thursday, October the third.

5. Mr. and Mrs. Clarence Harper wish to announce that the dinner planned for next Saturday has been postponed until the following Saturday, November the fifth, owing to the fact that Mr. Harper has been unexpectedly called out of town.

Bear in mind that these are *formal* notes, correct only when engraved invitations have been sent out.

How to Break a Formal Dinner Engagement

If a dinner engagement must be broken, the hostess should be notified at once by letter or by telephone. The reason for not being able to attend should be given.

Dear Mrs. Prescott:
Mr. Houghton has been called to Chicago by the sudden grave illness of his mother. I'm quite sure he won't be back in time for your dinner on Thursday.
We are both extremely sorry to break our engagement at this late date. We hope that you and Dr. Prescott will understand and forgive us.
With many regrets,

Sincerely yours,
Florence T. Houghton

Inviting a Friend to Fill an Empty Place at Dinner

When a hostess finds herself short one dinner guest, due to the fact that someone was unable to come at the last minute, the usual thing is to call on a friend to fill in the gap. If time is short, she telephones; otherwise she writes a note frankly explaining the situation and asking the friend to fill in as a special favor.

Dear Bill:
I hope you have no plans for this Wednesday night, the twelfth—as I'd like you to fill in at my dinner party. One of my guests has just telephoned that he can't come because of illness.
I'm putting it to you very frankly, Bill—as you can see! I need another guest; and Frank and I can think of no one we'd rather have than you.

So will you overlook the informality of this invitation and make us both very happy by accepting?

Dinner is at seven, and we do hope you can come!

Sincerely,
Thelma Cranston

Such an invitation is more likely than not to be acknowledged by telephone, as there is usually no time to respond by letter. However if there is time, a cordial and friendly note is indicated—one that either accepts with grace, or that gives some very good reason for not accepting:

Dear Thelma:

Of course you can count on me for Wednesday night! I'm very glad to come. You know I always look forward with great pleasure to your dinner parties.

Thanks to you and Frank for asking me!

Cordially,
Bill Stevens

Dear Thelma:

I certainly wish I could accept your tempting invitation for Wednesday night! I always enjoy your dinner parties so thoroughly. However I've already accepted an invitation for that evening, and I couldn't possibly make a change in plans at this late date—much as I might like to! I'm sure you understand.

My very best to you and Frank, and thanks for asking me.

Cordially,
Bill Stevens

INFORMAL DINNER INVITATIONS AND ACKNOWLEDGMENTS

A note inviting people informally to dinner is always written by the hostess for her husband and herself. It is addressed to "Mrs." only (not "Mr. and Mrs.")—but the note itself always includes mention of the husband.

Dear Mrs. Carter:

Will you and Mr. Carter have dinner with us on Friday, the fourth of September, at seven o'clock?

We do hope you can come, as it's such a long time since we have had the pleasure of seeing you.

Sincerely yours,
Margaret B. Prescott

Such a note of invitation should be acknowledged promptly, with a definite acceptance or regret. The answer should be a specific "Yes, we'll be delighted to come!"—or "So sorry! We can't come because . . ."

Dear Mrs. Prescott:

Mr. Carter and I will be delighted to dine with you on Friday, the fourth of September, at seven o'clock. How very nice of you to ask us!

We are looking forward with great pleasure to seeing you and Dr. Prescott again.

Sincerely yours,
Marjorie Carter

In declining a dinner invitation, the reason for not being able to accept should be given. And of course it's courteous to say how sorry you are:

Dear Mrs. Prescott:

Mr. Carter has been at his branch office in Montreal for the past two weeks. I kept putting off this note, hoping he'd get back in time for your dinner party. But now I must regretfully write that he'll still be out of town on Friday, September fourth—and we therefore cannot accept your kind invitation for dinner on that day.

I'm so sorry to miss an evening with you and Dr. Prescott. And I know Mr. Carter will be just as sorry as I am to miss such a delightful occasion. Thank you for asking us!

Cordially,
Marjorie Carter

Always bear in mind that even to an intimate friend, an invitation should be an *invitation*—not a minor detail lost in a long account of local news and family gossip. Any invitation assumes greater significance, appears far more important to the person who receives it, when it's sent as a special and separate communication . . . instead of just part of a chatty letter. Here, for example, is how one might invite a close friend to dinner:

Peggy, dear:

Get out that busy little engagement book of yours and make note of a date with us for Tuesday, November the second. Dick and I are having some of our very special friends for dinner that evening—and naturally the party wouldn't be complete without you and Fred.

Now don't tell us you have something planned for that evening, because we just won't take "no" for an answer! The Reeds and the Whitneys are coming, and perhaps we can play some bridge afterward.

Dinner is at seven, as usual. We'll be looking for you two charming people at that time, so don't disappoint us!

Affectionately,
Susan

If you cannot accept a dinner invitation, you must explain why—even to a very close friend. It's neither necessary nor desirable to make long, involved explanations; but your note should sound as though you were genuinely sorry:

Dear Susan:
I wish we could accept your invitation for November second. I certainly hate to miss an evening with you and Dick . . . and Fred feels the same as I do about it.
But unfortunately we've already accepted an invitation for the second, and we can't very well get out of it. Fred's partner and his wife are celebrating their tenth wedding anniversary that evening, and we've promised to be with them. I'm sure you understand.
You were sweet to ask us, Susan. I know we are missing a wonderful evening, and I do wish we could be with you!

Affectionately,
Peggy

WHEN A DAUGHTER ACTS AS HOSTESS IN A MOTHERLESS HOME

When the daughter of a household acts as hostess for her father, she does not send out dinner invitations in her own name. She makes it clear that she is acting for her father. For example:

Dear Mrs. Jennings:
Father wishes me to ask if you and Mr. Jennings can dine with us on Wednesday, March the third, at seven o'clock.
We hope you can come, and look forward to seeing you.

Sincerely yours,
Ellen Hunter

The response to any invitation should go to the person who writes it. Therefore acknowledgment of the invitation above must go to the daughter, not the father.

ACCEPTANCE

Dear Miss Hunter:
Mr. Jennings and I are delighted to accept your father's kind invitation for Wednesday, March third, at seven o'clock.
We are looking forward with great pleasure to seeing you both!

Cordially yours,
Martha P. Jennings

REGRET

Dear Miss Hunter:

I'm so sorry, but a previous engagement prevents us from accepting your father's kind invitation for Wednesday, March the third.

Please tell him that Mr. Jennings and I thank him for asking us, and we deeply regret that we cannot come.

Our kindest regards to you both,

Sincerely yours,
Martha P. Jennings

FORMAL LUNCHEON INVITATIONS AND ACKNOWLEDGMENTS

Formal third-person invitations are used only when the luncheon is a large and ceremonious affair . . . as, for example, to announce an engagement, to celebrate a wedding anniversary, to present a debutante daughter, or perhaps to honor some special guest. Such socially important luncheons warrant the dignity and formality of engraved invitations. They are sent out two or three weeks in advance, and are similar in phraseology to dinner invitations:

Dr. and Mrs. John Edgar Prescott
request the pleasure of

Mr. and Mrs. James T. Millard's

company at luncheon
in honor of their daughter
Miss Laura Prescott
on Saturday, November the second
at one o'clock
277 Park Avenue

Please respond

Such an invitation should be acknowledged at once with a definite acceptance or regret. The wording should follow the same formal wording as the invitation.

As a rule, luncheons are not given jointly by a husband and wife, except for special occasions like the above. Most men cannot attend social functions in the middle of the day; and luncheons are therefore generally planned for women alone and are issued in the name of the hostess alone. The name of the host does not appear unless he is to be present at the luncheon, and men are to be included among the guests.

Following is the standard form of invitation for an elaborate formal luncheon for women—whether at home, club or hotel. It may be engraved for a large number of guests; but should be handwritten if only six or eight guests are invited:

Mrs. Franklin J. Pierce
requests the pleasure of
your company at luncheon
on Friday, September the seventh
at one o'clock
Ten Sutton Place

Please respond

ACCEPTANCE

Mrs. Wayne H. Klint
accepts with pleasure
Mrs. Franklin J. Pierce's
invitation for luncheon
on Friday, September the seventh
at one o'clock

REGRET

Mrs. Wayne H. Klint
regrets that a previous engagement
prevents her from accepting
Mrs. Franklin J. Pierce's
invitation for luncheon
on Friday, September the seventh

When a large and elaborate luncheon is given by two or more women, the invitations are generally engraved, and the names of all the women appear on it:

Mrs. John E. Prescott
Mrs. Frederick G. Blanchard
Mrs. James Mathes
request the pleasure of
your company at luncheon
On Wednesday, April the eleventh
at half past one o'clock
The Royal Plaza

Please reply to
Mrs. John E. Prescott
277 Park Avenue

Your reply to the above invitation should list all the names of the hostesses, exactly as in the invitation. But the envelope should be addressed only to the person whose name and address are indicated in the lower left corner. If no name and address are given, the envelope should be addressed to *all* the hostesses and sent to the hotel, as it can be assumed that arrangements have been made to receive them there.

INFORMAL LUNCHEON INVITATIONS AND ACKNOWLEDGMENTS

For simple, informal luncheons, a telephone call is more likely than not to be the only invitation. But there are many who prefer writing personal notes of invitation, like the following:

Dear Alice:
Can you come to luncheon on Tuesday, May the sixth, at one o'clock?
My sister, Janet, is here on a brief visit and I'd like to have you meet her. She's the sister who lives in Texas; I'm sure you've heard me speak of her many times.
Doris and Suzanne will be here, and perhaps we can play some bridge after luncheon. So do say you'll come! I know you'll enjoy meeting Janet, and she's most eager to meet you.

Affectionately,
Eileen

ACCEPTANCE

Dear Eileen:
Of course I'll come to your luncheon on Tuesday, May sixth! I'll be there promptly at one, and I'm certainly looking forward to it.
It will be nice meeting your sister; I've heard so much about her. But most of all, Eileen, I'm looking forward to seeing you. It's been a long time since I had that pleasure.

Affectionately,
Alice

REGRET

Dear Eileen:
I'd love to come to your luncheon and meet your sister, but unfortunately I can't. Tuesday, May sixth, is the day of Judy's recital; and naturally all the mothers will be there. I couldn't possibly let Judy down; she'd never forgive me if I weren't there to hear her play.
So much as I'd like to, Eileen, I can't say "yes." I'm sure you understand. Please express my regrets to your sister and tell her I hope to have the pleasure of meeting her some other time.
Thank you so much for asking me!

Yours affectionately,
Alice

SUPPER INVITATIONS AND ACKNOWLEDGMENTS

As a rule, supper parties are very informal. Guests are more often than not intimate friends or members of the family; and invitations are usually telephoned.[3] But a written note of invitation makes the occasion seem more important:

Dear Barbara:
We're having some friends in for a buffet supper on Sunday night, April the tenth—and of course we want you and Tom.
We'll have an early supper and play bridge afterward. So come at six, if you can. The Petersons and the Cortwrights will be here, and I know you always enjoy their company.
Bill and I are looking forward to seeing you; it's been a long time since you've been here!

Affectionately,
Claire

Ordinarily your presence at the supper party is all the acknowledgment necessary to an invitation like the above. Of course if you like to be especially courteous and considerate, you may write a brief note to let your hostess know you'll be there; but it isn't actually required. However if you cannot attend the party, you must reply at once, by telephone or by note:

Dear Claire:
I wish we could come to your buffet supper on Sunday, the tenth—but we're going to a wedding that evening. One of Tom's friends at the office is being married, and we have already accepted the invitation.
I'm awfully sorry, Claire. Tom and I hate missing your parties—they're always such fun. But thanks so much for asking us; and we hope to see you both real soon.

Affectionately,
Barbara

If an elaborate and ceremonious supper party is given for some special occasion, the invitations should of course conform. Either visiting-card invitations should be used[4] or invitations should be engraved in third-person style, as for a formal dinner or luncheon.[5]

[3]For invitations by telephone, see page 122.
[4]For visiting card invitation to a buffet supper, see page 50.
[5]For formal supper dance invitation, see page 309.

4. DANCE AND PARTY INVITATIONS AND ACKNOWLEDGMENTS

THE word "ball" is rarely used on invitations nowadays, except for a large public subscription dance or a charity affair. For ordinary social invitations, formal or informal, the word "dance" is used.

Invitations for formal dances are usually engraved, and are sent out two to three weeks in advance. Following are the most familiar and acceptable forms:

Mr. and Mrs. Wilbur T. Cantrell
request the pleasure of your company
at a small[1] dance
Wednesday, the first of June
at ten o'clock
The Sherry-Walton

Please reply to
485 Park Avenue

The fill-in-type of invitation, with the guest's name written in by hand, is somewhat more personal and many people prefer it. Instead of "at a small dance" in the body of the invitation, the word "Dancing" may be used in the lower right corner.

Mr. and Mrs. Wilbur T. Cantrell
request the pleasure of

Dr. and Mrs. John E. Prescott's

company on Wednesday, the first of June
at ten o'clock
The Sherry-Walton

Please reply to   Dancing
485 Park Avenue

[1]The phrase "a small dance" frequently appears on formal invitations, regardless of the size of the function.

The most formal invitation of all is the "At Home" with "Dancing" in the lower left or right corner. It may be used whether the dance is for twenty or thirty people in a private house or for several hundred people, with an entire floor of a large hotel engaged for the purpose:

Mr. and Mrs. Elliot Rogers
At Home
Tuesday, the third of March
at ten o'clock
The Stafford Arms

Kindly send reply to   Dancing
96 High Terrace

When a dance is given in honor of an important guest, the name of that person should appear on the invitation. Either of these two forms is correct:

Dr. and Mrs. John Edgar Prescott
request the pleasure of your company
at a dance in honor of
Miss Julia Powell
Thursday, the eighth of September
at ten o'clock
The Ritz-Crown

OR

To Meet
Miss Julia Powell
Dr. and Mrs. John Edgar Prescott
request the pleasure of

Mr. and Mrs. Foster Kendrick's

company on Thursday, the eighth of September
at ten o'clock
The Ritz-Crown

Dancing

Invitations for formal masquerade or costume dances are exactly like those for any other formal dance, except that "costume dance," "masquerade," or "fancy dress" appears somewhere on the invitation to show what kind of dance it is. For example:

Mr. and Mrs. Elliot Rogers
request the pleasure of your company
at a costume dance for their daughter
Miss Emily Rogers
Friday, the ninth of March
at nine o'clock
The Rivercrest

OR

Mr. and Mrs. Elliot Rogers
request the pleasure of your company
at a small dance
to be given at their home
on Friday, the ninth of March
at nine o'clock
96 High Terrace

Please respond   Fancy Dress

If a special kind of costume is to be worn, it should of course be
indicated on the invitation.

DEBUTANTE DANCES AND DINNER DANCES

Following is the usual form of invitation for a dance in honor of a
debutante daughter:

Mr. and Mrs. Harrison Barclay
request the pleasure of

Miss Laura Prescott's

company at a dance in honor of their daughter
Miss Elizabeth Barclay
Tuesday evening, October the second
at ten o'clock
Nine East Sixtieth Street

R.s.v.p.

Instead of the above, a formal "at home" invitation may be used. The name of the debutante appears below that of her parents at the top of the invitation:

Mr. and Mrs. Harrison Barclay
Miss Elizabeth Barclay
At Home
Tuesday, October the second
at ten o'clock
Nine East Sixtieth Street

Please respond   Dancing

Or if the dance is at a club or hotel, the following type of invitation may be used:

Mr. and Mrs. Harrison Barclay
request the pleasure of your company
at a small dance in honor of their daughter
Miss Elizabeth Barclay
on Tuesday, October the second
at ten o'clock
The Ridgewood

By far the most popular type of entertainment for a debutante is a dinner dance. As a rule, two groups of guests are invited: one group for dinner and dancing, another for dancing only. When this is the case, two sets of invitations are issued: dance invitations for those who are to come after dinner; and invitations like the following for those who are invited for both dinner and dancing:

Mr. and Mrs. Harrison Barclay
request the pleasure of your company
at dinner
in honor of their daughter
Miss Elizabeth Barclay
Tuesday, October the second
at eight o'clock
The Ridgewood

Please reply to   Dancing at ten
Nine East Sixtieth Street

Supper Dance Invitations

When a formal supper party with dancing is given for a special guest or for a debutante daughter, engraved formal invitations are indicated. Following are two examples: the first for a supper dance at home to introduce a debutante daughter, the second for a supper dance at a hotel, to introduce a new daughter-in-law.

Mr. and Mrs. Harrison Barclay
Miss Elizabeth Barclay
request the pleasure of your company
at a supper dance
Tuesday, October the second
at half past ten o'clock
Nine East Sixtieth Street
The favor of a reply
is requested

To meet
Mrs. Martin Caldwell
Mr. and Mrs. William G. Caldwell
request the pleasure of your company
at a supper dance
on Thursday, September the fifth
at ten o'clock
The Waldmore
R.s.v.p.
Twelve University Place

Tea Dance Invitation

The invitation for an afternoon tea with dancing is generally a formal "at home" with the name of the hostess and her guest of honor at the top:

Mrs. William G. Caldwell
Mrs. Martin Caldwell
At Home
on Thursday, the fifth of September
from four until seven o'clock
The Glenbilt
Dancing

Acknowledging Formal Dance Invitations

Formal invitations should be answered in formal third-person phraseology, and preferably in the same decorative spacing.

TYPICAL ACCEPTANCES

Dr. and Mrs. John E. Prescott
accept with pleasure
Mr. and Mrs. Wilbur T. Cantrell's
kind invitation to be present
for dancing
on Wednesday, the first of June
at ten o'clock
at the Sherry-Walton

Mr. and Mrs. Henry Armstrong
accept with pleasure
Mr. and Mrs. John Emmett's
and
Mr. and Mrs. Raymond L. Smith's
kind invitation for dancing
on Tuesday, the fifth of October
at ten o'clock
at the Lynncrest Country Club

Miss Laura Prescott
accepts with pleasure
Mr. and Mrs. Harrison Barclay's
invitation to a dance in honor of
Miss Elizabeth Barclay
on Tuesday, October the second
at ten o'clock

TYPICAL REGRETS

Dr. and Mrs. John E. Prescott
regret that they are unable to accept
Mr. and Mrs. Wilbur T. Cantrell's
kind invitation for dancing
on Wednesday, the first of June
at ten o'clock
owing to a previous engagement

Mr. and Mrs. Foster Kendrick
regret that they will be unable to attend
Dr. and Mrs. John E. Prescott's
dance in honor of
Miss Julia Powell
on Thursday, the eighth of September
as they will be out of town

Mr. and Mrs. Peter Worth
regret that owing to illness
they are unable to accept
Mr. and Mrs. Elliot Rogers'
kind invitation to a costume dance
for their daughter
Miss Emily Rogers
on Thursday, the ninth of March

SUBSCRIPTION DANCES AND CHARITY BALLS

The use of the word "ball" is correct only on invitations to public subscription or charity dances. As attendance to such dances is by paid subscription, no formal acceptance or regret need be written. The return of an enclosed form or card with a check for tickets is the only acknowledgment required or expected.

The Entertainment Committee of the Midvale Club
requests the pleasure of your company
at a Ball
to be held at the club house
on Friday, the fifth of September
at ten o'clock
for the benefit of
The Midvale Hospital

Tickets five dollars

OR

The pleasure of your company is requested
at the
Annual Masquerade Ball
of the Midvale Advertising Club
to be held at the Fairview Hotel
on Tuesday, the fifteenth of September
at half past ten o'clock
for the benefit of
The Children's Aid Society

The subscription is three dollars
for each person

Dance invitations issued by a club usually list the names of the patrons or patronesses. They may appear on the face of the invitation, as shown below; or they may be listed separately on the inside of the invitation.

The pleasure of your company is requested
at a
Spring Dance
on Saturday evening, the second of June
at ten o'clock
The Terrace Club

Patronesses

Mrs. Thomas Ames   Mrs. Curt Mumford
Mrs. John Halliday   Mrs. Anthony Farrell
Mrs. Arthur Hurst   Mrs. Charles Preston

Please send reply to
Dance Committee   Tickets five dollars
The Terrace Club   for each person

As a rule, the invitation to a subscription dinner dance gives the name of the person through whom reservations can be made:

The Graduating Class of 1938
Hahnemann Medical College and Hospital
invites you to attend a
Dinner Dance
at
The Stratvue-Belmont
Wednesday, the fourth of October
at half past seven o'clock
Make reservations through
Miss Margaret Baker   Tickets five dollars
11 Rittenhouse Square   for each person

INFORMAL DANCE INVITATIONS AND ACKNOWLEDGMENTS

Invitations for informal dances may be by telephone or by note. It is always more gracious to write a friendly note instead of telephoning, if there is time to do so. The note may be as brief as you like, but it should be cordial.

Dear Harriet:

We are having a little dance on Saturday, September the fourth, to celebrate our tenth wedding anniversary. Can you and Steve come?

The dancing starts at nine—and I hope you'll be here! We'd like all the members of our original bridal party to be with us that evening. Keith and I are looking forward with great pleasure to seeing you both.

Cordially,
Annette

Dear Julie:

My brother Richard will be home for the Thanksgiving holiday next week. Mother has asked me to invite a few friends to a small, informal dance she is giving for him on Friday evening, the twenty-third, at nine o'clock.

I'd like very much to have you and your brother George come. There'll be dancing until eleven, and a buffet supper afterward. I think I can promise you a good time, and I know Richard will be delighted to see you both.

So *do* come if you possibly can!

Affectionately,
Pat

ACCEPTANCE

Dear Annette:

Can it really be ten whole years? It doesn't seem possible! Of course Steve and I will come and help you celebrate. In fact, we wouldn't miss it for anything.

So count on us for Saturday, September the fourth, at nine o'clock. I just can't tell you how much we're looking forward to it!

Congratulations and our very best wishes to you and Keith on your tenth anniversary.

Affectionately,
Harriet

Dear Pat:

I'd love to come to your dance for Richard on Friday, the twenty-third —but the whole family's going to Boston for Thanksgiving to be with my grandmother, and we won't get back until Sunday.

It was swell of you to ask me, Pat, and I'm awfully sorry to miss it. George is as disappointed as I am. He says to be sure and thank you for asking him.

We hope Richard will still be here when we get back, and that we'll have a chance to say "Hello" to him. In the meantime, please give him our very best regards!

Affectionately,
Julie

REQUESTING AN INVITATION FOR A FRIEND

One may request an invitation to an informal dance for a relative or friend, but never for one's self. A letter making the request might read somewhat as follows:

Dear Alice:

We have a friend from California visiting us this week; and as he doesn't know anyone else in town, we don't like to leave him alone for an evening.

So may we bring him to your dance on the eighth? He's a most charming and congenial person, and I'm sure you and Paul will enjoy meeting him.

But if you'd rather not have an extra guest, Betty—please say so! We'll understand; and we'll get him a ticket for the theater or something for the evening of the dance.

Affectionately,
Jane

A courteous hostess will reply at once, inviting the stranger or explaining why she cannot do so. For example:

Dear Jane:

Of course bring your friend to the dance on Friday the eighth! We'll be delighted to meet him, and to have him spend the evening with us.

Paul and I are looking forward with great pleasure to seeing you.

Affectionately,
Alice

OR

Dear Jane:

I certainly wish I could include your friend among my guests for Friday, the eighth; but I can't! I have already invited more people than I can comfortably accommodate.

I'm sure you understand, and that you will come to the dance anyway —as Paul and I are looking forward to seeing you.

Affectionately,
Alice

INVITATION FOR AN INFORMAL COCKTAIL PARTY

Dear Mary:

Can you and Bob come for cocktails on Thursday, May the tenth, from four to six?

It's a long time since we have seen you; so do come if you can! Quite a few of your friends will be here.

Cordially,
Anne

For a Formal Cocktail Party

Dr. and Mrs. John Edgar Prescott
At Home
Tuesday, June the fifth
from four until six o'clock
277 Park Avenue

Cocktails

It is not necessary to acknowledge an invitation to a cocktail party, unless a reply is specifically requested. You accept by attending; but if you cannot attend, a brief note of regret should be sent at once.

For an Informal Tea Party

Dear Mrs. Carter:
Some of your good friends and mine are coming for tea on Wednesday, April the sixth, at four o'clock. I hope you can join us.
Rita Martell will be one of the guests, and she has promised to sing for us. So do come if you possibly can.

Sincerely yours,
Myra T. Cranston

For a Formal Tea

Mrs. John Edgar Prescott
Miss Laura Prescott
At Home
Tuesday afternoon, October second
from four until seven o'clock
277 Park Avenue

For Garden Parties

Mr. and Mrs. Harold G. Fox
At Home
in the garden
Thursday, June the twenty-eighth
from three to six o'clock

Dear Helen:

We'd like our friends to see our garden—it has never been as lovely as it is now. So we're having tea on the lawn next Thursday, June the twenty-eighth, from three to six o'clock.

We hope you and Fred can come. It's been much too long since we've had the pleasure of your company!

Affectionately,
Janet

Acknowledgment of a tea, reception or garden party invitation is not necessary, unless requested. You accept by attending. But if you cannot attend, you send regrets at once—in traditional third-person phraseology for a formal invitation, in the form of a brief friendly note for an informal invitation.

NOTE: For wedding invitations and acknowledgments, see Part III, Chapter 3. For invitations to bridge parties, showers, christenings, house and week-end parties, children's parties, etc., see the chapters on these specific subjects.

5. LETTERS OF CONGRATULATION

MAKE it a point to write letters of congratulation promptly, as soon as you hear the news of an engagement, marriage or birth. Don't wait until your interest has cooled off. A note of congratulation always sounds more enthusiastic and sincere if it's written when you are still excited by the news.

CONGRATULATIONS ON AN ENGAGEMENT

It is not considered good form to congratulate a young lady on her engagement. The man is congratulated—the lady is sent good wishes for her happiness.

Dear Harriet:

What wonderful news! I just can't tell you how delighted I am to hear of your engagement to Floyd Sanders. Let me be among the first to wish you every joy and happiness.

I think Floyd's a lucky chap to have won a marvelous girl like you; please tell him for me that I congratulate him!

Affectionately,
Barbara

Dear Floyd:

We've just heard the news about you and Harriet. I can't say we were exactly surprised, as we've been expecting it for some time. But we're certainly pleased and delighted—and very happy for both of you.

Bill and I send you our warmest congratulations. We wish you and Harriet every good fortune, and a lifetime of happiness together.

Sincerely,
Patricia Ames

CONGRATULATIONS ON MARRIAGE

Dear Katherine:

It was certainly a pleasant surprise to receive the announcement of your marriage in this morning's mail. Let me wish you the best of luck, and every possible happiness.

My congratulations to you and Mr. Fenton; and may life bring the best of everything to both of you!

Sincerely,
Ruth Banning

Dear Katherine:

You and Jimmy have certainly taken all your friends by surprise! I was thrilled and delighted to hear the news.

I hope you'll write and tell me all about the wedding, Kathy. I'd love to hear about it.

In the meantime, my best wishes to you both—and may you always be as happy as you are right now!

Fondly,
Janet

Dear Mrs. Fenton:

This is to wish you and Mr. Fenton every happiness in your marriage.

Mr. Thomas joins me in wishing you both great joy and success in your life together.

Sincerely yours,
Martha P. Thomas

CONGRATULATIONS ON A WEDDING ANNIVERSARY

Dear Lenore:

Is it really five years since you and Dan were married? It just doesn't seem possible!

Fred and I send congratulations, and our sincere wishes for your continued happiness.

May the next five years bring you even greater joy and contentment!

Affectionately,
Claire

Dear Anne and Ted:

Congratulations on your tenth wedding anniversary! Bill and I send you both our love, and our very best wishes for the future.

Too bad there's a continent between us; it would be wonderful to see you and give you our congratulations in person. But I'm sure you know we are thinking of you today, and wishing you everything good and fine in life.

We hope you will have many, many more anniversaries, each one happier than the one before!

Affectionately,
Doris

Dear Mrs. Owens:

I have just learned that you and Mr. Owens are celebrating your fiftieth wedding anniversary in a few days. I take pleasure in adding my good wishes to those of your many admiring neighbors and friends.

Surely this must be a very proud milestone in your long and happy life! I know of no other two people who have accumulated so many friends along the way, who have so completely won the respect and affection of everyone in the community.

Sincere congratulations from Mr. Sanborn and myself. We wish you both many more years of happiness.

Cordially yours,
Julia T. Sanborn

CONGRATULATIONS ON A BIRTHDAY

It's gracious and thoughtful to write personal notes to your friends on their birthdays, instead of sending ready-made greeting cards. There is no objection to such cards, of course; they are universally used—and at least they show that you have not forgotten the day. But no printed sentiment, however eloquent, can possibly mean as much as a few sincere words in your own handwriting.

Dear Judy:

I'm thinking of you on your birthday, and wishing you the best of everything—now and always! Congratulations, my dear, and many happy returns of the day.

Next time you come into town to do some shopping, call me and I'll meet you for lunch. It's been much, much too long since we have seen each other!

Affectionately,
Caroline

Dear Aunt Emily:

I wish you didn't live so far away! I'd love to see you and be with you on your birthday.

But as I can't, I'm doing the next best thing: I'm sending you a little gift I hope you'll like. And with it go my love, my congratulations, and my very best wishes for the coming year.

I hope you'll have many, many happy birthdays, Aunt Emily—and that you'll never lose the cheerful outlook and gay spirits that have made you so well-loved by all the family.

John and the children join me in sending congratulations. Love from all of us,

Paula

Dear Harold:

My brother tells me it's your birthday. So I'm sending congratulations and my best wishes for many happy returns of the day!

Sincerely,
Mary Lou

Dear Mary:

Congratulations on your birthday! May I take you to dinner and the movies to celebrate? I'll telephone Tuesday to find out what evening you prefer; and in the meantime—happy birthday to you!

Cordially,
Jack

Congratulations on the Birth of a Child

Dear Helen:

I've just heard the wonderful news. I'm so glad it's a girl, because I know that's what you wanted—and I can just imagine how happy you are.

Congratulations to you and Pete, from both of us! And best wishes to the little newcomer. Bill joins me in wishing you two proud parents a lifetime of joy and pleasure in your new daughter.

Affectionately,
Alice

Dear Mrs. Kinney:

Heartiest congratulations to you and Mr. Kinney on your new son. I hear he is quite a handsome young fellow, and I'm looking forward to seeing him when you return from the hospital.

Mr. Elliot joins me in sending congratulations and best wishes.

Sincerely yours,
Francine Elliot

CONGRATULATIONS ON GRADUATION

Dear Marc:

I understand you have received your doctorate in philosophy from Princeton University. May I offer my congratulations?

Your brother has told me of your interesting plans for the future, and I certainly wish you every success. All your old friends here in Midvale are very proud of you!

Cordially,
Bob Fleming

Dear Edwin:

Your mother has just told me of your graduation from Dartmouth, and I should like to add my congratulations to the many you are receiving.

Please accept my best wishes for your future success and happiness. I am sure you will distinguish yourself in whatever you undertake.

Sincerely yours,
Margaret Crawford

Dear Claire:

Congratulations on your graduation from Vassar. I have been hearing on all sides how brilliantly you distinguished yourself.

And congratulations also on that exciting radio job in New York! I know it's what you've always wanted to do, and I'm sure you'll be a great success.

I'm sorry, as all your friends are, that you are leaving Midvale; but I'm glad you have this opportunity, and I wish you the best of luck!

Sincerely,
Roger Haskins

6. LETTERS OF THANKS

EVERY gift, however trifling, should be acknowledged with a note of thanks. The truly gracious person also makes sure that every favor or courtesy, every kindness or attention on the part of a neighbor or friend—certainly every letter of condolence or congratulation—is given prompt and gracious acknowledgment.

A thank-you note should have the ring of sincerity, achieved only when you really *feel* grateful and appreciative. So don't put off writing your note of thanks. Write it quickly, while the glow is still with you. Then you won't need to grope for words; trying to sound sincere; the words will come of their own accord.

Notes of thanks should be written by hand. Well-bred people do not use printed cards or forms. Only public officials or celebrities may be forgiven the use of printed thank-you cards; as following large public funerals or receptions there may be hundreds, or even thousands, of persons whose flowers, expressions of sympathy, or congratulations, etc., must be acknowledged. But surely in private life any courtesy or kindness which deserves thanks deserves the warmth and friendly expression of a personal message.

For Wedding Gifts

It's a wise bride who promptly acknowledges each wedding gift as it arrives, instead of letting the thank-yous pile up and become a problem. She personally acknowledges *all* gifts, including those to her husband from business associates who are strangers to her.

To a Relative

Dear Aunt Mary:

I just don't know how to thank you and Uncle Fred for the simply gorgeous little boudoir clock you sent us! It's one of the loveliest wedding gifts we have received.

Kenneth is as delighted with it as I am, and we both want you to know how much we appreciate your generosity.

Do come and visit us soon, Aunt Mary, and see how beautiful the clock looks on our dresser.

With love,
Cynthia

To an Intimate Friend

Betty, dear:

What a magnificent dinner cloth! I'll be just about the proudest hostess in all New York when I use it.

Thank you, darling—for Kenneth and me. It's a wonderful gift, and I hope you know how much we appreciate it.

We're looking forward to seeing you at the wedding.

Affectionately,
Cynthia

To a Neighbor

Dear Mrs. Walsh:

How sweet of you and Mr. Walsh to send us a gift—and such a handsome one! We're simply thrilled with the salad bowl, and you can be sure we'll take great pleasure and pride in using it.

Many thanks to you both, from my fiance and myself. We hope you will come and see us when we are settled in our own home.

Cordially yours,
Cynthia Clark

To a Business Associate of the Groom

Dear Mr. Marshall:
Thank you so much for the handsome tray you sent Kenneth[1] and me. It's one of the most useful gifts we have received—and you can be sure we'll use it with great pleasure and pride.

Sincerely yours,
Cynthia Clark

FOR SHOWER GIFTS

It's courteous to acknowledge shower gifts individually, with a brief but cordial note of thanks.

Dear Julia:
I must thank you again for the beautiful guest towels. I was so excited at the shower on Saturday that I'm sure I didn't express myself adequately.

The towels are simply lovely, Julia, and I'm thrilled as I can be with them. I always said you have wonderful taste!

I'm looking forward to seeing you on the twelfth.

Affectionately,
Sally

A special note of thanks goes to the hostess who planned the party and provided the refreshments:

Dear Elaine:
It was sweet of you to give a shower for me, and I appreciate it more than I can say. I don't know how you managed to keep it such a secret! It was a complete surprise to me, and a thrill I'll never forget.

Walter and I are overwhelmed by the wealth of lovely linens we have suddenly acquired. Your luncheon cloth is especially lovely, Elaine. I am *doubly* indebted to you—for the party and for your generous gift!

Thanks from both of us, for everything.

With love,
Sally

[1]Use of the first or last name here depends upon the degree of intimacy between the persons involved.

For Christmas Gifts

Dear Aunt Martha:

I'm simply thrilled with the beautiful umbrella you sent me for Christmas. How did you know I needed one?

Thank you very much, Aunt Martha. I'll think of you with affection every time I use my lovely new umbrella.

I hope you had a wonderful Christmas, and that you'll come to Midvale real soon.

With love,
Doris

Dear Bob:

As you can see, I am writing this note on the handsome stationery you sent me for Christmas. It was sweet of you to remember me, Bob, and I appreciate it very much.

I hope you had a pleasant Christmas. My best wishes to you and your family for a very happy New Year.

Sincerely,
Evelyn

For Birthday Gifts

Dear Alice:

You have a real talent for selecting gifts! The scarf is just exactly what I needed to go with my new suit. I'm delighted with it—and with you, for remembering my birthday.

Many thanks, Alice—for the scarf, and for your very charming birthday wishes.

Affectionately,
Hazel

Dear Arthur:

I must admit I was flattered that you remembered my birthday!

Thanks for the perfume; it's one of my favorites. And thanks especially, Arthur, for your good wishes.

Sincerely,
Hazel

For Wedding Anniversary Gifts

The wedding anniversaries that are most frequently celebrated, and for which friends and relatives customarily send gifts, are:

> 1 year, Paper
> 5 years, Wood
> 10 years, Tin
> 15 years, Crystal
> 20 years, China
> 25 years, Silver
> 50 years, Gold
> 75 years, Diamond

Such gifts should, of course, be graciously acknowledged by a written note of thanks. The note is written by the wife, for her husband and herself.

Dear Emily:

How wonderful of you and Jim to remember our anniversary! Dave and I were quite overcome when the beautiful vase arrived this morning. It's standing on the piano now, filled with roses—and it makes the whole room look festive and important.

It's hard to believe that Dave and I are married for fifteen years. It certainly doesn't seem that long. And to think that you remembered, Emily! I appreciate it more than I can say.

Many thanks to you and Jim, from both of us.

> Fondly,
> Annette

For Baby Gifts

Dear Eric:

After all you have already done for us as the baby's godfather—to send such a magnificent gift! Really, Eric, we are quite overwhelmed.

The silver bowl and cup are beautiful, and I know that some day Patsy will be very, very proud of them. I just don't know how to thank you for your generosity.

Fred and I deeply appreciate your many kindnesses to us; and we hope you know how happy we are that you are Patsy's godfather.

> Affectionately,
> Claire

Dear Mrs. Sloane:

How very thoughtful of you to send a gift for the baby! Mr. Nichols and I certainly appreciate it.

The quilt is lovely—just about the prettiest one I've ever seen. And it happens to be the one thing I needed! So thank you very much, and do come and see the baby now that we are home.

Cordially,
Claire Nichols

THE BREAD-AND-BUTTER LETTER

When you receive hospitality at the home of a friend for a week end or longer, courtesy requires that you write a note of thanks within a day or two after your return home. Even though you may have personally thanked your hostess before leaving, a so-called "duty" note is expected of you. This has become known as a "bread-and-butter" letter because it thanks the hostess for the hospitality she provided.

Dear Rosalie:

I just can't tell you how much I enjoyed the week end at Pine Ridge! Every minute of it was perfect; I can't ever remember having had a better time anywhere.

It was good of you to invite me, Rosalie, and I hope you know how deeply I appreciate your hospitality. Many thanks to you and Ted for a really wonderful week end!

Affectionately,
Lenore

THANKS FOR A LETTER OF CONDOLENCE

Every message of condolence should be acknowledged by personal note. Printed thank-you cards are sometimes used, but are not considered good form except for public officials or persons of prominence who receive an overwhelming number of letters from strangers.

The reply to a note of sympathy need not be written as promptly as other notes of thanks. It may be mailed any time within six weeks after receipt of the flowers or note of sympathy. It can be brief to the point of saying nothing more than a simple "Thank you for your kind expression of sympathy." Or it can be as wordy as one's feelings and impulses at the time prompt. To an intimate friend, one might write:

Dear Margaret:

Thank you for your wonderful letter of sympathy. No one but you, who knew Betty so well—and loved her as we all did—could have written with such kindness and understanding.

Your letter meant more than I can say, and I'll always remember it with gratitude. Nor will I ever forget your many kindnesses to my sister during her illness.

> Sincerely
> Alice

A woman who has lost her husband may find it difficult to write notes of thanks even to her most intimate friends. She may ask a son or daughter, or some other close relative, to acknowledge the flowers and messages of sympathy she received.

Dear Mrs. Merton:
Mother has asked me to write to you, as she cannot do so herself right now.
She would like you and Mr. Merton to know how much she appreciates the flowers and the letter of sympathy you sent. You have both been very kind.

> Sincerely yours,
> Elizabeth Keenan

Thanks for Letters of Congratulation

Dear Kate:
Your letter made us both very happy. Thank you so much for your good wishes. If our life together proves only half as rosy as you predict, we'll be well content!
Tom joins me in hoping you'll come often to see us in Rosedale. We expect to be at home after November first.
Thanks again, and with affectionate greetings from us both,

> Cynthia

Dear Dr. Prescott:
I was very pleased to receive your note of congratulation on my election as president of the state medical society.
Thank you for writing; I deeply appreciate your good wishes.

> Sincerely yours,
> Thomas P. Edmonds, M.D.

7. LETTERS OF CONDOLENCE AND SYMPATHY

THERE is probably no time when a letter can mean so much and be so deeply appreciated as when death strikes. It always helps to know that friends are sympathetic and understanding. A few sincere and well-chosen words can give comfort even to the most grief-stricken, can renew the faith and courage of those cruelly hurt and embittered by their loss.

A good letter of condolence is like a handclasp, warm and friendly. It is written with dignity and restraint, not filled with gushy sentiment. It is *brief,* for this is no time to be wordy. It doesn't dwell on details of the illness or death, nor quote "comforting" passages from poetry or the bible. It doesn't touch on memories that reopen the floodgates of pain and sorrow.

Often, in a note of condolence, it's not so much what you say as what you *don't* say that counts. Surely there can be no comfort in a letter that says, "What a pity—she was so young to die!" or "What will you do now? You'll be lost without him!" It's better not to write at all than to write so tactlessly. A letter of condolence is written for one purpose only: to give comfort.

It shouldn't be difficult to write a good letter of condolence if you are genuinely moved to sympathy by a friend's misfortune. The important thing is to write *promptly,* as soon as you hear the news. If you write while your heart is filled with sadness, your letter will have the ring of sincerity to it.

On the Death of a Parent

Dear Marjory:

I was grieved and shocked to hear of your great loss. I know how you adored your mother, and I only wish there were something I could do or say to comfort you in your sorrow.

Walter and I send heartfelt sympathy to you and to your family. We hope you will call on us if there is anything we can do to help.

Affectionately,
Janet

Dear Miss Jenkins:

I wish to express my deepest sympathy on the death of your mother. I know what a great loss this must be to you—and I only hope that time will quickly soften the blow.

Sincerely Yours,
Leonard T. Cushing

Dear Paul:

I have heard the sad news and wish to offer my condolences. I know how devoted you were to your father, and sympathize with you deeply in your loss.

But you have the consolation, Paul, of knowing that he went quickly, without pain or suffering—which is a great blessing.

Margaret joins me in sending affection and sympathy. I am sure you know that if there is anything we can do, you need only to call on us.

Sincerely,
Alex

Dear Paul:

We were shocked and grieved to hear of your father's sudden death. Fred and I send heartfelt sympathy to you and your family.

Sincerely,
Ethel

My dear Hartley:

I was indeed sorry to hear of your loss when I returned to the office this morning. Please accept my sincere sympathy.

Cordially yours,
Jonathan P. Fredericks

On the Death of a Husband or Wife

Dear Marion:

Our hearts are filled with sympathy for you in this hour of trial. How I wish there were something we could do or say to help!

But all we can do is send you our deepest sympathy, and hope that time will soon ease your sorrow.

With love from Jim and myself,
Helen

Dear Mrs. Whitmore:

We have just learned of your husband's death and hasten to offer our condolences.

Mr. Kent and I feel for you in your great sorrow, and we sincerely wish there were some way we could help and comfort you. If there is, will you call on us? We hope you look upon us as your friends as well as your neighbors.

With profound sympathy from us both,
Sincerely,
Florence Kent

Dear Mark:

I was shocked and grieved to hear of Virginia's death.

I well realize what this great loss must mean to you, and I know there is little I can say to lessen your grief. But I'd like you to know that you have my deepest sympathy.

Sincerely,
Rosalind

Dear Mark:

My thoughts are with you today, and I wish I knew how to comfort you in your grief. If only sharing your sorrow could take some of it from you!

Arthur and I send our heartfelt sympathy; and we hope you know you can always call on us if there is ever anything we can do to help.

Affectionately,
Laura

Dear Mr. Mansfield:

I am extremely sorry to learn of the death of your wife. Please accept my sincere condolences.

With warmest personal regards,

Sincerely,
Richard T. Mason

On the Death of a Child

A message of condolence to grief-stricken parents should be very brief, and should avoid mention of any subject that may give pain.

Dear Edna:

There are just no words to express our shock and grief. Our hearts are filled with sympathy for you and Joel. Will you please let us know if there is anything we can do?

In deepest sorrow and affection,

Clara and Jack

Dear Edna and Joel:

We know that words are little consolation to you at a time like this. But Fred and I want you to know that our thoughts are with you, and that you have our love and deepest sympathy.

We hope and pray that time will soon ease the pain.

Affectionately,
Mabel

Dear Joel:

All of us here at the office have been profoundly touched by the news of your son's death. We hope you count us among those who share your grief, and would gladly share your burden if that were possible.

We send our profound sympathy to you and Mrs. Corbett. I'm sure you know we all stand ready to help if there is anything we can do.

Sincerely,
Edgar Hollis

On the Death of a Brother or Sister

Dear Laura:

Your brother's death has come as a great shock to all of us who knew and admired him.

I know how devoted you always were to your brother, and how keenly you must feel his loss. I wish I knew how to comfort you; but all I can do is give you my love and my sympathy—and hope that time will soon ease the pain.

Please give my condolences to your mother and to the rest of the family.

In sorrow and affection,

Margot

Dear Jane:

News of your sister's death has just come to me, and I hasten to send deepest sympathy to you and the family.

I hope you are finding some small measure of comfort in the fact that she went quickly, without suffering—as she would have wished.

Is there any way I can help? You know I would gladly do anything I can.

Sincerely,
Philip Ansell

When Someone Is Killed

Dear Edith:

I can find no words to express my shock and grief.

Jerry and I send you our heartfelt sympathy, and we beg you to let us help you in any way we can.

In deepest sorrow and affection,

Marcia

Dear Frank:

We are heartbroken by the tragic news. We can only hope and pray that time will quickly soften the cruel blow.

Ed and I are standing by to help. Will you have someone call and let us know what we can do?

In deepest sympathy,

Julia

8. GREETING-CARD ETIQUETTE

No greeting card, printed with somebody else's sentiments—however beautifully or eloquently expressed—can ever take the place of an intimate personal message in your own handwriting. So on birthdays and anniversaries, and especially to those you love best and miss most—always take time to write a letter instead of sending a card if you possibly can.

And you know, of course, that nothing but a personal note of thanks will do for a gift or favor received—for an expression of sympathy or condolence. To use a printed form or card as a substitute for a written message at such a time is neither gracious nor sincere—and is certainly not in good taste.

But at Christmas time and other special holiday times of the year—that's another story! To friendly and social-minded people all over the world, greeting cards serve a real and useful purpose on such occasions. They are busy little harbingers of love and good cheer. They tell distant friends they are not forgotten—rekindle fond memories and affections—pleasantly renew and strengthen old ties.

So by all means send out greeting cards—lots of them!—at Easter, Christmas, New Year. *Especially* at Christmas. As annual messages of good will—when it would be impractical if not impossible to send personal greetings to all one's many relatives, neighbors, and friends—Christmas cards represent a gay and charming convenience, surely a custom to be encouraged.

When to Send Christmas Cards

One of the most important pointers anyone can give you about the etiquette of greeting cards is simply this: *mail your cards to reach their destination in time.* Cards that arrive even so much as one day late lose much of their effectiveness.

Christmas cards that are to be printed or engraved with your name should be ordered early. At the time you place your order, ask to have the envelopes delivered as soon as possible—or better still, take them with you. Then you can address them leisurely, a few at a time, while waiting for the cards to be delivered.

Even cards addressed locally should be mailed at least five days in advance to assure their delivery before Christmas. Cards addressed out of town should be mailed a week to ten days ahead of time; and those going abroad should be mailed anywhere from two weeks to two months in advance, depending on where and how they are going.

Just bear in mind that postal facilities all over the world are taxed to the extreme before Christmas, and the only way to be sure your greetings reach relatives and friends in time is to mail them early.

To Whom to Send Cards

A Christmas card is a greeting of friendliness and cheer, and may properly be sent to anyone you have ever known and want to remember—from the most intimate friends to the most casual acquaintances. After all, no one can possibly object to a friendly greeting at Christmas; but on the other hand, sensitive people may be offended if they are forgotten.

So whenever you are in doubt whether or not to send someone a card, send it. It is never a mistake to be thoughtful and kindly. Just be sure you don't send cards to complete strangers for the purpose of making their acquaintance, soliciting their business, or currying their favor. Such cards violate the true spirit and tradition of Christmas.

Some people send Christmas cards to everyone they know, in business as well as socially. Some send cards only to relatives and close friends. There's no rule about it; you send cards to whomever you wish . . . including even Junior's teacher and the family doctor, if you are so inclined.

A good idea is to keep a list of those you want to greet at Christmas time, adding to it as your circle of friendship and acquaintance widens. Check the list from year to year against the list of those from whom you have received cards, so that you will not fail to return the courtesy.

But if you receive a card from someone to whom you have not sent greetings, don't make the mistake of sending that person a card after Christmas. Such an obviously late arrival is no compliment to the person who receives it. If your greetings and good wishes cannot be sent in time to arrive before Christmas, they should not be sent at all. Nor should a New Year's card be sent to "make up" for the omission. The only courteous thing to do is to send a personal note of thanks, expressing pleasure at having been remembered and extending good wishes for the coming year. No one ever resents a friendly personal message, whenever it arrives; but a Christmas card that is clearly an afterthought is not always well received.

What Kind of Cards to Send

Christmas cards are of such wide and staggering variety that no one can possibly suggest the best type or style to choose. There are so many styles: gay, colorful, simple, serious, religious, elaborate, scenic, artistic, symbolic—even humorous! The choice is entirely a matter of personal taste and preference. Just bear in mind that good taste is essentially simple, and try to avoid any extremes of size, color, design, or sentiment.

Next to good taste and sincerity, the most important factor in guiding your choice of Christmas cards should be *suitability*. Don't send a comic novelty card to a college professor, nor a photograph of the kiddies to a casual acquaintance. *Consider the person to whom the card is going.* Surely a gay and lighthearted greeting that shouts "Merry Christmas" to a friend in mourning—or a frivolous skating or skiing scene to one who is a hopeless invalid—is unsuitable and unkind.

There are two broad general types of Christmas cards: the intimate or informal type (which may be almost anything!)—and the formal card which is conventional in design and dignified in treatment. Most people who send out a large number of cards each year use both types: informal cards for their relatives and intimate friends, formal cards for their business associates and less intimate friends.

Both types may be either printed or engraved with the sender's name; but it's just as good taste to sign your name to the cards in your own handwriting. In fact, some people consider the handwritten signature more personal and friendly.

How to Sign Christmas Cards

There is no rule about whose name comes first on the joint Christmas card of a husband and wife. When cards are printed informally with the first names, the form generally used is "Frank and Betty Duncan" (following the conventional "Mr. and Mrs." sequence, with the "Mr." first). But when the cards are signed by hand, either "Frank and Betty" or "Betty and Frank" may be used, as preferred. Usually the person who does the writing courteously places his or her own name last.

However when children's names are added, the father's name always comes first. "Frank, Betty, and Mary Lou" is better than "Betty,

Frank, and Mary Lou." Informal cards to friends may be signed "The Duncans"—meaning the whole family. Or one may sign even more informally as "The Duncans—all Four" or "The Duncans—Frank, Betty, Mary Lou, and Tim."

The printing or engraving of names on formal Christmas cards follows the rules for the engraving of names on visiting cards. The title of "Miss," "Mrs.," "Mr. and Mrs."—or whatever the case may be—precedes the signature and is properly a part of it. Formal cards are never engraved with first names only, or even with first and last names, but always with the complete title and signature: "Dr. and Mrs. John Edgar Prescott."

It is considered somewhat better form to put engraved or printed names on formal cards at the head of the message instead of at the end of it. For example, "Dr. and Mrs. John Edgar Prescott wish you a Merry Christmas and a Happy New Year" is better than "A Merry Christmas and a Happy New Year from Dr. and Mrs. John Edgar Prescott."

How to Address Christmas Cards

Christmas cards are properly addressed to "Miss Mary Wilson" or to "Mr. and Mrs. Frank Duncan." If children are included in the greeting, "Our love to all of you!" or "Love to the children" may be written in ink below the printed message on the card.

There is no longer any objection to the use of the convenient phrase "and family" in addressing greeting cards (but do not use it for addressing invitations!). A card addressed to "Mr. and Mrs. Frank Duncan and family" includes their two small children, Mary Lou and Tim. But for grown children, either separate cards should be sent or "Greetings and love to Mary and Tim" may be written in ink on the card.

Christmas greetings addressed to a doctor at his home should include his wife, whether you know her or not. It is an unspeakable rudeness to send a card to a professional man at his home and leave his wife out of your good wishes. So be sure your envelope is addressed to "Dr. and Mrs. Thomas Blank."

A card sent to a business associate whose husband (or wife) you don't know may be sent to him alone, if it's addressed to his office or place of business. If it's sent to his home, and you know that he is married, address the envelope to "Mr. and Mrs."

OTHER GREETING CARDS

The same few simple rules of courtesy and good form that apply to Christmas cards apply, of course, to all other greeting cards. Whether for Easter, Mother's Day, or whatever the occasion, be sure the cards you send out are *suitable*, in *good taste*, and expressive of your *true sentiments*. Be sure to sign and address them properly, and to send them out so they reach their destination in time.

Greeting cards give charming evidence of your affection and esteem; so use them generously. But use them only for the purpose for which they are intended: the remembrance and greeting of friends on special days of the year. Do *not* use a printed, decorated, or novelty card of any kind as a substitute for a written note of thanks or a message of condolence. Such cards are utterly lacking in dignity and taste.

QUESTIONS FREQUENTLY ASKED ABOUT GREETING CARDS

Question: Is it good form to write personal messages on greeting cards?

Answer: Yes, especially to friends who are ill or in sorrow. A message added by hand always makes a card more intimate and welcome.

Question: Are brightly colored envelope linings in good taste for Christmas cards?

Answer: Envelope linings may be as gay as you like, for Christmas cards and all greeting cards.

Question: May one who loves flowers use summer scenes, like birds and gardens, on Christmas cards?

Answer: Yes; but of course a scene or decoration symbolic of winter and of Christmas time is more suitable.

Question: Is it good form to use family photographs on Christmas cards?

Answer: Family photographs are fine for doting grandparents and other intimates, and especially for friends who live at a distance and rarely see the family. But don't send pictures of your children or your house to people who aren't likely to be interested; they'll only think you are showing off.

Question: Are homemade greeting cards in good taste? I enjoy making my own.

Answer: There is no objection to making your own cards if you are capable of doing a reasonably good job. Friends appreciate the extra effort that goes into a card you have designed or decorated yourself, but only if it is attractive. A crudely made card has no appeal.

Question: Should people who are in mourning send out Christmas cards?

Answer: That is entirely up to them and their own feelings in the matter. Those who have suffered a recent bereavement generally do not send out cards; but they may if they want to. It is never improper to send good wishes to one's friends.

Question: May one send out Christmas cards without any signature, enclosing a personal visiting card instead?

Answer: This is an extremely formal and impersonal type of greeting, and is suitable only for clients, customers, and business associates. It is not a gracious way to greet friends.

Question: Is it permissible to sign Christmas cards in red or green ink, to match the decorations?

Answer: Yes. It's permissible to sign names and also write messages in colored ink on informal Christmas cards. (But remember that colored inks are tabu for social correspondence.)

Question: May an engaged couple send out Christmas cards together?

Answer: Yes, an engaged couple may send joint cards to relatives and intimate friends. But they should be informal cards, signed or printed with the first names only, "Mary and Tom." They should not be formally engraved, "Miss Mary Smith and Mr. Thomas Brown."

Question: Is there any objection to the use of post cards for Christmas greetings?

Answer: It is not considered good form to send a personal message of any kind on an exposed card. It should always be enclosed and mailed in an envelope.

Question: May a small gift like a handkerchief or a bookmark be tucked in the envelope along with the Christmas card?

Answer: Why not? It sounds like a charming and delightful idea. Just be sure it *is* a small gift, not a bulky one; and that the envelope carries sufficient postage.

Question: Is it good form to acknowledge a Christmas gift on a Christmas greeting card?

Answer: No, it is definitely *bad* form. One should write a separate note of thanks.

Question: Do married people ever send out greeting cards separately?

Answer: Only to business associates—never socially.

Question: Is it considered presumptuous to send a Christmas or New Year greeting to someone you don't know but greatly admire, like a public figure or celebrity?

Answer: Not at all! Everyone enjoys receiving good wishes that are kindly and sincerely meant.

PART VI

The Social Graces

1. CONVERSATION

TO BE able to talk well is one of the most desirable of all the social graces. There are few attainments that can give greater satisfaction in one's contact with people. Good talk is, in fact, one of the most useful and fundamental pleasures of life; and those who cannot express themselves readily and with ease are at an obvious disadvantage.

One of the first essentials of agreeable conversation is a soft, well-modulated tone of voice—a voice that does not grate harshly on the ears of others. A rich, warm voice has distinct magnetism, is often even more compelling than physical beauty.

THE IMPORTANCE OF A PLEASANT SPEAKING VOICE

We all know the power of a pleasant voice to impress people, to win and hold their interest, to inspire their trust and understanding. We have all, at one time or another, fallen beneath the spell of an irresistibly beautiful speaking voice. But we know, too, that voice can affect people unfavorably. A shrill, high-pitched voice can be as irritating as the squeak of chalk on a blackboard. A raspy voice, a nasal twang, can repel people as surely as bad manners or an untidy appearance.

In view of this great power of the voice to attract or repel, it's astonishing that so few people make any effort to improve the way they speak. We hear harsh, unpleasant voices on all sides. We hear strident, irritating voices wherever we go. A really lovely voice, rich and full-toned, is such a rarity in ordinary conversation that to hear one is always a pleasure, and clearly a great social advantage to the person who possesses it.

So if your voice has any harsh or unpleasant qualities—if it is thin, flat, nasal, high-pitched or shrill—make every effort to correct and improve it. Take whatever steps are necessary to eliminate the disagreeable qualities. The voice is capable of great improvement, and is well worth whatever time and effort you put into it.

You will find it helpful to listen critically and creatively to the voices of other people. Don't hesitate to copy the qualities you admire. You can learn more that way than from any book. Listen to the voices of fine actors and to the distinguished voices on radio and television, especially the news commentators. They have trained voices, voices with charm and personality.

Read aloud whenever possible; it's excellent practice. Train yourself to speak slowly, distinctly, and in a soft, well-modulated tone.

Take some singing lessons if you can, even if you never expect to sing a note. Singing is wonderful training for the speaking voice.

The point is that your voice can be magnetic, or it can be irritating. It can be sheer delight to listen to, or it can grate unpleasantly on people's nerves. It can win friends, inspire trust, create sympathy and understanding—or it can actively repel people and make you disliked. It's all up to you; because your voice, like your personal appearance, is what you make it.

GESTURES AND MANNERISMS

There can be no objection to an occasional gesture in speech, if it is simple, natural, and unaffected. But well-bred people do not pound on the table to emphasize what they are saying, do not continually shrug and gesticulate. They do not keep a finger carefully leveled at the person to whom they are talking, nor dig a finger into his ribs to illustrate a point.

If you have a certain way of nodding when you speak, of smiling a little, or lifting your voice at the end of each sentence—these are pleasant and often charming, mannerisms. Don't do anything to change them.

But to wet your lips continually while you are talking to people is an unpleasant and offensive mannerism. So is clicking your teeth, putting your face close to another person's, grabbing him by the arm or lapels as though to force him to listen.

Just as irritating are such habits as drumming on the table while others are speaking, cracking your knuckles, stroking your chin or cheek. Some people are forever slapping their thighs for emphasis, or striking the palm of one hand with the fist of the other. Some affect a maddening drawl, some nervously cough or clear their throat every few minutes, some prefix every remark with "Listen," close every remark with "See what I mean?"

These are all unpleasant mannerisms; and if you recognize any of them as your own, decide to put an end to them. They are just careless habits of speech—and like all habits, can be overcome by will power and persistent effort.

PRONUNCIATION

Nothing is so conspicuous in speech as a flagrantly mispronounced word. Nothing is more embarrassing than to have a word slip from your lips, and to realize an instant later that you have mispronounced it.

The rules of cultivated speech are exact and precise. It's true there are distinct traits of pronunciation in various sections of the country. A Philadelphian is likely to say "haow" for "how" and "caow" for "cow." A Bostonian is almost certain to say "haht" for "heart" and "bawn" for "born." Some people say "watter" for "water," "wawsh" for "wash," "thot" for "thought," "hyar" for "here." Such differences merely indicate the part of the country one is from, and are more fascinating than otherwise.

But whether a person hails from Charleston or New York, from Chicago or Kalamazoo, if he says "boid" for "bird," "ersters" for "oysters," "cherce" for "choice," "figger" for "figure," "et" for "ate," there's no mistaking his illiteracy!

So if you are in doubt as to the correct pronunciation of a word, *don't use it.* Substitute a familiar word instead. But remember the word on which you stumbled, and look it up in a dictionary at the first opportunity. Write it down on a piece of paper and carry it around with you. Find opportunity to use it in your conversation; and by using it, make it your own. There's an old saying that if you use a word correctly three times, it's yours for the rest of your life.

There is no better way to correct and improve your pronunciation, apart from daily association with cultivated people, than to establish an intimate and friendly relationship with your dictionary. Resolve never to let a written or spoken word pass you by until you know what it means, how to spell it, and exactly how to pronounce it. For remember: whatever other social graces you may have, without the ability to speak as well-bred people do, you lack the most important asset of all. A cultivated way of speaking is the final test of a lady or gentleman—the passport to good society.

It would be impossible, of course, to give a full and comprehensive list of the words that are frequently mispronounced. Many useful books on the subject are available at public libraries; and those who need more help than is given here would do well to pursue the subject further. But here are some of the most glaring crudities of all—pronunciations that are unmistakably illiterate and should be avoided at all costs.

DON'T SAY

genil-man	for gentleman		progrum	for program
guvment	for government		yuh	for you
samitch	for sandwich		jest	for just
pitcher	for picture		chawklit	for chocolate
eggsit	for exit		chillun	for children
yeah	for yes		perduce	for produce
ketch	for catch		idear	for idea
colyum	for column		sumthin	for something
merridge	for marriage		tee-jus	for tedious
fillum	for film		Febuery	for February
strenth	for strength		amachure	for amateur
farn	for foreign		grajate	for graduate
fambly	for family		uv	for of
becuz	for because		deef	for deaf
awright	for all right		reconize	for recognize
tamarra	for tomorrow		attack-ted	for attacked
litter-cher	for literature		drownd-ded	for drowned
liberry	for library		architek	for architect
Eye-talyun	for Italian		praps	for perhaps
mee-jum	for medium		usally	for usually
Omurican	for American		yestiddy	for yesterday

Not all errors in pronunciation are as crudely obvious as these. Many are simply the result of sloppy, careless speech. In the rush and hurry of modern life, people often mutilate their words—drop letters, clip off syllables, run sounds together. They say "puddin" for "pudding," "gonna" for "going to," "ivry" for "ivory," "yarnot" for "you are not." The only way to correct such slovenly habits of speech is to practice talking slowly and deliberately, making a conscious effort to sound every syllable.

Some Suggestions for People with a Foreign Accent

Foreign-born people living in the United States who wish to identify themselves with American life and American activities should be able to speak the language intelligibly and correctly.

This does not mean that a foreign accent is necessarily objectional. Quite on the contrary—an accent often adds character and distinction to one's speech. But an accent must not be confused with a crude, illiterate way of speaking.

If a foreign-born person says "Give to me my hat" (instead of "Give me my hat")—or "I must try this to do" (instead of "I must try to do this")—it's not the *accent*, but the careless use of the language that grates unpleasantly on the ears.

Foreign-born people should make every effort to learn correct, grammatical use of the language as quickly as possible—to learn the forms of speech, and above all the proper pronunciation of words. This can be accomplished only by sustained and determined effort. A good dictionary is indispensable; and one should use it *daily*—not only for the exact meanings of words, but for their spelling and pronunciation. The dictionary habit is of immense value to foreign-born people interested in learning to speak the language properly.

It is helpful also to listen attentively to people who speak English well. Give particular attention to their diction, inflections, and use of words. Make an effort to learn familiar American colloquialisms, and the idiomatic use of words and phrases. Be careful how you translate the idioms of your language into English; for often the entire structure of a sentence must be turned around to make sense to American ears. If self-study, reading, listening to others, and systematic practice at home are not enough, it is advisable to take some private or class instruction in English. The sooner you learn to speak correctly, the sooner you will enjoy the full benefits of your American life.

As for the accent itself, all you can do is hope that it will gradually disappear. Sometimes it does, very quickly; but in other cases it never completely disappears. However, it doesn't really matter. A foreign accent is no more offensive than the regional accents people have right here in various sections of the country. Southerners have an unmistakable accent of their own—midwesterners have theirs—New Yorkers certainly have theirs. If your diction and pronunciation are correct, your choice and use of words grammatical, the inflections of your voice pleasant and agreeable, there is no need to worry about a native accent.

There are a certain few English sounds that seem to be especially difficult for the foreign-born. Among the most troublesome are *th, sh, ng, w,* and *b.* We often hear foreign-born people say *dis* for *this, srewd* for *shrewd, brink* for *bring, vell* for *well, crip* for *crib.* We urge those who have been misusing these sounds to make a sincere effort to correct themselves. The best way is to make a list of words for each sound, and practice reading them aloud daily—until they no longer present any difficulty.

Following is a list of errors made frequently by foreign-born people.

Find those characteristic of your race, and make every effort to eliminate them from your speech.

ah for er	AS	feathah for feather
oi for ir	AS	thoid for third
e for a	AS	cen't for can't
b for p	AS	cab for cap
p for b	AS	crip for crib
th for fth	AS	fith for fifth
w for wh	AS	wat for what
k for g	AS	rink for ring
g-g for g	AS	ring-g for ring
w for r	AS	twy for try
r-r for r	AS	r-r-ring for ring
sr for shr	AS	srew for shrew
z for s	AS	thiz for this
z for th	AS	zis for this
d for t	AS	lidle for little
e for i	AS	leetle for little
d for th	AS	dem for them
v for f	AS	vrom for from
v for w	AS	vind for wind
w for v	AS	wice for vice

THE CHOICE USE OF WORDS

Good expression depends not only on voice and pronunciation but on the proper choice and use of words. So watch your language! Avoid vague, stilted, misleading, unlovely, or inappropriate forms of expression. Say what you have to say simply and concisely, in words that come easily and naturally to your lips.

The modern way of talking is lively and fast-moving. It is casual, sometimes colloquial, often slangy and colorful. But among people of good taste and good judgment it is never pompous or affected.

The well-bred person is careful to avoid pretentious language. He never uses elaborate, bookish words when simple ones will do. He doesn't purchase a residence; he buys a house. He doesn't attend a banquet; he goes to a dinner. He doesn't retire, arise, perform ablutions, partake of the morning repast. In good plain everyday language he goes to sleep, gets up, washes, has breakfast.

Remember, the finest English in the world is simple English, uncluttered and direct. Always try to say what you have to say in short words that clearly express your meaning. Crisp, familiar words are always more expressive than flowery, high-sounding language.

As undesirable as pretentious speech are the crudities of expression which instantly betray lack of breeding. Among them are words like *punk, lousy, goofy, savvy, scram.* These are not accepted forms of slang or provincialism; they are crudities which should be avoided.

Abbreviations like *phone, photo, auto, movies, frat* for fraternity, *tux* for tuxedo, *kids* for children, *wire* for telegraphed—even *O.K.* and *Hi!*—although they are not the most cultivated forms of expression, are now widely used. They are recognized and accepted as characteristic forms of speech, as American as hot dogs and popcorn. But *gent* for gentleman and *hubby* for husband remain offensive crudities, abhorrent to the cultivated ear.

Words like *swell, hunch, dandy, humdinger, cutup, lots* (for many), *tops* (for superior)—are considered colloquialisms, and there is no objection to their occasional use. But be careful to avoid overworking a pet word like *swell,* or a pet phrase like *sure thing!* or *you bet!* The frequent repetition of a favorite word or phrase can be very tiresome to those who must listen to you.

The Use of Slang

Slang is a lively, colorful, amusing, sometimes grotesque, but always expressive part of the American language. But it's important to distinguish between slang that is low and coarse and slang that is vivid, provocative, and in good taste. Crude slang is usually transitory and short-lived; it serves its brief purpose and is gone. But clever and useful slang expressions, drawn from every phase of modern life, are the vital "feeders" of language, keeping it supple and timely.

It should not be difficult to distinguish between coarse expressions and good American slang. Some words and phrases clearly reflect the gutter and all. it typifies; others reflect new and interesting ways of life, new customs, fads and ideas. Words like *jerk, moll, mug, punk, rats, baloney, hooey* are crude and undesirable, and no well-bred person uses them. But words like *baby-sitter, highjacker, huckster, hoofer, disc jockey*—words like *scoop, blurb, plug, debunk, weasel words,* like *mike fright, zero hour, soap opera* and *hair-do*—are timely and expressive, and are used by the most cultivated people.

Many slang expressions are unmistakably the lazy vulgarisms of the illiterate. But just as many are clever figures of speech, conveying shades of meaning that formal language could not do as well. For example, *sez you, drop dead, button your lip, spit it out, smell a rat* are impossibly vulgar. But *thumb a ride, in the groove, hold everything, hit the jackpot, tell the world, on the spot* are lively, colorful phrases that streamline conversation and give it a characteristically American sparkle and tang.

Many of our most interesting slang expressions are picturesque compounds which tell in a single quick phrase what might otherwise take a whole sentence to explain. Our language is full of expressive combinations like *has-been, pay-off, also-ran, hide-out, walkie-talkie, juke box, sob sister, best-seller, plug-ugly, hard-boiled,* and new ones are coined almost daily. Their use adds spice to conversation, and often helps express a thought or idea more vividly. But don't overdo the use of any kind of slang; and don't use stale or overworked phrases that have lost their piquancy.

Frequent Mistakes in Grammar and in the Use of Words

We cannot even begin to cover the essential principles of grammar. That would take a big book by itself! But here are the mistakes people make most frequently, and that one should be very careful to avoid.

Wrong	Right
It was *me* that telephoned.	It was *I* that telephoned.
I do not believe it was *her*.	I do not believe it was *she*.
She objected to *me* going out.	She objected to *my* going out.
Jane coming here was a surprise.	*Jane's coming* was a surprise.
She meant it for you and *I*.	She meant it for you and *me*.
This is *her* speaking.	This is *she* speaking.
It *won't* rain, I *don't* believe.	I *don't* believe it will rain.
Imagine *him* doing that.	Imagine *his* doing that.
I am *laying* down.	I am *lying* down.
It's not *us* who are to blame.	It's not *we* who are to blame.
I just *seen* her.	I just *saw* her.
She *got* married yesterday.	She *was* married yesterday.
They *learned* the baby to talk.	They *taught* the baby to talk.
Them people said they would **help**.	*Those* people said they would help.
Don't blame it *on* me.	Don't blame *me* for it.
She's *different than* I am.	She's *different from* me.
Can I go now?	*May* I go now?
Leave him alone!	*Let* him alone!
I'll *bring* him the letters.	I'll *take* him the letters.
Who do you *want* to see?	*Whom* do you *wish* to see?
Will you *loan* me your book?	Will you *lend* me your book?
Mary *don't* like candy.	Mary *doesn't* like candy.

Wrong	*Right*
They don't want *none.*	They don't want *any.*
Just between you and *I.*	Just between you and *me.*
Everyone's entitled to *their* opinion.	Everyone's entitled to *his* opinion.
Neither Bob nor Bill *have* come.	Neither Bob nor Bill *has* come.
He *done* it all by himself.	He *did* it all by himself.
No one came *beside* me.	No one came *besides* (or *except*) me.
You go now and I'll come *after.*	You go now and I'll come *afterward.*
Where are they *going to?*	Where are they *going?*
The mirror is *broke.*	The mirror is *broken.*
Was you a good girl today?	*Were* you a good girl today?
She likes *those* kind of clothes.	She likes *that* kind of clothes.
If I *was* you.	If I *were* you.
For *who* is he painting it?	For *whom* is he painting it?
Divide it *between* the three *of* you.	Divide it *among* the three of you.
I don't want *none.*	I don't want *any.*
They *affected* an entrance.	They *effected* an entrance.
He climbed the fence *easy.*	He climbed the fence *easily.*
I'm *anxious* to go abroad.	I'm *eager* to go abroad.
The *two twins* are going with us.	The *twins* are going with us.
I *would* like to go.	I *should* like to go.
I *told* him to do me a favor.	I *asked* him to do me a favor.
He behaved very *bad.*	He behaved very *badly.*
They went *in* the room.	They went *into* the room.
Her mother's a *widow woman.*	Her mother's a *widow.*
Why do you never go *nowhere?*	Why do you never go *anywhere?*
You shouldn't *of did* it.	You shouldn't *have done* it.
I wish I had *wrote* to her.	I wish I had *written* to her.

WHAT CONSTITUTES GOOD CONVERSATION

A pleasing voice, good diction, skill and facility in the use of words —all are highly important requirements of the well-bred personality. But they fall short of their essential purpose if they are not used effectively in conversation.

Some few lucky individuals are "born" conversationalists to whom the knack of ready speech comes easily and with natural charm. But rarely does this useful ability sprout by itself. Many people, even those who are glib and talkative among their intimates, become tongue-tied in a roomful of people. But today there is no need for anyone to be so handicapped. With so much going on in the world, so much that is new and exciting to talk about, no one need be inarticulate at any time, in any company. There are certain simple conditions that nourish the art of conversation, that unfailingly help to develop this useful and pleasurable attainment; and these we shall now consider.

As social relationships are intended to be pleasant and relaxing, conversation that is on a strictly social basis should be pleasant and relaxing, too. No one enjoys listening to "peeves" or complaints, to a long recital of worries, troubles, or grievances. In general, it's best to avoid gloomy subjects like illness, death, or disaster, unless those talking are personally involved and it would be unnatural not to discuss what is foremost in all their minds. But don't unnecessarily introduce a gloomy or distressing subject in social conversation. Keep it on a cheerful note. Avoid controversial subjects like religion and politics, unless you can discuss them without treading on people's toes or hurting their feelings. Talk that stems from friendly social contact should be *friendly* talk, not contentious or provoking.

To be interesting and enjoyable, conversation should be on a reciprocal basis. The really good conversationalist knows when to listen. He knows how to draw others out and get them to talk with spirit and animation. He doesn't try to impress people with his own importance, doesn't try to prove himself wittier or cleverer than anyone else. On the contrary, if he's smart he lets others shine—maneuvers the conversation so that *they*, and not he, appear to advantage.

Unless you are having a tête-à-tête with an intimate friend, it is best that you speak as little as possible about yourself. Try to acquire the knack of putting yourself in the other person's place, of seeing things from his point of view. Failure to recognize and fully appreciate this human element in conversation—failure to see things from the other person's point of view—is the cause of much of the dull, boring, uninteresting talk we hear on all sides.

People like to feel important, and they resent very much any implication that they are not important. Always bear that in mind in conversation. Don't talk continually about yourself—about your plans, your problems, your experiences. Reverse the process and let others talk about *their* interests, *their* hobbies, *their* plans and experiences. Ask questions that show you are interested. Listen responsively, with all your attention. You'll be considered very interesting and clever, though you do little of the actual talking. It's a quick, sure way to increase your popularity; for there isn't a person in the world who doesn't enjoy talking about himself and feeling important while doing so.

One of the most important rules of successful conversation is to think before you speak. Too many of us impulsively blurt out remarks that hurt, irritate, or embarrass others. If you make it a firm rule to think first, you won't say careless, unkind things that tend to make you unpopular—and that you may later have cause to regret.

A very useful quality in conversation is to be able to disagree with others without being rude or unpleasant about it. Lively discussions are the very breath and substance of good talk. They give it tone and sparkle. In fact, some of the best talk is based on friendly controversy; for discussion of a subject on which two or more people have differing views is often very stimulating. But the important thing is to keep discussion on a friendly basis, to keep it amiable and calm. It must not be allowed to become violent or disagreeable. Unpleasant arguments are out of place when people come together socially—are not conducive to good satisfying talk.

WHAT TO TALK ABOUT

Your conversation is a reflection of the things you see, hear, read, experience, and think about. To talk well, you must be reasonably well informed. You must have a wide range of general knowledge from which you can draw at will, and a good stock of information based on your observations and experiences.

Nowadays no one need ever be at a loss for a subject to talk about. New and interesting things are happening all the time, and the possibilities for lively conversation are practically limitless. Everything that happens to you or to the people you know, everything you read or hear about, can be grist to your conversational mill. Just train your mind to be alert and receptive. Make an effort to develop your sense of observation. Make a mental note of any interesting or unusual thing you see or experience, to use in conversation when the opportunity presents itself.

The full-bodied flavor of conversation calls for many ingredients. The reason many people are poor conversationalists is because they are absorbed in one or two things, and can talk of nothing else. Because they are greatly interested in bridge, golf, gardening, tropical fish, they think everyone else must be. The worst offenders are the talkative mothers of child prodigies, politicians, music lovers—people so wrapped up in their single dominating interest that they always manage to maneuver the talk in that direction. Few things are more boring in this world than a couple of specialists or hobbyists who get in a huddle and talk all evening about their particular interest, to the exclusion of everyone else.

The good conversationalist has a lively, versatile mind. He can talk

with equal facility on many subjects. He always has something interesting to contribute to the general discussion, whether the subject
intimately concerns him or not.

As to what to talk about, no one can tell you that. It depends on
so many personal factors. Just bear in mind that *no conversation is
good conversation if it fails to interest the listener*. Therefore don't
talk exclusively about yourself. Keep the listener in mind. What are
his interests, his hobbies? What exciting or interesting news can you
give him? What would he most enjoy hearing about?

Naturally you wouldn't talk to a neighbor's teen-age boy the same
as you would to a dignified, elderly friend of the family. You must
consider the person to whom you are talking. People are different,
their tastes and interests are different—and obviously the best talk is
that which is keyed to the listener's point of view.

Far easier than telling you what to talk about is telling you what
not to talk about—what subjects to avoid as boring, unsuitable, or in
bad taste. Here there can be neither doubt nor contention; for certain
subjects are plainly objectionable, and can never be otherwise:

It is never good taste to give all the involved and boring details of
your illness or operation. Keep the unpleasant facts to yourself. Don't
talk about diseases or obstetrical problems at the dinner table. Don't
itemize your ailments or symptoms at any time, as that doesn't make
good conversation.

Don't talk about how much money people have, except in a very
broad, general way. Don't always put a price tag on everything—how
much this cost, how much that cost. Don't discuss your financial
problems or boast of your financial success. Listeners dislike both.

Don't rave about your children, except to a doting grandparent or
an intimate friend who has children of her own. It usually bores
people to have to listen to prattle about other people's children.
Furthermore, the bright sayings of children never sound quite so
bright outside the boundaries of their own indulgent homes. So
remember—grandma adores hearing all about Junior's accomplishments, but nobody else does!

Try not to fill your conversation with details of your domestic
affairs, especially complaints about servants. It may relieve your injured feelings to indulge in a long tirade about your maid's insolence
or incompetence, but it doesn't make suitable conversation. Your
friends may sympathize with you in this or any other domestic difficulty, but they get very tired of hearing about it.

It is not advisable to discuss business reverses in general social conversation. There may be times, of course, when you feel you must
confide in someone who will sympathize and understand. But don't

make it a practice to talk about your personal business problems socially.

Don't make your conversation a running commentary on the disappointments of life, the mistakes you made, the "bad breaks" you got. Nobody likes to listen to that kind of negative talk. Keep your disappointments to yourself—or for private discussion with your family or few intimate friends.

It is not good taste to brag about successful relatives, or boast of celebrities you have met. Even worse is to brag about illustrious ancestors. Intelligent people admire you for yourself, not for the nebulous prestige of some long-gone relative.

Ordinarily religion is a subject to be avoided on social occasions, for many people are mentally immature and cannot keep their feelings under control. They let their prejudices spout through, bluntly treading on people's toes and ruffling their tempers. It's wise, therefore, to avoid religious discussions except with the most intimate friends. This doesn't mean you need to hesitate to express your ideas and convictions freely and honestly, when the occasion calls for it. But don't ever be the one to enkindle difficult religious controversies at a dinner or party where people have come together for a good time. And if the subject of religion is brought into the conversation, make it a point to avoid flat statements as much as possible. A truly sophisticated and cultured man or woman of the world is never heard to condemn a race, a creed, or an individual who happens to look, speak, or think differently from himself.

Politics can be another difficult subject if it's allowed to get out of hand. In general, it's best not to talk about your political views unless you are specifically asked about them.

Don't discuss art, literature, music, or any subject as an authority unless you know enough about the subject to speak with authority.

Don't indulge in long personal reminiscences that have no special interest for the company. Reminiscing can become a habit, if you let it—very satisfying to your soul, but very boring to others. Young people usually get restless and uneasy when you start off with "I remember when . . ." Older people get annoyed; they want to do the reminiscing themselves! So when you find yourself launching off on a long personal narrative, stop yourself and ask: "Are they interested? Do they really want to hear about it?"

Don't talk endlessly about your personal experiences in the war. If the general conversation concerns the war, or if there's some logical reason to relate an unusual or dramatic wartime incident, that's another matter. But you can get quite a reputation as a bore if you always talk about your personal exploits.

Don't monopolize a conversation. Thomas Carlyle used to say that if there was anything in the world he despised it was to sit at a dinner table and listen to a guest smugly delivering a monologue to the extreme limit of boredom. "Take me away!" he implored. "To sit still and be pumped into is never an exhilarating process."

Don't go to the other extreme and be a discouraging "door slammer," letting the conversation die every time it reaches you. Keep the conversational ball rolling. The life and charm of conversation depend on the free interchange of thoughts and ideas, on easy friendly talk in which all share.

One final word of warning: Don't attempt repartee unless you are deft and skillful in the art. It's very easy to offend in repartee, and to cause yourself embarrassment. Beau Brummell is said to have made many enemies by his conversational faux pas. For example, a hostess once asked him if he would "take a cup of tea." "Thank you," he said, "I never take anything but physic." "I beg your pardon," his hostess retorted, "you also take liberties." Although the records don't say, it's reasonable to assume he was never invited to that particular house again.

2. PERSONAL APPEARANCE

SURELY no one needs to be convinced of the immense importance of personal appearance! We all know that the world takes us at face value, and that the way we look influences people quite as much as the way we talk or act among them. Those who are careless of their appearance—who are dowdy or untidy, or who wear clothes that are conspicuously unsuited to the occasion or otherwise in bad taste—are clearly at a disadvantage. For as long as the world continues to judge by appearance (often, unfortunately, regardless of more enduring values!) the way we look must be given careful thought and attention.

Well-bred people make an effort to appear at their best at all times, socially and in business. Their "best" doesn't necessarily mean elaborate or expensive clothing, furs, and jewels. Quite on the contrary: the best appearance often calls for utmost simplicity in dress, for quiet good taste combined with flawless and unmistakable personal grooming.

It isn't necessary to have a great deal of money to spend on clothes to look well dressed. It isn't necessary to have a large wardrobe, with many changes. A few good dresses, a few good suits, can provide the basis of excellent grooming and appearance for a wide variety of occasions.

The whole question of good taste in dress can be summed up in a singe word: *suitability*. What you wear should be suitable to the occasion, to your circumstances, to your age and to your type. Clothes that are not suitable are not acceptable, however flattering they may be to the wearer.

CORRECT DRESS FOR WOMEN

The first thought that pops into most women's minds when they receive an invitation or plan to attend a social function of some kind is "What shall I wear?"

Naturally everyone wishes to look as attractive as possible, and at the same time be appropriately dressed for the occasion. No one relishes the idea of being either conspicuously overdressed or underdressed. To be too elaborately or formally dressed for an occasion can often be very embarrassing, but it is perhaps an even greater faux pas to appear in conspicuously casual clothes when formality is indicated.

No well-bred woman ever appears at a luncheon or tea in slacks, for example, or in riding breeches, or even in tweedy country clothes that are out of place among the delicate afternoon dresses of the others. Simplicity is good taste, of course, at any time. When in doubt, one should always wear simple clothes in preference to elaborate ones. But there's a great difference between simplicity and a careless unconcern about dress—between conservative clothes and clothes that are unconventional.

Actually there should be no problem about what to wear. The proper clothes for various types of functions are clearly defined. For all daytime affairs, women wear street-length clothes—as dressy as the occasion calls for—and always with hat and gloves. For any type of informal social activity in the evening, they wear the same sort of clothes they would wear in the afternoon—a little dressier perhaps, but still street length, and still with a hat. For formal but not particularly gala occasions, they wear what is known as a "dinner dress"—which has a long skirt but covered shoulders, and sometimes even has long sleeves. For very formal, ceremonious evening functions, they wear their most elegant evening gowns—décolleté and as elaborate as they wish. Hats are not worn with dinner gowns or evening gowns; long or short gloves are worn, but are always removed for eating.

These are the general classifications as to types of clothes. Following is more specific information on correct dress for various occasions.[1]

[1]Clothes for weddings, funerals, travel, business, etc., are discussed in the chapters on those subjects.

For Dinners

It's traditional to "dress up" for a dinner party, even if it's a quite simple one. To an informal dinner in a private home or club, you wear one of your most flattering afternoon dresses—partyish, but street length. If the hostess specifies "formal," wear a dinner dress or evening gown—depending on the character of the function and what the other guests are likely to be wearing. If it's an important social function, a formal sleeveless evening gown is indicated. With it one should wear furs or a cloth evening wrap. It is not good form to wear an ordinary daytime coat—especially a sports coat—over an evening gown.

For Teas and Receptions

For any type of daytime reception—whether it's a debutante luncheon, an afternoon tea, or even an elaborate wedding reception—women wear street-length dresses. Long skirts are not correct for before-dinner functions, though the hostess at an afternoon tea may wear a long "hostess" or "tea" gown if she wishes. Hats and gloves are worn by guests to afternoon teas and receptions; and hats are kept on through the afternoon.

At evening receptions, a woman's dress depends on the formality and importance of the occasion. For a simple reception, a dinner dress is adequate; but for a very formal ceremonious debutante ball or wedding reception, formal evening dress should be worn.

For Cocktail Parties

Both informal street-length clothes and formal evening dress are correct at cocktail parties. Guests who come directly from a business office cannot be expected to return home to dress; therefore they come as they are, in ordinary daytime clothes. On the other hand, guests who plan to go to the theater or to a dinner party afterward may be obliged to come in evening clothes or not at all. A cocktail party is therefore a function at which one dresses as convenient.

For Dances

Dances are generally evening functions—usually formal, though not necessarily so. But formal or not, dances call for gay, colorful clothes, attractive to look at and in keeping with the occasion.

Unless a dance is definitely informal in character, or unless it's a public function with "dress optional" stipulated in the invitations, evening dress is required. For dancing, choose a dress that is glamorous but *comfortable*, that permits freedom of motion and makes dancing a pleasure, not an ordeal. Avoid wearing a gown that keeps slipping off your shoulders or catching in your heels. Avoid metallic fabrics that feel scratchy and unpleasant to a man's touch, and bulky front ornaments like buttons, buckles, and misplaced posies that get in the way and tend to annoy your dancing partner. Choose a dress that is flattering in motion—free-swinging and graceful—neither too tight nor too long. A gown doesn't need to sweep the floor to look flowing and lovely; it can be a full inch off the floor and be just as effective.

And by the way, if it's a country club or resort dance and your partner is wearing a white tuxedo, be very careful not to use dark make-up that rubs off and leaves marks. Women who leave traces of powder or lipstick on men's clothing are not very likely to be popular at a dance.

For Bridge and Card Parties

For an afternoon card party, you dress as for an afternoon tea—in one of your most flattering daytime dresses or in a costume suit. Unless you are receiving, it's correct to wear a hat and keep it on.

Dress the same for an evening card party unless it follows a formal dinner. At an informal evening card party in a private home, women customarily remove their hats; in a club or hotel, they remove their hats or not, as they wish.

For the Theater and Opera

Women dress for matinees as they do for any afternoon function —in attractive street-length clothes.

In New York and most cosmopolitan cities, evening clothes are worn to first nights at the theater and to opening nights at the opera —and in box and front orchestra seats all other nights during the height of the season.[2] Long dresses are never out of place in the evening at the theater or opera; but street-length clothes are also correct for routine theatergoing when there is no particular occasion for formality—and especially when rear orchestra or balcony seats are occupied.

Extremely décolleté gowns are not in good taste at any time in orchestra seats at the theater. Well-bred women wear semiformal dinner gowns; or if they are going on to a ball or some important

[2]The New York social season begins in November (traditionally with the National Horse Show at Madison Square Garden) and ends at New Year's. During this period are concentrated a series of important society events including the Junior Assembly, the opening of the Metropolitan Opera, first nights, balls, parties and benefits.

social function afterward, they wear a small jacket or cape over their décolleté, to be removed later.

Women who occupy boxes at the theater or opera, especially on opening nights, wear their most lavish gowns and jewels—for they come to be seen as well as to see. Décolleté is customary and good form in boxes, but a wrap should be worn over the gown when entering or leaving the theater, and during intermission.

For Concerts and Musicales

Whether you dress formally or informally for an evening concert or musicale depends on the character of the function and the custom of your particular community. If it's traditional for everyone to attend in formal clothes, it's better taste to conform than to come in ordinary street clothes. But if no one ever "dresses" for such functions in your town, it would be an affectation for you to do so.

For Restaurants and Night Clubs

The clothes a woman wears to a restaurant or hotel dining room depends entirely on the type of place it is, the particular function she is attending, and of course the time of day.

For luncheon or tea in a public dining room she dresses as she would for the same type of function in someone's home: in street-length clothes and always with a hat and gloves. It's best to avoid elaborate or extreme clothes in public dining rooms as they are likely to attract too much attention.

For dinner in an ordinary restaurant, street-length clothes are generally best. If one is going to the theater or opera afterward, or to a formal dance or party, it's advisable to dine in a hotel dining room or club. Evening clothes are too conspicuous for the average restaurant, though in better-class restaurants in large cities, tuxedos and dinner dresses are frequently seen.

Informal dinner parties at hotels or clubs do not ordinarily call for long dresses. But some of the better hotels and clubs do require formal dress regardless of the type of function, especially on Saturday night. If there is any question about it, the smart procedure is to check beforehand and make sure.

Though a few of the more famous night clubs require all patrons to be in evening dress, the general run of night clubs do not. At the average night club, on a weekday evening, one sees as many street-length dresses as long evening gowns; for nowadays many people go out for the evening directly from business, without going home to change. On Saturday nights it's traditional to "dress" for dining and dancing, but not every club or hotel has a firm rule about it. Persons in ordinary street clothes who are refused admission to a night club or public dining room where formal dress is required, should leave at once, quietly.

For Country and Sports

Naturally a more casual and informal type of dressing is expected in the country and in small suburban communities than in the city. But the basic rules of suitability must be observed regardless of where one lives or how informal one's way of life may be.

Nowadays nearly everyone wears slacks in the country—on the village streets, in the small community shops, and even when visiting neighbors informally. However, casual country life is no excuse for slacks worn to luncheons or teas, bridge parties, or other social functions. Simple sports clothes may be worn; they are, in fact, more appropriate for the country than dressy afternoon frocks. But conspicuously unsuitable attire is never in good taste, anywhere.

Kerchiefs may be worn instead of hats for riding, walking, sports, and all informal purposes. But hat and gloves should be worn even to the simplest little village church; and of course a hat is always required for a daytime wedding reception or formal garden party.

For a summer dance at a clubhouse or in the country, women usually wear gay and colorful dinner dresses of some sheer material like organdie or cotton lace—in preference to more formal fabrics and styles. Elaborate décolleté doesn't fit into a simple country setting.

There are two types of sports clothes: those worn for active sports in which one participates—and those for spectator sports. The most important consideration in either type is comfort; sports clothes should provide complete ease and freedom of action. And they should, of course, be worn with suitable low-heeled shoes.

"Spectator sports clothes" is simply another name for country clothes—like sweaters and skirts, casual cotton or linen dresses, separate jackets of flannel or tweed. They are the sort of clothes that can be worn from morning to night in the country, except when one is going to a function like a garden party or an elaborate tea.

CORRECT DRESS FOR MEN

Casual as life is these days, there are still a few occasions that call for "white tie and tails"—most formal of all evening attire for men.

Traditionally, men are supposed to wear full dress when women wear elaborate décolleté evening gowns, and dinner jackets when women wear dinner gowns. But the modern trend is to wear "tails" only for the most formal and ceremonious functions, such as important formal dinners, balls, elaborate evening weddings, and opening night at the opera.

Full dress for men includes a tail coat with black silk or satin lapels, white waistcoat (single or double-breasted), a stiff-bosomed shirt, wing collar, and white bow tie. Aside from the facing of the lapels and wide braid on the trousers, there should be no trimming whatever.

As important as the suit itself are the accessories that go with it, for a single wrong accessory can ruin the entire effect. With formal evening attire, a gentleman wears white gloves, black dress oxfords, black silk socks, and a top hat or the convenient "opera" hat which is collapsible. If a flower is worn in the buttonhole, it should be white. The final touch is a fine white linen handkerchief folded casually into the breast pocket. The overcoat worn with a full-dress suit should be black or very dark blue. If a muffler is worn with it, only white or black-and-white is correct.

The dinner jacket, or tuxedo, is a conveniently useful garment. It can be worn nearly everywhere and for nearly every type of evening function except those of extreme formality. Actually it's a typical English dinner coat, the name "tuxedo" deriving from the fact that it was first introduced in this country at the Tuxedo Club to provide something less formal than the swallowtail.

Tuxedo clothes differ from full dress in the cut of the coat, the use of a black tie instead of white, and somewhat narrower braid on the trousers. Lapels or shawl collar are of silk or satin, but there should be no other trimming on the coat. A single-breasted tuxedo is worn with a white or black waistcoat, the white being considered a little more formal. No waistcoat is worn with a double-breasted tuxedo. Either a stiff-bosomed or softly pleated white shirt is correct. A wing or turned down collar, black bow tie, black dress oxfords or pumps, plain black socks, and a white handkerchief complete the details. The overcoat should be black or very dark blue, and with it most men wear a black or gray Homburg, but a top hat is also correct. Gray suede gloves are generally worn.

White or gray tuxedos, instead of black, are often used for resort wear and aboard ships on a tropical cruise. They are worn with somewhat lighter-weight black trousers than those ordinarily used for a black tuxedo. All other details are the same, except that a maroon bow tie may be worn instead of black, if one wishes.

For formal morning and afternoon functions—especially weddings (and at church on Easter morning)—some men still cling to the cutaway or morning coat with striped trousers. But more and more the trend is away from formal daytime dress for men. Nowadays a dark conservative business suit is considered correct for almost every type of function. Pallbearers frequently wear cutaways at a funeral; and in Washington cutaways are seen a great deal at formal public functions. But the average man today has little use for formal morning attire.

The correct cutaway coat is black, with plain or braided edge. Usually it is worn with a matching waistcoat, but at spring and summer weddings it may be worn with a white piqué or sand-colored double-breasted linen waistcoat. The trousers should be gray-and-black striped, or black with a fine white line. A wing collar, black oxfords, black socks, and either a black-and-white or gray bow tie complete the ensemble. Four-in-hands and ascots may also be worn with cutaway coats, but are considered less formal.

As a compromise between the formality of a cutaway and the informality of an ordinary business suit, many men now wear a plain black or dark gray suit coat with striped trousers for important daytime functions. All other details remain the same, except that a black or gray derby hat is worn instead of a silk hat. This semiformality of dress is acceptable for all but official and highly ceremonious occasions. It's especially desirable for luncheons, teas, receptions, and afternoon parties, as it's more important-looking than ordinary business clothes, and therefore more complimentary to the host.

For all informal daytime and evening functions, a business suit is correct. Well-dressed men wear clothes of conservative pattern and cut, avoid "flashy" accessories.

For sports and informal wear in the country, men can forget their conservatism and indulge their fancy for bright socks and ties, gay sweaters and jackets . . . livelier colors and styles than would be considered good taste in town. Sports clothes should be worn for sports, not for other purposes—golf clothes are for golf, riding clothes for riding. Obviously it is not good taste to wear them for effect only. Slacks and sports shirts are acceptable for all routine country and resort wear, without coat or tie. But both coat and tie should be put on before going into the dining room. A well-bred man never dines in shirt sleeves or without a tie, in his own home or anywhere else. A tweed or flannel jacket worn with well-tailored slacks is correct attire for informal country dances, bridge parties, afternoon teas, and in fact any simple unpretentious country function. A dark coat with white or gray flannel trousers is correct for semiformal occasions, and for church in the country.

Questions Frequently Asked About Dress

Question: What should a woman, dining alone in a large metropolitan hotel, wear?

Answer: She should dress inconspicuously and wear a small hat. Loud or dazzling clothes are especially bad taste on a woman dining alone in a hotel. She may wear a dinner dress, if she likes; but she should avoid a backless or extremely décolleté gown.

Question: May a girl who is going to a dance with a man shorter than herself wear low-heeled shoes? Or must high heels always be worn with a dance dress?

Answer: Ordinarily, high heels are more suitable with dance clothes. But when a girl is taller than her partner, she is wise to wear low heels.

Question: May a woman wear an evening gown when her escort is wearing an ordinary business suit?

Answer: It is not good form to do so. She may wear a semiformal dinner dress (long skirt and covered shoulders) if he wears a plain dark blue suit with a starched collar and black bow tie or plain tie. But if she wears formal evening clothes, he should dress formally too.

Question: Does the hostess at an afternoon reception in a hotel keep on her hat?

Answer: Yes.

Question: How does a woman dress for a formal "At Home" in honor of an important visiting celebrity?

Answer: Exactly as she would for any formal daytime function, in street-length afternoon dress—perhaps a little more elaborately than she would dress for an ordinary tea or bridge party.

Question: Is it considered bad taste to wear a fur jacket over slacks?

Answer: Yes; slacks call for a casual sports jacket.

Question: Does a woman speaker at an afternoon club meeting wear a hat?

Answer: Yes.

Question: Is it bad form to telephone one's hostess to find out whether daytime or evening clothes should be worn?

Answer: Not at all. It's the sensible thing to do if you are in doubt.

Question: Do men still carry a cane when they wear full dress?

Answer: Only if they wish; there is no firm rule about it. If a stick *is* carried, it should be of plain malacca or other wood, with little or no ornamentation.

Question: Do ladies wear hats to informal Saturday night parties when elaborate but street-length dresses are worn?

Answer: Whether the dress is simple or elaborate is no factor. Hats are properly worn with street-length clothes, on Saturday night or any other night. It's true that nowadays many women in suburban communities and small towns go hatless, day and night; but that doesn't make it right. In cosmopolitan cities like New York, well-dressed women always wear hats with street-length clothes—do not wear hats with dinner or evening clothes.

Question: Are evening gowns ever worn in the balconies of theaters?

Answer: Not as a rule. But on gala first nights in New York, evening gowns are seen all over the theater—even in the balcony.

Question: Must men's dress shoes be patent leather?

Answer: With formal tails, yes. With a tuxedo, preferably but not necessarily.

Question: When does a woman wear a train?

Answer: When trains are in fashion for formal décolleté "ball" gowns, worn to elaborate functions.

Question: At large public formal receptions do people keep on their gloves?

Answer: On very formal occasions, men as well as women shake hands with gloves on.

Question: Is it considered bad form to go without stockings in the summer?

Answer: On city streets, and at even the most informal social functions in town, bare legs are in bad taste on all except the very young. In the country and in small suburban communities, it is not objectionable to go without stockings.

Question: Are spats still worn, and if so, when are they correct?

Answer: Spats were once very popular with formal morning coats, or cutaways. But they are rarely worn now, and are not considered especially smart. At fashionable weddings, white or sand-colored spats are still occasionally worn by the groom, best man, and ushers, for a more gala effect; but otherwise they are almost never seen any more.

Question: When long gloves are worn as part of a formal costume, should they be removed before going in to dinner, or may they just be tucked in at the wrist?

Answer: They should be removed. It is a breach of etiquette to eat with gloves on.

Question: What kind of hat does a man wear with a white tuxedo?

Answer: A straw or panama, or none at all.

3. TELEPHONE AND RADIO COURTESY

ALL of us use the telephone; but few of us ever give thought to the all-important matter of telephone courtesy.

The first thing is to answer the telephone *promptly*. You wouldn't keep friends waiting impatiently at the front door; don't keep them waiting at the other end of your telephone.

Answer the telephone *pleasantly*. Don't be impatient or gruff just because the person at the other end can't see you. Put a smile in your voice. Be friendly!

Answer the telephone *courteously*. Don't be rude, curt, abrupt—no matter how irritating the situation may be. If the call is for someone who isn't at home, be polite and helpful about it. Suggest taking the message, or having the person call back. If it's a wrong number, just say so. Don't get angry about it.

Answer the telephone *intelligently*. Be brief, concise, to the point. Don't go into a long discussion about unrelated subjects. Don't gossip. The person at the other end may be very busy, but too polite to cut off the flow of long-winded chatter. Remember: the telephone is an instrument of convenience, to speed and facilitate communication—not a gadget for the amusement of those with a lot of time to waste.

Answer the telephone *clearly*. Always speak directly into the mouthpiece, with your lips about half an inch away. And pronounce each word plainly, distinctly, for slurred words and dropped syllables are doubly difficult to understand on the telephone.

Don't shout on the telephone; it isn't necessary. Just speak in a quiet, normal tone of voice, as you would to a person in the same room with you. You aren't talking over a long line or wire, you know. The delicately sensitized transmitter conveys the vibrations of your voice as easily over a long distance as over a short one. So speak softly, without raising your voice—but speak clearly, distinctly, and directly into the transmitter.

COURTESY IN MAKING TELEPHONE CALLS

Try not to call people at mealtimes or other inconvenient times of the day. A call that is an interruption is no more welcome to the person who receives it than an untimely visit.

When you call someone's house on the telephone, give your name at once. If a butler or maid answers the phone, give your full name:

"This is Mrs. Frank Thompson. May I speak to Mrs. Curtis, please." Don't ask for an adult member of the family by a first name. And don't ask, "Is Mrs. Curtis home?" until you announce your own name.

If there are no servants and you do not recognize the voice of the person who answers the telephone, you say: "This is Mrs. Thompson. I'd like to speak to Mrs. Curtis, please."

If there are several daughters and you want to speak to one of them, you ask for her specifically—not as "Miss Curtis," but as "Miss *Joan* Curtis."

If it's the home of an intimate friend and you recognize the voice of the person who answers, you say: "Hello—Patricia? This is Alice Thompson. How are you? May I speak to Joan, please." It's rude not to greet the person who answers the phone when you know all the members of the family.

If you are calling Mrs. Curtis socially and she herself answers the phone, you say, "Hello, Mrs. Curtis. This is Alice Thompson." You do not say "Mrs. Thompson" unless you are considerably older than she is. Or if it's a business call, you say, "This is Mrs. Thompson of the Wide World Travel Bureau."

Of course if it's an intimate friend you are calling and you recognize her voice at once, you naturally drop all formality and greet her as you would in person: "Joan, darling—this is Alice! How are you?"

A man calling a woman socially says, "This is Peter Cushing"—not "Mr. Cushing." Only when a man calls a woman on business is it correct to say, "This is Mr. Cushing of Stern Brothers." But when calling a man, he'd be more likely to say, "This is Cushing of Stern Brothers."

Don't play guessing games when you call someone on the telephone. It's childish and ill-mannered to say, "Guess who this is!" In these busy days people just don't have the time or the patience to guess who is calling. And even people with all the time in the world to waste are likely to be annoyed when they are challenged to "guess who it is." The first and most fundamental rule of telephone courtesy is to state who you are and why you are calling. Anything else is inconsiderate . . . and therefore rude.

IF SOMEONE PUTS IN A CALL FOR YOU

It is extremely bad manners to have someone put in a call for you, and then keep the person at the other end waiting until it's convenient for you to answer. By such procedure you imply that the other person's time is less valuable than your own—certainly a rude affront, whether intended or not!

There's no objection, of course, in having someone call a number for you. But you must stand by and be ready to pick up the receiver as soon as the connection is made. A person who has been interrupted in the middle of whatever he happened to be doing and called to the telephone should not be kept waiting unless it's absolutely unavoidable (as sometimes happens in business). In that case the person who asked that the call be made should explain the delay and apologize for it as soon as he is able to take the wire.

COURTESY IN ANSWERING TELEPHONE CALLS

In a private home, "Hello" is still the most convenient and practical way for members of the family to answer the telephone. Servants are generally instructed to say "Mrs. Blank's residence." But many families prefer not to throw wide the doors, so to speak, and announce whose household it is until they know who is calling. The method of response by a servant must therefore depend upon the family's personal preference, and upon the needs and desires of the particular household.

In business, of course, it saves time to say, "Stern Brothers—Mr. Cushing speaking." And in the combined home and office of a physician it helps avoid confusion to say, "Dr. Benton's office" or "Dr. Benton's residence," as the case may be.

But for a woman in her own home to answer, "Mrs. Clark's residence" is stiff and formal . . . and somehow a little pompous. "Mrs. Clark speaking" leaves the lady of the house with no chance of retreat if it happens to be a persistent salesman calling. "Hello"—pronounced with a rising inflection as though you were asking, "Who is there?" —leaves it squarely up to the person at the other end to announce who he is and what he wants. If he says, "This is John Trenner; may I speak to Mrs. Clark, please?"—she answers, "This is she."

If a servant answers the telephone, it's correct to ask, "Who is calling, please?" The person should give his or her name at once, and the reason for calling: "This is Mrs. Oliver Preston. I'd like to talk to Mrs. Clark about next Sunday's bazaar." But if the caller curtly retorts, "Never mind who's calling! I want to talk to Mrs. Clark personally," whoever answers the telephone should say, "I'm sorry. I cannot interrupt Mrs. Clark unless you tell me your name."

When an intimate of the household calls and recognizes the voice of the maid who answers the telephone, she says, "Hello, Kate. This is Mrs. Brent. May I speak to Mrs. Clark, please." The well-trained maid replies, "How do you do, Mrs. Brent. Just a moment—I'll call Mrs. Clark."

If it's the dinner hour, and especially if there are guests for dinner, the maid should say, "I'll see if Mrs. Clark can come to the telephone." And if it's awkward or inconvenient for Mrs. Clark to leave the table at that time, she may instruct the maid to take the message or to tell whoever is on the telephone that she will call back a little later.

Of if there is no maid, Mrs. Clark herself may say to a friend who telephones at an inconvenient time, "Can I call you back in half an hour, Kathy? We're at dinner"—unless, of course, it's an important call that cannot wait. Being frank about a call that's inconvenient is by no means a rudeness, and should not be so interpreted. On the contrary, it's rude to interrupt and delay dinner for no better purpose than chatting with a friend on the telephone.

Don't Let Small Children Answer the Telephone

In a well-managed household, the telephone is always answered by a responsible person: never by a maid who cannot speak the language, nor by a small child who knows only a few half-intelligible words. Few people nowadays have the time or inclination to hang on while Junior is coaxed to "Say 'Hello' to Aunt Lillian!" It may be awfully bright and precocious of the youngster, but it's also time-consuming— and often very boring.

When the youngster is old enough to talk like a human being and to take messages properly, that's another story. But until that happy time, answer the telephone yourself . . . and impress upon your growing child that the telephone is an important means of communication, not an amusing play toy.

Invitations by Telephone

For many informal types of parties a telephone call is likely to be the only invitation. One simply calls up about a week or so ahead of time and says, "How about coming for bridge next Tuesday afternoon"—or "We're having a buffet supper Sunday night. Can you and Ted come?"

It's not good manners for the person who receives a telephone invitation to hesitate about it, as though weighing its possibilities for enjoyment, and to say "Well, I'll have to let you know . . ." The courteous person accepts or declines at once—graciously.

Never preface an invitation with, "What are you doing Sunday night?" That puts the other person on the spot, so to speak—doesn't give him the right of choice. If he says "nothing" and is then invited to a bridge game (which game he detests and would much rather avoid) he cannot very well refuse. If he says he has an engagement for that evening, and then learns he was to have been invited to something he'd like very much, he cannot change his mind without embarrassment.

So don't say, "What are you doing Sunday night," but "We're having a party Sunday night; would you like to come?" In this, as in everything, show your friends the same courtesy and consideration you would expect from them.

Paying for Calls on Other People's Telephones

The question of whether or not to pay for a call made on a friend's or neighbor's telephone is sometimes embarrassing to people, but it shouldn't be. There is no reason to feel that the neighbor or friend will resent proffered payment for the call. A debt incurred must be paid; and certainly a call made on somebody else's telephone is a debt. A single local call made by a visitor or house guest can be overlooked. But several calls made in the course of a visit—and certainly every long-distance call—should be paid for.

Upon completing a long-distance call, a visitor should immediately call back the operator and ask for the toll charge. She should then either pay the hostess at once, or make a note of the date and the number and pay for all her calls at the time of leaving.

Payment for calls is good practice, and an experienced hostess takes it as a matter of course. She knows that guests in her house cannot feel free to use the telephone as much as they like or need unless they are permitted to pay for the bills they run up. It is not good manners to make a fuss about it; but when, through a mistaken sense of hospitality, someone does make a fuss, it's best to drop the subject and later on send a little gift "for the courtesy of using your telephone for so many of my personal calls!"

Postscripts on Telephone Courtesy

Always keep a pencil and pad right next to the telephone. Then you won't have to keep people waiting while you rush off to find something to write on.

If you must refer to a letter or bill that you can't put your hand on instantly, or search for an address or telephone number that you have misplaced, don't keep the person on the other end waiting. That is thoughtless and inconsiderate behavior. The courteous procedure is to say, "I don't have the information right here, but I'll find it and call you back in a few minutes." Or if there is no urgency about it, "I'll find the bill [or the letter, or the recipe, or whatever it may be] and mail it to you today."

If the telephone rings just when the baby wakes up and demands attention, or the decorator arrives with your new drapes, or your young hopeful falls off his bike and comes bawling into the house, don't answer and say "Wait a minute!" It's more courteous not to answer the phone at all than to keep someone waiting indefinitely. If you do answer and can't listen at the moment, explain the circumstances very briefly and say, "I'll call back in a few minutes." Then do so! To say you'll call back and not do it is an unforgivable rudeness.

When you put in a long-distance call, stay right in the room and near the telephone. Don't wander off and make it necessary for someone to go searching for you when the connection is completed.

When you get a wrong number, don't curtly demand, "What number is this?" Ask instead, "Is this Sterling 4600?" Upon being informed that it is not—whether rudely or otherwise—just say you are sorry and hang up.

Don't call "Information" for a number you can easily find for yourself in the telephone book. Others who really need information—perhaps urgently—may be kept waiting by your unnecessary call.

After using the telephone, people with colds should at once wipe out the mouthpiece with tissue or a clean handkerchief. This is for the protection of others who use the same instrument. Unfortunately it's a custom few observe, but which *all* should be encouraged to do as a simple, basic courtesy to others.

Needless to say, well-bred people never listen in on other people's telephone conversations—whether by accident or design.

RADIO AND TELEVISION COURTESY

There are just a few basic rules of radio and television courtesy that everyone should know. But these few rules are important.

Everyone knows, of course, that it's bad manners to keep a radio blaring loudly at night when it's likely to disturb others who want to sleep. But unfortunately many people are still guilty of this thoughtlessness. Radios that are kept on after ten o'clock—especially in apartments where there may be sleeping children right next door—should be tuned down to the point where they cannot possibly be classified a disturbance.

A radio right next to an open window, or carried out into the garden, can be very annoying to neighbors at any time of the day—if it's kept going full blast. No one objects to the muted sounds of music and of voices. But the loud, staccato report of a fight or game, or the frenzied rhythm of a jazz band, can be maddening to a neighbor who wants to read, study, think . . . or just relax in peace and quiet.

Portable radios are a fine convenience—wonderful for picnics, boats, and out-of-the-way places. But don't take a portable radio into a hotel card room or writing room, where it's bound to disturb others. Don't use it on a plane, or on any public conveyance where people are busy with their thoughts or trying to read. If you take a portable to the beach, don't sit right next to others; try to find a spot where your radio won't be likely to annoy anyone—and keep it tuned down.

Don't carry on an animated conversation in a room where others are trying to listen to a favorite radio program.

Don't turn on the radio or television in a room where people are playing cards or reading, unless you ask their permission first and are quite sure you won't be disturbing them.

Don't ever turn on the radio or television in somebody else's house unless you have secured permission to do so—or unless, of course, you are a house guest and the equipment is in your own room.

If you invite neighbors or friends for a special television program, let them occupy the best seats, just as you would if they were your guests at the theater. Don't invite more people than you can comfortably accommodate. If they must crowd one another to see the screen, you have invited too many. If you have guests for the evening and there's a choice of television programs, let your guests make the choice. Their preference comes first.

When the Arrival of a Guest Interrupts a Favorite Program

If you are listening to a program when an unexpected guest arrives and you want very much to continue listening to it, just say so. It's much better manners to say, "Hello, there! Come in and listen to the rest of this program with me!" than to turn it off and be irritable about it the rest of the evening.

But of course when expected guests arrive, the radio or television must be turned off at once—however interesting the program may be, however eagerly the family may have been waiting to hear it.

An observant guest, however, will notice *how* the radio is turned off —whether it's done eagerly, or with reluctance. And if she sees that it is snapped off with wistful regret, she says at once, "That was an interesting program! Don't turn it off—let's all listen to it together." Her friends will enjoy her visit all the more for her tact and considereration.

4. THE QUALITIES THAT MAKE YOU A WELCOME GUEST

SOMEONE once asked Eleanor Roosevelt, when she was living in the White House, what quality in a guest she considered least enjoyable. She answered without an instant's hesitation, "Selfishness!"

Selfish people are seldom popular, and do not make welcome guests. Here, as in every other personal relationship, consideration for others is important—consideration for one's hosts, and for the pleasure and convenience of the other guests.

For example, it is selfish and inconsiderate to arrive late, as that makes it difficult for the hostess and unpleasant for the other guests. Always make it a point to arrive *on time*, within ten minutes of the hour specified—neither earlier nor later, unless of course it's unavoidable.

It's especially important to arrive on time when you are invited for a meal. If you arrive too early, the hostess may still be busy with last-minute preparations, or with final touches to her own appearance. If you come late, the roast may be ruined or the salad beginning to wilt —and the hostess is probably wondering why she ever invited you in the first place!

The selfish person who thinks only of his own convenience, his own comfort or pleasure, ignoring responsibility to his hostess and her guests, is ungracious in the extreme. And whatever other qualities he may possess, a *selfish* guest is not likely to be very popular in other people's houses.

As inconsiderate as arriving too early or too late is coming in sloppy clothes, looking too carelessly or casually dressed for the occasion. That is an affront to the hostess, as it implies you do not consider her hospitality important enough to warrant dressing up. It isn't necessary to wear new or elaborate clothes; but it *is* necessary to look well groomed and attractive.

The considerate guest does not, of course, wear rubbers into the house, tracking mud on the carpets and floors. Rubbers and dripping raincoats should always be removed in the entrance hall. He does not push past a maid or butler at the door, but removes outer wraps first and waits to be announced or ushered in. He shows pleasure on arrival, is smiling and affable, clearly delighted to be there, friendly, and eager to meet everyone.

It is most selfish of all to disappoint friends who are expecting you, to telephone at the last moment and say you aren't coming. That's unforgivable, unless there has been some sudden emergency like illness or an accident. Once you have accepted an invitation and the hostess is counting on you, it's your obligation to be there or at least to let her know far enough in advance so that she can invite someone else.

BE CHEERFUL—NOBODY LIKES A KILLJOY

An important fact to bear in mind is that being entertained in someone's home is not merely accepting a treat. It's accepting a *responsibility*.

As a guest at a party, you are expected to contribute to the general fun and good fellowship, to be cheerful and friendly, co-operative, good company. That means being lively and animated, whatever your mood may be. It means being pleasant and agreeable, whoever the other guests may be. It means being amiable about the evening's activities, joining in the fun whether it appeals to you or not.

You can't be good company if you sit around moping all evening, nursing a grouch. Nor do you contribute to anyone's enjoyment of the evening by talking endlessly of your symptoms, complaining about your personal problems. *Be cheerful!* People go to parties for a good time, and the best-liked guests are those who *help* them have a good time.

So keep your troubles to yourself. Leave your moods, your peeves, your bad temper at home. Start out with the idea that you are going to like everyone at the party, and that you are going to do everything you can to help make the party a success.

HELP MAKE THE PARTY GO

One of your major responsibilities as a guest is to contribute intelligently to the conversation, *to help make the party go*. This doesn't mean monopolizing the talk, but holding up your end of it by keeping it lively and interesting. Instead of trying to "shine" and make a hit yourself, concentrate on getting others to talk and on making *them* feel important.

Nothing can be more distressing to a good hostess than to have a guest sit in stony silence, looking either shy or bored—and clearly boring everyone else. So don't ever let yourself sit in one corner all evening, listening while others talk, waiting to be entertained. Remember that you are expected to be an active participant, not just an observer.

Don't Take Liberties in Other People's Houses

One of the worst offenses of all is to take liberties in a house where you are being entertained.

Don't use the telephone in someone else's home for long-distance calls. An invitation to a party does not include unlimited use of the telephone. If you *must* use the telephone for a long-distance call, be sure to check with the operator, find out the cost, and pay for the call.

Don't ever wander from room to room in someone's house, curiously looking around, picking up things and examining them.

Don't open a closet, desk drawer, or cabinet, however well you may know your hosts. Well-bred people respect other persons' privacy—and their property.

Don't use a piano or organ in someone's house without first asking permission.

Don't help yourself to liquor unless you are specifically invited to do so.

Don't go into the kitchen unless the hostess asks you to, or insist on helping if she prefers doing things herself.

Don't give orders to servants in other people's houses—that's a serious breach of manners! And don't get familiar with the servants in your friends' homes, even if you know them a long time. Be courteous, be friendly—but don't be familiar.

Don't search in your hosts' medicine cabinet for aspirin or headache pills. If you need anything, ask for it.

Don't take books down from library shelves and leave them carelessly on a table or chair. Put them back where they belong.

Don't put wet glasses or burning cigarettes where they can do damage.

These are simple, ordinary courtesies, yet it's amazing how many people blithely ignore them. If you want to be a welcome guest, be courteous and considerate—and *don't take liberties.*

Show Your Appreciation

Too many people take hospitality for granted, accepting it as their due. But the guest everyone loves to entertain is *appreciative* of hospitality, and doesn't hesitate to show it. It isn't necessary to be gushy about it; but a simple expression of gratitude for a good time is always well received.

When you have been generously entertained in someone's house, *show your appreciation*, even if it's nothing more than a sincere "Thank you" when you are leaving. If you like to be especially courteous and thoughtful, write a little note in the next day or so to say how much you enjoyed the evening.

Don't Overstay Your Welcome

We are all familiar with the guest who never knows when to leave —the "bitter ender" who stays on and on until everyone else is gone . . . and then stays on some more to talk things over!

Gluyas Williams calls them "night-blooming guests" because they seem to come to life at midnight and grow brighter and fresher with each passing hour, regardless of the fact that their hosts are practically expiring.

Never risk overstaying your welcome. Decide what is the best time to leave, and when that time comes—*go!* Don't dawdle, keeping your host and hostess standing in an open doorway, making unnecessary last remarks. When you are at the door, have said goodbye, and have thanked your host and hostess for a good time, take your leave promptly. Long, awkward leave-takings are an ordeal for everyone.

5. THE QUALITIES THAT MAKE YOU A GRACIOUS HOST OR HOSTESS

Successful entertaining is one of the highest of social attainments. Few things give a man or woman greater satisfaction than entertaining graciously and well, with ease and self-possession.

Entertaining isn't a matter of money, a big house, servants, material possessions, social position. It is entirely a matter of spirit and personality—a genuine interest in and liking for people, and a desire to please them. It is a fine art made up of many things, but above all it is a matter of heart. Its essential purpose is to enjoy the company of your friends and to see that they enjoy yours. Its aim is to provide fun, gaiety, and relaxation, to share your house and everything in it.

So whatever the nature or purpose of any gathering in your house, be sure your heart is in it! Look upon it as an opportunity to give people a good time, not as an unpleasant duty or a burden. For only by enjoying the party yourself, and enjoying the people who have come at your bidding, can you hope to function as a charming, gracious hostess.

Choose Your Guests Carefully

A very important factor in entertaining is to show care and judgment in the selection of guests. Even with the best intentions in the world, a woman fails dismally in her role of hostess if she brings together people who bore or annoy each other, or who have violently opposed viewpoints and ideas. No hostess can always be right, of course. But any hostess can avoid turning her party into an open battlefield if she's careful not to invite people who dislike each other or are known to be incompatible.

Always try to invite guests who are congenial, preferably with some interest in common, and with at least reasonably similar tastes and ideas. Don't invite to the same intimate little party people who like nothing better than to sit and talk all evening, and people who simply must play games or be unutterably bored. Don't invite to the same dinner party sophisticated career people who like to talk of world affairs and simple homebodies who tend to be uneasy in such company, who would much prefer talking about their own familiar everyday lives.

Inviting congenial people who enjoy the same sort of things, and who are likely to be comfortable and happy in each other's company, is a large part of the success of any party.

Plan Your Parties to Suit the People You Invite

You naturally entertain in different ways for different people. For your very intimate friends, you entertain frequently and informally— Sunday night buffets, card parties, simple little dinners. For important social occasions you may want to entertain more elaborately, perhaps more formally. But always your purpose should be the same: to give people a good time, to enjoy their company and see that they enjoy yours.

Don't make a practice of inviting people who never drink to cocktail parties, nor people who do not enjoy cards to card parties. Invite them to something they can join in and enjoy, even if it's nothing more than an evening of good, friendly talk.

Don't invite friends to a picnic unless you are reasonably sure they *like* picnics. Many people do not.

Don't invite friends to a concert or musicale unless you feel certain they *like* music and enjoy listening to it. Not everyone does.

Don't invite a busy doctor for dinner on an evening when he has late office hours. Find out when he does *not* have regular hours, and plan your party for that evening.

Don't invite an avowed gourmet to a careless "potluck" supper, an expert bridge player to sit in with beginners, a teen-ager to dine with elderly friends of the family. Such invitations may be generous and hospitable, but they are not wise.

A gracious and accomplished hostess not only has the good judgment to invite the right people, but also makes a point of inviting them to the *right kind of function*.

Invite Guests Well Ahead of Time

In these busy days, invitations are often hurriedly and haphazardly given, sometimes almost at the very last moment. But unless it's for a very informal card party or get-together, planned on the spur of the moment when friends happen to meet, invitations should be issued at least two or three weeks in advance. For however welcome it may be otherwise, an invitation received just a few days before the occasion cannot be considered gracious or thoughtful.

Once you have arranged a party and invited your guests, don't make any sudden last-minute change in plans unless absolutely necessary. To inconvenience half a dozen or more people for your own pleasure or in your own interest is basically bad manners; and something not even a close friend soon forgets.

How to Greet Guests on Arrival

Making friends feel welcome and at ease is the essence of hospitality.

In a gracious home guests are made to feel welcome the instant they arrive. The way the door is opened, the way they are greeted, the way they are ushered in and presented to guests already there—all tend to make them feel special and important. They are given the impression that their arrival has been eagerly awaited.

Whoever opens the door to admit guests should be instructed to open it wide, and to greet the visitor with a friendly smile. To open the door a crack and peer out suspiciously never fails to make a bad impression on arriving guests. A door widely opened is the traditional gesture of welcome; and when guests are expected, this should be the unfailing custom of the household.

On formal occasions, a hostess always stands by the door to greet her guests, and the host stands near by. Both shake hands with every guest on arrival. On informal occasions, host and hostess may be seated with other guests; but both always rise and go forward to greet new arrivals. In a household where there are no servants, either host or hostess may go to the door; but *both* should always rise to greet the guests and shake hands with them. Half-grown children of the family rise when guests enter the room, but do not necessarily shake hands.

The important thing is to make guests feel welcome. A cold, stand-offish greeting can be devastating to a shy guest, or to one who is sensitive. So always make your greeting as cordial and friendly as you can.

A Good Hostess Is Relaxed and at Ease

People go to parties to relax and enjoy themselves. But they cannot relax if there's a sense of strain and worry in the air, if the hostess is tense and harried, and keeps disappearing into the kitchen every few minutes with a faraway, troubled look in her eye. Her uneasiness soon communicates itself to her guests; and though they realize it's for their own welfare that she is nervous and concerned, it's not a pleasant feeling.

Try to make your entertaining as calm and effortless as possible. Complete all preparations well before your guests arrive, and greet them looking rested and cheerful. Don't worry about the refreshments, the appearance of the house, your own appearance, *anything!* A nervous, worried hostess is never a good hostess.

On the other hand, try not to be overzealous in your role of hostess. Don't let your generous instincts run away with you and make you "fuss" over your guests. If the party is going well, the talk lively and interesting, the guests having a good time . . . just sit back and relax. Don't keep jumping up every few minutes to empty ashtrays, pass candy, or cigarettes, refill glasses. Courteous attention to the needs and wants of your guests is fine, of course; but it should be *unobtrusive*. Too much attention can be annoying, and is usually the sign of a hostess who is not quite sure of herself. The less you worry about how the party is going, the more your guests are likely to enjoy themselves.

A Good Hostess Is Tactful

No guest should ever be made to feel uncomfortable or embarrassed, regardless of the circumstances. A gracious hostess is very careful not to look shocked or annoyed no matter what happens.

If an ornament or a piece of furniture is damaged, or a fine cup or glass broken, a well-bred hostess passes it off lightly, doing or saying what she can to put the guest who caused the damage at ease. Then she quickly and tactfully changes the subject, diverting everyone's attention to something else, sparing her guest as much embarrassment as possible.

In a gracious household, a guest is never rebuked for anything—not even for shocking or distressing conduct. He may be taken aside by the host or hostess and privately requested to stop whatever objectionable thing he is doing. He may not soon be invited again (in fact, is very likely never to be invited again!) But he is never censured or rebuked.

A tactful hostess does not talk about previous guests in her home, does not tell about amusing faux pas they made—or in any way hold them up to ridicule. Nor does she complain to guests at her table about the high cost of food or the difficulty of entertaining without servants. She is careful to avoid any remarks that may make her guests feel uncomfortable.

A tactful hostess doesn't try to outshine her guests, but gives them a chance to shine. She does what she can to put nervous or self-conscious people at ease. She draws out shy people, gets them to join in the conversation. She never lets a guest sit alone and neglected on the side lines, but insinuates him into a lively and animated group—deftly, of course, without seeming to.

The accomplished hostess tries to ward off unpleasantness at her parties. If an argument develops and a guest is forced into an embarrassing or unhappy position, she skillfully diverts the discussion and changes the subject. She never lets a guest be subjected to any deliberate unkindness in her house, if she can possibly prevent it.

Above all, a tactful hostess shows *equal courtesy and consideration to all guests*. She does not cater to special or important guests to the point of making others feel neglected or ignored.

Don't Force Entertainment on Guests—Let Them Do What They Like

The greatest charm of any hostess is her alert interest in all her guests. But interest can be carried to extremes; and when the zeal to amuse one's guests reaches the point of *forcing* entertainment on them, it ceases to be charming and becomes an annoyance.

When three or four people are sitting in a group talking, don't feel it's your duty to rush in and break it up, to insist on bridge or dancing. Let them talk, if that's what they want to do.

If guests are sitting around in quiet contentment, sipping their drinks, talking, or perhaps listening to music, don't try to force charades or home movies on them! Save your movies and your games for a bored or restless party, a party that isn't coming off quite as it should. A mood is a fragile thing; and when the mood of your guests is relaxed and contented—*let it be.*

Don't insist on herding your guests to the basement playroom for a television program when they are obviously more interested in continuing their game of gin rummy.

Don't suddenly snap off a television program, or a radio symphony concert to which everyone is listening with delight, and announce: "Well, that's enough of *that!* Let's play bridge." It's up to your guests to decide when they have had enough.

Don't "rescue" the guest who has wandered into your library and is browsing through your books, coyly shouting to him, "Ah, there you are! All by yourself, you poor thing! Come right on out and play gin with the Bartons." The chances are he hates card games, loves browsing through books, and wishes you'd go away and stop being such a diligent hostess.

Guests can be bored beyond words by too much attention from the hostess—too much effort to amuse and entertain them. So don't be continually and obtrusively on the heels of your guests, guiding them, directing their activities, fussing over them like a busy mother hen with her chicks. Give them plenty of freedom to use their own initiative, and to enjoy themselves as they like best.

Consider the Problems and Preferences of Your Guests

If you are an especially gracious hostess, you will try to remember the individual problems and preferences of your guests, so that you can add in every way possible to their enjoyment.

If a guest doesn't like a soft chair, try to remember it and give him a straight-backed chair. If he is known to dislike cats, or is allergic to cat's fur, keep your pet securely out of sight for the evening. If a certain guest never drinks, keep that fact in mind—and remember to serve him fruit juice or tomato juice when you serve the others a cocktail. If another cannot drink coffee at night, don't wait to be reminded of it but serve him some other beverage instead.

Guests are always grateful when you remember their food preferences. This doesn't mean it is necessary to pamper the food fads of everyone who comes to your house. But if a friend has a favorite meat, or vegetable, or dessert, try to have it the night he is a guest for dinner. Or if someone cannot eat a certain food because of an allergy or food idiosyncrasy, remember it and don't serve it the night that friend is at your table. Such thoughtful, kindly attention is the mark of a truly gracious hostess.

PART VII

Etiquette in Public Places

1. ON THE STREET

As we have repeatedly emphasized all through this book, courtesy is simply consideration for others: for their rights, their feelings, their well-being, and their dignity as fellow human beings.

This basic principle applies as much to strangers and casual acquaintances as to our most intimate friends—to our conduct in public places as in private drawing rooms.

General Rules of Good Behavior in Public

One of the first and most important rules of good behavior in public is to avoid making oneself needlessly conspicuous. Well-bred people do not attract attention to themselves by loud talk or laughter, by rude or boisterous actions. Good manners in public, as in private, stem from thoughtful consideration of others.

Courtesy, the simple little civilities we all expect and like to be shown, is what makes the wheels of our everyday lives turn smoothly and pleasantly. Remember that people are quick to recognize courtesy and eager to respond to it. So in public places and on the street, among strangers as among your own personal friends, be courteous. Try not to annoy or inconvenience anyone in any way. Never walk directly and deliberately in front of an oncoming person, but move a little to one side. Don't carry an umbrella or stick carelessly, especially going up a flight of stairs. Avoid getting into the way of people who are obviously hurrying to get somewhere. Remember to keep to the right in passing; and don't walk three or four abreast, making it difficult for others to pass. These may seem like minor and unimportant details, and perhaps they are. But they add up to the sum total of well-bred, courteous behavior in public.

When greeting people on the street, bear in mind that a quiet, unobtrusive manner shows good breeding. You can be cordial without making yourself conspicuous. By all means greet your friends with a cheery "Hello!"—but don't shout it so that strangers turn to see what has happened. Never yell a greeting to someone halfway down the street, nor elbow others rudely out of the way to catch up with an acquaintance in the crowd.

And while we are on the subject of crowds, don't lose sight of the fact that when you are *in* a crowd you are *part* of it . . . and please be a good-natured part of it! Don't be so rudely impatient that you make it even more unpleasant for those around you. Don't shove or push; don't glower at people who cannot help crowding close. An understanding smile goes a long way toward making everyone feel better.

If you meet friends on a busy thoroughfare, don't stop to talk to them right in the way of everyone passing by. Walk on together, or move off to one side where people won't have to make a detour around you.

Don't talk about family affairs or discuss people by name in a public place so that others can overhear what you are saying. It is very discourteous to talk about personal or private affairs, your own or anyone else's, in a loud tone of voice.

If you stop someone on the street to ask directions, remember to say "please" and "thank you." If you are a man, raise your hat; if you are a woman, give your most gracious smile. It takes very little effort to be polite, but it pays enormous dividends, often works magic with strangers. Few can resist the charm of a genuinely *courteous* personality.

Some Things Well-Bred People Never Do

There are certain things that people of good taste and good manners never do in public. Some of these are so obvious as to be scarcely worthy of mention. Others are not quite so obvious, and should be emphasized for the benefit of those who wish to avoid rude, offensive behavior among strangers.

These are some of the things so plainly obvious that it's almost embarrassing to mention them: Well-bred people never cough, sneeze, or yawn without instantly covering the mouth. They do not eat on the street, clean or file their nails in public, comb their hair or pick their teeth in the presence of others. If they chew gum at all, they do so inconspicuously. If they powder their noses, they do so quickly and briefly—without attempting a complete make-up job. Any major repairs to the personal appearance should be done in *private*, not in public.

Well-bred people don't slam doors in people's faces. They don't try to push ahead of others on a waiting line, or edge in ahead of their turn at a telephone booth or information desk. They never deliberately take unfair or unkind advantage of anyone, stranger or not, for they know that such behavior does not contribute to an attractive, desirable personality.

Well-bred people try to be poised and controlled in public, regardless of the circumstances. They don't lose their temper at the least little thing. They don't argue or bicker in a loud tone of voice, pick quarrels, noisily berate waiters and others who serve them—or in any way attract unfavorable attention to themselves or to others.

Well-bred people do not make a public display of their emotions, do not kiss and embrace in the presence of others. They do not appear on city streets or in public places without stockings, without a tie, in shorts, with curlers in the hair—or otherwise unsuitably or inadequately dressed. They don't think it's "smart" to ignore No Smoking or No Admittance signs, for they realize they are often placed there for their own comfort and protection.

The truly courteous never stare or point at people, nor make personal comments about them. They are careful not to ridicule anyone or make fun of those who are different from themselves.

SHAKING HANDS

The handshake is a natural and instinctive gesture of friendliness. It dates back to primitive times when cave men extended the weapon hand, unarmed, to show friendly and peaceful intentions.

There were once firm rules of etiquette concerning the shaking of hands—such as when it was proper to shake and when not, whose hand went out first, and so on. But such precise regulations have little place in the modern world. People nowadays are inclined to be pleasantly informal and spontaneous about such things.

The rule used to be that when a man and woman meet in public, the woman offers her hand first; but today, more likely than not, both hands go out in a simultaneous gesture of greeting. At any rate, it's no longer a fixed convention; it doesn't matter whose hand goes out first —or whether they shake hands at all. A nod and cordial smile serve the same friendly purpose.

Two men meeting on the street or in a public place generally shake hands. But two women usually do not; they merely nod and smile in greeting. Strangers usually but do not necessarily shake hands on being introduced.[1]

[1] For more on this subject, see page 19.

RAISING OR REMOVING THE HAT

Raising the hat is a traditional gesture of courtesy and respect. In general, a man always raises his hat on meeting or taking leave of a lady. But there are many other occasions when a man is called upon to raise or lift his hat in public, or to remove it entirely and hold it in his hand. For example:

When he gives his seat to a woman, or picks up something she has dropped, or performs any little service or courtesy for her.

When someone gives a seat to the woman he is accompanying, or performs some service or courtesy for her.

When the woman he is with bows to someone, or is greeted by an acquaintance in passing.

When he is walking with a woman and a male acquaintance of his greets him.

When a woman addresses him to ask for information or directions; and again when she thanks him for his help.

When he must pass in front of a woman in a narrow passage, or hurry ahead of her through a door. (He says "I'm sorry" or "I beg your pardon" and lifts his hat.)

When a woman makes way for him in a crowded subway or bus so that he can reach the door. (He says "Thank you" and touches the brim of his hat.)

When he is in the elevator of a hotel, apartment house, or club and there are women present.

When he greets a minister, a very old or very distinguished man, or a superior in office.

When the American flag is passing or the national anthem is played. (The hat is held in front of the left shoulder.)

When he is at a funeral, or in the presence of death.

GOOD MANNERS WHEN A MAN AND WOMAN MEET

When a man meets a woman acquaintance on the street, he raises his hat, bows, and smiles pleasantly in greeting. If they stop to talk, he removes his hat and holds it in his hand, regardless of the weather. If she is a woman of his own age, he replaces his hat as they stand talking. But if she is an older woman, he does not replace it unless she suggests that he do so.

If he is smoking a pipe or cigar when they meet, he holds it in his hand during their conversation. If he is smoking a cigarette, he throws it away. It's rude for a man to smoke while he stands talking with a woman, unless she herself urges him to do so.

Often, if they are going in the same direction, they walk on together. But the suggestion should come from her, not him. Of course if they walk together, he replaces his hat.

If a woman's arms are full of packages, a gentleman will naturally offer to carry them for her. She should graciously accept his offer, for it would be awkward and embarrassing for him to walk unencumbered while she struggled along with her burden. But if it's a small package which she is perfectly able to manage without help, she should do so.

On Walking with a Woman

Traditionally a man walks on the outside, nearest the curb—though the once-logical reasons for this practice have long since ceased to exist. When roads were muddy lanes and runaway horses a daily menace, a woman needed the protection of a man walking beside her next to the road. Though the need is now gone, the custom lingers on; and a gentleman still clings to the curb side when walking with a lady.

He does not, however, link his arm in hers. He does not grasp her firmly by the elbow. He offers the protection of his own arm only when there is some very good reason for it.

For example, a man offers his arm to a lady when they are crossing a busy or dangerous thoroughfare, or when there is likelihood of becoming separated in a crowd. He offers his arm when the pavement is icy or uneven, or the road rough or bumpy, or whenever there is danger or difficulty in walking. He may support her by the elbow for a moment to help her up or down a curb; but otherwise his arms are at his own side.

On Walking with Two Women

It was once the rule that a gentleman *always* walked on the curb side of the sidewalk, whether with one woman or several. But since the ladies no longer require protection from runaway horses and mud-spattering lanes, the rule has ceased to have any significance—and is gradually coming to be disregarded.

Today when a man walks with two women, he walks *between* them (if he is sensible and not too tradition-bound!), so that he can talk easily to both and give both the same attention. If he is with a group of ladies, he lets the curb take care of itself and devotes himself to the pleasure of their company, walking wherever is most pleasant and convenient for all concerned.

On Streetcars, Buses, and Subways

There is probably nowhere that rudeness more quickly betrays itself than in a public conveyance, where people are often crowded in great discomfort and have more reason than ordinarily to lose their tempers and forget their manners. But neither is there any place where simple courtesy can mean so much, and win such grateful response.

It's true that in the scramble and confusion of the rush hour there is little time or chance for elaborate politeness. But there is always time for a smile instead of a scowl, for a friendly attitude instead of a disagreeable one. There is, in fact, no better opportunity to display good manners than when the general tendency of others is to be rude and thoughtless.

So even when the only way to get aboard is to be jammed along with the crowd, be pleasant about it! Don't add to the confusion and discomfort by shoving, pushing, or squeezing ahead of people. You'll get on just as well—better, in fact. For by giving those ahead of you a chance to get on or off first, you stand a better chance of getting on or off yourself. Crowds always move more quickly and efficiently when people co-operate and are orderly.

Following are some suggestions for courteous behavior on subways, streetcars and buses:

Don't hold up a line of hurrying people while you fumble for your fare; have it ready.

Don't try to get on while outcoming passengers are trying to get off. Give them a chance, and you'll get on more easily and pleasantly yourself.

Don't block the doorways if you can help it. Always try to move down toward the center of the car.

Don't take small children and big packages on subways or buses during the rush hours. Go at an off time instead.

Don't rush for a seat ahead of an old or infirm person who needs it more than you do.[2]

Don't pile bags or briefcases near the door or in the aisle where people may trip over them.

[2]See page 9 for the etiquette of giving up one's seat in a subway or bus.

Don't occupy more seat than you are entitled to; keep packages and small children on your lap.

Don't spread out your newspaper in a crowded subway or bus, to the discomfort of those around you.

Don't cross your feet when someone is standing in front of you. People don't like to have shoes wiped off on their clothes.

Don't put your feet on the empty seat opposite; the next one who sits there may be wearing new clothes. (Would you like it?)

Remember: *It pays to be polite.* Courtesy is contagious. Try being pleasant and agreeable toward strangers next time you are on a bus or subway, and see what happens. See how eagerly people respond to friendly, courteous overtures . . . there is usually so little of it in public places where it is needed most.

In Public Buildings

It's just as necessary to be courteous and thoughtful of others in public buildings as elsewhere, perhaps even more so.

One of the most important rules to bear in mind is never to stop in a doorway or busy corridor to talk, making it difficult for others to get by. People who must stop to talk should find a spot where they will not be in anyone's way.

In the lobbies and corridors of an office building, a man may keep on his hat; but he removes it, of course, as soon as he enters a private office. In a public building like a museum or library, a man always removes his hat the moment he enters.

The elevator of an office building is in the same category as the corridor and street. Men generally keep their hats on even when there are ladies present; but naturally a gentleman always removes his hat when a lady he knows walks in.

It's always "ladies first" of course going through doors, down aisles, into and out of elevators, and so on. But this isn't always possible in the crowded elevator of an office building. As a rule the men step aside and let the ladies out first *only if they can do so easily and conveniently.* Otherwise they avoid confusion and delay by stepping out quickly in turn.

At museums, exhibits, memorial buildings, art galleries, and the like, a quiet attentive manner is the first essential—combined with a strict policy of *hands off.* In some museums, notably the Museum of Science and Industry in New York, visitors are encouraged to press buttons, turn cranks, move gadgets, and otherwise operate the exhibits for their interest and instruction. But unless the exhibits are clearly and unmistakably so marked, visitors should under no circumstances touch or handle them. Rare and costly paintings, sculpture, tapestries, and objects of art can be easily damaged by inquisitive fingers. Small children should not be permitted to run wild in a museum or art gallery; they should be held by the hand and carefully restrained from touching what is not supposed to be touched.

In libraries, especially in the reference rooms where people go to read and study, *quiet* is the first rule of conduct. It's rude and inconsiderate to disturb the readers by whispering, rattling papers, moving about a great deal, talking loudly, or laughing.

People who avail themselves of the use of a public library should know its rules and be guided by them. They should take excellent care of the library's property, should never damage or mutilate a book in any way. When reference books are taken from the shelves, they should be replaced exactly where they came from or left on the table for a librarian to take care of. A misplaced reference book can be a great annoyance and waste of time to the next person who must use it.

It's a great privilege to be able to examine rare old books and manuscripts at public libraries, and those who enjoy this privilege should have the courtesy to examine them with extreme care. They should bear in mind that old books and papers are fragile and easily damaged, and sometimes impossible to repair or replace.

Store Etiquette

For etiquette in stores and shops, and etiquette in a doctor's office, see pages 503 to 505.

In Church

The keynote of good manners in church is reverence. Loud talking or laughing, waving to people, primping, rattling papers or squirming around restlessly or curiously—all these are out of keeping with the dignity of a church.

Well-bred churchgoers make it a point to be on time, as late arrivals are disturbing to the worshipers as well as the clergyman. If unavoidably late, they enter quietly and take a seat in the rear.

Men always remove their hats in the vestibule, the moment they enter the door. They do not replace them until they are leaving the vestibule and going out into the street.

Women should dress suitably (never in sweaters or slacks!) and should wear hats and gloves. Conspicuous make-up and strong perfume are out of place in church; and jangling charm bracelets are usually an annoyance to everyone around.

It's courteous for those who arrive early to take central seats so that others can be seated without too much disturbance. Those who pass others in a pew to get to their seats always face the altar and say "Excuse me" or "Sorry" (very quietly) as they pass.

Elaborate greetings before or during services are in very bad taste. If neighbors and friends are greeted at all, it should be with an almost imperceptible smile and nod of the head. The time for friendly talk is after the services when people meet outside the church.

Whispering during services is rude. Tapping with feet or fingers is irritating—a habit one should guard against and control. Giggling, motioning to friends, passing notes are very bad manners in church, not to be tolerated even in irrepressible teen-agers.

Unless there's a very good reason for it, no one should leave a church before the service is over. If one knows that it may be necessary for him to leave early, he should take a seat in the last row, and should leave as quietly and inconspicuously as possible.

Well-bred people do not congregate in the aisles and doorways after a church service, blocking the way of people who want to leave. They wait until they are outside before they engage in lengthy conversations.

Men should not take out cigarettes and put them in their mouths until they are outside the church and on the street.

ETIQUETTE OF THE HIGHWAY

There can be no question about the fact that courtesy prevents accidents and that courteous drivers are safer, more dependable drivers. Indeed, the toll of accidents is high every year largely because of the lack of courtesy in driving. And the toll will continue high until motorists realize that safe driving is not just "legal" driving; it is also careful driving based on consideration for others on the road.

The rules and regulations of driving vary in different states, and every motorist should, of course, acquaint himself with the rules of the locality in which he is driving. But courtesy in driving is something that cannot be legislated; it depends on the motorist alone. Even a skillful and experienced driver cannot be considered a safe driver unless he also drives courteously.

Following are some basic rules of road courtesy. Many are legal re quirements as well—but all of them add up to *safer driving*. Sensible motorists will follow these suggestions, for nowhere is courtesy more reciprocal than on the road.

Suggestions for Motorists

If you like to drive slowly, courtesy demands that you stay well over to the right and let faster cars pass. Don't "hog" the road.

Don't drive too slowly where there is no opportunity for others to pass. You may be holding up someone who is ill and on the way to the hospital, or someone who must make a plane or train.

Don't confuse the driver behind you by putting out your arm to point at the scenery or shake the ashes from your cigar.

Hand signals differ in different states. Acquaint yourself with local rules and customs, and try not to give false signals.

Don't wait until the last moment to give a signal. Always give the driver behind enough time to prepare himself for whatever turn you plan to make.

Don't crowd the car ahead of you. Keep a courteous distance—a *safe* distance.

Weaving in and out of traffic is dangerous; and yet there are times when you must cut out or you must cut in. Sometimes it's difficult to draw the line between reckless "weaving" and proper driving. The only way to judge is for the driver to ask himself if *he* would want others to cut him under the same conditions. If not, he should stay in line until a better opportunity for cutting presents itself.

Don't use the horn unnecessarily. Use it for warning or for signals only—not to give vent to your anger or impatience. Never keep a finger on the horn; that's as ill-mannered and undignified as turning to glare or snarl at another motorist.

At night, dim your headlights when there is an oncoming car (unless they are equipped with non-glare glass.) If your lights blind the driver, you endanger your own life as well as his.

Don't try to "beat the light." Traffic experts say many accidents are caused that way. Slow down when you see that the light is about to change; and don't start up again until the red light is green.

Give the pedestrian a fair chance when he's caught midway across the street and the light changes. Don't make him sprint for safety. (Do you like it when you're a pedestrian?)

Don't speed through puddles on rainy days so that bystanders on the curb are spattered with mud.

Don't monopolize parking space meant for two cars.

Suggestions for Pedestrians

Don't dart across the street from behind a parked car. Oncoming drivers cannot see you, and if you are hit it's your own fault.

Cross at intersections only, and with the light when there is one.

If you must walk in a road at night, always stay well over on the left side—facing oncoming cars.

If you are wearing dark clothes and must cross dark or dimly lit highways, tie a white handkerchief around your arm so that motorists can see and avoid you. It's a sensible precaution.

Don't lose your temper and shout or swear at a rude driver. It doesn't do any good . . . and it certainly isn't characteristic of poised, well-bred behavior.

2. AT THEATERS AND OTHER PUBLIC AMUSEMENTS

THOUGHTLESS behavior at the theater and other places of public amusement is perhaps even more noticeable than anywhere else, for the boisterous or offensive actions of one person can completely ruin the enjoyment of a performance for everyone in the vicinity.

Although the suggestions that follow are specifically for the theater, they apply as well to the movies, concerts, operas, lectures, and all forms of entertainment—except sporting events and the circus. These have a liberal and wholly informal etiquette of their own!

ARRIVING AT THE THEATER

It is not good manners to arrive late at the theater for the purpose of "making an entrance." Latecomers are disturbing to the performers and to the audience.

As a rule, tickets for the theater are purchased in advance. When they are not, or when the tickets are to be picked up at the box office, one man in the party attends to this while the others wait in the lobby, keeping well to one side so that they do not block the entrances. In the case of a man and woman attending the theater together, she may wait in the lobby—or if the line is a very long one, she may prefer to walk slowly beside him instead of waiting alone.

When a large number of people enter the theater in one party, the person with the tickets goes first. But when a man and woman enter together, she precedes even though he has the tickets.

Men generally check their overcoats as they are too bulky to hold. If a coat is not checked, it should be removed before going down the aisle. Women who remove their coats either hold them or let them hang over the back of the seat—being very careful not to disturb the people sitting in front or behind.

GOING DOWN THE AISLE

After a man and woman have entered the theater, and he has removed and checked his coat, he finds an usher and hands him the tickets. The usher leads the way down the aisle, followed by the woman and then the man. In a very dark or very crowded theater, the man may go first to help her; but when they reach their seats, he always steps aside and lets her enter first.

When there are several people in the group, the person with the tickets goes first. If there is to be a definite plan of seating, it should be arranged before they go to their places. For example, the host of a large theater party should tell the guests at the back of the theater, *before they start down the aisle,* how they are to sit—so that they can proceed in that order and take their places with a minimum of confusion.

The hostess of a large party of women precedes them down the aisle, and courteously stands to one side when they reach their places, letting them enter and take seats in any order they wish. She does not attempt to direct their seating arrangement from the aisle, as that usually creates a great deal of commotion and makes the party conspicuous.

If the curtain has already gone up and the performance started, the least that latecomers can do is to be extremely quiet on the way down the aisle and in taking their places.

SEATING ARRANGEMENTS

The lady or ladies in a party enter the row of seats first, unless it's a very large party and more convenient for each couple to enter in turn. The formalities of precedence are disregarded in a public place like a theater.

The proper way to enter is facing the stage, being careful not to tread on the toes of those already seated or brush against the heads of people in front. If someone *is* bumped or disturbed in any way in passing, a polite "I'm sorry!" is required. A man entering the row after ladies *in his party* have been seated, turns to face them instead of the stage as he slips by to his own place further on.

Men rise from their seats to let other people pass; but a woman may remain seated unless she has a heavy coat in her lap and it's clearly difficult for anyone to get by. Courteous people say "Thank you" to those who get up to make room for them—not necessarily to each person in the row, but to several at a time in passing. When the performance is in progress, men often do not rise but merely turn their knees to one side to provide passageway. This is a courtesy to those behind, who would otherwise have their view of the stage momentarily cut off.

When a man and woman attend the theater together, the man usually occupies the seat nearest the aisle. If they have the last two seats in a row, the rule has always been that he must take the aisle seat. However, like so many other rules that serve no useful purpose in modern life, this too is gradually being relaxed. If a woman is short and can see better from the end seat, there's no reason in the world why she shouldn't sit there—unless of course she is a member of a theater party which is observing the traditional formalities.

As a rule, a group of two couples are seated with a man on either side and the two women between. But there are no fixed rules for seating groups of people. They sit any way they find pleasant and agreeable.

In boxes at the theater or opera, the women occupy the front chairs —the men those behind. A courteous hostess always gives the best seat to the oldest or most distinguished guest, taking the least desirable position for herself. The host usually takes the seat directly behind his wife.

CONCERNING WOMEN'S HATS

A tiny woman wearing a postage-stamp hat may keep it on if she wishes. But anyone whose hat is even remotely likely to interfere with the view of persons behind—especially if it's a hat with towering feather, flowers, or bows—should remove it as soon as she is seated, *and without waiting to be asked.*

If a woman's hat is small and inconspicuous but she nevertheless wishes to be polite, she may turn to the person behind and ask, "Is my hat in your way?" If assured that it is not, she smiles and says, "Thank you." But if the person behind says, "Yes, it is," she removes it at once without further comment, and without looking pained or annoyed about it. The person behind should of course thank her for removing it.

A woman who is thoughtless enough to keep on a large, obstructing hat in the theater or at the movies may be asked by the person behind —man or woman—to remove it. But she should be asked courteously and in a pleasant tone of voice; there is no reason to be rude or offensive just because she is. The well-bred way is to lean toward her and say in a friendly tone of voice, loud enough for *her* to hear but no one else, "Would you mind removing your hat?" or "Will you remove your hat, please?" If she is less rude than she seems, she will say, "I'm sorry"—and remove the offending hat at once. But even if she removes it unwillingly and ungraciously, the person behind should thank her.

A shy person who hesitates to ask the owner of an offending hat to take it off may ask the usher to do so.

THEATER ETIQUETTE

During a performance, well-mannered people are quiet and attentive—not only out of courtesy to the actors, but consideration for those around them.

They do not talk, hum, whistle, drum on the arm of the seat, beat time to the music, or in any way disturb the people around them who have paid for an evening's entertainment and are entitled to enjoy it.

They do not rattle paper, crunch nuts or candy during the performance, tear open cellophane packages, audibly chew gum, or jingle an armful of noisy bracelets, for they know how such sounds can distract and annoy their neighbors.

They try to avoid coughing and clearing the throat as much as possible, remembering to take along some type of lozenges if they are subject to throat irritation.

They are aware that voices carry both ways across the footlights, and if they are near the stage they are very careful not to make personal remarks about the actors. It's never courteous to be unkind . . . and unfavorable comments can wait.

If they have seen the play or picture before, they do not ruin it for others by telling in advance every interesting or exciting thing that's about to happen.

They laugh heartily, but not *boisterously* (there's a big difference!). A hearty laugh is rich and pleasant, makes others want to chuckle. A boisterous laugh is loud and noisy, makes people want to hold their ears.

If they are in the smoking section of the theater, they are careful not to blow smoke in people's faces or drop ashes on their clothes.[1]

In brief, they are courteous, well-mannered individuals, quiet and attentive, and considerate alike of the actors and the audience.

Asking Someone to Stop Talking

Of all the things that can annoy people at the theater or movies, loud talking is perhaps the worst. Who hasn't sat, at one time or another, near a thoughtless person who talked, talked, *talked* all through a movie or play—ruining it for everyone around?

In the days of the silent movies, signs used to be flashed between the reels saying, "Quiet, please!"—a not-too-subtle reminder that talking created a disturbance. But there are no such reminders today; and if you are unfortunate enough to find yourself sitting in front of a Talker—and if you cannot change your seat—there is only one thing to do: Turn around and ask the offender, *very pleasantly and amiably*, please to stop. You might say, "I'm sorry, but I can't hear while you talk. Do you mind—?" Or, "Excuse me, but would you mind very much not talking? I can't hear anything." Don't let yourself get angry about it; don't glare; and above all, don't become involved in an unpleasant argument that makes you conspicuous. Make your request courteously . . . and if the Talker still persists, you must either resign yourself to a lost evening, or ask the usher to do something about it.

If, on the other hand, you are the one who has been thoughtlessly talking too much, and someone turns around to ask you to stop, be gracious about it. Whether you are asked rudely or politely—be gracious. Say you are sorry and stop talking, and you'll both enjoy the evening a great deal more.

During Intermissions

People who go out to smoke between the acts should make it a point to be back in their seats before the curtain goes up again.

If a man is with a woman who does not smoke, he may leave her during one intermission—but only one. It would be rude to leave her alone several times during the evening.

At the opera, it's customary for a gentleman who is a guest in one box to visit friends in another during intermission. The visit must end as soon as the lights are lowered for the curtain, and he should be

[1]For general smoking etiquette, see pages 404 to 410.

back in his own box by the time the music begins. Women do not visit other boxes.

LEAVING THE THEATER

One should never get up and start putting on wraps while the actors are still on the stage. It's rude to the actors, and especially rude to those whose view of the stage is cut off in the closing moments of the play.

People who must leave early should do so as quietly and unobtrusively as possible, putting on their wraps after they are out of the aisle and at the back of the theater.

When the play is over, people should leave their seats as quickly as possible so as not to hold up or inconvenience others. There can be no fixed precedence in the aisles because of the crowds; people in groups walk out together any way that happens to be convenient, but of course with the ladies always going first through doors.

AT SPORTING EVENTS AND THE CIRCUS

It goes without saying that the rules which apply to the theater and opera are completely out of keeping with the circus and with indoor or outdoor sporting events. Here noise and talk, loud cheering and shouting are all very much a part of the picture . . . and it would seem very dull and strange without them!

However, a few words of caution: "Rooting" for a team is one thing; yelling at the players or at people in the audience and making a noisy nuisance of oneself is quite another. Popcorn and peanuts are a cheerful part of circus life; but dropping shells on people's clothes, being careless with cigarettes, letting ice cream drip on the people in the seats ahead are bad manners and always will be—at the circus or anywhere else.

3. RESTAURANT AND NIGHT-CLUB ETIQUETTE

IN THE better-class restaurants and hotel dining rooms, men do not take their hats and coats to the table but check them at the door. A woman may check her coat with the dressing-room attendant, if she wishes; but usually she wears it to the table and drops it over the back of her chair. If she is wearing a hat, she keeps it on. It is most emphatically *not* good form for a woman to remove her hat at the table and run her hands or a comb through her hair.

The headwaiter is the official "host" of the dining room. He greets guests as they arrive and shows them to a table. Well-bred people do not saunter into the dining room by themselves and try to find a desirable table, but wait at the door for the headwaiter to seat them. If they do not like the table to which he takes them, they ask for another; but if no other is available, *they do not make a fuss about it.* A woman especially does not complain audibly about the table; if for some reason she doesn't find it comfortable or to her liking, she says so to the man accompanying her and he speaks to the headwaiter about it.

The important thing to bear in mind is that it is never good manners to make a scene in public, regardless of the circumstances. Well-bred people prefer to walk out rather than attract the unfavorable attention of other diners.

SEATING THE PARTY

Women always precede men entering a dining room. When there is just one couple, the headwaiter leads the way, followed by the woman and then the man. When there are several in the party, it is customary for all the women to go first and the men to fall behind; but it is also correct for them to follow the headwaiter two by two, the men beside the women. When a woman entertains a group of her friends at a luncheon or dinner in a public dining room, she follows the headwaiter to the table, then stands to one side and indicates to her guests how they are to be seated. But a woman who has invited just one other woman to lunch or dine with her, naturally lets her guest go first, and insists that she take the choice seat.

When a man and woman are shown to a table in a restaurant, the headwaiter draws out the "best" chair for the woman, and usually helps her with her coat after she is seated. The man stands by until she is comfortably settled (helping her with her coat if the headwaiter hasn't done so), then takes the seat opposite.

A woman lunching or dining with two men sits between them. A man dining with two women does likewise, unless one of them is his wife—in which case he sits opposite her with their guest between them. In a party of four, the women always take seats opposite each other; and after seating them and helping them with their coats, the men take the places between. If a man is giving a party for six or more, the women stand at the table until told by their host where to sit.

Many restaurants and night clubs nowadays have bench or "sofa" seats against the walls. It's proper for a man to sit beside a woman or opposite her, as he wishes. As a rule when there's a floor show or other entertainment to watch, he sits beside her. When there are four or more people in the party, the women sit against the wall, the men sit facing them.

ORDERING

When a man and woman dine together in a restaurant, the courteous procedure is for him to ask her what she would like to have—and perhaps make suggestions as to what he thinks she might enjoy, or what he knows from past experience is especially good in this particular place. She decides what she would like (without changing her mind half a dozen times!) and tells *him*, not the waiter. He gives the order to the waiter, being careful to mention her choice of each course first. There is no fixed rule that says a woman may not give her order directly to the waiter, if she wishes; but as the man is her host, it is more courteous to let him function as such and do the ordering for both of them.

When there's a large group at the table, the most practical way is for each person to order individually, although sometimes one person orders for all if he can do so without too much confusion.

A dinner party is, of course, in a different category than casual restaurant dining. A woman who entertains a group of people at dinner in a restaurant or hotel dining room makes all her arrangements ahead of time. She decides on the menu, pays for everything in advance, and all her guests are served the same food, just as they would be in her own home.

At a large dinner party in a first-class restaurant, each dish is usually presented to the host as soon as it is brought from the kitchen. *He is not expected to help himself.* He merely looks at it, nods approval of its appearance and preparation, and the waiter then serves it to the guests.

When ordering from a restaurant menu, it's entirely proper to ask the waiter to explain what a certain dish contains or how it is made. But some people ask to have practically *everything* on the menu explained, and that is not good manners!

Those who are unfamiliar with the meaning of foreign words frequently seen on American menus are referred to the list at the end of this chapter.

RESTAURANT MANNERS

The subject of table manners has been discussed in another part of this book.[1] And of course good table manners are the same in a restaurant or night club as they are anywhere. However there are some rules which apply specifically to public dining rooms.

For example, do not call a waiter "garçon." That is an affectation which no one admires, and which the waiter usually resents. If you wish to attract the attention of a waiter in a restaurant, keep looking in his direction until you catch his eye—then beckon him with a lift of the chin. If it's impossible to catch his attention, and if he is within hearing distance, call, "Waiter, please!"—or it may be necessary to clap your hands once or twice to attract him. But do not tap noisily on the edge of a glass, and do not whistle to him.

If you smoke at the table, use an ash tray; and if there is no ash tray on the table, ask for one. Don't use a saucer as a substitute, or flick the ashes on the floor. But even worse than either of these is the very offensive habit of "dunking" a cigarette in the dregs of a coffee cup! Be careful not to leave your cigarette smoldering in an ash tray as the acrid smell of a dying cigarette can be very distressing to diners near by.

If you drop a piece of silver or a napkin, don't pick it up. Leave it where it has fallen, and when the waiter comes to the table again ask him to replace it.

It isn't good manners to reach a fork or spoon across the table and "taste" something from somebody else's plate. It may be fun at picnics, but it's not the best behavior in a public dining room.

A woman dining with a man should not ask the waiter for an ash tray, more coffee, a glass of water—or whatever it may be she needs. She should tell her host, and he will call the waiter and ask him to bring it.

Gloves and purses do not belong on the table; they should be kept on the lap. A woman who has a number of books or packages with her should check them before entering the dining room, if possible; otherwise she should ask for an extra chair on which to put them. She should not pile packages on the table.

Although the fleeting use of a powder puff is not objectionable, a woman should not make major repairs in her appearance at the table. It is neither good taste nor glamorous to wield a lipstick or apply rouge in public. Beauty is more enchanting when it's mysterious.

[1] Pages 51 to 67.

A man always rises when a woman leaves the table or returns to it. He half-rises and bows when someone across the room bows to him or others at his table. He rises to a standing position when a woman stops at the table, and remains standing until she leaves. (If she is courteous, she does not remain more than a moment or so.) He also rises when a man stops at the table to greet someone in his party. A woman, once seated, does not rise to meet or greet anyone—except perhaps a very old or very distinguished woman to whom she wishes to show special courtesy.

An unmistakable characteristic of well-bred people in restaurants and other public places is their *consideration for those who serve them.* They do not complain every few minutes about the service or the food. They don't let trifles annoy them; they try to be patient and understanding.

PAYING THE CHECK

When you entertain a group of people at dinner and the check is presented to you, try to glance over it as quickly and unostentatiously as possible. Naturally you want to make sure it is correct and you are not being overcharged; but to study it at great length and check each item before your guests can be very embarrassing to them.

If you find a mistake in the check, don't become annoyed or discuss it with your guests. Just beckon the waiter, point it out to him very quietly and courteously, and let him take care of it. If there is any disagreement about it, don't argue. Wait until after your guests leave the table, then see the headwaiter and have the matter adjusted before you pay your check.

When a group of men and women dine together, but not as guests of one person in the party, they may ask the waiter for separate checks if they prefer it that way. But it is considered somewhat better form for one person to pay the check and tip the waiter, and for the others to give him their share later, after they have left the table. The customary procedure is to divide the total equally and not attempt to figure out each person's individual check.

A woman who entertains friends socially in a restaurant or public dining room, and who does not make arrangements and pay for everything beforehand, may give one of the men in the party whom she knows well somewhat more than sufficient money to pay the check and tip the waiter. He later makes an accounting to her and returns whatever is left over. At a business luncheon or dinner, the most graceful way is to take her guest or guests to a club or restaurant where she has a charge account and sign the check. Otherwise she just pays the check casually and without embarrassment; nor need the men in her party feel awkward or embarrassed about having her pay the check, for this is done quite as a matter of course nowadays, and is considered entirely proper and in good form.

The Etiquette of Tipping

Tipping has been variously described as a bore, a nuisance, an imposition, and even a racket. But however true all this may be, and regardless of how you personally may feel about it, tipping in restaurants and public dining rooms is a universal practice—and it's necessary to conform because salaries are based on it, and waiters and waitresses depend on tips to make up the major part of their income. Here and there efforts are being made to abolish the system; some of the better-class restaurants and hotels do not permit tipping and compensate their waiters accordingly. But unless "no tipping" is clearly specified, well-bred people conform to the common practice and tip according to the prevailing standards.

The amount of the tip depends on a number of factors. Where you are has a great deal to do with it. Tipping is higher in New York, for example, than in small towns—higher in luxurious hotel dining rooms and night clubs than in simple restaurants. You can roughly estimate the size of the tip by taking ten per cent of the check as a basis, and adding whatever extra you feel the waiter deserves for courteous attention and good service. Ten per cent is the very least you can leave with dignity anywhere, for any kind of service; but in a good restaurant, and certainly in a night club or hotel dining room, ten per cent nowadays is a very lean gratuity. For example, on a $20 check for a party of four, a ten per cent tip is only $2. That might be more than enough for a careless or disagreeable waiter; but in a better-class restaurant or hotel dining room where one has lingered over the meal and received excellent service throughout, it could hardly be called adequate. A tip of fifteen per cent, or $3, would be more nearly correct.

Obviously it's impossible to give any one general rule on tipping restaurant or night-club waiters. In some places a fifty-cent tip for dinner for two would be considered quite generous. In other places, like elaborate night clubs, a dollar tip is the very least one can leave for two persons, even though they have had only a drink or a sandwich apiece . . . the idea being they have taken up space that might otherwise have been given to someone who would have spent more money. The size of the tip depends on these five factors:

1. The type of place.
2. The amount of the check.
3. The quality of the service.
4. The number of people in the party. (The more people, the larger the tip.)
5. The time spent at the table. (The longer you linger, the more generous you should be.)

It is neither good form nor a sign of sophistication to tip excessively. Well-bred people tip for service, not for effect. They make it a point to compensate generously those who serve them well; but they are careful to avoid overtipping or "cash-flashing" as it is called, for throwing money about to make an impression is bad manners.

Tips should be given quietly and inconspicuously, and without comment except perhaps a word or two of appreciation when warranted. A tip thrown noisily on the table is an insult. A tip waved in the air to a waiter or headwaiter is an affront to dignity.

Night-Club Etiquette

A "night club" is not, strictly speaking, a club but a place for eating, dancing, and entertaining; and, in the case of the more famous clubs, a place to see and be seen.

In a general way, of course, the etiquette of night clubs is the same as that for restaurants or any other public place for dining and dancing; but there are a few points that should be emphasized.

At most night clubs it is necessary to make reservations in advance. The procedure is to telephone the headwaiter, tell him the number of people in the party, and reserve a table. It is not necessary to tip the headwaiter unless the party is a large one and special preparations are required in advance.

It is not necessary to drink at a night club. It is neither adult nor well-bred to drink for effect, or to drink more than one should. It is especially bad manners for young people to show off by drinking more than is good or proper for them.

Don't check your manners with your coat. Being in a night club doesn't give you the right to be rowdy or boisterous. Tables are usually close to each other in a night club; and rude or offensive behavior can be very annoying to those near by.

A woman at a night club should not talk to strangers at an adjoining table. She should not leave her own party to join friends at another table. She should not accept an invitation to dance from a stranger . . . nor from a friend at another table if it means her escort will be left sitting alone. She should not become overfriendly with the musicians, overtalkative with the waiters.

It is not good manners to smoke on the dance floor, to chew gum, to hum or whistle audibly to the music. It is not good manners to call to people across the room; or to stop and chat with friends on the floor, blocking the way of the other dancers. A woman should not dance in her coat or furs, and should not wear a large hat that bumps into people as she dances by.

It goes without saying that gentlemen do not make personal comments to the entertainers, and are very careful not to do or say anything that may embarrass the women in their party.

THE MEANING OF FRENCH WORDS FREQUENTLY SEEN ON MENUS

It's always a good idea to know what you are ordering. If you have difficulty with the words on the menu when you go to a restaurant, night club or hotel, this list will help you. It gives the meanings of the French words and phrases seen most frequently on American menus.

à la carte	according to the bill of fare; each part of the meal chosen and paid for separately
à la jardinière	with spring vegetables
à la king	meat or fowl served in a sauce to which mushrooms and pimientos or green peppers have been added
à la maître d'hôtel	with a thin butter sauce
à la Marengo	with olive oil
àlamode (or à la mode)	pie or cake "à la mode" is served with ice-cream; beef à la mode is braised and simmered
à la reine	literally "cooked to a queen's taste"; soup prepared "à la reine" contains white meat of chicken cut in tiny pieces or pounded to a pulp
à la Russe	according to the Russian fashion; individual portions
à la vinaigrette	with a sauce of oil and vinegar, sometimes flavored with cucumber
apéritif	a small amount of alcoholic liquor taken before a meal to stimulate the appetite

au buerre	with butter
au fines herbes	with parsley and butter
au fromage	with cheese
au gratin	prepared with grated bread crumbs and (or) cheese
au jus	meat served in its juices or cooked in stock
au lard	with bacon
au vin blanc	with a white-wine sauce
blancmange	a dessert made from gelatinous or starchy substances and milk, flavored, and usually shaped in a mold
boeuf à la mode	beef simmered in a sauce
bouillabaisse	a fish chowder, elaborately seasoned and made from at least two kinds of fish
bouillon	a clear broth
braised	seared and browned in fat, then simmered in a small amount of moisture
café au lait	coffee with hot milk
café noir	black coffee
canapé	an appetizer made of plain or toasted bread topped with a delicacy like caviar or liver paste
carte du jour	menu for the day
champignons	mushrooms
châteaubriand	a steak, well done
compote	stewed fruit
compotier	dish for stewed fruit or candy
consommé	a strong clear broth
croutons	bread cut in small squares and either toasted or fried; usually dropped on top of soup
cuisine	the kitchen; also the manner or style of cooking
déjeuner	breakfast
déjeuner à la fourchette	literally, breakfast "with a fork"—or including meat
de la maison	a specialty of the house; a dish made from the chef's own recipe
demitasse	a small cup of black coffee served at the end of the meal
du jour	special dish for that particular day
en buffet	served from a buffet
en casserole	served in a small earthen dish
en coquille	served in the shell
en gelée	jellied
en tasse	served in a cup
entrée	originally meant a side dish served before the roast. But today, as used on American menus, it means the main course of the meal

entremets	side dishes or relishes served with or after the main course
filet de sole	a choice cut of the sole fish, without bones
filet mignon	small choice piece of beef tenderloin, usually served with a sauce
flageolets	small beans known as "baby lima beans"
fondant	a soft icing
frappé	frozen to a mushy consistency
fromage	cheese
gâteaux	small cakes
genévoise	hot sauce with mushrooms
glacé	a frozen dessert; a glacé fruit is glazed or candied
haricot	stew with vegetables
haricot vert	string beans
hollandaise sauce	sauce made of butter, egg yolks, and lemon juice
hors d'oeuvres	small delicacies and appetizers served at the beginning of a meal, usually with cocktails
jambon	ham
julienne	a clear soup containing thin strips of carrots, onions, etc.; also used to designate vegetables cut in thin strips
jus	gravy
légume	vegetable
madrilène	essence of tomato
mayonnaise	a salad sauce of oil, egg, vinegar, and spices
menu	bill of fare
parfait	an ice-cream dessert served in a tall, thin parfait glass, usually topped with whipped cream
parmentier	potato soup
pâté de fois gras	a paste made of goose livers
patisserie	a shop that sells French pastry; but as used on menus, it designates the pastry itself
petite marmite	a soup made of brown stock and a few large pieces of vegctable or meat, served in a small earthenware pot, or marmite
petit pois	small peas
petits fours	little fancy cakes usually served at the end of a dinner with the demitasse
plat du jour	the day's specialty
poisson	fish
pommes de terre	"apples of the earth"—or potatoes
potage	a thick soup
pot au feu	beef stew with vegetables
poulet	chicken
prix fixe	a one-price or fixed-price meal

purée	a food such as peas, prunes, apricots, etc., that has been rubbed through a sieve; also means a thickened soup
quenelles de poisson	fishballs
ragoût	a stew of any meat, usually thickened and well seasoned
rémolade	sauce of olive oil, vinegar, and mustard
ris de veau	sweetbreads
rissolé	browned by frying in deep fat
romaine	a long-leafed lettuce
rôti	roast
salmis	meat cut in small pieces, served in thick sauce mixed with red wine and chopped mushrooms
sauce piquante	a sauce of herbs
sauté	browned in butter
soufflé	dish of beaten eggs, milk, etc., baked
table d'hôte	a restaurant meal of several courses for which you pay a fixed price regardless of what you order (as contrasted with à la carte)
veau	veal
vin ordinaire	an inexpensive wine
volaille	poultry or fowl
vol-au-vent	patty or pastry shell filled with meat, fowl or fish, usually creamed

4. SMOKING AND DRINKING ETIQUETTE

IT's truly amazing how many people who are considerate and well-mannered otherwise are positively *boorish* when it comes to the matter of smoking! Many of them commit dozens of little smoking discourtesies every day, often without even realizing it. It's for their guidance that the following suggestions are made—to help them avoid these unwise and unpleasant smoking habits at home and in public.

GENERAL SMOKING COURTESY

In broad general outline, the code of courteous behavior for those who smoke is (1) to consider their own dignity, (2) to consider the feelings of others around them, (3) to consider the hazards of smoking and carefully avoid all damage to property and all danger of accident.

For example, if you talk to people with a cigarette dangling from the corner of your mouth—that's *undignified*. If you smoke in a sick-room, an infant's nursery, or in the presence of an elderly person who is made wretched by it—that's *inconsiderate*. If you lay a cigar or cigarette on the edge of a table and forget about it, letting it burn a charred groove or perhaps even start a fire—that's *destructive* and unwise. And bear in mind that some people are made physically ill by the smell of tobacco, many have delicate throats and sinuses which are irritated by smoke.

There are a few simple and obvious rules of smoking courtesy:

Don't carry a lighted cigarette carelessly, especially in a crowded elevator. You may touch someone's coat or dress and damage it.

Don't blow smoke directly toward a person; that's as rude as cough-ing or sneezing in his face.

Don't flick your cigar or cigarette so that the ashes blow on some-one near you.

Don't talk with a pipe or cigarette in your mouth—nor dance with a cigarette in your hands.

Don't strike a match against furniture or statuary—nor grind out a cigarette against lamp bases or ornaments.

Don't smoke when smoking is forbidden, or hazardous, or offensive.

SMOKING IN PUBLIC PLACES

Nowadays smoking is permitted in nearly all public dining rooms and restaurants, in hotel lobbies, and in waiting rooms and airline terminal buildings.

Smoking is *not* ordinarily permitted in museums, libraries, public exhibition buildings, and auditoriums. Recently it has been prohibited in many large department stores and beauty parlors because of the fire hazard. As a rule, signs designate whether or not smoking is per-mitted, and one should be guided accordingly.

At concerts, the opera, and the theater, smoking is generally per-mitted in the lobbies only, during intermission. It is not only bad manners but *against the law* to violate these smoking regulations.

At the movies, smoking is generally permitted in a special section set aside for the purpose—like the mezzanine. Only smokers should occupy these seats, as they will not be annoyed by the smoking of others around them. But even in a section set aside for smokers, one should be very careful about letting a thin column of smoke (espe-cially from a smelly pipe or cigar!) blow directly into a neighbor's face. That can be extremely distressing, even to a smoker. If possible, the smoke should be directed downward or upward . . . or at least in some way diverted from its steady, persistent curl in one direction. One should be careful also about flicking a cigarette too close to a neighbor's knee, as few things are more annoying than to have one's lap used as an ash tray!

Smoking is never permitted in church, nor during religious or ceremonial proceedings like a christening or funeral.

Smoking in Public Conveyances

There is ordinarily no smoking on streetcars or busses, unless a special section has been set aside for the purpose—in which case it is always clearly indicated. There is, of course, no smoking on subways. Ignorance of the law is no excuse; there are signs posted in every car.

On trains and ships, smoking is permitted in some sections—prohibited in others. One should find out what the regulations are and smoke only where smoking is permitted.

Strict regulations govern smoking at airports and on planes, for here the hazards of fire are greater than elsewhere. No smoking is permitted on the ramp or field, or when boarding the plane. Aboard, no smoking is permitted before the take-off, during the take-off, on landing, and whenever the *No Smoking* sign is on in the plane. *Only cigarettes should be smoked* in flight, as cigar and pipe smoking can become very offensive in the close quarters of a plane . . . especially to those who are inclined to be airsick. Naturally a considerate passenger doesn't smoke at all if someone near him is obviously uncomfortable and would be likely to be made even more so by the smell of tobacco.

A gentleman does not smoke when riding in a closed taxicab with a lady. The odor of tobacco in a small closed-in place like a cab has a way of clinging unpleasantly to one's clothing, and even to one's hair and skin.

Smoking in Your Own House

The fact that you are in your own house is no excuse for smoking carelessly and offensively. Flipping ashes and matches about, leaving cigarettes to smolder and smell in an ash tray, or squashing them out in a flowerpot or vase, is just as bad manners in your house as in someone else's.

Make it a practice never to use anything for a lighted cigar or cigarette but an adequate ash tray. If there isn't one right at your elbow, go and get one before you light your cigarette. Don't ever put a cigarette on the edge of a table, a mantel, or a piece of furniture. Don't lay it even for an instant on the top of a book. Such careless smoking habits are destructive and hazardous.

When you are through with your cigarette, put it out completely. Don't let it smolder in an ash tray, the fireplace, or anywhere. Even if this weren't dangerous, it's highly offensive to other members of the household. The stale odor of a smoldering cigar or cigarette can cling for days to the upholstery and draperies of a room, making it unpleasant for everyone.

Don't litter your nice-looking fireplace with burnt-out matches and stubs. That doesn't add to the charm of your living room.

Don't toss matches or cigarettes out of the window. That doesn't add to your popularity with the neighbors.

Don't leave matches where small children can get at them. (That isn't etiquette—it's just plain common sense.)

It hardly seems necessary to add that smoking in bed is a dangerous and unwise habit. If you need a good-night cigarette, smoke it before getting into bed—and avoid the risk of setting the mattress on fire.

SMOKING IN OTHER PEOPLE'S HOUSES

The rules of courteous smoking behavior are even more stringent in other's people's houses. Be very careful not to damage rugs, tables, upholstery. You may joke all you like about ashes being good for the rugs . . . but your hostess won't think it's funny. Neither will she take kindly to brown scars on her lovely marble mantel, burns at the edge of her fine coffee table, matches and stubs dropped into delicate porcelain vases.

Before you start to smoke, look around for an ash tray. If there aren't any around, ask your hostess for one. If she hesitates or says quite bluntly that she doesn't have any, don't smoke. It is bad manners to smoke in the house of someone who clearly objects to the habit.

A gentleman does not smoke a pipe in somebody else's living room, unless the hostess herself, knowing he is a pipe smoker, suggests it. A pipe is for outdoors in the country, or beside one's own hearth. A well-bred person does not inflict it on others without their permission.

If you are a guest at dinner, don't smoke if no provisions for smoking have been included in the table setting. In some conservative households, smoking during dinner is not approved; and if you see neither cigarettes nor ash trays on the table, you can assume such is the case. It would be an offense to your hostess, under these circumstances, to take out your own cigarettes and smoke them during the meal. If you *must* smoke, wait until the dessert is served, and if by that time no cigarettes have been put on the table or passed, ask the hostess for permission to smoke one of your own. Of course if each place is set with cigarettes when you sit down, and if there are plenty of ashtrays and lighters in evidence, you may start smoking at once, if you like—even before the first course is served. But don't grind out your cigarettes in anything but an ash tray. It's inexcusable to use your hostess' fine china for this purpose.

In the homes of intimate friends, there is naturally no formality about smoking. Whether cigarettes are provided or not, people accustomed to smoking in one another's houses do so at the table or anywhere else, without thinking about it.

Suggestions for the Host and Hostess

When preparing for a party, the hostess should see to it that there are plenty of ash trays—big roomy ones—strategically placed to protect her possessions from careless smokers. Tiny ash trays may be attractive, but they are impractical for parties. All trays should be emptied frequently during a party.

The hostess who sees a guest pick up a delicate or costly ornament to use as an ash tray need have no hesitancy in taking it away from him. She shouldn't make a fuss about it, of course—shouldn't be tactless or rude—but just very matter-of-fact. She should smilingly hand him an ash tray and say, "I think you'll find this more convenient."

People often ask whether or not the hostess should supply the cigarettes for a party. It is naturally expected that some cigarettes be provided—on the dinner or buffet table, and on the coffee table in the living room. But it is not necessary to provide every popular brand in lavish quantity. Chain smokers, and those who smoke a special or unusual brand, should bring their own.

The hostess who is not herself a smoker may not realize how distasteful dry, stale cigarettes can be. She should not use cigarettes left over from a previous party, but should always provide fresh ones. And the host who hides his best cigars, handing out second-rate ones to his guests, is anything but hospitable! It's better not to offer any cigars at all than to inflict inferior ones on guests.

Smoking Outdoors

Always be very careful about striking a match outdoors. Don't strike it directly *toward* someone near by, especially if it's a windy day—as the head of the match may fly off and land on that person's clothes.

Don't throw matches and burning cigarettes about when you are camping or picnicking. Such careless smoking habits cause many forest fires every year.

Don't attempt to strike a match and light a cigarette while driving. That's very unwise—and likely to worry others riding in the car with you.

Don't litter someone's well-kept lawn with discarded match books, crumpled cigarette packs and other smoking debris. If there's no convenient way to dispose of them at the moment, keep them in your pocket or purse.

Don't scatter matches and cigarette stubs on golfing greens and fairways, and in the club house. It is never good manners to leave an unsightly trail of ashes and charred matches behind you.

The Woman Who Smokes

Nowadays women everywhere smoke as freely as men do; and there's no objection to it provided they maintain their dignity and avoid offense to others.

It's not dignified, for example, for a woman to walk along the street smoking a cigarette. It may not be wrong, actually, but it is a habit that's neither charming nor feminine, and an intelligent woman always considers appearances.

Women smoke as publicly as men, of course, in restaurants and night clubs, during intermission at the theater, in hotel lobbies, in waiting rooms, on trains and planes—everywhere, in fact, except on city streets. However, one should bear in mind that the attitude toward women smoking in public varies widely in different sections of the country. What may pass unnoticed in New York or Chicago may cause lifted eyebrows in Little Village. The woman who visits a community where smoking in public is looked upon with disapproval or distaste, should be understanding and gracious enough to do her smoking in private.

The woman who smokes should avoid careless or sloppy smoking habits that offend people. She should never talk with a cigarette in her mouth, nor dance with a cigarette in her hand, nor hold a cigarette and coffee cup at the same time. Such actions do not help make a woman more popular or appealing!

Needless to say, the woman who smokes regularly should carry her own cigarettes and not forever "borrow" them from others. But if she is with a man and he offers her one of his cigarettes, it's better manners to accept it than to say, "I have my own" (unless, of course, his brand is positively distasteful to her). And she should always let him light her cigarette; it's a courtesy a man expects to perform for a lady, and it's somewhat disconcerting to have her do it herself.

DRINKING ETIQUETTE

The etiquette of social drinking—or "civilized drinking," as Julian Street calls it—is very clearly defined. Some things are correct and acceptable, others are not—and there's no mistaking which is which.

Drinking in moderation for enjoyment and sociability (just as one eats fine foods at dinners and parties for the same pleasant reasons) is correct and acceptable. But drinking in excess to show off or make an impression most emphatically is not.

Asking for fruit juice when the host serves cocktails is correct and acceptable. But asking for scotch instead, or saying "I never drink cocktails—do you have any wine?" is rude and inexcusable.

Drinking when liquor makes one sick, or loud, or unruly, or in any way offensive, is neither well-bred nor wise; and people who are unpleasantly affected by liquor should learn how to say a firm but friendly "No!"

The line of demarcation between what is right and what is wrong is sharply drawn in the matter of drinking behavior; and every intelligent, socially mature person is careful to observe the rules.

HOW TO REFUSE A DRINK

Before all else, let us make it quite clear that *it is not rude to refuse a drink*. For some reason, many people are under the impression that to refuse a drink socially is somehow an affront to the hostess. It is nothing of the sort. No one ever need feel embarrassed or hesitant about refusing a drink, any more than one would feel embarrassed about refusing foods which are distasteful or to which one is allergic.

Young people especially seem to hesitate to say "No." Perhaps it's because they think drinking is expected of them, and that they may be less popular if they refuse. But actually, no one admires a person who drinks because he's *afraid* not to, because he feels he must keep up with the others and do as they do or not be accepted by them. In this day and age, the people we admire and value most as friends are those with the courage of their own convictions. They drink if they want to; but they *don't* drink if they don't want to—no matter how much they are urged or coaxed.

The important thing is to know how to refuse. A simple, courteous "No, thank you" should be adequate; but if friends insist (as they certainly shouldn't!) one might say, "I'd rather not, if you don't mind —it doesn't agree with me." Or, "Thanks—but I'll take some tomato juice or fruit juice instead." An experienced hostess always provides a non-alcoholic beverage for those who don't like liquor or are too young for it. But even if no soft drinks or fruit juices are offered, it is permissible to ask for them.

One should be very careful not to look or sound critical when refusing a drink. However strongly you may object to drinking, don't feel you must show your disapproval to the hostess. Just be friendly and casual about it. There's no need to take a drink if you don't want to; but surely there's no need to be a "wet blanket" about it, either!

People who don't drink often hesitate to accept invitations to cocktail parties; but there's no reason for it. They can go to such parties and enjoy the company of their friends without feeling obligated to drink if they don't want to. In most smart circles today there are some who drink and some who don't; and the do's and don'ts have a fine time together. It's easy enough for nondrinkers at a cocktail party to avoid the embarrassment of being continually asked, "Aren't you drinking?" by holding a glass and at least appearing to be drinking along with the others.

When a toast is proposed at a wedding or reception, even those who don't drink should raise the glass to their lips and go through the motions. It would be conspicuously rude not to make the gesture of joining in the toast.

REFUSING WINE AT THE TABLE

At the table it is proper to say "No, thank you" before any wine is poured into your glass; but it is *not* good manners to put your hand over the top of the glass and say "None for me!" when a servant, or the host, is about to pour wine into it. Nor is it good form to turn the wineglass upside down when taking your place at the table. That's an unnecessarily rude way of saying "No."

If you don't want any wine, the only proper way to refuse it is to say "No, thank you"—without any elaborations such as "Wish I could!" "I never drink wine," or "What is it—sherry? No, thanks!" Such remarks are ungracious and uncalled for.

If the host insists on pouring wine in your glass after you have refused it (which is bad manners on *his* part!)—just let it stand. Don't push it aside, or try to give it to someone else, or keep making apologetic remarks about not drinking it.

DON'TS FOR DRINKERS

Don't drink to excess at any time, under any circumstances. This is not a matter of etiquette but of good common sense. Drinking more than you should is no credit to you; it never wins the respect or admiration of others, but only their pity or contempt. Moderation in drinking, as in smoking and everything else, is the sign of intelligent, civilized living.

Don't boast about your ability to drink a great deal "without showing it." That's neither adult nor admirable. It's just plain childish *showing off*, which no one admires.

Don't help yourself to a drink in somebody else's house, unless invited to do so. Even though the liquor is openly displayed on a bar, table, buffet, or cabinet—wait until it is served, or for an invitation to serve yourself.

Don't ask your host or hostess for a drink, unless you are in the home of intimate friends. Don't ask for a *second* drink nor suggest another round of cocktails before dinner. Such suggestions must come from the host, not the guest.

Don't ask for some other kind of drink when cocktails are served (unless you want plain fruit juice or a soft drink). If you don't like cocktails, just say "No, thank you." Don't ask for rye or scotch instead. But of course, if your host or hostess says, "Would you prefer scotch?" that's a different matter. You are then at liberty to accept or refuse, as you see fit.

If you don't like the drink you have been served, just put it aside quietly. It isn't necessary to make any remarks about it. You don't need to drink it if you don't want to; but neither do you need to offend your host by making a face and demanding, "What *is* this, anyway?" Rudeness is never smart or "cute" in any company.

Don't leave a drink on the edge of a chair where it can easily be knocked off. Don't leave a drink on the floor where someone may step on it or kick it over. Don't put a wet glass on the unprotected surface of a table, bookcase or cabinet. If no coasters are provided, put your empty glass on a tray or doily—or carry it out to the kitchen, if necessary—but don't put it down carelessly where it can cause damage to furniture or rugs.

In a public dining room, don't feel you must order something to drink just because your friends do. Drinking or smoking for effect is never good manners, in a man or woman. Order a drink if you want it, but only if you want it—for no other reason. Remember: no one need ever drink, at any time, unless he wants to.

SUGGESTIONS FOR THE HOST AND HOSTESS

It isn't necessary to serve a drink to every casual visitor. Nor is it sophisticated graciousness to insist on guests' drinking when they don't want to, or when they have obviously had enough. Drinks should be offered to guests, never forced on them.

It goes without saying that the kindly, well-intentioned host never serves alcoholic drinks to young boys or girls. When drinks are being served, at least one non-alcoholic drink like tomato juice or grape juice should be served for the young people, and for those who do not drink.

The host who wants to control the drinking in his household should never announce generously to his assembled guests, "Just help yourselves!" There is usually at least one person at a party who can't resist the appeal of alcohol and will "help himself" until he has to be helped home. That certainly doesn't contribute to the success of a party. The host himself should dispense the drinks . . . intelligently. It isn't necessary to offer your guests a choice of drinks. If it's a very small group, you may mention two or three of your specialties and ask each guest to name his. But for a crowd, just serve one kind of drink —choosing one that is likely to be popular with most of your guests.[1]

As a rule, only one round of cocktails is served before dinner; sometimes two—but rarely more than two. The host himself should mix the drinks and not relegate this duty to one of the guests. The mixing may be done in the pantry; but part of the fun of casual drinking is in mixing the ingredients in front of the guests.

At a cocktail party, drinks are served continuously throughout the afternoon or evening. But an intelligent hostess who understands her responsibility to guests does not encourage excessive drinking.

The hostess who wants to protect her furniture and rugs should provide plenty of coasters, trays, and napkins. If she sees a drink left

[1]For the correct service of wines and liquors, see pages 155 to 168.

precariously on the arm of a chair or on the floor, she may remove it to a place of safety—but *pleasantly*, with a smile, not with a reproachful glance at the offender.

5. TRAVEL ETIQUETTE

To TRAVEL happily and well is a fine art, calling for a combination of attributes and abilities . . . not the least of which is taking things as they come, and getting on pleasantly with other people along the way.

The very first principle of enjoyable travel is to be a "good sport" —to accept with grace whatever turns up and not let little things annoy you. If you are traveling for pleasure, be sure to make it a pleasure! Travel with a relaxed spirit and an open mind, receptive to the joys of brief encounters and ignoring the *unpleasant* things as much as possible. Remember that fussy travelers who worry and fret about everything, who are easily irritated and have neither patience nor poise, never get any real fun out of travel.

Make up your mind beforehand that you won't be as comfortable as you are at home. Bad coffee, lumpy mattresses, noisy elevators outside your bedroom door, poor food, rude fellow travelers—all these are part of the price you must pay for the immense pleasures of travel and of seeing the world.

So whether it's just a week end of skiing or a world cruise touching at every great port—*relax and enjoy it*. Start out with the idea of taking everything in your stride, with the determination to be friendly, pleasant, and well mannered, come what may. Expect considerably less than perfection, and you may be agreeably surprised to find how very close you may come to perfection at times.

FIRST STEPS

Travel nowadays has been greatly simplified. All the complicated details of schedules, connections, reservations—even arrangements for sight-seeing in distant places—can be turned over to a local travel agent. Qualified agents not only buy your tickets and make your hotel reservations, they help you plan your trip so as to get the greatest possible enjoyment from it.

Unless you are a seasoned traveler with very decided ideas about where to go and what to see—or unless you have unlimited time and funds at your disposal—your best buy in travel today is one of the so-called "packaged" trips. These are not the old-fashioned tours or group affairs, but are arranged for you individually by a steamship company, railroad, airline, or travel agent. Everything is carefully planned and taken care of for you, depending on how much time you have and the amount of money you wish to spend. You know before you start just where you are going and how, what you will do when you get there, and how long you will stay. Everything is paid for in advance, and you are assured of accommodations wherever your trip takes you.

If you prefer to make your own plans, be sure to arrange for all reservations and attend to all details well ahead of time. Avoid last-minute rushes, as that's not the way to start a trip with pleasure and with poise.

The simplest and safest way to handle money for traveling is by means of traveler's checks, which are spendable all over the world. You can buy them in any bank, American Express office, Railway Express agency, or the ticket window of railroad, bus, and airlines. Traveler's checks are honored where you are unknown and where you would have difficulty cashing your own personal checks; and they avoid the necessity for carrying around and risking the loss of large sums of money.

CLOTHES FOR TRAVELING

When you have decided where to go and have made your reservations, the next important step is to plan your wardrobe and start packing. The normal impulse is to pack all you own; but if you are wise, you will keep your travel clothes down to a minimum and avoid burdening yourself with excessive baggage.

Women especially are always confronted by the big problem of what to take and what to leave behind. If they are wise and experienced in the ways of travel, they begin with the basic essentials and add interchangeable accessories—making one outfit do the work of two or three. They plan "separates" (skirts, blouses, jackets, slacks, etc.) that mix and mingle in endless variety, and make very good travel companions. They avoid bulky clothes that can be worn only with their own special accessories.

A good basic suit is the main essential for a woman traveler, with the right shoes, hat, gloves, and bag to go with it. These same accessories should go with at least one or two of the basic daytime dresses in the wardrobe—dresses which can also be worn with other accessories to change their general effect and appearance. A casual coat that can be worn over a dress or suit is, of course, a requirement for travel of any kind.

Whatever else is included naturally depends on where you are going and what you plan to do when you get there. *When in doubt, leave it behind.* It's better to take too little than too much, for wardrobes can always be replenished along the way if necessary—but a dud in your trunk or suitcase is a nuisance.

Certain types of clothes are better travelers than others; they do not crush easily, keep their shape and their crispness, and arrive looking as well as when they departed. Silk jersey travels superbly well. So does silk shantung. Many of the new crease-resistant cottons and linens are excellent travelers; and the modern synthetic fabrics which pack like a dream and shake out like new are a great convenience.

The important thing is to avoid fabrics that wrinkle easily and are likely to need pressing on arrival. It's wise also to avoid very bulky fabrics that take up too much room. A quilted bathrobe, for example, takes up far more room than it's worth; a sheer woolen robe, or a silk or cotton negligee, serves the same useful purpose and takes up no more space than a dress. A bouffant evening gown practically fills a suitcase by itself; but a long skirt and several gala blouses take up little space and provide a number of interesting changes for dinner and dancing.

Never take large hats when traveling; they unpack looking battered and limp. Take washable white cotton gloves instead of kid ones, and nylon underwear that rinses out like stockings. Remember to take a laundry bag so that soiled clothes won't come into contact with clean ones.[1]

How to Pack

Included in the fine art of traveling is the knack of packing clothes properly, so that they look well en route and arrive none the worse for their experience. Here are some suggestions you will find helpful:

Before you pack so much as a handkerchief, wipe out the inside of your bags with a cloth soaked in toilet water or cologne. This not only removes the dust, but when you open your bags they have a lovely fresh scent instead of a stale one.

Always put heavy things like shoes and purses at the bottom of the bag, lighter things on top. Arrange the shoes around the sides of the case (tucking small jars, socks, etc., inside them), and pack the purses

[1]Suggestions for clothes on trains, planes, aboard ships, etc., are in the parts of this chapter devoted to those specific subjects.

flat in the center. Fill in with belts, stockings, gloves, and small accessories until you have a fairly flat layer—then cover with two or three sheets of tissue paper and start packing your clothes.

The best way is to pack skirts and slacks first, putting tissue at the folds. Button up cardigans, jackets, and suit coats before packing them; then crisscross the sleeves in front and fold once. (Remember that the secret of keeping clothes from wrinkling is to use plenty of tissue!) Dresses should be folded lengthwise, then crosswise at the waistline. Blouses look best on arrival when they have been folded just once, crosswise at the waistline.

Keep your itinerary in mind and pack according to what you will need in transit. For example, don't tuck your sun glasses way at the bottom of the bag if you are likely to need them to protect your eyes from the glare of the sun while traveling. Put them in a side pocket where you can get at them without disturbing everything else in the bag; or keep them out until the last and put them at the top among your handkerchiefs and lingerie.

If you don't have a fitted traveling case with jars and bottles for your cosmetics, use a waterproof beauty kit for the purpose. And use small sizes of your indispensables. Huge jars and bottles take up a lot of room and add to the weight. Unless you are going to a remote island or jungle, you'll be able to buy refills and replacements as you need them.

Pack tightly, filling in the corners as well as you can—for when clothes slide around they become wrinkled. If the bag isn't full, strap down the contents to keep them securely in place.

Two very sensible precautions in packing are to tip scissor points with Scotch tape or adhesive, and to seal lotions and perfume bottles with colorless nail polish to keep them from opening and emptying out over everything.

TRAIN TRAVEL

Train reservations are made in person or over the telephone at the railroad depot, city ticket offices, transportation desks of hotels and department stores, or through a travel agent.

A reservation should be made in advance, unless it's for a very short trip; and you specify exactly what kind of space you want. For daytime travel there are coach seats or parlor-car seats. For night travel there are tourist sleepers or Pullmans. Pullman accommodations include upper berths, lower berths, roomettes, bedrooms, compartments, and drawing rooms. A roomette is a very small room, occupied by one, and has the advantage of being completely automatic so that the passenger can retire whenever he wishes without waiting for the porter to make up the bed. A bedroom may be occupied by one or two persons, a compartment by one to three persons, a drawing room by one to four persons. Two persons may occupy a lower berth for the price of one berth.

When you make your reservation you will be told when to call for your ticket, and you pay for it at that time. A free baggage allowance of 150 pounds per person is permitted; and your baggage may either go on the train with you—or you may ship it in advance by producing your railway ticket at the baggage room of the depot.

It is not advisable to take a dog with you when you travel—by train or any other way, except perhaps in a private car. But if you must take a dog or other pet with you, it travels as baggage in the baggage car; and it must be crated or muzzled. A very small dog may be taken into a pullman drawing room, compartment, or bedroom in a basket or container—but not on a leash.

For an overnight train trip, pack all your essentials in one small bag so that you can leave the rest of your baggage intact until you reach your destination. In the small bag pack your pajamas, robe, slippers, fresh underwear and handkerchiefs, toilet articles, and whatever you think you will need to make yourself comfortable and to keep yourself fresh and clean on the train. Experienced travelers pack their toilet articles in a small waterproof kit which they can carry back and forth with them to the dressing room.

Well-bred people dress conservatively on a train, avoiding loud colors and extreme styles. A knitted suit that sheds dust and doesn't wrinkle is ideal for a woman traveler. A simple dress worn with a good-looking casual coat is always appropriate and always in good taste. Comfort is of course a very important factor when one must sit for hours, as on a train; and one should bear that point in mind when selecting an outfit for the journey.

Train courtesy is the same as courtesy anywhere else in the world— based on consideration and a friendly regard for others. Courteous travelers do not spread their luggage in the aisles for others to trip over. They do not encroach on space belonging to fellow passengers, are careful not to annoy or inconvenience them in any way. They do not demand more service or attention than they are entitled to; and are never rude to porters, waiters, or others who serve them. They do not open or shut windows without first asking those around who might be made uncomfortable. And although they are friendly and pleasant, they are reserved—never forcing their company or their conversation on strangers.

The person who has the lower berth of a section is entitled to the seat facing forward. If a woman has been unable to get a lower berth, the man who has the other half of the section may offer to exchange with her—and she may accept or not, at her own discretion. But it's a courtesy on his part and deserves a gracious "Thank you" whether she accepts or not.

When you are ready to go to bed, you ring for the porter to make up your berth (or your bedroom or drawing room, as the case may be). If the train is crowded, it may take some time before he gets to you; but if it does, don't become annoyed about it.

Passengers who occupy roomettes, bedrooms, compartments, and drawing rooms on a train have their own private toilet facilities. Passengers who occupy berths use a public dressing room at the end of the car. The dressing room is small and must be used by many people; therefore it is rude for any one person to monopolize it, and especially rude to leave it in a messy condition. Passengers are expected to dress partially in their berths, then go to the dressing room in a robe and complete their toilet as quickly as possible.

The two qualities that distinguish an experienced woman traveler are her courtesy and poise. A woman who has traveled a great deal doesn't engage in petty bickerings with the porter about her bags, with the waiter about her food, or with fellow passengers about the use of the dressing room.

A woman traveling alone should not ask a fellow passenger to perform little services for her, such as opening a window or adjusting her luggage. If she wants something done, she should ring for the porter and ask him to take care of it. She may engage in conversation with anyone she wishes, of course, man or woman—for friendly encounters are one of the great joys of travel. But she should not permit a strange man to pay for her meals or any of her purchases on the train.

Children should be kept busily and happily occupied with books and games so that they do not annoy other passengers. They should not be permitted to shout, run wild through the aisles, eat between meals, make frequent unnecessary trips to the water cooler, climb on the seats—and perhaps even on the passengers! It's true that long trips are tiring and small children difficult to control; but it should be very carefully explained to them that only the space they have paid for on the train belongs to them and that they must not intrude on the space and quiet belonging to other passengers.

You tip on a train as you tip anywhere else, for service and not for effect. If the service is exceptionally courteous and attentive, you tip generously; otherwise you give the minimum tip possible—or none at all, if none is warranted. Following are the average tips for train travel.

Use these figures as a basis, and give more or less according to the amount and quality of service you receive:

To the red cap or porter who carries your luggage to the train, the usual tip is 15¢ per bag, with a slight additional tip if he carries it and stows it on board. Thus if you have two bags and he carries them to the train, you give him 30¢. If he carries them to your room or seat on the train and puts them on the luggage rack, you give him 40¢ or 45¢.

To the parlor-car porter who handles your bags and brushes your clothes, you give 35¢. If he performs other small services like bringing a card table or getting cigarettes, you give him 50¢ when you reach your destination.

To the Pullman porter who makes up your berth, a tip of 50¢ per night is considered adequate. If you occupy a bedroom or drawing room, you tip a little more—perhaps 75¢ a night. If you travel with a child, give the porter an extra tip, for children require extra service and attention. You tip the Pullman porter at the end of your trip, as you are leaving the train.

Waiters who serve drinks in the lounge car are tipped 10¢ to 15¢ a drink. Dining-car waiters are generally tipped about 25¢ per person for a simple meal—35¢ to 50¢ per person for an elaborate dinner.

TRAVEL BY SHIP

If you are planning a trip abroad or a cruise at home, the first step is to see about your reservations. To secure a good choice of cabin, you should make your reservations well in advance—months in advance if the trip is to be made during the busy season. If you must return at a certain date, it's wise to arrange for return passage at the same time.

Reservations for cruises and ocean voyages are made at ship's lines, transportation desks, or travel agents. You state whether you wish a single or double cabin, with or without bath or shower, upper or lower deck, inside or outside accommodations, and whatever other specifications may be necessary. Most ocean-going liners have first, second (or "tourist"), and third class travel. Most cruise ships, however, have only one class of travel and passengers have the "run of the ship."

If you are going abroad, you will need a passport, which you can secure by going to the nearest Federal District Court or to a government passport agency. You will need your birth certificate or naturalization papers and two 3″ by 3″ white-background passport photographs.

In addition to the passport, you will need visas for the countries you expect to visit. A visa is a disembarkation permit, and can usually be secured without any difficulty through your travel agent or the steamship company with which you book passage.

The seasoned voyager "travels light," for excessive baggage is always a burden. Hand baggage is easier to transfer from place to place in a foreign country; and if it's possible to get along without trunks, it's advisable to do so. But when trunks are taken, they should be well within the stateroom limitations (you can get this information from your travel agent or steamship company), and they should be sent to the pier at least a day ahead of time. Hand luggage may also be sent in advance, but usually accompanies the traveler when he goes to the pier.

All trunks and all hand luggage should be carefully marked with the name of the passenger and steamer, date of sailing, stateroom or cabin number, and whether or not it is wanted in the stateroom. Heavy trunks are sometimes checked for through-passage, and are not opened or used aboard; but hand luggage is always kept in the stateroom. It is wise to have everything insured.

Passengers can make arrangements to take their cars abroad if they wish. Application must be made to the steamship company which will give all necessary information about insurance, foreign licenses, and the courtesies of foreign automobile clubs.

On the day of sailing, plan to arrive at the pier an hour or more ahead of time, especially if it's a big ship and a busy sailing. As you walk across the pier, you claim your baggage and are almost automatically moved through the various formalities of embarking.

As a rule, there are friends to see you off and wish you *bon voyage*. If so, you will be occupied with them until almost the time the ship sails; but as soon as you are free to do so, there are a number of things to take care of. *Don't feel you must take care of everything at once.*

Some time between sailing and the first meal aboard, see the dining-room steward and arrange with him for the seating of your party. As soon as convenient, see the deck steward and make arrangements for deck chairs and steamer rugs. Check your money, jewelry, and valuables with the purser; and, if necessary, arrange with him for the exchange of United States currency into foreign currency. The purser is the information bureau, the bank, and the postmaster of the ship. But remember that he has many duties and responsibilities, and that there are many passengers aboard with "problems" and questions to ask, so don't take up his time unnecessarily.

Places at the captain's table are obtained only by invitation. It is considered a great honor to be asked to sit at the captain's table, and it is therefore not proper to request the privilege. Sitting at the captain's table involves certain formalities which are not otherwise required, such as always being on time for meals, not beginning until the captain is seated, and remaining at the table until he leaves. Any passenger invited to sit at the captain's table who does not wish to conform to these requirements may courteously decline the honor, explaining that he or she plans to rest and relax on this voyage and prefers not to observe any of the more rigid formalities.

Well-bred people do not venture where they are not permitted aboard ship. They do not, for example, climb to the bridge uninvited. They do not explore parts of the ship ordinarily barred to passengers, such as radio rooms, control rooms—or any section of the ship marked "No Passengers Allowed."

Dress aboard ship depends on the part of the world you happen to be in. On a tropical cruise, you naturally wear light, summery colors and fabrics—sports clothes and so-called "play" clothes. But on a transatlantic crossing, you dress more conservatively—in darker colors, and in clothes that have less of a "holiday" air to them. Casual skirts and jackets, knitted two-piece outfits, suits and simple dresses are indicated for daytime wear. Women should avoid big, floppy hats that catch the wind—only small, close-fitting hats are appropriate aboard ship. And they should remember to take along sensible low-heeled shoes for promenading on slippery decks.

It is not proper to dress for dinner the first night out, even on the biggest and most luxurious liner. Nor is it proper to dress the last night before arrival . . . when trunks are (or should be!) locked and in the hands of the steward. Other nights aboard ship, men wear tuxedos and women dinner dresses for dining and dancing—unless it's a very small cabin ship, or an informal cruise ship, in which case people wear dinner clothes or not as they please.

The most gala and important social event aboard transatlantic liners is the captain's dinner, which is usually held the second night before landing. There is an especially elaborate menu, followed by entertainment and dancing—and sometimes by a masquerade ball. Women wear their most formal and elaborate evening gowns for this occasion.

The same general rules of courtesy apply aboard ship as anywhere else—only here even more so, for people are in close daily contact and rude behavior is soon unpleasantly apparent to everyone. Well-bred people are careful not to be noisy or boisterous, not to disturb other passengers when they are reading or resting, not to occupy deck chairs belonging to others. They are friendly and cordial in all contact with strangers; and at least interested, if not actively co-operative in, all shipboard activities.

There are more people to tip aboard ship, and tipping is usually higher, than almost anywhere else. It isn't practical to suggest exact amounts to give, as your tips should be in proportion to the luxuriousness of the ship, the type of accommodations you occupy, the attention you have received, and the service you have demanded.

The persons to be tipped are the dining-room and stateroom stewards, the deck steward, the steward who serves midmorning coffee or bouillon or afternoon tea on deck—and if you do not have a private bath, the bath steward. If there is a swimming pool and you use it regularly, you are expected to give the attendant a tip at the end of the voyage.

The best way to figure the amount of your tips is to allocate approximately 10 per cent of the price of your ticket for tipping purposes, and divide the amount according to the service and courtesy you received. For example, if your passage or cruise costs $500, set aside about $50 for tips and divide it among the various stewards as you think best and most fair. If you were a bad sailor and had special attention, you should remember to reward with special generosity those who looked after your comfort and well-being.

On an ocean crossing, tips are given at the end of the voyage. On cruises of more than two weeks' duration, dining-room and stateroom stewards are generally tipped at the halfway point and again on reaching the destination.

People who can afford to tip generously should do so, of course; but unnecessarily lavish tipping is a form of exhibitionism and should be avoided.

Before disembarking, it's courteous to seek out those with whom you have been friendly, bid them good-by, and exchange cards if you wish.

If you are entering a foreign country, the purser will explain the best and most efficient method for going through customs.

TRAVEL BY PLANE

If you are serious about seeing the world, you'll take to the air; for nowadays the airlines carry you swiftly and comfortably almost anywhere you wish to go. You can travel on giant sleepers to Brussels, Buenos Aires, London, Mexico. You can not only snooze between New York and Paris, but even have breakfast in bed! You can take an all-expense tour by air to Cuba, Hawaii, Bermuda, and all the many fascinating places you have wanted to see and that are now no longer "too far away."

Flight reservations may be made at the airport, but are usually made much more conveniently at airline ticket offices in town. Most of the airlines have representatives at centrally located hotels for the purpose of giving information and accepting reservations. On practically every major airline in operation today, reservations must be made in advance.

There are at this writing no reserved seats on planes. Passengers take whatever places are available—and first come, first choice. Many people prefer the front and rear seats because of better visibility; but otherwise all seats are about equally desirable, and well-bred people don't rush or crowd into the plane to get special locations. A passenger traveling alone should not take one of a pair of seats when a single is vacant, if by so doing he deprives two passengers of the pleasure of sitting together. Many people thoughtlessly do this on a plane, not realizing how rude and selfish it makes them appear to other passengers.

On the day of the flight, you appear at the airport with your baggage, usually coming by bus or limousine from the airline terminal or a hotel in town. (Your plane fare ordinarily does not include the limousine fare, which is usually collected en route to the airport.) A uniformed porter takes your bags to a desk where they are weighed and placed on the plane, and you are given numbered checks with which to claim them later. As your bags are not available during the flight, be sure to keep with you whatever you will need aloft—but be sure that what you keep is strictly within airline regulations. Passenger-service representatives are always on hand to give you whatever information you may need, and to direct you through the necessary departure formalities.

Each passenger is allowed 40 pounds of baggage free on his ticket; for any baggage weight in excess of 40 pounds, there is a small extra charge.[2] It is therefore necessary to weigh every item you take—not only in ounces, but in terms of its usefulness and importance to you on the trip. And be sure to use lightweight airplane luggage, otherwise the bags themselves will take up most of the 40 pounds! Dogs, cats, birds, or other live animals may not be taken aboard without special arrangement and permission.

Passengers should remain in the waiting room until the plane is ready to take off and the "all aboard" signal is given. Unforeseen conditions sometimes cause a delay, which well-bred people accept good-naturedly—realizing that planes cannot possibly arrive and leave with the regularity of trains. Flying schedules are subject to weather condi-

[2] On international flights, passengers are allowed to carry a slightly higher baggage weight without extra cost.

tions, and every airline reserves the right to delay or cancel flights without notice.

All rules aboard the plane are for your own safety and comfort, and must be rigidly observed. Smoking is not permitted while walking across the field or entering the plane, or during a take-off or landing. (Watch the "No Smoking" sign above the pilot's door.) Passengers must be seated before the plane begins taxiing across the field; and safety belts must always be fastened when taking off or coming in for a landing. While the plane is aloft, passengers may get up and move about if they like; but they must not venture into the pilot's cabin or any part of the plane where they are forbidden to go.

The rules of courtesy in a plane are dictated by common sense and are for your own personal comfort as much as for smooth and pleasant relationship with your fellow passengers. For example, women should not wear pungent, oppressive perfumes, and men should not smoke smelly pipes or cigars.[3] For in the confined space of a plane, even with modern air conditioning, strong scents are intensified and can cause great distress to a passenger with a squeamish stomach. Loud talking and boisterous laughter are inconsiderate to other passengers who may be trying to concentrate on important work they have taken with them, or on books they are reading. With people in such close proximity, only quiet and subdued behavior can be considered right and proper. Children especially should be kept under control, and prevented as much as possible from disturbing those around them.

Airsickness, like seasickness, is largely mental. When you board a plane, decide that you will not be sick, that it isn't necessary to be sick, that you are going to thoroughly enjoy the flight. And the chances are, you will. If not—don't be further upset by embarrassment. Just ring for the hostess and she will give you whatever you need to make you more comfortable.

You don't dress in any special way for air travel. Just wear the same kind of clothes you would on a train: conservative in color and style, and of fabrics that do not crush or wrinkle easily. A suit is always an excellent choice—with a coat or fur wrap which can be worn or discarded as one flies into varying climates.

When the plane reaches its destination and comes in for a landing, keep your seat. Do not unfasten your safety belt or stand up until the plane comes to a complete stop. Wait until it is your turn to go out; it's an unwritten law of plane etiquette for passengers to disembark in the same order they are seated.

Tipping is not customary on planes. You tip the porters who handle your bags at departure and on arrival, on about the same scale as rail-

[3]For more about the etiquette of smoking in planes, see page 406.

road redcaps. But the highly trained hostess and other members of the crew are *not* tipped.

To get your baggage after leaving the plane, give the checks to a porter and he will attend to it for you. Don't become impatient if the bags don't appear at once; it takes some time to unload the plane. But presently the porter will arrive with your bags in tow, will see you to a taxi or to the airlines limousine . . . and you'll be on your way.

At Home Abroad

There can be only one guiding principle for correct behavior when you are a visitor in another land among other people. You must act with the same courtesy as you would when visiting in the home of a friend. Surely you wouldn't laugh and jeer at a friend whose house and way of life are different from your own. It's just as rude, and just as *unfriendly*, to ridicule people in another country whose habits, customs, dress, and speech are different from what you are accustomed to.

When you visit a friend, you go with the idea of enjoying her hospitality. You should visit a foreign country in the same friendly spirit: *to enjoy its hospitality*—which means its people, its ideas, its traditions, and whatever else it has to offer that is new and different to you.

To enjoy a country, you must know and understand its people. You cannot learn to understand people by being rude or unkind, by acting lofty and "superior." Good manners are the same the world over; and courtesy attracts courtesy among strangers in foreign lands as surely as it does right here among your own friends.

If you can, learn a little about a country and its people before you go there. A bit of preliminary reading can add a great deal to your understanding and appreciation, and is bound to make you a more welcome visitor. It doesn't matter if you cannot speak the language. Courtesy and a friendly smile speak a universal language which people everywhere understand.

To be at home abroad, be that rarity among tourists: a well-bred American visitor. Be gracious, agreeable, and thoughtful of others, and you'll be thoroughly liked wherever you go.

6. HOTEL AND RESORT ETIQUETTE

IN THE "good old days" it was possible to get on a ship or train, go where your fancy led, and be reasonably sure of getting good accommodations when you got there. But nowadays you can't take that chance. If you want to be sure of good accommodations, you must make your reservation well in advance and get your confirmation before you pack so much as a handkerchief. The visitor to a city like New York or Washington who arrives without a firm reservation at a hotel is likely to spend the first few hours frantically trying to find a place to sleep. Don't try it!

When you write to a hotel for a reservation, state clearly the date and if possible the hour of your arrival, the number of persons in your party, and the approximate length of your stay. Specify exactly what accommodations you want: single or double room or suite, with or without bath, inside or outside, desired exposure if that is important to you—and if it's a resort hotel, whether you wish to be in the main building or a nearby lodge or cabin. Request a confirmation by letter or wire.

Hotels operate on either the "American" or the "European" plan, or both. The American plan means all meals included; the European plan means accommodations only, meals paid for separately. In making a reservation at a hotel which operates under both plans, be sure to state which you prefer. In a city like Los Angeles, Washington, or New York, where your activities are likely to keep you away from the hotel much of the time, the "European" plan is more practical. But at a resort hotel where you return regularly for meals, the "American" plan is usually more satisfactory.

ON ARRIVAL AT THE HOTEL

When you arrive at a hotel, a bellboy takes your luggage into the lobby and waits with it near the desk. You go directly to the desk, give your name to the clerk, and he locates your reservation and assigns your room.

Nowadays most hotels use individual registration cards instead of the old-fashioned "registers." These cards call for a street address as well as the city, and are useful for forwarding mail after you have left the hotel. It is important to sign your name and address legibly, as a hotel cannot give you good service insofar as mail and messages are concerned unless you do.

After you have registered, the clerk hands the key to the bellboy who leads the way with your luggage and takes you to your room or rooms.

Under no circumstances should a woman traveling alone go to a hotel without luggage. Even though she intends to remain only over-night, she should carry a small handbag with her.

How to Sign the Registration Card

The head of an arriving party signs the registration card, while the others wait to one side. For example, a man arriving with his wife and two children would sign for all of them: "Mr. and Mrs. Frederick Jamison and two children"—followed by the complete address. If the children are grown and will receive mail and telephone messages in their own names, he signs: "Mr. and Mrs. Frederick Jamison" and on the line immediately below, "Miss Anita Jamison, Mr. Carl Jamison" —followed by the home address.

The form "and wife" following a man's name is improper and should not be used.

A man alone signs "Frederick Jamison" without the "Mr." But a woman alone signs "Mrs. Frederick Jamison." An unmarried woman signs "Miss Anita Jamison."

When there is a maid or nurse in the party, the head of the family signs, "Mr. and Mrs. Frederick Jamison, two children, and nurse (Laura Blake)." The name of the nurse or the maid should be given, otherwise there will be confusion if mail or messages come for her.

Room Services

When you want information or service in a large modern hotel, you usually telephone from your room. If it's to inquire about mail or packages, to give the name of a visitor you are expecting, or to request that the people in the next room be told to tune down their noisy radio, you ask for "the desk, please." If you have any inquiries about luggage, or if you have a package to be mailed, you ask for "the por-ter's desk." If you wish to inquire about plane or train schedules, or make reservations, you ask for "the transportation desk." For a taxi, or to get your car from the garage, you call "the starter" and tell him when you would like it to be at the door. For magazines or newspapers to be sent to your room, you call "the newsstand." And of course if you want breakfast in your room, or any food or drink brought to you, you ask for "room service."

Women who like their morning coffee before they are completely dressed for the day may receive the waiter in pajamas and negligee. There is no impropriety involved. It is done all the time—even by the most sedate and old-fashioned ladies.

Receiving Guests at a Hotel

It is no longer considered irregular for a woman to receive visitors of the opposite sex in her hotel suite or private sitting room, nor for a man to receive women visitors under like circumstances. But when there is just a bedroom, it's better taste and better judgment to receive visitors in the public sitting rooms of the hotel.

Many hotels do not approve of men and women visiting each other in their rooms, and well-bred people naturally conform to such regulations wherever they find them. On the other hand, some of the newest and finest hotels today have bedrooms arranged and furnished to look like sitting rooms—so that one-room occupants may receive and entertain their friends at luncheon, tea or dinner without embarrassment. The hotel is a temporary home; and the modern trend is to make the individual accommodations homelike, permitting guests to receive and entertain friends as casually and conventionally as they would anywhere else.

Personal behavior is of course a very important factor. Well-bred people do not receive visitors of the opposite sex at unconventionally late hours, do not have noisy drinking parties in their rooms, are careful to avoid any actions that seem questionable or improper.

Visitors who are expected generally go to the guest's room without being announced. But friends who call unexpectedly should have themselves announced from the desk in the lobby by telephone.

In the Hotel Dining Room

At large and luxurious hotels, guests often "dress" for dinner, the men wearing tuxedos and the women dinner gowns. In some hotels dinner clothes are required at all times, in others on Saturday night only. But in the great majority of hotels, large or small, people dress as they please for dinner (just so long as they observe the ordinary conventions and do not appear in slacks or sweaters!).

In a large city hotel, a woman generally wears her hat into the dining room with daytime clothes. But at a resort or summer hotel, hats are not worn except by "transients" who are passing through and have stopped off for a meal. Women at resort hotels should bear in mind that Sunday night is traditionally an *informal* night, and it is not correct to wear formal clothes.

It's entirely proper for a man or woman dining alone to read a book or magazine at the table. It's better than sitting idly while waiting to be served, and much more polite than staring at people! But women should not knit in any hotel dining room, and men should not figure their income tax on the tablecloth.

Good manners are the same in a hotel dining room as anywhere else, with perhaps a little extra emphasis on patience and friendly good nature. There can be a temporary congestion in a busy kitchen just as there is before the cashier's window at a bank; and well-bred people take that into consideration. They know it is not fair to expect perfect service every time, and they make allowances if they occasionally must wait for something they have ordered—and that a dozen others may have ordered at exactly the same time.

Most of the better-class hotels have discontinued the practice of having guests paged in dining rooms. If you expect a message or a telephone call during dinner, inform the headwaiter—and he will quietly come to your table and let you know when you are wanted.

Checking out of the Hotel

As a rule you are asked upon registering how long you expect to stay. But whether you are or not, you should inform the desk clerk, as soon as you are sure of your plans, just when you expect to leave. Reservations for your room cannot be accepted if the desk clerk doesn't know how long it will be occupied.

At resort hotels, reservations are almost always made for a specified period—from a week end to an entire season—and guests are of course expected to arrive and leave on schedule. At a popular resort during the busy season, guests cannot expect to stay even a day longer than the reservation calls for, as someone else has the room or rooms reserved from that date and would be inconvenienced on arrival.

A few hours before you check out of a hotel, stop at the cashier's desk or telephone from your room and ask that your bill be prepared and made ready for you by a certain time. All hotels have a "check-out" time; and if you keep your room beyond that time, you are charged for an extra day.

When you are all packed and ready to leave, you telephone for a bellboy to carry down your luggage. Then you go to the cashier's window and pay your bill, leave your key at the desk or give it to the bellboy, and depart.

TIPPING AT HOTELS

Extravagant tipping is considered poor taste in a hotel just as anywhere else. But the waiter or bellboy who adds a bit of his own personality to his services and who is exceptionally courteous and attentive, deserves a more generous tip than one who is careless or indifferent. So use your own judgment, and tip as much as you think is proper and fair.

Bellboys are generally tipped 25¢ to 50¢ for taking luggage to your room, depending on the number of pieces. (The 10¢ tip is a thing of the past, even for a single suitcase!) If you arrive with a carload of bags, coats, golf clubs, books, fishing-tackle, and so on—including a movie camera and a portable radio which must be handled with special care—a dollar tip is not too much for getting everything safely out of the car and into your room.

Baggage porters are usually tipped 35¢ to 50¢ for handling a trunk —more if it's very heavy or very cumbersome.

Bellboys are given 10¢ to 25¢ for delivering ice water, newspapers and magazines, packages, telegrams, cigarettes, and so on to the room. Page boys and hat-check girls are tipped on about the same basis. Doormen also are tipped 10¢ to 25¢ for special services, like calling a taxi.

In a luxurious hotel, the chambermaid who takes care of a room occupied by two persons generally receives a weekly tip of $2. In a simpler hotel, a dollar tip is adequate. For an overnight stay at a hotel, many people do not tip at all; others, more generously inclined, leave from 25¢ to 50¢ on the dresser for the chambermaid. People who occupy elaborate suites in a hotel should tip according to the work involved and the kind of service given.

Hotel waiters are tipped on the same basis as waiters everywhere— ten percent of the bill plus something extra for extra courtesy and attention.[1] The more expensive the hotel, the bigger the tips as a rule.

At a resort hotel where you have the same waiter for every meal, $3 to $5 a week per person is the usual range—depending on the type of place. A tip of $10 a week for a couple in a very elaborate and expensive hotel is not excessive. Of course half that amount would be adequate—perhaps even generous—in some small country hotels.

[1]See page 399 for tipping waiters.

People usually tip the headwaiter in a resort hotel for an especially desirable location in the dining room, and for extra service or courtesy during their stay. Elevator operators are also frequently tipped at the end of a long stay in a hotel. And of course at camps, ranches, or lodges, it's customary to tip a guide, boatman, stable boy, caddie—or anyone else who has performed special services and contributed to the enjoyment of one's vacation.

Questions Frequently Asked About Etiquette in Public Places

Question: If a man meets a woman acquaintance on a streetcar or bus, should he offer to pay her fare?

Answer: Yes; and since the amount is so trifling, she may accept. But if she has it in her hand and prefers to pay it herself, she may say, "Thank you, but I have it ready."

Question: Is it wrong for a woman to smoke on a city street?

Answer: Not "wrong," necessarily, but in rather bad taste, and not exactly characteristic of a lady.

Question: If a seat is offered to a woman in the subway and she is getting off at the next station, should she take it anyway to be polite?

Answer: No, but she should be very gracious about it. She should say something like, "Thank you very much—but I'll be getting off in a moment."

Question: Do men in uniform doff their caps to women on meeting them in the street?

Answer: No. Men in uniform, including policemen and firemen, do not lift their caps; they salute instead.

Question: What is the proper way to dispose of chewing gum?

Answer: Eject it from your mouth into a small piece of paper, wrap it securely, and throw it into a wastepaper basket or container.

Question: If it is raining and a man and woman are walking together under one umbrella, who should carry it?

Answer: The man usually carries it.

Question: If a man meets a woman acquaintance in a bookshop, should he offer to pay for the books or magazines she has just purchased?

Answer: No. Should he make the mistake of offering to pay for them, she should courteously refuse.

Question: When a young man and woman attend church together, does he make her contribution to the collection box, or does she make her own?

Answer: A woman is expected to make her own contribution, and the man makes his.

Question: If a man meets a woman acquaintance in a restaurant and she invites him to sit at her table, is he obligated to pay her check?

Answer: No. The man pays the check only when he specifically invites the woman to dine with him.

Question: Is it bad form for a woman to knit while listening to a lecture?

Answer: It's discourteous to the lecturer.

Question: If a woman is asked to remove her hat in the movies and she refuses to do so, what should one do?

Answer: Such rudeness is almost unbelievable. One's only recourse is to change seats, if possible—otherwise complain quietly to an usher. Under no circumstances should one become involved in a noisy dispute, which is an even more conspicuous display of bad manners than refusing to remove a hat.

Question: May a woman invite a man to attend the theater as her guest?

Answer: Yes. She secures the tickets in advance and gives them to him before the arrival at the theater.

Question: Should a woman wear a hat when she goes into the dining car of a train?

Answer: She may wear a hat or not, as she wishes.

Question: Is it good taste for women to go to a hotel cocktail lounge at night unattended by men?

Answer: It is not good taste, and many hotels do not permit it.

PART VIII

Getting Along with Your Family

1. GETTING ALONG WITH YOUR FAMILY

"THERE'S no place like home" . . . to show kindness, courtesy, and a fine consideration for the rights and feelings of others.

We tend to take our families for granted. We don't bother to show them even the ordinary routine courtesies we give strangers. We are thoughtlessly rude and ungracious, often saying things we wouldn't dare say to an outsider. We take liberties with their privacy and their possessions . . . ignore their feelings and their pride. . . . Why? Surely our loved ones deserve at least the same courtesy and consideration we accord strangers. If anything, we should be even more thoughtful of them; for it's the loved ones with whom we associate intimately in our daily lives who suffer most when we are rude or unkind.

So be sure your etiquette is not for "show" alone, that it is not just a brittle finish on the surface of your personality. Don't save your smiles, your gracious behavior, for people outside your home. A great deal of your time is spent at home with your family, and much of your own happiness and peace of mind depends on your ability to avoid friction and discord in your intimate family relationships. It's true that home is the place to relax and be yourself, but that doesn't mean being grumpy, sulky, rude, inconsiderate, unkind! Getting along pleasantly and agreeably with those you *can't get along without* is the very essence of a mature, attractive, well-bred personality.

Furthermore, habitual courtesy and good manners at home are the best possible training for easy grace and charm of manner in contact with others. So if for no other reason than to train yourself for good behavior in public, try to be always as courteous and considerate to the members of your immediate household as you are to those outside it.

THE EVERYDAY COURTESIES OF FAMILY LIFE

The simple little civilities are so often forgotten in the closeness of family life. But they are very important. It takes so little effort to say "please" . . . so little effort to say a cheery "good morning" . . . to smile . . . to be pleasant, agreeable, *polite*. But what enormous returns you get in family happiness and harmony! How quickly jangled nerves relax, how instantly ruffled feelings respond to a simple act of kindness! Often a single thoughtful word or action can change the entire mood of a household, can impart a glow that lingers for days.

Don't be content just to *feel* affectionate toward the members of your family. *Show* your affection. Show it in the dozens of pleasant little ways that come up every day in every family circle.

Take time to admire the new suit or dress some member of the household is wearing.

Take occasion to bring home flowers, candy, or a new book now and then.

Take every opportunity that presents itself to be unselfish and cooperative, to be encouraging, to be patient, tactful, kind. For these are the basic qualities of family courtesy. These are the qualities that enrich and beautify family relationships.

Above all, bear in mind that courtesy is *consideration*—in little things as in the more important ones. Don't keep the radio blaring when other members of the household are trying to sleep. Don't whistle or hum a tune when someone else in the room is trying to read or concentrate. Don't bang doors, shout messages from upstairs or from room to room, interrupt when others are talking.

You can't excuse bad manners at home on the grounds that it's "just family." Rude, ill-tempered actions are *never* excusable. No one has the "right" to be cranky, irritable, overbearing, unreasonable—even in the bosom of his family.

Don't be unpleasant about answering the telephone and taking down messages. Don't be ungracious about helping when help is needed. Don't make a rush for the best seat in the living room, monopolize the best light, insist on your own comfort and convenience regardless of others. Don't talk of disagreeable or disturbing things at the table. Don't continually criticize and find fault—*especially* don't criticize a member of the family before outsiders! Keep up a standard of dress as well as manners; don't let yourself become sloppy and careless of your appearance. These are all part of the everyday courtesies of family life.

And don't leave the bathroom untidy—that's an important part of family courtesy, too! A ring in the bathtub is as rude as shouting "shut up" or slamming a door in someone's face. Always leave the bathroom neat and presentable for the next person; hang up the towels and washcloths, rinse out the basin, put the soap and other accessories exactly where they belong.

RESPECT THE PRIVACY AND POSSESSIONS OF ALL MEMBERS OF THE FAMILY

Be sure to respect the privacy of all members of your family if you want the same courtesy and consideration from them. Don't go into closed rooms without knocking, or eavesdrop at the door, or stand by and listen during a personal telephone conversation. Don't barge unannounced and uninvited into the living room when some member of the family is entertaining guests.

Letters, of course, are strictly private. Never read a letter or card addressed to another member of your family, however close that person may be to you. Reading a message not intended for you is more than discourteous; it is essentially dishonest.

It is important also to respect the possessions of all members of your household, even the youngest. Parents should not throw out anything belonging to a child without first consulting the child and getting permission to do so. In this way the youngster learns by example to respect the property of others, and is more likely to grow up with a sense of courteous consideration for the members of his family.

Don't borrow wearing apparel or other personal belongings without permission. If you do borrow something, return it promptly and in good condition. Don't open drawers or closets that don't belong to you; and above all, don't open and read private notebooks or diaries. No tie or relationship, however intimate, warrants sly snooping or prying into another person's possessions.

REFRAIN FROM RIDICULE AND SARCASM

The truly courteous and well-bred person is never deliberately unkind. And ridicule is just that—a deliberate unkindness. It's especially unforgivable when the cruel barb of ridicule is directed at a member of the family, for then the offense is against *affection* as well as breeding.

Make it a practice never to belittle or make fun of anyone, young or old. Children are just as sensitive as grown-ups, and their developing young personalities can be seriously thwarted by personal affronts and indignities, by being shamed before others, ridiculed in the presence of their friends. Never be guilty of making a child the butt of a cruel joke for the amusement of the rest of the family. Never be guilty of hurting anyone unnecessarily, especially those who love you and depend on you for happiness.

FAMILY QUARRELS AND COMPROMISES

Naturally the people with whom you live in close daily contact can provoke you more than the people you see only occasionally, and from who you are separated by a polite wall of reserve. Therefore it's doubly important to watch your temper at home, to exercise restraint and self-control. Don't be touchy and quick to take offense. Don't flare into anger over trifles. Don't go about with the proverbial chip on your shoulder, ready for an argument at any provocation.

Too many people let off emotional steam by giving in to bursts of temper and annoyance at home. The family may be understanding and forgiving of such outbursts; but obviously they do not make for happiness or harmony, and they should be controlled. It's well to talk things over at home, to ask for advice—and even for sympathy when it is needed. But don't make your family suffer for your jangled nerves and ruffled feelings. Try not to be overly possessive in your family relationships. Try not to be jealous, dominating, demanding—for these qualities often destroy the delicate balance of family affection and understanding.

Don't expect perfection from those close to you. That's the cause of so much family tension and discord! Husbands, wives, sons, daughters—maiden aunts and mother-in-laws!—all are plain ordinary human beings, like everyone else, with the faults and frailties of human nature. If you expect them to be without flaw or fault—there's bound to be friction in the family circle.

Don't correct your children any more than can be helped in the presence of servants or outsiders. Don't criticize your husband (or wife) publicly, or apologize for his (or her) manners or appearance. Never create a family scene when guests are present.

There are quarrels in every family, of course; and often a good healthy quarrel helps clear the atmosphere. But keep family quarrels private, behind closed doors; and get them over with fast. Don't let them drag on and on. Don't be afraid to admit that you are wrong; don't be too proud to apologize, too stubborn to give in. Often to lose a family argument or fight is really to win it.

So make the little compromises that family life demands, and make them graciously! Be generous in arguments, understanding in emotional crises, helpful in times of worry or stress. Laugh often, complain seldom, ridicule never—be courteous, fair and kind—and at least you'll have the basic formula for a happy family life.

DIFFICULT FAMILY RELATIONSHIPS

Any deviation from normal or customary circumstances tends to make family relationships more difficult. When there is a stepchild or adopted child in the family, when parents are divorced, when two families live together, or when a foreign bride comes to live in her American husband's critical and perhaps disapproving household, great tact and patience are required to avoid clashes of temperament and misunderstanding.

But however difficult or unusual the family relationship, simple kindness is often the best solution to whatever psychological problems there may be. With kindness there is bound to be affection and understanding; and on this sound basis there cannot long be real unhappiness in any home.

WHEN A YOUNG COUPLE LIVES WITH PARENTS

For a young couple to live in the home of parents is always a difficult and often a distressing situation. Rarely can the delicate personal adjustments of intimate living under one roof be made without some antagonism and friction.

The most trying relationship, as a rule, is when a young wife must live with her husband's family. This is certainly not difficult to understand. Becoming a "mother-in-law"—traditional butt of the jokesters —is a psychological step down for a devoted mother. Coming as a bride to another woman's house is by no means easy for a girl starting a new life of her own. Both must be tolerant and understanding of the problems involved; and each must be willing to meet the other halfway, to compromise and co-operate, to be considerate and kind. It takes an immense amount of tact and good will; but a happy relationship can be achieved if those most involved are willing to make the necessary adjustments.

The bride who, through force of circumstances, must live with her husband's parents, should accept the arrangement good-naturedly and without resentment. The attitude with which she takes her place as the fourth member of the family is extremely important. She cannot be bitter or antagonistic in her heart without the others knowing it. She cannot be grudging and unpleasant without making the delicate adjustment more trying and difficult for herself. Instead of giving in to petty annoyance—which gets her nowhere and only threatens her own happiness—she should devote her thoughts and energies to planning ahead toward the time when she will be proud mistress in her own home.

The first stumbling block is the matter of addressing her mother-in-law. The relationship is more likely to get off to a good start if the bride can use the word "Mother" naturally and easily, without having it get self-consciously stuck in her throat every time she tries to say it! But if "Mother" means only her own mother to her, and she simply cannot use the term for anyone else, she should find some acceptable substitute. If there is a family pet name or term of endearment she can use, she is fortunate in having it ready-made for her. Otherwise she must work out the problem for herself, finding some acceptable designation for the older woman. An *affectionate* way of addressing a mother-in-law is the first important step toward a smooth and happy adjustment of this difficult family relationship.

A young woman living with her husband's parents should try, as much as possible, to take her place as a member of the family and adjust herself to the ways of the household. She should realize that it is hard for the mother to give up her son and accept second place in his affections . . . hard for her to open her house and her heart to a young woman who was previously a total stranger to her. She should therefore make allowances for any shortcomings, should try to understand any little flare-ups of irritation or impatience. She should be generous and forbearing, never letting herself forget for one instant that this is her mother-in-law's house, and that by every law of courtesy, kindness, and good breeding her mother-in-law must be recognized as mistress in it. However she should *not* relinquish her right to a life-pattern of her own. She should *not* subordinate her relationship with her husband to placate the feelings of a selfish or resentful mother-in-law. Her attitude should be courteous and affectionate, but by no means subservient. That is why living together takes so much tact and good will on the part of both.

Frequently it is the mother-in-law who is most to blame for problems of maladjustment. She may be so fiercely possessive—so resentful of sharing her son's affections with another—that she loses all sense of proportion. She becomes critical and arrogant toward her son's wife, interferes whenever she can, is often unreasonably jealous. In extreme cases she may even develop a martyr complex and be full of sorrow and pity for herself, expecting the rest of the family to be sympathetic.

But no really intelligent woman permits herself such childish reactions. She realizes that her son is entitled to a happy life of his own, and she does not try to prevent him from having it. When he marries, she abdicates as graciously as a queen, opens her arms and heart to the bride in her household, does everything possible to make her feel welcome and at home. She is careful not to criticize or find fault. She refrains from giving advice and suggestions unless they are asked for. She guards against being overly sensitive, easily hurt. She does not harbor grievances, but talks things over and tries to reach a mutually agreeable understanding. She scrupulously keeps her hands off the marriage—*does not interfere*—lets the young people have a life of their own in her house, and thereby establishes a fine and enduring relationship with them.

It isn't nearly as difficult, as a rule, for a son-in-law to become adjusted to his wife's parents. A man does not usually object to calling his mother-in-law "Mother"—nor does he as bitterly resent advice and suggestions. But in-laws should nevertheless be considerate of a man's feelings and dignity, should be very careful not to criticize or interfere. The perfect in-law relationship is one of trust, affection, and courteous restraint.

Any young couple obliged to live with parents should do so with the avowed intention of "getting along"—of making a success of it. The *desire* for a happy relationship is half the battle. Only by a friendly, unselfish attitude of give and take on the part of all concerned can the difficult adjustment be made to a new life under the same roof with one's parents.

WHEN AN OLDER PERSON LIVES WITH A MARRIED CHILD

Perhaps an even more delicate situation than that of a young couple living with parents is that of a parent living with a married son or daughter. Older people are often extremely sensitive; and in their determination not to become a burden or make a nuisance of themselves, they tend to go to the other extreme. They become introspective and self-centered, consumed with self-pity, and oversensitive to the point of imagining slights and insults. That makes it difficult for everyone in the household.

Naturally it isn't easy for an older person, accustomed to first place in a home of his or her own, to fit into the household of a young couple. It isn't easy to relinquish one's life pattern and adjust oneself to somebody else's mode of living, somebody else's family routine. But if it must be done, it should be done cheerfully, without resentment or bitterness, and with the firm resolve to make a success of the difficult relationship.

In-laws who live with a young couple should not expect or demand special attention or consideration because of their relationship. They should not expect to be included in every family activity, should not invariably be present when young guests are being entertained. They should not take sides in family quarrels, nor interfere in strictly private family affairs. Young people have the right to their own lives, their own friends, their own interests and ideas.

The reason older people are often a problem in their children's homes is because their lives are empty and idle. They have little or no outside interests. As a result, they concern themselves too much with what is going on in the family—they are almost always present, whoever is visiting and whatever the family may be doing, and they are moodily plaintive and hurt if they think they are being left out of things.

A man or woman living with a married child can easily avoid this state of affairs by maintaining outside interests and refusing to become bored. *It's never too late in life to take up a new interest or hobby.* Anything that takes an in-law out of the house at regular intervals, away from the family to interests or hobbies of his own, enriches his life, makes him a better-adjusted individual—and vastly improves his position and relationship with the rest of the family.

There's an old saying that no house is big enough for two women, and this is especially true when a mother lives with her married son. It is often extremely difficult for her to relinquish his care and well-being to a younger and less experienced woman. She criticizes and interferes in spite of herself, and it is just this well-meant but bitterly resented interference which has given the term "mother-in-law" its unflattering connotation.

The all-important thing for a mother-in-law to remember is that her son's house is not *her* house, however welcome she may be to share it with him and his wife. She should be pleasantly willing to help when help is needed or requested, but she should not arbitrarily take over any part of the routine or management of the household. The lady of the house is entitled to run and manage it in her own way, whether she is twenty or sixty—and however poorly or inexpertly she may do so.

The wise mother-in-law does not give advice unless she is asked for it. She does not criticize the young wife's cooking, housekeeping or taste in interior decorating. If there are young children, she does not interfere in their upbringing and is especially careful not to pamper and spoil them. If there is an infant in the family, she does not pick it up, rock it, or do anything the young mother does not wish or approve. This simple courtesy seems very difficult for many older women to practice. On the basis of age and experience alone, they seem to rate themselves as authorities and all younger women as fools in the matter of child rearing and training. Many an otherwise pleasant relationship breaks up and founders on the reef of this one smug fallacy.

On their part, married children should be generous and understanding of the parent who lives with them. They should realize that, at its best, this is not a happy arrangement; for every person, young and old, likes to feel rooted in a place of his own. To even the most dearly loved and deeply welcome mother or father, being an in-law in the house is far from easy . . . and at times can be most distressing to one who is sensitive and proud. One should therefore be unfailingly courteous and friendly to an in-law in the household, considerate of his or her feelings—never guilty of an intentional rudeness or affront. A resentful attitude toward a parent-in-law never escapes the notice of others who may be present . . . and certainly never wins their admiration or respect.

In all family relationships, whatever their nature or problem, simple kindness is the greatest courtesy of all. With kindness there is bound to be affection and understanding—the twin keys to family contentment.

When Two Young Couples Live Together

The two-families-under-one-roof situation is rather familiar nowadays; and sometimes it is successful, but more often it is not. When four people of different temperament and personality live together, run and manage a household together, share expense, experience, and the very pattern of their daily lives, they must be pretty close to perfect to escape occasional conflict and clashes. If there are children, the relationship is even more involved; and only by a deep-rooted sense of fairness, and by unceasing consideration on both sides, can a smooth and amicable relationship be maintained.

When two families decide to live together, either for economic purposes or for some other equally good reason, the first step is to sit down and work out the best plan for their needs. There should be a set of "house rules" by which all agree to abide; and there should be complete understanding about the duties, responsibilities, rights, privileges, and routine activities of every member of the combined household. Unless such a definite plan or schedule is worked out, the two-in-one household is not very likely to function successfully.

The most feasible plan, when two couples live together, is for both to contribute equally to the family budget, and for one person to make all purchases and keep accounts. Sometimes this responsibility is rotated, so that one month one wife does the marketing and keeps the records—the next month the other wife takes over the responsibility. All expenses for food and household supplies are meticulously halved; and of course all other expenses are fairly and squarely divided, down to the last penny. The details of the two-family budget must be carefully worked out to suit the needs of the particular household; but whatever the arrangements may be, an exact record of expenses must be kept, and the accounts should be balanced at regular intervals.

Although efficient handling of the household funds is very important, it is no more so than a carefully thought-out plan for division of the work. There can be no harmony in a household where there are recurring arguments about who does what. Household duties should be divided according to ability, preference, and convenience. The wife who is the better cook of the two may prefer to take over that responsibility in preference to washing or cleaning; but if both wives like to cook and want to cook, a rotating plan agreeable to both must be worked out. Perhaps one week one wife would have the kitchen entirely to herself, and the next week the other wife would have it, and so on. The same plan could be worked out in regard to all other household duties. Big jobs like washing windows, cleaning up the attic or cellar, spring cleaning, etc., should be done together. It's more fun that way, quicker, and the fairest way to share the work.

Even in a pattern of life so closely woven and integrated, the two couples can easily maintain their own interests and hobbies, and entertain their own friends. All that's necessary is for their plan to include a definite schedule for staying in and going out. Certain nights should belong to one couple for entertaining or other personal interests, certain nights to the other couple. Each should respect the other's privacy, either going out for the evening or keeping to their own quarters. There will be times when they entertain jointly, of course—in which case they share the cost. But expenses for personal entertaining, hobbies, and the like are taken care of by the individual couple.

If there are children, each couple should willingly act as sitters for the other, on specified evenings, so that there is a fair division of free time. This should all be part of their basic schedule or plan.

Couples living together should maintain a strict policy of hands off where young children are concerned. They should not interfere in the training or discipline of each other's youngsters, but should rather try in every way to uphold each other's principles and ideas.

Clearly the double design for living is difficult and complicated, and offers many problems. But it can be happy and successful if all concerned are good sports, fair-minded, generous, and considerate. Add to this simple good manners—and the good sense to respect each other's intimate and private lives—and you have a workable formula for two-families-under-one-roof.

WHEN A FOREIGN WIFE LIVES IN AN AMERICAN HOME

Personality clashes and problems of adjustment are sometimes especially difficult when a foreign wife lives in an American home with her husband's people. Much unhappiness can be avoided by a friendly spirit of helpfulness and co-operation—and a willingness on both sides to understand customs and a way of life different from one's own.

A young woman (or *anyone*, for that matter!) who comes from another country to live in the United States should learn the ways and customs of the people around her as soon as she possibly can. Obvious little differences—as in table manners, for example—tend to make her conspicuous and set her apart from the others. She must make a sincere and willing effort to adjust herself to her new surroundings, to dress and conduct herself as much as she can like the people around her. This doesn't necessarily mean changing her personality. It means *conforming*—fitting herself into the American picture. It means adopting the country, the people, and the way of life she accepted along with the man she married, and learning to live as others do in the place she now calls "home."

A foreign wife in an American home should be very careful of her *attitude* toward her husband's family. She shouldn't hold herself aloof, resentful of outward differences between them—quick to imagine mockery and insults where none are intended. She should be gracious and affable, showing by her friendly interest that she *likes* her new relatives and wants them to like her. She should take her place as an affectionate member of the household, not behave as though she were a guest at a hotel, entitled to deference and expecting to be waited on. That attitude is bound to offend her husband's family and make her an outsider among them.

It is equally important for the relatives of a foreign wife to be kind and understanding in *their* attitude toward her. They should realize that many things are strange and difficult at first in a new land; and they should make things easier for her by being helpful and encouraging. They should make her feel welcome, desired. They should respect her "oddities," overlook her little mistakes of uncertainty and inexperience. They should refrain from correcting her in public, from criticizing her at any time—never by word or action causing her to be embarrassed. They should try to make her feel an intimate part of the family circle, letting her share in the routine activities of the household, feeling useful and accepted. They should praise her; admire her progress; ask her opinions; show interest in her problems. But never, never should they be guilty of making fun of her, to her face or even among themselves!

To ridicule people for any reason at all is, of course, rude and unforgivable. But to ridicule people solely because their dress, speech, manners, habits, customs, or even their ideas or beliefs are different from one's own is the greatest discourtesy of all.

Only by affectionate understanding, and the practiced habit of tolerance, can personality clashes and unhappiness be avoided in a household where a foreign husband or wife lives with American relatives.

When Parents Are Divorced

For a discussion of problems concerning children of divorced parents, see pages 251 and 252.

The Stepchild and the Adopted Child

No family relationship is difficult if it is staunchly held together by the bonds of love and understanding. Not even the traditionally unhappy stepchild relationship need follow its familiar—and outrageously false!—pattern. Cruel stepmothers may flourish in fairy tales; but they do not exist in the enlightened American home. Nowadays the most awkward family problems are easily adjusted by kindly and intelligent handling; and even the most bitterly unhappy and resentful adolescent stepchild is often quickly won over by simple affection.

An infant stepchild naturally presents no immediate problem. And one can easily avoid future emotional crises by bringing up the child exactly as though it were one's own—receiving complete love and trust in the normal course of events, by the simple virtue of earning and deserving them.

But with an older child, more delicate personal adjustments are necessary. The first task of a stepmother or stepfather is to break down the invisible barriers of resentment and distrust and to win the friendship of the child. This takes great patience and understanding; for fits of temper, sulking, and even dishonesty are all part of a child's instinctive reaction to the adjustment he is called upon to make. Often the adjustment is too difficult for his years—especially if he is angry, jealous, or in some way emotionally disturbed by the new parent's position in the household. It is very important to make allowances for the child's behavior at this time, to be gentle, sympathetic, and unfailingly *kind*. It is very important to get off to a good start, to make a friend of the child, to win his confidence and respect. Once you have taken this first difficult hurdle, love and trust soon follow, and the family relationship is established on a sound, happy basis.

A stepmother who has children of her own should guard carefully against showing them any preference or partiality. She should never, by the slightest word or action, show greater feeling or affection for one child than another. Stepchildren should be treated at all times and in all circumstances exactly the same as natural children. There can be no compromise with this attitude, and no qualifications. Anything less than complete impartiality is a threat to family unity and happiness.

The same is true of an adopted child. If he is taken into one's home, he must also be taken into one's heart—receiving complete and unqualified love and devotion. Of course a child by legal adoption is actually as much the son or daughter of parents as a child by birth. In fact, birth certificates now give the adopted parents' names. But the family attitude toward an adopted child is what really counts. Unless the youngster is treated exactly like a natural child—unless he is given exactly the same impartial love and understanding—there can be no real or lasting joy in the relationship.

Whether an adopted child should be told the facts of his relationship depends on factors beyond the province of this book. However, it is our opinion that, in general, a child *should* be told—and at an early age, so that he grows up with an awareness and acceptance of that fact. There is always a feeling of betrayal and shock when a child learns from outsiders that he is "just adopted." How much better to be told by his parents that he was chosen from all the children in the world because they loved him at first sight and wanted him for their own. No tactless outsider can hurt a child fortified by that knowledge.

PART IX

Etiquette for Children

1. GROWING UP WITH GOOD MANNERS

MANY devoted parents feel they are doing their job when they feed and clothe their children, teach them to walk and talk. Loving a child, providing for his physical well-being, and giving him an education are all vitally important of course, but they are not enough. One of the most significant tasks any parent faces is to prepare the child for smooth and agreeable relationship with the rest of the world. For in that direction lies much of the child's future happiness and fulfillment.

The youngster who grows up without a basic training in good behavior is handicapped from the start. Likewise the child who has been trained like a little puppy to do and say certain polite things when strangers are about is at a disadvantage. For children whose manners are neglected are bound to suffer for it later in life, are bound to be awkward and uncomfortable among people, and often very unpopular.

Principles of courtesy and consideration for others should be thoroughly ingrained in a child's developing personality. Good manners should be a matter of simple instinct, natural and unstudied. This isn't possible if the child is expected to be well-behaved only part of the time, when there's important company around—when he's on display, so to speak. The child with part-time company manners is at best a self-conscious, uneasy youngster, likely to do or say the wrong thing through sheer nervousness. At worst, he is an insufferable little exhibitionist.

Children, like adults, are most at home in what they are accustomed to do; and those who grow up with good manners as part of their daily lives find it as natural to do and say the right thing as to breathe. Sensible parents see to it that their children acquire good manners while they are still very young; for it is then, in their formative years, that they absorb quickly, unconsciously, and *by imitation*.

EARLY TRAINING

As soon as the child is old enough to understand, discipline and training should begin. Even an infant can be made to realize that there are persons in authority who must be obeyed. It is always a great temptation for an indulgent parent to yield to a child. It is so easy to stop a fit of crying or of childish temper with a toy or some other bribe. But such appeasement is costly in child training, is often disastrous to the child's developing personality. A habit once established is difficult to overcome; and the child who is permitted repeatedly to make a nuisance of himself to get what he wants, will have a hard time overcoming his selfishness and bad manners later on.

A little patience with children in the beginning pays far greater dividends than buying an hour's peace with candy or a toy, or overlooking a rudeness or discourtesy because it's "cute." Someone must teach a child the difference between right and wrong. Someone must be the interpreter of the laws of civilized living, must show the youngster that rudeness and bad manners bring their own unpleasant consequences. There are rules in every well-ordered household; certain things may be done, others may not—and these the child should know and understand, and no violation should be overlooked.

Of course a child should be told *why* he must not do or say certain things. To demand blind obedience from a youngster may make him sullen and resentful. He should be told that shouting indoors is unkind because it disturbs people who are trying to read or think —that gulping food at the table is wrong because it's unpleasant and offensive to others.

It goes without saying that one must have the grace to overlook tiny faults that cannot possibly grow into bad habits. One must not nag youngsters until they fear to act naturally. Children need plenty of wholesome, normal outlets—outdoor play with other children, opportunities for making and doing things by themselves. Wise parents expect children to be lively and noisy in their play, and do not attempt to repress them. But these same wise parents are careful to discourage at the start any tendency to be rude and boisterous in public places, to annoy or interrupt people, to show off or take advantage.

Make no mistake about it: *early training is important.* The character and personality of your child are very largely what you yourself make them during the formative years.

Relationship Between Parent and Child

It is natural for a child to look to his parents for guidance and approval. Often surprising results can be achieved through the simple expedient of a word of praise when it is warranted, a compliment when it is deserved. Most children are quick to respond to praise; and parents who have their children's interest at heart will not overlook this means of stimulating them to better manners.

And by parents we mean *both* parents. So often the task of training the child in courtesy and behavior is left entirely to the mother. But it's the father who is frequently (to the child, at least) the hero of the household; and as such, what a tremendous influence he can have by setting a good example!

For just as children absorb ideas, opinions, fears, prejudices, likes, and dislikes from their parents, they absorb good manners and careful speech. Children's perceptions are more acute than is generally realized; and little that goes on in a household is lost on small observers. If what they see is gracious and mannerly, if what they hear is courteous and well-bred, they grow up with a great advantage. For what children observe in their parents, they imitate—what they become accustomed to in their home, they do instinctively outside of it. To get children off to a good start, parents must set a good example, must make themselves models of everything they wish their youngsters to be and become.

From your own observations, you know how imitative a child is, how he tries to do exactly what the grown-ups around him do. If you slam doors instead of closing them gently, you can be sure your child will slam doors, too. If you shout at him for being untidy instead of patiently explaining the importance of being neat, why shouldn't *he* shout at his brothers and sisters, or his friends? If you open his mail and listen in on his telephone conversations, you must expect him to grow up to be a snooper—with no respect for other people's property or privacy.

If necessary, you must *exaggerate* your own good manners to demonstrate to your growing child the importance of courtesy and consideration for others. For the kind of person he will become depends so very much on the influence you, his parents, exert on him in childhood.

The First Things Every Child Should Be Taught

No matter how adorable they may be otherwise, the young of the species are little savages as far as manners are concerned; and politeness is something which must be slowly grafted onto their young personalities. But there are few things in this world more appealing than a well-mannered child; and the mother who realizes this fact will not indulgently permit her young son or daughter to grow up undisciplined.

Training doesn't need to be a rigid blueprint of dos and don'ts. The best kind of training is that which makes children realize and understand the broad general principles of kindness and consideration toward people. The first thing they should be taught is that there are *rules for living*, just as there are rules for a game of baseball or tennis, and that it's not only easier but a lot more fun to know the rules and live up to them. They should be made to understand that breaking the rules is being a bad sport; and that children who are bad sports are never very popular.

It's neither practical nor *possible* to teach children everything they need to know about polite behavior all at once. Nor is it wise to attempt to teach everything in precise detail. For example, it's more essential for a youngster of six or seven to know he must not slump, play, dawdle, be greedy, noisy or messy at the table, than to know how to use every piece of silver correctly. The details can come later; it's the basic principle of *being a fit table companion* that's important.

But even very small children can be taught a little of everything they will need to know as mature, well-bred men and women. It takes time and it takes patience, for it can be accomplished only through sustained and persistent effort. To a busy mother with three or four lively children underfoot, and no one to help her with the physical care they involve, this may sound like a tremendous job. And it is! But it's one of the most important jobs any mother can have, for it lays the foundation of a well-ordered, happy life for her children.

Following are some of the simple, basic things children should be taught as soon as they are old enough to understand. Parents who wisely insist on these small basic courtesies every day, within the family circle, aren't very likely to be faced by serious problems of conduct or behavior later on.

Almost as soon as they can say anything at all, children should be taught to say "please" and "thank you." They should be made to understand that when they bump into people or inconvenience them, they are expected to say "excuse me" or "I am sorry." If they hear these small civilities every day within the family circle, they will learn to say them as a matter of course, without being constantly reminded.

Children should be taught from the earliest possible age that courtesy is kindness, and that it is not kind to ignore a friendly greeting, to interrupt people who are talking, to cross directly in front of people in a room or push ahead of them in a crowd. They should be taught that it is not kind to contradict older people, or to ask them personal questions or make personal remarks. They should be taught a little about tact, and the importance of not hurting people's feelings. *They can be made to understand.* It is amazing how much even a six-year-old can understand if you take the time and trouble to explain.

Children who are allowed to disregard the rights and feelings of others, who are allowed to be rude and thoughtless in their speech and actions, aren't just growing up *without* manners. They are growing up with *bad manners.* And the longer their bad manners are tolerantly overlooked, the more difficult they become to correct.

No youngster should ever be allowed to barge into a room without knocking, open drawers or closets not his, take another child's toys or books without asking. One of the very first things a child should be taught is respect for the privacy and property of others—beginning with his own small sisters and brothers.

Children should be taught not to bring their outdoor manners into the house—slamming doors, shouting upstairs, racing through the halls. They should not be permitted to come to the table with dirty hands or uncombed hair. Much can be accomplished by insisting on the same standards of neatness and quiet behavior when the family dines alone as when there is "company" at the table.

Even a very small boy can be taught to let his sister enter a room first, to hold her chair, and to wait until older people are seated before taking his own place. He can be taught to remove his hat to a lady, and to give his hand readily in greeting, like a gentleman. Such manners in a child are a tribute to the mother's influence and training . . . and to the father's courteous example in the home.

2. *LEARNING TO LIVE LIKE A GROWN-UP*

THERE are many things a child must learn on the way to becoming a grown-up; and much of it he learns outside the home, in school and in church, and from ever-widening association with others. But most of it comes from the experiences of daily living within the family circle, and from the unfailing influence and example of those closest to him: *his parents.*

The family is the child's first community and first social unit. It is within the boundaries of the household and in the family relationships that the child should learn the laws which govern orderly grown-up living in the larger world outside.

As the child grows older and must learn to adjust himself to adult standards and proprieties, it should be impressed upon his mind that there are certain factors by which he will be measured and judged all through life. Among these are his personal appearance, his speech, his table manners, and his attitude toward people. Whatever else he may or may not need to know, these are the more conspicuous factors of a well-bred adult personality; and in these phases of his development he should receive especially careful training and instruction.

Habits of Neatness Should Begin in Childhood

One of the important things children must learn is that people do not live in a hodgepodge of confusion and disorder, that they keep their surroundings neat and tidy and put things in their proper places.

Neatness is not something children are ordinarily born with. It is something that parents must teach them and encourage in them until it becomes a habit.

Children should not be permitted to leave a room littered with toys, to leave clothes in an untidy heap on the floor, to leave rubbers, schoolbooks, balls, and other possessions anywhere they please around the house. They should be taught to put each thing in its proper place—toys and books where they belong, clothes hung up neatly in the closet, soiled things in the laundry bag or hamper. It takes time and patience, and often great perseverance to teach children these things; but it's well worth the effort, for it's during these important years of growing up that lifelong habits of neatness can be instilled.

Personal Neatness Is Important, Too

Neatness does not apply to a child's surroundings alone, but to his appearance as well. Training in this direction is extremely important, and cannot begin too early. Children should be instructed in habits of personal cleanliness as soon as they are old enough to understand, and as they grow older should be taught step by step how to keep themselves well groomed and presentable.

As early as possible, children should learn to brush their teeth, take care of their own hair, scrub their nails to keep them clean. Later they should be taught to brush their clothes before hanging them away, and to wipe the dust from their shoes before putting them in the closet. A mother who wisely insists on these things in her young son or daughter helps the child grow up with the lifelong habits of personal neatness and grooming which are characteristic of well-bred people everywhere.

CHILDREN'S CLOTHES SHOULD BE SIMPLE AND COMFORTABLE

The matter of children's clothes requires little comment, for all that's necessary is that they be comfortable and in good taste. Extreme or elaborate clothes are of course unsuitable for small children, and sensible mothers avoid them. They avoid also (even for parties and special occasions) clothes so dressed-up and fussy that the child feels conspicuous and cannot be comfortable.

It's a grave mistake to dress a child, boy or girl, in clothes that are unusual, or in some way different from those to which his playmates or schoolmates are accustomed. Being forced to wear clothes that look strange to other children can have a withering effect upon a youngster—so much so, in fact, as to warp the entire future pattern of his life. Psychologists tell us that between the ages of six and twelve, when a child is learning to adjust himself to life outside the home, he wants more than anything else to conform, to be like everyone else. The clothes a child wears during this period should be the same kind his friends wear. And it's far more important that they be comfortable and in simple good taste than showy or "smart."

LEARNING TO SPEAK WELL—AND TO EXPRESS IDEAS

As the child's developing character and personality reflect the influence of the home environment, so does his speech usually reflect the speech of his parents.

Very little of what is said around him escapes the growing child. There's a great deal of truth in the old saying that "little pitchers have big ears"—and not only have they big ears, but a sensitiveness which often makes them permanently influenced by what they hear in the home and outside of it. How often do we hear a child blurt out some unfortunate word or phrase that one of his parents let slip in a moment of anger or impatience! The child is quickly hushed, and the parents are shocked or annoyed, as the case may be . . . little realizing they themselves are to blame. *The danger is that children may hear things they do not blurt out but keep to themselves—fragments of adult opinions, prejudices, and ideas, which accumulate in their young minds and remain to color their thinking and their ideals throughout life.*

It is for this reason that what the child hears in the home is so vitally important. It's only natural that as a child grows up he will interpret the world outside in accordance with the experiences and conceptions gained at home. Intelligent parents realize this and are careful what they say and how they express themselves in the presence of their children.

To speak well is of course one of the most useful and distinguishing qualities anyone can have. Children should be made to realize this, and encouraged to express themselves from an early age. As soon as they have any ideas of their own, they should be allowed to contribute them to the general conversation—and should be listened to politely and with attention. What they have to say may be quite unimportant; but what they gain in the way of poise and self-expression is very important indeed. Busy mothers may scoff at the idea of listening politely to "childish prattle," not realizing it's prattle only because they have never encouraged the child to talk any other way. There's a vast difference between talking *to* a child (usually to warn, scold, nag, or demand an explanation!) and holding a friendly conversation *with* him. The boy or girl who grows up encouraged to enter into family talk—whose ideas, however childish, are listened to and discussed—has a tremendous advantage over the child who is rudely shut out of conversation by parents who don't like to be "interrupted."

Because most parents are so busy and most children so active, the enforced leisure and comparative quiet of the meal hours offer an ideal opportunity for training in speech and self-expression. The conversation should be kept within the range of the child's comprehension, without "talking down" to him. It should be kept on a high level for example's sake, avoiding such familiar themes as criticizing the neighbors and gossiping about relatives or friends. Parents should make it a point to talk of interesting and pleasant things at the table; and should give even the littlest ones their turn to say what they saw or did during the day.

To instill in children a love and appreciation of fine English, and to teach them to talk properly and well, parents should of course watch their own choice and use of words. They should be very careful of their pronunciation and grammar, and even the tone of voice. Parents who habitually talk in loud, harsh tones can influence their children's voices to take on these same undesirable qualities.

For American-born parents who are well educated, and to whom the use of good English comes easily and naturally, the task is comparatively simple. But for foreign-born parents who have an accent difficult to overcome, the problem is a little more complicated. The child is bound to acquire some of the characteristics of the parents' speech; and the only way to counteract this is to see that he is given the opportunity to hear perfect English whenever possible. He should be present whenever there are visitors who speak the language well; and he should be encouraged to play with children who have no trace of accent in their speech.

Learning to Eat with Good Manners

Table manners must be taught to children with great patience and care. For though *eating* is as old as man himself, *dining* is comparatively recent—the product of a highly advanced civilization. It is only natural that the child should revolt against using a knife and fork when fingers are so much more convenient!

Of course, children from two to six cannot be expected to have good manners at the table. While they are learning to feed themselves, they should eat alone or with other small children. They will surely spill food and get their fingers into it, for it's the only way they can learn. A small child needs to be shown many times how to hold his spoon and cup, and how to handle his food properly. But that is learning to *feed* himself, not how to eat with good manners. Manners can come a little later, when the child isn't engrossed in the serious business of getting food safely to his mouth.

But even then, a child should not be expected to master quickly and easily all the intricacies of the knife and fork, and other details of table behavior with which even adults sometimes have difficulty. He should be taught slowly, patiently and with steady determination that the whole idea of eating nicely is to make it pleasant for others to be at the same table with him.

Serious training in table manners should begin as soon as a child has graduated to the use of a knife and fork and can handle them neatly. The time to do this depends on the child; he may be ready at three, or he may not be ready until he is four or five. But the earlier the better, for if training in table manners begins when the child is still very young, he will learn the essentials almost as naturally as walking.

One of the first fundamentals of table etiquette children should be taught is that they must come to the table looking neat and clean, without toys or pets to keep them company, and for one purpose only: to eat their meal—not to play, have fun, or show off before visitors or the family. They should be made to understand that quiet, orderly behavior is expected at the table and that certain rules must be observed if they wish to enjoy the company of others. The punishment for disregarding these rules should be eating alone.

We emphasize again that *infinite patience* is required, and that the process of teaching children to eat with good manners is a slow and painful one. Never lose your temper at the table. Never coax, bribe, threaten, or nag—for such methods do more harm than good. The only proper training is to teach the child step by step what he must know, to set him a good daily example by your own perfect table manners, and to correct him firmly but without annoyance when correction is necessary. You can always accomplish more with a child by talking things over with him in a friendly way than by losing your temper. You can always win a child's confidence and co-operation more readily by treating him as an equal than by shaming him before others—especially outsiders. But of course if a youngster persists in being unruly or unmanageable, he must be sent from the table. He must be made to realize that to eat with grown-ups he must conform to grown-up standards.

These, then, are the two essentials in teaching a child to behave properly at the table: *discipline* and *example*. And of the two, example is perhaps the more important—for no child can be expected to eat with any better table manners than he observes in those around him.

Elsewhere in this book we have discussed the general rules of table etiquette, and they are of course the same for children as for adults.[1] But following are some suggestions that parents may find helpful in the training of young boys and girls:

Children should be taught to walk quietly into the dining room, not run—and to wait by their chairs until grown-ups are seated. They should be taught to sit up straight, in the center of the chair—not slumped in one corner of it—and to avoid moving and squirming about as much as possible. They should not begin to eat before everyone is served.

It's important to teach youngsters that food should be eaten in small mouthfuls, slowly and quietly, and that it is bad manners to talk with food in their mouths. They should not be permitted to bend way over the plate, to wave implements in the air, to prop themselves on their elbows. They should understand that it's rude and offensive

[1]See pages 51 to 67.

to smack their lips, lick their fingers, sip noisily from a glass or spoon.

Children should be taught that it's not good manners to jab a slice of bread with a fork; they should take it from the tray with their fingers. They should not lay a slice of bread on the palm of the hand and butter it all at one time; the proper way is to break off and butter a small piece at a time. They should not push back their plates when they have finished but leave them where they are. They should not play with the food, do tricks with the table appointments, drum on the plate or table.

Well-bred children do not criticize what is being served at the table, do not loudly express their likes and dislikes in food. They say "No, thank you" instead of "I hate carrots!" They don't ask, "What's for dessert?" but wait until it's served. They don't talk about unpleasant things at the table; and they don't monopolize the talk —they give others a chance.

Children should not be permitted to gulp their food and rush through a meal because someone is waiting to play, or because there's "something good" on television. They should not leave the table before everyone else does, unless it's for something very important—in which case they politely ask to be excused.

3. CHILDREN'S PARTIES AND PARTY INVITATIONS

CHILDREN's parties are usually to celebrate birthdays—or holidays like Christmas, Thanksgiving and Hallowe'en. For children of high-school age there are also little dances and supper parties, which are, however, in a somewhat different category than the small-fry functions we are here considering.

Children's parties should be in the afternoon, and preferably a week-end afternoon if the youngsters are of school age. For very young children, three to six o'clock is the usual time for a party. Boys and girls should not be allowed to attend evening parties until they are at least sixteen. Youngsters from twelve to sixteen are often permitted to attend supper parties which last until eight or nine o'clock; but arrangements must always be made to see that they get home safely. Very young children should never be permitted to go home unattended from a party; older children should not be permitted to go home unattended after dark.

The two chief features of children's parties should be simplicity, and a surprise combined with suspense. Children are delighted beyond measure when a special surprise is promised. It may be a Jack Horner pie filled with gifts, an exciting game with prizes, a treasure hunt, movies—anything that is likely to be greeted with shouts of pleasure and excitement.

Good parties are gay and spontaneous, not too organized, provide plenty of simple entertainment, familiar foods served in festive ways, lots of laughter—and no stomach-aches. The party that is not so good is a frenzy of squealing and bickering among the youngsters—usually because there is not enough to keep them amused and entertained— an orgy of excitement and fancy and unfamiliar food, followed by sleepless nights and stomach-aches for the children, headaches and solemn vows of "never again!" for the parents.

The Kind of Entertainment Children Love at Parties

Small children can have a wonderful time with very, very little . . . if they are not supervised too much by adults. Their capacity for laughing, cutting up, and having fun is enormous. Just provide the hospitality, the food, the favors, and the games, and the youngsters will take care of their own good time.

Children are easy to please, and are happiest when they can be natural and have fun in their own way. The simplest kind of entertainment is best at parties; and when youngsters get to be seven or eight, they should be allowed to take over personally. Too much adult management, unless it is very skillful, destroys the "party" feeling and tends to make children feel stiff, unresponsive. Of course very small children must be supervised, but it should be done in a way that does not make them feel "herded" or managed against their will. And whoever is in charge should watch the children for signs of restlessness, quickly switching from the waning interest of one game to the exciting anticipation of the next. Children should never be forced to continue a game when they are obviously bored with it, as that only makes them rebellious and difficult to manage. The whole trick of keeping very young tots happy and amused at a party is to provide a lot of simple, amusing things to do, to keep them busy and absorbed so they have no time to squabble among themselves or get into mischief.

Anyone who plans a birthday or holiday party for three-year-olds, or in fact any tots up to the age of six or thereabouts, should bear in mind that youngsters love doing things with their hands. They cannot be expected to sit around and behave like miniature adults, playing together quietly and eating their refreshments like little ladies and gentlemen. They are excited, keyed up, off schedule, perhaps nervous and upset in a strange house among strange people. *They must be kept busy and amused.* They must be kept interested and happy; otherwise whatever else the party may or may not be from an adult viewpoint, it is certainly no fun for the little ones themselves.

What can young children be given to do with their hands at a party? There are so many things youngsters love to do that keeping them amused and entertained should really be no problem at all! Here are a few suggestions; you can probably think of a dozen more. Give each child an old magazine and a pair of plastic scissors (that cut paper but nothing else!) and explain that there's a prize for the little boy or girl who cuts out the prettiest pictures. Or give each child a box of clay and some molds to experiment with; it's good fun. So is a little pan filled with damp sand, and a box containing the makings of a miniature garden. So are beads and strings for the youngsters to make their own favors of costume jewelry. Children love showing grown-ups what they have made all by themselves. Of course, if you object to a temporarily disordered room, you shouldn't have parties for small fry. For the fun children have at a party is often in direct ratio to the amount of mess they leave behind them. It isn't reasonable to expect three or four-year-olds to be tidy; though naturally one should not tolerate or encourage deliberate destruction of property— whether it's the child's own toys or the possessions of others. Intelligent adults know where to draw the line.

When young guests arrive at a party, it's wise to engage them at once in some game or group activity . . . until they become accustomed to each other and to the strange surroundings. Joining in and doing what all the others are doing gives a shy young arrival a sense of *belonging*, of being part of the group, and helps to avoid the sulks and tantrums which spoil so many children's parties. Group games for tots should be very simple and easy to follow, quick-moving, and full of fun and action. Each child should be given a chance to participate; and the game should last only as long as it keeps the youngsters interested and amused.

An easy way to get things off to a good start is to seat the youngsters in a circle on the floor and give them a big soft ball to toss around the ring, from one child to the next. They love it, wait eagerly for their turn and shout with glee when they catch the ball. When they become bored or restless, just put a wastepaper basket in the center of the circle and let each child try in turn to toss the ball into it from his seated position.

For youngsters of eight or nine there are guessing games, donkey games, telling fortunes, anagrams, musical chairs, treasure hunts. Any public library can provide books of new and exciting party games for children. It always adds to the fun if there are prizes for the winners.

For children of twelve or thirteen you may want to provide somewhat more sophisticated entertainment, though it isn't necessary. Nowadays even pre-teen children have very definite ideas of their own and prefer to manage their own party games and entertainment without adult interference. For a very special occasion, however, it's possible in large cities to engage a puppeteer, magician, animal act, or some other type of entertainment suitable for a children's party.

Don't make the mistake of planning anything for teen-agers. Just provide plenty of food . . . and let them take care of their own fun! Boys and girls of high-school age are extremely self-sufficient. They resent having older persons watch them or tell them what to do. So teen-age parties should be managed without seeming aid from grown-ups. It's wise for grown-ups to be present, but unobtrusively—in another part of the house—to help if needed but not to act as chaperons.

PARTY DECORATIONS

Children's parties do not require elaborate decorations. Simple, inexpensive paper things that can be discarded after use are best. Naturally anything that's bright, gay, and colorful delights children and adds to the festivity of the occasion.

In decorating a room or table for a children's party, bear in mind that youngsters are far more impressed by grotesque balloons floating from the ceiling than a Sèvres bowl filled with orchids. Plan your decorations to amuse and delight the children, not to impress their mothers.

For birthday parties, there are usually fancy hats for the young guests, little paper candy baskets which they can carry home as souvenirs, and birthday decorations on the table. Sometimes the birthday cake is used as a centerpiece; but more often it is brought in at the proper moment and placed ceremoniously before the birthday child while everybody sings "Happy birthday to you!" It is traditional for the child to blow out the candles on the cake and make a birthday wish.

Holiday parties naturally take their decorative note from the occasion itself—turkeys and perhaps Indian decorations for Thanksgiving, holly and Santas for Christmas, and so on. A good way to keep small children busy and happy at Christmas parties is to provide each one with a miniature tree and a box of tiny ornaments, and let him decorate it himself and take it home as a souvenir. And of course singing carols is fun, and should be part of every Christmas party. In fact, singing familiar tunes of any kind always helps make a party successful—for children love participating in things as a group.

Hallowe'en is a gala occasion in the eyes of children, and a wonderful time for a party. Masquerades are a favorite, as children delight in dressing up and pretending to be something fearsome like a witch or ghost. At this point we should like to inject a word of warning to parents. Every year scores of small children lose their lives when they light up Hallowe'en pumpkins, and their flimsy masquerade costumes catch fire. *No child should ever be permitted to light a candle in a pumpkin.* The fun isn't worth the great risk. Before permitting a child to attend a Hallowe'en party, parents should make sure that there will be no lighting of pumpkins and no opportunity for the youngster to find and use matches without permission.

WHAT TO SERVE AT CHILDREN'S PARTIES

An important part of any party, especially for children, is the refreshments. Whatever is served should be simple and wholesome, and preferably familiar, as young children are chary of eating something they have never seen or tasted before. The trick is to serve these familiar foods in unusual and interesting ways, to give them a "party" look and make them seem different.

For example, sandwiches can be cut in the shape of animals. Creamed chicken can be served in cute little individual casseroles (some of them come in the shape of chickens and turkeys). Ice cream can be served in flower or animal forms. Anyone with a little imagination can think of dozens of ways to serve everyday foods in ways that are appealing to a child. Even ordinary cereal, wisely served as the main course of a birthday luncheon for the diaper set, can be decorated with raisin "faces" to enchant the young guests. Just serve a plate of steaming cereal to each child, with raisins for the eyes, nose, and mouth, so the youngster sees an exciting "face" in the plate and not just an ordinary, everyday food. It makes all the difference in the world in their response to it!

As a rule, it's better to have small children for lunch or early supper than to fill them full of ice cream and cake between meals—and perhaps make them ill by throwing them off their regular schedule. But with children of six or more, midafternoon refreshments are usual at parties. The important thing is to serve simple foods, not rich or "fancy" things that are likely to interfere with dinner later on.

Children always enjoy helping themselves more than being served.

So when they are old enough to manage without grown-up help—certainly by the time they get to be nine or ten—refreshments may be served buffet style at parties. It's convenient for the hostess, and usually a lot of fun for the youngsters. They love being served tomato or fruit juice from a tray, like grown-ups, and then helping themselves to sandwiches, salad, relishes, and other good things to eat from a gala buffet table. It's different from what they are accustomed to in their everyday routine, and therefore adds to the fun and festivity.

An excellent idea for children from ten to thirteen is a "box supper." Refreshments are wrapped and packed individually in identical boxes, and each box elaborately decorated to suit the occasion. The boxes are numbered, and the children pick from a hat to find which box is theirs. Though the food in each is the same, the favor or "prize" is different, so there's an element of surprise and suspense combined with the refreshments. The children sit wherever they like and eat right out of their party boxes; or they can sit around a table and serve themselves from the box. Milk, hot chocolate, or soda is served separately. This type of easy, informal serving at children's parties has many advantages—especially in a servantless house. The boxes can be prepared well ahead of time, the young host or hostess helping to pack, wrap, and tie them. The mother can then relax and enjoy the party instead of spending all her time in the kitchen getting the food ready and serving it.

Of course no birthday party, whether it's for tots or sophisticated teen-agers, is complete without a cake. And the more beautiful it is, the better, for it's meant to be symbolic of all that is good, sweet, rich, and beautiful in life for the young person who has become a year older. Gadgets are now available that make a cake sing "Happy Birthday" at the proper moment; and some cakes are baked with individual favors in them for the youngsters. But such elaborate novelties aren't really necessary. A homemade birthday cake lovingly decorated with the child's name and age—and fitted with the appropriate number of candles to blow out and make a wish on—serves the traditional purpose just as satisfactorily.

CERTAIN LITTLE MATTERS OF PARTY ETIQUETTE

Children cannot be taught too early to be agreeable, considerate little hosts at their own parties. This is never successfully accomplished by a lot of last-minute "don'ts" and dire threats just before the party. The only way is to show the child by consistent day-by-day example that in *his* house guests always come first—that a guest's interests, comforts and desires must be considered before those of the family. A child should grow up with this awareness of a guest's right to courtesy, so that it becomes instinctive and almost "second nature" with him to be generous and considerate toward young visitors at all times, not only at parties. A child so taught and trained from earliest years rarely needs to be warned or reminded about it on special occasions.

Youngsters of five or six should know that at their own parties they must be on hand to greet each guest, to say "Hello, Jimmy!" or "Come on in, Grace!" and take the newcomer in to join the others. They should never be permitted to remain engrossed in a game while a new arrival stands shyly in the doorway. No one expects a child of that age to be formal or prim about social conventions; but surely a child of six is old enough to understand that guests must be greeted on arrival and made to feel welcome.

Introductions are not necessary among very small children. But older children at a party should at least know each other's first names; and if they are strangers to each other, the young host of seven or eight should certainly know enough to introduce them. All that's necessary is to say "Mary, this is Tom" or "Tom, this is my cousin, Bill."

If a young guest arrives while a game is in progress, the newcomer should be included at once, if possible—even if it means starting all over again. A child can be made to feel very shy and unhappy if he is left out of a game at the very beginning, and it often spoils the whole party for him.

The well-bred child doesn't insist on dominating his party, playing only the games *he* wants to play, selfishly imposing his will and whims on the others. He considers the wishes of his guests before his own, lets them decide what games to play and how to play them. If his young guests are bored with a game and want to play something else, he cheerfully agrees. If they suggest playing something he doesn't like or enjoy, he joins them anyway and says nothing about it. It goes without saying that he never takes a prize at his own party, even if he wins it. He knows that would be poor sportsmanship, that prizes are for guests only.

Young guests at a birthday party should present their gifts with a friendly "Happy Birthday"—not just hold out the package and say "Here!" The child who receives the gift should say "Thank you" and place it aside with his other birthday presents to be opened later. He should not tear off the wrappings then and there to see what it is. Of course if it's not a party, if there's only one child and one gift, the package may be opened at once; and the child who receives the gift should be taught to show pleasure even if it's a disappointment.

At a birthday party, gifts are usually placed on a table or desk, according to prior instructions. Later all the children sit in a circle while the birthday child opens each exciting package in turn, reading the name on the card aloud (or mother does this if the child is too young). Each little guest should be thanked in turn for his gift as it is opened, examined, and admired. It's important to make youngsters realize, just as soon as they are old enough to understand, that they must show equal appreciation and enthusiasm for all gifts, whatever they may be. In some homes children are not permitted to open their birthday packages until all the young guests are gone; but it's always more fun (and just as good custom) to open them at the party and let those who brought the gifts see the pleasure with which they are received.

A well-bred child doesn't rush to the door as each guest arrives to see if there's a package for him, never asks for a gift or shows disappointment when none is given. If a youngster comes to a birthday party without a package, the little host or hostess should be taught not to remark about it. Children old enough to think about presents are old enough to be taught they must never ask for them, or show an excess of greedy interest in what guests bring.

When the party is over, the young host or hostess should stand at the door and say good-by individually to each departing guest. An exceptionally courteous child will say, "Thank you for coming," or "Thank you for the nice present."

Departing youngsters should say, "Good-by, Barbara—it was a wonderful party." Or to the child's mother, "Goodbye, Mrs. Martin—thank you for a very nice time."

CHILDREN'S PARTY INVITATIONS AND ACKNOWLEDGMENTS

Children's party invitations are usually in the form of gaily decorated cards with blank spaces for filling in the date, place, hour, occasion, and so on. Even very young children should be permitted to fill in and address their own party invitations, as it gives them a sense of social responsibility. But it's wise to check on the time, date, and other essential data to make sure it's entirely correct. Otherwise youngsters may arrive on the wrong day or at the wrong hour.

When printed cards of invitation are not used, notes are written—either by the child or by his mother. Naturally a child of three or four needs to have his invitations written for him. Here is an example:

Dear Mrs. Clinton:

Bobby will be four years old on Saturday, May 5th, and I'm having a little birthday party for him.

I know he won't be happy unless his pal, Dickie, is at the party; so I hope you will let him come.

If you bring Dick about three, he'll be just in time for the fun. I'd like you to stay and have tea with the other mothers at five. But if you can't stay, I'll see that Dick is safely delivered to your door no later than six o'clock.

Sincerely yours,
Anna T. Walsh

Dick's mother promptly writes a friendly note of acceptance or regret. If her little boy cannot attend the party, she explains why in her letter.

Dear Mrs. Walsh:

Dick is thrilled and excited about Bobby's birthday party. Of course he'll be there—with his best party manners, I hope!

I'll bring him at three and call for him about six, so you won't need to bother about getting him home.

I'd like very much to stay and have tea with the other mothers, but I have a previous appointment for the afternoon and I can't very well get out of it. Thanks for asking me.

Sincerely yours,
Laura Clinton

Dear Mrs. Walsh:

I haven't told Dick about the birthday party because I know how disappointed he would be not to go. But he is scheduled to take a series of allergy tests on May 5th and unfortunately the date cannot be changed.

I am sure you understand, and that you and Bobby will forgive Dick for not being there.

Thank you for Dick and myself for your gracious invitation. And many happy returns of the day!

Sincerely yours,
Laura Clinton

As soon as a child is old enough to write his own invitations, he should be permitted to do so. Don't tell him the *exact words* to write; just make whatever helpful suggestions you think are necessary. Let the invitations be natural and childish.

Dear Nita:

Next Sunday is my birthday. I will be eight years old. I am going to have a cake with eight candles. Can you come to my party? It starts at two o'clock. Good-by, but don't forget to come.

Helen

Dear Tom:

Please come to my birthday party on June 6 from 2 to 5 o'clock. I'll be nine years old so I am inviting nine boys. My dad is going to show movies. I hope you can come to my party.

Your pal,
Arthur Wade

Dear Patsy:

Mother said I can have a party for my birthday. It's next Friday. Can you come at four and stay for dinner? My dad is going to drive all the girls home around eight. I hope you can come.

Joan

Notes of Acceptance

Children's party invitations are not, as a rule, as conscientiously acknowledged as adult invitations. They don't need to be. Sometimes the mother telephones to say the young guest will be there. Sometimes the child's presence on the day of the party is the only acknowledgment. It's always more gracious, of course, to write a note of acceptance, and youngsters should be encouraged to do so. But there's no question about the need for acknowledgment when a child cannot attend. In that case a note of regret must be sent at once, explaining why the invitation cannot be accepted.

Following are specimen letters of acceptance and regret to guide the young beginner in his social duties.

Dear Helen:

Yes, I can come to your birthday party. My mother will bring me on Sunday at 2 o'clock. I love parties and I am glad you are having one.

Nita

Dear Arthur:

Thank you for inviting me to your party. I am very glad to come. The movies sound wonderful. I'll see you on Saturday.

Your pal,
Tom

Dear Joan:

Your party sounds like lots of fun! I'll be there on Friday at four, and mother says I can stay until eight as long as someone takes me home. I am looking forward to it.

Your loving friend,
Patsy

NOTES OF REGRET

Dear Gladys:

I'm sorry I cannot come to your party on Sunday. My grandma is coming and I haven't seen her in a long time. Thank you for asking me. Happy birthday.

Your friend,
Mildred

Dear Claire:

I'm just getting over a sore throat, and mother doesn't think I'll be well enough to go to your party on Friday.

I'm awfully sorry. I know I'll miss a very good time.

Love and congratulations on your thirteenth birthday.

Lenore

PART X

Teen-Age Etiquette

1. GENERAL TEEN-AGE ETIQUETTE

THERE is probably no one in the world who needs to know the conventions and proprieties more than a teen-age boy or girl. Of course the teen-agers themselves would be the last to admit it. They would, in fact, scoff at the very idea of etiquette.

But have you ever seen anything more pathetic than a teen-age boy on his first date trying to act completely adult and sophisticated . . . and not knowing quite how?

Have you ever watched a teen-age girl getting ready for her first big "formal," wondering what to wear and how to act, and hoping she'll make the right impression?

No—they don't give a hoot about behavior, these bright young moderns. But when they start dating, going to parties, and coming smack up against the proprieties—that's when the agony begins! That's when they want to know exactly what to do, say, write and wear, that's when they want to be, in their own colorful and characteristic phrase, "in the groove."

To teen-agers who want to know the basic fundamentals of good manners, we make the following general suggestions.

IT TAKES GOOD MANNERS TO BE GOOD COMPANY

A girl doesn't need to be good-looking to be popular. It's more important to be good company—which means being a good sport, taking an interest in people and in things outside herself, contributing to the talk and the fun, and being a lady.

A boy doesn't need to be handsome to make a hit. It's more important to be poised and sure of himself, to know how to act in company—to be friendly, casual, civil, and considerate. Gentlemen are always preferred.

However you personally may feel about it, the fact is that good manners pay off. To be popular and well liked by those who really count, you must have "what it takes." And a very large part of what it takes is just plain, simple, garden-variety courtesy—which costs nothing at all and takes practically no effort.

The first and most important rule for public behavior is to attract as little attention to yourself as possible: in dress, in speech, and in actions. Try never to make yourself conspicuous in any way. Have fun —but don't be noisy about it. Leave that to the kindergarten set, where it belongs. Keep your voice down and your laughter under control; there's no need to disturb others just because you're having a good time. It's more adult to be restrained and not advertise your presence to everyone within hearing distance. Of course if you're at a ball game, that's another thing again; a little plain and fancy shouting is in order. But on the street, at the movies, and in public places in general, act your age and avoid making yourself conspicuous.

It isn't smart to look sloppy, speak carelessly, act like a rowdy, be offensive or rude to older people. It certainly isn't smart to act or speak in a way that reflects unfairly on the influence of your home and your parents.

Don't walk along the street eating; it's not good manners. Don't shout across the street to your friends; it's better form to cross over and join them. Don't swing along the street three or four abreast, making it difficult for others to get by; that's kid stuff . . . and not at all courteous.

Why be courteous? Why be thoughtful of others? *Because you can't get by with bad manners.* You may say "Nuts!" as inelegantly as you please. You may scoff at courtesy and call it old-fashioned. But of this you can be certain: If you don't have good manners, you are going to miss them pretty badly some day—just when you need them most. If you don't acquire habits of courtesy and good breeding, you can count on many a blunder and embarrassment later on.

RUDENESS NEVER MADE ANYBODY POPULAR

When you are entertained at someone's home, be careful not to overstay and wear out your welcome. When the time comes to leave, do so promptly and courteously. Say your good-byes and go at once; don't lag. If it was a special party (not just a friendly informal visit), remember to send your hostess a note of thanks. Don't dash off any old thing; take a little pains with your note and make it sound sincere. People who take the trouble to entertain you deserve appreciation, and always enjoy receiving it.

It's very rude and ungracious to criticize someone whose home you have visited. Never make disparaging remarks about the furnishings, the food that was served, or members of the family. To make fun of someone whose hospitality you accepted and enjoyed is inexcusable.

The essence of good manners is adaptability. If you are a guest in a humble home, have the grace and tact to enjoy its simple hospitality without boasting about your own elegant possessions. If you are a guest in a great house, don't let yourself be too impressed by its magnificence. Try not to be awed by a standard of living above which you are accustomed, nor contemptuous of a standard below your own. Remember that in the world of today people are judged by what they are, not by what they have.

Well-bred teen-agers out "on the town" are never rude to waiters or others who serve them. They keep their monkeyshines for the playroom or back yard, behave properly in a public restaurant or theater. They never shove ahead of others on a line, nor jostle and annoy people standing near them. A girl doesn't enjoy being out with a clown; it's so much more fun being with a suave young gentleman.

At the theater, well-bred teen-agers are careful not to disturb people who, like themselves, have paid money to enjoy the performance. They know it's bad manners to talk, giggle, whistle, or crackle paper during the show. They know it's unfair to keep on an obstructing hat and make the person behind go through contortions to see the stage or screen.

At home, well-bred teen-agers are agreeable, co-operative, responsible members of the household. They take pleasure and pride in their family relationships; and participate, when required, in family activities. They do not regard their parents as old-fashioned merely because they are older. They never correct or contradict their parents before outsiders. They are prompt for meals, don't bring books or magazines to the table when they are eating with the family, never sit down before their parents or start eating before everyone else does. They do not "borrow" their brother's or sister's belongings without permission, read mail or messages not intended for them, listen in on private telephone conversations. They are desirable members of the family team: fair, unselfish, and considerate.

At school, well-bred teen-agers are punctual and attentive. They wear suitable clothes, and they wear them *neatly*. School is school—a place of learning and of dignity—and clothes should be in keeping: simple, sturdy, and in good taste. Smart girls and boys save their fancy clothes for evening dates, their "faddy" clothes for picnics and jamborees. They give their teachers the courtesy and respect to which they are entitled. They never feel it is necessary to "run with the pack," to bully or taunt someone who is disliked, persecuted, left out of games. They are more likely than not to be especially kind to someone who needs kindness so badly. They play fair in games and sports. They win without gloating, lose without annoyance and without making excuses.

Most well-bred young moderns have a basic honesty of thought, an intellectual integrity, which is most refreshing. They refuse to accept other people's fixed ideas and prejudices. They are open-minded and tolerant—think things through for themselves. They respect the right of every individual to his own beliefs and ideals. They do not consider themselves better or superior to other people because their beliefs are different.

DATES AND DANCES

A teen-age boy who has a younger sister should take her to parties and dances occasionally. They can learn much from each other in the way of social graces. Being together, dancing together, chatting together will give them a poise and assurance far beyond their years— an advantage they would not have otherwise. The boy who is accustomed to paying little courtesies to his mother and sisters is more fortunate than he realizes. He is not likely to be awkward and make embarrassing blunders when he takes somebody else's sister to a party or dance.

The teen-age boy who is new at dating should try to pick a partner who likes approximately the same things he does. If she's just pretty and not especially compatible, they won't enjoy each other's company. It takes two to make a date click and be fun; and the two should at least be able to talk about the same interests.

So if you would rather skate or bowl than do anything else in the world, don't date a girl who hates both but simply adores dancing. It's better tactics to date a girl who likes bowling or skating, too, or who is at least willing to go your way and learn.

When you call a girl for a date, have something definite in mind. It's up to you to suggest where to go or what to do. Girls don't like vague "take-a-walk" dates; they like to know where they're going so they can tell how to dress. Never call a girl on the telephone and ask, "Doing anything tonight?" That puts her in an awkward position. If she says "No," you may invite her to a bridge party to which she'd rather not go. If she says "Yes," she may miss out on a movie she'd like very much to see. Put your question courteously and properly: "Would you like to go to the movies with me tonight?"

Never beg a girl for a date, no matter how important it may be to you. If she turns you down, take it in your stride. Be casual and worldly about it—not juvenile.

Don't be late for dates. If it looks as though you are going to be late, take a minute to telephone and let her know. That shows you are thoughtful and polite, and worth any girl's while.

It is theoretically the girl's privilege to ask a boy to call, if she wishes him to do so. But most boys nowadays do not hesitate to ask if they may call when they meet a girl they like and wish to continue seeing her. This is now considered entirely proper. However a boy should never ask a girl to call on *him*; that just isn't done! Of course if it's a party, that's another thing again; but a young man never asks a girl alone to come to his house.

The first time you call on a girl, you naturally want to make a good impression on her family; and there's no surer way than to be gentlemanly and polite. Being polite means more than just saying "Good evening" instead of "Hi." It means taking off your hat the instant you walk through the door. It means acknowledging introductions properly: smiling and bowing slightly as you say "How do you do" to her mother, stepping forward and shaking hands with her father—looking directly at them and not at the floor. It means making some pleasant and casual remark to the girl to put her (and yourself!) at ease, so you don't just stand grinning at each other and feeling foolish.

Don't stay too long the first time you call on a girl. And when you leave, be sure to include her family in your good-byes. Once you get up to leave, don't linger in the doorway twisting your hat; that's always a sign of social inexperience. Thank the girl for a pleasant evening, ask her for a date if you wish, say goodbye—and go.

When you take a girl out, call for her at her house—don't arrange to meet her at some convenient corner. If you call for her in your dad's car, be courteous enough to get out and ring her doorbell. It's very rude to pull up in front of the house and honk the horn. When you're ready to leave together, open the door of the car and help her in before you take your own place. Or if there's no car, be very gallant and protective walking beside her on the street, remembering to help her up and down curbs. Little courtesies like that make a girl feel precious and desirable . . . and show that you know what's expected of a gentleman.

Before you leave your house, be sure to check on your appearance. Are your shoes polished? Is your hair neat? The lad who looks sloppy is no prize to a girl on a date. She dresses up for you, so return the courtesy and call on her looking like a beau. That calls for a clean shirt, a pressed suit, a respectable-looking tie, and a freshly scrubbed look. Whatever else a girl may overlook in a boy she likes, you can be sure she'll never overlook or forgive *dirty nails.*

For an informal party or dance, no special kind of clothes are required. But for a formal function, you are expected to wear a regulation dinner jacket in winter; a white dinner jacket, or a dark coat and light trousers, in the summer. A girl wears a simple party dress to informal dances, an evening gown to formal affairs. If she has good taste, she chooses clothes that are suitable—avoiding extreme styles and deep décolleté.

At a party or dance, the first duty of a boy and girl—after they have left their wraps in the dressing rooms—is to go *together* to their host and hostess and greet them. This is an essential courtesy which is all too often overlooked by careless teen-agers.

A boy must dance first with the girl he has taken to the party. Thereafter he may dance with anyone he wishes, but he should be sure that his date has partners and does not sit alone and neglected while he has a good time. He is expected to return to her between dances and attend courteously to all her wants during the evening. If there is a supper after the dance, they go in together.

"Cutting in" is an accepted practice among young people at a dance; however, like any other privilege, it becomes rude and offensive when it is abused. When cutting in, the boy lightly touches the shoulder of the girl's partner. The partner either relinquishes her at once and steps aside, or he smiles and says "Next time around." He *must* make the change next time around; and he may not cut in again on that girl until someone else has claimed her as a partner. In other words, he does not cut in on the same boy who has cut in on him. The girl always says "I'm sorry" when she leaves one partner for another. She should not show marked preferences but should be equally friendly and pleasant to all.

Casual teen-agers rarely use the precise and formal phrase, "May I have this dance?" They are more likely to say just "Dance?" or "Shall we?"—with a smile that adds politeness to their words. At the end of a dance, the boy always thanks his partner; she does not thank him. He does not leave her standing in the middle of the floor but returns her to her friends or to where she was sitting.

It's very rude for a girl to refuse to dance with a boy on the plea of being tired—and then dance with someone else. If she doesn't want to dance with him for some reason, she should deftly invent an excuse for escaping—like going to the dressing room to fix her hair—and she should skip that dance completely. Boys notice when a girl is unnecessarily rude or unkind to someone at a dance, and it doesn't add to her popularity with them.

Getting a girl home safely, in person and *on time*, is a very important part of a date. A boy should never ask someone else at a party to take home the girl he brought, except in a sudden emergency. If her parents have specified that she must be home by a certain hour, he sees to it that she gets there in time. Of course he takes her right to her door and waits until she is safely inside before leaving. If members of her family are still up and she invites him in for something to eat or drink, he may accept if he wishes. But if it's late and everyone is asleep, it's better judgment on her part not to invite him, and better manners on his part, if she does ask him, not to accept.

It's a good idea for boys and girls in their early teens to travel in groups at first, instead of going out on individual dates. It broadens their social experience; they learn many things they need to know from contact with various types of people; and they acquire the poise and confidence that are so important to them later on.

2. SOME SPECIAL TEEN-AGE PROBLEMS

ONE of the major problems of every teen-ager is to have fun, to be popular and a "good sport"—and at the same time observe the proprieties.

Can a girl drink, and pet in a parked car, and still be the kind of girl who inspires a real moonlight-and-roses romance? Can a boy scoff at the conventions, make his own sweet rules, and act just as he pleases, without being ostracized by the families in his community who count most?

The answer is "No!" No matter how many exceptions rush to your mind—no matter, even, if everybody else you know does these things —the answer is still "No!" And it's not based on any old-fashioned ideas of morality, either. It's based on simple principles of common sense—with which every intelligent young person who wants a well-ordered, balanced, and *happy* life will agree.

ABOUT SMOKING

There is no objection to smoking if you *like* to smoke, and if your parents have given their permission. But to smoke for effect, to look grown-up and sophisticated, is just plain showing off. It makes you look like a "smarty" to your friends; and if anything, more juvenile than grown up.

So don't start smoking just to show off or keep up with the crowd. Don't defy your parents and "sneak" cigarettes before you have their consent. Wait until you are old enough and until your parents approve; then if you *must* smoke, do so casually and in moderation.

The very earliest you should start to smoke, if you do so at all, is sixteen. If your parents object, wait until you are eighteen. You owe them that courtesy and consideration. And before you start what may become a lifelong habit, weigh these considerations: Smoking stains the fingers and the teeth. It makes clothes and breath offensive. It adds up to a lot of dimes out of your allowance every week; and if you take the time to figure up what smoking for thirty or forty years is likely to cost you, you may find the amount rather staggering. So take your time about deciding whether or not to smoke, and think it through carefully. Remember that smoking is not a sign of being grown up; at least half the adults in the world never touch a cigarette at all.

But if you happen to belong to the other half, please learn to smoke properly and observe the rules of smoking etiquette.[1]

Smart Teen-Agers Do Not Drink

To young people who want to know about drinking, our suggestion is to wait until you are out of your teens. Never mind what everybody else does; you be the smart one! It's time enough to start taking a sociable drink now and then when you are twenty; but if you insist on starting sooner, at least talk it over with your parents and come to some pleasant agreement with them as to when, where, and how much. If they give their consent to a glass of beer or a glass of wine on certain special occasions, be fair and live up to your part of the bargain.

Don't feel you must take a drink at a night club or restaurant just because the waiter asks, or because others in your party are drinking. It is never necessary to take a drink at any time, under any circumstances, unless you want to. Don't feel you must order a drink to appear mature; it's just as sophisticated to order a ginger ale or a "coke." Drinking is no prerequisite to becoming an adult; and it's not only bad manners but very poor judgment for a teen-age boy or girl to drink for effect.

One thing more about drinking; you don't need it to have a good time. Smart teen-agers take their fun straight, without paying for it in headaches and upset stomachs.

[1] Pages 404 to 410.

Why Petting Is Unwise

The reason many teen-age girls pet is because "everybody else does" and they're afraid of being unpopular, of missing out on good times! But petting is a high price to pay for popularity. The girl who pets to fill up her date book is courting trouble; for it doesn't take the fellows long to get on to her dating reputation and take advantage of it.

The objection to petting is not that it's necessarily wrong, but *cheap*. If a girl pets with every boy who takes her to a movie or dance, she doesn't rate herself very high; and if *she* doesn't, nobody else will! A girl who thinks so little of herself that she gives her kisses to all comers may wake up to a startling realization some day. She may discover that her kisses have lost their romantic value—that they mean nothing at all to the one-boy-in-the-world who really counts.

If a girl is smart and socially mature, and a credit to her well-bred parents, she's clever enough to have lots of dates and good times *without* petting. She's always such good company, such fun to be with, so pleasant and so interested in everyone, that a boy counts himself lucky just to rate a date with her. And with all her good spirits and gaiety, she's always such a *lady* that no lad even dreams of taking liberties!

Suggestions to the Teen-Age Girl

The qualities that make a girl popular are difficult to define, and there are so many of them! Everybody knows it's not just good looks alone—nor wit or poise alone—nor even that elusive and desirable quality known as charm. Actually it's a combination of all of these, with many more added. But of all the things that go to make up a lovable and attractive personality, there is perhaps nothing more important than the good manners and courtesy which stem from a liking for people and an interest in them, and the desire to be liked in return. For even with beauty and talent and every other attribute, a girl cannot be popular if she is completely wrapped up in herself and shows neither interest in nor consideration for other people.

Courtesy expresses itself in many little ways, easily overlooked by a girl who is inexperienced. The following suggestions are to help her avoid what may seem like rudeness or ill-breeding, but which is usually only lack of social knowledge and unfamiliarity with social forms. These paragraphs are addressed to the teen-age girl, for whom they are written.

Play straight with your dates. Don't break a date because something better to do has come along. The lass who does *that* often enough finds herself sitting at home with her knitting! If you absolutely must break a date for some reason, call the boy and explain. Ask him to release you—and when he does, be sure to thank him courteously.

If you want to be a credit to your home and your parents, don't "sneak" dates. If your parents disapprove of a boy you are seeing, accept their more mature judgment and don't go out with him. But if you do, don't make a secret of it. One of the worst things you can do is to deceive your parents.

When you go out with a boy, come home with the same one. Don't let somebody else take you home because you like him better. Boys soon get to know about things like that!

If you know your parents are sitting up waiting for you, and you can see you'll be an hour late or more, take a minute to call them and let them know. It's thoughtless and unkind to let them worry. Another thing: boys notice how a girl treats her parents—so don't think it's smart to "talk back." The boys won't admire you for it.

One of your greatest personal assets, whether you realize it or not, is your smile. If you want people to like you, be cheerful and smiling as much of the time as you can. Don't let little things get you down. Take disappointments in your stride . . . and remember that a reputation for unfailing good spirits is a wonderful thing to have.

If you meet someone you like and you want to know him better, invite him to a party at your house. But never pursue a boy—that's very bad tactics! Don't call him on the telephone unless he asks you to. And don't be possessive. Boys don't like girls who act as though they own them.

Make it a point to be on time for your dates. It's bad manners to keep people waiting—even when it's just the boy down the street whom you've known all your life. Be ready and waiting when he calls for you; that's the courteous way.

Don't criticize one boy when you are with another. He'll wonder what you say about *him* when you're with somebody else.

Don't boast about your conquests. That's childish—and doesn't fool anyone.

Don't write love letters to half a dozen different boys. The day may come when you'll be sorry. And don't read your love letters to the girls! That's something nice girls just don't do. A letter written for you alone isn't meant to be shown around; it's private, and privacy should always be respected.

Be natural. Nobody likes a girl who is always putting on an act and pretending to be something she is not. Avoid silly fads. Don't go in for phony speech tricks and fake accents. Just be yourself—it's easier, and a lot more appealing. Remember that one of the qualities everybody admires most is *sincerity*.

The world takes you at your own estimate of yourself, so rate yourself high! Don't go out with anybody, just for a date. Don't go around with boys and girls who have no character, no common sense, and no manners. Set a high standard for yourself and live up to it. If you don't think you rate the best, who will?

Don't monopolize the conversation when you're with a group of people. Listen attentively when others talk. Let them see that you are interested. Make them feel that what they're saying is important. A good listener is always popular.

Don't whistle, hum, or keep up a stream of small talk when you are dancing with a boy. It's irritating, like chatting in the movies when he wants to watch the picture. A smart girl knows when to be quiet.

If the boy who invited you to the prom sends a corsage, wear it even if it doesn't go with your dress. Put it in your hair or tie it on your wrist—but wear it! And don't tell him he should have called you and asked the color of your dress. (There's nothing a boy hates more than to be made to feel dumb and unsophisticated!) Thank him sweetly, wear it proudly—and have fun.

Suggestions to the Teen-Age Boy

A recent survey among teen-age girls shows that their pet peeve is boys who smoke, drink, get "fresh," and show off in general to make an impression. The only impression they make, say the girls, is a very bad one.

Make no mistake about it—the girls like boys who are gentlemen and know how to behave. They don't like to be made conspicuous by a boy whose actions are rowdy and undisciplined, whose manners and speech are crude. They don't like to be seen with a boy who looks sloppy and acts silly.

If you're smart, you'll dust off the monkeyshines and act like an adult. That means being quiet and poised in public places, and watching your manners and your speech. There's nothing "sissy" about being polite. You can be the star quarterback on the football team and still act like a gentleman.

When you're out with a girl, don't forget the little courtesies that show you know what's right. Walk on the outside; hold her chair; help her with her coat. She'll love it! Masculine protectiveness is always a delight to a girl.

Be sure you know where you're going when you take a girl out. Don't start looking for a restaurant at the last minute.

Don't chew gum or smoke a cigarette when you're dancing with a girl.

If you're a poor dancer, don't keep apologizing for it. Do the best you can, and learn to dance better as soon as possible.

When you're out with a girl, don't talk about other dates. Give her your rapt attention, and all of it, if you want to make a hit with her.

Don't break a date at the last minute unless there's a very good reason for it. And even if you break an arm or something, *don't stand a girl up.* Call her on the telephone, or get somebody else to do it and explain the circumstances.

Always try to look neat and well-groomed, be friendly and agreeable, act like a gentleman and show consideration for others, and you'll have no trouble being popular.

PART XI

Club Etiquette

1. CLUB ETIQUETTE

THERE are many different kinds of clubs, and many long-established customs and traditions of club behavior. But good manners are the same in clubs as anywhere else in the world, based on thoughtful restraint and consideration for others. In clubs, however, the basic rules of courtesy are intensified. For a club is for the pleasure and convenience of many, and rude or selfish behavior on the part of one member does not long go unnoticed.

In general, the rules for behavior in a club derive from the same broad principles of courtesy and good taste which govern the behavior of ladies and gentlemen in the drawing room of a private house. But each club has its own special rules and regulations, and it is the duty of every member to know what these rules are and to observe them scrupulously.

The well-bred man or woman is punctual for club meetings, reasonably regular in attendance, interested in club activities, unfailingly loyal to club principles, customs, and ideals. He enjoys but does not abuse his rights and privileges. He is as careful of club property as his own, and is friendly and courteous to all members, new and old.

It goes without saying that the well-bred club member pays his dues promptly. If the time comes when he can no longer afford to be a member, he resigns while he is still in good standing—certainly before he has allowed dues and perhaps other debts to accumulate. He never uses his club for business purposes, nor exploits it in any way for personal gain. He is careful not to discuss the intimate or private affairs of his club, or of any of its members, with outsiders. If he has reason to criticize an officer or member of the club, he does so only within the framework of the organization, and in the manner prescribed in the by-laws. In all club dealings and activities he is fair, open-minded, aboveboard, and sincere.

These are the simple basics. But there are countless "unwritten" laws of club etiquette which in some cases are even more sacred to the organization than the traditional rules of courtesy. It's up to each club member to know what the customs of his particular club are, and to be guided by them.

How to Join a Club

There are several ways to join a club, the method depending on the type of club it happens to be. Membership in some clubs may be had simply by walking in and paying dues. Other clubs require formal application, which is then passed on by a committee or voted on by a board of governors. Still others require sponsorship, letters of endorsement, special abilities or qualifications. Then, of course, there are some clubs that cannot be joined by application at all; one must be formally *invited* to become a member.

Before attempting to join a club, therefore, it's important to find out all you can about it—what the requirements are and exactly how to go about becoming a member. As a rule, it is only political clubs, civic and service clubs, and some athletic organizations and country golf clubs, which are open to general membership. That is, anyone may join by walking in and paying dues. But to join a purely social club of high rank and distinction, a literary or professional club, or one of the exclusive men's clubs, is a very different matter. The usual procedure is to have one's name "put up" for membership by a friend, and seconded by another friend—both members of the club. The name is then posted on the bulletin board in the club house.

As soon as a person's name goes up, it is the duty of his sponsor and seconder to write letters of recommendation to the board of governors. Other members who see the name on the board, and who know and like the applicant, may also write letters of endorsement. On the other hand, if any member has reason to believe that the applicant is undesirable and should not be accepted, it is his privilege to write to the governors of the club and tell them so. All letters are read at the next meeting of the board, when the name of the would-be member comes up for election.

When an applicant has been voted on and elected to membership, he is promptly notified by mail. Included in the notification is the amount of his initiation fee and dues, which he must mail at once. He may then consider himself a member of the club, and may use its facilities as little or as much as he likes.

A person who is not well known in the community, or who is unpopular with some of the members of the club, may not be elected to membership the first time. His name may be put up a second time when he is better known in the community, or when the sponsor feels that the original objection to him has been overcome. But a man or woman *twice* turned down for membership in a club should not be proposed again.

It is not considered courteous to ask anyone but a very close personal friend to propose one's name for membership in a club, or even to second it. It's awkward to place a conscientious member who does not know you well in the position of refusing. Furthermore, sponsorship involves considerable time, effort, and responsibility, and no one but an intimate friend should be expected to take it on. It's always best when the suggestion to join a club comes voluntarily from a friend, who then offers to act as sponsor—and perhaps suggests someone to second him.

To join a club *by invitation* may mean several things. You may be invited when a club is just starting to be one of the founders or charter members. Or, if you are a distinguished citizen or prominent in the field that a certain well-established club represents, you may be invited by the board of governors to become a member. In small, informal clubs it's common practice to let suitable people know that they would be welcome as members.

An invitation to join a club may be accepted or not, as one sees fit. It's no affront to refuse; but a gracious note of explanation and appreciation should be sent to the board of governors, or the chairman of the membership committee.

THE NEW MEMBER

One of the first and most important duties of the new member of a club is to secure a copy of the bylaws or "house rules" and study them carefully. He should make himself familiar with all the customs and traditions of the club and guard against any violations. He should also learn the names of the officers and of the other members as quickly as possible.

Customarily, the new member goes to the club for the first time with his sponsor or seconder, or with some other established member who knows his way about. This isn't required, of course, but it's usually very helpful—especially in a large city club where there are likely to be unwritten laws of conduct that must be explained.

In all but a very few cosmopolitan clubs, it is customary for older members to approach and speak to a new member, introducing themselves and making him feel welcome. But the new member should on no account approach older members who are strangers and make himself known to them. He should be careful not to impose on older members in any way, and should particularly avoid annoying them by asking too many questions or expecting too much help or advice. The best strategy, in the beginning, is to be an alert observer rather than an active participant, to learn all one can about the routine and procedure of the club by looking on and listening. He can also learn by asking questions of personal friends, or of those whose official status in the club makes them a logical source of information.

COUNTRY CLUBS

In general, country clubs, golf clubs, yacht and beach clubs, fishing and hunting clubs, are not as exclusive as men's top-ranking city clubs. Some are; a few are even more exclusive, and one must meet the most exacting social requirements to get into them. But these few are not representative; there are thousands of country clubs with very simple requirements.

The big difference between city and country clubs—apart from their basic purpose, of course—is in their membership privileges. A city club extends membership privileges to no one but the member himself. A country club extends its privileges, the use of its clubhouse and other facilities, not only to the member but to his family and friends.

Most country clubs have resident members and non-resident members. A resident member lives on the grounds, or within a certain specified distance from the club. Non-resident members live beyond the specified distance, but enjoy exactly the same privileges and the same use of the clubhouse and facilities.

The average country club requires an initiation fee and the payment of yearly dues. However, some clubs grant "season privileges" to people who have come to spend the summer or winter in the vicinity of the club. Sometimes sponsorship is required even for a season's membership, but usually it is not. There is rarely an initiation fee for this type of membership; and one does not pay regular dues like regular members, but a season's subscription for the right to use the clubhouse, grounds, and facilities.

At most country clubs, members may entertain guests as often as they wish. However, the number of guests permitted at any one time is usually limited, and members should be careful not to break the rule. Any abuse of a privilege is bad manners.

Country clubs are on the whole considerably less formal than city clubs. But well-bred people are careful to observe the rules and regulations and to dress, speak, and conduct themselves at all times, under all conditions, with good taste and decorum.

Regarding Good Manners in a Club

As we have already pointed out, good manners are the same in a club as anywhere else; but there are some special points of club etiquette that should be emphasized.

Never interrupt a private conversation between members of a club, even if you know them well.

Never carry on an animated conversation in a reading room or library where people are trying to concentrate.

Never interrupt a club member who is absorbed in a book or busy writing a letter. People go to their clubs to relax, and to get away from interruptions.

Never appear in the club rooms carelessly or unsuitably dressed. If shorts, halters, bathing attire, etc., are not permitted, don't wear them. A good club member does not break the rules.

Don't put your feet on club furniture, ashes on the floor, wet glasses where they can do damage. Don't abuse club books or magazines, or misuse any of the club facilities.

Don't use club stationery for business letters.

Don't use your club as an office, to conduct business affairs. It's proper to entertain customers or clients at lunch or dinner in your club; but it is *not* proper to hold meetings there for business purposes only.

An unmarried man, or a man who lives at his club, may use the club address on his visiting cards and note paper. But the address of a married man is his *home*, and he should not use his club as an official address.

The Non-active Member

In almost every club there are at least a few members who, for one reason or another, do not take part in club activities or affairs. They may have joined originally because they were urged to do so by friends. They may have joined to show their good will toward the club, or their approval of its aims and ideals. Or they may have merely wished to contribute to the club to the extent of paying their dues.

In any case, members who joined with no intention of becoming active—or members who no longer *can* be active due to ill health or the press of other duties—should not be criticized for remaining in the background. They should not be censured for failing to attend meetings regularly, work on committees, buy or sell tickets, or participate in other club affairs. As long as they continue to pay their dues regularly, and are in no way disloyal to the club or a discredit to it, they have the right to remain non-active members in good standing.

As for such members themselves, they need not feel it is bad manners or poor sportsmanship to refuse to hold an office or function on a committee. It is their privilege to refuse if they feel they haven't the time or energy for it. But it definitely is discourteous to keep finding fault with those who do take over an office or some other club responsibility and try to do the best job they can.

Guests at a Club

Practically every club allows its members to invite guests and to extend certain courtesies and privileges to them.

Men's clubs have private dining rooms in which members may give stag dinners for their friends; and most of them have private dining rooms and sitting rooms where women guests can be entertained. Some men's clubs exclude women entirely, never permit them to cross the threshold for any reason, at any time.

In women's clubs there are usually no special rooms for men, who are customarily entertained in the general lounge and dining room.

The bylaws of a club invariably specify the guest privileges, and sometimes stipulate that guests may be entertained for the day only. In others they may be put up for several days, or even for several weeks at a time. The procedure is either to take the visitor directly to the club, write his name in the visitors' book, and make arrangements personally for his guest privileges, or to write to the secretary for a visitor's card of introduction. The secretary sends the card directly to the stranger, inviting him to use the club privileges and facilities for a certain specified time—*as guest of the club, through the courtesy of his friend.*

That last phrase should serve as keynote to the guest's conduct and attitude during his stay. As a *guest of the club,* he must not abuse the privileges so graciously extended him, and should be careful to observe all the rules and regulations. And as a guest *through the courtesy of his friend,* he must not permit that friend to assume further obligations in his behalf. He must pay his own bill, either arranging at the club office to have it given to him directly, or asking his friend for it at the end of his stay.

Guests at a club should never make themselves conspicuous in any way, should never attract undue attention to themselves or infringe on the rights of regular members.

The guest who is curt or inconsiderate to a member of the club is *doubly* rude—to the member, and to the friend who secured the guest privileges for him. He does not deserve to be invited again.

A visitor who has guest privileges has, in effect, all the rights of a regular member, except that he cannot give a dinner in the private dining room. And obviously a visitor cannot introduce others to the club nor ask guest privileges for them.

If a guest at a club wishes to invite several members to dinner, it is better to take them to a restaurant or a hotel dining room than into their own club dining room.

A guest at a club is expected to tip servants and attendants, unless the rules of the club forbid all tipping (by members as well as guests).

How to Resign from a Club

It is considered rude simply to drop out of a club and not submit a formal resignation.

The member who wishes to resign should write a letter to the secretary of the club, informing him of the fact and asking that the letter be presented at the next meeting of the governors or directors. Although it is not necessary to give a reason for resigning, it is certainly more courteous to do so.

Letters of resignation, like all club correspondence, should be brief, courteous and to the point.

Suggestions for Club Officers

It is important for officers of a club to know the exact requirements of their posts, and to take their responsibilities seriously. No well-bred man or woman will accept an office for the sake of prestige or personal gratification—and then deliberately evade the work that goes with it.

We cannot go into a detailed discussion of the various officers of a club and their specific duties, nor even touch upon the rules for conducting a meeting according to the best parliamentary practices. That information is readily available for those who need and want it, in books dealing exclusively with the subject. Our concern here is solely with the manners, personality, and general attitude of club officers.

All officers, of course, should be thoroughly familiar with the constitution and the bylaws of the club. They should know enough about parliamentary practices and procedure to conduct themselves properly in club meetings and to discharge their duties efficiently and well. In the matter of attendance and promptness, they should set a good example; and in their devotion to duty, as well as their loyalty to club principles and ideals, they should be an inspiration to the others.

The presiding officer of a club should be its presiding genius— prompt, conscientious, diligent, and sincere. He (or she) should be well liked and *good to look at*. This doesn't necessarily mean good looking, but neat, well groomed, smiling, and agreeable.

The presiding officer of a club should plan the meeting beforehand and try to be prepared for whatever important matters may come up. He should be equally fair to all members, permitting no personal angles to obtrude in the conduct of a meeting or in any of the club affairs. He should be tactful and courteous, never lose his temper or show irritability toward anyone. He should preserve order and maintain dignity by adhering strictly to the rules. He should be impelled only by what is best for the organization.

The presiding officer should not take sides in a debate, unless he has something really vital and important to add to the discussion. In that case, he should turn over the chair to a subordinate officer and talk from the floor.

When the presiding officer serves as toastmaster, he should be brief and complimentary. He shouldn't try to explain what the speaker is going to say; his job is simply to *introduce* the speaker and set the stage for him. He always stands while making the introduction, and remains standing until the speaker begins. He then resumes his seat, rising again at the end of the address to thank the speaker in behalf of the club and to introduce the next speaker.

SUGGESTIONS FOR COMMITTEE CHAIRMEN

If you accept the chairmanship of a committee, you should do so with a full understanding of the duties involved and a willingness to put in all the time and work necessary to fulfill those duties and achieve the committee's purpose.

In handling your committee duties, be courteous and tactful. Don't let yourself be influenced by personal likes or dislikes—be very careful not to show preferences or prejudices. A committee must work together harmoniously to achieve its aims. It's the chairman's job to see that all members work together smoothly and efficiently, as a unit, without bickering.

There are likely to be some disturbing incidents; there always are in committee meetings. Take them in your stride. Don't lose your temper, become irritable or impatient. If you were named chairman, it was because you were considered to have somewhat more tact and executive ability than the others. The time to show these qualities is when the meeting becomes difficult and trying.

Don't give a long speech when you are reporting on the work of the committee and what has been accomplished. Just give the facts, and keep the minor details within the committee itself. And be sure to give credit to the other members—don't take all the glory for yourself.

A woman who presides over a club or committee should dress neatly, smartly. She should avoid frills, clanking jewelry, odd-looking hats, veils, exotic make-up. She should dress like a successful business-woman, not like the belle of a party. And she should strive to be gracious and poised, to be soft-spoken and calm, to express herself at all times, under all circumstances, courteously and *to the point*.

PART XII

Business Etiquette

1. HOW TO BE WELL LIKED IN BUSINESS

NO ONE can deny that good manners, in man or woman, represent a very valuable business asset. It's just as important to be well liked in business as in social life, perhaps even more so. The man who is tactless and rude may get ahead in his job, may even become an outstanding success in his particular field. But he will find the going harder than the man who has less ability but more personal charm—the man whose good manners and agreeable personality win him friends all along the way.

If you were a manufacturer of soap, perfume, or breakfast cereal, you would naturally package your product *attractively*. Why should you do any less for yourself? Why should you let offensive manners or careless speech make you unattractive to the people with whom you spend so much of your time in close business relationship?

It's not so much for the sake of others as for *your own sake* that you should be courteous and well-bred in business. Don't make the mistake of thinking that tact, consideration, a gracious and kindly manner are only for the purpose of pleasing others. They react unmistakably to your advantage as well. Good manners smooth the way for you, make your daily contacts more pleasant, influence people and win their good will.

Many men can trace their quick success to an ability to mix easily and well with others, to win their confidence and friendly co-operation. This calls for unfailing courtesy and tact in all business dealings, large and small, for consideration of people's feelings and a strong sense of fair play, and, most of all, an understanding tolerance and patience for others' shortcomings.

GETTING ALONG WITH YOUR BUSINESS ASSOCIATES

The importance of thoughtful courtesy in business relationships cannot be overemphasized. There are so many little things that can come up in the course of a day to irritate, annoy, or harass busy people who are trying to concentrate. Loud talking or laughing, unnecessary interruptions, taking time to tell smutty stories or spread silly gossip, using the telephone for long and distracting personal calls—these are only a few of the "little" things that sometimes loom large in the petty irritations of the day.

Much of the friction and unpleasantness of business contact could be avoided by the exercise of just a little of the courtesy and consideration usually reserved for social life. It's a sad fact that some of the most charming individuals socially, people who seem to possess all the necessary graces when they are with their personal friends, are complete boors in business.

Within the organization, a courteous and helpful attitude on the part of men and women toward those beneath them is of immense importance. The chronic grouch and faultfinder never gets the wholehearted co-operation that a likeable "boss" does.

In outside contacts, courtesy has a real dollars-and-cents value, as every intelligent person well knows. A curt letter, an abrupt or tactless answer on the telephone, can destroy good will that may have taken years to establish.

To get along well with business associates, it's important to rise above the petty annoyances of the day's routine and avoid unpleasant outbursts of temper or impatience. Even in the most trying situations, try to hold yourself well in hand, to remain good-natured and calm. If you win a point, win it without losing the esteem of your associates. If you insist on getting your way in a certain situation, get it without arousing antagonism or resentment and without destroying good will. Bear in mind that courtesy and restraint are evidence of emotional stability; and that to control others, you must be able to control yourself.

Keep yourself aloof from office gossip and intrigue as much as possible. Be friendly to everyone, but don't make intimates of those with whom you associate solely on a business basis. Don't let your emotions obtrude in your business life. Never let yourself be envious, suspicious, resentful, or jealous of anyone.

Ambition is a fine thing to have, but not if one is scheming and aggressive to an obnoxious degree, determined upon self-advancement no matter by what means or at whose cost. With ambition there should be modesty and a spirit of friendly co-operation with others. Don't ever try to "lord it" over anyone or appear superior. Don't take credit for a good job someone else has done, or put the blame for your mistakes on others. Never let anyone say you are unfair, unjust, or unprincipled, for these are not the traits of a well-bred personality, in business or outside of it.

Don't correct or criticize your business associates in the presence of others. Point out their errors to them in private, and without being patronizing or superior about it. It's never good tactics to make anyone feel shamed or humiliated before his fellow workers.

You'll get along much better with people, in any situation, if you consider their feelings. Instead of saying, "*That's wrong!*" or "*This is no good!*" learn to say, "*Don't you think it would be better this way?*" or "*Let me show you how I would do it.*"

It won't improve your business relationships to tread on people's toes, to interfere in their jobs or try to assume their responsibilities. Be especially cautious about going over your immediate superior's head. Don't take liberties, curry favor, ignore company policies. The tactlessly aggressive individual is never popular, in any organization.

An almost infallible way to get along with people is to make them think well of themselves, to make them feel important. Nothing can win their good will more quickly and completely. But don't try to do it with flattery, as intelligent people always see through insincerity and resent it. You can, however, encourage your business associates to talk about themselves; you can show an interest in their personal accomplishments; you can ask their opinions and advice; you can welcome their criticisms, show appreciation for their help or suggestions, admire and praise a job well done.

"Make other people like themselves a little better," wrote Lord Chesterfield to his son, "and I promise you they will like you very well."

The Well-bred Businessman

The well-bred man in business is quiet, soft-spoken, and reserved. He is never loud or boisterous, never rowdy or offensive, never any less a gentleman in his office than he is in a social environment.

He does not talk to a lady with his hat on or with a cigar in his mouth.

He doesn't remain "planted" in his chair when a woman visitor is ushered in to see him. Whether it's a typist to see him about a job or a world-famous celebrity to sign a radio contract, he has the courtesy to get up and greet her properly.

He doesn't receive visitors in shirt sleeves or with his tie off. Nor does he rudely continue with what he's doing after someone has been ushered in to see him, letting the person stand awkwardly by until he's ready to look up.

He doesn't keep visitors waiting in an outer office for long periods of time, unless it's absolutely unavoidable. The busier he is, the more he realizes how important time can be to others . . . and he doesn't waste it needlessly. If he cannot see a caller reasonably soon, he is gracious enough to let him know—and to leave it up to him whether he wants to wait or return at some more convenient time.

It goes without saying that the well-bred man in business does not make unwelcome advances to girl employees. He does not drink during office hours, nor immoderately at any time. He does not habitually cadge cigarettes, borrow from fellow employees, sponge on people, accept "gifts" that are clearly bribes. In other words, he does not do any of the things that would stamp him as crude and undesirable in social life.

The well-bred man in business is honorable and discreet. He doesn't discuss confidential business matters with outsiders.

He is appreciative. He doesn't take everything for granted. He's as polite to the office boy as to the president, never feels that a friendly "Thank you" is out of place or unnecessary.

He is straightforward and loyal. He doesn't continually grouse to friends and associates about his job, his superiors, his salary. If he has a legitimate complaint to make, he carries it to the proper authorities. If he is dissatisfied or unhappy in his job, he either does what he can to adjust the situation, or makes a change. But as long as he continues to hold his job and accept his salary, he does not criticize or condemn his employers.

The well-bred man in business is always carefully groomed, always immaculate, for he knows how important appearance is. He avoids loud or conspicuous clothing, dresses in conservative good taste. His suits always look well brushed and pressed, his linens spotless, his shoes shined. He himself is always beyond reproach—never in need of a shave, a haircut, or any other personal attention.

The Well-bred and Successful Businesswoman

Modern women have gone into practically every business and profession, and have made their mark in all of them. Recent surveys show that a large percentage of the key jobs in all fields today are held by women; and there is a growing tendency to entrust to them important executive posts to which they would not even have aspired twenty or twenty-five years ago.

These are serious-minded women who don't spend half an hour in the rest room every morning fussing with their hair and talking about last night's date. These are worldly, well-bred women who don't gossip, waste time, evade responsibility, and concentrate on making romantic conquests. Whatever talents or abilities they may possess, you can be sure they have this one trait in common: *They all know how to get along with people.* They are tactful and gracious, poised and controlled, as mature and intelligent in handling themselves as they are in handling others.

This doesn't mean that to be successful in business a woman must be grim about it, must take herself so seriously that she loses all sense of perspective. She doesn't need to be any less feminine and charming in her office than outside of it. In fact, feminine charm is one of her major personal assets, and she is careful not to lose or destroy it.

But there's a difference in being gracious and charming to all people, in all situations—and deliberately using one's charms for personal gain. The well-bred woman in business does not make a practice of resorting to feminine wiles or coquetry to achieve her aims. She doesn't let the fact that she is a woman influence her business relationships. She doesn't expect or demand special consideration because of her sex, nor take unfair advantage of it in any way.

The well-bred woman in business is wisely circumspect in her conduct. She is careful not to do or say anything that will get her talked about unpleasantly. She is friendly to everyone, but familiar with no one, and too sensible to let herself become emotionally involved where no real or lasting attachment is indicated. She is dignified and reserved, but always pleasant, focusing her attention on the job and not on personalities. It's her own life after dark, but during business hours she is a businesswoman . . . and conducts herself accordingly.

A successful businesswoman learns to keep her business and social activities apart. She doesn't take her private life to the office with her in the morning. She doesn't discuss her personal affairs with business associates, except in a very general way. She doesn't let outside interests interfere with her job or her working attitude—doesn't write personal letters, receive personal visitors, make long personal telephone calls during business hours. She is no temperamental prima donna, expecting people to cater to her whims. She avoids fits of depression and the "blues," as far as she is able to; keeps her moods and feelings under control; tries not to be oversensitive and "touchy," taking every trifling incident as a personal affront and making an issue of it. She is above envy or jealousy of her associates. She never puts on airs or considers herself above her job. She tries to avoid unpleasant clashes of personality, handling even difficult or offensive people with restraint and composure—for she knows that to lose her temper is to lose her own serene advantage.

Above all, she is honorable and discreet. She does not talk about her employer's private or personal affairs. She does not divulge business or professional secrets. She is prompt for appointments, can be counted on to keep her word, is in all things dependable and trustworthy.

Top-ranking businesswomen are always well groomed, smart-looking. They give as much thought to the way they look during business hours as in social life; but they dress *suitably*. They don't wear glamorous clothes or exotic make-up to the office, avoid the overuse of elaborate jewelry and strong perfume. They dress attractively but not conspicuously, in clothes of good quality and good taste. They are more interested in looking fresh, clean, and immaculately groomed than merely appearing in the latest fashions.

At the Front Door of Business

To arrange an interview with someone you have never met before, the best plan is to write a letter, state your business briefly and clearly, and ask for an appointment. Or if it's more convenient to do so, telephone and speak directly to him or his secretary, arranging a time that is mutually agreeable. But don't call on a busy man without letting him know you are coming, and expect to be admitted. You may be, if you are important enough. But it's more courteous to make an appointment, and you'll be more welcome if you do.

The people at the front door of business, those who meet and greet the public—the receptionist, the telephone operator, the executive's private secretary—play an important role. For theirs is the first contact with outsiders, and theirs the responsibility for avoiding unnecessary antagonisms. No caller, whatever his business, should be treated rudely. No one should ever be turned away with some such curt remark as *"Mr. Graves is tied up"* or *"Mr. Graves can't see you."* It's so much more tactful and gracious to explain the situation and say something like, *"I'm sorry but Mr. Graves is in an important meeting right now. Would you like to leave a message?"*

It's never necessary to offend people, to be insolent or brusque. The person at the switchboard or reception desk should be unfailingly courteous to everyone. Sometimes this takes great patience and tact, especially when a visitor is officious or rude, taking it as a personal affront to be kept waiting. But there's nothing to be gained by arguing about it and being rude in return. A courteous response is always the best strategy in handling unreasonable anger or annoyance.

Use of the Telephone in Business

We have already discussed telephone etiquette in an earlier chapter.[1] The same general rules of courtesy apply to the use of the telephone in business. However we should like to add a few suggestions that apply specifically to business telephoning.

In the first place, it isn't necessary to shout into the telephone. This can be very annoying in a busy office where people are trying to concentrate. Always talk slowly, distinctly, and in a quiet tone of voice, not only because it's less disturbing to others around you, but because it's the most efficient way to use the telephone. A loud voice is never as clearly transmitted as a soft one. If you do not mumble or slur your words carelessly, the person at the other end will have no difficulty understanding you, even though you talk in little more than a whisper.

The good telephone voice has life and tone. It has warmth and personality. It sounds friendly, interested, helpful.

A cold, expressionless tone of voice is no asset in business—any more than it is in social life. People who talk in a weary monotone —or who sound impatient, indifferent, or annoyed—do not represent themselves or their firm to advantage on the telephone.

Although "Hello" is still often the most convenient way for members of a family to answer the telephone in a private home, it is not the best way in business. The person who answers the telephone should identify the firm and himself at once. A telephone operator would say, "*Wade and Company*" or "*Murray Hill 4–9100.*" But an individual in the organization would say, "*Wade Brothers, Mr. Jones speaking*" or "*China Department, Miss Hillary speaking.*"

A man calling a woman on business says, "*This is Mr. Evans of the Rogers Company.*" To a man he would be more likely to say, "*This is Evans of the Rogers Company.*"

A young woman calling either a man or woman on business says, "*This is Miss Pearce of Chadwicke and Company.*"

If someone asks for Mr. Smith, don't retort with "*Who's this?*" or "*What's your name?*" That sounds curt and unfriendly. Say, "*May I ask who is calling, please?*" or "*May I tell him who is calling?*"

Don't waste a busy man's time by having your secretary call him and then keep him waiting until you finish with some other business. That is tactless and rude. If you have someone put in a call for you, be sure you are right there ready to pick up the receiver as soon as the connection is made.

[1]See page 362.

Don't keep someone waiting a long time while you look up a letter or a record. If you don't have it conveniently at hand, suggest that you call him back in a few minutes with the information.

Don't slam down the receiver on a telephone when you have completed your conversation. It's like slamming a door—rude, noisy, and unnecessary. Put the receiver down *gently*.

If you expect to be away from your telephone, be sure to leave word where you are going and how long you will be gone; also whether you can be reached. It's annoying to people who call to be vaguely informed that "Mr. Harris isn't here" or "Mr. Harris is out." It's better if your secretary can say, "Mr. Harris is out of the office right now, but he'll be back in about an hour. Would you like to leave a message for him?"

Some Helpful Suggestions when Applying for a Job

The personnel director of an important organization says, "If young people realized how frequently the failure to secure a job was due to appearance, they would certainly be far more careful about how they dressed for an interview."

Beginners who seem promising from all other aspects are often turned down because they look slovenly and untidy, or because their clothes are in bad taste. Employers feel, and rightfully so, that the person who is careless in his physical make-up is likely to be careless in the details of his job.

The way you look and how you conduct yourself are important in any business interview, but especially so when you are applying for a job. Appearance is regarded by every intelligent employer as a key to character and personality; and well-mannered, courteous people are in demand in every business.

Here are some suggestions men may find helpful when applying for a job:

Don't go into an interview carrying a lighted cigarette.

Don't ever appear for an interview with the smell of liquor on your breath.

Don't carry a cane or wear spats when you go for an interview; many employers consider such things an affectation.

Don't chew gum.

Don't go in squinting; wear glasses if you need them.

Don't wear an odd or unusual piece of jewelry. It tends to distract the attention of the interviewer.

Don't apply for a job when you have an unpleasant, sniffling cold.

Don't go to an interview obviously needing a haircut or shave.

Don't appear without a hat; carry it if you prefer not to wear it—but don't go to the interview without one.

Don't use loud scent or greasy pomade on your hair; and avoid "trick" mustaches that attract attention.

Don't wear lodge emblems or political buttons when you go for an interview.

Here are some suggestions women may find helpful when applying for a job:

Don't wear ankle socks or sloppy shoes.

Don't wear ornaments or flowers in your hair.

Don't wear a giddy hat that distracts the interviewer's attention.

Don't wear a veil; the interviewer wants to see your face.

Don't let your hem hang or your slip show. Always examine yourself critically in a full-length mirror before going out to see a prospective employer.

Don't go for an interview in run-down heels or ripped stockings.

Don't appear in an office dressed as for a party and expect to be considered seriously for the job.

Don't wear soiled gloves to an interview.

Don't go in smoking, or with the smell of tobacco on your breath.

Don't carry a dripping umbrella into a private office; leave it outside.

ETIQUETTE OF THE INTERVIEW

Always arrive on time for an interview—preferably well ahead of time than even one minute late. When you are admitted, approach with a smile and a cheerful "Good morning, Mr. Brown." (If the door is closed, be sure to knock before entering.) Don't offer your hand unless the interviewer offers his. If he is talking on the telephone when you enter, you may unobtrusively take a chair or stand by and wait for an invitation to be seated. Don't sit too close to the interviewer; if there are two chairs—one beside the desk and one opposite—take the chair opposite unless you are directed to do otherwise.

It is not considered good form to take off your coat unless you are asked to do so. Keep your hat and personal effects in your hands or on your lap; don't put them on the desk or the floor. Don't attempt any familiarity or anything that might be interpreted as familiarity, such as offering the interviewer a cigarette, leaning your elbows on his desk, handling things on his desk, slouching in the chair, or conspicuously crossing your legs.

It's best for a woman not to smoke during an interview, even if she is offered a cigarette. A man, however, may accept a cigarette if it is offered to him and if the interviewer himself is either smoking or intends to light a cigarette.

You are not likely to encounter rudeness in high places. But you may; and, if you do, it's important to conceal your resentment. If the man behind the desk keeps you waiting deliberately and unnecessarily, or if he looks up as you enter and barks, "Well, what do you want?" just state your business as courteously as you can. Don't let his rudeness affect your attitude, and keep you from showing yourself to best advantage.

The telephone may ring during the interview. It may ring many times in the office of a busy executive. Don't look annoyed. Just continue after each interruption, bridging the gap with an appropriate question or remark. It isn't necessary to leave the room if a personal call comes in while you are there; if the interviewer wants you to step out for a few moments, he will tell you so. But be careful not to give the appearance of listening intently; try to busy yourself with a notebook or magazine while he is talking. And be sure that you never make reference to anything you overhear in a telephone conversation.

While you are talking, the prospective employer is studying and appraising you. So don't fidget. Don't smooth your hair, twirl your handkerchief, finger the buttons on your coat. Don't keep opening and closing your pocketbook, or crossing and uncrossing your legs. Sit back quietly and relaxed. Look at the interviewer squarely; don't let your eyes wander out of the window or to the floor. Control the tone of your voice; *keep it down*. Nervousness may make your voice high-pitched and unpleasant unless you guard against it.

Always be honest and straightforward in an interview. If you are asked your age, state it plainly and without hesitation. If you are asked why you left or lost your previous job, answer truthfully and without rancor. It's tactless to complain about a previous employer or to imply that you were treated unfairly. Even if that happens to be a fact, avoid mention of it, for your chances of getting the job are greatly lessened by criticism of a former employer. Nor will an intelligent girl use the ancient and unconvincing excuse that she left her job because the boss was "fresh." Maybe he was, but it's best not to mention it.

When you feel that everything has been said that needs to be said, take your leave—and take it promptly, without dawdling. You can be certain no busy executive is going to feel kindly disposed toward you if you overstay your welcome and waste his time. Don't try to prolong an interview after it has clearly come to an end; don't continue to plead your cause or try to persuade him to make an immediate decision. Express your appreciation for the courtesy received, leave definite means by which he can communicate with you, either by letter or by telephone, and make your exit. To leave promptly, gracefully, and graciously is to leave a good impression behind—with a better chance of getting the job.

STORE ETIQUETTE (FOR PERSONNEL)

Don't argue with fellow employees in the presence of a customer. Such conduct reflects discreditably on you and on the store.

Don't keep a customer waiting while you finish telling a fellow clerk about last night's date. That's thoughtless and ill-mannered.

Don't assume superior airs with a customer. Never say, "But madam, nobody uses *that* any more!" If "that" is what the customer wants and you do not have it, just say so—politely. No other comments are necessary.

Don't call a customer "honey" or "dearie." Such terms are extremely offensive.

Don't try to high-pressure a customer into buying something she doesn't want. If you do, you can be sure she'll give you a wide berth in the future—and perhaps avoid the store as well for permitting such tactics.

Don't ever say to a customer, "My, you're short!" or "You're rather stout, aren't you?" Such remarks are tactless and uncalled for. The customer knows her own shortcomings and doesn't like to be reminded of them.

Don't discuss irrelevant personal matters with a customer. She didn't come into the store to talk about your daughter's wedding or your Aunt Agatha's recipe for plum pudding. She came in to buy something.

Don't ever snap "I'm busy!" to a customer who asks for directions or information. You are paid by the store to do a job, and part of your job is to be courteous to customers.

Don't interrupt an employee who is taking care of a customer, unless it's unavoidable. Even then, be sure to apologize first to the customer for the interruption.

Don't contradict customers or argue with them. Sometimes they are very unreasonable; sometimes they are impossibly rude and offensive. But arguing only makes things worse. The best way to handle a difficult customer is with dignity and restraint, refusing to lose your temper and waste your own emotional energy.

Store Etiquette (for Customers)

Don't ever be rude or condescending to a salesperson. It doesn't add to your stature as a controlled, well-bred individual.

Don't monopolize a salesgirl's time if you are "just looking" and have no intention of buying.

Don't handle fragile merchandise that is easily damaged. Teach youngsters to keep their hands off things in a store. Watch out where you put your packages or dripping umbrella. Be careful not to get lipstick or perspiration stains on clothes you try on. Often soiled or damaged merchandise cannot be sold and represents a real loss to the store.

Don't seat a small child on a glass showcase and let him dangle his feet against it. Children cannot be taught too early to be careful of other people's property.

Don't try to be waited on before your turn. Well-bred people never take unfair advantage of others.

Don't lose your temper or make a scene, regardless of the circumstances. You can usually get far more satisfaction by explaining things calmly and in a pleasant tone of voice. And a smile almost always softens resentment, puts things on a more agreeable basis all around.

Don't make a fuss about something that is clearly unavoidable. If you must wait for your change or your package, do so gracefully. Losing your temper and being rude to the salesgirl won't help whatever's holding things up behind the scenes—it will only make things unpleasant for you and the salesgirl both. Remind her you are waiting, if you wish, or ask her to see what she can do about hurrying things a bit. But do it courteously.

Don't be irritable or impatient with salespeople, especially during busy holiday seasons. Serving an exacting and often unreasonable public from morning to night is a tiring and nerve-racking job. It's not only bad manners but thoughtless and unkind to add to the burden.

Don't forget to say "please" and "thank you" to the people who serve you in stores. It's ordinary courtesy, expected of the well-bred.

Etiquette at a Doctor's Office

Always telephone for an appointment with a doctor or a dentist.

If you cannot keep an appointment, telephone in ample time to cancel it—not ten minutes before you are due but the day before, or at least the morning of the same day.

Be prompt; arrive a few minutes before you are expected—not an hour early or an hour late.

Don't litter the waiting room with ashes or matches. If there are no ash trays in evidence, you can assume that smoking is not desired.

Don't tear pages out of magazines. Don't take magazines or books away with you from a doctor's waiting room—or any waiting room. That is stealing, plain and simple; it cannot be dignified by any other name. If there is an article or picture in which you are interested, make a note of it and get your own copy.

Don't take dogs to a doctor's office.

Don't let your child put sticky hands on the walls or furniture, or tear up magazines.

Don't make the doctor's office a rendezvous for personal friends, asking them to meet you there.

Don't try to gossip with the office nurse about other patients, or about the doctor.

Don't use the doctor's telephone for incoming or outgoing calls, except in an emergency.

Don't risk being offensive; always take a shower, use a mouthwash, put on immaculately clean undergarments when you go to a doctor's office. This is all part of the broad, general picture of courtesy and consideration for others.

Don't take advantage of a doctor's good nature. He's a busy man, has many calls to make and patients to see, and when you make unreasonable demands upon his time, you are cheating others of attention they should be getting. A talkative patient who keeps a doctor tied up when others are waiting is not only rude but selfish.

Questions Frequently Asked About Business Etiquette

Question: Should a man rise when a woman employee comes to his desk?

Answer: The exigencies of business make this impractical. He rises only for outside visitors—not for women on the staff who "pop" in and out without formality.

Question: Is it wrong to give a gift to one's superior?

Answer: Only if it's given as a bribe to win favor. But there is no objection to a friendly birthday or Christmas gift to someone you like, regardless of his position in the organization. Most people love to receive gifts. If there is any question about a gift being in good taste, making it a group gift from several people is a convenient alternative.

Question: If a woman real-estate agent takes a man client in a taxicab to see a distant site, who pays the fare?

Answer: She does, of course. It would belittle her position in the business world for him to insist on paying. She should have the money ready as they reach their destination, and hand it as unobtrusively as possible to the driver.

Question: When a woman in business is hostess to a man, a customer or client of her firm, how can she pay the lunch or dinner check without causing him embarrassment?

Answer: She can take him to a restaurant where either she or her firm has a charge account, and sign the check. Or she can arrange for the lunch or dinner beforehand, paying for it when the arrangements are made. Or if the check must be paid at the cashier's window, she can ask him to excuse her for a moment just before they leave, go to the window and pay the check, then return to the table and leave with him. Of course, the easiest way out is to take a male associate along from the office and let him take care of the bill.

Question: How can one get rid of an unwelcome visitor without offending him?

Answer: Arrange with someone to call you in ten minutes or so to say you are wanted at once in another office.

Question: Should a man's wife give his secretary a gift at Christmas time?

Answer: Only if she knows her well and particularly wants to remember her.

Question: Should a note of thanks be written for a gift presented by the firm?

Answer: By all means! Even if it's a regular bonus, distributed to all employees, a letter of thanks to the head of the firm is gracious— and very welcome to him.

Question: Should a secretary rise when her employer comes to her desk to give her instructions?

Answer: It's a mark of respect and courtesy to do so, and good practice —though not very common in most offices.

Question: When a secretary enters a man's office in response to his summons to take dictation, and there is no chair near his desk—should he get up and place it for her?

Answer: No. She should place the chair where she wants it. A man is not expected to show his secretary the personal attention he would show her in social life.

Question: Is it appropriate for a man to call his secretary by her first name?

Answer: If he has known her for many years and wishes to call her by her first name, there is no objection to it. However, it's more dignified to call her "Miss Blank" in the presence of clients or other outside visitors.

Question: Should a young woman employee get up when she is introduced to an important new male executive?

Answer: Yes, if she can do so easily and without confusion. But if she is barricaded behind office equipment, she should just nod and say "How do you do" in acknowledgment of the introduction.

Question: Is it bad form for a woman to travel with her employer and stay at the same hotel he does?

Answer: This is a frequent occurrence nowadays when so many women hold important executive positions and are required to travel a great deal with clients, employers, etc. All that's necessary is for both to conduct themselves with the utmost decorum. It's advisable for them to occupy rooms on different floors and to hold meetings and conduct business affairs in public rooms of the hotel instead of in their own private rooms.

Question: Is it necessary for a man to stand when a woman visitor to his office gets up to leave?

Answer: Yes; and he also goes to the door with her—or even to the elevator—if he is courteous.

PART XIII

Highlights of Military and Official Etiquette

1. HIGHLIGHTS OF MILITARY AND OFFICIAL ETIQUETTE

WASHINGTON has an etiquette of its own, and a social life which sets it apart from any other American city. It is an involved and exacting social pattern, in which even trifling rules assume astonishing importance. These rules must be known and understood by newcomers who expect to take part in the life of the capitol or engage in its social activities.

The great difference between Washington society and that of other American cities is its complicated *protocol system*. This is a formula that decides who shall be seated next to whom at official dinners and who shall be announced before whom at official receptions. Washington takes this matter of precedence very seriously. It's practically an exact science; every important official is graded according to an established rule, and there is no deviation from this rule. If there is any question about who outranks whom, the protocol division of the State Department is the final arbiter.

A visitor who expects to participate in the official life of the city and who needs advice or assistance should write to his senator or congressman. If he wishes to see him personally, he should write or telephone his private secretary and arrange for an interview. A woman new to the Washington scene who expects to be presented at the Executive Mansion, attend embassy dinners and other ceremonial functions, should make every effort to acquaint herself with the formalities—engaging a social secretary if necessary. Before giving a dinner or reception to which persons of various ranks have been invited, a Washington hostess who is not sure of her seating arrangement should submit her list to someone who is qualified to pass on the "protocol ratings" of her guests.

EXISTING ORDER OF PRECEDENCE IN WASHINGTON

Following is the general order of precedence in Washington at the present time. No list is issued by the State Department, and therefore this cannot be considered "official." Furthermore, the rating and order of precedence change in certain minor particulars from time to time. However the following is as authoritative as possible.

1. The President of the United States. (Preceded only by the head of a foreign government in this country. Abroad the President takes first position.)
2. The Vice-President, *in the absence of the President.*
3. A special ambassador directly representing the head of a foreign government on a special mission.
4. The Chief Justice.
5. Foreign ambassadors in the order of their length of residence in the country.
6. The Vice-President. (When not representing the President, he ranks as head of the Senate and is placed below the Chief Justice—who as head of the Supreme Court of the United States outranks the Senate.)
7. The Speaker of the House of Representatives.
8. The Secretary of State.
9. Ministers representing foreign governments.
10. Associate Justices of the Supreme Court.
11. The Secretary of the Treasury.
12. The Secretary of Defense.
13. Attorney General.
14. Postmaster General.
15. Secretary of the Interior.
16. Secretary of Agriculture.
17. Secretary of Commerce.
18. Secretary of Labor.
19. Governors of states.
20. Senators (according to length of service).
21. Representatives.
22. Secretary of Army.
23. Secretary of Navy.
24. Secretary of Air Force.
25. Army chief of staff (if 5-star rank).[1]
26. Naval chief of operations (if 5-star rank).[1]
27. General of the army (5-star rank).
28. Fleet admiral (5-star rank).
29. General.
30. Admiral.
31. Lieutenant general.
32. Vice-admiral.
33. Major general.
34. Rear admiral.
35. Charges d'affaires.
36. The solicitor general.

[1]Otherwise following 5-star officers.

37. Brigadier general.
38. Commodore.
39. Undersecretary of State.
40. Undersecretary of Treasury.
41. Assistant secretaries. (According to length of service).
42. Lieutenant governors.
43. Presidents of state senates.
44. Speakers of state assemblies.
45. State justices, mayors, and state senators (ranked according to length of service).
46. Counselors, military and naval attaches.
47. State representatives or assemblymen.
48. Foreign first secretaries.
49. Federal Reserve.
50. Interstate Commerce Commission.
51. Secretary of the Smithsonian Institution.
52. Director of the Pan-American Union.
53. Foreign second and third secretaries.

A wife or widow is given the precedence to which her husband's rank entitles him.

In an American house, the ranking foreigner is given precedence. In a foreign embassy, the ranking American or any other stranger is given precedence.

MILITARY AND NAVAL PRECEDENCE

Army officers take precedence over naval officers of corresponding rank. This is because the army was the earliest force in the service of the nation. Following are the corresponding ranks of the army, navy and air force. Rules and customs for members of the United States Air Force follow, in general, those for the United States Army. The highest ranking officer is a four-star general. Changes in nomenclature of ranks and grades are expected.

ARMY	NAVY	AIR FORCE
General of the army	Admiral of the fleet	
General	Admiral	General
Lieutenant general	Vice admiral	Lieutenant general
Major general	Rear admiral	Major general
Brigadier general	Commodore	Brigadier general
Colonel	Captain	Colonel
Lieutenant colonel	Commander	Lieutenant colonel
Major	Lieutenant commander	Major
Captain	Lieutenant	Captain
Lieutenant	Lieutenant junior grade	Lieutenant
Second lieutenant	Ensign	Second Lieutenant

Enlisted men are graded as follows. (These lists are not arranged to show corresponding ranks).

ARMY	NAVY	AIR FORCE
Chief warrant officer	Chief warrant officer	Chief warrant officer
Warrant officer (3 grades)	Warrant officer	Warrant officer (j.g.)
Master sergeant	Petty officer, chief	Master sergeant
Sergeant first class	Petty officer, first class	First sergeant
Sergeant	Petty officer, second class	Technical sergeant
Corporal	Petty officer, third class	Staff sergeant
Private first class	Seaman	Sergeant
Private	Seaman apprentice	Corporal
Recruit	Seaman recruit	Private, first class
		Private

HIGHLIGHTS OF WASHINGTON ETIQUETTE

Following are some of the traditional rules and customs which official Washington takes very seriously. Only the highlights can be given. Anyone who expects to take an active part in the social life and activities of the capitol, and who is not familiar with the conventions, should make a study of Washington etiquette. It's a special (and somewhat staggering!) subject in itself.

All newcomers to Washington who expect to join in the ceremonious life of the capitol, and particularly all officials and their families and all foreigners of distinction, call first at the Executive Mansion. They do not expect to be admitted; the call is a formality—to pay their respects to the President and his wife. They merely leave their cards and go at once.

When a personal interview with the President is desired, the custom is to write to his private secretary asking that a date be set. This note is written after the formal call has been made and cards left. Anyone who has an appointment at the White House must keep it and must be on time. Calls are generally limited to about ten minutes.

An invitation to lunch or dine at the White House is a command, and automatically cancels any previous engagement. It should be acknowledged the day it is received, by hand—and the acceptance should be left at the door, not sent by mail.

Acknowledging an Invitation to Dine at the White House

Mr. and Mrs. Thomas P. Daly
have the honor to accept
the kind invitation of
The President and Mrs. Blankname
for dinner on Thursday, the sixth of May
at eight o'clock

Note of Regret to a Deserted Hostess

Mr. and Mrs. Thomas P. Daly
regret extremely
that an invitation to the White House
prevents their keeping
their previous engagement for
Thursday the sixth of May

At White House dinners, the President enters first with the wife of the most distinguished guest. The President's wife does not enter last as do other hostesses, but follows immediately after the President with the most distinguished guest. Others follow according to rank.

At any ceremonial function at the White House, guests remain standing until the President and his wife are seated—and rise when the President and his wife rise. The President is addressed as "Mr. President" or "sir"; his wife is addressed as "Mrs. Blankname."

Guests invited to the White House must arrive at least ten minutes before the hour specified. They are expected to be standing in the drawing room when the President makes his entry. The President makes a tour of the room, shaking hands with each person in turn; and it is not considered proper for guests to make any comments or try to engage him in conversation at this time. They merely bow as they shake hands, and remain silent unless he addresses them—in which case they answer briefly and to the point.

People who have been entertained at lunch or dinner at the White House must make a courtesy call within three days, leaving cards but not asking or expecting to be admitted. Neither the President nor the President's wife make formal calls or return visits.

There are many formal duty calls to be made by a newcomer to the official life of Washington. The wife of a new official, after making her first call at the White House, calls on the wives of all who rank above her husband. Most of these visits are made on fixed "reception days," and it's essential to know what these days are and to conform to them. For example, Monday is the official reception day of the wives of the Justices of the Supreme Court and of the commanding officers of the Navy Yard and the Marine Barracks. Tuesday is the day to visit the wives of the representatives. On Wednesday the wife of the Vice-President receives—also the wives of the cabinet officers and the Speaker of the House. Thursday is senators' day; and Friday is the day when the wives of the diplomats officially receive. The hours for formal duty calls are from four to six.

MILITARY ETIQUETTE

A rigid etiquette regulates military social life, and any hostess who entertains officially should be careful to observe these regulations. One of the firm rules is that commissioned officers and enlisted men should not be invited to the same function. However this does not apply to informal, unofficial entertaining when a hostess may invite any one she pleases.

Even so, it is not the best judgment to invite high-ranking commissioned officers to dine at the same table with enlisted men. Mixing up officers and privates socially may prove awkward to them, if not to the hostess.

In conversation, brigadier generals, lieutenant generals, and full generals are all addressed as "general." Army officers are addressed socially by their military title: "Colonel Rogers," "Major Brown," etc. First and second lieutenants are addressed as "lieutenant." Doctors may be addressed either by their military or naval title, or as "doctor." A chaplain is called "chaplain" regardless of rank.

Warrant officers are all introduced as and called "mister"; noncommissioned officers are introduced and addressed by title (as "Corporal Green," "Sergeant Fiske"). Privates are introduced as such, and may be addressed as "Private Jones" or "Mr. Jones."

Naval officers are addressed socially by their naval titles. However any officer in command of a ship, when he is aboard his ship, is called "captain" by his own men and by visitors from ashore. Rear admirals, vice-admirals, and full admirals are all addressed socially as "admiral." Senior and junior grade lieutenants are both addressed as "lieutenant." Petty officers and enlisted men in the navy are introduced as and called "mister."[2]

[2]For written forms of address, see Appendix, page 521.

In making introductions, the person of lower rank should be presented to the person of higher or senior rank. When two officers of equal rank are introduced, the younger man is presented to the older. A hostess who is not sure how to introduce an army or navy officer may smile and ask, "How shall I introduce you?" That's always more courteous than introducing him improperly.

Whenever men in uniform are present and music is available, it's customary to play the national anthem. Everyone rises, and the men in uniform stand at attention.

If a toast is made to the President, to an important foreign dignitary, to an officer, etc., everyone present must drink to it. But men in uniform do not drink a toast to their own branch of the service; that is like drinking to themselves.

A good hostess does not encourage excessive drinking among men in uniform while they are guests in her home.

Formal receptions are often given in honor of distinguished army and navy men, or visiting dignitaries from other countries. There is a receiving line with the senior officer's wife first in line, the visiting dignitary or guest of honor second, and the other officers following in the order of their rank. If the officers' wives are in the receiving line, they stand beside their husbands.

An aide or officer is appointed to stand some distance ahead of the line, near the door, to announce people as they arrive. Guests go immediately down the line, receiving introductions and exchanging greetings with those they know. Then they join any one of the groups they wish in the reception room. Individual introductions are not necessary; guests at a reception mingle freely and talk with whomever they like, whether strangers or not.

At large receptions it is not necessary to seek out the guest of honor or other important persons to say good-by. The usual procedure is to stay an hour or two and leave—unless, as is frequently the case, a dance follows the reception.

An officer at a formal dance is expected to ask the following for at least one dance: the hostess, the woman guest of honor, his dinner partner (if dinner preceded the dancing), and the wife of his commanding officer. These women should receive his attention before any civilian guests.

Hospitality extended to an army or navy man and his wife need not be returned. However a gracious note of thanks is due the hostess and certainly should not be overlooked.

MILITARY WEDDINGS

There is nothing quite so romantic as a full military wedding with flashing sabers and glistening braid. Before planning such a wedding, a girl must be reasonably sure of two things: first, that the groom will be able to get leave and be present at his own wedding, and second, that he is not likely to be sent abroad at a moment's notice. It is wise to make arrangements for the leave several weeks in advance, if possible. An enlisted man does not make plans to marry without the knowledge and consent of his superior officer.

When the groom is an officer, the invitations and announcements give his title. The generally accepted rule at present is that for the rank of captain or above in the army—lieutenant senior grade or above in the navy—the title is used before the name. For example:

Captain Richard Farnham
United States Army

For officers under these ranks, the title goes on a line directly below the name. For example:

Harold Brighton
Lieutenant, junior grade, United States Navy

If the groom is in the regular Army or Navy, the wording "United States Army [or Navy]" appears in the line below his name. But if he has been called into the army or given a temporary commission, the positioning is the same but the wording is "Army of the United States"—or for the Navy, "United States Naval Reserve." In the case of a private or noncommissioned officer, the name is on one line and the branch of service is designated below it. For example:

Frank Jenson
Signal Corps, United States Naval Reserve

OR

James Hamilton
Coast Artillery, Army of the United States

The title of "Mr." is not used in military invitations or announcements.

ARMY OFFICER'S WEDDING INVITATION

Colonel and Mrs. Winthrop Hale
request the honor of your presence
at the marriage of their daughter
Marilyn
to
Captain Thomas Brent
United States Army
on Tuesday, the tenth of May
at four o'clock
Christ Church
Santa Barbara, California

NAVAL OFFICER'S WEDDING INVITATION

Mr. and Mrs. Ward Sewall
request the honor of your presence
at the marriage of their daughter
Janet Kay
to
Theodore Creighton
Ensign, United States Navy
on Thursday, the seventh of June
at twelve o'clock
Saint Paul's Church

The problem of whom to invite to a military or naval wedding is sometimes a difficult one to the bride and groom. They invite their relatives and friends, as usual; but in addition they invite, as a rule, the groom's superior officer and as many of his fellow officers or friends in the ranks as they feel they would like to have. They come in uniform of course, which adds to the color and pageantry of the wedding.

In a military wedding, it's desirable for all men in the bridal procession to be in uniform. An officer generally selects a fellow officer as his best man; but whether he is of higher or lower rank is of no special significance.

At the wedding of either an enlisted man or officer, the regimental colors of the groom are usually displayed. But otherwise the details of the wedding do not differ substantially from those of any other wedding. The bridal party enters the church the same as for a civilian ceremony, the ushers (if they are in uniform) depositing their caps and coats in the vestry and putting on their gloves before taking their places in the procession.

The groom, and all army or navy men in the bridal party, must be in regulation uniforms. The groom does not wear a flower in his lapel, as that is not considered good military form. He does not wear or carry his hat; he leaves it in the vestry and the best man gets it and hands it to him after the ceremony when the bridal couple leave the church.

The most dramatic and picturesque part of a military wedding is the recessional. An "arch of sabers" is formed by the ushers—either immediately after the ceremony is over, as the bride and groom turn from the altar, or on the steps of the church as the bride and groom walk through the door. The procedure is for one of the ushers to give the command ("Draw—sabers!" for the Army; "Draw—swords!" for the Navy), and the ushers instantly form the arch. Only the bride and groom walk beneath the arch; it is not proper for other members of the wedding party to do so. The flower girls, maid of honor, and bridesmaids wait until the bride and groom have passed under the arch and the order to "return—sabers!" has been given.

At the wedding dinner or supper following the ceremony, army and navy officers and their families should be seated according to their rank. The groom's commanding officer and his wife are usually seated as guests of honor at the bridal table.

It's the custom at a military wedding for the bride to cut the first slice of her wedding cake with her husband's saber—his hand over hers. It is also customary to drink a toast to the bride, the signal being given by the best man. When the toast is proposed, the ushers again draw sabers (at the command of "draw!" and cross them over the bride's head (at the command of "sabers!") Everyone then lifts his glass and drinks to the health and happiness of the bride.

If an army or navy chaplain performs the wedding ceremony, no fee should be offered, as he will not accept it.

ETIQUETTE OF THE FLAG

Americans who love and honor their country's flag display it, not only with pride, but with full knowledge of the etiquette and customs surrounding it.

For example, the flag should not be hoisted before sunrise or allowed to remain up after sunset. At sunset, when the flag is lowered, civilian spectators should stand at attention and uncover their heads. Military or naval spectators are required by regulation to stand at attention and give the military salute.

When lowering the flag, care should be taken not to let it touch the ground. The flag is supposed to be hoisted quickly, lowered slowly. When it is to be flown at half staff as a sign of mourning, it should be hoisted to the top of the staff and then lowered to position.

When the flags of several nations are displayed with the American flag, our flag should be both hoisted and lowered first and should be in the center of the group. If only two flags are displayed, our flag should occupy the position at the right.

When carried in a parade or procession with other flags, our flag should have the place of honor—on the marching right. It should be the same size, and carried at the same height, as all other flags.

The flag should not be used to drape an altar, hang from a balcony, or as a covering for a monument, tablet, or statue. It should be used as a distinctive feature of the ceremony, but not as a drapery.

The flag should never be draped over the hood or top of a car; should never be displayed on a float unless it is flying from a staff; should never be used for advertising purposes in any manner whatsoever. It should never be permitted to trail on the ground. When used on a speaker's platform, the flag, if displayed flat, should be displayed above and behind the speaker.

When the flag is used to cover a casket, it should be so placed that the union is at the head and over the left shoulder. The flag should not be lowered into the grave or allowed to touch the ground.

Following are the days when the flag is usually displayed:

Lincoln's Birthday	Feb. 12
Washington's Birthday	Feb. 22
Mother's Day	Second Sunday in May
Memorial Day	May 30
Flag Day	June 14
Battle of Bunker Hill	June 17
Independence Day	July 4
Defense Day	Sept. 12
Constitution Day	Sept. 17
Columbus Day	Oct. 12
Armistice Day	Nov. 11

When the color guard passes, men in uniform rise and stand at attention. Civilians are supposed to uncover and stand with the right hand over the heart. Following is the pledge of allegiance to the flag:

"I pledge allegiance to the flag of the United States of America and to the Republic for which it stands; one nation, indivisible, with liberty and justice for all."

Appendix

FORMS OF ADDRESS

M ANY alternate forms of address and salutation are permissible, especially in informal correspondence. But all these many variations of local usage cannot be included in the limited space available in this book. The chart following gives the forms in customary usage, and is as complete as possible for a book of this scope.

Forms of salutation beginning with *"My dear"* are not included in the chart. In all cases, *"My dear"* may be used instead of "Dear" for greater formality. (This applies to the United States only, as in Great Britain the reverse is true.)

The words *"honor"* and *"honorable"* are spelled according to the residence of the person addressed. In the United States, *"honor"* and *"honorable"* are preferred; in Great Britain *"honour"* and *"honourable"* are the preferred forms.

Social invitations to a married man of title or rank are addressed to the man *and* his wife. For example:

> Senator and Mrs. James Blank
> The President and Mrs. Blank
> Lord and Lady Blank
> Their Excellencies, the French Ambassador
> and Mrs. Blank

When the wife is the person of title or rank, the husband's name is still written first on the envelope and inside address. For example:

> Mr. John and the Honorable Mary Smith
> Mr. Frank and Dr. Margaret Symonds
> Mr. George and Lady Mary Blakely

The use of the word *"to"*—as in *"To his Grace, the Duke of York"* —is optional. There is no hard and fast rule about it; you may use it or not, as you prefer. Our own choice is for the simpler form: *"His Grace, the Duke of York."*

In addressing an envelope, the phrase *"His Excellency"* may be abbreviated to "*H.E.*," and "*Their Excellencies*" may be abbreviated to "*T.E.*" But in general, abbreviations should be avoided—especially in the salutation of a letter.

Old feudal phrases of courtesy like "*My Lord*" and "*Your Lordship*" are not used in the United States. But they should be used by an American writing to dignitaries of foreign countries entitled by tradition to such forms of address.

Rank or Title	Address the Envelope	Begin the Letter
Abbot	The Lord Abbot of Fieldston or The Right Reverend Abbot Blank	Dear Father Abbot: My Lord Abbot:
Air Force Officers	Like army and naval officers	
Alderman	Alderman John Smith	Dear Sir: Dear Mr. Smith:
Ambassador (American)	His Excellency the American Ambassador to Great Britain American Embassy London, England or The Honorable[1] John D. Smith American Ambassador to Great Britain American Embassy London, England	Sir: Your Excellency: Dear Mr. Ambassador:
Ambassador (British)[2]	His Excellency the Ambassador of Great Britain British Embassy Washington, D.C. or His Excellency Sir John Farbish Ambassador of Great Britain British Embassy Washington, D.C.	Sir: Excellency: Your Excellency:
Archbishop (Anglican)	His Grace the Lord Archbishop of London	My Lord Archbishop: Your Grace:

[1]"*Honorable*" or "*The Honorable*" may be used; both are correct.
[2]Same general form is used in addressing ambassadors of other foreign countries.

Rank or Title	Address the Envelope	Begin the Letter
Archbishop (Catholic)	The Most Reverend John Smith Archbishop of St. Louis *or* The Most Reverend Archbishop Smith (Followed by postal address)	Most Reverend Sir: Most Reverend Archbishop: (In England:) Your Grace: My Lord: My Lord Archbishop:
Archdeacon:	The Venerable John Falten Archdeacon of New Orleans	Venerable Sir:
Army Officers:	Always address letters to army officers in accordance with their exact rank. (In the salutation, however, you drop the qualifying adjective—such as the "lieutenant" in "lieutenant colonel." In other words, letters to both "Lieutenant Colonel Phillips" and "Colonel Pryor" would begin "Dear Colonel ———.") A retired army officer is addressed by his title, with "U.S.A., Ret." following his name. A doctor, dentist, or clergyman may be addressed either by his professional degree or his army rank, unless he is in an administrative capacity—in which case the army rank is always used. Lieutenant General John Fiske Commanding Officer Army of the United States 3rd Corps Area (Followed by postal address) Major General John Crane, U.S.A. Commanding Officer, 2nd Tank Corps	Sir: (formal) Dear General Fiske: Dear Colonel Pryor: Dear Sgt. Blank: Dear Corporal Smith:

Rank or Title	Address the Envelope	Begin the Letter
Army Officers:	Colonel Arthur Pryor Medical Corps, U.S.A. Major Thomas Quinn, U.S.A., Ret. (Postal address only) Captain James T. Ballard Field Artillery, U.S.A. Lieutenant Peter Adams Coast Artillery, U.S.A. or Peter Adams Lieutenant, Coast Artillery, U.S.A. Corporal Henry T. Smith 5th Quartermaster Corps, U.S.A. or Henry T. Smith Corporal, 5th Quartermaster Corps, U.S.A.	
Assemblyman	The Honorable John B. Rogers Member of Assembly Albany, New York or Assemblyman John B. Rogers The State Capitol Albany, New York	Sir: Dear Sir: Dear Mr. Rogers:
Assistant Secretary (Assistant to a cabinet officer)	The Assistant Secretary of Commerce Washington, D.C. or Honorable John B. Hansen Assistant Secretary of Commerce Washington, D.C.	Sir: Dear Sir: Dear Mr. Hansen:
Associate Judge of a Court of Appeals	The Honorable John Clearly Associate Judge of the Court of Appeals Albany, New York	Sir: Dear Sir: Your Honor: Dear Mr. Justice:
Associate Justice of a State Supreme Court	The Honorable Frank Parsons Associate Justice of the Supreme Court Albany, New York	Sir: Dear Sir: Your Honor: Dear Mr. Justice:

Rank or Title	Address the Envelope	Begin the Letter
Associate Justice of the Supreme Court of the United States	The Honorable Edward Brent Associate Justice of the Supreme Court Washington, D.C. or The Honorable Edward Brent Justice, Supreme Court of the United States Washington, D.C. or Mr. Justice Brent Supreme Court of the United States Washington, D.C.	Dear Sir: Dear Mr. Justice: Dear Justice Brent:
Attorney General	The Honorable The Attorney General of the United States Washington, D.C. or The Honorable John Lane Attorney General of the United States Washington, D.C.	Sir: Dear Sir: Dear Mr. Attorney General:
Baron	The Right Honourable Lord Blakely or The Lord Blakely	My Lord:
Baroness	The Right Honourable the Baroness Cleve or The Lady Cleve	Madam:
Baronet	Sir John Holt, Bt. (or Bart.)	Sir:
Bishop (Anglican)	The Right Reverend the Lord Bishop of Sussex or The Lord Bishop of Sussex	My Lord Bishop: My Lord:
Bishop (Catholic)	The Most Reverend Thomas Hall Bishop of Chicago or The Right Reverend Bishop Hall	Your Excellency: Dear Bishop Hall:
Bishop (Methodist)	The Reverend Bishop John Smith	Dear Bishop Smith:

Rank or Title	Address the Envelope	Begin the Letter
Bishop (Protestant)	The Right Reverend Michael Vale Bishop of Cleveland	Right Reverend and Dear Sir: Dear Bishop Vale:
Cardinal	His Eminence John, Cardinal Blank	Your Eminence:
Chief Judge of a Court of Appeals	The Chief Judge of the Court of Appeals Albany, New York or The Honorable Myron F. Brown Chief Judge of the Court of Appeals Albany, New York	Sir: Dear Sir: Dear Judge Brown:
Chief Justice of a State Supreme Court	The Chief Justice Supreme Court of the State of New York Albany, New York or Honorable Patrick Gilmore Chief Justice of the Supreme Court Albany, New York	Sir: Dear Sir: Dear Mr. Chief Justice: Dear Mr. Justice Gilmore:
Chief Justice of the United States	The Chief Justice of the United States Washington, D.C. or The Honorable John Blank Chief Justice of the Supreme Court of the United States Washington, D.C. or The Chief Justice Washington, D.C.	Sir: Dear Sir: Dear Mr. Chief Justice: Dear Mr. Justice Blank:
Clergyman	The Reverend Frank Hall or Reverend and Mrs. Frank Hall or (if a doctor of divinity) Reverend Dr. Frank Hall	Dear Sir: Reverend Sir: Dear Mr. Hall: Dear Dr. Hall:
Commissioner of a Government Bureau	The Commissioner of the Bureau of Education Department of the Interior Washington, D.C.	Sir: Dear Sir: Dear Mr. Commissioner:

Rank or Title	Address the Envelope	Begin the Letter
	or The Honorable Dwight Kelley Commissioner of the Bureau of Education Department of the Interior Washington, D.C.	Dear Mr. Kelley:
Congressman	See Representative in Congress	
Consul	The American Consul at London London, England or Mr. John Smith American Consul at London London, England	Sir: Dear Sir: Dear Mr. Smith:
Countess	The Right Honourable the Countess of Blank or The Countess Greystone	Madam: Dear Lady Greystone:
Deacon	The Reverend Deacon Black	Reverend Sir:
Dean (Ecclesiastic)	The Very Reverend the Dean of Barth	Very Reverend Sir: Sir:
Dean of a College or University	Dean Albert S. Frank School of Business Columbia University New York, N.Y. or Albert S. Frank, Ph.D. Dean of the School of Business Columbia University New York, N.Y. or Dr. Albert S. Frank Dean of the School of Business Columbia University New York, N.Y.	Dear Sir: Dear Dean Frank: Dear Dr. Frank: Dear Mr. Frank: (if he does not hold a doctor's degree.)
Delegate (Member of the House of Delegates of a State Legislature)	The Honorable John F. Weylin The House of Delegates Charleston, West Virginia	Sir: Dear Sir: Dear Mr. Weylin:

Rank or Title	Address the Envelope	Begin the Letter
Duchess	Her Grace, the Duchess of Kent	Madam: Your Grace:
Duchess of the Royal Blood	Her Royal Highness the Duchess of Kent	Madam: May it please your Royal Highness:
Duke	His Grace, the Duke of Blank	My Lord Duke: Your Grace:
Duke of the Royal Blood	His Royal Highness the Duke of Kent	Sir: May it please your Royal Highness:
Earl	The Right Honourable the Earl of Blank or The Earl of Blank	My Lord: Sir: Dear Lord Grayson:
Earl's wife	See "Countess" above	
Governor of a State	The Honorable the Governor of Michigan Lansing, Michigan or His Excellency The Governor of Michigan Lansing, Michigan or His Excellency, John E. Tarr Governor of Michigan Lansing, Michigan or The Honorable John E. Tarr Governor of Michigan Lansing, Michigan	Sir: Dear Sir: Your Excellency: Dear Governor Tarr:
Head of a State Department	The Secretary of State[3] The State Capitol Topeka, Kansas or The Secretary of State State of Kansas Topeka, Kansas or The Honorable John C. Blank Secretary of State The State Capitol Topeka, Kansas	Sir: Dear Sir: Dear Mr. Blank:

[3]Some states (like Pennsylvania and Massachusetts) use the term "Commonwealth" instead of "State." The first line in that case would read: "The Secretary of the Commonwealth."

Rank or Title	Address the Envelope	Begin the Letter
Instructor in a College or University	John T. Rice, Ph.D. Department of Economics[4] Harvard University Cambridge, Massachusetts or Dr. John T. Rice Department of Economics Harvard University Cambridge, Massachusetts or (if the instructor does not hold a doctor's degree) Mr. John T. Rice Department of Economics Harvard University Cambridge, Massachusetts	Dear Sir: Dear Dr. Rice: Dear Mr. Rice: (if he does not hold a doctor's degree)
Judge of a Federal District Court	The Honorable Frank Preston United States District Judge Eastern District of New York Brooklyn, New York	Sir: Dear Sir: Dear Judge Preston:
Justice of the Supreme Court	See Associate Justice of the Supreme Court of the United States	
King	The King's Most Excellent Majesty or His Most Gracious Majesty, King George	Sir: May it please your Majesty:
Lady:	The title "Lady" is held by all peeresses under the rank of Duchess. It is also held by all daughters of dukes, marquises, and earls, and by the wives of baronets, knights, and lords of session. The envelope is addressed: Lady Florence Heath or Lady Heath or The Honourable Lady Florence	Madam: My Lady: Your Ladyship:

[4] If "Instructor" is substituted for "Department," "in" is used instead of "of." For example: "Instructor in Economics" (but "Department of Economics.")

Rank or Title	Address the Envelope	Begin the Letter
Legislator	The Honorable Arthur James The State Legislature Albany, New York or The Honorable Arthur James Member of Legislature The State Capitol Albany, New York	Sir: Dear Sir: Dear Mr. James:
Lieutenant Governor of a State	The Lieutenant Governor State of Wisconsin Madison, Wisconsin or The Honorable Edward Doyle Lieutenant Governor of Wisconsin Madison, Wisconsin	Sir: Dear Sir: Dear Mr. Doyle:
Lord of Session	Honourable Lord Overton	My Lord:
Marchioness	The Most Honourable the Marchioness of Blankton	Madam:
Marine Officers	Like Army and Naval Officers. The appropriate designation —U.S.M.C. (United States Marine Corps)—should follow the branch of the service in which the person addressed is engaged. For example: Colonel Roy Tait Medical Corps, U.S.M.C.	
Marquis	The Most Honourable the Marquis of Blank or The Marquis of Blank	My Lord Blank:
Mayor of a city	The Mayor of the City of Chicago City Hall Chicago, Illinois or The Honorable John F. Blank Mayor of the City of Chicago City Hall Chicago, Illinois	Sir: Dear Sir: Dear Mayor Blank: Dear Mr. Mayor:

Rank or Title	Address the Envelope	Begin the Letter
Minister (diplomatic) American	His Excellency The American Minister Stockholm, Sweden or His Excellency Carl Hawks American Minister Stockholm, Sweden or The Honorable Carl Hawks American Minister Stockholm, Sweden	Sir: Your Excellency: Dear Mr. Minister: Dear Sir:
Minister (diplomatic) foreign	His Excellency The Swedish Minister The Swedish Legation Washington, D.C. or The Honorable James Fount Minister of Sweden The Swedish Legation Washington, D.C.	Sir: Your Excellency: Dear Mr. Minister: Dear Sir:
Minister of religion	See clergyman, priest, rabbi	
Monsignor	The Right Reverend Monsignor Blank	Right Reverend Sir: Dear Monsignor:
Mother Superior of a Sisterhood	Reverend Mother Superior or Reverend Mother Mary (followed by initials designating the order) or Reverend Mother Superior Mary (without the initials designating the order) or Mother Mary, Superior Convent of the Blessed Virgin	Reverend Mother: Dear Reverend Mother:
Naval officers:	Always address letters to naval officers in accordance with their exact rank. (In the salutation, however, you drop the qualifying adjective—such as the "Rear" in "Rear Admiral." In	Sir: (formal) Dear Admiral Bailey: Dear Captain Blank: Dear Cadet Holt:

Rank or Title	Address the Envelope	Begin the Letter
Naval officers:	other words, letters to both "Admiral Bailey" and "Rear Admiral Shannon" would begin "Dear Admiral ———.") A doctor, dentist, or clergyman may be addressed either by his professional degree or his naval rank, unless he is in an administrative capacity —in which case the rank is always used.	
	Admiral James K. Bailey Chief of Naval Operations Navy Department Washington, D.C.	
	Rear Admiral Thomas Shannon New London Submarine Base New London, Connecticut	
	Captain John Blank, U.S.N. U.S.S. Missouri Pensacola, Florida	
	Lieutenant Commander John Wagner Medical Corps, U.S.N. Philadelphia Navy Yard Philadelphia, Pennsylvania	
Nun	See Sister of a Religious Order	
Pope	His Holiness the Pope His Holiness, Pope Pius XII	Your Holiness: Most Holy Father:
Postmaster General:	The Honorable the Postmaster General Washington, D.C. or The Honorable William Kane The Postmaster General Washington, D.C.	Sir: Dear Sir: Dear Mr. Postmaster General: Dear Mr. Kane:
President of a College or University	John Smith, LL.D. (or Lit.D., D.Sc., etc.) President of Dartmouth College Hanover, New Hampshire or	Dear Sir: Dear President Smith:

Rank or Title	Address the Envelope	Begin the Letter
	Dr. John Smith President of Dartmouth College Hanover, New Hampshire or (if he holds no doctor's degree) President John Smith Dartmouth College Hanover, New Hampshire	
President of a Theological Seminary	The Reverend President John K. Hancock Western Theological Seminary Austin, Texas	Dear Sir: Dear President Hancock:
President of State Senate	The Honorable Richard Daly President of the State Senate of Kansas The State Capitol Topeka, Kansas	Sir:
President of the Senate of the United States	The Honorable The President of the Senate of the United States Washington, D.C. or The Honorable Thomas Fenton President of the Senate Washington, D.C.	Sir:
President of the United States	The President The White House Washington, D.C. or The President of the United States The White House Washington, D.C. or The President Washington, D.C. or President John Blank Washington, D.C. or	Sir: Dear Mr. President:

Rank or Title	Address the Envelope	Begin the Letter
President of the United States	His Excellency The President of the United States Washington, D.C.	
President's wife	Mrs. John Blank The White House Washington, D.C.	Dear Mrs. Blank:
Priest	Reverend James E. Murphy or Reverend Father Murphy	Dear Father: Reverend Father: Dear Father Murphy:
Prince of the Royal Blood	His Royal Highness Prince Charles	Sir:
Princess of the Royal Blood	Her Royal Highness the Princess Mary	Madam:
Professor in a college or university	Professor John Smith Department of Mathematics Northwestern University Evanston, Illinois or John Smith, Ph.D. Professor of Mathematics Northwestern University Evanston, Illinois or Dr. John Smith Department of Mathematics Northwestern University Evanston, Illinois	Dear Sir: Dear Professor Smth: Dear Dr. Smith:
Queen	The Queen's Most Excellent Majesty or Her Gracious Majesty, the Queen	Madam: May it please Your Majesty:
Rabbi	Rabbi Kenneth Bogen Temple Emanu-El Fifth Avenue New York, N.Y. or Reverend Kenneth Bogen or Reverend Kenneth Bogen, D.D. or Dr. Kenneth Bogen	Reverend Sir: Dear Sir: Dear Rabbi Bogen: Dear Dr. Bogen: (if he holds a doctor's degree)

Rank or Title	Address the Envelope	Begin the Letter
Representative in Congress	The Honorable John Smith The House of Representatives Washington, D.C. or Representative John Smith The House of Representatives Washington, D.C. or (if sent to his home) The Honorable John Smith Representative in Congress (followed by postal address)	Sir: Dear Sir: Dear Congressman Smith: Dear Representative Smith: Dear Mr. Smith:
Secretary of Agriculture	The Honorable The Secretary of Agriculture Washington, D.C. or The Honorable John Smith Secretary of Agriculture Washington, D.C.	Sir: Dear Sir: Dear Mr. Secretary:
Secretary of Commerce	The Honorable The Secretary of Commerce Washington, D.C. or The Honorable Thomas Crane Secretary of Commerce Washington, D.C.	Sir: Dear Sir: Dear Mr. Secretary:
Secretary of Labor	The Honorable The Secretary of Labor Washington, D.C. or The Honorable Philip Dale The Secretary of Labor Washington, D.C.	Sir: Dear Sir: Dear Mr. Secretary:
Secretary of State	The Honorable The Secretary of State Washington, D.C. or The Honorable Lee Thompson Secretary of State Washington, D.C.	Sir: Dear Sir: Dear Mr. Secretary:
Secretary of the Interior	The Honorable The Secretary of the Interior Washington, D.C.	Sir: Dear Sir: Dear Mr. Secretary:

Rank or Title	Address the Envelope	Begin the Letter
Secretary of the Interior	or The Honorable Frank Dash Secretary of the Interior Washington, D.C.	
Secretary of the Navy	The Honorable The Secretary of the Navy Washington, D.C. or The Honorable Thomas Cary Secretary of the Navy Washington, D.C.	Sir: Dear Sir: Dear Mr. Secretary:
Secretary of the Treasury	The Honorable The Secretary of the Treasury Washington, D.C. or The Honorable Williard Ball Secretary of the Treasury Washington, D.C.	Sir: Dear Sir: Dear Mr. Secretary:
Secretary of War	The Honorable The Secretary of War Washington, D.C. or The Honorable Philip Jenks Secretary of War Washington, D.C.	Sir: Dear Sir: Dear Mr. Secretary:
Senator	The Honorable John Blank United States Senate Washington, D.C. or Senator John Blank The United States Senate Washington, D.C. or (if sent to a home address) The Honorable John Blank United States Senator (followed by home address)	Sir: Dear Sir: Dear Senator Blank:
Sister of a religious order	Sister Mary Angela or The Reverend Sister Angela	Dear Sister Angela: Dear Sister:
Speaker of the House of Representatives	The Honorable The Speaker of the House of Representatives Washington, D.C.	Sir: Dear Sir: Dear Mr. Speaker:

Rank or Title	Address the Envelope	Begin the Letter
	or	
	The Speaker of the House of Representatives Washington, D.C.	
	or	
	The Honorable Frederick Knight Speaker of the House of Representatives Washington, D.C.	
State Representative	The Honorable Peter Blank The House of Representatives The State Capitol Jefferson City, Missouri	Sir: Dear Sir: Dear Mr. Blank:
State Senator	The Honorable John Smith The State Senate Trenton, New Jersey or Senator John Smith The State Capitol Trenton, New Jersey	Sir: Dear Sir: Dear Senator Smith:
Undersecretary of State	The Undersecretary of State Washington, D.C. or The Honorable Robert Corey Undersecretary of State Washington, D.C.	Sir: Dear Sir: Dear Mr. Corey:
Vice-President of the United States	The Honorable The Vice-President of the United States Washington, D.C. or The Vice-President Washington, D.C. or The Honorable Michael Brent Vice-President of the United States Washington, D.C.	Sir: Dear Sir: Dear Mr. Vice-President:

Index

Index

A

Abbreviations: signature, 283; speech, 345; states, 288–89

Accent, foreign, 342–44; list of mispronunciations, 344

Acceptances and regrets, 289–316. See also Invitations

Accessories, house, 80

Accidents, table, 64

Acknowledgment: condolence, notes of, 267; flowers, 267; invitation to dine at White House, 513–14

Address, forms of: army officers, 514; chaplain, 514; doctors, 514; naval officers, 514; President, 513; President's wife, 513

Adopted baby, 446–47; announcement, 254

After-dinner coffee, 113, 115, 117, 159. See also Coffee

After-dinner drinks, 159

Afternoon tea. See Tea

Air Force, Army, Navy, corresponding ranks, 511

Air Force, enlisted men, grades, 512

Airplane travel, 423–27; clothes, 425; courtesy, 425; luggage, 424, 426; reservations, 424; seats, 424; smoking, 406, 425; tipping, 425

Airsickness, 425

Aisle: garden wedding, 240; home wedding, 239

Altar: club wedding, 241; garden wedding, 241; home wedding, 239; hotel wedding, 241

Ambassador, introductions, 14

Ambition, business, 494

American home, foreign wife in, 445–46

Anniversaries, wedding: invitations to, 211, 295; list, 324

Announcements: baby, adopted, 254; birth, 253–54; death, 259–60; military title, use of, 516; wedding, 184, 201–2

Announcements, sample: adopted baby, 254; death, 260; wedding, 202

Answering telephone, 362, 364–65

Apéritifs, 156, 157; cocktails, 165

Apologizing at the table, 67

Appearance, personal, 352–61

Appetizer wines, 156, 157

Apples, eating, 55

Applying for job, 500–1

Archbishop, introductions, 14

Army, Air Force, Navy, corresponding ranks, 511

Army, enlisted men, grades, 512

Army officers: addressing, 514; precedence, 511; wedding invitation, 517

Artichokes, eating, 55, 60

Asparagus: eating, 55, 60; serving, 170

At home, formal, dress, 360

At-home cards, 32, 47; bride, 48–49; bride and groom, 202

At-home day, 27, 28, 29, 47–49

Attendants, wedding, 184–85

Awnings, 107

B

Babies: adoption announcement, 254; christening clothes, 257; gifts, 32–33, 257–58; gifts, acknowledging, 324–25; showers, 258; visits to, 32–33

Bachelor: dinner, 190, 245; host to unmarried women, 170

Bacon, eating, 55

Baggage porter, tip, 431
Ball: charity, 311–12; use of word, 305, 311. *See also* Dance
Ballroom etiquette, 139–40
Banana, eating, 55
Banquet cloths, 79
Bar glassware, *diagram*, 167
Bare legs, 361
Basic furniture, 72
Basic silver, 72–74
Bathroom linens, check list, 80
Bedroom linens, check list, 79–80
Behavior, basic social, 1–67
Behavior, in public, 379–81
Bellboy, tips, 431
Berries, eating, 55
Berth: lower, seat, 419; making up, 419
Best man: bridal table, 243–44; bridegroom's father, 248; costume, 230–32; duties, 184–85; flowers, 230, 231, 232; recessional, 237; responsibilities, 222; toastmaster, 244; wedding ceremony, 237
Bible, bride's, 218, 225
Birth: announcements, 253–54, from foreign country, 253; parents divorced, 253–54; congratulations, 319
Birthday: children's gifts, 465–66; children's parties, 462, 464, 465–66; congratulations, 318–19; gift acknowledgment, 323
Bishop, introductions, 14
Black band, 268
Black-bordered cards, 51
Blue garter, 218
Bone china, 75
Bones, picking up, 59
Born with a silver spoon in one's mouth, 258
Bottles, sealing with nail polish, 417
Bouillon served in a cup, eating, 56
Bouquet: bridal, 225; bridesmaids', 221
Box supper, 464
Boxes, opera and theater, clothes for, 356
Boy: dance, taking girl to, 476; girl, calling on, 475; girl, taking home, 477; girl, taking out, 475, 481; small,

envelope addressing, 287, 288; teen-age, suggestions to, 481–82
Brandy glass, 164
Bread, serving, 112, 114
Bread and butter: eating, 54, 58–59; letter, 155, 325; plates, 58, 106, 112, 114, 119
Breakfasts, 126–28; English manner, 127; family, 128; setting, *diagram*, 127; wedding, 194, 242; wedding, military, 518
Bridal: consultants, 221–22; dinner, 189–90; party, gowns, 221; procession, 184; procession, children, 234; showers, 178–79, 245; table, 243–44, *chart*, 243; traditions, 218. *See also* Bride
Bride: at-home cards, 48–49; bouquet, 225, throwing, 218–19, 244; bridal table, 243–44; cake, 186, 190; costume, garden wedding, 226–27; garter, 218–19; gift book, 212, 213; gifts, thanking for, 212, 213; girl, called bride for one year, 247; giving away, by young brother, 248; giving away, when parents are divorced, 249; gloves, 246; honeymoon, leaving for, 244–45; in mourning, 246; lifting over doorstep, 220; living with parents, 439–41; outfit, 222–27; owner of wedding gifts, 248; parents' financial responsibilities, check list, 191; processional, 237; receiving line, recessional, 237; 242–43; teacup tradition, 220–21; toast, military wedding, 518; trousseau, personal, displaying, 248; veil, 219–20, 224–25, 227; visiting, 31–32; wedding arrangements, 181–82; wedding ceremony, 237; wedding rehearsal, 190
Bridegroom: bridal table, 243–44; costume, 230–32; costume, military wedding, 518; financial responsibilities, check list, 191–92; flowers, 230, 231, 232; honeymoon, leaving for, 244–45; receiving line, 242–43; recessional, 237; responsibilities, 188, 189, 222; wedding ceremony, 237
Bridegroom's father: best man, 248; receiving line, 242
Bridegroom's mother, receiving line, 242–43

Bride's father: costume, 232-33; duties, 247; processional, 237; wedding ceremony, 237

Bride's mother: entrance at church, 236; receiving line, 242-43

Bridesmaids, 184; bouquets, 221; bridal table, 243-44; costumes, 221, 227-29; in mourning, 228; luncheon, 190; processional, 237; receiving line, 242-43; recessional, 237; sisters of groom, 245; wedding ceremony, 237

Bridge: dessert, 147; ethics, 145-46; good manners, 144-45; luncheon, 141-42, 146; prizes, 144; supper, 147-48; tea, 147. See also Bridge parties

Bridge parties, 140-48; afternoon, 143; clothes, 355; equipment, 143; hostess, 141, 142; informal luncheon before, 121; invitations, 141; players, 142-43; refreshments, 146-47

Brunch, 128

Budget, two-family, 444

Buffet: service, 124-26; table, 124-25

Burgundy, sparkling, 156; to ice, 162

Buses, etiquette, 384-85

Business: ambition, 494; associates, getting along with, 493-95; callers, meeting, 498; etiquette, 493-507; etiquette, questions and answers, 505-7; introductions, 12, 16, 25; telephone etiquette, 499-500

Business card, use for social purposes, 45

Businessman, courtesy, 495-96

Businesswoman, well-bred successful, 496-98

Butler: addressing, 89; duties, 83

Butter, on vegetables, 59

Butter knife, 58; placing, 104, 106, 114

C

Cake: bride, 186, 190; eating, 54-55, 61; wedding, 185-86, 244

Calls: condolence, 27-28, 30, 35; duty, 26-27, 39; obligation, 27-39; sick, 27-28, 30, 33-34; unexpected, 37-39; Washington, formal duty, 513-14; White House, courtesy, 513; White House, formal, 512

Canapés, cocktail party, 149

Canceling formal dinner invitations, 296-97

Candles, on table, 102, 119

Cane, with full dress, 360

Captain's dinner, transatlantic liners, 422

Captain's table, sitting at, 421-22

Card-leaving rules, 43

Card parties, 140-48; clothes, 355. See also Bridge parties

Card tables, 143

Cardinal, introductions, 14

Cards: at home, 32, sample, 47, 48, 49; Christmas, 331-35; congratulations, sample, 45; debutante daughter, sample, 46; double, 51; gift acknowledgment, sample, 213; greeting, general, 335; greeting, questions and answers, 335-37; informal, 51; introductions, sample, 24; invitations, 49-51, 149, 289-90, 304; message on, sample, 44; sympathy, sample, 45; visiting, 26-27, 29, 39-51. See also Visiting cards

Cars, taking abroad, 421

Carving meat, 114, 116, 125

Casserole dinner, 117

Catholic Church: christening, 256; funeral flowers, 260

Caudle, christening, 257

Celery, use of salt, 66

Centerpieces, 102-3, 118

Ceremonial function, White House, 513

Chairmen, committee, suggestions, 490-91

Chairs: arrangement, 70; card tables, 143

Chambermaid: duties, 86-87; hotel, tip, 431

Champagne, 155-57, 159; christening, 257; glass, 164; to ice, 162; weddings, 183, 244

Chaplain, addressing, 514

Charity balls, 311-12

Charts: bridal table, 243; receiving line, 242; wedding, 237

Chauffeur: addressing, 89; duties, 84

Check list: bathroom linens, 80; bedroom linens, 79-80; bridegroom, financial responsibilities, 191-92;

bride's parents, financial responsibilities, 191; china, 76; flat silver, 73–74; glassware, 77–78; kitchen linens, 79; linens, 79–80; table linens, 79; wedding plans, 188

Checkout time, hotels, 430

Cherries, cocktail, eating, 61

Chewing gum: disposing of, 432; using, 6

Children: adopted, 446–47; and parents, relationship between, 451; art gallery, 386; bad manners, 453; birthday gifts, 465–66; bridal procession, 234; clothes, 455; divorced parents, 251–52; entertainment, 460–62; etiquette for, 449–70; first things to be taught, 452–53; hospital visits, 33; imitative, 451; learning to live like a grownup, 453–54; mourning clothes, 268; museum, 386; neatness, habits of, 454; neatness, personal, 454–55; ridiculing, 437; self-expression, 456; speech, 455–57; stepchild, 446–47; table manners, 457–59; telephone, answering, 365; traveling on trains, 419; two families under one roof, 444; well-mannered, 452–53. See also Children's parties

Children's nurse, duties, 87

Children's parties, 459–69; birthday, 462, 464, 465–66; Christmas, 462; decorations, 462–63; etiquette, 464–66; games, 461; hour, 459; invitations, 466–69; refreshments, 463–64

China: buying, 75–77; check list, 76; essential, 74–77

Christenings, 254–57; Catholic Church, 256; church, 256; decorations, 256; font, 256, 257; home, 256–57; invitations, 255–56; robe, 257

Christmas cards, 331–35; acknowledging gift on, 336; addressing, 288, 334; business associate, sent to, 334; celebrity, sent to, 337; choice of, 333; colored ink, 336; engaged couple, sending out, 336; envelope linings, 335; family, 333–34; family photographs on, 335; formal, 333; gift enclosed in, 336; homemade, 335; husband and wife, 333; informal, 333; list, 332; married people, 336; mourning, sent by those in, 336;

post cards, 336; printing or engraving of names, 334; professional man, sent to, 334; signing, 333–34; summer scenes, 335; to whom to send, 332; visiting card enclosed with, 336; when to send, 331–32

Christmas gifts, acknowledging, 323

Church: christening, 256; contribution, who makes, 433; decorations left after wedding, 246; dress, women, 387; engaging for wedding, 181; funeral, 263–64; good manners in, 386–87; wedding, 182, 234–39

Cigarettes, supplying for a party, 408; See Smoking

Circus, courtesy, 394

Clergyman: christening, 256, 257; envelope addressing, 287; fee, wedding, 246; signature, 282; visiting card, 41; wedding ceremony, 237; wedding reception, 243

Clothes: airplane travel, 425; "at home," formal, 360; best man, 230–32; boy, in bridal procession, 234; bridegroom, 230–32; bridegroom, military wedding, 518; bridesmaids, 221, 227–29; bridge party, 355; card party, 355; children's, 455; cocktail party, 354; concerts, 356; conservative, 353; dance, summer, 357; dances, 354–55; dinner dress, 353, 354, 355, 356; dinner, formal, 353, 354; dinner, informal, 354; dress, train on, 361; funerals, 262, 263, 265, 266; hotel dining room, 429; maid of honor, 221, 229–30; men's country, 359; men's daytime, 359; men's evening functions, 359; morning coat, 358, 359; mothers, at wedding, 233–34; mourning, 259, 267–68; musicales, 356; night clubs, 356; opera, 355; packing, 416–17; pallbearers, 359; receptions, 354; restaurants, 356; Saturday nights, dining and dancing, 356–57; ships, 422; spectator sports, 357; Sunday night, 430; teas, 354; teen-agers, 473, 475; telephoning hostess when in doubt, 360; theater, 355; theater balconies, evening gowns worn in, 361; traveling, 415–16; unconventional, 353; ushers at wedding, 230–32; woman

dining alone in hotel, 360; women, 353-57
Club: address, use of, 487; country, 486; country, guests, 486; duties of new member, 485; etiquette, 483-91; guests, 488-89; introductions, 16; joining, 484-85; manners, 487; non-active member, 487-88; non-resident member, 486; officers, suggestions for, 489-90; presiding officer, 490; resident member, 486; resigning, 489; sponsorship, 485; tipping, 489; wedding, 241
Coats: checking, 390, 394; theater, 390
Cocktail lounge, women alone, 433
Cocktail parties, 148-50, 413; canapés, 149; clothes, 354; hour, 148, 149; informal invitation, 314, acknowledging, 315; non-drinkers, 411; quantity of drinks, 171
Cocktails: before dinner, 109, 165-66, 413; fruit, leftover juice, 65; glasses, 166; luncheon, 118
Coffee: after-dinner, 113, 115, 117, 159; at afternoon tea, 168; buffet supper, 125-26; dance, informal, 134; luncheon, 120; sugar and cream, 170
Colloquialisms, 345
Color guard, passing, 519
Color scheme, furniture, 71
Colored tablecloths, 101
Coming-out party, 136
Commercial letterheads, 272
Committee, subscription dance, 136
Committee chairman, suggestions, 490-91
Communications, informal, 289
Compartment dishes, 169
Compromises, family, 438
Concerts, clothes, 356
Condolence calls, 27-28, 30, 35
Condolence letters, 261, 326-30; acknowledging, 267, 325-26
Confetti, wedding, 219
Congratulation calls, 32-33
Congratulations: birth of a child, 319; birthday, 318-19; bride and groom, 247; engagement, 316-17; graduation, 320; letters of, 316-19, thanks

for, 326; marriage, 317; wedding anniversary, 317-18
Convalescents, visits to, 33-34
Conversation, 339-52; good, 347-52; opening, 20-21; subjects to avoid, 350-52; what to talk about, 349-52
Cook, duties, 85
Cordials, 159, 162
Corks, wine, 160, 161; drawing, 164
Corn, eating, 55, 60-61
Correcting a friend in public, 7
Correspondence: formal, stationery, 269; informal, stationery, 269; social, 269-337
Corresponding ranks, Air Force, Army, Navy, 511
Corsage: bride, 225; mother at weddings, 233
Costume ball, 168, 306
Country clothes: men's, 359; women's, 357
Country clubs, 486
Country-house stationery, 271
Country wedding, transportation, 200-1
Couple, parents living with, 439-41
Couples, living together, 443-45
Cover, place setting, 103
Cremation, 266
Crepe: streamers on door, 261; veils, 267
Crowds, 380
Crudities of expression, 345
Crystal glassware, 77
Customers, store etiquette, 504
Customs, going through, 423
Cutaway coat, 358, 359
Cutting in, dancing, 139-40, 476

D

Damask tablecloths, 101
Dances and dancing: clothes, 354-55; cutting in, 139-40, 476; debutante, 307-8; dinner, 308; etiquette, 139-40; floor manners, 401; formal, 134-35; informal, 133-34; invitations, 305-16, formal, acknowledging, 310-11, informal, 312-13, issued by club, 312; make-up, 355; masquerade, 168, invitation, 306-7; officer, at formal dance, Washington, 515; partners, 139, separating, 169; programs, 171;

refusing to dance, 139; "small dance," use of phrase, 305; subscription dance, 135–36, 311–12; subscription dinner dance, invitation, 312; summer clothes, 357; supper dance, 138–39; supper dance, invitations, 309; tea dance, invitation, 309; teen-agers, 474–77, 480, 481; use of word, 305; wedding, 244

Dates, teen-agers, 474–77, 480, 481

Daughter, hostess for father, 300–1

Daughter-in-law problems, 440–41

Days when flag is displayed, list, 519

Death, 259–67; announcing, 259–60; cremation, 266; friends and neighbors, conduct, 261–62; house, procedure in, 260–61, 266–67; women of the family, conduct, 261. See also Funerals

Debutante: dance, 307–8; dinner invitation, 296; introducing, 136–37; parties, 136–37; visiting cards, 46

Debuts. dances, 137 38; dinner, 138 39; group, 136–37, 138; luncheon, 137; outdoor, 137; winter, 137

Decanter, wine, 165

Decorations: bridal table, 243; children's parties, 462–63; christening, 256

Dentist, introductions, 14

Dessert: bridge, 147; course, diagram, 105; serving, 112, 115, 117; wines, 156, 159

Diagrams: bar glassware, 167; breakfast setting, 127; courses, dinner, 105; luncheon, setting, 119; seating arrangement, dinner, 104. See also Charts

Dictionary habit, 341, 343

Dining car, hat worn in, 433

Dining room: entering, 109–10, 113, 118; hotel, 429–30; public, entering, 395

Dining table, seating oneself, 65

Dinner: announcing, 109; bachelor, 190; bridal, 189–90; casserole, 117; cloths, 79; cocktails before, 413; coffee service, 113; courses, diagram, 105; dance, 308; dance, subscription, invitation, 312; debut, 138–39; dress, 353, 354, 355, 356; engagement, breaking, 297; formal, 106–13; formal, clothes, 353, 354; guest, filling

in, 297–98; guest list, 107; guests, arrival, 107–8; hour for, 107; informal, 113–17; informal, clothes, 354; introductions, 15–16, 17; latecomer, 66; parties, 106–17; parties, restaurant, 396; partners, 109–10, 113; planked, 96; planning, 107; seating arrangement, diagram, 104; serving, 111–12; serving without a maid, 115–17; table behavior, 53; table setting, 103; waiting for, 108–9; White House, 513; wines, 157, 158, 159, 171. See also Dinner invitations

Dinner invitations: acknowledgment, 291–301; engraved, 290; formal, 290–300; handwritten, 290; informal, 298–301

Dinner jacket, 358

Dinner service, gift to bride, 221

Disabled, courtesy to, 4–5

Dishes: compartment, 169; helping to wash, 39; stacking, 114, 116

Divorce, 249–52; announcements, 250; bringing suit, 249–50; meeting socially after, 251; property division, 250–51. See also Marriage

Divorcée: bridal veil, 225; envelope addressing, 285; matron of honor, 247; name, 251; remarriage announcement, 206; signature, 282; visiting card, 42; wearing first husband's rings, 249, 251

Doctor: addressing, 514; envelope addressing, 285–86; introductions, 14; signature, 282; visiting card, 41

Doctor's office, etiquette, 504–5

Door, crepe streamers on, 261

Doormen, tip, 431

Double card, 51

Double-ring wedding ceremony, 187; groom's ring, 248

Double wedding, 203; brides attending each other, 248

Dress: correct for men, 357–59; correct for women, 353–57; good taste in, 353; questions and answers, 360–61. See also Clothes

Dressing room, train, 419

Drinkers, don'ts for, 412–13

Drinks and drinking: etiquette, 410–14; evening drinks, 166–68; host,

suggestions, 413; hostess, suggestions, 413; night clubs, 400; refusing drinks, 410–11; teen-agers, 478
Duke, introductions, 14
Dunking, 66
Duty calls, 26–27, 39

E

Earthenware, 75
Easter cards, 335
Eating, etiquette, 51–67
Eggs: boiled, eating, 128; breakfast, 127
Elbows on table, 67
Elevators, etiquette, 8
Elopement, announcements, 202
Employment agencies, 90–91
Engaged couple: behavior in public, 176–77; relatives and friends, meeting, 176
Engagement, 173–81; announcing, 174, 245; broken, 179–81; congratulations, 316–17; gifts, 177; length, 179; newspaper notices, 174–75; parents' disapproval, 173; questions and answers, 245–49; ring, 175; ring, wearing at wedding, 246
Engraved stationery, 270
Engraving, sample, godfather's gift, 258
Enlisted men, grades, Air Force, Army, Navy, 512
Entertaining: etiquette, 69–171; modern, 94–100; questions and answers, 168–71; simple, 95–97; successful, 372–78; Washington, 515; without servants, 95–97, 115
Entertainment, children, 460–62
Envelope: inserting letter, 273; punctuation, 285; spelling, 285. See also Envelope, addressing
Envelope, addressing, 284–89, diagram, 284; boy, small, 287, 288; divorcée, 285; doctor, 285–86; "Esquire," use of, 286; family, 288; father and son, 287; girl, small, 287; husband and wife, 286; "Junior," 286; men, 286–87; men, two or more, 287; minister, 287; priest, 287; rabbi, 287; servants, 287; sisters, 287–88; widow, 285; woman, married, 285–86; women, 285; women doctors, 285–86

Episcopal Church, funeral flowers, 260
Equipment, bridge party, 143
Evening meal, name of, 168

F

Family: breakfast, 128; compromises, 438; courtesies, everyday, 435–37; envelope addressing, 288; getting along with, 435–47; happy life, formula for, 438; privacy and possessions, 437; quarrels, 438; relationships, difficult, 439–47
Fancy-dress dance, invitation, 306
Fans: bride, 225; bridesmaids', 228
Fare, man paying for woman, 432
Father and son, envelope addressing, 287
Fee: clergyman, at wedding, 246; military wedding, 518
Finger bowl, 62–63, 112, 115, 120
Finger foods, 54–55
Fish bones, removing from mouth, 62
Flag: carried in parade, 519; days when displayed, list, 519; etiquette, 518–20; lowering, 519; pledge of allegiance to, 520; use of, 519
Flat silver: check list, 73–74; engraved, 217
Floor coverings, selecting, 71
Flower girls: costumes, 234; weddings, 185, ceremony, 237, processional, 237, recessional, 237
Flowers: acknowledging, 267; best man, 230, 231, 232; bridegroom, 230, 231, 232; bridesmaids, 228; debutantes, 137, 138; funeral, 260, 261–62, 265; table decoration, 102; ushers, 230, 231, 232; weddings, 186, 223, 225
Flying schedules, 424
Font, christening, 256, 257
Food: eating, 53, 59–60; finger, 54–55; fork, 56; left on plate, 65; passed by servants, 63; prepared at table, 123; spoon, 55–56; unfamiliar, 66
Food and wine, 157; list, 158
Footman, duties, 83–84
Foreign accent, 342–44; list of mispronunciations, 344
Foreign countries, courtesy in, 426
Foreign wife, in American home, 445–46

Fork: placing, 104; use of, 56–58
Fork foods, 56
Foster parents, 447
Frappé, liqueurs, 159
French words, on menus, *list*, 401–4
Fruit cocktail, leftover juice, 65
Fruit knife and fork, 55
Fruit pits, 62
Fruits, eating, 55
Funerals, 259–67; arrangements, 259; church, 263–64; costume, 262, 263, 265, 266; flowers, 260, 261–62, 265; home, 265–66; house, 264–65; "omit flowers," 260; private, 260; procession, 264; services, 262, 266. *See also* Death
Furniture: basic, 72; buying, 69–72; color harmony, 70, 71; open stock, 72; period or style, 70; proportion, 70–71; quality, 70, 71–72

G

Gambling, 144
Games, children's parties, 461
Garden luncheons, 121–22
Garden party, invitation, 315; acknowledgment, 316
Garden weddings, 240–41; bridal costume, 226–27
Garter, bride, 218–19
Gesture, speech, 340–41
Gift book, bride, 212, 213
Gifting infants, custom of, 258
Gifts: babies, 32–33, 257–58; babies, acknowledging, 324–25; birthday, acknowledging, 323; birthday, children, 465–66; bridal shower, 245; Christmas, acknowledging, 323; convalescents, 34; engagement, 177; hostess, 169; returning after broken engagement, 180; sent with visiting card, 44; shower, acknowledging, 322; to business superior, 505; to husband's secretary, 506; ushers and best man, 189, 190; wedding. *See* Wedding gifts
Girl: boy calling on, 475; boy taking home, 477; boy taking out, 475, 481; dance, boy taking girl to, 476; dance, refusing to, 476; small, envelope ad-

dressing, 287; teen-age, suggestions to, 479–81
Glassware: bar, *diagram*, 167; brandy, 164; champagne, 164; check list, 77–78; cocktail, 166; crystal, 77; essential, 77–78; table setting, 104–5; wine, 163–64
Gloves: bride, 226, 246; bridesmaid, 229; debutante, 137, 138; eating with, 361; long, removing, 361; men, 358; men, at wedding, 232; public formal receptions, 361; removing, 20; women, 353, 354, 356, 357
Godmother, 256, 257
Godparents, 254–55, 256, 257; accepting, 255; gifts, 258; proxy, 255
Going-away outfit, 216
Golden apple, myth, 220
Governess: addressing, 89; duties, 88
Graduation, congratulations, 320
Grammar, frequent mistakes in, *list*, 346–47
Grapefruit: eating, 55; squeezing juice from, 66
Grave, services, 266
Gravy, sopping up, 59
Greasy food particles dropped on tablecloth, 66
Greeting cards: birthday, 318; etiquette, 331–35; general, 335; personal messages on, 335; questions and answers, 335–37
Group debuts, 136–37, 138
Group introductions, 13–14
Guest list: debutante party, 136; wedding, 183
Guest of honor: dinner, 109, 118; introductions, 15; invitation to meet, 293, 294; seating, 103; serving, 111; subscription dance, 136; tea, formal, 132; toast, 165
Guest room, 152–54
Guests: announcing, 108, 113; appreciation, showing, 372; bridge party, 140–41; choosing, 373–74; christening, 257; club, 488–89; country clubs, 486; dance, 139; dining rooms, paging in, 430; dinner, 53; dinner, filling in, 297–98; dinner, remaining after, 170; dressing, 369; forcing entertainment on, 377; greeting, 374–75; helping hostess, 123, 169; home

wedding, 239; hotel, receiving in, 429; house party, 151–55; late arrival, 110; night-blooming, 372; overstaying, 372; problems and preferences of, 377–78; punctuality, 369; radio programs, interrupting, 368–69; rebuking, 376; receiving line, wedding, 243; responsibilities, 370–71; right to courtesy, 465; taking liberties, 371; tea, formal, 132; telephone calls, paying for, 366; uninvited, 36–39; waiting for dinner, 108–9; wedding, at church, 235–36, 239; wedding, reception and ceremony, 194; welcome, 36, 369–72; White House, 513

H

Hallowe'en party, 463
Handwriting, difficult, 271
Handwritten letters, 271
"Happy is the bride the sun shines on," 220
Hat: dining car, worn in, 433; men, raising, 8, 382; men, removing, 385, 386; women, 353, 354, 355, 356, 357, hotel reception, 360, hotels, 430, refusing to remove, 433, removing, 29, 395, speaker at afternoon meeting, 360, theater, 391–92, with street-length clothes, 361
Head of the table, 170
Headdress, bridal attendants, 228–29
Headwaiter, tip, 432
Heels, worn with dance dress, 360
Highball, mixing, 166–67
Highway, etiquette of, 387–88
Holiday greetings, addressing, 288
Home: christening, 256–57; teen-agers' behavior, 473; wedding, 182, 239–40
Honeymoon, bride and groom, leaving for, 244–45
Hope chest, 215
Hors d'oeuvres: cocktails, 166; serving, 109; wine, served with, 157
Hospitals: introductions, 17; visits, 27, 32–33
Hospitality, true spirit of, 69
Host: drinking, suggestions, 413; gracious, 372–78; guests, greeting, 375;

smoking suggestions, 408; theater party, 390
Hostess: bridge party, 141, 142; buffet party, 126; dance, 139; daughter, for father, 300–1; deserted, note of regret to, 513; drinking suggestions, 413; entering dining room, 110; gift, 169; gracious, 372–78; guests, receiving, 108, 113, 118, 375; house party, 151, 152–55; serving dinner, 169; shower, thanking, 322; smoking suggestions, 408; tactful, 376; tea, formal, 132–33; theater party, 390; uneasy, 375–76; Washington, 509
Hostess-alone serving, rules for, 115–16
Hot biscuits, eating, 58
Hotels: American plan, 427; arriving, 427–28; calling at, 47; checking out, 430–31; dining room, 429–30, clothes, 429; etiquette, 427–32; European plan, 427; guests, receiving in, 429; luggage, 427, 431; registration, 427–28; registration card, how to sign, 428; reservation, 427, 430; room services, 428–29; stationery, 270; tipping, 431–32; wedding, 241
House, funeral, 264–65
House guest, 151–55
House parties, 150–55
Household: duties, two-family, 444; large staff, 82–89; linens, 78; one-maid, 82, 89–90
Housekeeper: addressing, 89; duties, 82–83
Housemaid, duties, 86–87
Husband and wife: envelope addressing, 286; seating, 168
Husband's secretary, gift to, 506

I

Ice, served with meat course, 65
Ice cream, eating, 55–56
Ice-cream cake, eating, 61
Infants, gifting, 258. See also Babies
Ink, colored, 271, 336
Interior decorating, 69–72
Intermissions, theater, 393
Introductions, 10–26; acknowledging, 19; ambassador, 14; archbishop, 14; awkward pause, 20–21; bishop, 14; business, 12, 16, 25; cardinal, 14;

cards, 24; ceremonious, 14–15; club, 16; daughter, 12; daughter-in-law, 13; daughter's friends, 12; dentist, 14; distinguished people, 14–15; doctor, 14; duke, 14; form of, 10; formal, 10, 14–15; formal dinner, 15–16, 17; group, 13–14; guest of honor, 15; guests, 13, 15, 16; hospital room, 17; husband, 12; indirect, 18; judge, 14; letters, 22–26; luncheons, 13, 15, 17; meeting again after, 21–22; men, to women, 10–11; men, two, 10–11; men, younger to older, 10–11; mother-in-law, 12–13; names, 20, 22; officers, 14, 514, 515; oneself, 17–18; parties, 13, 15; party, children, 465; phrases, suitable, 10–11, 17–19; phrases to avoid, 11; President, 14, 15; priest, 14; privates, 514, 515; public places, 15–17; purpose of, 10; relatives, 12–13; relatives-in-law, 13; resorts, 17; restaurant, 16; rising, 19; royalty, 14; senator, 14; servants, 18; shaking hands, 19–20, 21; shipboard, 17; sickroom, 17; social 10–26; social function, 17; strangers, 15, 17; street encounters, 15, 17; taking leave, 21; tea, formal, 132; theater, 15, 16; when not to make, 16; when to make, 15–16; wives, 12; women, two, 10–11; women, unmarried to matrons, 10–11; women, younger to older, 10–11; written, obligation of, 23, 25; younger groups, 13–14

Invitations: addressing, 288; club, issued by, 312; for friend, requesting, 314; general, 289–316; issued ahead of time, 374; issued in presence of others, 7; military title, use of, 516; "please reply," 296; R.s.v.p., 296; telephone, 365–66; visiting card, 49–51, 289–90, 304; writing, 278

   Acceptances, regrets, sample:
at home: with dancing, 306, 308, 309
bridal shower, 178
bridge: luncheon, 142; party, 141
charity ball, 311
children's party, 466–69
christening, 255–56
cocktails, 149, 314, 315
dance, 305–16; costume, formal, 307;

debutante, 138, 307, 308; formal, 135, 305, 310–11; honoring important guest, 306; informal, 134, 312–13; issued by club, 312; supper, 309
debutante party, 137
dinner, 289–301; daughter hostess for father, 300, 301; debutante, 296; formal, 290, 291, 292, 293; formal, canceling, 296–97; formal, postponing, 296–97; honor of special guest, 293–95; informal, 298–301; special occasion, 295
dinner dance, 308; subscription, 312
garden party: formal, 315; informal, 316
house parties, 150–51
luncheon, 118, 120, 301–3; formal, 301–3; formal, given by several women, 302; informal, 303
supper: buffet, 124; dance, 309; party, 122, 304
tea, 129, 132, 309, 315; dance, 309; formal, 132, 315; informal, 315
wedding, 183–84, 192–212; army officer's, 517; bride, second marriage, 206; bride with divorced parents, 205; bride with no parents, 205, 206; bride with one parent, 204; bride's home, 198; church, 195, 196; church and reception, 197; double, 203; home of relative or friend, 199; informal, 209–10; married business associate, 248; naval officer's, 517; outdoor, 199–200; reception, 195, 196, 197, 199; special, 202–6; to whom sent, 248
wedding anniversaries, 211
week-end parties, 150–51
White House, 512, 513

J

Jacket over slacks, 360
Jewelry: bridal attendants', 230; bride's, 224
Jewish synagogue, funeral flowers, 260
Job: applicant etiquette, 501–3; applying for, 500–1
Jr. and 2nd, use of, 283, 286
Judge: introductions, 14; visiting card, 41

K

Kerchiefs, wearing, 357
Kissing, at altar, 246
Kitchen linens, check list, 79
Kitchen maid, duties, 85
Kitchen parties, 96–97
Knife: butter, 58; placing, 104; salad, 61; use of, 56–58
Knife and fork, using: American method, 56–57; European method, 57
Knitting, at lecture, 433

L

Lace tablecloths, 101
Lady's maid, duties, 87
Language, pretentious, 344
Latecomer at dinner party, 66
Leaving the table, 65
Letter of introduction: acknowledging, 25; presenting, 24–25
Letter writing: appearance, 271; body of, 277–79; bread-and-butter, 155, 325; business, closing phrases, 279; condolence, 261, 278, 326–30; condolence, thanks for, 325–26; congratulation, 316–19; courtesy, 274–75; envelope, inserting letter, 273; folding letter, 273; form of address, 277; grammar, 278; gratefully yours, use of, 280; handwritten, 271; heading, 276; introduction, 22–26; language, 274; love, closing phrases, 279, 280; page sequence, 273; paragraphing, 278; parts of, 275–83; personal, closing phrases, 279–80; respectfully yours, use of, 280; salutation, 276–77, degrees, holders of, 283; formal, 277, informal, 277; signature, 281–83; social, closing phrases, 279, 280; social asset, 269; spacing and arrangement, 272; spelling, 278; sympathy, 326–30; tact, 274–75; thanks, 278, 320–21; typewritten, 272; undersize, 270; well-written, 273–74, 277–79
Letters, sample: baby gifts, acknowledging, 324–25; birth of a child, congratulations, 319; birthday congratulations, 318–19; birthday gifts, acknowledging, 323; bread-and-butter letter, 325; bridge party invitation, 141; Christmas gifts, acknowledging, 323; condolence: brother's death, 330, child's death, 329, husband's death, 328, parent's death, 327–28, sister's death, 330, someone killed, 330, wife's death, 328–29; congratulation, thanks for, 326; dinner, filling empty place, 297–98; dinner engagement, breaking, 297; dinner invitation, canceling, 296–97; engagement, congratulations on, 316–17; engagement party, canceling, 180; godparent, invitation to act as, 254; graduation congratulations, 320; introduction, 23–24, 26; introduction, indirect, 26; invitation for friend, requesting, 314; maid's reference, 94; marriage congratulations, 317; shower gifts, acknowledging, 322; sympathy, reply to note of, 325–26; wedding anniversary, congratulations on, 317–18; wedding anniversary, invitation, 211; wedding anniversary gifts, acknowledging, 324; wedding gifts, acknowledging, 321–22; wedding invitation, informal, 209–10, acknowledgment, 210–11; week-end invitation, 150–51
Lettuce, salad decoration, 65
Lighting, card party, 143
Linens: buying, 78–80; check list, 79–80; monogrammed, 168, 217; requirements, 78–80
Liqueurs, 159, 162
Liquors, 155–68
Livery of footmen, 83–84
Lobster, eating, 61
Luggage: airplane, 424, 426; hotel, 427, 431; ship, 421; train, 418; woman traveling alone, 428
Luncheons, 117–22; bridesmaids', 190; bridge, 141–42; cocktails, 118; debut, 137; formal, 117–20, 301–3; formal, invitations, 301–3; garden, 121–22; given by several women, 302–3; hour, 117, 121; informal, before bridge party, 121; informal, invitations, 303; introductions, 13, 15, 17; invitations, 118, 120, 301–3; outdoor, 122; parties, informal, 120; service, 119–20;

setting, *diagram*, 119; table, formal, 118; table, setting, 103, 119; table behavior, 53; wine, 157

M

Maid: addressing, 89; addressing employers, 92–93; dismissing, 93; dress and behavior, 92–93; engaging, 90–91; kitchen, duties, 85; lady's, duties, 87; leaving, 93; parlor, duties, 86; references, 94; relationship with, 91–92
Maid of honor, 184; bridal table, 243–44; costume, 221, 229–30; function, 229; processional, 237; receiving line, 242–43; recessional, 237; wedding ceremony, 237
Make-up: bridal attendants, 229–30; bride's, 224; dances, 355; in public, 6, 397
Mannerisms, speech, 340–41
Manners: club, 487; growing up with good, 449–53; restaurant, 397–98; table, 51–65; table, children, 457–59; table, questions and answers, 65–67
Marriage. *See* Weddings
Masquerade, invitations, 306
Matron of honor, 184; divorcée, 247
Meat, carving, 114, 116, 125
Men: business suit, wearing in evening, 360; carrying woman's packages, 383; clothes, see Clothes; coat in theater, 390; courtesies to a lady, 7–10; dress shoes, 361; envelope addressing, 286–87; envelope addressing, two or more, 287; guest of woman, at theater, 433; guest of woman, in business, 506; hat, removing, 7–8, 382, 385, 386; in uniform, lifting cap, 432; in uniform, toast, 515; introductions, 10–11; job, applying for, 500–1; meeting woman on street, 382–83; mourning, 268; offering arm to woman, 9, 383; outdoor clothes, removing, 29–30; paying for woman, 432; paying for woman's purchases, 432; rising, general rules, 7; rising for woman employee, 505; rising for woman visitor to his office, 507; rising in restaurant, 398; shaking hands, 19, 20, 21, 381; signature, 281, 282; signature, degree, use of, 283; smoking, 382–83;

with two women, seating, 395; with two women, walking, 383–84; with woman, walking, 383
Menservants, 83–85, 88; addressing, 89
Menu: breakfast, 127; bridge tea, 147; buffet, 125; cocktail party, 148, 149; dance, formal, 135; dance, informal, 134; dinner, formal, 110–11; French words, *list*, 401–4; luncheon, formal, 119; luncheon, informal, 121; luncheon, outdoor, 122; party, planning, 99; supper party, 123; tea, formal, 132; tea, informal, 131
Military: announcements, title, use of, 516; etiquette, 514–15; invitations, title, use of, 516; precedence, 511–12; weddings, 516–18; weddings, breakfast, 518, whom to invite, 517
Military and official etiquette, 509–20
Minister. *See* Clergyman
Monograms: linen, 217; silver, 217; stationery, 270
Mother: christening costume, 257; wedding costume, 233–34
Mother-in-law: addressing, 440; problems, 440–41, 442
Mother's Day cards, 335
Motorists: courtesy, 387; suggestions for, 388
Mourning: dress, 259, 267–68; men, 268; visiting cards, 51
Museum, children, 386
Music: dance, formal, 135; dance, informal, 133, 134; house funeral, 265; weddings, 186–87
Musicales, dress, 356

N

Nail polish, sealing bottles with, 417
Name: divorcée's, 251; introductions, 20, 22
Napkin: cocktail, 148, 150; placing, 104, 119, 125; use of, 62–63
National anthem, playing, 515
Navy: enlisted men, grades, 512; officer, addressing, 514; precedence, 511–12; wedding invitation, 517; wedding, whom to invite, 517
Navy, Army, Air Force, corresponding ranks, 511

Neatness: habits in childhood, 454; personal, children, 454–55
Neighbor, calling on a new, 30–31, 35–36
New Year's card, 332
New York, social season, 355fn.
Newspaper notices: death, 260; engagement, 174–75; engagement, broken, 180
Night clubs: bench seats, 396; clothes, 356; etiquette, 394–401; reservations, 400
"No house is big enough for two women," 442
Non-active member, clubs, 487–88
Non-resident member, clubs, 486
"Not at home," phrase of convenience, 30
Nursemaid, duties, 87–88

O

Office stationery, 270
Officers, Army and Navy: highest ranking, United States Army, 511; introductions, 14, 514, 515; mixing socially with privates, 514; visiting card, 41; Washington formal dance, 515
Officers, club, suggestions for, 489–90
Olive: cocktail, eating, 61; pit, 62
One-maid household, 82, 89–90
Open stock: china, 76; furniture, 72
Opera: box seats, 391; boxes, visiting, 393–94; clothes, 355
Orange blossoms, 220, 224
Oranges, eating, 55
Outdoor: debuts, 137; luncheons, 122; tea, formal, 133; weddings, 240–41
Overnight train trip, 418
Oyster fork, placing, 104

P

P.P.C. card, 45–46
Packing clothes, 416–17
Page, costume, 234
Pallbearers, 262, 264, 266; clothes, 359; procedure, 263
Paper napkins, 170
Parasols, bridesmaids', 228
Parents: and children, relationship between, 451; couple living with, 439–41; divorced, 252; living with married children, 441–43
Parlor maid, duties, 86
Parsley, eating, 66
Parties: birthday, children, 462, 464, 465–66; bridge, 140–48; card, 140–48; children's, 459–69; Christmas, children's, 462; clothes, 354, 355; cocktail, 148–50, 314, 413; debutante, 136–37; dinner, 106–17; dinner, restaurant, 396; etiquette, children, 464–66; games, children's, 461; garden, 315, 316; Hallowe'en, 463; house, 150–55; introductions, 13, 15; invitations, 305–16; kitchen, 96–97; luncheon, 117–22; menu, planning, 99; planning, 373–74; prenuptial, 189; preparations for, 97–98; supper, 122–23, 304, 309; tea, 315–16; teen-age, 462; two successive, 98–99; week-end, 150–55; when to give, 97
Passport, securing, 420
Pastries, eating, 55
Peaches, eating, 55
Pears, eating, 55
Pedestrians, suggestions for, 389
Pencil, writing in, 271
People, greeting, on street, 379
Pepper shakers, 106
Personal appearance, 352–61
Personal neatness, children, 454–55
Personal trousseau, 216
Personnel, store etiquette, 503
Petting, teen-agers, 479
Photograph, newspaper, 175
Picking up bones, 59
Pickles, serving, 112
Pie à la mode, eating, 61
Pineapple, eating, 55
Pipe, smoking indoors, 407
Pits, removing, 62
Place cards, 106, 110, 113
Place mats, 101, 118
Place plate, 119
Planked dinners, 96
Plated silver, 73
"Please reply," 296
Pledge of allegiance to the flag, 520
Politeness, pattern for, 5–6
Popovers, eating, 58
Porcelain, 75

Portable radios, 368
Portraits, wedding, 246
Post cards, used for Christmas cards, 336
Postponing formal dinner invitation, 296-97
Potato, eating, 55, baked, 60
Pottery, 75
Prayer book: bridesmaids', 228; wedding, 221, 225
Precedence: army officers, 511; military, 511-12; naval, 511-12; order of, Washington, D.C., list, 509-11
Prenuptial parties, 189
President, U.S.: addressing, 513; introductions to, 14, 15; personal interview with, 512
President's wife, addressing, 513
Presiding officer: club, 490; toastmaster, serving as, 490
Priest: envelope addressing, 287; introductions, 14
Privacy and possessions, family, 437
Privates, army: and officers, mixing socially, 514; introductions, 514, 515
Prizes, bridge, 144
Problems, teen-age, 477
Procession: funeral, 264; wedding, 191, 236, chart, 237; wedding, home, 240
Pronunciation, illiterate, 341, list, 342
Property, division, in divorce, 250-51
Proxy godparent, 255
Public, good behavior in, 379-81
Public behavior, teen-agers, 472, 473
Public buildings, etiquette, 385-86
Public library, etiquette, 386
Public places, etiquette in, 379-434, questions and answers, 432-33
Pudding, eating, 55-56
Pullman accommodations, 417
Purse, bride, 226

Q

Quarrels, family, 438
Questions and answers: business etiquette, 505-7; dress, 360-61; engagements and weddings, 245-49; entertaining, 168-71; greeting cards, 335-37; public places, etiquette in, 432-33; table manners, 65-67; weddings and engagements, 245-49

R

R.s.v.p. (abbreviation), 296
Rabbi, envelope addressing, 287
Radio: courtesy, 367-69; portable, 368; programs, guests interrupting, 368-69
Rattles, baby, 258
Real china, 75
Receiving, tea, formal, 132
Receiving line: Washington, 515; weddings, 242-43, chart, 242
Receptions: acknowledgment of invitation, 316; clothes, 354; Washington, days for, 514; Washington, formal, 515; wedding, 182-85, 194, 241-44
Recessional, wedding, 238-39; chart, 237; garden, 241; home, 240; military, 518
Red carpets, 107
Red table wines, 156
References, giving, 94
Refreshments, children's parties, 463-64
Registration card, hotels, how to sign, 428
Rehearsal, wedding, 247
Relationships: difficult family, 439-47; parents and children, 451
Religious discussions, 351
Reservations: airplane, 424; hotel, 427, 430; ship, 420; train, 417
Resident member, clubs, 486
Resort: etiquette, 427-32; introductions, 17
Restaurants: bench seats, 396; check, paying, 398-99; check, paying for woman, 433; clothes, 356; dinner party, 396; etiquette, 394-401; introductions, 16; manners, 397-98; ordering, 396; party, seating, 395-96; table, finding, 395; tipping, 399-400
Rice, throwing, 219
Ridicule, 437, 446
Ring: engagement, 175; wedding, 187
Ring bearer, weddings, 185; costume, 234
Road, courtesy, 387-88
Rolls: eating, 54, 58-59; on the table, 66
Room services, hotel, 428-29
Roomette, train, 417-18

Rose petals, wedding, 219
Royalty, introductions, 14
Ruled stationery, 270

S

Sabers, arch, military wedding, 518
Sailing, formalities of, 421
Salad: eating, 61; knives, 61; serving, 112, 115, 116, 120
Salad course, diagram, 105
Salt: dishes, 106; helping oneself to, 66
Sandwiches, eating, 59
Sarcasm, 437
Saturday nights, clothes, dining and dancing, 356-57
School, teen-agers, 473
Seasickness, 425
Seating arrangement: dinner, diagram, 104; theater, 390-91
Seats: airplane, 424; church wedding, 235-36; giving up, 9-10; lower berth, 419
Secretary, office: chair, placing for, 506; calling by first name, 507; rising for employer, 506
Senator, introductions, 14
Servants: addressing, 89; duties, 81-94; envelope addressing, 287; introductions, 18
Service: luncheon, 119-20; plate, 103, 111, 112, 114, 119, 168; tea, 129
Service jitters, avoiding, 63
Services, funeral, 266
Serving dishes, 63, 111
Shaking hands: introductions, 19-20, 21; men, 381; women, 381
Ships: clothes, 422; dressing for dinner, 422; introductions, 17; luggage, 421; reservations, 420; tipping, 423; travel, 420-23
Shoes, old, throwing, 219
Showers: baby, 258; bridal, 178-79, 245
Sick calls, 27-28, 30, 33-34
Sickroom: etiquette, 33-34; introductions, 17
Signature: abbreviations, 283; daughter and mother, same name, 283; degree, use of, 283; divorcée, 282; doctor, 282; initials, 283; "Junior," 283; letter, 281-83; men, 281, 282; min-ister, 282; mother and daughter, same name, 283; typed, 272; widow, 282; woman, married, 281-82; woman, unmarried, 282
Silver: basic, 72-74; buying, 72-74; flat, check list, 73-74; monograms, 217; plated, 73; sterling, 72-73; table, rules for, 52; table setting, 103-4, 114
Silver sixpence in shoe, 218
Silverware: dropped, 64, 397; wiping at table, 65-66
Sisters, envelope addressing, 287-88
Slacks, jacket over, 360
Slang, use of, 345-46
Slippers: bridesmaid, 229; worn with wedding gown, 246
Smoking: airplanes, 406, 425; at home, 406-7; at table, 397; during dinner, 407-8; etiquette, 404-10; host, suggestions, 408; hostess, suggestions, 408; in bed, 407; men, 382-83; other people's houses, 407-8; outdoors, 409; pipe, indoors, 407; public conveyances, 406; public places, 405-6; teen-agers, 477-78; theater, 392, 393; woman, on street, 432; women, 409-10
Social: behavior, basic, 1-67; correspondence, 269-337; graces, 339-78; introductions, 10-26; life, military, 514; season, New York, 355fn.
Something old—something new, 218
Son-in-law, 441
Soup: appropriate, 168; course, diagram, 105; eating, 56; serving, 114, 120
Spaghetti, eating, 61
Sparkling wines, 156
Spats, when worn, 361
Speech: children, 455-57; gesture, 340-41; mannerisms, 340-41
Sponsorship, club, 485
Spoon: long-handled, 56; use of, 55-56
Spoon foods, 55-56
Sporting events, courtesy, 394
Staff: big house, 82-89; ideal, 81
Stand-up supper, 124
States, abbreviations, list, 288-89
Stationery: colored, 269-70; correspondence, formal, 269; correspondence, informal, 269; country-house,

271; engraved, 270; hotel, 270; mono-grammed, 270–71; office, 270; ruled, 270; typewritten letters, 272
Stepchild, 446–47
Stepfather, task of, 446–47
Stepmother, task of, 446–47
Sterling silver, 72–73
Stocking-throwing, 219
Store etiquette: customers, 504; personnel, 503
Stories, repetition, 7
Street: behavior, 379–84; greeting people, 379
Streetcars, etiquette, 384–85
Subscription: dances, 135–36, 311; dinner dance, 312
Subway: etiquette, 384–85; seat, offer of, 432
Successful businesswoman, 496–98
Sugar bowl, 169
Sunday night: clothes, 430; supper, 122, 123
Supper: dances, 138–39, 309; parties, 122–23, 304, 309; stand-up, 124; Sunday night, 122, 123
Sympathy, letters of, 326–30

T

Table: accidents, 64; behavior, 53–54; bridal, 243–44, chart, 243; buffet, 124–25; card, 143; clearing, 116; head of, 170; hostesses, 133; leaving, 65; tea, 129, 131
Tablecloth, greasy food particles dropped on, 66
Table coverings, 101–2
Table decorations, 102–3, 118
Table linens, 78; check list, 79
Table manners, 51–65; children, 457–59; questions and answers, 65–67
Table setting, 100–6, 113–14; basic procedure, 103–6; harmony, 100
Table silver, rules for, 52
Table ware, 74–77
Tact, importance, 6–7
Taking leave, group of strangers, 21
Talking, modern way of, 344
Tasting, from another's plate, 397
Taxicab fare, woman paying, 506
Tea: afternoon, 128–33; coffee at, 168; bridge, 147; cloth, 129–30; clothes,
354; dancing, 137, 309; formal ceremonious, 131–33; formal outdoors, 133; hour, 129; informal, 130–31; informal invitation, 315; acknowledgment, 316; invitations, 129; preparing, 130; service, 129; spike, 133; table, 129, 131; tray, 129, 130; wagon, 115
Teacup tradition, bride, 220–21
Teen-agers: adaptability, 473; boy, suggestions to, 481–82; clothes, 473, 475; dances, 474–77, 480, 481; dates, 474–77, 480, 481; drinking, 478; etiquette, 471–82; girl, suggestions to, 479–81; home, 473; parties, 462; petting, 479; problems, 477; public behavior, 472, 473; school, 475; smoking, 477–78; theater, 473
Telephone: answering, 362, 364–65; calls, courtesy in making, 362–64; calls, guests, paying for, 366; children answering, 365; courtesy, 362–67; courtesy, hints, 366–67; etiquette, business, 499–500; invitations, 365–66; voice, 499
Television, courtesy, 367–69
Theater: aisle, going down, 390; aisle seats, 391; arriving, 389–90; balconies, evening gowns worn in, 361; box seats, 391; clothes, 355; coats, men, 390; coats, women, 390; entering, 389; entering row of seats, 390–91; etiquette, 389–94; intermissions, 393; introductions, 15, 16; leaving, 394; seating arrangements, 390–91; smoking, 392, 393; talking, 393; teen-agers, 473; women's hats, 391–92
Themes, table decorations, 102–3
Tipping: airplanes, 425; amount, 399; baggage porters, 431; bellboys, 431; chambermaid, hotel, 431; club, 489; debut dinner, 139; doormen, 431; excessive, 400, 423, 431; headwaiter, 400, 432; hotels, 431–32; house guest, 155, 171; restaurants, 399–400; shipboard, 423; train, 419–20; waiters, 431
Toast: bride, military wedding, 518; bride and groom, 244; groom to bride, 190; guest of honor, 165; joining in, 411; men in uniform, 515;

prospective bride and groom, 245; Washington, 515

Toastmaster, presiding officer serving as, 490

Toothpick, use of, 64

Traditions, bridal, 218

Train: berths, 417, 418, 419; clothes, women, 418; courtesy, 418; dogs on, 418; dressing room, 419; luggage, 418; overnight trip, 418; reservations, 417; tipping, 419–20; travel, 417–20

Training, importance of early, 450

Transatlantic liners, captain's dinner, 422

Travel: agent, 414; airplane, 423–27; clothes, 415–16; etiquette, 414–26; "packaged trips," 415; planning, 414–15; ship, 420–23; train, 417–20

Traveler's checks, 415

Tray buffets, 126

Trips, "packaged," 415

Trousseau: bride's personal, displaying, 248; considerations, 217; meaning of word, 215; modern, 215–17

Tuxedo, 358; hat worn with, 361

Two-families-under-one-roof, 443–45; budget, 444; household duties, 444

Typewritten letters, 272

U

Umbrella, who should carry, 432

Undersize letters, 270

Uniforms: chauffeurs', 84; maids', 85, 86, 87, 92

United States Army, officer, highest ranking, 511

Ushers: ballroom, duties, 170; bridal table, 243–44; flowers, 230, 231, 232; military wedding, 518; processional, 237; recessional, 237; wedding, ceremony, 237; wedding, costume, 222, 230–32; wedding, duties, 185, 235–36, 239; without bridesmaids, 248

V

Valet, duties, 88–89

Vegetables, butter on, 59, 60

Veils: crepe, 267; wedding, 219–20, 224–25, 227

Visas, securing, 420–21

Visiting, etiquette of, 26–39

Visiting cards, 26–27, 29, 39–51; address, change of, 45; at-home day, 47–49; Christmas card, enclosed with, 336; colored, 40; congratulation, 44, 45; debutante daughter, 46; engraving, 40; friend at a hotel, 47; gift, sent with, 44; good form in, 40; introductions, 24; invitations, 49–51, 149, 289–90, 304; Jr. and 2nd, use of, 42; messages, 43; modern uses, 43–45; mourning, 51; names, 41; P.P.C., 45–46; sizes, 40; styles, 40; sympathy, 44, 45; titles, 41; traditional use, 42–43; uses, 39–40

Visitor, office, unwelcome, getting rid of, 506

Visits: bride, 31–32; dropping in, 37–39; formal: arrival, 29–30, brevity, 28, hours for, 27–28; friends in the country, 39; informal, 36–37; length of, 38–39; new mother, 32, 257–58; new neighbor, 30–31, 35–36; "not at home," 30; returning, 35–36; sick or injured, 33–34; unexpected, 37–39; when not to stay, 37–38

Voice: pleasant speaking, 339–40; telephone, 499

W

Waiter: attracting attention of, 397; tip, 431

Waitress, duties, 86

Washington, D.C.: calls, formal duty, 513–14; entertaining, 515; etiquette highlights, 512; hostess, 509; precedence, order of, list, 509–11; protocol system, 509; receiving line, 515; reception days, 514; receptions, formal, 515; toasts, 515

Water glasses, 111, 114, 116

Watercress, eating, 66

Watermelon, eating, 55

Wedding: arrangements, 181–82; attendants, 184–85; attendants, informal home, 247; breakfast, 194, 242; breakfast, military, 518; cake, 185–86, 244, military, 518; ceremony, 238; chart, 237; church, 234–39; church, admission card, 197–98;

clergyman, fee, 246; club, 241; country, home, 200; country, transportation, 200–1; dancing, 244; date, setting, 181; day, 234–45; flowers, 186, 223; garden, 240–41; guest lists, 183; guests, reception and ceremony, 194; home, 198–200, 239–40; hotel, 241; hour, 182; informal, procedure, 247; leaving for church, 235; march, 190, 221; military, 516–18; music, 186–87; naval, whom to invite, 517; outdoor, 199; plans, 181–92, check list, 188; portraits, 246; procession, 191, 236–38; processional, *chart*, 237; questions and answers, 245–49; receiving line, 242–43, *chart*, 242; reception, 182–85, 194, 241–44; reception, after honeymoon, 247; reception, private home, 243; recessional, 238–39, 240, 241, 518, *chart*, 237; rehearsal, 190–91, 247; ring, 187; toasts, 244; train and direction cards, *sample*, 200–1; veil, 219–20, 224–25, 227

Announcements and invitations, 183–84, 192–212; army officer's, 517; bride, second marriage, 206; bride with divorced parents, 205; bride with no parents, 205, 206; bride with one parent, 204; bride's home, 198; ceremony, 194; church, 195, 196; church and reception, 197; double wedding, 203; elopement, 202; engraved, 192; envelopes, 192; home of relative or friend, 199; informal, 209–10; issuing, 193; mailing, 194; married business associate, 248; naval officer's, 517; outdoor, 199–200; parents separated or divorced, 193; recalling, 180, 207; reception, 195, 196, 197, 199; special, 202–6; to whom sent, 248; wording, 193–94; year, 193

Costumes, 221–34; men: civil, 232; formal daytime, 230; formal evening, 231; informal, 223; informal daytime, 231; informal evening, 231; parsonage, 232; summer, 231–32; women, 223–24, formal, 223; garden, 226–27; gold slippers, 246

Gifts: acknowledged in bride's absence, 213; acknowledging, 213,

321–22, system for, 212; bride's preference, 245; displaying, 214; exchanging, 215; returning, 247, 248
Wedding anniversaries: congratulations, 317–18; gifts, 324; invitations, 211, 212; *list*, 324; reception, 211
Week-end parties, 150–55
Welcome guest, 369–72
White House, Washington: call, courtesy, 513; call, formal, 512; ceremonial function, 513; dinners, 513; guests, 513; invitation to, 512; invitation to, acknowledging, 513
White table wines, 156
Widower, funeral procession, 264
Widows: bridal veil, 225; envelope addressing, 285; funeral procession, 264; marriage, 249; mourning, 267–68; signature, 282; visiting card, 41; wearing first husband's rings, 247
Wife, foreign, in American home, 445–46
Wineglasses, 163–64; filling, 112, 163, 165
Wines, 155–68; and food, 157, *list*, 158; appetizer, 156, 157; care and handling, 160–61; corks, 160, 161; drawing, 164; decanting, 165; dessert, 156, 159; dinner, formal, 157; dinner, informal, 157; dinner party, 171; host's glass, 164–65; luncheon party, 157; pouring, 165; red table, 156; refusing at table, 411–12; sediment, 160–61; sequence, 159; served with dinner, 112; service, customs, and traditions, 164–65; sparkling, 156; spoiling, 161; storage, 160; temperatures, 161, *list*, 162; white, table, 156
Wine cellar, 160
Winter debuts, 137
Wives and husbands, seating, 168
Woman, business, hostess to man, 506
Women: clothes: church, 387; club meeting, 491; correct, 353–57; evening gown, with man in business suit, 360, on train, 418, traveling clothes, 415; cocktail lounge, 433; doctors, envelope addressing, 285–86; employee, introduction to, 507; envelope addressing, 285; gloves, 353, 354, 356, 357; guest of honor, 109, 118; hat: hotel reception, 360, in

hotels, 430, removing, 29, 395, speaker at afternoon meeting, 360, theater, 391–92, when to wear, 353–57, with street-length clothes, 361; introductions, 10–11; job, applying for, 501; leaving cards, 43; man carrying packages, 383; man paying for, 432; man paying for woman's purchases, 432; man, walking with, 383; man's arm, holding, 9, 383; married, envelope addressing, 285–86; married, signature, 281–82; meeting man on street, 382–83; men's

courtesies to, 7–10; night clubs, 401; restaurant check, paying, 398; rising, in restaurant, 398; shaking hands, 20, 21, 381; smoking, 409–10; smoking on street, 432; taxicab fare, paying, 506; theater, coats, 390; traveling alone, 419, luggage, 428; traveling with employer, 507; two with man, walking, 383–84; unmarried signature, 282; visiting card, 41; with two men, seating, 395

Words: choice use of, 344–45; frequent mistakes, 346–47; pronunciation, 341